# Psychoanalysis, Behavior Therapy, and the Relational World

# Psychoanalysis, Behavior Therapy, and the Relational World

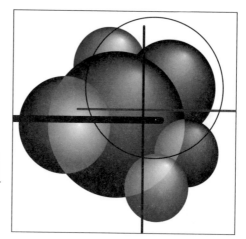

# Paul L. Wachtel

AMERICAN PSYCHOLOGICAL ASSOCIATION
WASHINGTON, DC

First printing March 1997
Second printing November 1997

Published by
American Psychological Association
750 First Street, NE
Washington, DC 20002

Copies may be ordered from
American Psychological Association
Order Department
P.O. Box 92984
Washington, DC 20090-2984

In the UK and Europe, copies may be ordered from
American Psychological Association
3 Henrietta Street
Covent Garden, London
WC2E 8LU England

Typeset in New Caledonia by GGS Information Services, York, PA

Printer: Data Reproductions Corp., Rochester Hills, MI
Cover Designer: Janet Minker, Bethesda, MD
Technical/Production Editor: Catherine R. Worth

**Library of Congress Cataloging-in-Publication Data**

Wachtel, Paul L., 1940–
    Psychoanalysis, behavior therapy, and the relational world / Paul
L. Wachtel.
        p.   cm.—(Psychotherapy integration)
    "Including the complete original text of Psychoanalysis and behavior
therapy."
    Includes bibliographical references and index.
    ISBN 1-55798-409-3
    1. Behavior therapy.   2. Psychoanalysis.   3. Eclectic
psychotherapy.   I. Wachtel, Paul L., 1940–   Psychoanalysis and
behavior therapy.   II. Series.
RC489.B4W32   1997
616.89'142—dc21                                          96-53417
                                                           CIP


**British Library Cataloguing-in-Publication Data**
A CIP record is available from the British Library

*Printed in the United States of America*

*For Ellen*

# CONTENTS

# PART TWO:
# THE RELATIONAL WORLD

# PREFACE: PSYCHOANALYSIS, BEHAVIOR THERAPY, AND THE RELATIONAL WORLD

THIS volume is at once a new edition of *Psychoanalysis and Behavior Therapy* and a new book in its own right. Rather than rework the original chapters of the book, as is often done in new or revised editions, I have chosen instead to republish the book in its original form and to add an entire new seven-chapter section (Part Two: The Relational World) that addresses developments, findings, and perspectives from the time of the original publication to the present.

This decision was premised on several considerations. Certainly not irrelevant was the sheer difficulty of the task of revision. *Psychoanalysis and Behavior Therapy* was written to be a single, coherent whole. Its logical structure, language, transitions, the order of the arguments, and so forth, were composed in such a way that it would have been difficult to "slip in" a new theoretical consideration here, a new finding there, a new application elsewhere. Some books are written modularly, in effect, with sections that are almost independent of each other. My own writing in general, and *Psychoanalysis and Behavior Therapy* in particular, is more organic in style. To "update" a piece here or there would unravel the entire thread of its structure, in which the transitions from one point to the next were crucial both aesthetically and logically. Had I intended a merely "cosmetic" updating (for example, inserting extra references with more recent dates at the points where references are already cited, or putting in an occasional new sentence or modifying footnote), perhaps this course might have been feasible. However, as will be clear to the reader, my aim is a more serious and substantial reexamination of the possibilities for an integrative approach to psychotherapy and of the theoretical synthesis that has evolved in the course of my work. The seven new chapters included in this edition seem better suited for this task.

My decision about how to approach the task was based as well on the gratifying reception the book has received since its original publication and on the helpful input of Dr. Gary VandenBos, Executive Director of

Publications and Communications, at the American Psychological Association. Gary was kind enough to articulate the issue in a way I could not permit myself to do: The book had become a "classic" that continues to be read and cited, and, therefore, the scholarly and research community would best be served by a form of publication in which a new generation of students, clinicians, and researchers could have available, along with the new material, the complete original volume with its original pagination. In the form presented here, references to particular points in the book that are cited in other work may be checked out in detail, even as the book is thoroughly updated in light of developments both in my own clinical and theoretical efforts and in the several lines of thought from which its integrative model has drawn.

The fact that Part One and Part Two of this book were written at different times offers an opportunity for an unusual resolution of the ongoing problem of how to take into account that the human race consists of two genders without writing sentences riddled with phrases such as "The therapist must direct his or her attention to his or her role in his or her patient's experience." In Part One, written before issues of gender in language had filtered into the awareness of most writers, the traditional pronouns "he" and "his" were used to refer to generic persons. Therefore, in Part Two the pronouns "she" and "her" will be similarly used.

This solution is consistent with the intent of publishing the complete text of *Psychoanalysis and Behavior Therapy* in its original form while still attending to the concerns that have led to the reexamination of linguistic habits that had long been traditional and unexamined. Moreover, this particular solution to the question of how to overcome the bias implicit in old language patterns, by offering a contrast between the acceptable forms of two decades ago and the concerns of the present, has the additional advantage of calling attention even more fully to the change in our consciousness and of calling attention as well to the ways in which, often without recognizing or articulating it, we are shaped by social and historical forces.

The Preface to the original edition (included in this volume) enabled me to offer my gratitude to a large number of individuals and institutions who contributed to shaping my ideas over the years. In writing the new chapters for Part Two, I accumulated further debt, which I am pleased to acknowledge. Since its founding in 1983, the Society for the Exploration of Psychotherapy Integration (SEPI) has been a source of constant stimulation and continuing education for me, and has as well as provided a "home" for those of us who have left the safe waters of the orientation in which we were raised to explore new integrative possibilities. The dedication to open-minded consideration of other people's ideas that is SEPI's very foundation is contagious; its meetings have provided more substance and less "ego-tripping" than any others I have attended.

Several SEPI members provided particularly helpful feedback on the new chapters in Part Two. It is a pleasure to acknowledge the input of Hal Arkowitz, Kenneth Frank, Marvin Goldfried, Stanley Messer, and Jeremy Safran.

The contribution of Annette DeMichele to this new edition is almost beyond description. More than a research assistant, Annette was virtually an alter ego throughout the writing, providing editorial assistance of almost uncanny perceptiveness. If I were a multiple personality, the authors of all my previous books would be green with envy for how much easier Annette made writing this new edition.

Finally, I once again thank my wife Ellen for her loving support, but now I must acknowledge her as a colleague and coauthor as well. My appreciation of the strong affinities between the point of view at the heart of this book and the theoretical perspectives that guide most work in family therapy was enriched greatly by discussions with Ellen that drew on her deep understanding and creative applications of systemic approaches. Our first collaborative effort in articulating this convergence was our joint book *Family Dynamics in Individual Psychotherapy*, for which she was in all respects (except age) the senior author. Subsequently, we have conducted numerous joint workshops on the integration of individual and family therapy, on the related topic of intervening in the vicious circles that characterize unhappy lives, and most recently on the much neglected topic of what therapists actually say (or what they should say) to move from understanding people's difficulties to effectively helping them change. This last collaboration derived from her valuable and insightful chapter on therapeutic communication with couples that extended the purview of my last book, *Therapeutic Communication*. In all of these joint efforts, I have never failed to learn something new. It seems that virtually every time we do a workshop together, there is some new subtlety to be grasped that further enhances my work with individuals and couples seeking to improve their lives.

The theory presented in this book has at its core the concept of vicious circles. It points the therapist or researcher to examine the cyclical patterns in people's lives, the ways in which our actions and perceptions interact with the actions and perceptions of the people I call the "accomplices" in our life patterns and the ways in which these interactions tend to reproduce once again our familiar experiential world and the behavior that reinitiates the cycle. For this reason I have come to call the theory *cyclical psychodynamics*. It is a theory in which unconscious thoughts and inclinations play a codetermining role with the actual overt behaviors that constitute our interations with others. The vicious circle or self-perpetuating interaction cycle is the key unifying concept that permits the integration of observations and methods from viewpoints that had otherwise seemed antithetical.

As I have continued to explore the implications of this theoretical viewpoint, it has become clear that its application is not bounded by the task of integrating psychodynamic and behavioral approaches to psychotherapy. As a contribution to psychodynamic theory in its own right, it will be of interest even to some psychodynamic clinicians who have little interest in the behavioral point of view but who regard a transactional perspective on psychodynamic theory as illuminating. Cyclical psychodynamic theory has been the foundation for a variety of explorations in theory and clinical practice that, while rather centrally concerned with the use of active intervention methods in an integrative psychodynamic model, explore as well a range of issues—such as transference, resistance, neutrality, conflict, and the concept of an inner world—close to the heart of contemporary psychodynamic thought (e.g., Wachtel, 1987). The theory has been central as well to the efforts my wife and I have made to bring together individual and family systems perspectives. It can even be seen to underlie the work I have done in the realm of social analysis and social criticism—my analysis of the psychological consequences and contradictions of the consumer way of life (Wachtel, 1989) and a book currently in preparation examining the cyclical processes and vicious circles that characterize race relations in America.

At a conference a number of years ago, the aphorism occurred to me upon hearing a description of a case that "the self becomes what the self has wrought." Our actions do not simply reflect our inner psychological state; they contribute to shaping that state in its ongoing evolution. Psychological change and development are a result neither of inner change alone nor of new behavior alone, but of the way in which the two continually intersect in the living of a life. That notion lies at the heart of cyclical psychodynamics, and it perhaps provides a useful point of departure for the reader as he or she begins to read this book and to consider its implications.

# FOREWORD

## Gerald C. Davison, Ph.D.

S EVERAL years ago a clinical psychologist from "the city" (as Long Islanders refer to Manhattan) telephoned and expressed an interest in seeing someone *do* behavior therapy, in contrast to *talking about* behavior therapy. The man calling from New York University, where he was teaching at the time, had been working for years in a generally psychodynamic fashion, and yet had already assimilated an amazing wealth of information about behavior therapy. Clearly he knew more about the literature of my approach than I did about his!

So Paul Wachtel came out one Tuesday afternoon to watch me, from behind a one-way screen, interviewing a client as part of my training seminar for Stony Brook's Postdoctoral Program in Behavior Modification. After I closed the session, I returned to the seminar room for the usual rehash with the four postdocs. But this time it was *different,* and much better. After following our discussion for some time, Wachtel gradually began to talk about what he saw, what he thought I was trying to do at various times during the session, and what he would have done differently. It was mind boggling. His comments, and the ensuing discussion, made vivid that we see what we are prepared to see, and that we act as therapists within a sometimes narrow set of parameters that are set by our theoretical biases. But what was especially fascinating about Wachtel's contributions to the discussion was the manner in which his interpersonal-ego-analytic suggestions seemed to complement some of the behavioral plans that I was pursuing at the time with the client.

He attended several other seminars, and my respect for his disciplined creativity continued growing. I then began to read some of his manuscripts, including the chapters that comprise this book. I have never experienced greater intellectual exhilaration.

To comment on but a few themes of the book: Wachtel inveighs against what he poetically refers to as the "woolly mammoth" view of psychopathology that characterizes psychoanalytic theory. According to this view, a repressed conflict remains "frozen" in the psyche and must be unearthed by the analyst if true progress is to be made in the here and now. The neurosis is assumed to derive from unsuccessful efforts to deal with the encapsulated residues from the past which, because of their isolation from the ego, continue to make primitive demands. The challenge he issues to his psychodynamic colleagues—including contemporary ego analysts—is to forsake this view and concentrate instead on altering current behavior patterns. Not only may this more efficiently help the client, but it can also change the nature of the childhood conflicts themselves. For if an adult is fearful of sexual relationships because of childhood traumata, might not this buried fear be altered by changing the adult patterns? This proposal, which seems eminently reasonable to me, leads Wachtel to urge his psychodynamic colleagues to avail themselves of recent developments in behavior therapy. Behavior change, as many of us have been arguing, is not irrelevant to cognitive change.

But think not that Wachtel's brief is only with his psychoanalytic friends, for he turns his incisive mind to how clinical behavior therapists might benefit from a careful study of contemporary analytic thought. Behavior therapy, he aptly points out, is arid as to the *content* of human life. Our strengths lie much more with functional relationships, and we have been somewhat weak in paying systematic attention to the *what* of behavior. Wachtel proposes that behavior therapists might take some clues from analytic theorizing regarding the *kinds* of problems people tend to develop. For example, psychoanalytic theory assumes that children have strong and ambivalent feelings about their parents which are unpleasant enough to be repressed (forgotten thoroughly). Consider then the assessment activities of a typical behavior therapist working with a male client who appears excessively fearful of heterosexual relationships. In most instances the focus in therapy will be on reducing these anxieties via systematic desensitization and/or rational restructuring techniques. If behavioral deficits appear to be part of the clinical picture, we might also focus on the teaching of social skills. All well and good. But Wachtel, from his psychoanalytic perspective, would suspect that such a client may also be angry at women, a reaction stemming from childhood conflicts with his mother. (We behavior therapists, if forced to do so, will translate this into "stimulus generalization," but no matter.) This hypothesis would lead him to inquire into the client's feelings about mother and into possible anger toward women. This altered perspective should generate clinical data quite different from those collected by a behavior therapist whose thinking is not influenced by analytic theorizing. The behavioral intervention will differ under these two circumstances.

This is a small sample of Wachtel's argument. I consider *Psychoanalysis and Behavior Therapy* one of the few really significant books published in clinical psychology or psychiatry in the past twenty years. It will become, I believe, a milestone in the literature that attempts to explicate the ways people become unhappy and worse, and the ways professionals can try to help them. It drives home the simple but oft-neglected point that none of us has a corner on the truth. We have accomplished much, but our ignorance is much greater than our knowledge. Most importantly, we may have to alter some of our cherished assumptions if we are to achieve nontrivial advances. Wachtel brilliantly and eloquently proposes a way to enhance that understanding.

Some of his suggestions will trouble many readers, but we should be grateful to him for disturbing our complacency. He is a good scientist and therefore expects disagreement with his admittedly speculative ideas. But he is also an insightful artist who can properly sense a vital integrity in the major thrust of his proposed integration of behavior therapy and psychodynamic thinking.

I have read this book—which makes me envy the reader who is about to begin it.

GERALD C. DAVISON
*Professor of Psychology and Psychiatry*
*State University of New York at Stony Brook*
*Past-President, Association for Advancement of Behavior Therapy*

# FOREWORD

## Hans H. Strupp, Ph.D.

$\mathbb{D}$R. WACHTEL has written an important, timely, and forward-looking book, which outlines clearly the direction in which psychotherapy practice and research must move in the years to come. He has broken new ground in the long-term endeavor to amalgamate divergent theoretical viewpoints and to move toward the ultimate goal of establishing psychotherapy as a unified discipline. He is one of the relatively rare people who are fully conversant with psychodynamic as well as behavioral principles and techniques, and he succeeds in surmounting partisan debates by being thoroughly knowledgeable, appropriately critical, and fair-minded. Though his predilection seems to be for psychodynamic therapy, and he retains admiration (in my opinion, appropriate) for its substantive contributions, he is a psychodynamicist who takes behavior therapy and its teachings seriously.

The greatest failing of psychoanalysis over the years—one that marks a radical departure from Breuer and Freud's seminal work in the 1880s—has been its scant regard for empirical data and the nitty-gritty of the patient-therapist interaction. There have been few meticulous descriptions of the interventions which are instrumental in therapeutic change. With rare exceptions, psychoanalytic writings have dealt with higher order abstractions and metapsychological excursions. We never knew *exactly* what went on between Freud and his patients, but perhaps what Freud said to them between the time they got off the couch and passed through the door of his consulting room was as much a part of his therapeutic influence as the "interpretations" he advanced while they were in the recumbent position. A few intrepid pioneers, like Franz Alexander and Thomas French, recognized the importance of examining in detail the patient-therapist interaction, but we still have scant information on how psychoanalytically oriented psychotherapy—by far the most prevalent form practiced today—is *typically* carried out. It is clear that Freud never practiced psychoanalysis in the manner advocated in his writings, and today, more than ever, there exists a vast hiatus between actual psychoanalytic practice and enshrined principles. But by and large, psychoanalytic therapy has undergone few fundamental changes, let alone advances.

What behavior therapy has contributed, beyond challenging technical innovations, is a new and abiding regard for empirical data, a serious concern for the need of testing techniques in the crucible of research, and a critical attitude toward generalizations advanced from the armchair.

By this time, one might expect numerous critical analyses of what these two major viewpoints have to offer, and how one might enrich the other. Clearly, there is wheat and chaff in both. Yet few comparative analyses have been made so far, and for many years the polemics centering on slogans and clichés—"the medical model," "symptom substitution," "diagnosing," "the unconscious," "spontaneous remission"— have deterred advances. Moreover, few analytic practitioners and theorists have immersed themselves in a systematic study of behavior therapy; conversely, behavior therapists have evinced gross ignorance about the essence of psychoanalytic therapy. The time is indeed ripe for a thoroughgoing examination of how both forms of psychotherapy actually operate, and for studies of their commonalities and differences and their respective potentialities and limitations with particular patients.

Dr. Wachtel has made a promising beginning in this area, one that no doubt will be pursued and expanded in the foreseeable future. It cannot be otherwise if the field is to advance. For the time being he has adduced further evidence that behavior therapists, for example, use inferences—how can they help it?—and that analytic therapists "influence" and "reinforce" their patients in a variety of ways. In numerous respects he has pressed the inquiry further than others before him. In the end, there may be unbridgeable gaps between the two viewpoints, which need to be studied and documented further. But more important is Dr. Wachtel's argument for openmindedness, and his recognition that all of us are engaged in a scientific enterprise that is characterized by flux, uncertainty, and evolution. A psychotherapeutic system, as analysts as well as orthodox behavior therapists should have learned, is not a dogma but a set of provisional hypotheses in need of testing, refinement, and further testing. When perceived as dogma, concepts and terms become reified with disastrous consequences.

For example consider that most empirical of formulations, the "transference." What can be more crucial than what goes on between a therapist and a patient in the "here-and-now"? What can be more important than what a patient (often unwittingly) attempts to do with the therapist (as a representative of adult reality) in the context of a particular session, how he or she views and relates to the therapist, distorts reality by virtue of defenses and childhood fantasies, and enacts the totality of the neurotic problems that constitute the "illness" for which cure is sought? Timidity, hostility, obsequiousness toward the therapist, neurotic patterns of all kinds—these are data more real, potentially more meaningful, and more down-to-earth than a reading on a psychogalvanometer or a cheek mark on a rating scale. The fact that we still have a hard time measuring these phenomena should not detract from the realization that the true data of psychotherapy are to be found in the patient-therapist interaction.

Yet transference phenomena are among the "X-rated" (Wachtel's apt phrase) psychoanalytic concepts as far as most behavior therapists are concerned, and most psychoanalytic authors, for their part, have done too little to explore more fully that richest of all goldmines. Transference phenomena represent a common pool of empirical data second in importance to none. But only a handful of psychoanalytic authors, Dr. Merton Gill for one, have stressed the overriding significance and the mutative effect of "analyzing" these contemporary transactions, which always take precedence over interest in "the past."

The emphasis of behavior therapists on empirical data has had a powerful impact upon research in psychotherapy and strengthened the future of psychotherapy as a scientific discipline. In a day and age in which new systems and techniques have inundated the area on the one hand, and where consumers, legislators, and the public at large demand accountability from the mental health professions on the other, Dr. Wachtel's book represents a welcome plea for rationality, sanity, and hard evidence in the therapeutic marketplace.

HANS H. STRUPP
*Distinguished Professor of Psychology*
*Vanderbilt University*

# PREFACE: PSYCHOANALYSIS AND BEHAVIOR THERAPY

THIS BOOK has a rather ironic origin. It began with an invitation to a symposium that never got held, and with an effort to write for that symposium a paper that would put those behavior therapists in their place. At the time I was convinced that behavior therapy was foolish, superficial, and possibly even immoral. My training—excellent and encouraging of critical inquiry in most respects—had left me with an aversion to behavior therapy that was based, I now recognize, not only on any close examination of what behavior therapists do, but on a strong sense of "us" and "them."

In preparing to administer the *coup de grace*, I was forced for the first time to really look at what behavior therapy was and to think carefully about the issues. What I saw and what I thought surprised me. I found things to quarrel with, to be sure; but I also found much that was impressive, sophisticated, and intriguing, and—perhaps most surprisingly—I began to realize that the particular version of psychodynamic thought toward which I had been groping for a number of years dovetailed to a remarkable extent with what a number of behavior therapists were doing.

My paper on why behavior therapy was bad and unworthy of the interest of the psychoanalytically initiated has become a book on why behavior therapy is good and crucial to the development of psychodynamic thought. Instead of slaying the philistines I have embraced them. I have not, however, become a "convert" to behavior therapy. As that term is currently used, it tends to imply a clinical approach and point of view that is opposed to and dismissive of psychoanalytic thought. Few behavior therapists have more than a passing familiarity with the range of psychoanalytic formulations and observations; they comfortably dismiss a caricature, while never really making the acquaintance of a major tradition in man's thinking about man. My own formative experiences in the field were within the psychoanalytic tradition, and my respect for the richness and importance of this tradition has not been diminished by my increasing recognition of what has been inflicted on it by those who purport to be its friends and custodians.

Two main themes underly the arguments in this book. Firstly, in order to help, we must *help*. The stance of minimal intervention, which, for a variety of reasons, has characterized most clinical practice in the psychoanalytic tradition (as well as much work conceived of in terms such as "client-centered," "humanistic," or "existential"), is one of the main targets of the critiques offered in this volume. On both substantive and ethical grounds, I try to make a case for the appropriateness of *active intervention* in a patient's troubling life patterns, and to confront the argument that such intervention either compromises the degree of change that can be achieved or treats the person in an inhumane, disrespectful way.

Secondly, I argue for an approach to personality theory that substitutes for the traditional psychoanalytic imagery (e.g., "archaeological" layering, superficial surfaces that mask deep and genuine inner cores) a conception of cyclical events that confirm themselves by a complex set of feedback processes in which the cooperation of other people is essential. Personality is a process, not an onion. While there are certainly important ways in which our manifest behavior may disguise crucial things about ourselves, the peeling of layer after layer is not the essence of either getting to know someone more fully or helping the person to change. I have tried to show in this volume that what analysts have observed about human self-deception and the multitude of meanings in human affairs can be incorporated in a framework that does not imply that behind the facade of everyday life lurks an "inner reality," separate from and impervious to the events of our adult lives. I do not dispute the critical role of childhood in shaping our later personalities, nor the importance of those feelings and events that Freud forced us to recognize as important features of those early years. But I try to outline a different way of conceiving of development than Freud suggested and to spell out its implications for the therapeutic enterprise.

It will be apparent to some readers that many of the ideas and methods propounded in this book are consonant with developments in other theoretical and therapeutic traditions. The links between the point of view developed here and those of family theorists and family therapists seem to me particularly worthy of future exploration. The present focus on psychodynamic and behavioral conceptions should not be taken to imply that these are the only two orientations to personality theory and to psychotherapy that are of value. Psychodynamic and behavioral approaches are, however, perhaps the two most influential sources of clinical practice and theory today. Moreover, there are few junctures in the field where mutual antagonism and misunderstanding have been as great, and thus where an integrative effort presents as much challenge—or as much opportunity.

This is a clinical and theoretical book for clinicians and personality theorists. It presents verbatim clinical examples bearing on the practice of psychotherapy, and it examines a number of issues that I think are crucial in personality theory. It is not, however, intended strictly for professionals. I believe that this will be a useful supplementary text for students in graduate and advanced undergraduate courses in abnormal psychology, personality, and personality theory, and it is my hope that it will be of value to the interested layman as well. How to conceive of human behavior and/or human nature and how the person develops and changes are not, after all, matters of interest just to students of a particular discipline. Many of the issues discussed here have an important bearing on the possibilities for social change and for how such change can be brought about. For reasons of space and focus, I have decided not to discuss these matters in this book, but they seem to me intimately related to the issues that *are* discussed, and I hope the reader will be moved to think along these lines.

This book presents little new "data" in the sense that that term is typically used in the field of psychology, though it does present clinical observations to bolster and illustrate the points made. It thus departs from a strong tradition in psychology that stresses data over theory and certainty over speculation. The issues in the study of personality and personality change do not seem to me to have reached that point of clarity at which much data collection has yet been fruitful (though it has certainly been plentiful). We need a good deal more critical thought about how to conceptualize the issues, about what is worth knowing, and about the various ways in which what has been observed thus far can be understood. We need to examine more closely the assumptions that underlie our questions. For our questions are our destiny: once we have framed a question, the answer already lies in wait, concealed as the statue is in the sculptor's block of marble. The experimenter tends to be more literal than the sculptor in insisting that what is revealed has been there all along, but no less than the sculptor does the experimenter influence what emerges by how he hacks away at the task with his favorite tools.

Psychology has been obsessed with answers. This book is concerned mainly with questions. Though I have a definite point of view about psychological matters, and though I suggest some ways of doing therapy that derive from that point of view, I have no hard data to persuade the skeptic. But I do try to raise hard questions—about the data accumulated up to now, and about the kinds of data needed if facts are *really* going to replace debate in determining how to deal with neurotic misery.

An author's first book provides an opportunity to acknowledge many debts that have accumulated over the years. The first of those debts was accrued during my undergraduate days at Columbia, where I encountered the very special sort of intellectual stimulation that Columbia provided and that has led me ever since to dare to tackle "big issues." As a graduate student at Yale I was fortunate to have had many teachers who helped me to avoid the false dichotomy between clinical and research approaches to our field. Sidney J. Blatt played a particularly prominent role throughout my years at Yale, and Seymour B. Sarason continually stimulated me to broaden my view of the clinician's role and modes of thought. My understanding of psychoanalytic thought and its clinical application was given a firm foundation in extremely valuable courses and seminars with George Mahl, Ernst Prelinger, and Roy Schafer. The influence of John Dollard, who taught my first course in psychotherapy and was my first therapy supervisor, will be obvious to the professional reader of this book. Dollard and Miller's presence at Yale during the years I was there had an extremely important role in providing me with a model for viewing psychoanalytic and learning concepts as compatible and complementary.

Since leaving Yale I have been fortunate to have had the opportunity to learn from many colleagues of unusual sophistication and talent. At Downstate Medical Center, Jean G. Schimek provided me with a model of respectful irreverence for psychoanalytic orthodoxy and many valuable and sophisticated critiques of my early efforts to write on aspects of psychoanalytic theory. The Research Center for Mental Health at New York University, under the directorship of George Klein and Robert Holt, and later of Leo Goldberger, provided me with a setting in which the very latest trends in psychoanalytic thought were a daily menu and with an array of colleagues hard to match for intellectual capacity and knowlege of psychoanalysis. A staff seminar led by Merton Gill on the role of the analyst's real behavior in the patient's transference reactions was particularly stimulating at the point when the ideas for this book were just beginning to take shape.

During those same years my training in psychoanalysis and psychotherapy in the New York University Postdoctoral Program provided me with an opportunity to receive clinical training that was not limited by the mold of any one theoretical position. The atmosphere of the program, under the direction of Bernie Kalinkowitz, was one in which many diverse flowers could grow. My supervisors in the program, Sabert

Basescu, Ruth-Jean Eisenbud, George Kaufer, and Herbert Zucker, all approached clinical work from a different point of view, and each taught me to see things I had not seen before. George Kaufer, in particular, was a mentor to me throughout those years, and it is perhaps the greatest measure of his special qualities that he could give me so much support in writing a book whose conclusions are so different from his own. Emmanuel Ghent, too, provided a very special kind of support and a freeing influence during those years.

During the years in which my work on this particular project proceeded, two major sources of aid and stimulation were invaluable. One was the atmosphere created by my students and colleagues in the Ph.D. Program in Clinical Psychology at City College. I have benefited from an atmosphere in which my ideas could be challenged without rancor and praised without embarrassment. The second major source of help was provided by a number of behavior therapists who were willing to discuss their work with me and to let me observe their work firsthand. I particularly wish to acknowledge the stimulation and cooperation provided by Gerald Davison and Arnold Lazarus and the valuable training provided by Joseph Wolpe and his staff at the Summer Institute in Behavior Therapy at Temple University. A grant provided by the Research Foundation of the City University of New York enabled me to attend the Summer Institute, and a travel grant from the American Council of Learned Societies enabled me to participate in an International Symposium on Interactional Psychology in Stockholm, where my ideas about personality theory were further clarified. Those sources of support are gratefully acknowledged, as is the opportunity provided by Dr. Otto A. Will, Jr., to use the library and interact with the staff of the Austen Riggs Center in Stockbridge, Massachusetts, during the final summer of writing.

A number of friends and colleagues read all or parts of the manuscript and provided valuable feedback even when they viewed things from rather different premises. It is a pleasure to thank Arthur Arkin, Marvin Goldfried, Ronald Murphy, I. H. Paul, Russell Rodewald, Jean Schimek, and Lloyd Silverman for their contributions in this regard.

Finally, a very special acknowledgement: it is frequent at this point in a preface for the author to refer to the sacrifices made by his spouse and children, how they tolerated his single-minded devotion to his work, and so on. To be sure, my wife Ellen has had much to put up with during the years I was writing this book, and has had to deal with moods that varied with the progress of the work but that all had their impact on her. And she *has* encouraged this effort (including providing espe-

Preface: Psychoanalysis and Behavior Therapy

cially insightful comments on every chapter). But she did not play the role of the patient idolizer stepping aside for something more important. To her, nothing is more important than *living*. Thanks to her, living was not put aside to write this book, and our son and daughter have not had to substitute a father's success for a father's loving attention. The list of preoccupied weekends where book won out over family is short, and in its place is a long list of loving interactions that sustained me in this effort. For this I am deeply grateful, and I lovingly dedicate this book to her.

# PART ONE

*Psychoanalysis and Behavior Therapy*

# 1

# *Introduction*

---

Psychotherapy is not just a technical activity performed by a practitioner. Psychotherapies have existed throughout history, and they have always been rooted in philosophical views of human nature and man's place in the universe. The theories that guide contemporary psychotherapeutic efforts both reflect and shape the culture's view of human potential and of the good life. This book is centrally concerned with the relation between theory and therapy. While its main focus is on psychotherapy, it is equally a book about personality theory. My premise is both that psychotherapy must be understood in light of the theories that guide it, and that therapeutic practice provides a unique opportunity to test the mettle of a theoretical perspective and to discover its implications in action.

Among the theories that guide psychotherapeutic work, psychoanalysis has been particularly dominant in our culture for many years, shaping the layman's view of human nature as much as the therapist's view of how to proceed with his technical task. The development of psychoanalysis originally represented a major breakthrough in man's understanding of himself. It shattered a great deal of hypocrisy and turned a searching eye on old and worn assumptions. Today, however, the vitality that had been so characteristic of the psychoanalytic movement is not as evident. Like so many revolutions, both political and intellectual, this one too has produced a new establishment, which jealously protects the given view of things. There are those who would make of psychoanalysis an immovable, granite-like monument to Freud rather than a vital, flowing continuation of the probing activity it was as Freud practiced it.

There are, to be sure, creative voices still to be heard within psychoanalysis. In recent years, a number of prominent psychoanalytic thinkers have raised fundamental questions about the basic terms and concepts used by Freud and elaborated upon by men like Hartmann and Rapaport. But even in these noteworthy efforts one sees little, as yet, that would lead us actually to do anything very differently. There has not been much change in psychoanalytic techniques over the past two decades.

The new ways to deal with people's problems have largely come from elsewhere. Group and family approaches, approaches stressing bodily and sensory awareness, community approaches, and other viewpoints and perspectives have evolved significantly in recent years. Practitioners of these approaches often have rather strong disagreements with the classical psychoanalytic approach, and they clash with traditional practitioners on matters of ethics as well as pragmatics. Nonetheless, there remain lines of communication between these points of view. Psychoanalysis can be seen as the soil from which many of these approaches grew. Many of the major figures in these new therapies were originally trained psychoanalytically, and their work may be seen in some respects as an outgrowth of psychodynamic thought that has now achieved independence from its origins and challenges the parent theory.

Behavior therapy, on the other hand, is a major new trend that has developed largely *in opposition to* psychoanalysis, and the mutual distrust between proponents of the two points of view is considerable. Psychoanalysts and behavior therapists seem to agree on scarcely anything except the joint conviction that they have little to say to each other and that the two points of view are fundamentally incompatible.

At their most extreme, it is indeed correct that the two approaches are widely divergent. Classical Freudian drive theory and radically Skinnerian behavior modification have little in common. But the heirs of Freud are many, and the behavior therapy movement has many rifts and controversies concealed beneath the opposition to psychoanalysis which most behavior therapists share.

Not all those whose thinking has been nourished by Freud have swallowed him whole. The contributions of Erikson, Horney, Sullivan, Alexander, and others suggest a framework responsive to the observations on which psychoanalysis is based, yet potentially able to make use of newer methods and perspectives provided by behavior therapists.* On the other hand, the findings of learning researchers can be seen as consistent with, and shedding new light on, much that has been reported by psychoanalysts, as Dollard and Miller (1950) first showed more than twenty years ago.

It is my general premise that psychodynamic and behavioral approaches to psychotherapy, and to the understanding of personality, are far more compatible than is generally recognized, and that an integration of the concepts and observations accumulated by these two approaches can greatly enrich our clinical work and our understanding of human behavior. The work of the behavior therapist promises to provide that which has been most lacking in psychoanalysis: a means to actively intervene in the human dilemmas that psychoanalysis has enabled us to understand so keenly. The psychoanalytic point of view, on the other hand, has made its greatest contribution in revolutionizing our understanding of the meanings latent in our thoughts and acts. Its strength lies in discerning hidden strivings and revealing the enormous complexities of our affective life, not in a causal analysis of our behavior. The value of recognizing psychoanalysis as most basically a psychology of meanings has been stressed increasingly by contemporary psychoanalytic writers, who are far more distant from the crude tautologies embodied in terms such as "psychic energy" and "cathexis" than most behavior therapists realize.

Psychoanalysis has yielded a body of observations quite different from those provided by the learning lab or those made by clinicians doing behavior therapy. The clinician working from a psychodynamic framework is guided to notice different things from the behavior therapist. It is my experience that workers guided by either of these two broad frames of reference tend to have only a rather superficial knowledge (and sometimes none at all) of the important regularities observed by those guided by the other viewpoint.† Each defends his or her own

---

* It may be jarring to some readers to see these names together, since they belong to differing political groupings in the organization of psychoanalytic thought. Further, some of these thinkers and their followers might object to my suggestion that their ideas are compatible with behavior therapy. The reader is asked to withhold judgment on these matters until the central arguments of the book are presented.

† In the body of this book, this rather global distinction will be refined, and the in.-portant differences among psychodynamic thinkers and among behavior therapists will be considered. The global dichotomy is sufficient for our present purposes, because the boundary of ignorance is rather sharply drawn. Those of differing viewpoints in behavior therapy may disagree with each other, but they are aware of the basis for the other's view in a way they are not when regarding psychoanalysis. Among psychodynamic thinkers, the same is true if the appropriate and obvious transpositions are made in the sentence.

position by caricaturing the other, and by so doing avoids any basic change in viewpoint.

I am not advocating that behavior therapists adopt a little psychoanalysis or psychoanalysts use a little behavior therapy. My hope is, rather, that in trying to develop a frame of reference that encompasses the observations (and the directions for observation) that have accrued from both traditions, a newer, more complete and integrated approach will be achieved. One fruit of such an integration would be, I hope, the development of more effective ways to do psychotherapy. And we can anticipate that a sounder understanding of the development and maintenance of personality will also have implications for preventing personality disorders and for efforts at social change.

Psychodynamic and behavioral points of view are characterized not only by concern with different data but also by rather different epistemologies. The two (different data and different epistemologies) are, of course, not independent. Frequently, what are considered solidly established facts of observation by psychoanalysts are regarded as unfounded speculation and unverifiable inference by behaviorally oriented workers. Psychoanalysis is indeed greatly in need of clarification in this regard. I shall have occasion later on to refer to some of the recent efforts that have been made by psychoanalytic thinkers to clarify these matters. The articulation of what is data and what is theory in psychoanalysis has been recognized as a major challenge by a number of psychoanalytic writers.

Many other epistemological and methodological issues will concern us as we proceed. Of particular concern will be the reliance of psychoanalytic thought, for most of its history, on the selective recollections by analysts from huge masses of data that could in fact be organized in an enormous number of ways. A corollary concern is the question of the degree to which these data should be seen as the responses of patients, highly dependent upon their analysts, picking up subtle cues and giving back what is expected.

My own position on these matters is a more skeptical one than that of most psychoanalysts. Freud had a tendency to present his brilliant hunches and speculations as certainties already proved, and this tendency has persisted in much of the psychoanalytic literature. Far too much is taken as *demonstrated* by observations which would be more properly regarded as raising intriguing questions. Far too few thinkers over the broad range of psychoanalytic thought have much respect for evidence obtained outside of the patient-therapist interaction, particularly if it contradicts accepted assumptions.

But despite the methodological problems with psychoanalysis, the strictures of methodological behaviorism seem to me unacceptable. It is no accident of phraseology that I refer to an integration of psychodynamic and *behavioral,* rather than *behavioristic,* points of view. The term "behaviorism" connotes to me a methodology of "thou shalt not," an emphasis on avoiding certain kinds of concepts or ways of thinking. While embodying some important warnings, such a philosophy seems to me too severe; it requires us to disavow valuable conceptual tools and ignore important experiences.

By a *behavioral* approach to psychotherapy I refer primarily to an approach that focuses on the manifest events of the patient's life, and to a body of techniques (to be elaborated later on) that seem of value in bringing about change in particular distressing patterns of behavior. These techniques tend to be inspired by a number of more or less related conceptual models in which the notion of learning is very central. The patient's difficulties are seen as learned responses to particular situations, and the therapy is seen as a way of helping the patient to unlearn these responses and/or to learn new, more adaptive ones.

In its more general terms, such a description of psychotherapy is unexceptionable. Psychoanalytic therapy also is a learning experience, and the psychoanalytic theory of neurosis—especially since Freud's revised view of anxiety (Freud, 1926a)—can readily be shown to be a learning model. Behavioral approaches, however, tend to focus on more specific responses to more specific situations, and to posit that changes in particular troubling behavior can often be effected permanently without a complete reorganization of the personality. Thus, in one instance of the many confusing tricks of language in this area, the behavioral point of view can be seen as more *analytic* in its approach than is psychoanalysis.°

Most, though not all, behavioral methods in psychotherapy are based on what is generally designated as a stimulus-response point of view. To the extent that this implies a view of man as a passive reactor to environmental events, or that it carries the implication that "stimuli" can best be understood as physical quanta of energy impinging on receptors, or that it implies that it is not of value to examine the motives, feelings, and cognitions that influence our behavior, this volume is opposed to such a view. I believe, however, that it is perfectly possible to use most of the psychotherapeutic methods developed by behavior therapists without holding such attitudes. Indeed, the majority of the behavior

---

° No value judgment is intended here in either direction. The substantive question of when it is useful to look at specifics in isolation and when it is better to posit an integrated system will concern us considerably as we proceed.

therapists I have met do not view man or psychology in this fashion.

The more sophisticated among behavior therapists recognize that there is often only a loose, analogic connection between the methods they use and the learning experiments on which the methods are purportedly based. The various models of learning derived from experimental research serve only as stimulating guiding metaphors for much of the clinical work in the behavioral tradition. I believe that these metaphors have been rather rich and provocative and that they have led to important advances. But they can be mischievous when the connection between clinic and laboratory is exaggerated or misconstrued for purposes of polemic or myth. Such is unfortunately not infrequently the case, perhaps because among the most prominent figures in the behavior therapy movement are psychologists who are almost exclusively experimental researchers, with little or no clinical experience. Things look neater from that perspective, and case reports generally do not communicate the subtleties necessary to understand the gap between laboratory and clinic.

Behavior therapists are often effective precisely because they are *not* behavioristic in any narrowly construed way. In their clinical work they find it necessary to make inferences and to concern themselves with what their patients want and feel as well as what they do. Most of the practicing behavior therapists with whom I have discussed this issue have acknowledged privately that what they actually do looks quite different from what one would expect from reading the literature. (This, incidentally—though not unimportantly—is also true of psychoanalytically oriented therapists.) If instead of talking of stimuli and responses, with their pretension to a precision that clinical realities do not permit, we refer simply to learned ways of experiencing and dealing with situations, we are left with a framework both flexible and useful.

The clinical investigations of behavior therapists have greatly advanced our understanding of how our behavior is coordinated with the events occurring in our lives; and, as we shall see in later chapters, they have provided valuable guidelines to the clinician who would inquire in this direction. This behavioral work nicely complements that of the interpersonal school of psychoanalysis, which has undertaken a similar task in a different way. Behavior therapists have developed (based on their behavioral analyses) ways of intervening in troubling interpersonal patterns that represent a substantial departure from anything practiced in traditional therapies. Additionally, while not quite the experimenters-with-the-single-case that the literature implies, they have been considerably more scrupulous about evaluating their concepts and their results than has been traditional among psychotherapists.

This introduction is not the place to try to substantiate the contention that integrating psychodynamic and behavioral views will take us further than efforts to develop either of these approaches in isolation. In fact, as the wary reader might well suspect, this entire volume will not provide unequivocal evidence either. That must await years of creative innovation and careful evaluation by a great many clinicians and investigators. The burden of the present volume is to make a gamble in this direction seem enticing, and to indicate in a rough way how one might proceed. If the reader, of whatever persuasion, gains a clearer view of the unacknowledged assumptions and possible limitations of his own view, and a greater interest in exploring previously alien directions, the book will have achieved its purpose.

*Theoretical Considerations*

# 2

# *Psychoanalysis:*
# *From Medicine to Psychology*

───────────

Fᴿᴏᴍ our current vantage point, it may seem largely an historical accident that psychoanalysis began as an outgrowth of medicine. Today, the associations of psychoanalysis with medicine are rather arbitrary and cause much confusion. The current activities of the psychoanalyst resemble those of the physician far less than they do the activities of many other professions and disciplines. In fact, a great deal of the way the psychoanalytic relationship is structured may be seen as explicitly designed to *differ* from the traditional doctor-patient relationship. Further, it is ironically the case that the chief challenge to psychoanalysis today, the behavior therapies, represents in many respects a return to the doctor-patient relationship from which psychoanalysis departed. I say ironically, because one of the most common complaints lodged against psychoanalysis by behaviorally oriented writers is that psychoanalysis follows an outmoded "medical model" or "disease" conception of psychological disorder. I shall examine the substance of this issue later on, as well as some of the economic and sociological conflicts that are expressed in the language of the "medical model" debate.

For the present, however, I shall begin with an examination of how Freud made the transition from physician to psychological theorist, and of the baggage he gathered on that journey. It was not really altogether capricious that the origins of psychoanalysis were in medicine. For one thing, psychoanalysis is concerned with secrets. The thoughts, feelings, and experiences that are of most interest to psychoanalysts are not the kinds of things one would readily tell another. Rather, they are things we do not ordinarily even tell ourselves. To be privy, then, to receiving the data upon which psychoanalytic theory is based, one would have to be an extraordinarily trusted figure. The image of the wise, kindly doctor is probably better suited than that of most professions for encouraging in people a sense that they might dare to communicate those unseemly thoughts or memories that do slip into awareness.

The role of the priest was perhaps one of the few that matched that of the doctor in engendering trust and raising the expectation of a wise and understanding response to the divulgence of shameful and guilty thoughts. Most of the crucial data from which psychoanalytic theory was constructed were probably reported in the confessional box long before they were reported on the couch. Certainly there is little that Freud found in the id that would have shocked Augustine, and Freud's shattering of the myth of childhood innocence would no doubt have seemed to the Christian saint a rather dated rerun.

The clergy shared with the medical profession another characteristic that likely is crucial in eliciting the kind of data from which psychoanalytic theory was constructed: they dealt with people in desperate need of help. In a traditional society, it is likely that only imminent danger to one's body or one's soul could pry loose from good citizens those evil thoughts they had been taught to suppress almost from the first dawning of their consciousness. Whether the propagation of Freud's ideas, or other modern developments, have brought about a real or fundamental change in people's views of themselves or their genuine tolerance for deviance is difficult to determine. It does seem to be the case that at least the ways we *present* ourselves to others are different today than they once were. There are segments of our society in which the person who claims he has never felt lust for his mother or hatred for his son is damaging his good name.

Even today, however, there are many secrets we would probably not reveal to others unless great suffering or threat of suffering motivated us. Perhaps this is why it is so frequently reported that people who enter therapy under the push of considerable anxiety derive more from it than those who are more comfortable when they begin (Luborsky et al., 1971). At any rate, it does appear that Freud heard things from his patients that he would not have been told were he not their only hope for relief. Had he been only a researcher and not also in the helping role of the physician, his findings might well have been less controversial—and also less exciting.

Yet another related consideration makes it more understandable that psychoanalysis was developed by a physician. Freud's discoveries centered on the psychology of disavowed psychological elements. He studied those psychological processes not recognized by their possessors as part of their personalities. It is not surprising that those psychological events least readily acceptable as such should frequently find their expression in seemingly nonpsychological ways, such as complaints about somatic functioning. Many of the people Freud saw early in his career could only say what was troubling them by saying something was wrong with their bodies or their nervous systems. Those whose complaints were more frankly psychological predominated only later.

The latter group might seem at first thought a more likely stimulus to psychological theorizing. In recent years, in fact, they have been. Schizoid, narcissistic, and obsessional tendencies, deeply embedded in the patient's character, are the focus of much current psychoanalytic theorizing.

But the importance of *disowned* feelings and wishes, and the potential of such to create difficulties for us, is more starkly revealed when the disowning is more complete. Even today, the psychoanalytic treatment of obsessionals or people with character disorders is thought by many to be far more difficult than that of hysterics. With hysterics, it is easier to know what they don't know. Their naiveté is far more complete and more striking. Those patients who can more readily psychologize their feelings present considerable problems both for treatment and for conceptualization. If the challenge to which a theorist must rise is to discover the importance of something *absent* (or at least apparently absent), that discovery may be somewhat easier when the absence is at least more total, and hence potentially more striking, than when it is subtle. The man who tells you he is afraid but distorts how much he is afraid, or who acknowledges anger while hiding still more anger, presents greater problems in detection than the man who makes the striking claim that no angry or fearful thought has ever crossed his mind.

## ANNA O.

The absences or lacunae with which psychoanalysis is concerned today are different from what they were initially. Today, psychoanalysts are concerned with an enormous range of phenomena that occur without (or with partial) awareness. Wishes, fantasies, fears, moral judgments—all these and more fall within the province of psychoanalytic inquiry. They are of interest to the psychoanalyst because they can be hidden, influencing our behavior and conscious experience although absent in our reports of ourselves and our histories.

Initially, however, the focus of psychoanalytic inquiry was much narrower. In the very first cases seen by Freud, the aim was specifically to recapture absent *memories*. Once the patient remembered the appropriate event, with appropriate strong emotion, the symptom was expected to disappear. If it reappeared again, then it was assumed that the event recalled was not the original pathogenic occurrence but only a later associatively connected one, and the search continued for the earlier memory—with the confidence that if *it* was recaptured, the cure would be permanent and complete.

Such a view derived originally from empirical observation. Breuer's experiences with his famous patient, Anna O., in the early 1880s (Breuer and Freud, 1895) first suggested the value of this approach. Breuer's efforts with this patient did not originate primarily from a theoretical predilection. Rather, they were more in the nature of serendipitous findings. The "cathartic" technique was discovered by Anna O. herself at least as much as by her physician. Rational and intentional efforts at cathartic treatment only followed the observation that Anna seemed to feel better after relating to others some of the fantasies and hallucinations she experienced in the altered state of consciousness she was prone to undergo. On the days this expression did not occur, relief was not evident. Gradually Breuer assumed the role of regular listener as Anna reported her fantasies and images in an autohypnotic state. This "talking cure"—"chimney sweeping," as she called it—offered slow and moderate gains.

The specific emphasis that came to be placed on recovering the memory of the *original occurrence* of the symptom was also a result of a serendipitous observation. On one occasion, Anna began to speak about her English governess, whom she intensely disliked, and then told Breuer with much disgust of once having entered her room and seen the governess's dog drinking out of a glass. Though greatly disgusted, she said nothing at the time in order to be polite. Having told Breuer of this incident, with the kind of intense anger she had held back at the time that it occurred, she asked for a drink of water, drank a great deal, and then awoke from hypnosis with the glass at her lips. For quite a while before this she had been suffering from a phobic inability to drink, despite terrible thirst, and had been living on liquids from fruits alone. After she remembered this incident, the symptom completely disappeared and did not return.

Following up this rather striking observation, Breuer then developed with Anna the procedures that became the starting point for Freud's work. While Anna was in a hypnotic state, he would focus on evoking the memory of the earliest occasion associated with each of her symptoms. He found, however, that it was usually impossible to proceed directly to the original event, and that even if he could recapture it, such a direct assault on the target had little therapeutic benefit. Rather, he found he had to proceed gradually and systematically back from more recent occasions until the original event was finally recalled.° When this event was related with appropriate strong affect, the symptom disappeared.

## THE EARLY THEORETICAL FOCUS

A guiding principle was thus introduced rather early in the development of psychoanalytic thought: if improvement does not occur, or if the improvement is temporary, search further back into the patient's history. This would appear to be an empirically based generalization, compelled by the data rather than by any preconception of the investigator. Given the early observations that presented themselves to Breuer and then to Freud, it was indeed a reasonable assumption to make.

But the distinction between theory and data is not an easy one to make. Data and theory generate each other in complex ways. We shall soon examine rather critically the emphasis of psychoanalysis on the past, and consider alternative ways of understanding clinical observations. But for now, let us review the early developments in theory that followed from this line of inquiry.

At first, the forgotten events that were recovered appeared to represent a wide range of incidents one might have reason to prefer to forget. The "traumatic" memories reported in the *Studies on Hysteria* ( Breuer and Freud, 1895) included such things as being yelled at by a much admired and secretly loved boss for letting a visiting lady kiss the children;

° The reader may wish to consider this observation again when systematic desensitization is discussed later in the book.

sitting exhausted with worry at the sickbed of a child and fearing waking the child; having dead animals thrown at one by brothers and sisters; and self-reproach when, attending to a sick father, the patient had a desire to be at a neighbor's house from which dance music was coming. As is well known, it soon became striking to Freud—and even to Breuer, whose fear of the transference and countertransference events, we are told, had made him hesitant to pursue this line of inquiry—how many of these traumatic memories had a sexual content. Even where the situations that were recovered did not at first appear to be sexual ones, the procedure of seeking earlier and earlier memories until the symptom permanently disappeared ultimately began to lead to this kind of content.

As Freud (1914b) described it in *On the History of the Psycho-analytic Movement*, the sexual traumas first appeared to be adult ones, and the idea of infantile sexuality did not occur to him. "At first one merely remarked that the effect of current experience had to be traced back to something in the past. Only inquirers often find more than they bargain for! One was drawn further and further back into the past; one hoped at last to be able to halt at puberty, the period in which sexuality is traditionally supposed to wake. But in vain; the tracks led on still further backwards, into childhood and into its earliest years." (p. 299)

## THE NEUROTICA

By 1896, Freud's explorations had reached the point at which he was prepared to assert that all hysteric and obsessive-compulsive patients had had a traumatic sexual experience in childhood, which they had repressed and which they could remember only under the special conditions of the treatment used by Freud. By that time, the treatment he used had changed considerably from his first, hypnotic methods. The process of free association was now the major means of tracing back the roots of the neurosis.

In his second paper on the "defense neuropsychoses," Freud (1896) asserted that for every case of hysteria there was an experience of passive seduction, with actual excitation of the genital organs. "In every case a number of pathological symptoms, habits, and phobias are only to be accounted for by going back to these experiences in childhood, and the logical structure of the neurotic manifestations makes it impossible to reject these faithfully preserved memories which emerge from childhood life." ° (p. 159) Later traumas were seen as capable of producing hysterical symptoms only if they re-awakened the memory-trace of such a childhood incident, which instead of being consciously remembered is repressed and its affect discharged by means of such a symptom.

Obsessional symptoms were also attributed to a childhood sexual experience, but these were active experiences in which the child was the aggressor and experienced considerable pleasure. The obsessional symptom itself was described at one point in the paper as a form of self-reproach and later, more fully, as a "compromise-formation between the repressed and the repressing ideas." (p. 163) Freud suggested that such sexual activity in childhood tended to follow upon a still earlier experience of passive seduction.

There is a certain beauty to this early theory. In contrast to the rather baroque over-elaborateness of later developments in psychoanalytic thought, it is simple and direct. It is built on readily identifiable empirical observations. Little inference is required to decide whether a hypothesis has been confirmed or not. Whereas there can be considerable disagreement among observers as to whether a particular dream and its associations point to oedipal conflict, one could expect quite high agreement as to whether a patient reported a specific seduction experience in his childhood and whether the symptom disappeared when the experience was finally remembered.

We may also note that a number of features that remained important in psychoanalytic thought were already apparent in this quite early theory. The idea of a quantity (here of "affect," later of "energy") needing to be discharged and capable of being displaced is already evident, and it remained a key image in Freud's theorizing. Also already apparent and destined to remain central in psychoanalytic thought are the notion of intentional repression from consciousness and, relatedly, the notion of counter-forces empirically tied to resistance in treatment. And, of course, we see a strong emphasis on the idea of sexuality being at the root of neurotic problems.

Despite its several virtues, however, the theory had to be abandoned.

---

° Note again Freud's tendency to assert as unequivocal his conclusions from his observations. Since in this instance he himself later acknowledged he had drawn the wrong inference from the data, it may perhaps give us pause in considering the utter certainty with which Freud, and many modern analysts, regarded his later efforts to order a body of data pregnant with meaning but far from unambiguous in its implications. Excessive certainty is the most serious difficulty that has plagued psychoanalysis.

Over a period of several years Freud came to recognize that it could not be true as stated. In a letter of September 21, 1897, he elaborated some of the reasons for his growing doubts about the theory he had come to call his "neurotica." He noted that the analyses that he was performing with his patients were not complete or successful. Patients were running away, and the partial successes he did achieve could be explained in other ways. Additionally, his theory would have led him to conclude that perverted acts against children were prevalent to a degree that strained its credibility. Hysteria itself was found to be far more frequent than expected, and "perversion would have to be immeasurably more frequent than hysteria, as the illness can only arise where the events have accumulated and one of the factors which weaken defense is present." (Freud, 1887–1902, p. 216) A third consideration for Freud was his growing conviction that the unconscious does not distinguish between fact and fantasy. Finally, his skepticism about his theory was also furthered by the finding that even in the deepest psychoses and most confused states of delirium, such memories did not emerge.

## RECONCEPTUALIZATION

Eventually, of course, Freud found a way to come to terms with the clear indications of error in his formulations and yet salvage the important insights he had begun to gain into the role of unconscious processes. But what he accomplished was not a mere salvage job. Freud's reconceptualization of what he had heard reported by his patients was a stunning intellectual tour de force, perhaps the single most brilliant stroke of his lifetime. What had seemed at first like an imminent defeat turned out instead to be the crucial step in expanding the legitimate range of his theories from a limited number of specific aberrations to the entire realm of human psychological functioning.

Freud had tried to expand his perspective even before recognizing that his "neurotica" was in error. His posthumously discovered Project for a Scientific Psychology (Freud, 1895) was an effort to develop a general psychology based on neurological concepts and on a number of general assumptions that he retained throughout his lifetime in one form or another. (For example, there was his model of the nervous system as a tension-reducing apparatus, with corollary assumptions of displaceable energy quanta and of the need gradually to develop the capacity to delay discharge in the service of ultimately safer and more complete gratification.) This 1895 effort has been judged in recent years (Pribram and Gill, 1975) as an impressive approximation to our current knowledge of the nervous system. It is also of great interest to many analysts as an early effort to elaborate upon the assumptions which the psychoanalytic point of view was based on. But as a general psychology its value is rather limited, and Freud himself chose not to publish it. So long as Freud held to the view expressed in the second "defense neuropsychoses" paper (Freud, 1896), the very logic of his theory questioned the relevance of his observations for psychological problems in general. For he was claiming to be observing the vicissitudes of reactions to particular traumatic incidents, and the relevance of such observations for persons who did *not* experience childhood seductions was not apparent. The nature of the theory required it to remain primarily medical, a theory of neurosis but not of the mind in general. In contrast to the *developmental* point of view characteristic of current psychoanalytic theory, the life-history considerations of this early theory represent merely an *etiological* point of view. Similarly, there is really no adaptive point of view here (Rapaport and Gill, 1959), only a pathological one.

Environmental events were taken into consideration by Freud at this time (more so in fact than in later versions of psychoanalytic thought, until the advent of psychoanalytic ego psychology), but only as unfortunate accidents that happen to the individual, not as adaptational dilemmas the individual must learn to deal with. Theory was essentially concerned with the untoward consequences of a small class of events. It gave relatively little attention to the rest of human existence.

But once Freud made the leap of construing his patients' reports not as accounts of actual events, but rather as hazy and somewhat altered glimpses at the wishes and fantasies of their childhood, the situation was drastically altered. His new theory suggested that the vantage point offered him from behind the psychoanalytic couch provided a view of a universal dilemma confronting the developing human being. The actual occurrence of childhood seductions could not be postulated as part of the history of every person, but the need to deal with the intense feelings and longings developed in the crucible of the family could be and was. Once his patients' reports were conceptualized by Freud as fantasies, his patients could be viewed not as unfortunates who had had experiences that set them apart from the rest of us, but as individuals whose efforts to resolve common human problems were particularly unproductive.

## THE PERSISTENCE OF EARLIER VIEWS

If Freud's reconceptualization of his patient's reports represents a crucial turning point in the development of psychoanalytic thought, it is nonetheless the case that the earlier view had a fateful effect on Freudian thinking which has never been completely altered. That is, the search for rejected memories gave a distinctly historical cast to psychoanalytic thought. By definition, memories refer to something previous rather than to what is currently going on. The patient's current life situation and the way he or she is living life right now appear largely as irrelevancies from the viewpoint of a theory of the pathogenic effect of unassimilated memories. Even more so is this the case when the theory stresses *childhood* memories. From such a perspective, adult personality and life style appear to be the inevitable results of something that happened years ago and are of interest, if at all, only as signs of what must have happened at the time things *really* mattered. To alter the patient's difficulties in any lasting and extensive way would seem to require an uncovering of the residue of the past. To attempt to intervene at the level of current functioning and current influences would appear futile.*

This emphasis on the past was reduced hardly at all by Freud's reconceptualization of his patient's reports as fantasies instead of veridical memories. They were still seen as *childhood* fantasies, and were understood as persisting because of conditions present at the earlier time rather than because of anything currently happening. It is readily understandable that such should be the case. For one thing, there was a historical dimension to the order of events recalled by Freud's patients and to the kind of revelation that had a potent therapeutic effect. That is, his patients spent relatively little time thinking about their childhoods early in the analysis, whereas increasingly more aspects of their childhoods occurred to them as the treatment proceeded. Further, the tendency for symptoms to disappear, and for their disappearance to be more than momentary, seemed to be correlated with the increased attention to the patients' childhoods. It thus appeared that "earlier was deeper" (in the sense of requiring more active and extended digging to become apparent), and that access to earlier experiences was a crucial factor in therapeutic success.

---

* This was less true in considering those difficulties Freud classified as "actual neuroses," in which current sexual practices could be crucial. But it was decidedly the case with his view of the "psychoneuroses," which were of greater interest to Freud and were far more the model upon which his general theory rested.

A second factor important in the persistence of the idea of the past in psychoanalysis was the lack of success when working in terms of the present. Early in the development of Freud's work, efforts were made to bring about change by concentrating on what was currently going on; but suggestion, advice, cajoling, and appeals to will power all seemed to provide only temporary change at best.*

Finally, the continuation of the old way of thinking may be understood in terms of the conservative nature of theory-building. In any scientific endeavor, one can expect changes in basic theory only when they appear absolutely necessary. One might expect this to be even more the case in as intensely personal a science as psychoanalysis—personal both in the sense of dealing with a uniquely affect-laden and value-relevant subject matter, and in the sense of being to an unprecedented degree the creation of just one man.

## LATER DEVELOPMENTS

For a while, psychoanalytic thought focused almost exclusively on detailing the contents and transformations of secret fantasies and on the sequence of childhood desires that were thought to be biologically given. Reactions to actual events and situations in a person's life were given scant attention, except as they were considered exacerbating factors in arousing predetermined desires too early or too intensely, or in frustrating such desires excessively. The enormous amount of adaptive learning going on throughout life that was not readily conceived of as simply arousing or frustrating drives was of little interest. As Rapaport (1960) put it, "The theory of instinctual drives . . . preoccupied [Freud] for a long time at the expense of all his other empirical discoveries and conceptual inventions. And when he turned his attention to other discoveries and conceptual inventions, psychoanalysts and others found it hard to give up this old exclusive preoccupation which they had come to share with him." (pp. 176–7)

According to Rapaport, this excessive concern is no longer characteristic of more sophisticated Freudian thinkers familiar with develop-

---

* The techniques of behavior therapy are thought by some analysts to be no more than the superficial manipulative efforts that Freud tried and found lacking. When these are examined more closely in later chapters, it should become clear how they differ from the methods Freud tried and why they are likely to prove of value in a way that these early attempts did not.

ments in ego psychology. Rapaport claims that the theoretical developments put forth by Hartmann and by Erikson permitted an integration of knowledge about adaptation, learning, and social interaction with earlier psychoanalytic propositions about instinctual vicissitudes and infantile fantasies. He further claims that developments in the interpersonal and "culturalist" approaches to psychoanalytic thought by writers such as Horney and Sullivan fail because they do not achieve such an integration but instead reject earlier insights.

Arlow and Brenner (1964) also see the development of ego psychology as providing momentous new possibilities for psychoanalytic thought. The authors spell out in some detail the implications for clinical practice of the "structural theory" first outlined in *The Ego and the Id* in 1923. In their discussion they point to a number of significant—and progressive—changes in psychoanalytic understanding and technique that follow from the developments in psychoanalytic ego psychology. Among these are: appreciation of defenses as unacknowledged *activities* of the individual, which are important to examine in detail; recognition of the specific and partial nature of regressions and of the pathological involvement of adaptive functions in conflict; and understanding of the way in which the regressive phenomena of psychosis can serve to defend against anxiety.

It is noteworthy, however, that Arlow and Brenner, despite their emphasis on the new perspectives provided by the structural theory, nonetheless retain a major feature of psychoanalytic thought which, as we have seen, has its origins in the very earliest period of psychoanalytic inquiry and conceptualization: the emphasis on understanding by means of a search of the person's past. The route is more indirect now, involving a detailed analysis of resistances instead of a direct push to remember in spite of them. The content sought now is wishes and fantasies, rather than memories of actual traumas. But as in the neurotica, the patient is still essentially conceived of as suffering because something from his or her past continues to press disturbingly for recognition, despite the patient's efforts to continue as though it weren't there.

In the next two chapters we shall critically examine the emphasis on the past in psychoanalytic thought. The aim of this criticism is not simply to purge our thinking of earlier ways of viewing things. To be sure, I do regard the current psychoanalytic view of the past as being a remnant of the early efforts at theory-making described in this chapter, and I believe that our newer understanding of what Freud really was observing when his early patients told him what "happened" to them requires a different conceptual strategy. But in addition, I believe it is essential to take into account and make use of important developments in therapeutic practice that derive from nonpsychoanalytic sources. It is my contention that the sharp separation of psychodynamic viewpoints and behavioral viewpoints in particular has hampered the development of both approaches and prevented the emergence of a maximally effective integrated psychotherapeutic approach.° As I shall try to show in the next chapter, the persistence of an old emphasis on the past is one of the major obstacles to such an integration.

---

° The integration of developments in group and family therapy with contemporary psychoanalysis—an important and worthwhile task in its own right—also requires a reconsideration of the psychoanalytic view of the past.

# 3

# The Historical

# and the Intrapsychic

 

 

$\mathbb{T}$HE Freudian view of the role of
the past in present psychological functioning presents a major obstacle to
any effort to integrate psychoanalytic and behavioral approaches. The
judgment of many analysts that the inclusion of behavioral methods in
their therapeutic repertoire would make the therapy more superficial is
based in large measure upon their understanding of how past experiences and modes of psychological functioning influence current experiences and behavior.* We will therefore begin our examination of the
possibilities of integration with a consideration of the historical dimension
in psychoanalytic thought. We will then look at how this aspect of psychoanalytic theory has led analysts to reject a wide range of therapeutic
interventions that, in the present view, may be of considerable potential
value for their patients.

Psychoanalysis is not unique in its emphasis on the importance of childhood and in its effort to understand a person's feeling and behavior in

---

\* This is of course not the only basis for the skepticism of psychodynamic thinkers
toward the value of behavioral approaches. Also very important are the emphasis on
insight and understanding in producing meaningful change, and a variety of related
conceptual and ethical issues. These will be considered in later chapters.

terms of that person's life history. A wide range of psychological theories would suggest that early experiences are likely to establish lifelong patterns unless certain unusual subsequent events occur. The precise way in which psychoanalysis treats the historical perspective in psychological inquiry is, however, quite distinctive, and controversial as well, especially in its explanation of the uniquely powerful influence of childhood experiences. There are many ways of understanding the continuities between early behaviors and experiences and those of later life, and many ways of conceiving of the seeming inappropriateness of much of day-to-day adult behavior to current realities. What is particularly characteristic of the psychoanalytic approach to these problems is its postulation of the persisting influence of certain childhood wishes and fears *despite later experiences that might be expected to alter them.* Repression, in the psychoanalytic view, does not merely prevent the individual from being aware of what is being repressed; it also prevents the repressed desire or fantasy from "growing up," from changing in the course of development as do unrepressed desires or fantasies.

The analyst readily acknowledges that the child's conscious, unrepressed strivings may be altered or redirected as his values change and his conception of morality matures. New information and the dictates of logic often lead us to alter conscious choices and to give up efforts to achieve goals once highly prized. However, those motives that do not appear to be represented in consciousness seem far less responsive to the modifying influences of rational thought and contradictory information. The fantasies and yearnings for the mother that often become apparent in the course of the psychoanalytic treatment of adult males seem appropriate for a naive four-year-old, whose most important gratifications primarily depend on mother, who has little experience with other women that would temper his queenly image of her, and who has hardly begun to develop the adult's complex view of people as having mixed strengths and weaknesses, beauties and warts. Though he consciously knows that she is now a middle-aged woman who is probably far less attractive than most women he meets, though he can readily report that she is often a tiresome nag and that he doubts she has given his father a good time in bed, though he knows that many others could gratify him far more than she could, he shows unacknowledged signs of longing for her with the same fervor he did when she was all the world to him, the holy center of his child's universe. His desire seems unmodified by his conscious perception and understanding of the realities of his life and the limited possibilities for gratification with his mother.

## THE NOTION OF DISSOCIATED SYSTEMS

Freud's attempt to account for the persistence of such seemingly anomalous desires relied heavily on a conception of dissociation or disruption of integration in psychological functioning, as explained below. The apparent unmodifiability of certain aspects of our psychological life (in particular those aspects that were unconscious), in contrast with the responsiveness of much of our psychological functioning to changing circumstances, prompted Freud to build his model of mental functioning around an image of separate psychological systems, often influencing our experience and behavior in conflicting ways and thereby introducing disharmony into our efforts to find gratification and safety in the world.

In his earliest writings, when he was still concerned primarily with unconscious memories rather than wishes or fantasies, Freud (along with Breuer) indicated that repressing the memory of a traumatic event not only kept it out of awareness but also prevented its interaction with the person's other ideas and memories. By remaining encapsulated and unintegrated with the rest of the person's mental functioning, it did not participate in the processes whereby memories of emotionally arousing events typically lost their original affective intensity. Unrepressed memories underwent a wearing-away of the associated affect through such "discharge" paths as crying, laughing, moving about, and taking action, as well as thinking things through.* The last-named served to discharge the affect associated with an idea both by relieving the push to think about it and by modifying its implications through comparison, putting things into perspective, and so on. Repressed memories, on the other hand, by not undergoing such processes, remained fresh, retaining in an unmodified way their original significance and intensity. The unconscious memories were viewed as "timeless," in contrast to memories of unrepressed events, which gradually lost their preoccupying significance as new events took center stage in the person's continuing life history.

Freud's description of the persisting influence of the past is reminiscent of the tales of woolly mammoths found frozen in the Arctic ice, so perfectly preserved after thousands of years that their meat could be eaten by anyone with a taste for such regressive fare. Freud was extremely im-

---

* We need not concern ourselves here with the thermodynamic model implied by such terms as "discharge." Freud's tendency to utilize a concept of psychological energy has been critically examined on a number of occasions and found to be less intimately related to the structure of psychoanalytic thought than had previously been supposed. (See Holt, 1965, 1967; Klein, 1967; Loevinger, 1966; Schafer, 1972, 1973; Wachtel, 1969.)

pressed with the "freshness" and vividness of the memories revealed after digging through layers of resistance. Their lack of access to the usual associative pathways was seen as preserving them.

Some observations from other quarters tend to support the view that memories can somehow be stored in ways that lie dormant for years and then are extraordinarily powerful and vivid when they see the light of day. Penfield, for example, has reported that patients described memories of almost hallucinatory vividness when certain regions of the brain were stimulated during surgery (Penfield and Roberts, 1959). Although his emphasis on localization of function has been questioned, and though many modern accounts of memory stress reconstruction rather than storage of exact copies of past experiences, observations of this sort do seem convergent with the kind of observation that so impressed Freud.

In a somewhat different vein, a friend and colleague of mine scared the wits out of her husband and several nurses when, on recovering from anesthesia following the delivery of her child, she began to speak in gibberish while appearing to believe she was communicating. Fortunately a resident was around who happened to speak Hungarian and who readily identified the sounds she was making as decent, if somewhat simple, Hungarian sentences. She had been born in Hungary and spoke Hungarian for the first few years of her life, but came very early to the United States and as an adult spoke unaccented English and knew no Hungarian. Upon fully recovering from the anesthesia she proceeded to communicate in excellent English again, and to this day remains, in everyday life, blissfully ignorant of how one would ask the time of day in Budapest.

Such examples suggest that whatever the exact means of storage and the exact process of recall, there are ways in which some record of past experiences can be stored for long periods of time without being subject to the kinds of wearing away or fusing of memory traces that so distress students at exam time and interest experimental investigators of memory. The bearing of such observations upon the Freudian view of the "timeless unconscious," however, is far from clear. Even at this early point in Freud's theorizing, when he thought his patients suffered from memories of actual events, the memories he was referring to were far from dormant. To push our metaphor a bit further, the woolly mammoths Freud saw frozen in the paleolithic layers of the psyche were trumpeting loudly enough to wake the dead, and they certainly disturbed the sleep of the living. The memories were not accessible to consciousness, in Freud's view, but they were very active indeed. A continuous effort was thought to be needed to keep them from becoming conscious.

## REPRESSION AND UNINTEGRATED
## SEXUAL DEVELOPMENT

Freud's theoretical emphasis eventually shifted away from concern with repressed memories of real events and toward repressed fantasies associated with unacceptable wishes and urges. The theoretical account of how the unconscious remained "timeless" was thereby changed and elaborated. However, the emphasis on repression as preventing integration as well as consciousness remained. In the *Three Essays on the Theory of Sexuality* (1905), Freud presented a picture of the development of the sexual drive in which he postulated that, early in life, a number of separate longings and urges developed which under ideal circumstances were integrated into a unitary genital urge at puberty. Thus Freud saw the complex nature of adult sexuality (in which full sexual activity and pleasure included oral and anal aspects as well as the involvement of the genitals, and in which sadistic, masochistic, exhibitionistic, and voyeuristic activities and pleasures were also readily apparent) as the integration of a variety of relatively separate motivational tendencies apparent in the child.

The successful integration of these "component instincts" was seen by Freud as interfered with by repression. When a component drive was repressed, it was separated from the rest of the course of development. It persisted unconsciously in isolation while the rest of the instinctual life continued to be gradually shaped and molded by processes of development and by the increasing influence of reality-experiences upon the nature of desires and the people, times, and places toward which such desires were directed. Thus, as Freud saw it, while the rest of our desires were "growing up," those that were repressed—and thereby prevented from being integrated with the rest of the personality—remained active in their original primitive form.

## DISSOCIATED SYSTEMS AND EGO PSYCHOLOGY

The close relation in Freud's thought between repression, the persistence of past psychological tendencies in unmodified form, and the conception of separate psychological systems is particularly evident after 1923. In that year Freud published *The Ego and the Id*, in which his theorizing was recast in what has come to be called the "structural theory." In that work he distinguished between "the coherent ego and the repressed which is split off from it." This latter aspect of our psychological functioning Freud designated as the id.*

Freud's conceptualization of these separate systems or structures was not intended by him as a formal theory. In the preface to *The Ego and the Id* he stated quite clearly that what he was presenting there "[did] not go beyond the roughest outline." It is important to recognize this, because current references to the "ego" in psychoanalytic works often treat this term not as an initial conceptual groping toward understanding of the organization and structure of psychological processes but, rather, as an entity given by nature. Questions are directed toward what the ego is like rather than whether it is useful to conceive of an ego.

Such tendencies in psychoanalytic writing obscure the issues Freud was attempting to grapple with. The "ego" for Freud, when he was at his clearest and most consistent, was not an actual entity whose properties were to be studied. It was a tentative conceptual effort to bring together several theoretical issues that Freud sensed might be related. Implicit in Freud's writings one can see several definitions of the ego rather than one. These were not conflicting or incompatible definitions but, rather, foci or nuclei—vantage points from which the organization of psychological processes could be glimpsed. We must briefly examine these differing approaches to the ego concept in order to see clearly in what way Freud's use of this concept is relevant to our understanding of the psychoanalytic approach to the past, and what alternative approaches are available to us.

## ASPECTS OF THE EGO CONCEPT

The ego was designated by Freud as that part of the mind which was coherent and organized. "[The] ego is an organization and the id is not. The ego is, indeed, the organized portion of the id." (Freud, 1926, p. 97) In referring to an organized entity, Freud was trying to come to terms with the fact that successful adaptation requires a coordinated effort in which various psychological processes must function together as a unified

---

* The id is not, however, strictly coterminous with the repressed (see Gill, 1963; Schur, 1966).

system (much as synthesis and organization are characteristic of, and perhaps even define, life processes in general).

Though we may separately conceptualize such processes as motivation, perception, memory, and so on for purposes of study and discussion, our survival depends upon these various aspects of our ongoing adaptational activity functioning together, as a system. When we are hungry, we must remember where to look for food, we must see the food in front of us, we must bring the food to our mouths, and so on. If processes of motivation, memory, perception, and motor learning were not coordinated, this could not happen. We would be no more likely to search for food when our bellies were empty than when they were full. We would be no more likely to initiate movements toward the food we see than toward any other object in our visual field. We would, in short, simply not function in a way that would enable us to survive.

The property of organization or coordination in psychological functioning, then, was represented in Freud's theorizing by conceptualizing an organized *system*, the ego. From this perspective, the id is defined by its separateness from this organization. Psychological processes conceived of as part of the id are not coordinated with the adaptational activities of the "ego" system. Fuller elaboration of what this means requires us to consider a second focus of Freud's conceptualization of the ego.

The ego was described by Freud as that mental system which *starts out from perception,* or as he put it at another point, "that part of the id which has been modified by the direct influence of the external world." °
He goes on to say that "[for] the ego, perception plays the part which in the id falls to instinct."

From this perspective, the ego is conceived as a system of psychological processes whose functioning is responsive to environmental events. That is, what happens "out there," at least as it is represented by our perceptual activity, has a considerable influence on just what thoughts are thought, what desires are aroused, what desires are acted upon, and so on, *if those thoughts, desires, or other psychological processes or events are part of the ego system.*† Fantasies or wishes that are part of the id, however, and therefore by definition are not participating in the coordination and organization of the ego system, are *not* conceived as influ-

---

° This way of putting it implies that initially there was just id—that is, that all of the psychological processes that constitute the ego are modifications of original primitive instincts. Increased recognition of the problems with such a formulation led to Hartmann, Kris, and Lowenstein's (1946) postulation of an original undifferentiated ego-id.

† The activities of the ego are, of course, in the psychoanalytic view, responsive to influences other than environmental events as well, such as the arousal of id desires and prohibitions of the superego.

enced by what we perceive of real external events. In other words, they are not subject to reality testing. As conceived by Freud, these wishes and fantasies persist (unconsciously) despite being grossly unrealistic.°

They also are conceived as persisting despite being quite at odds with other important goals or ideas of the person. To mix theoretical metaphors, one might say that cognitive dissonance theory holds only in the ego. The ego, as an organized psychological system, is subject to the constraints of logic. Holding inconsistent ideas or wanting incompatible things creates a strain, and leads to alterations of one or another part of the system. But as Freud conceives it, id wishes or fantasies are not similarly organized. Incompatible wishes and ideas considerably at odds with other things we know persist without modification if they are not part of the ego system.

Still another perspective on what Freud was getting at in his conception of the ego as a system and the id as separate from it is provided by attending to the names Freud gave to these constructs. The latinate terms "ego" and "id" obscure the phenomenological implications of the original names, *das Ich* (the "I") and *das Es* (the "it"). Thinking of *das Ich* as the I instead of as the ego highlights the view of the ego as an organization of psychological processes including, and strongly infused with, the feeling of self.

This is not to say that all psychological processes conceived as part of the ego system are experienced as part of the self, or acknowledged as what "I" am doing. On the contrary, the very observations that were most prominent in Freud's decision to recast his theory in terms of ego, id, and superego involve "ego processes" not experienced as self. The activities referred to by psychoanalysts as defense mechanisms are conceived of as part of the ego system, yet they are often not acknowledged by the patient as something he or she is doing. A tendency to try very hard to be nice when unacceptable hostile urges are stirred, or to become preoccupied with an irrelevant intellectual issue when a strange and disturbing feeling is aroused is not likely to be part of the self-image of the person who exhibits such a tendency.

Yet the intimate conceptual link between the ego system and the experience of self is readily apparent in Freud's writings in more ways than his assigning the name *das Ich*. For example, he stated that the ego is "first and foremost a body ego" (Freud, 1923, p. 27), pointing to the

---

° Id fantasies or wishes are not *completely* unresponsive to environmental events. They may, for example, be stirred or triggered by such events. But, in the Freudian view, they are not permanently *changed* by current happenings, no matter how inconsistent with current perceptual input they may be (see Chapter 4, pp. 42–43).

young infant's explorations of its own body as the beginning sense of self that is very much at the core of the developing organization of the ego.

Additionally, the action of the ego as the system from which the defenses emanate points to the ego as a system closely linked to self-feeling. From the earliest period of psychoanalysis, Freud was attuned to efforts of individuals to cast out from their experience that which did not fit with their sense of who they are or want to be. The ego system is by no means synonymous with the sense of self, which is but one aspect or portion of the ego construct; but the sense of self is nonetheless a very crucial feature distinguishing the ego as a system from the id, which is excluded from it.

## FURTHER IMPLICATIONS OF THE
## STRUCTURAL MODEL

In Freud's later formulations, then, those tendencies that are defended against are not merely kept unconscious. They are also dissociated from the coordinated system of processes maintaining the individual's adaptation, rendering them relatively unresponsive to new environmental input and not able to be experienced with a quality of self-feeling.° In fact, from the perspective of the structural theory, it became increasingly apparent that certain ideas and strivings that were at least somewhat in awareness might still be best conceptualized as belonging to the id, and as having problematic consequences quite comparable to those of some more fully unconscious strivings.

Repression from awareness was seen more clearly as but one kind of defensive activity directed toward threatening ideas and inclinations. Individuals relying on isolation and intellectualization as defenses, for example, are often able to verbally report desires or fantasies which other individuals are not able to verbalize at all. These verbal reports, however, tend to be affectless, not integrated with other mental processes in the same way as tendencies not defended against. The intellectualizing individual may tell us, for example, that he knows that a particular wish or

---

° It is necessary to recognize that the theory does not postulate *absolute* separation between the systems. Freud notes, in commenting on a figure he devised to represent this theoretical model, that "the ego is not sharply separated from the id; its lower portions merge into it." Without *some* communication between systems, one would have no way of accounting for the ability of repressed drives to influence behavior and create disturbance.

fantasy he is reporting is illogical or at odds with what he knows is in his best interests. Yet it is also clear that knowing it is illogical in no way changes his ideas in this case. The logic that is a modifying or regulating influence coordinating most of his ideas seems to bounce off this particular one, as if it were not part of the regulated system of thought.

Further, the idea defended against by isolation or intellectualization, while sometimes able to be in awareness, is nonetheless not experienced with a sense of it being part of the self. It is often experienced as a kind of inference, as something observed from outside rather than felt from within. ("It looks like I must be wanting . . . ," "I guess that means I'm trying to . . . ," "I seem to be feeling . . ." rather than "I want . . ." or "I feel . . .") Thus the idea remains "it" (Es) rather than "I" (Ich).

Just such observations led Freud to change his description of the aim of the psychoanalytic process from "making the unconscious conscious" to "where id was, let ego be." It is not enough that an idea be conscious. As we saw above, an idea can be conscious, at least to some extent, and still functionally be part of the id.* That is, it can still be excluded from the modifying influences regulating those processes that are part of the organized adaptational system Freud called the ego. Such apparently conscious yet defended-against ideas have psychological implications for adaptation similar to those ideas that in Freud's older theory were part of "the unconscious." They are peremptory and unrealistic because they don't change over time in response to new environmental input and are not modified by being put into perspective in the way ideas more familiar to us in our day-to-day living frequently are. Whether they become conscious is thus less important than whether they become part of the ego, that is, whether they are tamed by being integrated into a coordinated adaptational effort.

## PSYCHOTHERAPEUTIC IMPLICATIONS

This ego psychological model is certainly far more sophisticated than the model of dissociated memories in Freud's earliest psychoanalytic writings. It opened psychoanalytic concern to an enormously widened range of

---

* The question of what is "conscious" is not a simple one. Horney (1939), for example, talks of unconscious tendencies when a person is aware of some trend in his behavior but not of its pervasiveness or full implications for his functioning. Also, the distinction between "intellectual" and "emotional" awareness is a common though not very clear one in the psychoanalytic literature (see Chapter 6).

phenomena. But in many respects, it remains just a more sophisticated version of the "woolly mammoth" model.

This is particularly so with respect to the therapeutic technique of psychoanalysis. The large body of research on perception, cognitive styles, and adaptational strategies that has been undertaken in the name of psychoanalytic ego psychology has had little impact on the theory of neurosis and even less on psychoanalytic technique. Analysts do pay far more attention now to the details of how the patient keeps some of his inclinations dissociated (that is, to the actual processes and activities of defense), and they are concerned with assessing how the patient's problems are exacerbated by defects in ego functioning such as faulty thinking, faulty reality testing, faulty impulse control, and so on. But the crux of the neurotic's problems is still thought to be the split in psychological functioning caused by his defending against childhood inclinations (and therefore the persistence of unintegrated remnants of childhood that are impervious to the effect of new life experiences).

The continuity between modern formulations and the original view of the preservation of memories is especially clear in a passage from Stone (1961), which is particularly significant in that Stone's volume represents one of the major attempts within the classical psychoanalytic tradition to modernize the role of the therapist. Stone writes that "true transference . . . retains unmistakably its infantile character. However much the given early relationship may have contributed to the genuinely adult pattern of relationships (via identification, limitation, acceptance of teaching, for example), its transference derivative differs from the latter, *approximately in the sense which Breuer and Freud (1895) assigned to the sequelae of the pathogenic traumatic experience, which was neither abreacted as such, nor associatively absorbed in the personality.*" (p. 67; italics added)

The implications for therapy of this view of the intrapsychic preservation of the past are considerable. The patient's neurosis is seen as deriving most essentially from his continuing and unsuccessful efforts to deal with internalized residues of his past which, by virtue of being isolated from his adaptive and integrative ego, continue to make primitive demands wholly unresponsive to reality. It is therefore maintained that a fully successful treatment must create conditions whereby these anachronistic inclinations can be experienced consciously and integrated into the ego, so that they can be controlled and modified. The vehicle for such an effort is the "transference neurosis," a shifting of the patient's neurotic preoccupations toward the person of the analyst. The transference neurosis, in its intensity and inappropriateness, reveals and highlights the infantile origins of the patient's concerns. In his authoritative text on psychoanalytic technique, Greenson (1967) states that the transference neurosis "offers the patient the most important instrumentality for gaining access to the warded-off *past pathogenic experiences*. The *reliving of the repressed past* with the analyst and in the analytic situation is the most effective opportunity for overcoming the neurotic defenses and resistances. Thus the psychoanalyst will take pains to safeguard the transference situation and prevent any contamination which might curtail its full flowering. . . . All intrusions of the analyst's personal characteristics and values will be recognized as factors which might limit the scope of the patient's transference neurosis. Interpretation is the only method of dealing with the transference that will permit it to run its entire course." (p. 189–90; italics added)

Greenson, like Stone, does indicate that the analyst need not—indeed should not—be cold, aloof, and utterly unresponsive. Stone recommends a "physicianly commitment" on the part of the analyst to understand and help the patient, and Greenson devotes considerable space to describing how to facilitate a "working alliance" with the patient that enables the patient to cooperate in the difficult and frustrating task of being analyzed.

But though their positions modify some of the harsher interpretations of Freud's recommendation that the analyst be a "mirror" or a "blank screen," both Greenson and Stone recommend that this softening be undertaken only to the minimum degree necessary to enlist the patient's cooperation. Both books are replete with warnings about the limitations in therapeutic change that accompany any therapist activity that might distort or restrict the transference neurosis. Greenson states, for example, that "a mode of behavior or attitude on the part of the analyst other than that of consistent, humane nonintrusiveness obscures and distorts the development and recognition of transference phenomena" (p. 272), and adds elsewhere that "[e]very *deviant* school of psychoanalysis can be described by some *aberration* in the way the transference situation is handled." (p. 151; italics added)

The decision by an analyst to seek to evoke a transference neurosis and to eschew the wide range of therapeutic intervention thought to limit the transference neurosis, means the patient will experience a good deal of pain. For one thing, the transference neurosis itself can be a painful thing. Violent emotions, of an intensity more characteristic of children than of adults, appear, often incomprehensibly.* Further, it is generally agreed

---

* The classical idea that the transference neurosis *replaces* the presenting neurotic problems suggests that the sum total of suffering in this regard might not increase. Greenson notes, however, that the patient's neurosis outside of the analytic situation

that the transference neurosis cannot develop properly without a good deal of frustration. Additionally, the need for the analyst to remain as anonymous as possible (in order to be able to demonstrate to the patient that his reactions to the analyst are displaced from the past) requires that the analyst do little to actively intervene in the patient's life, other than through interpretation. Thus many interventions that could bring immediate relief for particular current distresses are eschewed. Finally, the strategy whereby change is intended to be brought about through the evocation and resolution of a transference neurosis includes a recognition that such a process requires years to be completed.

These privations are regarded as the course of choice, however, in cases in which the patient can stand them, because they are thought by analysts to lead to change that is far more extensive and more lasting than in any other kind of treatment. Such an evaluation follows rather directly from the view that the effective cause of the patient's current neurosis is *tendencies within the patient that were locked in, in the past, and that continue to exert a pressure unchanging in quality and intensity and unresponsive to anything happening in his current day-to-day living.*

If this view is correct, the most effective treatment would necessarily be one that enables the locked-in tendencies to be released so that they may be integrated with the rest of the personality and become subject to the limits of logic and reality, as are the patient's more mature inclinations. The classical psychoanalytic situation does seem to be a method *par excellence* for ultimately promoting the appearance of fantasies and strivings that are not directly expressible in any other way.

Within the classical framework, the only alternative to slowly and painfully uncovering the past within is to help the person to bury it more effectively and merely gain a respite from its disturbing pressures. Such a course of action may at times provide considerable relief to suffering individuals, and often in much less time and with far less suffering. In the view of most analysts, however, there is a substantial price paid for this less demanding treatment. For one thing, by helping the patient better ward off the past, rather than integrating it into his present personality, the patient continues to commit a substantial portion of his psychic resources to defensive activity, resources which in our complex era are sorely needed for the business of living. Attention paid to keeping oneself

---

often "merely pales and becomes relatively insignificant compared to the transference neurosis—only to reappear in the patient's outside life when another constellation dominates the transference picture." (p. 188) Elsewhere, he comments that "psychoanalytic treatment is a time-consuming, long-range, costly therapy that is by its very nature frequently painful." (p. 53)

in check cannot be paid to other matters, and some limitation in the richness or effectiveness of the patient's living can be expected.

From another perspective, it is pointed out that the comfort achieved by such "supportive" measures is achieved by again cutting oneself off from sources of pleasure and creativity that are part of our natural heritage. The infantile strivings are feared largely because they originally occurred at a time when the patient was both more dependent on powerful others and less able to control his impulses and to discriminate appropriate from inappropriate opportunities. If accepted and integrated into the adult personality, these inclinations, instead of being a threat, could be modified and expressed in a more mature form. The way would thus be opened to greater creativity and richness in living, rather than permanently barring such pleasures from the person's life.

Finally, therapeutic measures that do not uncover and resolve underlying conflicts are thought to produce change that is precarious. There is a potential for new disorders if anything disturbs the still-fragile equilibrium. Since the patient's adaptive capacities are already strained by the need to continually devote some energy to defense, the patient treated non-analytically is especially vulnerable to the occurrence of illness, loss of job, change in an important relationship, and so on.

The reader at this point is likely to point out that there is a wide range of psychoanalytically inspired therapies between the poles of classical analysis and strictly supportive therapy. But from the classical framework these therapies appear best understood as being varying mixes of the two elements of uncovering and support (the latter including such means as suggestion, encouragement, strengthening defensive efforts, advice by the therapist, manipulation of environmental circumstances, and so on).* If one examines, for example, the reactions of the psychoanalytic community to the efforts by Alexander and French (1946) to modify psychoanalytic technique, the most common criticism turns out to be that Alexander and French, although attempting an uncovering therapy, did not let the transference neurosis develop to the full extent. Modifications that (from the perspective to be discussed shortly) could be viewed as facilitating change and enhancing the effectiveness of psychoanalytically inspired efforts, appear from the classical Freudian perspective to be compromises, useful with many patients but never capable of yielding as deep or extensive change as classical analysis, if the

---

* Bibring (1954), in an influential paper, has suggested a somewhat more complex categorization, in which suggestive, abreactive, manipulative, clarifying, and interpretive techniques are distinguished.

patient is "analyzable." (Cf. Bibring, 1954; Eissler, 1956, 1958; Gill, 1954; Greenacre, 1954; Rangell, 1954.)

It is clear that from the classical Freudian frame of reference, the introduction of behavioral methods would appear particularly limiting. However effective they might be in bringing about change in important specific patterns of behavior and interaction, such methods would seem to ultimately limit the depth and extensiveness of change. They would limit the frustration that is essential to evoking a full transference neurosis (see especially Menninger, 1958) and would also substantially reduce the therapist's anonymity, which is seen as essential in both evoking and resolving the transference neurosis. The possibility that such methods could enable the process of change to be faster and less painful, and might even *increase* the depth of change, would from this framework appear a hopeless illusion.

There is another way of looking at the observations that analysts have made, however, one that does not provide such a discouraging picture of the possibilities of a breakthrough in therapeutic effectiveness or of the value of utilizing newer methods of intervention. The next chapter will consider such an alternative framework. It will argue both that this framework is capable of dealing with the full range of observations Freudian analysts have drawn on as the basis for their point of view, and that from the perspective of this alternate framework a far wider range of therapeutic activities may be considered without raising the specter of superficiality, incompleteness, or leaving something rotten still inside.

# 4

# *An Interpersonal*
# *Alternative*

$O$UR concern in the present chapter is with whether it is possible to account for the seemingly child-like quality of the fantasy life and secret strivings of neurotic patients without assuming that these are locked-in remnants of the past, which can be changed only by gradually uncovering layer after layer of intra-psychic structure. Putting it another way, we may ask: can the presence of these inclinations in the patient be accounted for by the way he or she is currently living, and might these manifestations change if the way of living changed?

The alternative presented below draws heavily on the formulations of Horney, Sullivan, and Erikson, but it departs from their views in impor-tant ways. Probably the most important departure is my conclusion that an understanding of the role of interpersonal events in perpetuating neurosis implies a need for more active intervention by the therapist in order for neurotic patterns to change. The path from interpersonally oriented psychodynamic theorizing to the interventions developed by behavior therapists is not a well-trod one. The reader is likely to want to examine carefully the reasoning that has led me along this unusual route.

## WISHES AS INDEPENDENT AND
## DEPENDENT VARIABLES

From the traditional psychoanalytic focus, an unconscious desire or fantasy is examined primarily as an independent variable—as something which, when present, has effects which are to be understood. But desires and fantasies can also meaningfully be studied as dependent variables— as being themselves effects. One of the valuable contributions of the interpersonal approach to psychoanalysis, and of some existential writers as well, has been to emphasize that we always live *in situations,* that our perceptions, our feelings, and our behavior are in response *to* something. Rather than globally describing someone as an angry person, or as often struggling with hostile impulses, it is useful to ask *when* hostile impulses are aroused or *when* a conflict is evoked.

One does see a concern for the circumstances that evokes an impulse among modern Freudian writers as well. Silverman ( 1972 ), for example, examines in fascinating detail the particular evoking conditions arousing forbidden wishes. In one clinical example, he discusses a symptom in a childless and unmarried woman. She could readily identify the point of onset of the symptom: she had been reading an article when it began. The content of the article seemed to bear no relationship at all to her conflicts or symptom. In the course of her analytic session, it occurred to her that the author of the article was named *Rothschild,* and that she had recently received a *birth announcement* from an old friend toward whom she had always experienced considerable jealousy and rivalry. The friend's married name was Roth and it seemed to both patient and analyst that the author's name, *Rothschild,* had, without her awareness, stirred up her hostile and jealous thoughts about the new *child of Roth.* Interestingly, when she first received the birth announcement, and consciously experienced jealousy of her rival and wish for her own child, no symptom occurred. Silverman suggests that the symptom was a consequence of such thoughts and feelings being aroused without her being aware of them.

Considerations of this sort by psychoanalysts reflect the growing concern in psychoanalytic ego psychology with the role of actual life events in influencing the clinical phenomena observed. But it is important to notice that even in this very modern example, the role of environmental events is to evoke something lying in wait to be released. Although broad theoretical statements by analysts may acknowledge a wide range of ways in which the actual events in the patient's world may be influential, in the concrete clinical examples in the literature one finds rather generally that when external reality is considered, it is primarily viewed as a source of triggers able to activate different parts of the already formed structure that is the personality.° One sees little emphasis on how that structure is perpetuated by the person's own actions and their consequences. The structure is more or less given. The assumption that an understanding of the major features of the personality must be sought in childhood rather than in the person's current life situation seems to have inhibited inquiry into self-perpetuating processes that are a continuing part of the person's personality.

If one does look closely from a somewhat different perspective, it is usually possible to see how the desires and conflicts which may dominate a person's life can be understood as *following from*, as well as causing, the way he or she lives that life. Consider, for example, the patient who seems compulsively to go out of his way to be active, independent, and responsible for others. Often such individuals are found to long unconsciously for dependent gratification, and to fear the extent of their passive yearnings. We need not, however, assume that the conscious attitudes are simply a defense against desires from the past. We may valuably examine how this very pattern of compulsive activity and responsibility *creates* the so-called oral needs: by constantly taking on excessive burdens and simultaneously denying himself almost any opportunity to manifest normal dependence, such a person is kept continually yearning for dependence to an unusual degree (as he also continues to pursue an excessively independent way of life because, in large part, of the frightening strength of these continually created longings). By de-emphasizing the longing as a simple perpetuation of the past, we may see how it is brought about in the present, both by the patient's own behavior and by the behavior he evokes in others.

Similarly, consider the patient whose excessive niceness and gentleness is seen as defending against extreme rage and vengeful desires. If, in the traditional fashion, we look back into his history, we may well seem to find sufficient justification and understanding of his situation from that direction. We may uncover in his history the presence of violent death wishes toward a parent, which he desperately attempted to cover

° Schafer (1972), in an important paper, has criticized the use by psychoanalysts of such terms as "internal," "external," and "structure" as leading to reification and obscuring the *actions* taken by people. I am in strong agreement with much that is presented in that paper. Since I am here trying to depict an established way of thinking, however, I shall use such terms, which are the terms in which these ideas are cast and which make them more readily recognizable. I do not view such terms as desirable in efforts to formulate new theoretical positions.

up; and we may be able to see a continuity in this pattern which seems to suggest that he is still defending against those same childhood wishes. We may even find images and events in his dreams that point to continuing violent urges toward the parent and may discern many other indicators of warded-off rage toward that figure.° If we look in detail at his day-to-day interactions, however, we see a good deal more. We may find that his meekness has led him to occupy a job that is not up to his real potential and that he silently and resentfully bears. On the job and in his other social interactions as well, he is likely to be unable to ask for what is his due, and may even volunteer to do things for others that he really doesn't want to do. One can see this excessively unassertive and self-abnegating behavior as motivated by the need to cover up his strong aggressive urges, and this would be correct as far as it goes. But it is equally the case that such a life style *generates* rage. Disavowed anger may be a continuing feature of his life from childhood, but the angry thoughts that disturb his dreams tonight can be understood by what he let happen to himself today.

Such a person is caught in a vicious circle. Having learned early to fear his angry feelings, he has built up overt patterns of behavior designed to squelch and hide them. Even the smallest assertion seems dangerous, because he senses an enormous reservoir of violence behind it.† Yet it is just such excessive restrictions upon his assertiveness that create the conditions for further violent urges. Ironically, his impulses are in large measure a product of the defense against them.

In one sense, he guards against his anger for good reason: as he is at any given moment, he *is* potentially explosive, he *is* resentful and full of (unacknowledged) hatred, he *would* be nasty and vindictive if he were not trying so hard to be otherwise. If he were not so frequently bending over backwards, if he could act with reasonable assertiveness and demand a fair return from others, he would discover that the underlying rage would diminish. But because at any given moment real aggressive inclinations and fantasies have accrued from his way of living, he is afraid to act assertively. So he once more squelches himself, thereby arousing the fierce resentment that will in turn motivate his further self-abnegation and lead once again to strong, if unacknowledged, resentment. In such fashion he perpetuates his personal myth that there resides within him an untouchable kernel of rage that is part of the essence

---

° See pages 56–60 for a discussion of why this might be the case.

† Here, as elsewhere in our discussion, the use of terms like sense, believe, fear, and so on, does not necessarily imply a conscious experience. See Schafer's (1972) discussion of the false issue raised when such terms are taken to mean a concern only with what is conscious.

of who he is. And to a substantial degree this myth may be subscribed to by his analyst, as well, in the analyst's view that the anger is "in" the patient from the past, rather than a response to his life circumstances.

### VARIABILITY IN THE PATTERN

Our understanding of such a life is further complicated if we look still more closely at the above patient's day-to-day behavior. We are likely to find that he is not really *always* a shrinking violet. It is rare for a person to behave the same way in all situations. We are likely to find a number of situations that he handles quite adequately and others that are especially troubling. Situations acquire varied meanings for people, and while some situations strongly evoke his conflict and anxiety, others may be no problem at all. It is easy for the patient to overlook this, because the situations he handles adequately are likely to be experienced by him (especially in the context of a therapy session) as just background, hardly worth noticing.

Thus patient A, who can easily hold his own in an intellectual discussion, may be unable to tell another person he doesn't like something the other is doing, or even to say, in discussing what restaurant to eat in, "No, I don't like Chinese food. Could we choose another place?" The first situation, which he handles adequately, is described by him in therapy as insignificant. "Sure I can talk out in formal situations. But when it comes to the real nitty-gritty of personal relationships, I'm a flop." *

Patient B, on the other hand, may have relatively little trouble expressing preferences about restaurants or annoyance about petty inconsiderate acts, but may compulsively agree with others when intellectual or philosophical issues are discussed. His claim may be, "Sure I can handle the trivia, but when it comes to a discussion of something important, I show how insubstantial I really am."

Each of these people may have some awareness that there are others who have trouble with what comes easily to him, but neither really appreciates that the other can be tortured about it in the same fashion that he is by his own aberrations. It is important, for several reasons, to recognize this often unacknowledged variability in the patient's behavior. Firstly, recognition by the patient that there are many ways in which he functions quite adequately, and that these may be just as "important"

---

* In this particular situation we are, of course, talking of a person who has achieved some insight into his way of living. With a different person, or perhaps at an earlier stage of therapy, we might find no awareness of a problem in this regard, only the claim that he tries to be nice to everybody but is mysteriously depressed, or plagued by headaches.

as the ways in which he is anxious or ineffectual, can itself be an important insight following from early therapeutic exploration. For some patients, their global condemnation of themselves as "neurotic" or a "failure" obscures the reality of their day-to-day functioning.° Secondly, moving from a global picture of the person's personality dynamics or interaction patterns to a more detailed consideration of the variations in that pattern leads to a fuller understanding, by therapist as well as patient, of the patient's way of living. Finally, as we shall see more clearly further on, examination in such fashion of the variability of the person's life style opens the way for greater reconciliation between the points of view of psychodynamic and behavioral workers (the value of which it is of course the burden of this volume to support).

Another variation in the functioning of the problematically unassertive patient is perhaps of even greater interest. Not only can we expect to find quite a few situations in which he functions quite adequately; we are also likely to see on occasion rather strong outbursts of anger. At times such behavior may be due simply to direct learning, through rewards and punishments, that anger is acceptable in some instances and not in others (see Bandura and Walters, 1963; or Mischel, 1968). But often it is clear that such angry outbursts are intimately connected with the excessive meekness that the person exhibits so much of the time.

An illustrative experience was reported by a patient who had a strongly dependent, clinging relationship to her boyfriend, whom she let take advantage of her in all sorts of ways. The boyfriend would often arrive very late when they had arranged to get together, usually apologizing quite casually. At times his lateness would cause her considerable inconvenience (he was never late if they were planning to do something important to him), but she would always respond to his minimal apology with a reassurance that she didn't mind, she wasn't uptight about such things. There were many indications that she was actually quite angry at his lateness, but she maintained that it was of no moment, and that besides, she didn't want to be a nag.

---

° For others, of course, the reality of their *problems* is what is obscured. With these people, who must compulsively present themselves in a positive light, one is constantly tempted to interject, "Then why are you in therapy?" Obviously one would approach such a person differently in some respects. But it is still important to know where they experience trouble and where they do all right.

It should also be noted that it is not being suggested here that simply pointing out where a person functions well will necessarily eliminate global self-condemnation. This is a complex matter, in which phenomena subsumed by psychoanalysts under the rubric of "the harsh superego" obviously play an important part. How such phenomena are conceived of here, and how they are seen as changed, will become apparent as the book proceeds.

On one occasion, when they had made plans to have dinner at the home of another couple, he arrived at her house about twenty minutes later than he had said he would. When he arrived, she exploded, screaming at him that he ruined her evening, that the other couple would never speak to her again, that he had no consideration for other people. She angrily and tearfully complained that he thought he could arrive whenever he pleased, that he came late all the time because he had no respect for her feelings.

Her boyfriend was at first a bit stunned by this outburst of rage, and then reacted angrily himself. He pointed out that he had mentioned he might be a little late (which was true) and that the other couple had said to come "around 7:30," and would hardly care if they came twenty minutes later. He then added that he was particularly furious at all this fuss about lateness because she had repeatedly told him she didn't care if he was late. How the hell could she now accuse him of being callous and inconsiderate after she had indicated so often that she wasn't uptight about when he arrived! He said he was sorry he was late, but that her screaming and yelling over something like that was ridiculous and that he thought she was crazy making such a fuss over nothing. At this she burst into tears, begged his forgiveness, and said she didn't know what had gotten into her.

Her angry outburst, rather than effectively putting an end to what was troubling her, instead served to confirm the very pattern she was trapped in. Since she had held back indicating to her boyfriend how she felt about his lateness, her reaction seemed "out of the blue." Instead of reflecting on how he had been treating her, her boyfriend was readily able to focus instead on her "instability." And she experienced the event as a confirmation that she was really "crazy" and "potentially violent," and that she was lucky to have a boyfriend who would put up with her. She threw herself even more intensely into the role of the good, understanding, faithful girlfriend and once again made minimal demands and covered over any dissatisfactions . . . thus accumulating grievances that would result in the next outburst.

## A COMPARISON WITH THE FREUDIAN VIEW

These considerations are likely to seem familiar to the psychoanalytic reader. He or she has seen such links in his practice and has probably discussed them with colleagues. Because they have such a familiar ring, he perhaps may feel that such a point of view is well represented in the psychoanalytic literature, that it represents part of what was added to psychoanalysis by the development of ego psychology, and that where psychoanalysis differs from other approaches is in integrating such a perspective into a broader and deeper framework rather than "reductionistically" emphasizing it to the exclusion of "hard-won" insights into the nature of primitive biological urges. I believe that the analyst who holds such a view will be surprised to reexamine the Freudian psychoanalytic literature with this focus and discover just how rarely the perspective described in the past few pages is included in either case reports or clinical descriptions. Put very plainly, the orthodox psychoanalytic journals hardly mention such a point of view on clinical data. While such a point of view is part of the common-sense understanding every analyst brings to bear on his work, it is not really well integrated into the *theory* that guides his work. This is especially true of the theory of therapeutic change, and it strongly influences the therapeutic options that seem "legitimate" to use.°

The absence of a genuinely interpersonal focus in psychoanalytic case reports follows a tradition begun by Freud. Fenichel (1940), in a review of Horney's *New Ways in Psychoanalysis*, claims that Freud's case studies are full of accounts of the vicious circles that Horney describes. I must confess that I have been unable to find very many such descriptions in my reading of Freud's case studies. Freud's genius lay in deciphering meanings—in discerning what is expressed by the patients' dreams, fantasies, associations, slips, and (to somewhat lesser extent) acts. Freud was not, however, a student of interaction sequences. When the patient's overt interpersonal behavior was the focus of his inquiry, it tended to be of interest as a further vehicle for expressing the underlying dynamics. Rarely was it examined for its *consequences*.

Even in his strong focus on the transference, which would seem to imply great attention to the interpersonal, it is evident that Freud did not look much at interaction sequences or consider how present behavior and its consequences perpetuate old patterns. The extreme degree of asymmetry in the analytic situation was designed to make it as clear

---

° Stone (1961, p. 18) points out that the analyst's theoretical conception of the analytic situation "has great influence and power, occasioning self-consciousness or even guilt, when its outlines are transgressed." Analysts of necessity will vary from the pure classical model; but if varied interventions are viewed as deviations from an ideal, rather than being integrated into the theoretical model and modifying our view of what the ideal is, then our effectiveness in applying new insights is severely limited.

as possible that the patient's behavior was not in response to anything that the analyst did, but stemmed instead from an almost inexorable assimilative process in the patient. The framework provided by Freud did not emphasize examining how the patient's behavior was a response to the current behavior of others, and it emphasized still less how the behavior of others could itself be seen as a function of one's own acts.

Modern analysts do give some attention to these matters, especially from the perspective of psychoanalytic ego psychology. Rapaport (1958), for example, in his discussion of ego autonomy, has stressed the concept of "stimulus nutriment." He has suggested that psychological structures often require environmental input to maintain themselves, and that without such "nutriment," patterned psychological actions do not persist in their current form. Elsewhere (Rapaport, 1960) he even states that "the vicious circle of neurosis crucially involves the fact that the patient persistently exposes himself to situations (stimulations) which tend to elicit his defensive behaviors and to reinforce his defenses, and avoids other situations which would tend to elicit alternative behaviors and thus would facilitate giving up his defenses." (p. 892)

But while such discussions make clear that the view presented here is not one that is alien to psychoanalytic thought, it is also necessary to recognize that Rapaport stops short of exploring the possibilities of the "stimulus nutriment" concept to the fullest. For Rapaport, while defenses and other ego structures are in part dependent upon environmental feedback, they are "maintained, *ultimately*, by *internal* (drive) stimulus-nutriment" (Rapaport, 1958, p. 737; italics added). The question of *whether drives or motives themselves require stimulus-nutriment* is never really seriously considered. In a sense, it is precisely this question that the alternative view presented here raises: what feedback events are required for the patient to persist in (unconsciously) wishing for the same things he did as a child? That is, what stimulus-nutriment is required to maintain those structures that psychoanalysis has designated as part of the id? ° Persistent pursuit of this question has major implications not only for theory but especially for therapeutic intervention.

An interpersonal perspective is also evident in the way modern analysts understand their own emotional reactions to their patients. The analyst's reaction is often used to provide the analyst with a sense of how other persons, significant in the patient's life, are likely to feel in inter-

---

° Again, I do not mean here to endorse the term "structure" (see footnote, p. 43), but rather to clarify the parallels and differences between Rapaport's view of how patterned psychological events are maintained and my own view.

acting with him or her. Even here, however, such insights on the part of the analyst are more likely to be used to highlight what the patient is *up to* than what he provokes or confronts: "You'd like me to feel sorry for you" or "You're trying to get me to help you," rather than "You get people to feel sorry and help you out, and so you never get the chance to learn and try things out yourself."

Following through on the latter way of understanding, the therapist might note that since the patient is deprived of chances to learn, he's left with the feeling that *all he can do* is get people sorry for him and hope they help. This further perpetuates the cycle. As long as he succeeds in eliciting help, he continues to *need* help. As we shall see, when the problem is viewed this way, the therapist is less likely to rely solely on interpretation. Helping the patient to undergo experiences that will help to break up the cycle, perhaps through actively learning certain modes in a protected situation, begins to look like a useful course. ( I shall discuss this further in Chapter 10. )

It may further be noted that even when analysts do pay attention to interaction sequences in the fashion I am emphasizing here, the very nature of the classical analytic situation guarantees that their attention to such matters must be fleeting at best. As I shall illustrate in later chapters, in order to get a detailed picture of just what led to what in a particular sequence in the patient's life, it is usually necessary to persistently ask probing and detailed questions of a sort not compatible with the emphasis on free association and nonintervention that one sees even in quite modern textbooks on psychoanalytic technique ( e.g., Greenson, 1967 ), or for that matter on psychoanalytically oriented psychotherapy ( e.g., Langs, 1973 ).

Yet unless a *great deal* of attention is paid to ongoing interpersonal processes, such processes are not likely to seem sufficient to account for the phenomena analysts observe. Only a detailed examination of the subtleties of interaction can provide a convincing alternative to the traditional psychoanalytic emphasis on the past. The Freudian tradition does not point inquiry in that direction.°

---

° The transference relationship in the classical analytic situation is no substitute for a detailed knowledge of the sequences in the patient's daily living. The ambiguous stance of the analyst, his efforts to minimize the kind of interaction with the patient that is characteristic of other kinds of relationships, make it extremely difficult to study, through this medium, the patient's way of responding to and affecting actual and manifest behaviors of other people. The analyst, by interpreting and by remaining silent much of the time, truncates interaction sequences and produces instead expressive monologues.

## AN ALTERNATIVE DEVELOPMENTAL MODEL

Viewpoints such as the one being presented here are often criticized in the psychoanalytic literature for lacking a "genetic point of view," and hence are seen as incomplete or reductionistic. To be sure, the approach described in this volume does place much less emphasis than does ortho-dox psychoanalysis on the need for the patient to understand his or her history in order to solve his or her neurotic dilemma. This approach is not, however, antidevelopmental. To question whether detailed under-standing of the history of a problem is necessary for therapeutic pur-poses is not to say that research and theory should not attempt to account for how such problems arise.

Indeed, preventing problems is ultimately far more humane and efficient than treating them once they have arisen. And for purposes of prevention, a knowledge of how problems develop—of the childhood roots and later transformations—is essential. More immediately, therapeutic work with children requires a sound knowledge of the modes of thought and action typical of various age groups, and of the concerns and di-lemmas children of various ages are likely to confront. It is thus no com-ment on the need for a developmental point of view in psychological theory to consider whether therapeutic work with adults may in fact be sidetracked by making that situation the arena for such research.*

A major focus on how the patient's current way of living perpetuates his problems does not imply that there are no continuities between present reactions and those of the past. The similarities are very clear. So, too, is the great importance of childhood in shaping the way of life that will be evident in the adult. Seeking correlations between childhood ex-periences and adult problems seems to me a valuable line of inquiry for research efforts, if not so crucial for therapeutic change.

But if connections or continuities are discovered, the question re-mains: how are these continuities mediated? The more traditional de-velopmental view in psychoanalysis is one that stresses the layering of residues of past patterns in hierarchical fashion. The imagery is archaeo-logical. The focus is on the early structuring of the personality; the per-sonality patterns attained by the end of the Oedipal period are seen as set and relatively unresponsive to changing conditions.

* There is also, of course, the important question of whether reconstructions from adult patients provide an *accurate* genetic picture. Even within psychoanalysis, the most vital approach to studying developmental issues involves child observation and longitudinal studies, rather than reconstruction.

A somewhat different view can also account for the tendency for early patterns to be maintained, but in addition it readily handles instances where change is instead rather striking. (More importantly, as we shall see as we go along, this view points to a wider range of ways in which change can be brought about.) This view emphasizes that the kind of experiences we have early in life, and our way of dealing with these experiences, strongly influences what further experiences we will encounter, as well as how we perceive those experiences and how we deal with them.

For example, the two-year-old who has developed an engaging and playful manner is far more likely to evoke friendly interest and attention on the part of adults than is the child who is rather quiet and withdrawn. The latter will typically encounter a less rich interpersonal environment, which will further decrease the likelihood that he will drastically change. Similarly, the former is likely to continually learn that other people are fun and are eager to interact with him; and his pattern, too, is likely to become more firmly fixed as he grows. Further, not only will the two children tend to evoke different behavior from others, they will also interpret differently the same reaction from another person. Thus, the playful child may experience a silent or grumpy response from another as a kind of game and may continue to interact until perhaps he does elicit an appreciative response. The quieter child, not used to much interaction, will readily accept the initial response as a signal to back off.

If we look at the two children as adults, we may perhaps find the difference between them still evident: one outgoing, cheerful, and expecting the best of people; the other rather shy, and unsure that anyone is interested. A childhood pattern has persisted into adulthood. Yet we really don't understand the developmental process unless we see how, successively, teachers, playmates, girlfriends, and colleagues have been drawn in as "accomplices" in maintaining the persistent pattern. And, I would suggest, we don't understand the possibilities for change unless we realize that even now there are such "accomplices," and that if they stopped playing their role in the process, it would be likely eventually to alter.

It is important to recognize, however, that it is not that easy to get the accomplices to change. The signals we emit to other people constitute a powerful force field. The shy person does many (sometimes almost invisible) things to make it difficult for another person to stay open to him very long. Even a well-intentioned person is likely eventually to help confirm his view that others aren't really very interested.

Thus, from this perspective, the early pattern persists, not in spite of changing conditions but because the person's pattern of experiencing and interacting with others tends continually to recreate the old conditions again and again. In many cases, the effects are subtle and not readily apparent without careful scrutiny. But on close inspection, each person may be seen rather regularly to produce a particular skewing of responses from others that defines his idiosyncratic, interpersonal world. Even in seemingly similar situations, we are each likely to encounter slightly different interpersonal cues that may render the texture of the experience critically different. We then act (again) in a way that seems appropriate to this particular state of affairs, and create the conditions for others to again react to us in the same fashion and thus again set the stage for the pattern to be repeated. Rather than having been locked in, in the past, by an intrapsychic structuring, the pattern seems from this perspective to be continually being formed, but generally in a way that keeps it quite consistent through the years. It may appear inappropriate because it is not well correlated with the adult's "average expectable environment," but it is quite a bit more closely attuned to the person's idiosyncratically skewed version of that environment.

Emphasis on such a cyclical re-creation of interpersonal events, and on the real behavior of "accomplices" in perpetuating characterological patterns, does not imply that the person is perceiving every situation "objectively." Most clinicians have seen abundant examples of patients' distortions of what is going on, particularly in transference phenomena. Such aspects of psychological functioning must be included in any tenable account of how neurotic patterns are perpetuated. But rather than relying on the metaphors that analysts have traditionally employed in conceptualizing such phenomena, I prefer to think in terms of the Piagetian notion of "schema." Such a notion implies that not only do we assimilate new experiences to older, more familiar ways of viewing things (as is implicit in the concept of transference), we also do eventually accommodate to what is actually going on.

Thus, as in transference phenomena, new people and new relationships tend to be approached in terms of their similarity to earlier ones; and frequently, particularly in the special conditions of the psychoanalytic situation, one sees what appear to be quite arbitrary assumptions and perceptions occurring. But in principle, I would suggest, accommodation is always proceeding apace and would, with non-reactive sources of stimulation, eventually lead to a fairly accurate picture of what one is encountering.° The problem is that other people are *not* non-reactive.

---

° Whether, and in what way, such a perspective is relevant to understanding the perceptions of psychotic individuals is not clear at this point, since understanding of the relative (and interacting) roles of experiential and biological factors is still a matter over which there is substantial disagreement.

How they behave toward us is very much influenced by how we behave toward them, and hence by how we initially perceive them. Thus, our initial (in a sense distorted) picture of another person can end up being a fairly accurate predictor of how he or she will act toward us; because, based on our expectation that that person will be hostile, or accepting, or sexual, we are likely to act in such a way as to eventually draw such behavior from the person and thus have our (initially inaccurate) perception "confirmed." Our tendency to enter the next relationship with the same assumption and perceptual bias is then strengthened, and the whole process likely to be repeated again.

Such a perspective enables us to understand both continuity and change in the same terms. In a large number of cases, this process of "distorted" perception leading to a skewing of responses from others, and hence to a "confirmation" of the problematic way of experiencing, continues for years and produces the phenomena so familiar to analytic observers. At times, however, a figure appears who, by virtue of his or her interpersonal history and personal force field, serves to intervene (for good or ill) in the developmental process rather than simply confirm present directions.° The patient's behavior may make this process unlikely to persist, but if it does, it can be expected that the patient will eventually accommodate to this new input and show substantial change in an important aspect of living. It is likely that many of the "spontaneous" cures that make the controls in psychotherapy research so tricky are the result of such accommodative processes.

By virtue of training and of orientation to the patient's behavior, the therapist is frequently in a particularly propitious position for changing, rather than confirming, the patient's previous modes of experiencing others—though as Wolf (1966) describes, this may not happen nearly as frequently as we might hope. The less reactive stance of the psychoanalyst, in particular (whatever its other limitations), does seem to reduce somewhat the likelihood of acting in the same confirmatory ways as previous accomplices in the patient's neurosis. The guarantee in this respect is far from ironclad, however (see especially Chapters 5 and 11). Frequently, the seemingly bizarre and unrealistic reactions of the patient toward the analyst are understandable as symbolizations of what is actually, though covertly, going on between them. Even where this is not the case, the seemingly anachronistic reaction need not be viewed as the triggering of a reaction pattern that was preserved in childhood in such

---

° Less dramatic instances of this sort, in which each person changes a bit, are common. Usually, however, the change is small, because each participant is free to leave rather than change. The more constrained to be together, the more each can alter the other.

a way that further possibilities of accommodating to new events were precluded. Investigation from the point of view advocated here frequently reveals that other figures throughout the person's life have participated in the kind of confirmatory process I have described, even if the analyst did not. Considerable working through is then necessary, because the disconfirming experience with the analyst is at odds with a long series of experiences that have produced expectations not readily relinquished after just one or two disconfirmations. Assimilative tendencies may be strong, even if not inexorable.

The earlier, hypothetical example of the two-year-olds was chosen to illustrate how striking continuities may be understood by a developmental model that stresses continuing responsiveness to current happenings. In actuality, the developmental course is likely to be more complicated and less unidirectional than was portrayed in the illustration. The likelihood of at least some disconfirming events, and the accommodation that can then occur, are likely to produce less monolithic differences than depicted thus far. Complexity is introduced by our ability to discriminate among the implications of different situations, especially when it is recognized that not only may our overt behavior differ from situation to situation, but so may our fantasies, wishes, and fears.*

The importance of conflict and defense further complicates the picture, introducing motivated misperceptions and peremptory behaviors, the meanings of which are poorly understood or misrepresented. As described early in this chapter and elsewhere in this book, patterns of conflict and defense can also be viewed not just as the expression of an intrapsychic state of affairs but also as part of a process in which feedback, skewed by the very processes the patterns maintain, plays a major role. Thus, processes of defense and processes of adaptation interweave complexly with the actual occurrences they produce or encounter. Finally, it is important to understand the role of innate constitutional factors and of endogenously developing changes in shaping the person's behavior and the world he encounters. The outgoing two-year-old who is so charming may become just a pain in the neck if, at age four, he exhibits an epigenetically programmed upsurge of intrusiveness beyond the ability of his parents and other important figures to tolerate (Erikson, 1963). The course of his development could then alter considerably.

---

* It must also be recognized, however, that interpersonal affect-laden situations are often exceedingly ambiguous, and that our power to discriminate in these situations is far less than in those where the cues are clearer. We must be aware of broad consistencies deriving from how we construe subtle interpersonal cues, as well as those discriminations and situational differences in our reactions that are also evident (cf. Mischel, 1973b; Wachtel, 1973a, 1973b).

Erikson has been particularly effective in illuminating how these various factors interact in the course of development.


## TIES TO "EARLY OBJECTS"


In describing this view of development, there is one more important issue for us to consider at this point. Frequently, psychoanalytic exploration reveals that, without awareness, the person remains tied in fantasy life and in secret strivings to figures from his or her early past. Typically, discovery of such a tie is viewed as accounting for the inhibitions and symptoms of the adult. The pull from the past is regarded as the causal influence. We shall now consider an alternative way of understanding this common observation.

As but one example, let us consider still another set of interlocked influences our two-year-old might encounter and then perpetuate. Suppose that he is not encouraged by his family to develop the skills that can help gain greater independence from them. This need not take the form of outright prohibition or interference. Indeed, the knot is often tighter when not readily visible, as when an ambivalent parent gives explicit encouragement to the child's budding independence but in subtle ways undermines it. Perhaps the mother, without noticing it, is more frequently warm and attentive when the child sweetly says "I love you, mommy" than when he shows her something he has put together. Perhaps she cuddles him when he stands apart from the other children ("to make him feel better, so he won't be afraid to play") instead of helping him to initiate play, or instead of joining in with the group of children until her child is comfortable there. There are many ways in which, through ignorance or unacknowledged intent, a parent can bind and cripple a child while thinking he or she is encouraging independence.

When such is the case, there is likely to be a point at which the child's fearful clinging is recognized as distinguishing him from his age peers. Not infrequently, the parental reaction is likely to be a nagging, complaining, or insulting one, motivated by parental anxiety, embarrassment, guilt, or desperation. Even if the parent does not come out with "What's wrong with you? Why can't you be like the other kids?" or some similar assault, the simple act of continuing to encourage participation in age-appropriate activities (when not accompanied by effective efforts to help the child accomplish the transition) can be experienced as punishment and cause the child considerable pain.

A child caught in such a developmental tangle is likely to remain more tied to his parents than most children his age. Having fewer alternative sources of gratification and security, he is likely to feel more than most the need to be mommy's or daddy's little boy. Not only is this likely to further impede the exploration and assertion needed to develop the skills that would get him out of this dilemma, it is also likely to make him quite fearful of expressing anger or disagreement toward his parents— and this in circumstances more likely than usual to arouse his anger. So we see an unhappy little child, afraid to venture forth, clinging to mother in a way that angers her (even as it also may gratify her), feeling frustrated and irritated and perhaps even sensing a grasping intent in the mother's harmful cloistering. Yet he desparately tries to be loyal and to be a "good boy" in order to at least maintain the security of his tie to mother. In so doing, he continues to prevent himself from developing the independence and expansiveness necessary for him to dare to loosen his hold on his mother or to feel able to cope with the complexity of his feelings for her.

In many instances, despite being confronted with such a dilemma, the child continues to grow. There are enough countervailing forces in innate developmental processes, as well as in the expectations and reward-structure of the larger social order—and even in other aspects of their own parents' behavior—to allow millions of children with such a history to grow up and become taxpayers, spouses, and parents—that is, in a very general way, functioning adults. It takes a rather extraordinary effort to inhibit cognitive and personality growth so completely that these rather minimal stigmata of "normality" are not achieved.*

But the situation I have described takes its toll. Such a person does not "make it" without pain and struggle, and usually he does not make it without paying a psychological price. In many respects he may advance along the way more slowly than his age-peers, getting there eventually but always feeling a little bit behind or a little "out of it," venturing less, mastering less, and thus again venturing less, and so on.

One such individual, whom I have discussed in more detail elsewhere (Wachtel, 1976) was, at the time he began therapy, a graduate student

---

* These criteria are meant simply to point to the *kind* of general achievements that tend to distinguish neurotic difficulties from more severe ones. It is in no sense meant to imply that individuals who do not marry, or do not have children, suffer from a serious personality disorder. My judgment on this would tend to be different, however, were the person completely lacking in human relationships.

with fairly substantial academic success, but he was almost completely unable to engage in even casual conversation with people at school without quite severe anxiety. His dreams and associations indicated rather strikingly the kind of intense ties to mother that are often stressed and elaborated upon in the psychoanalytic literature, and that are often viewed as the primary cause of current life difficulties. I was struck, however, by the cumulative effects of a life history in which the experiences necessary to develop social skills and ease with people did not occur; and I suggested that even if his conflicted ties to his mother were historically earlier, and thus primary in that sense, the present causal nexus was far more complicated. Since his mother was at that time just about the only person he could be with without experiencing incapacitating anxiety, it made as much sense to think of his current preoccupation with her as a function of his dismal life situation as it did to consider the reverse, and more traditional, interpretation. A chain of events had occurred in his life that left him tied to his mother in many different aspects of his being, and this state of affairs seemed destined to continue so long as he did not have alternatives readily available. Such considerations led to the conclusion that direct efforts to train social skills and reduce social anxiety might loosen those ties to his mother that seemed to "underlie" such anxiety.

Many other cases seen in therapy are quite a bit more subtle than the one just discussed, but not necessarily different in principle. The patient discussed above was so seriously and obviously hampered in an important area of his life that his ties to his mother were manifest (though certainly not fully conscious in all their ramifications), and the way his current life contributed to these ties was fairly obvious if one is willing to adopt such a perspective. With many other patients, however, the tie may be wholly unconscious, evident only in dreams and in the pattern of his associations. Further, he may seem to be struggling with these strong unconscious regressive wishes and fantasies while apparently functioning day to day in a rather successful and independent fashion.

Now, of course, if the patient is really living his present life completely freely and successfully he would have no reason to be in therapy, and his therapist would have no reason to attribute any neurotogenic importance to any Oedipal wishes and fantasies he discerned in the patient's productions. Something must be wrong in the patient's life, or such wishes and fantasies would be of no concern. In some instances, what at first is of concern are one or more isolated symptoms in an apparently otherwise psychologically healthy individual. In these cases, it is the symptoms that are viewed by the analyst as deriving from the conflict over the patient's continuing tie to figures from the past. Such was the classic picture of neurosis. Freud originally analyzed symptoms, not character.

With the more careful scrutiny of the patient's way of life that has resulted from modern developments in theory, it has become increasingly more difficult to find instances of pure symptom neuroses that have no characterological features. Indeed, one suspects that when such a state of affairs is evident, it is likely to be a case of the kind of simple conditioned reactions that were first put forth by behavior therapists as the model of all neuroses. But behavior therapists are increasingly recognizing that such simple neurotic responses are rarely as isolated from the patient's way of life as was first thought (e.g., Lazarus, 1971; Fodor, 1974), and certainly simple conditioned responses are not what analysts have in mind when they talk of neuroses.

In most instances, then, it is possible to find areas of inhibition, anxiety, or maladaptive behavior that are subtle equivalents of the more total and obvious life-impairment evident in the patient discussed a few pages back. The patient may, for example, evidence reasonable social ease and competence in general, but be inhibited in making sexual advances. Or he may be able to initiate sexual activity quite easily and "perform" adequately, but may not experience complete sexual release and satisfaction. Or perhaps the sexual aspect of sexual relationships is fully satisfying but does not seem linked to an intimate sharing of personal feelings.

Any of these limitations in living could, if found to occur in conjunction with evidence for disavowed ties to parental figures, be attributed to the effects of those ties. That has been the traditional psychoanalytic understanding of such observations. The implication drawn has been that one must work on untangling those ties in order to increase the patient's freedom in living. But again, it makes equal sense to consider, for example, how longings for the ideal mother of childhood might be fostered by a current life style that excludes fully satisfying experiences of intimacy and sensual satisfaction.

The lure of the Oedipal imagery is strengthened each time the person has an encounter that proves to be frustrating or disappointing. Whatever role the vicissitudes of feeling for mother may have played in starting the person on a life course that is in some important respects restricted in freedom, concrete interactions with later figures tend to be significant in perpetuating it. If one is anxious or hesitant about sexuality or intimacy, one teaches one's partners to be similarly inclined. Satisfying sexuality and the experience of intimacy require a mutual trust and understanding. If an individual enters a new relationship in a hesitant way, the partner cannot long continue to be open with him, and he will find confirmed again and again through his life that his defensiveness in such situations is "justified," since he is inevitably disappointed and finds his partners tensing up or closing off in ways that hurt (and lead him to again be hesitant the next time, and again evoke a complementary response from his partner).\*

In this view, then, Oedipal longings, while often "real," need not be the primary motor source for the patient's current difficulties. One can acknowledge the evidence for their existence, and even intensity, without necessarily viewing them as the crucial center. Instead one may see the conflicts generated in the family leading to a continuing series of experiences, which develop their own momentum and of which the Oedipal yearnings of the adult years are themselves a function. One would then expect that direct efforts to intervene in the events that perpetuate this vicious cycle would, if successful, lead to a diminution of the hold that Oedipal yearnings and fantasies have had on the individual. Painstaking examination of the interpersonal signals given off by the patient that disrupt mutual intimacy would become at least as important as the painstaking analysis of regressive fantasies; new methods to alter those signals and interactions, described in later chapters, would occupy a central position in efforts at change.


## THE HEURISTIC CHOICE OF MODELS


The two models—that of repression cutting off aspects of psychological development from influence by perceptual input, and that stressing the role of such input in maintaining old patterns (while stressing as well the way in which such input is likely to be generated by the very pattern it maintains)—are not necessarily mutually exclusive. In principle, each might be relevant to different cases. Even where the former is correct, the latter may be included as representing additional complicating factors (as in the concept of secondary gain). The clinical evidence and the rules for evaluating it are not yet precise enough to distinguish between these two ways of viewing neurotic functioning.

\* It should be clear that I am here describing something that does not necessarily go on consciously. Far from explicitly justifying a limited sex life on the basis of his partner's responses, the person may well extol both his partners and his sex life for quite a while. Only careful scrutiny may reveal the particular dissatisfaction or lack of freedom in the person's life.

Many psychoanalytic writers have in effect advocated taking both into account. They have suggested that an interpersonal point of view is only part of what is needed to understand neurosis, and that modern Freudian psychoanalysis, with the inclusion of recent advances in ego psychology, is more encompassing and hence superior. Of recent proponents of this view, Zetzel and Meissner's (1973, pp. 26–38) argument is among the most interesting, since it is based on illustrative clinical material and not just on the assertion that non-Freudians are superficial. In viewing the interpersonal point of view as incomplete, however, they seem to equate an interpersonal view with one that deals only with surface attitudes and adaptational issues and that pays little attention to conflict, defense, or unconscious processes. The interpersonal view described in this chapter would be quite concerned with the kinds of issues these writers regard as beyond the province of an interpersonal approach (e.g., a patient's fear of angry and hostile feelings and of surpassing his brother as being significant in motivating his more obvious—but also defended-against—passive dependent longings and fears). Where it would differ is in whether these unconscious conflicts need to be understood primarily in terms of the past.

Zetzel and Meissner tell us that, in dealing with his fear of his anger toward his bigger brother as a child, the patient they discuss "surrendered any attempts at open rivalry with the brother, and instead formed a strong passive and positive identification with him." This does not imply to me, however, that an understanding of the patient's current way of living will fail to reveal or elucidate his conflicted anger at his brother. I would expect that as a result of the compromise evolved in his childhood, the patient has created a life style in which anger and competition with his brother have no place, yet which (by virtue of his continued deference to his brother—apparently despite considerably greater actual competence) continually breeds such feelings. The frightening urge to destroy the (also-loved, and in some respects also-needed) brother is not surprising, given the patient's continuing efforts not to assert himself at all with his brother, and given, as well, the consequent continuing accrual of frustration and psychic injury. The continuation of these defensive efforts at excessive cooperativeness is in turn not surprising, given the (largely unconscious) destructive urges that any standing up to the brother would now stir—and given, as well, the patient's (not entirely incorrect) sense that his place in the social order of his job and family have come to be intimately tied to his role as the "nice" person who does the "right thing." Thus I would see the childhood conflict as leading to a life style that creates a vicious circle of stirring of and running from forbidden wishes that are by now the product of his current way of life, not of a separate internal reality. Such a view does consider unconscious conflicts at a variety of "levels," but it conceptualizes them in terms of the implications of current patterns of living rather than in terms of past experiences fixed by repression and defense.

In focusing on the current perpetuating processes and the feedback that maintains them, I am making a heuristic choice. I do not think that conceptualizations of dissociated systems are likely to prove entirely without merit. It does seem to me, however, that the traditional psychoanalytic approach has considerably overemphasized their role in perpetuating neurotic ways of living, and that this emphasis in itself reflects a vicious circle: with such a conceptualization as one's framework, the observations one is likely to make are those most likely to confirm the view of the encapsulated past preserved from influence, and hence to encourage one to continue observing in the same way. For as discussed in Chapter 3, the implications of this model have been taken to exclude certain kinds of inquiring and certain kinds of interventions. Deviations from the role of the therapist as a nonintrusive, carefully non-self-disclosing listener to free associations have been viewed as compromising the amount of change that can occur. And without inquiring and intervening in a more active way, the current feedback processes that maintain old patterns are not likely to come into sharp focus.

The traditional psychoanalytic stance does enable certain kinds of observations to be made that might not be possible with the active-intervention approach advocated in this book. As a research tool, however, the psychoanalytic method seems to me to have unearthed most of the riches it was developed to mine. The yield has been extremely rich, but after 75 years the likelihood of further surprises seems to me far less than it was when this extraordinary vein was first tapped. And as a therapeutic tool, its limitations seem to me to outweigh its advantages.

The Freudian psychoanalytic approach is not more "encompassing." Though its modern version does *in principle* stress both intrapsychic and interpersonal considerations, the implications of emphasis on the former have of necessity limited exploration of the latter. The Freudian and interpersonal models are distinguishable neither by a concern with unconscious processes and conflicts—which both stress—nor by avoiding the problem of excluding some potential observations and therapeutic tactics by focusing on others—which neither can avoid. Rather, they differ in the way in which persisting unconscious conflicts and "infantile" features are accounted for, and in the direction that new knowledge and improved therapeutic effectiveness are judged likely to be found. In stressing the role of interpersonal feedback processes (and thereby de-emphasizing the role of processes rendered impervious to feedback), I am placing a bet as to where the greater risk and potential lie. So, too, is the psychoanalyst.

# 5

# Some Therapeutic Implications
# of the Interpersonal View

A S we have seen, the model of the unintegrated past is closely associated with an approach to therapy in which interpretation is the strongly preferred intervention and in which other kinds of intervention are avoided wherever possible. Practical considerations of time and of money available; diagnostic considerations of the patient's tolerance for frustration and his ability to deal with new insights without disorganizing anxiety; and general human-relationship considerations, making it necessary at times to offer advice, support, or other noninterpretive aid—all these require analysts to intervene to varying degrees in ways other than by interpreting. These noninterpretive interventions, however, while often necessary, are nonetheless seen as potentially reducing the depth and permanence of the change that can be achieved.

If id wishes are essentially forces from the past that cannot be modified by current experiences and perceptions, then there are important limitations upon what can be accomplished by bringing about a change in the patient's current way of living. His day-to-day interactions are then of interest primarily as a reflection or expression of the intrapsychic state of affairs, not as a vital part of the causal or maintaining processes. Advances in ego psychology, in this context, have had the effect of leading analysts to be more sophisticated in how they manage the therapeutic relationship and go about evoking and "resolving" the transference neurosis.* They have not, however, led to a change in the emphasis on uncovering deeply buried wishes and fears and trying to demonstrate that their intensity comes from the past. They have led to a broader, less intellectual sense of what an interpretation is, and have pointed to greater understanding of how some noninterpretive maneuvers are necessary for interpretations to be maximally effective. They have not changed the view that interpretation is the "pure gold" of psychotherapeutic interventions, and that changes deriving from other sources are somehow base in comparison.

The interpersonal view presented in Chapter 4 views psychological conflict and primitive strivings and fantasies in quite a different fashion. I shall presently indicate what I see as the implications for psychotherapy of this important difference. Before doing so, however, it is useful to consider the psychotherapeutic recommendations of Sullivan and of Horney, since so much of the view presented in Chapter 4 derives from their work, and yet they largely come to different conclusions about the therapeutic process. In so doing, I will attempt also to indicate how these two thinkers, in different respects, failed to capitalize fully on the possibilities created by their own creative formulations.

Horney's view of the therapeutic process is in many respects a rather traditional psychoanalytic view. The patient's role is "to express himself as completely and frankly as possible . . . to become aware of his unconscious driving forces and their influence on his life . . . [and] to develop the capacity to change those attitudes that are disturbing his relations with himself and the world around him." (Horney, 1942, p. 101) Regarding the latter, Horney notes that lifting a repression frees the way for action, enabling the patient to begin to see his way out of the dilemma in which he has been blindly boxed in. For Horney, the major effort to bring about change is not directed toward "gross modification in action or behavior, such as gaining or regaining the capacity for public performances, for creative work, for co-operation, for sexual potency, or losing phobias or tendencies toward depression." According to Horney, such changes "will *automatically* take place in a successful analysis. They are *not primary changes*, however, but result from less visible changes *within the personality*." (Horney, 1942, p. 118; italics added)

How these internal changes occur is not clearly indicated by Horney. She talks of occurrences such as "gaining a more realistic attitude toward oneself instead of wavering between self-aggrandizement and self-degra-

---

* The word "resolve" is in quotation marks because it is a term which is often used to account for change in psychoanalytic writings, but whose meaning is far from clear. Chapter 6 will examine resolution of neurotic conflicts more closely.

dation, gaining a spirit of activity, assertion and courage instead of inertia and fears, becoming able to plan instead of drifting, finding the center of gravity within oneself," and so on. How such changes follow from the events of the psychoanalytic session, however, is left rather vague. She claims, for example, that the patient's "compulsive needs will be diminished as soon as any source of anxiety is diminished." As soon as a "repressed feeling of humiliation is seen and understood, a greater friendliness will result automatically, even though the desirability of friendliness has not been touched upon." (Horney, 1942, p. 119)

It is not clear what, precisely, is meant by "understood" here, or how such understanding leads to greater friendliness if the person is still (now consciously) afraid of humiliation. Neither does she indicate *how* a source of anxiety is "diminished." In a similar vein, she goes on to state that if "a fear of failure is recognized and lessened, the person will spontaneously become more active and take risks that he hitherto unconsciously avoided." But again, how is the fear of failure "lessened"? Horney's writings suggest that such a fear of failure, and the defenses built up to deal with it, would in fact make failure even more likely, for the patient is likely to have avoided experiences necessary to develop the skills required for success in important activities. Such being the case, insight alone may well not be sufficient to break into the vicious circle. The patient can justifiably feel that his or her fear of failure was once primarily irrational, but that his way of dealing with that fear was so debilitating that he now really does face the likely prospect of failure if he risks striving in the way others do.° Thus it would seem that not only does Horney's description of the therapeutic process leave a number of crucial issues unexplained, it also is challenged by the implications of some of her own insights.†

Let us now turn to a consideration of Sullivan's views of the therapeutic process. Sullivan's conception is harder to characterize, because Sullivan seemed to operate with two rather different views of how therapy proceeds. In some respects his accounts share many of the traditional features evident in Horney's writings on the subject. He viewed his job as helping the patient to understand more clearly how he lives his life and to enable him to integrate into his conscious view of himself those

---

° There are two different aspects of irrational fears of failure. One entails a compulsive need to succeed, which makes failure seem a tragedy rather than just a disappointment. The other is an excessively pessimistic estimate of one's probability of succeeding. The last few comments are directed to the latter. But the question of how fear is lessened applies to the former as well.

† Here, as elsewhere, challenging a theorist's description of how change occurs does not necessarily imply he or she has not in fact achieved therapeutic success, but only that the explanation of those successes is not fully satisfactory.

motivational tendencies which he had dissociated. Sullivan assumed that once the patient saw things clearly, he could handle things on his own. The therapist is described as proceeding

> along the general lines of getting some notion of what stands in the way of successful living for the person, quite certain that if we can clear away the obstacles, everything else will take care of itself. . . . I have never found myself called upon to 'cure' anybody. The patients took care of that, once I had done the necessary brush-clearing, and so on. It is almost uncanny how things fade out of the picture when their *raison d'etre* is revealed. The brute fact is that man is so extraordinarily adaptive that, given any chance of making a reasonably adequate analysis of the situation, he is quite likely to stumble into a series of experiments which will gradually approximate more successful living. . . . [The task of both patient and therapist is to] work toward uncovering those factors which are concerned in the person's recurrent mistakes, and which lead to his taking ineffective and inappropriate action. There is no necessity to do more. (Sullivan, 1954, pp. 238–39)

Thus, like Horney and like the Freudians, Sullivan stressed the prepotent role of insight in the process of therapeutic change, and in a number of places he implied that efforts to provide help other than in furthering insight could be infantilizing, disrespectful, and antitherapeutic. In this respect he was, as Horney, a traditional psychodynamic therapist. In one important respect, in fact, he was more traditional than Horney. Sullivan strongly emphasized intense scrutiny of the patient's history. Though eschewing the search for manifestations of infantile sexuality, and though extending the possibility of significant opportunities for change to a later time than in the traditional Freudian scheme, he nonetheless made the patient's understanding of his own past and how he had obscured it the keystone of therapeutic strategy. This is in substantial contrast to Horney's insistence that meaningful change could best be approached through understanding of how the person was currently living his life, and her view that concern with history often entailed an unwitting collusion on the part of the therapist with the patient's resistances, enabling him to keep concealed the current significance of some pattern in his life.

Sullivan revealed in a number of ways, however, another view of therapy quite different from the one we have discussed thus far, and far more compatible with the view being developed in this volume. At several points in *The Psychiatric Interview* (1954) Sullivan stresses the importance of a *"prescription of action"* as an essential element in consolidating the progress made in the course of the patient's and therapist's explorations. Such a view seems to provide a rather different picture from the recommendation that the therapist clarify where the patient obscures his understanding of the events of his life, then leave things up to the patient to work them out.

To some extent, one might attempt to reconcile these two views by noting that Sullivan distinguished the "prescription of action" from everyday advice-giving. A long footnote on pages 212–214 of *The Psychiatric Interview* emphasizes the general uselessness and even harmfulness of giving advice, except in certain unusual circumstances. And the one explicit example of a "prescription of action" in the text involves simply saying to a patient, when something remains unclear at the end of the session, "The business of how so-and-so came about is obscure. Well, maybe it will come back to you by next time." (p. 212)

Such a reconciliation is an uneasy one, however. Even in the last example, Sullivan goes on to justify the interviewer giving the patient "something to do" as follows: "whether or not the interviewer suggests homework, the patient will do some before the next session, and *the interviewer may have somewhat better judgment about what might be useful than the patient has.*" (p. 212; italics added) Shortly thereafter (though, it must be acknowledged, here referring explicitly to the situation in which the interviewer will not see the patient again), Sullivan suggests that the interviewer indicate "a course of events in which the interviewee might engage and which, in the interviewer's opinion, in view of the data accumulated, would improve his chances of success and satisfaction in life." (p. 212)

Sullivan's reluctance to give advice to patients would thus seem to be based in large measure on a recognition that most advice about what to do in any particular situation is based on personal values and hunches and is not in any sense objective or expert. For the therapist to use his privileged position to espouse his personal views about rather ambiguous and idiosyncratically determined human choices is an abuse. For him to use his professional knowledge and experience, however, to inform the patient of courses of action that are likely to have fairly predictable consequences, is not only acceptable but is his responsibility. It is this trend in Sullivan's thought that seems to be compatible with a more active, directive therapeutic orientation—and by extension, with the addition of behavioral interventions to psychodynamic inquiry.

At the time Sullivan was writing, the technology of psychotherapeutic intervention was considerably less developed than today. The interventions that characterize modern behavior therapy, in particular, were either not yet developed or were largely unknown. Sullivan had few potent options to consider in formulating the view that the therapist should essentially stick to uncovering and leave the rest to the patient.

He was largely registering a negative reaction to efforts of psychiatrists to pawn off on their patients subjective advice that had little effective therapeutic value and that often reflected a rather paternalistic attitude toward the patient.

Additionally, Sullivan was, I think, more immersed in the Freudian milieu of American psychiatry than is usually recognized. Despite his increasing divergence from the Freudian position in the language of his formulations and in certain important substantive areas, he continued in many respects to hold an essentially Freudian model of the therapeutic encounter. The virtue of minimal direct intervention has been a strongly held assumption of most therapists who recognized the importance of unconscious motivation in psychological processes. The distinction between exploratory and manipulative or supportive therapies is sharply etched in most psychoanalytic writings on therapy; and though Sullivan's theoretical formulations provide a foundation for transcending this distinction, much of his writing on therapy continues to reflect it.

At the same time, however, Sullivan's conception of the therapist as a participant observer introduces a novel element into the understanding of the therapeutic process. It implies the possibility of the therapist's participating in a much wider variety of ways. The therapist can never really be a "blank screen," nor can one ever see "the patient" in any abstract or isolated sense. One always sees the person *in a context,* and in psychotherapy the therapist is part of that context. He is as much a part of the context if he is silent and invisible as if he is face to face with the patient and overtly and discernibly responding to him.

In some respects it may be argued that, though the therapist inevitably is partly responsible for what the patient does and feels in the therapy room, by varying his own behavior as little as possible from moment to moment and hour to hour, a greater proportion of what happens is due to factors within the patient. Merton Gill (1954), one of the most astute writers in the Freudian tradition, observes that the "clearest transference manifestations are those which occur when the analyst's behavior is constant, since under these circumstances changing manifestations in the transference cannot be attributed to an external situation, to some changed factor in the interpersonal relationship, but the analysand must accept responsibility himself." (p. 781)

From an interpersonal perspective, however, the series of increasingly primitive and bizarre reactions in the course of an analysis would appear not as an exposure, through regression, of "layers of the personality," but rather as a view of the hierarchy of reactions this person has *to this particular kind of frustration.* One doesn't elude the limits of participant observation or, so to speak, undo the Heisenberg principle, by being constant. One merely limits one's direct observations about the patient to his way of dealing with one kind of situation only. The analyst is cautioned not to gratify the patient's transference demands or, in behavioral terms, to reinforce the patient's initial efforts in the situation. Not surprisingly, meeting with little reward for his first efforts, the patient resorts to others lower on his hierarchy of responses for that situation, until he has displayed his most desperately irrational efforts at trying to get some response from the person he has turned to for help.

Has one seen deeper into the personality in such an event? One could as readily suggest that what is seen thereby is not deep but improbable, that one is seeing ways of reacting that are quite uncharacteristic of the patient and that he tries only when all else fails. Further, in such an effort to go deep, one's probing is also narrow. By staying constant, the therapist assures that he will not directly observe the patient's reaction to most of the typical kinds of behavior he encounters daily. How does the patient feel and react when praised, or scolded, or challenged? The point is not for the therapist to systematically treat the patient in every conceivable manner that one human being can treat another in order to see how he reacts. The ethical, as well as practical, reasons for not attempting such an undertaking are obvious. But an interpersonal perspective on what is revealed in the psychoanalytic session does suggest (a) that a greater range of permitted therapist behavior will lead to a greater range of the patient's potential ways of being becoming manifest in the sessions, and (b) that at the very least it is necessary to recognize that what is revealed by remaining constant is not "the" true underlying personality, but those aspects of the patient's possible modes of adaptation that are likely to occur in a context of frustration and minimal feedback.°

## THE INTERPERSONAL PERSPECTIVE AND ACTIVE INTERVENTION

From an interpersonal perspective, there are a number of converging indications pointing toward the value of directly intervening in the patient's day-to-day problems in living. Firstly, as we have just seen, the

° One does of course get a picture of the patient's reactions to varied interpersonal cues from his descriptions of his interactions with *others*. But, as discussed in Chapter 7, obtaining sufficient information in this regard may require methods of inquiring quite different from the traditional psychoanalytic approach.

idea that by not doing anything conspicuous one sees the patient (and the patient sees himself) as he really is, with his inner workings not disguised by any misleading reference to external causes of his behavior, appears to be an illusory idea. Secondly, the therapist need not worry that by acting in such a way as to prevent a full therapeutic regression and the emergence of archaic desires, he will leave the underlying cause of the patient's problems untouched and still able to generate symptoms or distort the patient's character. From an interpersonal perspective, such desires are viewed as existing in such primitive and intense form only because a self-defeating cyclical neurotic process is going on. These unconscious urges and fantasies are as much a consequence of the neurosis as a cause. By intervening directly in the way the patient overtly interacts with others, one may never get to see the archaic manifestations observed by analysts in a regressive transference neurosis. But according to the view presented here, this would be the case not because the therapist has failed to discover what is really there, but because what has been done by the therapist has *changed* what is there.

Finally, it is important to consider the price paid for *not* intervening. If the neurotic process is largely maintained by a cyclical re-confirming of neurotic assumptions by the consequences they bring about, then there should be many points at which the vicious circles are appropriately interrupted. Interpretive efforts, aimed at insight into origins or even current motives, are but one of many ways of disrupting the destructive circle of events. Often such interpretive efforts may be undermined if they are not combined with efforts aimed more directly at bringing about new behavior in day-to-day situations. This topic will be discussed in more detail in Chapter 10. For now a brief illustration will suffice.

Consider, for example, a young man whose developmental history has led to considerable anxiety over sexual activity and inhibitions in learning the everyday social skills involved in approaching a woman who interests him. He is caught in a vicious circle in which anxiety over sexual arousal leads to avoidance of sexual situations, hence poor learning of skills of social intercourse, hence awkward and ineffective approaches to women, leading to rebuff and the intensification of his anxiety over sexual feelings. Such a cyclical pattern, repeated countless times, is likely to be far more responsible for his current fear of women than the exotic symbolic representations of his anxiety that finally "emerge" in his analytic sessions. The anxiety may well have begun when he was four years old and longed for his mother, but it persists because sexual activity continues to be a source of painful reactions from others. In some cases of this sort it may be impossible effectively to reduce the patient's anxiety through interpretive work in the therapy hour, unless rather definite efforts are also made to assure that he acquire the requisite social skills: his "insight," in the session, that his fears are "unrealistic" is countered by his experience, after the session, of approaching a woman and encountering failure.

Such a description, with its implication that the therapist may need to be a teacher of basic social skills and that his efforts to bring about understanding may falter if he is not sufficiently active in bringing about effective behavior, is not a congenial one for many dynamic therapists, including many who view themselves as interpersonal rather than Freudian in orientation. It is frequently assumed that, once inhibitions stemming from the past are understood, the patient can readily behave in a more socially appropriate fashion. In my view, such an expectation reflects a failure to appreciate the subtlety of interpersonal communication. I would contend that the interpersonally oriented therapist who holds such a view has not fully carried through on the implications of an interpersonal understanding of the events and phenomena explored by psychoanalysis. I shall attempt to demonstrate this more extensively in Chapter 10.


## SITUATIONISM, HUMANISM, AND INTERACTION SEQUENCES

The view presented in this and the preceding chapter strongly emphasizes the role of current actual events in influencing our behavior and even our motives, and it places considerable stress on the consequences of actions taken. Such a view can easily be confused with the approach that Bowers (1973) has aptly criticized under the label of "situationism," or with the single-minded emphasis on response consequences characteristic of some Skinnerians. It is therefore necessary to make clear how the present view differs, and in what sense it partakes of a "psychodynamic" orientation.

By "situationism," Bowers is referring to the metaphysical assumption made by many experimental investigators that behavior is essentially and ultimately controlled by external conditions and that individual factors of disposition or organism are of little or no importance. Situationism in this sense is similar to the position described by Chein (1962) as the view of man as an "impotent reactor," and it is often associated as well with the view that motives and cognitions are either epiphenomena with no influence at all upon events or are, at most, weak variables with only a very slight influence. It is a view often seen as incongenial with humanism, in its de-emphasis of human choice and freedom (see particularly Skinner, 1971); and incompatible with psychoanalysis, in its apparent contention that fantasies or motives are not really determiners of behavior but are, at most, "mental way stations," concern with which distracts from the more important task of relating behavior to environmental events.

By contrast, the view presented in Chapters 4 and 5 contests neither the reality of human choices nor the validity of motives and fantasies as determiners of behavior. The issue of how to conceive of choice and freedom will be taken up in some detail in Chapter 12. The role of fantasies and motives will be considered now.

To view the fantasies and motives discerned by psychoanalysts as responsive to the events of the patient's life is not to question the value of understanding behavior as motivated or as guided by cognitions and expectations. As indicated earlier, what is suggested by the approach put forth here is that motives and fantasies can usefully be examined as both cause *and* effect. The exclusive emphasis by some analysts on these phenomena as ultimate causes, and the exclusive emphasis by some behaviorists on their understanding as dependent (or sometimes also mediating) variables are both limiting approaches, and neither exclusionary focus is necessary.

In response to the events of our lives, we develop a view of the world and of what we wish to seek out. On the basis of these views and goals we take actions, whose consequences may confirm or modify the views and goals already held. From the very beginning, both *who we are* and *what happens to us* jointly determine how we act. Thus, the reactions of the newborn to the very first events of his life (and probably even his first vague perceptual organization of these events) are a function not only of environmental events but also of inborn characteristics of temperament and rudiments of cognitive style. As Bowers (1973) puts it, citing the work of Escalona (1968, 1972) and of Wiggins, Renner, Clore, and Rose (1971), "Right from the outset, the situation must be specified in terms of the particular organism experiencing it." (p. 327)

In emphasizing, then, that the events of one's life play an important role in determining what fantasies and motives are important for a person (and, as we shall see in the next chapter, what fantasies and motives must remain unconscious), I am not suggesting that we slavishly respond to some "objective" environment. The events that influence us must be understood as events *as perceived*. Psychodynamically inspired inquiry, in particular, has made clear that our perception of events, especially interpersonal events, is both active and motivated (see Wolitzky and Wachtel, 1973). It is also the case, however, that our perceptions are generally constrained within limits set by what is actually taking place, and that the motives for perceiving in particular ways, and the particular perceptual selection and organization manifested, are themselves responsive to life events (see Klein, 1958; Solley and Murphy, 1960; Wachtel, 1972).

What is posited here, then, is a continuing interaction between cognitions and motivations on the one hand and external events on the other. Strictly speaking, the two domains may not be completely separable. But for purposes of understanding the flux of events that constitutes a life, we must analyze the flux in terms of some discernible and roughly repeatable sequences. What is frequently overlooked is that the point at which we break into the flux to discern a sequence or undertake a functional analysis is essentially arbitrary. Only by tapping in at many points can we gain a rich and adequate understanding.

Experimentally oriented researchers are keenly aware of the dangers of explanations of behavior based exclusively upon inner, organismic constructs and unrelated to environmental events. Mischel, for example, says the following:

> Perhaps the most fundamental criticism of cognitive and phenomenological explanations is that they are incomplete and do not provide a sufficiently detailed and comprehensive analysis of the causes controlling behavior.° In Kelly's theory, for example, personal constructs are viewed as key determinants of behavior, but what determines the constructs that a person has? Offering the construct as a cause of the observed behavior may be an example of an unfinished causal explanation. Such unfinished analyses are found whenever mental states, perceptions, cognitions, feelings, motives, or similar constructs are offered as explanations of behavior while the determinants of the mental states themselves are ignored. (Mischel, 1971, p. 104)

As far as this goes, I would tend to agree with Mischel. But it is necessary to recognize that the environmental "determinants" of the mental states can themselves be seen as a function of the mental states. As I have described in more detail elsewhere (Wachtel, 1973b), the clear distinction between independent and dependent variables evident in psychological experiments is not accompanied by a similar clear distinction in real-life events. The events that *happen to* us are in large

---

° I presume that Mischel would also include psychodynamic explanations here.

measure brought about by us, and can be seen as consequences of the behavior generated by our cognitions and motives. Consideration of the degree to which individuals actively construct their perceptual world (see Bowers, 1973; Kelly, 1955; Neisser, 1967) also highlights the limitation of viewing the environmental events effective in influencing behavior strictly as independent variables. It suggests that one might just as correctly say that what the person notices of what goes on about him, and how he construes it, is a function of his motives and cognitive activities. This is particularly the case with the ambiguous interpersonal and affective events that play such a crucial role in the phenomena of interest to psychotherapists (see Wachtel, 1973b, pp. 328–30).

There is more than one way to skin a cat, and more than one kind of "unfinished causal explanation." Neither analyses starting from motives and thoughts and seeking overt expressions, nor analyses starting from observable events and treating motives and thoughts as a function of them are God-given. Nor is either "finished." In contending that psychoanalytic inquiry has insufficiently emphasized the responsiveness of (even unconscious) wishes and fantasies to actual events, I am not suggesting that man is a slave to the environment. Nor does insisting on the legitimacy of understanding people's actions as deriving from their desires and perceptions signify a return to empty concern with "will power" or to the circular, pseudoexplanatory way of using mental constructs that Skinner seems to believe is the only alternative to his way of analyzing psychological events.

Accounts of personality development from learning theory and psychodynamic perspectives need not be incompatible. Both approaches can be used as vessels for smuggling contraband metaphysical freight or as legitimate tools for discerning previously unseen connections between events. Learning experiments and psychoanalytic observation have each pointed to important coherences that can aid our understanding and our ability to help. We shall next consider how these differing insights can explicitly be brought to bear on each other.

# 6

# *Anxiety, Conflict,*

# *and Learning in Neurosis*

FURTHER consideration of how neurotic patterns of behavior are perpetuated or may be changed, and of the possibilities of integrating dynamic and behavioral approaches, requires closer examination of the concepts of anxiety and conflict. These have been central concepts in both Freudian and interpersonal thought, and the status accorded them in various learning-theory accounts of neurosis bears importantly on the question of how compatible dynamic and behavioral views can be. Dollard and Miller's (1950) formulations will be of particular interest to us in this chapter, both in relation to psychoanalytic formulations and to other learning-theory approaches.

In attempting to compare the role of anxiety in various efforts to understand neurosis, it is useful to note a line of development in psychoanalytic thought characterized by a shift in emphasis from viewing neurosis as caused by what we *want* to viewing it as caused by what we *fear*. Any theory that emphasizes conflict is, of course, likely to look at both wishes and fears; but in the early years of psychoanalytic inquiry, the forbidden wishes were of far greater interest than what made them forbidden. Anxiety was initially viewed by Freud simply as a discharge phenomenon resulting from repression. When the repressed wish did not achieve discharge in sufficient degree through symptoms, dreams, and other emergency valves, another form of discharge occurred: the direct conversion of libido into anxiety. It is likely that this formulation was aided by the frequency with which anxiety occurs in forms not directly experienced as fear. The appearance of such phenomena as rapid heartbeat, sinking stomach, sweating, and so on, often without the cognition of fear, readily lends itself to the metaphor of discharge.

But, as we know, Freud did eventually come to view anxiety as a *cause* of repression rather than its consequence. The state of apprehension generated by the arousal of particular impulses was seen as leading to the only kind of flight available from an internal danger: flight from awareness. The person learned to direct his attention elsewhere and, often, to develop elaborate schemes to assure that he would not become aware of, or openly act upon, these impulses. I am referring, of course, to the mechanisms of defense.

Following this reformulation of Freud's, the pervasive role of anxiety in psychopathology increasingly came to be recognized. Particularly important were the elaborations of the concept of *signal anxiety*. That is, no longer was anxiety viewed as only an experienced affect state or discharge phenomenon. Rather, anxiety came to be seen as a phenomenon whose effects were perhaps most important when they were silent or invisible. As the person learned to *anticipate* the events that led to distress and discomfort, quite minimal increases in the level of tension could lead to avoidance behavior and a redirection of attention and behavior. This avoidance then prevented re-examination of the possibility of danger, since extended contact with the source of fear was not allowed to occur. More basic than the preservation of old desires, then, was the preservation of old fears, for the former depended upon the latter (i.e., old fears kept defenses going, which in turn prevented the integration of the old wishes into the more mature ego).

The changes in Freud's view of anxiety, and particularly his formulations regarding signal anxiety, were major contributions to the emerging understanding of neurosis and character development. By the time that these conceptions were articulated, however, Freud's ideas about personality development and psychotherapeutic intervention had already taken shape in a quite definite way—Freud was 70 when *Inhibitions, Symptoms, and Anxiety* was published—and the impact of his new ideas about anxiety was constrained substantially. These ideas were essentially assimilated into an already-formed theoretical structure rather than forming the basis of a new structure, as they well might have.

The theoretical strategies of both Horney and Sullivan, in contrast, were largely worked out *after* the role of anxiety had been clarified, and both of their positions reflect this. Anxiety plays a considerably more central role in the theoretical efforts of Horney and of Sullivan than it does in Freudian theory, notwithstanding its importance to the latter as well. Much of the peremptory and irrational behavior that Freud attributed to the press of biological drives and their "derivatives" is, in the opinion of Horney (1939), best understood as behavior motivated by anxiety. For interpersonally oriented psychodynamic thinkers, Freud's later insights into the role of anxiety served as the basis for a rather major reorientation in understanding neurosis and character development. These insights were viewed as having more radical consequences for Freud's earlier formulations than were acknowledged by Freud or his more orthodox followers.

## THE CONTRIBUTION OF DOLLARD AND MILLER

Dollard and Miller (1950), in their reformulation of psychoanalytic ideas in learning terms, also took as a major point of departure the ideas about anxiety expressed in Freud's later writings.° Their formulations are critical to the present effort to bring together ideas and methods originating in the psychodynamic tradition and those clinical methods that have developed from attempts to change troubling patterns of behavior by a direct application of the concepts of learning research. Not only do Dollard and Miller provide a valuable foundation for any further efforts to integrate contributions from these two seemingly disparate realms, they also (as I will try to show later in this chapter) provide a basis for a clearer approach to such traditional psychoanalytic concepts as insight, conflict resolution, and working through.

### DOLLARD AND MILLER'S IMPLICIT CONCEPTUAL STRATEGY

Before considering some of the substantive features of Dollard and Miller's formulation, it is important to clarify some common misunderstandings of what they were trying to do. The terminology they use is

---

° For the non-professional reader it may be useful to know that Dollard and Miller are psychologists who were active in attempting to translate psychoanalytic ideas into terms which could be tested in the experimental laboratory. Dollard was an eminent anthropologist and sociologist before turning to the study of psychotherapy. Miller was a leading experimental researcher from the point of view of learning theory (and is currently one of the major figures in the study of bio-feedback procedures). Their book had a major impact when it first was published, but is less influential today. It will be obvious, however, that I regard it still as a valuable source of stimulating and clarifying ideas.

that of stimuli and responses, and this terminology has strong positive connotations for some and strong negative connotations for others. It is a terminology that derives originally from a laboratory tradition in which discrete, overt muscle movements or glandular secretions were related to discrete patterns of excitation presented to the sense organs. The adequacy of the stimulus-response approach has been challenged even for understanding relatively simple laboratory phenomena (e.g., Saltz, 1971), and its value for conceptualizing the complex events of human social behavior has been questioned most seriously. It has been claimed, with considerable justification, that the use of stimulus-response terminology in discussions of such phenomena as thoughts and images represents only the vaguest metaphorical extension of those terms (Breger and McGaugh, 1965).

Such criticisms are quite relevant to the not uncommon efforts to cloak particular conceptual strategies and laboratory models in the trappings of science and relegate all other approaches to understanding to a realm somewhere between fraud and superstition. These "scientistic" accounts treat clinically derived theories, especially psychodynamic ones, as at best well-intentioned efforts reflecting the inadequacy of pre-scientific thought. Their use of terms such as "stimulus" and "response" seems to imply, by contrast, a rigorous and precise analysis of clearly defined and measured events. Such anti-clinical and anti-psychoanalytic writers are indeed performing a bit of verbal sleight of hand when they sneak through the back door such phenomena and concepts as thought, image, or feeling, while the front door says, "Scientists at work: only stimuli and responses allowed. Psychoanalysts and clinicians prohibited."

Dollard and Miller, however, do not use stimulus-response terminology in the same fashion. To be sure, they do suggest that analysis in terms of stimuli and responses can clarify matters left ambiguous by traditional clinical theories, and they contend as well that their way of conceptualizing clinical phenomena renders hypotheses more testable than do traditional ways of talking about what patients do. But they are by no means hostile to psychoanalysis or dismissive toward clinical observation. Further, they use terms such as stimulus and response, not to evoke connotations of scientific precision, but to test out the limits of applicability of a conceptual framework that they feel has had a good deal of utility in the more modest context of laboratory experiments.

Dollard and Miller are under no illusion that by calling a tendency to sulk when insulted a "response to a stimulus," they are making it any easier to measure sulking or insulting. They use an S-R analysis not for its connotations but for its clues about the *functional properties* of psychologically relevant events.° This may be clarified by turning directly to their conceptual approach to understanding the implications of fear or anxiety.†

### FEAR AND ANXIETY IN DOLLARD AND MILLER'S ANALYSIS

Dollard and Miller suggest that fear can be fruitfully studied as a *response*. By so conceptualizing fear, they are essentially postulating that fear obeys the same laws as do external, readily observable responses. Starting with demonstrations that fear can be learned in the same way that other responses are learned, they proceed to establish other parallels as well. As they put it:

> Overt responses can be observed easily and have been fairly well studied. Many of their functional properties are known; they can be learned, generalized to new stimuli, extinguished, inhibited by conflicting responses, facilitated by summation, and so forth. Fear is more difficult to observe, but we are advancing the tentative hypothesis that it has all the functional properties of a response. (p. 68)

It is important to note that Dollard and Miller are talking here of tentative hypotheses. They are perfectly aware of drawing analogies from one realm of observation to another. The analogy is not being categorically asserted; it is being put forth as a working assumption, which will be retained if it proves useful. In what ways it *has* proved useful we will consider shortly.

First we must note, however, the other aspects of Dollard and Miller's approach to the analysis of fear. Fear can be studied not only as a kind of response. It may also be fruitfully viewed as a drive, in the sense that it energizes behavior and that its reduction is reinforcing; responses that reduce fear are likely to be strengthened and retained. Further, fear has cue properties, guiding and signalling what behavior is called for.

In Dollard and Miller's view, at the heart of most of the difficulties that bring people to therapy is anxiety that is attached to cues associated

---

° Although they are clearly committed to an S-R approach, their emphasis on functional properties, that is, on extensions of empirically observed relationships, will enable us later to consider how some of the perspective provided by their analysis can be useful even if a more cognitive learning theory is ultimately seen as more adequate than an S-R theory. Since they use an S-R analysis as a tool rather than as a battering ram for philosophical disputes with cognitive and psychoanalytic thinkers, we can consider the empirical utility of their propositions apart from their particular commitment.

† Dollard and Miller do not emphasize the distinction between fear and anxiety. They note that when "the source of fear is vague or obscured by repression, it is often called anxiety." (p. 63)

with the arousal of, and efforts to gratify, important interpersonal needs. As the person begins to feel inclined to approach someone sexually, or assert anger or disagreement, or seek protective succor or needed support or assistance, the cues associated with these inclinations evoke anxiety. Any activity which then diminishes those anxiety-arousing cues (or, I would add, diminishes *attention* to the cues) is strongly rewarded, for anxiety-reduction tends to be strongly reinforcing. °

Dollard and Miller note that there has been little really adequate research on precisely how anxiety comes to be associated with inclinations and activities so vital to successful functioning in our society, or why conflicts of this nature are so prevalent. But they venture to speculate in some detail how such anxiety could be learned, relying on what has been gleaned from clinical studies and on their knowledge of the literature on learning and of child-rearing patterns in our culture. Their analysis relies heavily on several features of human development and of child-rearing practices that have been central to the formulations of Freudian and neo-Freudian writers. They note, for example, the extreme helplessness of the human young and his or her vulnerability to the disapproval and mood changes of the parents as a result of the child's dependence upon them. They stress as well the relatively poor ability of the child to plan and anticipate and to recognize that a state of distress will come to an end. The child is thus confronted with events that are difficult to comprehend and that leave him with extreme states of misery or well-being. Dollard and Miller elucidate a variety of ways in which strong anxiety and conflict are particularly likely to be learned in the course of the early feeding situation, cleanliness training, early sex training, and situations in which the child is angry.

Anxiety that is associated with inclinations and feelings of almost inevitable importance in our society creates a particularly excruciating situation. When we learn to fear an external stimulus, we can often avoid it fairly readily.† But if anxiety is associated with our own strong inclinations, then we are also moved to approach what we fear, not simply to avoid it. The distinction between possible ways of coping with threats

---

° Seligman and Johnston (1973) have suggested that with persistent avoidance responses, it is often the occurrence of a safety signal rather than the avoidance of anxiety that is reinforcing. In their analysis, however, it is still necessary that certain cues be capable of producing fear if they do occur, and the main points in this chapter do not seem to be altered if one accepts their analysis.

† This is not always the case, of course. Elevator or travel phobias, for example, can interfere with one's social life and livelihood in a variety of ways and thus be a source of considerable conflict. But as noted below, behavior therapists have recently questioned whether the appropriate model for most such phobias really is just a simple conditioning of fear to an external stimulus.

that are external and those arising from within the person was frequently emphasized by Freud. It is also central to why Dollard and Miller's picture of neurotic distress emphasizes not just anxiety but conflict as well.

In principle, the contention by writers such as Wolpe (1958) and Eysenck (e.g., Eysenck and Beech, 1971) that anxiety alone is sufficient to produce most of the behavior evident in neuroses is probably correct. Dollard and Miller, too, despite their clear position that in most actual clinical neuroses conflict is readily discernable and central, would agree that intense anxiety alone, even without conflict, *could* produce neurotic behavior. Some phobias, for example, do seem to be simple conditioned-anxiety responses. Dollard and Miller in fact begin their discussion of phobias with a wartime case of a pilot who developed an intense fear of airplanes and anything connected with them, after a very traumatic experience in carrying out a bombing mission. Their account describes the conditioning of fear to cues associated with this terrifying experience.

But if some cases seem best understood as instances of fear conditioning to external situational cues, it must also be recognized that, outside of combat situations and occasional accidents, the conditions of everyday adult life are not likely, without some pre-existing characterological vulnerability,° to be anxiety-provoking to nearly such an extreme. Without some prior basis, the anxiety aroused by a social rebuff or poor performance on an exam would not be expected to be comparable to that evoked by the intense, prolonged, and life-threatening stress of combat. Mild or moderate anxiety would be expected by theorists of varying viewpoints (e.g., Eysenck and Beech, 1971; Dollard and Miller, 1950) to be extinguished in the course of day-to-day living, perhaps with the aid of friends and other informal therapeutic agents, but without the need for professional therapeutic assistance.

Thus, while Dollard and Miller are quite ready to acknowledge that

---

° There may, as Eysenck in particular has suggested, be variations in vulnerability due to biological factors as well as early experiences and character development. The former does not seem sufficient, however, to account for the specifics of just which kinds of stresses are magnified in which people.

The concept of incubation (Eysenck and Beech, 1971) has also been offered to account for how subtraumatic events can have such a powerful impact. Conceptualizing some such mechanism may well prove useful in understanding the cumulative effect of numerous subtraumatic events, and for understanding why neurotic fears often do not extinguish as readily as one might expect. Again, however, such an approach, if meant to *substitute* for notions of conflict and characterological vulnerability instead of to complement them, leaves unexplained the intricate connections between the various aspects of the patient's problems and life style. Eysenck, of course, is skeptical that such connections can be reliably shown to exist, and proposes a strategy of examining each problematic habit in isolation.

a simple fear-conditioning explanation may be adequate for some cases of combat neuroses (and hence that fear alone, without conflict, may in principle lead to neurotic behavior), they nonetheless maintain that in most cases seen for therapy, it is not a simple pairing of a stressful event with a previously neutral cue that is mainly at issue. Rather, the patient's problems appear most often to involve anxiety and avoidances associated with interpersonal events, and to derive in a complex way from the vulnerability of the child to parental disapproval or rejection and from the kinds of life experiences and adaptational strategies made likely thereby. Their approach stresses conflict and not just conditioned anxiety, because the anxiety in most clinical cases tends to be largely associated with the arousal of important motivational tendencies: the person is both drawn to a goal and afraid—that is, in conflict.

It is interesting that even where traumas such as auto accidents, getting caught in an elevator, and so on do play a role in bringing about a specific phobia, some behavior therapists report that there is frequently a characterological basis that determines whether the phobic reaction will persist. Fodor (1974), for example, emphasizes the frequent relationship between phobic reactions and a dependent, nonassertive life style (see also Lazarus, 1971; Andrews, 1966). And even the classic behavior therapy literature is not without case reports that seem to require consideration of conflict and not merely fears conditioned to external cues (e.g., Wolpe, 1969, p. 30 ff.). Further consideration of the nature of the fears associated with most clinical neuroses will be undertaken in Chapter 7.

LEARNING ANALYSIS OF REPRESSION

Central to Dollard and Miller's account of neurosis, as it is to Freud's, is the phenomenon of repression. Dollard and Miller illustrate a variety of ways in which anxiety can come to be associated with *thoughts*, thus leading to the avoidance of thinking certain things. For one thing, children are frequently punished for saying things in ways unacceptable to parents or for announcing intentions to act in disapproved ways. Such punishment may be overt and intended or it may be in the form of subtle gestures indicating parental disapproval or withdrawal, gestures of which the parent may well be unaware. Whatever the nature of the punishing event, the child can come to fear saying certain things and, by generalization, to fear thinking them as well. Dollard and Miller provide evidence that fear associated with spoken words can generalize to unspoken thoughts.

Fear can also be learned directly in connection with thoughts, without the mediation of spoken words and sentences. The thoughts a child is thinking just before committing a punished act can become fear-evoking, since like the act itself, they precede an aversive event. Additionally, parents can often pick up cues indicating the child's intent before he has acted or spoken. They may then stiffen and warn the child when he has done little overtly, and thereby attach fear to the thought itself, as well as interfering with the child's ability to discriminate clearly between the consequences of thoughts and overt acts.

Still another way in which thoughts are directly made frightening occurs when, as is frequent, the child is reprimanded or punished considerably after the act has occurred. The parent is then likely to remind the child what he did wrong, and the punishment or scolding occurs when the child is thinking about it or remembering it rather than when he is actually doing it.

In all these ways, thoughts can come to be anxiety-provoking, and thus the avoidance of such thoughts can become reinforcing. This highly motivated avoidance of certain thoughts is a central feature of repression. It is conceptualized by Dollard and Miller in terms of a response of *stopping thinking*.

In thus stretching the usage of the term "response," Dollard and Miller are again relying on a functional conception of stimulus and response. Labelling the events of repression as the response of "stopping thinking" does not magically render these events as easy to identify as pressing a bar or blinking an eye, and Dollard and Miller are well aware of this. Identifying the occurrence of the "stopping thinking" response requires the same kind of careful clinical observation and inference as the phenomenon demands in its traditional psychoanalytic appellation. The therapist needs to notice shifts in the direction of conversation, persistent avoidance of certain topics, signs of anxiety when such shifts or avoidance don't occur, and so on. Often this is not easy, because the stopping thinking is likely to be rather well rationalized and often subtle and/or disguised.°

But in linking these clinical observations to a learning theory framework, Dollard and Miller accomplish two things. Firstly, by conceptualizing a *response*, they are emphasizing that the person is *doing* something. In this they are amplifying a trend in psychoanalytic ego psychology, in which the older psychoanalytic imagery of defenses as counter-forces

---

° Once it addresses itself to a wide range of clinical phenomena, behavior therapy too requires substantial inference. The nature of inferences in psychodynamic and behavioral therapies will be taken up later in this book.

or as dams has largely given way to a recognition that defenses must be studied as activities of the ego. Clinically, analysts now stress that the patient must be shown what he is *doing* when he is defending, as well as being shown what he is defending against.

Secondly, Dollard and Miller's conceptualization of the "stopping thinking" response suggests, in similar fashion to the earlier illustration of fear as a response, that relations between events evident with simpler stimuli and responses may be discerned in this less accessible realm as well. Thus, one is led to ask what reinforces the response of stopping thinking and what events cue its onset. Similarly, one is led to look for parallels with more readily observable responses, and to consider whether ways of intervening that are effective with them might be helpful in dealing with repressions as well (see Chapters 8 and 9).

CONSEQUENCES OF REPRESSION

Dollard and Miller's analysis makes clear two particularly harmful effects of repression on the individual's efforts to live a rewarding and comfortable life. Firstly, as a form of avoidance, repression prevents the person from coming into contact with that which he fears, and thus prevents him from ever knowing if his fears are no longer justified. As life circumstances change, particularly in the course of maturation to adulthood, many things that were once a source of threat are no longer dangerous. But by persistently avoiding the anxiety-provoking cues, the individual never gets to discover this. He continues to be restricted by his early fears, thus limiting his opportunities for a variety of gratifications and often maintaining him in a state of distressing conflict.

Secondly, and at least as important, repression interferes with the higher mental processes, which are so crucial to optimal functioning. Dollard and Miller note a variety of ways in which repression has this effect. When the individual is unable to think and verbalize about things of importance in his life, he is deprived of the opportunities language and thought provide for making fine distinctions and for categorizing and conceptualizing in complex ways that go beyond immediate stimulus properties. Socially sophisticated equivalencies require language to represent them and are interfered with when there are inhibitions of language and thought. Further, words and thoughts are essential to a great deal of our planning and problem-solving and, by enabling us to represent past and future events, they free us from the control of immediately present stimuli. Additionally, repression interferes with the ability to accurately state what is troubling, and thus to get adequate help in dealing with the problem.*

In the analytic session, the consequences of repression are manifested as "resistance." The patient blocks, changes the subject, and does a variety of other things (motivated by the need to avoid thinking various fear-provoking thoughts) that prevent the analyst from getting a clear look at the patient's life and his inclinations.

For all these reasons, the individual who has learned to be afraid of and to avoid a fairly wide range of thoughts is considerably hampered in efforts to work out useful solutions to life problems. As Dollard and Miller put it, the person who uses repression extensively behaves stupidly.

### FEAR AND PSYCHOTHERAPY

Following through on their explication of the crucial role of fear or anxiety in generating neurotic problems, Dollard and Miller present an analysis of psychoanalytic psychotherapy in which reduction of fear is the central therapeutic process. The therapist creates an atmosphere and sets up a situation in which the patient is encouraged and facilitated in talking about things that arouse anxiety. He begins to talk about these things very tentatively and haltingly, anticipating some kind of negative or punishing response. When the therapist responds in an accepting manner, showing little or no discomfort and encouraging the patient to continue, some of the patient's anxiety is extinguished.

This extinction generalizes to related thoughts and reactions, so that a related thought previously just slightly too anxiety-provoking to be free of inhibition can now occur. In such a fashion, ideas and inclinations that were originally quite anxiety-provoking and hence quite strongly repressed can gradually be approached. Progressively more anxiety-provoking thoughts are in turn expressed and go unpunished. The patient's anxiety is thereby somewhat extinguished, and the extinction in turn generalizes to a still more conflicted response, enabling it to be disinhibited.

The process is of course slow and does not progress uniformly or continually. But if the general direction can be maintained in this way,

---

* I am personally skeptical that even an extended S-R framework will prove very useful in furthering understanding of the higher mental processes (though it may, by use of such strategies as treating complex Gestalts as "cues," be able to assimilate new understanding after the fact). But Dollard and Miller's account of how the higher mental processes are *disrupted* by anxiety and repression seems to me a useful starting point, even if one prefers a more cognitive approach to the processes themselves.

a number of important things happen. Firstly, as the anxiety associated with important inclinations begins to be extinguished, some of the reinforcement for the patient's symptoms begins to diminish; for as we saw, reduction of anxiety is one of the important motives maintaining symptomatic behavior.

As this process occurs, and the patient begins to be able to think about things previously repressed, there begins to be a reversal of the exacerbating influence of interference with higher mental processes. As the patient can begin to experience and formulate verbally some of the influences in his life, he is in a position to make better discriminations between safe and unsafe situations. Irrational anxiety is further reduced by the increased ability to verbalize and discriminate, and this reduction in turn leads to still further reduction in the stopping-thinking behavior of repression, hence to increased capacity to discriminate and reduce inappropriate anxiety still further, and so on. The reduction in interference with higher mental processes also enables the patient to begin to act more planfully and realistically in his day-to-day living and hence to further reduce some of the factors producing anxiety, conflict, and disturbingly high drive levels. Generally, the cycle of events in the course of therapy can be seen as the reverse of the interacting series of factors, described above, that produce and perpetuate the neurosis. As anxiety is the most basic factor in generating neurosis, extinction of anxiety is seen as the most central process in the therapeutic reduction of neurosis.

## ANXIETY AND CONFLICT RESOLUTION

Dollard and Miller's analysis provides a useful perspective on what is meant by "resolving" a conflict. The psychoanalytic literature is surprisingly devoid of clear definitions of this key term, which appears with such great frequency in discussions of therapeutic process. The term "resolution" tends to be used as if its meaning were self-evident. The question of what is meant by resolution, or *how* a conflict gets resolved, is rarely addressed. Yet the meaning of the term is far from obvious, and it can seem to explain far more than it actually does.

Though clearly not intended to imply a purely intellectual decision-making process, the term "resolve" does often seem to imply some kind of choice or decision that the person is able to make once he has a clearer picture of what the nature of his conflicts are. When defenses no longer obscure vital aspects of the patient's emotional life, and infantile fantasies are exposed to the light of rationality, the "reasonable ego" can appraise and choose effectively. Decision-making and rational analysis certainly are an important part of how we can come to make helpful choices and behave in ways that enhance our adaptation. Dollard and Miller also emphasize the importance of restoring efficient use of the higher mental processes to the patient; and use of these processes is not just an *outcome* of therapy, but is part of how therapeutic change occurs. The patient's ability to verbalize his experiences and the facilitating of discrimination between past and present conditions are crucial aspects of the process of change as well as of continued adaptive functioning.

But it is clear from Dollard and Miller's analysis that decision-making is only a part of what "resolving" a neurotic conflict entails. Even more crucial is the reduction of the avoidance tendencies that prevent the patient from reaching his goals and that make thinking seem a danger as well. Though the patient is certainly very much in need of becoming more conscious of his own motives, in light of Dollard and Miller's analysis it may be said that his actions are irrational and self-defeating not so much because of what he doesn't know as because he is *afraid*. Resolving his conflict means most of all reducing his irrational anxiety; then he will be free to think things through, to feel the full range of human emotions, and to carry through sequences of behavior that can lead him to his goals.

Dollard and Miller's emphasis on extinction of anxiety in the resolution of neurotic conflict is in principle quite compatible with (and in a sense merely a translation of) psychoanalytic thought on this matter. Certainly Dollard and Miller build on the position taken by Freud in *Inhibitions, Symptoms and Anxiety* (1926), and it is hard to imagine a modern analyst who would not claim to be centrally concerned with anxiety and who does not see reduction of unrealistic anxieties as a crucial aspect of his work. Yet if one examines discussions of conflict resolution in the psychoanalytic literature, one sees surprisingly little direct emphasis on anxiety reduction as the central feature.

For example, implicit in much psychoanalytic discussion of conflict resolution is the idea of renunciation as the means of resolving neurotic conflict. Once the patient becomes fully aware of what he has been seeking, he is in a position to give up his infantile strivings and turn elsewhere. A particularly clear example of this may be found in Dewald's *The Psychoanalytic Process* (1972), which also has the virtue for our purposes of being one of the very rare accounts in the psychoanalytic literature that provides fairly acceptable raw data. Dewald's book provides essentially verbatim notes, written by him during the sessions, of major portions of an analysis, as well as interpolated accounts of his thoughts about the sessions and the rationale for what he did and didn't do.

In discussing a session in which he interprets to the patient that her current lack of fulfillment with husband and children is due to her persisting wish for her father, Dewald states that when awareness of this wish "is ultimately fully appreciated and recognized by the patient, it will represent an important step towards final resolution of the neurosis, inasmuch as it then indicates to the patient that she carries within herself the potential for *renunciation* of the childhood demands *and thus for resolution* and cure of the neurotic suffering." (p. 375; italics added) Here we see also the close relation between the renunciation view of conflict resolution and the "woolly mammoth" model. The patient is seen as suffering from the results of a persisting childhood wish and fantasy. The causality is unidirectional (that is, there is no mention of how her current frustrations with her family might contribute to the persistence of the "childhood" longing). And the therapeutic aim is to bring to light this preserved bit of the past so that rationality can then override it.

In Dewald's summary overview of the "clinical theory of the therapeutic process," one finds such terms as "mobilization" of conflict, "revitalization" of conflict, and "reexperiencing" conflict; one reads of the need to "develop, explore and ultimately resolve" the transference neurosis; one sees references to "renunciation" and "active giving up" of infantile wishes and objects, and to conflicts being "subjected to the patient's mature secondary-process reasoning and reality-testing." What one does not see amidst all these phrases is the simple statement that resolving neurotic conflict involves, very centrally, the reduction of unrealistic anxiety.

The range of phrases Dewald uses to address the issue of how neurotic conflict is resolved is rather typical of the language one sees in the analytic literature on this topic, and his lack of explicit reference to anxiety reduction is hardly an idiosyncratic omission. To be sure, Freud did make clear in 1926 how anxiety plays a crucial role in neurotic conflict, and analysts certainly discuss anxiety frequently in all sorts of contexts. Nonetheless, the role of anxiety reduction has not really been well integrated into most psychoanalytic discussions of how the therapeutic process works. The persistence of highly evocative terms such as "mobilizing," "exploring," "reexperiencing," and "resolving" conflicts, and the concomitant persistence of an image of rational decision-making opposed to and transposing processes deeply emotional and irrational, prevents the role of anxiety reduction from being seen as clearly as it might. Thus, while Dollard and Miller's discussion in learning terms may be seen as merely putting into other language insights that Freud bequeathed to the psychoanalytic community, their approach to conceptualizing the therapeutic process clarifies and highlights the issue of anxiety reduction in a way far from typical of writings in the traditional psychoanalytic vein.

### ANXIETY REDUCTION AND WORKING THROUGH

The clarifying nature of an emphasis on anxiety reduction is also evident in discussions of "working through," another term that appears frequently in the psychoanalytic literature but that is rarely defined very clearly. The term is an important one in that it points to an aspect of therapy that is critical to the outcome of the process. But it is frequently used in a way that implies an explanation when it really is only a sign that one is needed. The concept of working through entered psychoanalytic thought fairly early, as it began to be recognized that merely remembering, or even remembering with a strong affective experience, did not usually produce lasting change. Freud noted in "Remembering, Repeating, and Working-through" (1914a) that beginning analysts forget that

> naming the resistance could not result in its immediate suspension. One must allow the patient time to get to know this resistance of which he is ignorant, to 'work through' it, to overcome it, by continuing the work according to the analytic rule in defiance of it. Only when it has come to its height can one, with the patient's cooperation, discover the repressed instinctual trends which are feeding the resistance; and only by living them through in this way will the patient be convinced of their existence and their power. . . . This 'working through' . . . is the part of the work that effects the greatest changes in the patient and that distinguishes analytic treatment from every kind of suggestive treatment. (pp. 375–76)

Working through, in this early use of the term, is not related to anxiety at all, but essentially to facilitating the patient's *knowing* something about himself. The earlier view that intellectual knowledge of what has been repressed will be curative has now been superseded, but the nature of the newer emotional or experiential knowing brought about by resistance analysis is not yet clear, nor is the process whereby change occurs.

Modern accounts of working through often have a fairly similar emphasis. Working through is described as a way of letting the patient see his conflicts from a variety of perspectives, of deepening understanding, of presenting the patient with the range of meanings evident in his psychic life, of elaborating insights through repetition, of permitting the ego to gradually absorb new experiences, and so on. Increasingly, however, it has come to be recognized that one of the central reasons, if not *the* central reason, that repetitive exposure to conflicted material is necessary is to enable inappropriate anxiety to diminish. Insight into what is desired but disavowed may still be sought, but the gradual unlearning of reactions of anxiety has been recognized as critical.

Unlike his account of conflict resolution, Dewald's discussion of working through does consider anxiety reduction, but in a highly rationalistic way, emphasizing rational appraisal and conscious scrutiny. According to Dewald, the "application of secondary process reasoning to the previously pathogenic primary-process fantasies permits the patient to recognize in the current situation the irrationality and unreality of the situations which previously had been unconsciously experienced as dangerous." He goes on to indicate that the gradual reduction and ultimate elimination of anxiety, guilt, shame, and so on are due to "repeated exposure to rational perception and conscious integration."

A somewhat less intellectualized picture of anxiety reduction in working through was provided by Schur at a psychoanalytic meeting on working through. Schur likened the task of the psychoanalytic patient to that of the child who "after having painfully learned about many dangers . . . is now required to learn that anxiety is unwarranted in so many situations." He then noted that the work of working through may be viewed as "an immediate complex repetition of a habituation process which enabled the child to unlearn his appraisal of danger." (Reported by Schmale, 1966, pp. 178–79.)

Dollard and Miller's discussion makes the role of anxiety reduction and its relation to repetition even clearer. As we have seen, Dollard and Miller's account of the interacting factors in neurosis implies that reduction of anxiety is critical. To some extent, this may be accomplished by fostering discrimination between safe and unsafe situations. In this sense they are talking about processes akin to those described by Dewald, and their discussion of how the elimination of repression enables increased use of higher mental processes is much like that of analysts who see abrogation of defenses as leading to appraisal of formerly unconscious fantasies by the mature ego.

But rational appraisal and discrimination are not the only ways in which anxiety is reduced. Repeated exposure to the cues that evoke anxiety, so that the anxiety response can be extinguished through lack of reinforcement, is also extremely important. (Recall that earlier we noted Dollard and Miller's contention that anxiety can fruitfully be viewed as a response and can be found to exhibit all the functional properties of the overt responses more readily studied in the laboratory.) Extinction of anxiety requires repeated exposure to the anxiety-provoking cues without the anticipated harmful reaction. The working-through process can thus be seen as a series of extinction trials. By talking over and over again about the wishes and fantasies he fears, the patient is exposing himself to the anxiety-provoking cues, which are largely response-produced cues associated with his own thoughts and behavioral inclinations. This repeated exposure enables the anxiety response to these cues to gradually be extinguished.

Responses are rarely extinguished with just one or two unreinforced trials, and anxiety is a response that has been found to be particularly difficult to extinguish. Thus, working through tends to be a prolonged process. Through repression and other kinds of avoidances, the patient has largely avoided exposing himself to the most anxiety-provoking cues; thus he has prevented the extinction of anxiety to cues that no longer realistically signal danger. The therapist's efforts at interpretation can largely be seen in this context as ways of getting the patient to expose himself to the dangers he has fearfully avoided. Since the "dangers" in this case are the patient's own thoughts and inclinations, the therapist must disrupt the patient's efforts to avoid certain lines of thought or to not notice certain aspects of his behavior and experience. The therapist's interpretations of defense or resistance are means of disrupting the effectiveness of these habitual avoidances, making likely more direct exposure to the fear-provoking response-produced cues. His interpretations of content represent a somewhat different means of facilitating exposure, in this case by eliciting rehearsal of the feared thoughts (see Dollard and Miller, pp. 289–301).

### INTELLECTUAL AND EMOTIONAL INSIGHT

We are now in a better position to see just how potentially significant was the shift in emphasis, noted earlier, from wish to fear as the central factor in neurosis. The emphasis on uncovering hidden wishes and fantasies, in the way in which it is discussed in much of the psychoanalytic literature, can be seen as the heritage of the early formulations discussed in Chapter 2: something from the past is buried, kept apart, and when it is fully known and understood, cure will ensue. In this view, working through is primarily understood as the elaboration of insight, the seeing of a more and more complex web of connections and meanings.

This way of looking at the therapeutic process must deal with the persistently reported observation that emotionless remembering and understanding tend to have little therapeutic value. The way of dealing with the problem traditionally has been to distinguish between intellectual and emotional insight. This seems to me a rather unsatisfactory solution. Precisely why emotional insight is therapeutic and intellectual insight is not cannot readily be addressed by means of this conceptual strategy. It provides a *name*, which helps point to an important distinction, but it gives little help in providing an explanation. Moreover, the decision about whether an insight is a real insight or only an intellectual one is not always easy to make at the time. Often, the decision is made retrospectively, when the patient does not change after voicing it. The difficulties with such circularity should be obvious.

The problem of intellectual versus emotional insight looks somewhat different from another point of view—one such as that which caused me to treat "working through" largely as a process of repeated exposure to anxiety-provoking cues, or repeated extinction trials. From this viewpoint one sees that insight in the course of therapy is not only a cause of therapeutic change but a consequence or sign of such change as well. Alexander and French (1946) stressed this point some time ago in their explication of the therapeutic effects of the corrective emotional experience, and Dollard and Miller's analysis points in a similar direction. Reduction in anxiety helps to eliminate repression and hence to facilitate thinking and memory. These changes are often manifested as "insights." They are not mere epiphenomena, in that they do contribute substantially to still further change—for example, by enabling the person to understand more clearly what he wants and how to go about getting it, by broadening the range of alternative ways of dealing with life situations that may be considered, and by fostering better discriminations between what is safe and what unsafe to do and, as part of that, between the consequences of thoughts and actions. But understanding the respective and interacting roles, in therapy, of insights and of exposure to cues that evoke anxiety enables us to understand somewhat better the problem of intellectual versus emotional insight.

At times, reduction in anxiety, or some other aspect of the therapeutic situation, enables the patient to verbalize about inclinations that he was previously too scared to acknowledge. Whether further change will follow upon this depends importantly on whether he merely emits words or whether he produces the whole complex of anxiety-provoking cues —words together with autonomic and other physiological reactions, muscular inclinations to act in certain ways, and cognitive representations of intentionality. That is, in many instances, the inhibitory anxiety is primarily attached to the *whole configuration* of cues, and exposure to merely the verbal component will do little to further the patient's freeing from neurotic constrictions. Some patients, in fact, particularly obsessional individuals, have learned a discrimination such that verbalizing *almost anything* can occur without anxiety, *so long as it is not in the context of emotional arousal and of an inclination to act on what is being said.* Thus, for such a patient, verbalizing even seemingly "significant" things is likely to be therapeutically fruitless unless the other cues to which anxiety is attached are produced along with the verbal cues.

In this light, intellectual versus emotional insight appears as a distinction whose importance derives from whether, or how thoroughly, the patient is exposed to those cues that really make him anxious. Since in most instances, anxiety is most strongly attached to a complex configuration of cues in which verbal, affective, cognitive, and motoric elements are all prominent, verbalizing without the other cues being present is unlikely to have much therapeutic value. Thus, "intellectual insight" is ineffective.


## THE ATTITUDE OF BEHAVIOR THERAPISTS
## TO DOLLARD AND MILLER'S WORK


Despite Dollard and Miller's emphasis on the application of learning theory concepts to clinical problems, their work has not tended to be very seriously considered by behavior therapists. It is sometimes viewed as a valuable early demonstration that learning concepts were relevant to the problems clinicians dealt with, but rarely as a contribution of enduring value. Indeed, it is not infrequently depicted as an unfortunate and misleading detour that delayed the advent of a really productive approach to therapeutic intervention.

Dollard and Miller's approach is certainly not without its problems. From the present point of view, for example, Dollard and Miller may be seen as focusing rather too exclusively on considerations deriving from an intrapsychic version of psychodynamic thought and not sufficiently on interpersonal feedback processes (see Chapter 4). Thus, while they are very helpful in understanding important aspects of conflict, anxiety, repression, working through, and insight, and provide valuable leads in dealing with the clinical issues which will be addressed in Chapters 8 and 9, their analysis provides far less help in dealing with the issues raised in Chapter 10, where interpersonal feedback processes are a central concern. Where Dollard and Miller do consider the role of the actual consequences of our social behavior, and how that feeds back to maintain the same neurotic pattern, they treat such considerations as "subsidiary" causal factors which, however important, are not at the heart of things. Even where they devote a whole chapter to the necessity of relieving neurotic conflicts in real life, and explicitly criticize Freud for failing to emphasize the acquisition of new responses outside the therapy hours, they do not approach the kinds of considerations of current life events stressed here (see Chapters 4 and 10). In light of the arguments presented in the preceding three chapters, it may well be that this was a significant reason why their analysis did not lead to the kinds of active intervention techniques that were later developed by behavior therapists, guided by many of the same (learning theory) concepts used by Dollard and Miller. Failure to explicitly and fully capitalize on the insights of interpersonal theorists regarding cyclical processes also was partly responsible for some confusing ambiguities in Dollard and Miller's presentation. [*]

Despite these problems and limitations, however, Dollard and Miller's way of understanding neurosis and the therapeutic process provides many extremely valuable aids to conceptualizing neurotic behavior and helping the patient to change it. In particular, they render traditional clinical concerns and discoveries in a form that makes it possible to reconcile and integrate them with the newer methods and perspectives of behavior therapists. In dismissing Dollard and Miller's work, writers on behavior therapy are unnecessarily limiting the considerations that guide their clinical practice, and they are failing to capitalize on all of the possibilities that a learning-theory approach to neurosis could provide.

I believe that the response of behavior therapists to Dollard and Miller's work cannot be viewed solely as a matter of objective scientific decision-making. At least part of the disinterest seems due to a strong *a priori* negative bias toward psychodynamic theorizing on the part of behavior therapists, a bias strong enough to encompass any theorist who is sympathetic to psychoanalysis. Bandura and Walters (1963, p. 30), for example, depict psychodynamic theorizing as a form of mystical demonology characteristic of the thinking of the Dark Ages.

---

[*] These ambiguities involve matters of therapeutic goals, of why anxiety is not extinguished as a result of partial exposure due to the approach aspect of the conflict, and other issues. They are discussed in some detail in a paper of mine now in preparation.

In part, analysts are themselves responsible for this excessively nega-tive view of their work. In many respects, Freud's warning that his observations rather than his theoretical speculations should be most highly valued has been ignored. The original terminology of psycho-analytic writing has tended to be retained by most psychoanalytic writers long after it has outlived its utility. It is a simple matter to find psycho-analytic papers (perhaps even the majority) that are dogmatic, circular, and teeming with assertions whose improbability is matched only by the paucity of evidence for them.°

But the unerring eye of behavioral critics in spotting absurdities in psychodynamic writings has not been matched by an equal ability to perceive the valuable contributions that have been made. The aspects of psychoanalytic thought focused upon by behavioral critics of psycho-analysis have tended to be the very ones that more sophisticated psycho-analytic writers have themselves recognized as needing change. But the behavioral critics seem ignorant of the solutions to these problems which modern psychoanalytic writers have suggested or of recent developments in psychoanalytic thought in general which carry it well beyond the crude reifications and vague energic metaphors in which psychoanalytic ideas were first expressed (cf. Holt, 1967b; Klein, 1967; Schafer, 1972, 1973a, 1973b; Wachtel, 1969, in press). In light of this strong attitude that psychoanalytic thought is thoroughly unscientific and without merit, it is not surprising that a work such as Dollard and Miller's, which explicitly acknowledges its debt to Freud, should be viewed rather unsympathetically and treated as an enemy to be conquered rather than a stimulus to further thought and exploration.

A second consideration relevant to understanding the negative attitude of behavior therapists toward Dollard and Miller's work is the latter authors' endorsement, in their volume, of psychoanalytic therapy as it was then practiced. Indeed, Dollard and Miller turn out to be among the extremely few writers who explicitly predict symptom substitution in a treatment that attempts to remove symptoms without dealing with their underlying causes. (It is quite surprising, in light of all that has been made of the symptom-substitution issue by behavior therapists, to discover just how rare reference to this issue is in the psychoanalytic literature—though it does seem to be implicit in much that is written.)

---

° It should be noted, however, that psychoanalysts have in no way cornered the market on mediocrity. Mischel (1973b), a staunch advocate of behavior therapy and critic of psychodynamic thought, has acknowledged that a substantial portion of studies by behaviorists are foolish and trivial. The creative thinkers in any intellectual orientation are a small minority.

As we shall see in Chapter 7, Dollard and Miller's prediction on this matter is really not inconsistent with what has been reported by behavior therapists, and is in fact quite similar to the position taken by Bandura and other writers on behavior therapy. But clearly their position at the time could be seen as contributing to a complacency about the state of the art and as discouraging direct efforts to deal with troubling behavior.[*]

Certainly, Dollard and Miller's contribution would have been greater had they sensed, as Wolpe and others later did, that a learning-oriented view of neurosis opened new therapeutic possibilities quite divergent from traditional psychodynamic methods. Wolpe and other therapeutic innovators in the behavior therapy movement deserve enormous credit for pioneering a major breakthrough in psychotherapeutic methodology. But Dollard and Miller's failure to make that particular kind of creative leap should not lead us to conclude that the principles they emphasized were not consistent with the innovations later developed. In fact, as we shall see in the next few chapters, those principles are extremely useful in providing a basis for the fuller and more effective utilization of the innovative methods that have arisen.

A third basis which has sometimes been offered for the critical attitude toward Dollard and Miller's work has been the contention that their work suffers "from the fact that they have relied heavily on a limited range of principles established on the basis of, and mainly supported by, studies of animal learning or human learning in one-person situations." (Bandura and Walters, 1963, p. 1) This criticism seems rather ironic, for many of the "principles of behavior modification" described by Bandura (1969) have their origins in the animal laboratories of Pavlov, Skinner, Hull, Tolman, Guthrie, and others, whereas the concepts of conflict and repression stressed by Dollard and Miller, and rejected by Bandura, have their origin in psychoanalytic observations of human beings revealing their most uniquely human aspects in an intensely social situation. Just which learning principles are valid and useful across species is an empirical issue, but to fault a theorist for relying excessively on animal research and then to proceed essentially to reject only those concepts of that theorist that originate from observations of uniquely human behavior seems rather strange.

---

[*] It is necessary to point out that Dollard and Miller's attitude toward psychoanalysis was hardly as uncritical and naively accepting as is often implied. Rapaport (1953) sensed quite definitely that their approach could potentially lead to rather wide divergence from standard psychoanalytic practice, though in his view it was the divergence that was a sign of naiveté.

Discussions of animal research abound in Bandura's (1969) volume, yet one finds hardly any discussion of Miller's important studies on conflict (see Miller, 1959). Certainly there are difficulties in translating these concepts to human social situations, as Bandura and Walters (1963) point out usefully and cogently; and experimental studies with humans that demonstrate clearly such phenomena as displacement, or the general principle—critical to Dollard and Miller's analysis of the effects of conflict—that the avoidance gradient is steeper than the approach gradient, are far from abundant.° But the wholesale dismissal of the concepts associated with the analysis of conflict seems to be a decision based more on ideology than evidence. There are certainly difficulties with uncontrolled clinical observation, but when carefully controlled animal studies converge so considerably with an enormous body of clinical observation of significant human interaction, it seems a rather defensive use of an epistemological position to treat as relevant only those studies involving both human subjects and experimental methodology. This is especially the case when many of the studies deriving from "social learning theory" require hardly less of a leap in applying them to the social behavior of concern in the clinic than is required in generalizing from the animal experiments cited by Miller.† (See Wachtel, 1973a, 1973b, in press.)

It may well be, as Lazarus (1973) suggests, that Bandura's presentation of the theoretical basis for behavior therapy is sounder than the earlier and simpler models that Breger and McGaugh (1965) criticized so effectively. But I would strongly take issue with Lazarus' contention, citing Bandura (1969), that "psychoanalytic and behavioral formulations are based on entirely different and irreconcilable models of man." Miller's demonstration of how readily psychoanalytic concepts can be reconciled with the principles of learning theory is as valid and conclusive for "social learning theory" as it was for the (putatively non-social) learning theory position preferred by Miller. The concepts central to Miller's analysis, such as reinforcement, extinction, generalization, discrimination, and so on are central for Bandura as well. And when Bandura's position on the nature of learning does differ from Miller's

---

° But see, for example, Brody's (1972) discussion of the work of Epstein and Fenz (Epstein, 1962, 1967; Epstein and Fenz, 1962, 1965; Fenz, 1964; Fenz and Epstein, 1967). Brody, whose volume is strongly anti-psychoanalytic and rather committed to Bandura's version of social learning theory, nonetheless acknowledges Epstein and Fenz's studies as raising serious questions about Bandura's downgrading of conflict.

† Additionally, it may be noted that Kanfer and Phillips (1970), in their equally prominent volume, claim that the model underlying behavioral approaches "assumes a continuity of behavioral principles across species and rests heavily on methodology and findings from animal research." (p. 91)

(as in a seemingly greater readiness to utilize traditionally "cognitive" concepts without translating them into S-R terms), his position seems rather closer to that of most psychodynamic thinkers than is that of Miller.

There is little in Bandura's approach that is in principle more "social" than that of Dollard and Miller. To be sure, Bandura stresses such "social" processes as modeling and imitation more than Dollard and Miller (1950) did, but that is hardly an emphasis alien to the latter authors, who, if they failed to fully exploit such concepts in their later volume, did devote an entire earlier book to just that topic (Miller and Dollard, 1941). Where Bandura does differ from Dollard and Miller regarding modeling and imitation, he is again closer to psychoanalysis than they are, in that he treats these phenomena in a more cognitive and representational fashion than Dollard and Miller do.

Bandura's vigorous rejection of psychodynamic concepts is in no way compelled by the logic of the theoretical position he follows. The kinds of analyses he prefers can be readily viewed as complementary rather than opposed to Miller's psychoanalytically inspired but learning theory-implemented analysis of conflict. Consider, for example, Bandura and Walter's critique of Miller's (1948) conflict analysis of displacement. As noted earlier, Bandura and Walters focus sharply on the difficulty in specifying *a priori* the dimension of similarity to the original goal object. After-the-fact explanations suggesting that a particular response occurred because it was different enough yet not too different may be plausible, but have limited utility and are difficult to prove or disprove. Bandura and Walters suggest instead a strategy emphasizing the specific effects of direct or vicarious reinforcement. In understanding the finding, for example, that aggressive adolescents tend to have parents who strongly punish aggression in the home, these authors reject the notion that the aggression shown outside is a displaced expression of the aggressive inclinations aroused by, but forbidden, in the home situation. They stress instead that the parents of such boys do encourage and reward aggression that occurs *outside* the home, and view this as indicative of discrimination training (aggression forbidden inside, rewarded outside) rather than displacement.

Similarly, they are critical of the scapegoat theory of prejudice, which views aggression toward "out groups" as a displacement of hostile tendencies closer to home that are dangerous to express. Here again they instead emphasize a more direct training in what responses are rewarded in what contexts. Through reinforcement, imitation, and discrimination learning, particular responses are learned to particular cues; and the responses learned to cues associated with the "out group" are aggressive ones.

In this fashion, Bandura and Walters provide a useful corrective to the excessively narrow range of variables discussed by Miller. As such, they provide a similar corrective to what is offered in the psychoanalytic literature by the ego psychologists and by interpersonal theorists. Freud seemed to have a persistent tendency to view those aspects of human behavior that he himself shed light on as being of central and overweaning importance, and to disregard or treat as secondary or superficial any explanation to which he did not contribute. It remained primarily for later psychodynamic writers to recognize that conflict and unconscious motivation were by no means all that was important in accounting for variations in human personality, and that factors familiar to students of learning, perception, social psychology, and so on were in many cases as important, if not more important, for understanding the behavior of their patients. Miller's discussion also focused too narrowly on conflict, and Bandura and Walters make a useful clarification.

But the factors emphasized by Bandura and Walters need not be viewed as contradictory to those considered by Miller. In developing a particular line of inquiry, Miller put aside for the moment more familiar modes of analysis; but concern with discrimination, reinforcement, and so on are hardly antithetical to his theoretical position. To some extent, Bandura and Walters seem to recognize this. They do not explicity and unambiguously reject Miller's conflict model or its application to displacement. Rather, they state that an "adequate social-learning model for the prediction of displacement must take into account a number of variables that are ignored in Miller's paradigm." (p. 20) This could be taken as an intent to include concern with conflict phenomena within a larger framework. But as noted earlier, Bandura's (1969) later volume is marked by an absence of concern with conflict; and Brody (1972), who is strongly supportive of Bandura's position, treats as a central feature of Bandura's point of view a rejection of the Miller conflict model and all of its implications.

Even, however, if the conflict model and the model of direct learning of particular responses to particular situations are recognized as logically compatible, one can reasonably ask if it is necessary or useful to combine them, especially since utilization of the conflict model generally requires a good deal of inference. As I have noted previously (Wachtel, 1973b), if one's views regarding psychological theory are based primarily on data from experiments, it may well appear that concern with conflict is unnecessary or irrelevant. Experiments are designed to simplify, and many aspects of the typical experiment make it appear quite sufficient to simply look at the reinforcement history of a particular response to a particular situation.

But in most real-life situations, the person finds an enormous range of potential reinforcers are available, for which a wide range of responses may be employed. A student sitting in a classroom may be reinforced by the admiration of his teacher if he speaks cogently and intelligently, may evoke the teacher's hostility but gain status with his peer group if he is sarcastic and smart alecky, may avoid the anxiety of risking a wrong answer if he is attentive but quiet, may gain still a different kind of gratification if he drifts into a reverie, and so on. All these response-reinforcement contingencies for that external situation, as well as many others, may have been learned by him through direct experience and observation of others. Knowing the contingencies he has experienced and observed is thus helpful, but it is far from sufficient. To know what he will do, we need to know a good deal about his motivation, and we need to recognize that the pursuit of some of his aims will be very likely to conflict with the pursuit of others. Concern with conflict and the multiplicity of human motivations may be ignored with minimal difficulty in the artificially restricted situation of the laboratory experiment—though even here, the work of Orne ( 1969 ), Rosenthal ( 1966 ), and others should give us pause—but it can be ignored only with great peril to the cogency of one's formulations when neurotic interpersonal behavior in everyday settings is to be understood.

The principles discussed by Bandura are useful but incomplete. They give little help in understanding just which of the multitudinous reinforcers available in everyday interactions will be sought, nor do they help in understanding the variety of ways in which conflicting aims are pursued. Effective behavioral clinicians are attentive to these matters. This becomes quite clear when one observes good behavior therapists work with neurotic patients, and is evident as well in that small portion of the behavior therapy literature that describes what actually goes on rather than presenting a neatly abstracted theoretical account of the case (see, for example, Lazarus, 1972 ). But the sensitivity of behavior therapists in this regard is implicit and often unacknowledged. There is little in the behavioral literature or in the behavior therapy tradition that is helpful in this effort or that even legitimatizes it.

Many of the most influential leaders of the behavior therapy movement encourage the pretense that there is little or no inference required in behavior therapy and that clinical practice is a rather straightforward application of laboratory principles, perhaps even something that can

readily be done by technicians. Guidelines for inference are not sufficiently addressed, because the need for inference is covered over. The
behavioral literature does not encourage the beginning clinician to learn
about conflict or to consider how to discern evidence of conflict in his
patients. It does not particularly encourage the search for multiple
sources of reinforcement (the psychoanalytic concept of over-determina-
tion) or for non-obvious and unacknowledged reinforcements (which, in
behavioral terms, is what is implied by psychodynamic writings on unconscious motivation). It doesn't emphasize the therapist's using his own
feelings, associations, and fantasies as a way of gauging the subtle affective communications from the patient, communications that give important clues as to why his interpersonal relations tend to proceed as they
do.*

All these and many more kinds of clinical thought and inquiry, which
are intrinsic to psychodynamic approaches, are probably often used by
practicing behavioral clinicians; they certainly are by the ones I've seen.
They are by no means incompatible with the main concepts of behavior
therapy. But they in large measure represent the same kind of under-
ground in the behavioral tradition that recognition of the therapist's role
as reinforcer, need for active intervention in the patient's day-to-day behavior, and so on do in the psychodynamic tradition. A full and explicit
statement of the basis for an approach which combines all of these activities and perspectives might still be called "social learning theory" if one
liked (or, perhaps, "psychoanalytic ego psychology," if that were one's
wont), but it would look different from Bandura's book and different
from any psychoanalytic work I know. In Part Two we will examine
some actual clinical activities in the light of a tentative glimmer of what
such an integration would look like.

---

* Goldfried and Davison's (1976) recent volume makes a substantial contribution
toward bringing clinical realities into the literature on behavior therapy.

*Clinical Considerations*

# 7

# *Psychoanalysis and*
# *Behavioral Analysis*

I<small>N</small> psychodynamic therapies, the assessment of the patient's personality and problems in living and the treatment of those problems are hardly distinguishable. To many dynamic therapists the joint effort by patient and therapist to articulate the patient's way of living his life, and to understand how it developed and why it causes problems, is the core of the therapeutic process. In a sense, the effort to understand *is* the therapy.

In contrast, behavior therapists distinguish rather clearly between the process of assessment and the process of therapy. On the basis of an initial assessment, specific intervention methods are employed.° Much of Part One of this book was devoted to the consideration of whether the use of such methods can be consistent with the views of personality and of the therapeutic interaction that have developed from the observations of Freud and later psychodynamic thinkers. We concluded that at least from an interpersonal psychodynamic perspective, such interventions could indeed be viewed as consistent; and we indicated that in some circumstances not intervening, when effective interventions were available, might well limit the patient's possibilities for change.

There is an appealing directness and practicality in the behavior

---

° This does not imply, however, that the behavior therapist's assessment of the problem cannot later be modified on the basis of new information, including the patient's reactions to the interventions that are tried.

therapist's emphasis on assessing the nature of the problem and then employing a specific intervention technique to change it. There are, however, a number of critical questions about this way of viewing therapy that must be addressed. First of all, one must consider how adequately behavior therapists, with their current assessment methods, do in fact (or potentially can) assess what is going on. Analysts, after all, seem to work for years on understanding the patient's difficulties. Secondly, one must ask how effective really are the various intervention techniques used by behavior therapists. What are their short-term and long-term consequences? Do they have undesirable side effects? Do they achieve specific narrow gains at the expense of preventing broader, more significant change? Thirdly, one must consider what ethical issues are raised when the therapist conceives of his role as not just facilitating a process of exploration and understanding, but also as engaging in direct efforts to change the patient's behavior.

The present chapter will primarily address the first question, that of evaluation and personality assessment. Examination of the specific interventions and the possibility of integrating them with a dynamic approach will be undertaken in Chapters 8 through 11. The ethical issues will be taken up in Chapter 12.

## CURRENT BEHAVIORAL ANALYSIS

Any behavior therapist is likely to agree that his treatment is only as good as his behavioral analysis. If his intervention efforts do not produce the desired result, he is likely to conclude that he had not adequately determined the variables influencing the behavior in question and will then seek to correct his assessment. The behavioral analysis is the crucial part of the behavior therapist's activity and the one requiring the greatest degree of skill.

The behavior therapist's concern is with the variables that are *currently* relevant in maintaining the patient's difficulties. Though some behavior therapists do take a detailed history (see particularly, Wolpe, 1969, Chapter 3), this is primarily to give some perspective or clues as to what to look for in the present; it is the present reactions to present events that are the focus. Writers in the behavior therapy literature frequently contrast this with the emphasis on history and understanding the past that is characteristic of dynamic therapists (see Mischel, 1968, p. 264). To some extent this distinction is a valid one. As we saw in Part One, however, psychodynamic therapists vary considerably in how much emphasis they place on understanding the past. The psychodynamic conception emphasized here, like that of Horney (e.g., 1939), is concerned primarily with the present consequences of the patient's characterological defenses and ways of interacting with others, and with the vicious circles that maintain maladaptive patterns. Thus, with regard to the issue of emphasizing past or present, it differs little from the approach taken by most behavior therapists.

There are some important differences, however, when it comes to precisely how the understanding of the patient's problem is actually arrived at and what the terms of that understanding are. I will first briefly describe some of the main features of behavioral assessment and contrast them with how the dynamic therapist proceeds. The issues raised will be examined as a basis for an integrated approach, and a way of working that has evolved for me over the past few years will be described.

### THE BEHAVIOR THERAPIST AS INTERVIEWER

Writers on behavior therapy frequently contrast behavior therapy with "verbal" or "interview" therapies (e.g., Bandura, 1969). It therefore came as rather a surprise to me to discover, in observing the work of a number of well-known behavior therapists, how much of the time in behavior therapy is spent in conversation. This is the case even in the more predominantly intervention stages of the therapeutic process (about which more later), but it is particularly true in the assessment stage.

The use of interviewing is, not surprisingly, considerably less in the more Skinnerian approaches to behavior modification. These predominantly operant conditioning efforts have been most typically used in working with psychotics, retardates, and autistic children, though they have in recent years been increasingly applied to a wide range of behavior problems in schools and families. Therapeutic efforts with neurotic adults, however, have tended not to be characterized by a predominantly Skinnerian approach. In terms of intervention, this has meant the employment of a wide range of techniques other than those based on simple operant conditioning models. In terms of assessment and conceptualization of patients' problems, it has meant a substantial emphasis on mediating events and even on subjective experience, as well as a tendency not to be limited by methods designed for laboratory research with animals.

It is this latter (I am tempted to say dominant) trend in behavior therapy that interests us here, and that I believe can be integrated with dynamic approaches in very promising ways. When working with patients of the sort seen by most dynamic therapists, behavior therapists, too, tend to talk to them. While direct observation of behavior in its natural setting is (in some respects—see below) more accurate, the gain in efficiency and flexibility when information is conveyed verbally by the patient is so great that most behavior therapists are quite willing to pay the price of being less purely behavioristic with patients who are able to communicate fairly well.

The behavior therapist's way of conducting the interview does differ in some important ways from the interviews conducted by dynamic therapists (though not nearly as much, I have found, as the advocacy literature would lead one to suspect). Mischel (1968), Kanfer and Saslow (1965), and other behavioral writers have stressed the value of *structured* interviews; and the interviewing done by behavior therapists certainly tends to be more structured than that of dynamic therapists. Not surprisingly, however, there are considerable variations within each group in how much structure is brought to bear in the interview. Among dynamic therapists, the way the early stages of the therapeutic interaction are set up is particularly varied—from therapists who start with a quite formal history differing little from that described by Wolpe (1969, Chapter 3), to therapists who listen with "evenly hovering attention" (Freud, 1912) from the first moment.

The interviews conducted by clinical behavior therapists are rarely strictly "behavioristic" in any meaningful sense of that term. The patient's verbal reports are rarely treated simply as behaviors per se, where their mere frequency is studied in relation to something else. Rather, they are listened to essentially as speech is listened to by anyone else, as the meaningful report by an intelligent observer of events that the speaker has been privy to and the listener has not. (This refers not only to subjective experiences, but also to events which in principle could be objectively observable but at which the patient was present and the therapist was not. Thus the patient might report what his mother-in-law said in their last fight, and the therapist does take it as information about the mother-in-law's actions and not just about the patient's tendency to say the words "My mother-in-law said . . ." and so on.)

This does not mean, however, that the patient's reports are listened to naively or with absolute credulity. In the above illustration, for example, the therapist might be expected to be appropriately skeptical about the accuracy of the patient's description and to make every effort to clarify where the patient's reported recollection might be incomplete, biased, or confused. The behavior therapist is quite concerned to assure that the referents of the patient's verbalizations are clearly understood, that the events to which his words refer are clarified and articulated. Thus, if the patient says he felt anxious when his girl friend was cold to him, the behavior therapist will want to know just what he means by anxious and just what he means by his girl friend being cold to him. Did he actually feel afraid something terrible would happen to him, did he experience painful tension in his neck, did his voice start to quaver, did he feel an intense desire to walk out, and so on? Similarly, precisely what did she do? Did she fail to laugh at his joke, did she push him away when he put his arm around her, did she "somehow just look tight" (and if so, can any of the cues that signal this be at all articulated)?

What at times seems to be lost sight of in behavioral writers' accounts of this (extremely valuable) way of listening and inquiring is that it is not the exclusive province of behavior therapists. I cannot say what percentage of dynamic therapists listen and inquire in this way, but I know I have been doing it for years, long before I had any interest in behavior therapy. One of the first things I was taught very early in my training in clinical psychology was that the therapist should always listen as if he were "naive," as if he did not know what the patient is referring to (even if he thinks he does). Thus he should continually question just what the patient means when he says he was "uptight," "copped out," "got depressed," and so on. Likewise, understanding just what such reactions were occasioned by had become second nature to me during a stage in my career when behavior therapy still seemed like an alien and dangerous menace. A good portion of the "insights" I have been able to gain in conjunction with my patients has come not so much from my knowledge of psychoanalytic theory (though, as I will argue later, that is certainly not irrelevant) as simply from listening more "naively" than I do in everyday conversation—from assuming I do not know what fairly simple statements refer to, and inquiring to find out. The answers are frequently surprising. (Perhaps this is why we don't ask such questions so readily in everyday conversation.)

SPECIFICITY AND NON-INTERVIEW METHODS

A related issue is that of the specificity of the formulations that are sought. Behavior therapists tend to see personality much less in "system" terms than do dynamic therapists. They seek instead to find specific stimulus-response connections. As Mischel (1968) notes, from the point of view of social learning theory it is expected that an individual's way of responding will vary greatly with different situations. Therapists operating from such a theory are unlikely to seek broad patterns of behavior (much less to relate them to early familial experiences), whereas many dynamic therapists do so.

I think the differences depicted in the behavior-therapy literature between dynamic and behavioral clinicians tend to be more real here than with regard to the issue of specifying the referents of the patient's utterances. I know very few experienced dynamic clinicians who do not in fact seek precise referents for patients' descriptions, but I know a good many whose conception of their patients' problems involves considerably greater concern with broadly relevant patterns than is the case for most behavior therapists.

There is, I think, something to be said for the emphasis of each group, and I will try to indicate how their respective strengths can be combined. There can be little question that behavior therapists have been particularly skillful in discerning how aspects of the patient's problem behavior vary from situation to situation. Not only does their theoretical framework particularly stress this, but their methods make it easy to assess as well. First of all, the keen (though unfortunately in some cases exclusive) concern for overt, observable behavior makes it easier to notice just when a problem behavior does or does not occur, and hence to relate its occurrence to particular kinds of events. Additionally, specific methods of obtaining observations, developed in the clinical tradition of behavior therapy, have not been employed by and large by dynamic therapists. These methods complement the interviewing aspect of the behavioral assessment.

Among these methods, a particularly useful one for discovering how the patient's functioning varies in specific ways is to request that the patient keep systematic records of particular aspects of his behavior or particular feeling states. The patient writes down every time the behavior occurs, or rates his mood at some regular interval, and indicates for each recording what has been going on immediately preceding. Such a procedure can provide a very valuable complement to the picture obtained from more traditional interviewing. The latter is quite subject to the distortion deriving from the patient's perceiving and remembering events in terms of his preconceptions (something which, in other contexts, dynamic therapists are quite aware of and even emphasize).

In my own work, I have found this kind of procedure particularly helpful with patients who claim to be always anxious or depressed. Often such patients are quite struck by what turns up when they are asked to chart their anxiety level through the day. Almost invariably they discover that they are not anxious nearly as continuously as they had conceived, and that in fact their anxiety level varies quite clearly with a number of kinds of situations. The "discovery" of substantial periods of their day when they function effectively and with minimal anxiety, as well as the increased articulation of what they are anxious about, have tended to encourage such patients, diminish resistance, and increase their cooperation in the therapeutic effort.

Other methods have also been used by behavior therapists to complement what is obtained from the interviewing per se. These have included direct observation of patient behavior in its natural setting, observations of the patient (often together with key figures in his life) in situations created by the assessor to make likely the evocation of particular aspects of the patient's repertoire, and role-playing procedures in which patient and therapist play out different aspects of the patient's day-to-day interactions. (The use of role-playing will be discussed in some detail in Chapter 10, where its employment as a way of implementing change will also be discussed.* )

The direct observation of patient behavior in its natural settings is perhaps the methodologically "purest" approach from a behavioral point of view. As we have noted, however, except for those behavior therapists of predominantly Skinnerian orientation, it has not been a way of proceeding that has been widely utilized. Outside of institutional settings, it tends to be very expensive and time-consuming to obtain direct observations, as Mischel (1968) has noted.

Additionally, observing human beings in natural social settings turns out to be a task that differs from the kind of observing done in an experiment to a far greater degree than much of the current rhetoric would suggest. To decide on the appropriate categories for recording and ordering observations is not a simple and straightforward task. There is an enormous, if not infinite, number of ways that the observational pie can be sliced, and precisely which set of categories is chosen will determine whether what is observed appears chaotic or orderly. Meehl (1973), writing from the perspective of both psychoanalytic clinician and hardheaded research psychologist, has recently emphasized anew the inevitable links between observations and theoretical presuppositions, the latter both influencing where one looks and how one organizes one's observations. Furthermore, as Goldfried and Sprafkin (1974) point out in their useful review of behavioral assessment methods and their methodological problems, obtaining accurate and reliable records from be-

---

* All of these common behavioral assessment methods are discussed in detail in Goldfried and Sprafkin (1974) and Mischel (1968), as are the epistemological and methodological issues that have recommended them to behavior therapists.

havioral observers is no easy matter when nontrivial events are to be recorded.

Despite the limitations, however, direct observation of the patient in his life setting can at times be a way for the clinician to observe aspects of the patient that would otherwise remain obscure. Though used infrequently by the behavior therapist who is engaged in an office practice with adult outpatients, it nonetheless remains an option for him that gives him added flexibility in his work. Moreover, it is on a continuum with less expensive methods such as role-playing life situations and enlisting the *patient's* participation as a behavioral observer by record-keeping and making charts or lists. Use of all these adjuncts to interviewing, as well as utilizing the particular perspectives on interviewing described above, enables the behavior therapist to notice a variety of contingencies and relationships between problems and life events that might be overlooked in traditional clinical practice.

Dynamically oriented therapists have tended to be skeptical of the value of such methods and to be concerned that whatever value they might have is more than offset by the limitations they place on the therapy. It has been suggested to me in several discussions, for example, that asking the patient to chart various aspects of his behavior or experience "plays into the patient's obsessional tendencies," and that behavioral methods in general, whether for assessment or intervention, seriously "distort the transference" and render it "unresolvable."

Regarding the latter concern, according to the view presented in Chapters 4 and 5, transference is in any event not really a reaction stemming solely from the past and unrelated to what the therapist "really" does or what he is like. Transference may always be understood as the patient's idiosyncratic way of construing and reacting to *what the therapist is doing*—and the therapist is never doing "nothing," even when he is being silent or reflecting back a question instead of answering it.

Some therapists maintain that they can learn all they need to know about the patient by observing reactions in the transference relationship, and they eschew the assessment methods used by behavior therapists on that ground, as well as on the ground that those methods make the transference "difficult to resolve." This seems to me particularly ironic because, to the degree that one learns about the patient primarily through his or her reactions to the therapist, it becomes especially important to offer a range of kinds of relatedness to respond to. To *restrict* how the therapist will interact with the patient (for example, "I will never give him an assignment, or suggest he look at anything in particular"), as part of a strategy of learning about him from how he reacts to the therapist, seems unwise unless one is committed to a rather exclusively intrapsychic model of a sort that would leave little room for the contribution of modern ego psychology.

It is interesting to note that, in a variety of ways, dynamically oriented therapists have deviated from the "don't do anything—you'll spoil the tranference" model in working with children and with psychotics. The ingenious and often courageous therapeutic efforts of individuals like Fromm-Reichman and Searles with schizophrenics contrast sharply with the restrictions analysts impose on themselves and their patients when working with less troubled individuals. And while a visit by an analyst to the home of an adult patient in order to observe the atmosphere in which he lives would be a *cause célèbre* in most institutes, Erik Erikson (1963) can report that he routinely did so with his child patients and remain (justifiably) one of the most influential of contemporary psychoanalytic thinkers. Excursions by dynamic therapists into family therapy and the treatment of couples have also been characterized by a loosening of the reins of orthodoxy. In such therapeutic efforts, the therapist does have an opportunity to directly observe how the couple or family interact with one another. Many dynamically trained therapists have recognized thereby the limits of restricting data-gathering to free associations, interviewing, and transference observations, and the considerable value of the additional perspective provided by direct observation of the patient in interaction with important life figures.

## VARIABILITY AND THE AFFECTIVE FOCUS OF DYNAMIC THERAPISTS

The methods and viewpoints just discussed enable behavior therapists to gain a much more articulated picture than is typical in psychodynamic approaches of how aspects of the patient's problems vary in differing contexts. It is important to recognize, however, that seeing behavior as responsive to varying events is not inconsistent with the theoretical perspective of most modern psychodynamic writers. Both interpersonal theory and psychoanalytic ego psychology are far removed from the crude id psychology of the early days of psychoanalysis, in which the relation between the patient's reactions and the events of his life was hardly considered (see Wachtel, 1973b, in press).

If dynamic therapists ask fewer "when" questions than behavior therapists (and in practice I think this is clearly the case), it is not because their theory of personality does not allow it. In part, it reflects features of the theories of *therapy* that tend to guide psychodynamic clinicians. As I tried to show in Part One, psychodynamic theories of therapy have not been modified by developments in ego psychology to nearly the degree that the theories of *personality* have. Conceptions guiding therapeutic work even by interpersonally oriented therapists tend to lead the therapist to seek to understand the patient's personality "structure" and its historical determinants, with only secondary consideration of the contexts in which it is variously manifested.

The lesser concern with the role of the situation by dynamic than by behavioral therapists is also likely related to a real feature of the phenomena that are of central concern in a psychodynamic approach. In focusing on affect, motivation, sense of self, and subjective experience, dynamic therapists work largely in a realm where variability is probably considerably less than in more manifest behaviors. As I have discussed in more detail elsewhere:

> The events focused on by analysts . . . tend to be those in which their patients' ability to discriminate is most challenged. Finely articulated alteration of response with stimulus changes, evident in studies where environmental events are readily discriminable, is not so evident where affective, interpersonal events are concerned. In the latter realm, early global and generalized predispositions may less readily become differentiated, and assumptions and reaction tendencies may apply to a wider range of situations. In Piagetian terms, analysts are likely observing phenomena where difficulties in perceptual discrimination make assimilation predominant, whereas [the emphasis on specificity by behavioral clinicians and researchers] applies to situations where a greater degree of accommodation and differentiation is possible. (Wachtel, 1973b, p. 329)

Nonetheless, there is still some variability with situations even in the realm of intimate, affective phenomena, and this variability is quite important. It is the rare individual who *never* expresses anger or can *never* get close to anyone to any extent. The somewhat sloppy (and all too frequent) clinical descriptions that imply this is the case essentially reflect the clinician's focus on a particular issue as of major importance for the patient. Such a description, when merely a shorthand, implies that the person is, say, inhibited in sharing feelings and letting loving or dependent feelings develop in a wider variety of situations than most, that his overall range of responsiveness is truncated or skewed, and so on. But within this restricted range, there are still circumstances that make it harder or easier, and particular people with whom he is more or less comfortable. The variations may well be complex and mediated by conflicting and interacting gradients, particularly including distortions and reorganizations of experience motivated by avoidance of anxiety. But if this variability can be understood, a better basis is available for intervening. Even where a dynamic is discerned that is broadly relevant over a wide variety of situations, articulation of its relationship to the actual events occurring in the patient's life, and understanding of where and how its disturbing role is intensified or diminished, is critical for maximum therapeutic effectiveness.

## INNER AND OUTER FOCUS: PERSPECTIVES ON EVIDENCE

As noted above, dynamic therapists tend to be particularly concerned with the patient's (manifest and inferred) thoughts, wishes, and fantasies, and with anxiety and conflict associated with them. In contrast with this concern with what (in learning terms) would be viewed as response-produced cues, most behavior therapists tend to stress environmental or situational cues as most relevant in the majority of cases. As Wolpe (1969) puts it, "The theme, or common core, of a neurosis is *usually* derived from extrinsic stimulus situations disturbing to the patient—like spiders or criticisms; *but sometimes* the core subsists in response-produced stimuli." (p. 107; italics added) There is thus some overlap. Behavior therapists do not *in principle* reject the possible role of response-produced cues, and modern dynamic therapists are cognizant of the need to consider the patient's reactions to environmental events as well as to his own wishes and thoughts. But the difference in emphasis, in preferred directions for inquiry and preferred hypotheses to explore, is quite plain.

The preference of behavior therapists for examining external stimulus sources of anxiety is not difficult to understand. The behavioral orientation in psychotherapy has derived from a tradition that emphasizes dealing with events that can be directly observed; behavior therapists are suspicious of the inferences made by dynamic therapists, which are often difficult to confirm in any reasonably certain manner, especially by the rules of evidence traditional in academic psychology. Though the notion of response-produced cues brings inner events into the framework of S-R theories, it is still much easier and more comfortable for S-R psychologists to relate directly observable responses to directly observable environmental events.

Clinical formulations hypothesizing that the patient's anxiety is due to cues associated with some inner striving or fantasy require a more complex web of observations and inferences for confirmation than do hypotheses that relate his anxiety to, for example, the physical distance of a spider or even to variations in the wording of a critical remark. One could, for example, independently vary the criticalness of a speaker's comment, assess the patient's consequent physiological reaction, and remain fairly well within the "objective" mode of inquiry ideologically most appealing to the leading voices in behavior therapy. But once one entertains the hypothesis that the anxiety is most accurately described as, say, a function of the patient's temptation to respond to the critic in a hostile fashion, the simple, straightforward experimental model can no longer be employed in quite the same way.

Even apart from the question of whether the "objective" physiological measure adequately gauges the patient's anxiety (a complex matter of concern in *any* formulation using the anxiety concept), there is the problem that the "independent variable" cannot really be independently varied by the experimenter or clinical assessor. As we shall later see in more detail in a different context, asking the patient to imagine himself acting in varying ways and then assessing his anxiety is far from fully equivalent to presenting varying stimuli in an "objective" experiment. When response-produced cues are considered in the clinical setting, the behavioral clinician is forcefully introduced to many of the ambiguities of inference and theory verification that he has scorned in the formulations of his dynamically oriented colleagues.

For two reasons, however, I believe it is a mistake for behavior therapists to try to defend their scientific virginity by not dallying with the "X-rated" constructs of psychoanalysis. Firstly, the clinical observations that present themselves to the clinician often seem most cogently understood in terms of the patient's fear of his own inclinations. The behavior therapy literature, heavily weighted with snake-phobia studies and discussions of laboratory models of conditioning, often gives the impression that the cues that evoke anxiety are largely a matter of accidental pairing and that patients' fears are largely independent of their mode of relating to others. Davison and Neale (1974), however, note that there is little solid evidence for such an accidental-conditioning view of human anxieties. Further, experienced behavioral clinicians are increasingly cognizant of the central role of interpersonal factors in their patients' problems (e.g., Lazarus, 1971; Fodor, 1974). These therapists' concerns are increasingly convergent with those of psychodynamic theorists who have emphasized characterological formulations.

Additionally, the efforts by some behavior therapists to maintain familiar methodologies and epistemologies by eschewing formulations that stress unacknowledged inclinations or fantasies have not been very successful when the complex fears and difficulties of clinic populations have been confronted. While some economy of inference may be achieved (perhaps at the expense of accuracy) by focusing on reactions to external events, the distance from original laboratory models and standards of precision is nonetheless substantial. Like it or not, the behavior therapist who is attentive to the data he confronts and to what he actually does must recognize that he cannot help but enter the murky waters of clinical inference. Consider, for example, the following description of how the behavior therapist identifies sources of anxiety in his patient:

> In current practice the selection of anxiety sources is based upon informally collected data, from interviews, case histories, and various personality tests, most of which were originally constructed for entirely different purposes. Although no reliability studies have been conducted in which different therapists select from the same protocols what they consider to be the critical sources of anxiety, it would come as no surprise to find low consensus, particularly in cases involving multiform problems. . . . The major controlling stimuli cannot always be identified solely through systematic examination of the objective characteristics of environmental events which may, in fact, be highly dissimilar. Rather, the common determinants are often revealed in detailed accounts of the thoughts and subjective reactions that clients experienced in anxiety-producing situations. . . . [T]he applicability of desensitization treatment is mainly limited by therapists' ingenuity in identifying sources of anxiety, particularly when the crucial stimulus determinates are obscure. This task is complicated by the absence of any objective criteria for determining the appropriate events for treatment. Let us consider, for example, a female agoraphobic who is unable to venture outside the household. Should one desensitize her to progressively farther anxiety-arousing excursions from the house? One might argue that her phobic behavior arises from a morbid fear of sexual encounters, apprehensions about abandonment and helpless exposure to crowds, or some other sources, and it is these contents that must be emphasized in the treatment.

This description was written not by a disgruntled psychoanalyst putting the behavior therapists in their place, but by a vigorous proponent of behavior therapy and passionate critic of psychoanalysis—Albert Bandura (1969, pp. 462, 464–65).

Bandura does not seem comfortable, however, with the recognition that psychoanalysis is not the only approach that has had to cope with the unreliability of clinical formulations and the complexities of clinical evidence. Despite his sophisticated depiction of the actual practice of systematic desensitization, and despite his many valuable discussions of the important role of cognition, personalized interpretation of events, private meanings, and so on, he nonetheless seems to lead us full circle back to the effort to restrict attention primarily to extrinsic sources of anxiety. Thus, immediately following the above quotation, he goes on to imply that psychodynamic formulations are seriously shaken by reports of success in using systematic desensitization with images of snakes without using images of phalluses, desensitizing claustrophobics to images of increasingly constricted space without considering fears of being left alone with dangerous impulses, and desensitizing acrophobics to images of increasing heights without considering fears of falling in self-esteem. When he indicates that it would be "most instructive" to compare the efficacy of desensitizing to phobic stimuli directly or to "hypothesized internal threats," he leaves the reader little doubt as to what he thinks the sensible bet would be.

In fact, however, the observations made to date are far from pointing unequivocally in the direction Bandura, along with many other antipsychoanalytic[*] behavior therapists, clearly prefers. Firstly, it must be pointed out that though Bandura refers to "laboratory studies" that provide evidence for the above-noted therapeutic successes with claustrophobics and acrophobics, the only study he cites in this regard (Lazarus, 1961) is hardly what the term "laboratory study" seems to imply. Lazarus' study was an interesting exploratory clinical study and recognized as such by its author. It compared a group desensitization procedure with interpretive group therapy and found much greater improvement in the phobics in the former group. *Both procedures, however, were administered by the same person, the author of the article.* The difficulties in drawing hard conclusions from such a report, in which the possibility of experimenter bias is especially acute and impossible to weigh, are certainly obvious. The evidential value of such a report is essentially little different from that of a series of case reports.

It is therefore interesting to note other case reports in which the "hypothesized internal threats" that Bandura views so derisively did seem important in bringing about therapeutic change. An interesting series of cases was reported by Feather and Rhoads (1972). [See also Rhoads and

---

[*] Bandura calls in a number of places for an end to fruitless partisan debates between proponents of "behavior therapy" and "psychotherapy" and asks that these "ill-defined partisan labels" be retired. Perhaps even greater progress would be made if we concerned ourselves less with partisan *labels* and concentrated instead on retiring partisan *attitudes*. It is hard for me to imagine a reader of Bandura's volume who would not agree that "anti-psychoanalytic" is an accurate label.

Feather, 1972.] One patient, who suffered from multiple crippling symptoms, had among other problems a severe driving phobia that had plagued him for ten years and that left him currently unable to drive. Efforts to desensitize him in traditional fashion, using images defined in terms of external stimulus attributes, proved unsuccessful. The patient feared that he would hit—or without realizing it had hit—pedestrians. A hierarchy was therefore first tried, which varied the number of pedestrians and their distance from the street in which he was driving; the lowest item on the hierarchy involved driving in an empty parking lot. This approach achieved very little.

In contrast, considerable success occurred when the patient was instead asked, while relaxed, to imagine *deliberately* running over someone. After imagining a number of scenes in which he pictured himself thoroughly enjoying increasingly more ghastly acts of aggression with his car, his anxiety diminished markedly and he was able to begin a graduated set of actual driving tasks that culminated, in two weeks, in his being able to drive anywhere in the city and even across the state.

Similarly, with this same patient, traditional desensitization of a fear of writing was first attempted. Feather and Rhoads report that they achieved "little success using a conventional hierarchy until it was discovered that his fantasies invariably went to revealing secret information. He was then asked to imagine *deliberately* disclosing all the secrets of his company by emptying all the file cabinets into the street. There was an almost immediate remission in his writing phobia, and he was instructed to begin writing at least six letters per day, which he did with little difficulty." (Feather and Rhoads, 1972, p. 505)

Precisely why this patient did not improve with more traditional hierarchies yet did improve with images of deliberate hostile acts cannot, of course, be determined with any degree of certainty from an uncontrolled case report. In the same way that objections could be made about the Lazarus study, the contention could here be made that the *wrong* hierarchy of external stimulus attributes was utilized, that the therapist communicated a biased expectation that one approach would work and another wouldn't, and so on. Nonetheless there is much in the details of Feather and Rhoads' report of this case to suggest that centrally implicated in this man's complex of difficulties were conflicted hostile and destructive urges that he had to take great pains to avoid acting on and recognizing; and, as in the other cases reported by these authors, the directing of therapeutic effort to the conflicted wishes and fantasies was followed by dramatic therapeutic change.

Feather and Rhoads are not in their report simply defending the traditional psychoanalytic view of neurosis and therapy against the behaviorist invaders. To be sure, their conception of the source of anxiety in this and the other cases they report is closer to the analytic model than to an accidental conditioning model. But Feather and Rhoads indicate clearly that the patient was not helped by years of psychoanalysis and may even have been made worse. They borrow from behavior therapy the utilization of relaxation training and the specific focus on the situation that gives the patient trouble. Where they differ from most behavior therapists is in their understanding of why the situation is troubling. Here they are keenly attentive to the patient's fantasy life and the evidences of warded-off inclinations and defensive efforts. Both the reports of what helped and what didn't and the internal consistency and coherence given to the material by Feather and Rhoads's explanation of the symptom complex lend support to such a way of approaching the material.

There is, of course, also a vast body of other clinical observations supporting the view that many of the problems patients bring to the clinic are centrally related to conflict and anxiety over one's own feelings and strivings, and that the most troublesome tendencies tend not to be in the patient's awareness. The view developed in Part One suggests that it may be more accurate to say that these tendencies are unconscious because they are troublesome rather than that they are troublesome because they are unconscious; but we have seen that the causality is probably in both directions (see Chapter 6, pp. 85–87). More germane to the present concern with assessing the sources of the patient's neurotic suffering is simply the consideration that, to the degree the patient's fears and avoidances are elicited by the signals of incipient behaviors that the patient doesn't know about, it is hard to identify the source of anxiety; and thus the kinds of clinical inferences made by analysts seem necessary. The interventions made on the basis of those inferences, however, need not be limited to what analysts have traditionally done.

## THE ISSUE OF "UNDERLYING" PROBLEMS

One of the most confusing and misleading issues in considering the respective emphases of dynamic and behavioral approaches is that of whether "symptoms" or their "underlying causes" are treated. The confusion arises from both sides. From the behavioral side, much of the confusion arises from the claim that is sometimes made that the symptom "is" the neurosis. Eysenck (Eysenck and Beech, 1971) has argued that his original comments in this regard (e.g., Eysenck, 1959) have been misunderstood. Rightly or wrongly, Eysenck's statement was understood by large numbers of both dynamically and behaviorally oriented clinicians as implying that each troubling bit of behavior could be treated separately, with little need to look at whether it was part of a larger pattern, or whether fears or cognitions not readily manifest played a role in maintaining it. It helped create an atmosphere in which dynamically oriented therapists could readily dismiss behavior therapists as clinically naive. After all, in their daily clinical work the former saw myriad connections among apparently disparate aspects of their patients' problems in living, along with clear indications of processes that were not immediately apparent and were difficult to make directly observable, yet that played a major role in the more manifest difficulties their patients complained about.

Eysenck's statement also became for a while a positively valued slogan for behavior therapists and probably led many behavior therapists to be reluctant to postulate underlying variables, lest they be tainted by association with psychoanalysis. Fortunately, this attitude by behavior therapists did not remain dominant very long. Sophisticated behavior therapists today have little difficulty in conceptualizing their patients' problems as understandable in terms of underlying causes as well as overt stimulus-response connections. Bandura (1969), for example, states, "Psychodynamic and social-learning approaches to psychotherapy are . . . equally concerned with modifying the 'underlying' determinants of deviant response patterns; however, these theories differ, often radically, in what they regard these 'causes' to be. . . ." (p. 49)

By and large I would agree with Bandura's assertion, though as indicated in Chapter 6, I would question whether the theories are really so radically different. In practice, however, the differences in focus of current dynamic and behavioral workers can be rather substantial, as this chapter should make clear. Bandura's contention that quite different stimuli are selected to focus upon by dynamic and behavioral therapists is consistent with the position taken here; not so his view that the focus of one of the two groups (the dynamic) is almost always wrong or irrelevant.

## THE ISSUE OF SYMPTOM SUBSTITUTION

The issue of underlying causes has been such a fruitlessly controversial one largely because it has become entwined with two other issues, which, though of some substantive importance, are also confusing and wrapped in rhetoric. One of these is the issue of symptom substitution. It is frequently implied by behavioral writers that grave doubt is cast on psychodynamic theories by the fact that new symptoms do not appear when a particular symptom is successfully treated in behavior therapy. These writers are correct, I believe, in contending that when reports of behavioral treatments first began to appear, most dynamically oriented therapists viewed such treatments as likely to be followed by symptom substitution (though, as noted in Chapter 6, it is striking how infrequently discussion of this issue is found in the psychoanalytic literature). They are not correct, however, in the view that these findings are in fact contradictory to the basic tenets of psychodynamic thought. The expectation of symptom substitution by dynamic therapists was in fact due to their misunderstanding of how behavior therapy methods actually worked. They paid too much attention to the "symptoms are the neurosis" rhetoric and not enough to what actually was taking place. As I shall discuss more fully in later chapters, methods such as systematic desensitization do not "take away" symptoms; they enable the patient to confront sources of anxiety that he had previously avoided. Even if the manifest cues that arouse anxiety are viewed as symbolically related to unconscious wishes and fantasies, one would expect that exposure to cues associatively linked to such wishes and fantasies—previously fearfully avoided and now experienced with no harmful consequences—would facilitate extinction of at least some of the anxiety associated with the fantasies and wishes themselves. (See Dollard and Miller, 1950; Weitzman, 1967; and later chapters of this volume.)

It is also important to recognize that symptom substitution—and even more frequently, symptom recurrence (Lazarus, 1971)—is not unheard of in behavioral treatments (Montgomery and Crowder, 1972). Bandura's analysis of the kinds of treatment efforts most likely to lead to an increase in other forms of maladaptive behavior is in fact almost entirely consistent with what would be expected—though phrased differently—by most psychodynamic theorists (1969, pp. 48–52). For example, where efforts are made to suppress undesirable defensive behavior without addressing the anxieties that have motivated it, or where maladaptive interaction patterns are dealt with by punishing them without helping the person find more adaptive ways to deal with the events of his life, then other problem behaviors are likely to become more prominent. Whether approached through suggestion, punishment, or extinction, treatment that tries to remove symptoms without understanding their basis is not likely to be free of complications.

## THE ISSUE OF THE "MEDICAL MODEL"

A second misleading issue that has been linked to that of "underlying causes" is that of the "medical" or "disease" model. Psychodynamic theories are frequently discussed in these terms by behavioral writers. It is not difficult to see on what this characterization is based. The founder of psychoanalysis was, of course, a physician, and though Freud (1926b) recognized that his was not a discipline for which medical training was necessarily the most appropriate, psychoanalysis has continued to be dominated by the medical profession, especially in the United States. This dominance, however, is not a rational one based on any close relation between psychoanalytic methods and concepts and those of medicine. It is, rather, a sociological or economic phenomenon in which a group in a position of power by virtue of historical conditions has striven to maintain that power.

Throughout its development, psychoanalytic thought has been creatively influenced by individuals who did not participate in the initiation ritual of medical school. Anna Freud and Erik Erikson come to mind as perhaps the most striking examples; but the knowledgeable reader will certainly be able to think of many others with backgrounds in areas other than medicine, who have also had very substantial influence on how psychodynamically oriented theorists and therapists think today.

There is, to be sure, a superficial resemblance between the terms used by dynamic therapists and those used in medical work. But the analogy is so loose that its continued emphasis by men who in other respects demonstrate keen critical and analytical skills is itself a phenomenon requiring explanation. At one time "symptoms" really were viewed as signs of a disease process, and the effort to "diagnose" did seem a meaningful one. It was Freud, however, who created the major alternative to this position, though his language continued in some ways to reflect where he had come from and how he earned his living. The continued use of the word "symptom" may be a poor choice of terms, but once dynamic thinkers are slapped on the wrist for sloppy verbiage,* it is useful to look also at the substance of what they do. As it is used today by psychodynamic thinkers, the concept of symptom in no way implies a "disease." The term refers to behaviors whose functional determinants are thought to include

---

* My use of the term "patient" throughout this volume may be criticized in this regard. The term is probably inappropriate, but having been brought up on "patient," I have never been comfortable using the term "client."

various aspects of the person as an ongoing psychological system, and whose change is therefore seen as often requiring a change in the system and not merely in immediate conditions of stimulation. This is not a medical model, it is a psychological one.

In some respects, *all* psychological theories make such "symptom" assumptions, as the quote from Bandura above indicates. Even the most radical Skinnerians can be seen in some respects to need such a view, at least to the extent that any behavior must be seen as a function of characteristics that have accrued to the organism and not merely as a function of the conditions of external stimulation. For example, in discussing efforts by Skinnerian-oriented writers to deal with avoidance behavior, Seligman and Johnston (1973) note that such writers seek to avoid any reference to what is going on inside the organism and refer to stimuli having become aversive rather than to the organism having become afraid.

> Such theories speak explicitly only of the *stimulus* as having become aversive. However, it is obviously the animal that has changed and not the stimulus. We are reminded of Mowrer's quip that if such theories are to be understood literally, we could take a stimulus that had been made aversive in conditioning one animal and use its termination to reinforce a naive animal's behavior. (pp. 86–87)

Various psychotherapeutic approaches differ not in whether they distinguish between "symptoms" and "underlying causes" (though their terminologies in this respect may differ) but in how much change is thought to be needed in a persisting state of the organism in order to bring about change in any particular aspect of the patient's complaint. As we have already seen, and will pursue further, behavior therapists do tend to assume that less extensive organismic change is needed for change in any particular aspect of behavior or experience. Dynamic therapists see more interconnections among events and postulate more complex mediation. But we have seen that this distinction is quantitative rather than qualitative and, further, that the differences are in substantial measure due to concern with different phenomena. As behavior therapists have increasingly become concerned with the kinds of patients and kinds of phenomena that have confronted dynamic therapists, their mediational concepts have begun to converge as well. (Cf. Goldfried and Davison, 1976; Mahoney, 1974; Mischel, 1973a; Wachtel, 1973b.)

Before leaving the issue of symptoms and diseases, it may be worth the effort to pursue one further confusing feature of the "medical model" debate. In several respects, the way of working typical of behavior therapists resembles that of the physician considerably more closely than does the dynamic therapist's approach. The behavior therapist first tries to assess what is causing the patient's suffering and then brings to bear his technical skills to change this state of affairs. He is explicit about informing the patient what he thinks is the trouble, tells the patient exactly what he intends to try to do about it, and is perfectly comfortable advising the patient as to what therapeutic regimen he thinks the patient ought to follow in order for improvement to occur. The dynamic therapist, on the other hand, approaches his patient in a quite different manner. He tends to be reluctant to advise or suggest anything, often avoids the explicit role of the authority or expert, and is ready to *interpret* all efforts of the patient to present himself for working on like a body on a surgical table. In a sense, his therapeutic activity is in large measure describable by the variety of ways in which he works to *avoid* falling into the conventional role of the doctor and all that that implies.

## NORMATIVE AND NON-NORMATIVE ASSUMPTIONS ABOUT PATIENTS' MOTIVES AND FEELINGS

I have already noted one reason for the preference of behavior therapists for focusing on extrinsic sources of anxiety: the (at least apparent) similarity to laboratory models that such a focus provides. A second source of this preference has suggested itself to me in my observations of a number of behavior therapists at work over the past few years, and it is something that can critically influence the way in which the therapeutic endeavor proceeds: behavior therapists have seemed to me to be far more likely than dynamic therapists to make normative assumptions about what the patient wants and feels. That is, they take the patient's description of his goals and his reactions to events largely at face value. They are therefore much more likely to perceive the patient as thwarted in a fairly single-minded pursuit of conventional and socially acceptable aims. Dynamic therapists, in contrast, are far more prone to see their patients as in conflict, wanting not only the expectable things they first say they want but a host of often odd, incompatible, and/or "unacceptable" secret things as well.

This difference largely reflects the well-known difference in the views of dynamic and behavioral therapists regarding unconscious motivation. In a certain sense, the dynamic therapist can be seen to approach the assessment of the patient's dominant motives and affective reactions more behavioristically than do most behavior therapists. The latter, bending over backward not to talk of unconscious motives, often will accept the patient's feelings and goals as being just about what the patient says they are; whereas dynamic therapists will often infer motives from observing consistencies in the patient's behavior, whether the patient professes the motive or not. Thus it is consistent with Mischel's (1968) contention that "there is no convincing evidence that unconscious processes play an important role in learning, discrimination, and performance" that he claims it is "unjustified to retain the psychodynamic belief that persons with problems cannot reach appropriate decisions about their desired goals without the benefit of interpretations about their unconscious processes from clinical 'experts.'" (p. 271)

Not only goals but also other aspects of patients' reports seem to be taken more literally by behavior therapists than by therapists who are dynamically oriented. For example, Wolpe (1958), describing a patient with a hysterical paresis that interfered with his work, says, on the basis of one interview, that the patient's "history *revealed nothing of significance*. He stated that he enjoyed his work and was happily married and that there were *no circumstances in his life that he found unpleasant*." (p. 190; italics added) There are no indications in Wolpe's report of anything like the skepticism with which almost any dynamic therapist would view such a report by the patient, nor is there any indication in his account of the course of therapy that such matters were ever again considered.

The following case, the treatment of which I was privileged to observe behind a one-way mirror, illustrates well the greater readiness of behavior therapists to make normative assumptions about what their patients want and feel. It also illustrates how this stems from a lesser degree of attention to the persistence of early patterns of behavior and perception and to the coherences in the clinical data highlighted by such a focus. The case seems a particularly useful one for our purposes, both because I did have an opportunity to observe the treatment directly and because the practitioner was not a straw man, either in the sense of being inexperienced or of being an adherent of a hard-line S-R view. Rather, the therapist was a particularly respected individual associated with the most clinically sophisticated and non-ideological branch of behavior therapy. Thus, while any illustration of this sort is of course subject to the specifics of the interaction between a particular patient and a particular therapist (and a particular Monday-morning-quarterbacking author), the illustration at least has the virtue of dealing with behavior therapy as practiced by a sophisticated and highly competent exponent.

The patient's presenting complaint was shyness and problems in sexual relations with women. He reported feeling little sexual desire but feeling that he "should" have such desires and that he felt something was wrong that he didn't. The case was conceptualized by the behavior therapist primarily in terms of fear of inadequacy. It was hypothesized that the patient had not learned early in adolescence the right techniques in meeting women, talking with them, making advances to them, and so on, and that this lack of acquired skill had had a compounding effect in several ways. Firstly, it made him anxious with women so that he tended to avoid contacts with them and hence tended to be deprived of opportunities to learn in the present what he had failed to learn earlier. Additionally, when he did on infrequent occasions approach a woman, his anxiety made him awkward and hesitant, he tended not to meet with success, and thus his anxiety tended to increase still further, and the vicious circle was maintained.

In line with this view of the patient's problems, the therapeutic effort centered on diminishing his fears of heterosexual encounters and building his skills in interacting with females. It was suggested that the patient read particular books that the therapist judged presented a more rational and reassuring view of sexual morality and sexual relations than the patient's current view. Additionally, modeling and role playing were introduced, along with direct suggestions as to how to handle particular situations. At one point, an attractive female graduate student was brought into a session as an assistant therapist to enable the patient to role-play talking with a woman in a more realistic context and to provide him with feedback about how his various efforts were perceived by a woman.

As should be evident to the reader by now (and will be even more so as we proceed), I have little objection to such a way of approaching a case per se. Unlike many dynamically trained therapists, I do not find that asking a patient to read a book, or bringing in a woman with whom he can practice social skills, necessarily raises my hackles (though I would certainly be concerned that this be done at the right time, with the right case, and so on, and that its meaning to the patient be considered fully [see Silverman, 1974]). I chose this case, rather, to aid in comparing the kinds of inferences made and formulations reached by dynamically and behaviorally oriented clinicians, and to illustrate how the conceptual tools and clinical directions deriving from the psychodynamic tradition provide an additional, complementary view of the patient's situation—one that is particularly likely to reveal the non-normative aspects of the patient's feelings and strivings.

The clinician faces a task much like an embedded-figures test: important things often fail to stand out from their context on initial scrutiny. The theoretical perspectives employed by the therapist determine what he will search for and what coherences he will be sensitive to. In the case under discussion here, a number of items that came up in varying contexts, sometimes with little emphasis, leaped out at me as a Gestalt at a certain point. In the course of history-taking, the patient mentioned that his mother had been periodically hospitalized for psychotic depressions. On another occasion, he mentioned in passing (in answer to a question about whether he had discussed some matter with his mother), "No, you couldn't really talk to her. She'd get depressed." On several other occasions, in referring to a girl with whom there seemed to be a possibility of a more intense heterosexual involvement than he had had previously, he described the girl as expecting a good deal of him. Still another time, he indicated that what he didn't like about this girl was her pouting and looking depressed. He said he felt he had to entertain her and had the thought, "What do you want out of me?" In light of these various observations, I tentatively formed the hypothesis that this man saw women as needy, draining, and demanding, and that he was reluctant to become closely involved with a woman because he felt he would have to offer support to her but would receive little in return—if he shared his concerns and worries, she would become depressed and simply add to his burdens.

Such a clinical hunch should be entertained with some caution. To treat the few tidbits that suggested it to me as "evidence" for it would be to prematurely fix and consolidate what should be a spur to further exploration. But these various bits and pieces did seem to me to hang together, and my set to discern links between past and present patterns of relationship made certain features of the patient's report stand out, though they were not particularly emphasized by him. I heard, for example, his report of this girl as "expecting" a lot from him in a different way when uttered by this man, whose mother became depressed when he shared his feelings with her, from the way I would have with a patient with a different history. Had the case been mine, I would have been inclined to examine much more closely the nature of the demand he experienced from this girl and his fantasies of what it would be like to get close to her. I would have considered whether the patient's self-proclaimed inadequacy and fumbling might be somewhat more complicated —not just a source of distress, but also a way of protecting himself from a worse fear: getting entangled with a dangerously demanding, leechlike woman who would suck the life out of him. If he were inadequate, then he would be less likely to get involved with a woman and would have an excuse for why he could not fulfill her demands if, as in this case, she pursued him.°

The behavior therapist who treated the case was not struck by the pattern that seemed evident to me. This could, of course, have been due to a number of specific factors, having little to do with our theoretical backgrounds, which influence what any particular therapist sees with any particular patient. (It was not, I must hasten to add, simply a matter of a more and a less perceptive clinician. However tempted I might be to accept such an interpretation, the therapist in this case was a man highly respected in the field and highly respected by me as well.) It seems to me that a major factor in our differing views of the case had to do with the normative assumptions made by the behavior therapist. He assumed that the patient clearly wanted to have sexual relations with women and to get closer to them and was simply being held back by fear of inadequacy. When it became clearer that the patient was not all that eager to get close to this girl, and that he had many complaints about her, the therapist suggested that she was probably the wrong girl for him. The idea that the patient was inaccurately or selectively perceiving this girl, or that he might have a propensity for choosing such females, was not entertained.

The point here is not that this patient necessarily needed to gain insight into the connection between his feelings about his depressed mother and his feelings about current women in his life.† Rather, the issue is that whatever the treatment approach—whether emphasizing interpretive or behavioral interventions (or a possible synergistic combination)—in

---

° Here again, the perspective deriving from psychodynamic thought need not be incompatible with proceeding behaviorally. One might still want to ask why he so fears a woman's demands that he would avoid developing social adequacy, and the treatment might well include assertive training in resisting the excessive demands some women might make on him. Throughout the therapy, as much of this book will illustrate, interpretive methods and a focus on unconscious processes can proceed apace with the active intervention methods and focus on overt action characteristic of behavior therapy.

† To be sure, such insights are not infrequently important in clarifying for the patient what he is dealing with and in helping to extend and consolidate gains made in other ways. Occasionally, they may even be a primary source of change in the patient's feelings and behavior. Both discrimination training and cognitive reorganization play a role in changing reactions to events. But seeing connections between past and present is not to my mind the major source of change in most cases. Even where the insight is an "emotional insight," a new way of seeing things tends to be tentative and unstable until acted upon and tested out experientially. And often such experiential relearning can proceed quite well without articulated insights (particularly insights about the role of the past). The insights often come later, and help to extend and consolidate the experiential learning taking place in the present (cf. Alexander and French, 1946; Wolf, 1966).

order to be maximally effective, it must be based on a full and accurate assessment of what the patient is up to. Important implications for how to proceed therapeutically can be drawn if the patient is understood in terms of the particular skew given by his family to the development of his dominant aims and interpersonal patterns, rather than in terms of normative assumptions based on shared, consciously-professed cultural values. For example, after several instances of "inadequate" social behavior by the patient that left his date upset and angry, the therapist said to him, "I assume you want to be nice to her," and proceeded to demonstrate better ways of handling the situation. If the patient also had feelings quite different from wanting to be nice to her, however, such a communication can make them still more frightening. It can also make the feelings less likely to become apparent and thus impede full and accurate behavioral analysis. Similarly, in discussing one girl who had shown interest in him despite the absence of behavior on his part that would ordinarily pass for warmth or charm, the patient said he didn't want to let her know that in fact he did not want to be her boyfriend; the therapist responded, with obvious certainty, that he understood that the patient did not want to hurt the girl's feelings. Perhaps this was so. But if in fact his reasons were more complicated (for example, conflict over *wanting* to hurt her, fantasies of her doing some kind of damage to him if he did not fulfill her expectations, and so on), such an emphasis by the therapist on the more conventional reason might again increase the patient's tendency to keep the full range of operative variables hidden.

There were in fact, it seemed to me, a number of signs that this patient did harbor quite hostile wishes toward women. On one instance, for example, he described taking this same girl on a date and spending the whole evening playing pool with some other guys while she sat in a corner. His overt message was "See, look how inadequate I am. I don't know how to act on a date." But the grin when he described this exile of the girl to the corner bespoke quite a different attitude.

Recognizing these hostile feelings is important for a number of reasons. For one thing, to the degree that hostility is an important unacknowledged motive for him, the patient is likely to act in ways that "inexplicably" undermine the therapeutic effort; and neither patient nor therapist will understand why, nor be able to alter treatment strategy accordingly.* Secondly, once these feelings are recognized, it is possible to iden-

---

* Frequently, for example, behavior therapists have reported to me that their methods work fine when the patient carries out the treatment tasks assigned, but that it is often a problem to get the patient to do so or to do it properly. The present

tify what they are in response to and hence to do something about the situation. Otherwise, events that are disturbing to the patient may not be labeled as such but may yet continue to contribute to the patient's tension and unhappiness. Additionally, it appeared to me that in this case the patient's hostility toward women represented a compounding factor in his social difficulties parallel to, but in addition to, those vicious circles in the case noted earlier (p. 127). Without being very clear about what he was doing, this man communicated a good deal of silent resentment toward women. His experiences of rejection with women were a likely important contributor to this resentment, but his resentful, mistrustful attitude was in turn a contributor to the rejection experiences in yet another vicious circle.

## ONE APPROACH TO INTEGRATION: AN ILLUSTRATION

The considerations discussed in this chapter have led me in the past few years to develop a style of working with patients that has elements of both dynamic and behavioral points of view. The particular way of working described here is not put forth as a model or ideal therapeutic approach. Judging from my own experience over the past few years, it is unlikely to be even my own approach for very long, for it is part of an evolving effort to find applications in practice for the theoretical considerations advanced in this book. Some aspects of how I now work with my patients seem to me to derive rather directly from these considerations; other aspects are probably historical accidents, related to my original training and personal predilections.

For example, the reader who is familiar with Lazarus's work (1971, 1976) on broad-spectrum or multi-modal therapy will recognize a good deal of overlap (though certainly also important differences) between the approach I am advocating and that developed by Lazarus. Yet Lazarus's work is likely to be perceived as a version of behavior therapy that liberally utilizes the contributions of dynamic therapists (as well as a good deal else), whereas my approach is likely to appear to be an essentially dynamic approach that has borrowed freely from behavior thera-

---

case had to be terminated after only eight sessions, due to extrinsic reasons, so it was not possible to tell whether the treatment would have been successful. At the point of termination, however, the behavior therapist was experiencing considerable frustration and annoyance at the patient.

pists. Starting from different points, the styles into which innovations are incorporated are also different.

My present initial approach to the patient is not readily distinguishable from how I practiced as a traditional dynamic therapist with an interpersonal orientation. (As the therapeutic relationship develops further, however, divergence from this approach becomes much more evident.) Thus, initially, I greet the patient, ask what brings him or her to see me, and prepare to listen. Throughout the course of therapy, a good deal of time is spent conversing, without this conversation being necessarily focused on a particular assignment the patient has taken upon himself to practice or a particular fear we are looking to desensitize. As I shall indicate, these latter kinds of efforts and foci do increasingly enter in, but typically within the context of a relationship in which my getting to know and experience the patient and his getting to know and experience himself is a major feature.

As I listen, I am set to perceive what the patient says (or does—I watch as well as listen) in terms of a variety of categories that my psychodynamic background has shown me to be useful. I listen carefully, for example, for indications of inclinations which the patient inhibits (e.g., the absence of expected sexual or assertive behavior, or blockages or changes of subject when certain themes are being discussed) or that he carries out in a disavowed manner ("I didn't mean to hurt him. I said it to be helpful, but he took it wrong." "He seduced me. I had no idea what he had in mind and by the time I realized it it was too late." "No, I certainly do not long to be taken care of! If I didn't have this terrible cold I'd never let her keep me in bed like this. But I've got a lot of responsibilities in my job and it wouldn't be fair to all those who count on me to let myself get run down.").°

I try to be attuned not only to what kinds of wishes or feelings the patient seems to be in conflict about (and/or not aware of), but also to how he keeps himself from knowing these things about himself and why he does so. Regarding the "how," I am set to perceive events as instances of the various defenses that have been conceptualized over the course of years of psychodynamic observation. Concepts such as repression, pro-

---

° In these, as in other examples to follow, the single illustrative statement by itself is clearly not enough to demonstrate the correctness of the clinical concept applied (though it should be enough to alert the clinician to *ask* if it is relevant). Whether the patient actually is conflicted about a particular inclination and/or acts on it while disavowing it must be determined by considering a variety of converging indications. It is a caricature of psychodynamic thought to suggest that a therapist would assert that such a conflict was important for a patient on the basis of one such statement. Taken just by itself, there is no way to evaluate whether the patient's explanation is believable or not.

jection, intellectualization, selective inattention, and so on are valuable tools to aid the clinician in noticing patterns that might otherwise escape his attention.

The utility of these concepts has not infrequently been questioned. A careful reading of the criticisms, however, reveals that they are often based on misrepresentation of the concepts, on an excessively restrictive notion of what constitutes appropriate evidence, or both. Holmes (1974), for example, claims that "there is no evidence that repression [exists]." (p. 650) In fact, he does not review, or even consider, all the evidence. What he examines is the *experimental* evidence, which he at a number of points implicitly equates with evidence per se. Interestingly, and ironically, in the very next sentence Holmes cites a proposition of Kuhn's (1962) regarding how scientific change comes about. Kuhn's work, of course, has never been supported by "experimental evidence"; it is based on examining events that occurred naturally and seeking to discern regularities in them.° He does not weigh the evidence in terms of statistics or controls in the usual sense, but rather in terms of seeking coherences that make the best order out of the wide range of specific instances that occur—much as evidence is weighed by the clinician. It is striking how often Kuhn is approvingly cited by psychologists who, in their own discipline, tend to be thoroughly dismissive of evidence of a non-experimental, convergent, interpretive sort. (For a discussion of such evidence, see Schafer, 1970; Wachtel, in press.)

Holmes's critique of repression—again, like much other anti-psychoanalytic writing—concerns itself only with the crudest version of the concept. Modern writings on repression do not limit themselves to selective forgetting; they are also concerned—perhaps even more so—with selectivity in what the person experiences in construing his own affects, plans, and intentions. Further, psychodynamically oriented theorists have gone well beyond the early formulations, which stressed fully articulated memory traces being removed from awareness (for example, Sullivan [1953] on selective inattention, Schachtel [1959] on infantile amnesia, Shapiro [1965] on repression and attentional style, and Schimek [1975] on mental representations). These writers would have little trouble with Holmes's explanation of selectivity in memory—Holmes does acknowledge that even the experimental literature strongly supports such selectivity—in terms of differential attention to certain events when they

---

° Kuhn's thesis has been challenged by other historians of science; but the equivocal nature of the evidence for different theoretical views is not limited to evaluations of non-experimental evidence, as should be clear to anyone familiar with the history of the controversies among proponents of the manifold theories of learning.

occurred and of the person's "set for viewing and interpreting his experiences, . . . which would influence associational patterns and recall." (p. 650) They would, however, take issue with Holmes's view that all that is at issue is that patients, unfamiliar with psychoanalytic concepts, have different expectations and patterns of association than the clinician. Converging lines of observation, analogous to the evidence garnered by Kuhn, point to the critical role of anxiety reduction and self-esteem maintenance in determining with what set a person views and interprets his experiences. (See also Erdelyi, 1974; Silverman, in press; Wolitzky and Wachtel, 1973 regarding *experimental* evidence bearing on this issue.)

To be sure, one can abuse the principles that have developed out of clinical observation.° The useful directive, for example, that vigorous protest by a patient that he does *not* feel or wish something may be an indication that he really does but is conflicted, can be used by a clinician to "prove" that his every wild guess or hunch is correct; either the patient acknowledges the accuracy of the interpretation or he denies it, thereby "confirming" it. This heads-I-win, tails-you-lose approach, however, is a caricature of the original clinical observation, not a legitimate application of it. The latter would require that the denial be conspicuously vigorous and that other lines of evidence point in the same direction. Even a particularly vigorous denial would not by itself be sufficient evidence. If, for example, the patient were reacting to the therapist's continuing to push a pet interpretation that has been rejected several times before, his high-volume denial would be an appropriate reaction and not a signal to place a bet on the therapist's hobbyhorse.

Thus, when I use a concept such as projection, for example (or at least when I use it as I think I use it, and would like to use it), I do not automatically assume that every complaint about another, or about me, is a projection. But when a patient experiences me as feeling or doing something that I don't think is the case, or when he interprets some other person's action in a way that seems unlikely or idiosyncratic, one question I am set to ask is: is this something the patient was himself inclined toward but conflicted about and is attributing to someone else instead? Needless to say, I consider other questions as well (including the possibility that, for example, the patient is accurately perceiving what I am up

---

° Disturbing questions about how clinicians use their concepts have been raised by Chapman and Chapman (1969). The matter of clinical inference is one in need of a long, hard reexamination. For now it may merely be noted that, as indicated above, the clinical activities of behavior therapists frequently face similar problems of inference, and that the decision of how inferentially to approach clinical material involves trade-offs (of the sort met in statistical decisions with Type-One and Type-Two errors).

to, and *I* am distorting). The confidence I have in different formulations depends again on how many other lines of evidence point in the same direction. (For example, is the motive attributed to the other person one that I have seen the patient disavow in other ways while acting in ways consistent with it? Is it a kind of human activity that he has shown he has a particular stake in saying he is free of? Has he recently dreamt of doing what he now says the other person did? And so on.) But the idea of putting the observations together in the formulation designated by "projection" comes from my immersion in psychodynamic thought. Without the set of concepts that that kind of training equipped me with, I would be unlikely even to think of the possibility of such a coherence in the data (or if only superficially familiar with the concepts, as probably every psychologist is to some extent, I would have little sophistication in knowing how to decide, as described above, whether my use of the concept in a particular instance was appropriate).

In attempting to evaluate what experiences and inclinations the patient tries to avoid or disavow, I am also concerned with *why* he does this. Here I am particularly interested in the patient's fantasies and expectations as to what would follow from full elaboration of the warded-off events. What does he think would happen if he reacted with open anger, or allowed himself to feel dependent on another, or engaged in frank and uninhibited sensuality? Sometimes he can (at least to some extent) answer such a question directly. But frequently, in my view, he is unaware of what fears or fantasies perpetuate his avoidance (as he may be of the avoidance itself, which he doesn't notice, explains in other terms, and so on). I am thus quite willing to infer what the fear or fantasy may be from a number of converging indications. The patient's dreams, daydreams, slips, associations, and so on are all sources of clues for this kind of inferential activity (which is, of course, subject to the same kind of dangers and evidential constraints as discussed above).

Generally, my use of dreams and fantasy material tends to stay closer to the "surface" than is true of many dynamic clinicians. This is neither because I seek more limited goals for my patients (see the discussion of Alexander's work in Chapter 3), nor because I completely reject the validity of the formulations about deeply repressed contents that are to be found in the psychoanalytic literature. I do feel that too many analysts are fast and loose when it comes to distinguishing between fascinating speculation and established findings; and that even where a regularity has been convincingly established for a particular patient, it is too frequently put forth as a universal without nearly sufficient justification. But my main reason for not plumbing the greatest of depths is strategic. I do not feel that one must necessarily discover and assimilate the most inaccessible and unwelcome of fantasies to effect extensive and lasting change. Nor do I believe that the degree of change is highly correlated with the recovery of such buried treasure. Further, I believe that the effort to discern these most archaic of psychic activities may divert from genuinely useful therapeutic activity or even preclude it (see Chapters 3 through 5).

Unlike many dynamically trained clinicians, I do not hold a strictly hierarchical view of personality structure, in which layer upon layer is conceived, with the "deepest" layers most crucial in keeping the patient as he is. Rather, I view repeated and interacting circles of events to be a generally more useful image for personality description than the peeling of an onion. While certain aspects of how a person behaves seem well described in terms of more obvious psychological events being reactive to and perhaps disguising less obvious ones, I find this conception to be only partially satisfying and at times misleading. In my experience, for example, excessive solicitousness, which may mask and be in reaction to a "deeper" or "underlying" hostility, is also quite as accurately described as a part of the processes that *cause* the hostility. By bringing about circumstances in which one's own needs are overlooked or given short shrift, such oversolicitousness for others can sow the seeds for feelings of resentment and hostility, and thus may be described as "underlying" the hostility every bit as much as it is a reaction to it. Though it is indeed important that certain portions of the cycle of events are more accessible to awareness than others, it is not necessarily most useful to think of the less aware portions as "deeper" or "lying behind" the more aware, if that concept implies more basic or genuinely causal.

Thus, in my conception of how neurotic patterns are perpetuated, it is generally important to have a good sense of what inclinations of the patient are inhibited, partially inhibited (pursued indirectly), or acted upon but disavowed.° Similarly, it is important to know something of the fearful or pleasurable fantasies which, without the patient's acknowledgement, seem to provide part of the cognitive basis for his avoidances and his active pursuits (see Irwin, 1971; Seligman and Johnson, 1973). But it does not follow that the more inaccessible such a fantasy or wish is to awareness, the more important it necessarily is. It does not constitute a rejection of the role of unconscious processes in human psychology to suggest that many analysts have justified their interest in the most exotic of

---

° In different terms, it is important to be aware of what kinds of reinforcements are regularly sought but not acknowledged as reinforcing, or what discriminative stimuli set the stage for both approach and avoidance.

mental products by the automatic assumption that such esoterica are necessarily most important. I share my colleagues' fascination with the extraordinary things patients reveal during the process of psychothera-peutic interpretation, but in many instances it has seemed to me that the revelation of these extraordinary mental activities has been a by-product of therapeutic change rather than its major cause (see Alexan-der and French, 1946).

At this time, it is not possible for me to state in any concise or reliable way just which unconscious wishes and fantasies are necessary to discern and which are window dressing (in traditional, hierarchical terms, "how deep to go"). The only guideline I can offer, vague though it is, is to seek for fairly dependable evidence that those hidden events which are sought play a fairly clear role in maintaining a frequent pattern of interpersonal interaction, and not to assume that any mental activity is *necessarily* important simply because it is unconscious (even "deeply" unconscious).

To return to those psychodynamic concepts which I have found valu-able in guiding my efforts at discerning coherences, I must note the influ-ence of the writings on character of Horney (1945), Reich (1945), and Shapiro (1965) upon how I watch and listen. While all three seem to me to err in the direction of assuming excessive, at times almost monolithic consistency, and (to varying degrees) to make other assumptions that seem to me rather questionable, all three authors, as well as a number of other traditional clinical writers, provide extraordinarily useful direc-tives to the observer who desires to be prepared to notice important, yet readily overlooked, patterning in a human life.

I am alerted to coherences of a different sort by the developmental schemes offered by Freud, Erikson, and Sullivan, and by others who have further elaborated these efforts. In using these notions in my own work, I am less concerned about establishing the actual genetic sequences with my patients than about being sensitized to notice certain things that vary together. Implicit in these developmental schemes is the idea that, in adult functioning as well, certain themes and issues tend to go together. Where particular conflict or intensity is associated with one feature of the hypothesized developmental stage, it is worth looking carefully for other expected features. It is of course essential to be open to *not* finding these other features as well, but this does not come down to a trivial either-it's-there-or-it-isn't. These conceptions are essentially probability statements, indicating those directions for search that are most likely to prove of value.

An analogy to other situations in which one must learn to perceive competently may be useful. The neophyte who listens to a concert or watches a football game tends to hear a mix of sounds with perhaps a vaguely discerned melodic line, or to see a jumble of men running aimlessly, falling, throwing red flags, and so on. When the ear or eye is trained to perceive, quite a different kind of event is perceived. The concert becomes a rich tapestry of interacting but separately articulated themes and instruments. The football game is perceived in terms of coordinated efforts by one group of men to advance, within a set of rule-governed actions, against the coordinated efforts of another group.

To pursue this latter sort of articulation just a bit further, one can consider what happens to our perception as we learn specific plays used by each team. Then, as we begin to notice what is being done by one or two men, we are alerted to expect and look for certain other actions by other men on the team and, if these occur also, to have a still firmer expectation of what all of them will do in the ensuing moments of action. "Diagnosing" a play is much like "diagnosing" a personality. In neither is any disease involved; in both there is a chance that being too set to see something on the basis of one or two signs will lead to error; but in both, when done skillfully, the likelihood of a correct guess is greatly enhanced by possession of these probabilistic concepts. Without them some errors may be avoided (particularly of the kind that make one look foolish), but overall success is reduced. (Of course, if the concepts are faulty, and/or the observer unwilling to note when he has been wrong, diagnosis will suffer.)

A further similarity is also important. In the realms of both football and psychotherapy, when one has accurately diagnosed what pattern has begun to be run, it is easier to disrupt it. To be sure, the football player can know more readily when he has erred (if only a "first down" could be called to alert the therapist to each time a patient has completed, without successful interruption, a neurotic action pattern!), but the principle is the same: those concepts and guiders of hunches should be retained which, while not perfect predictors, are useful enough to enhance the probability of picking up what is going on, what is likely to happen next, and what intervention is likely to turn things around.

USE OF THE THERAPY INTERACTION IN ASSESSMENT

Some of the most useful leads that I pick up in my therapeutic work come from examining how the patient and I interact with one another. The experiences of patient and therapist in the therapeutic session provide vital clues, especially to the affective subtleties and minimal cues that are central in the maintenance of neurotic patterns of living. In my work with patients I try to be particularly alert to the tone of what is going on between us. I look for hesitancy preceding his agreement to comply with a therapeutic request, or signs of annoyance accompanying his acceptance of an interpretation of what he is up to. I am alert to when he comes late to appointments, when he starts a session with a long silence, when he tells me he has read a paper of mine and likes (or doesn't like) it, and so forth.

Noticing this sort of thing has seemed important to me for a number of reasons. Firstly, as Silverman (1974) has illustrated, unrecognized patient reactions to the therapist or to what he is doing can be a source of considerable disruption to the therapy. Only by understanding the many levels on which the patient is experiencing the therapist is it possible to consider how to deal with or prevent such disruption.

Additionally, I am particularly attentive to the vicissitudes of the patient's reactions to me because his relationship to me is the one I know best, the only one I really know firsthand. Many of the more subtle ways in which he keeps neurotic patterns going may be much easier to discern through participant observation than as a third-person collector of data. Having been sensitized to a pattern in this special observational situation, I can then listen for it in accounts of his outside interactions, using this specific emotional knowledge to guide and educate my listening in much the same way as in the above description of how formal concepts aid perception. (This, incidentally, is also the main role in my work of knowing something of the patient's history. Knowing something about how his parents and siblings treated him, how he felt about them, what aspects of his experience he tended to truncate or deny, and so on, can alert me to similar kinds of patterns in his current life that might otherwise go unnoticed. I do not, however, strongly emphasize the patient's history, because I find that other ways of sensitizing myself are frequently more useful.)

The tranference reactions that the patient manifests within an active-intervention therapeutic approach will of course very centrally include reactions to the specific interventions. When the therapist introduces systematic desensitization, or role-playing, or behavior rehearsal, he is likely to evoke different kinds of feelings and fantasies than when he largely confines his behavior to silence and interpretation. The specific meaning of the intervention to the patient, however, is likely to be idiosyncratic. The interventions make a difference, but they make a different difference for each patient. Thus, some experience the use of such interventions as a sign of the therapist's caring and concern, some as a sign that they are "very sick" and require this special effort, some as indicative of the therapist's being controlling and manipulative, some as his running from intimacy from them, some as a sign he is willing to take risks and "really means it" when he indicates that they don't have to conform to others' expectations, and so on. Often, as might be expected, the positive and negative aspects are combined in a single conflicted perception, or alter at various stages in the treatment. One woman, whose parents had persuaded her to have a "nose job" when she was 16, associated to this past event when assertive training was suggested, and took it to mean that I wasn't satisfied with her as she was. Later the assertive training came to mean to her that, unlike her parents, I was not a critic who would stand aloof, saying what was wrong but unwilling to help her deal with it. It meant to her a willingness to honestly confront problems, but in a spirit of cooperative effort to solve the problems rather than as a depiction of unchangeable deficiencies.

Understanding the range of conscious and unconscious meanings that the intervention can have can be critical to whether or not the intervention succeeds. The topic of resistance is rarely addressed in the behavioral literature, but in my experience it is a common feature of active-intervention therapy, as it is of more strictly interpretive approaches. The prevalence of resistance derives from the anxieties that motivate neurotic patterns, and the fact that whatever gratification and relief from anxiety the patient has managed to achieve in his life has occurred largely within such patterns. By challenging the neurotic way of living and by confronting the patient with sources of anxiety (however gently the therapist may do either), he is a source of threat as well as hope. The use of active-intervention techniques can either diminish or increase the threat for any particular patient at any point. It is necessary to be clear about the meaning of the technique (and the technique in the context of whatever has occurred between the two people thus far) in order to know whether it is appropriate to introduce a technique at a particular point and/or how to deal with the patient's reactions once it is introduced. It is likely that many instances of patients who don't practice their relaxation exercises, forget to carry out an assertive training assignment, and so on are due to failure to deal with the meaning of the intervention to the patient. Therapeutic progress is never just a matter of isolated technical intervention.°

---

° In addition to the kinds of transference and resistance issues commonly discussed in the psychoanalytic literature, the important work of Frank and his colleagues (e.g., Frank, 1973, 1974) highlights the critical role of the patient's feelings and fantasies about the therapist as a factor in whether change can be brought about. See also Klein, Dittman, Parloff, and Gill's (1969) interesting discussion of their observations of the work of Wolpe and Lazarus, and the important contributions of Crisp (1966), Marks and Gelder (1966), Marmor (1971), and Sloane (1969).

USE OF "COUNTERTRANSFERENCE" FOR UNDERSTANDING

Not only am I attentive to my *patient's* reactions in the therapy sessions as a clue to patterns more general in his life, but to *my own* reactions as a source of clues as well. Though there is always a danger of excessively attributing to the patient a therapist reaction that is primarily the therapist's "own problem," I nonetheless rely a good deal on this source of clues. There is much possibility for error, but if one is continually questioning one's own motives and actions, and checking as well to see how what is surmised from within the session compares to what goes on outside, there is also much opportunity to correct and verify one's view and considerably enhance one's understanding of the patient and his difficulties.*

On one occasion, for example, I had been working for a while with a man who was rather severely suspicious and mistrustful of others. Not surprisingly, he saw me in a similar light, interpreting almost everything I did as designed to thwart and frustrate him. Knowing that he had experienced his father as being brutal and aggressive, and believing that my own efforts, even when momentarily frustrating to him, were primarily in his interest, I interpreted his reactions to me essentially as transference phenomena. I viewed his constant complaints of others' hostile and spiteful reactions to him in a similar light. There seemed to me a paranoid cast to his thinking that distorted others' actions to look like intentional affronts.

It thus came as a source of considerable enlightenment to me one day to recognize, in the course of a discussion of a possible appointment change, that in the guise of an effort to "understand" the request before deciding whether to try to fulfill it, I had really been provoking and frustrating this man. His perception of me as in conflict with him was, I had to recognize, correct, and my perception of him as distorting my innocent behavior was largely incorrect. I began to reflect on this, and recognized that on a number of occasions in the past I had acted similarly toward him. Further (I would still maintain), this kind of covertly spiteful, ungiving attitude was not at all typical of how I usually am with my patients.

My view of the troubling pattern in this man's life changed markedly after this experience. I reconsidered my view that his perception of others as spiteful and thwarting was a distortion, and wondered instead

---

* The traditional call for the therapist himself to have had an intensive therapeutic experience, while a bit repetitious by now, is still a sound recommendation in this regard.

if they, like me, had reacted to something about him by *really* wanting to get in his way, annoy him, and so on. I shared with him my recognition of how I had acted with him, how it differed from my usual behavior with patients, and what I thought it meant about how we ought to proceed. Our attention then turned toward examining, in much sharper detail, his behavior in the period just prior to the "offenses" by others of which he complained. Aided particularly by my attention to what he had been doing that had provoked my own unhelpful reactions, we were able to gain much greater clarity about what the sequences that characterized his difficulties in living were really like, and therapeutic progress increased considerably.[*]

### BEHAVIORAL FEATURES OF MY APPROACH TO ASSESSMENT

I have presented the preceding material in some detail in order to make clear how I view my way of working as reflecting my psychodynamic training, and to aid the reader with a behavioral orientation in evaluating the extent to which it differs from how he proceeds. As the clinical work of behavior therapists has become more sophisticated, it has become increasingly difficult to be sure what kinds of clinical thinking or action remain the province of dynamic therapists and are eschewed by behavior therapists, and what has been assimilated into the latter's work. I shall now indicate in what way my efforts at assessing the patient's problems partake of a behavioral approach or viewpoint, and how the dynamic and behavioral approaches interact. This aspect of the discussion will be somewhat briefer; I have already discussed some of the main features of behavioral assessment earlier in the chapter, and at various times almost all of these can be seen reflected in my work.

First of all, as noted earlier, I am from the very beginning strongly concerned with "when" questions. I try to be constantly alert to the danger of describing internal states or affective reactions in a vacuum, and make every effort to relate my inquiry into the patient's moti-

---

[*] This illustration is also relevant to the issues discussed in Chapters 3, 4, and 5. I cannot go into it in detail here, but I would maintain that what happened in this instance was not a simple "countertransference error," but rather a legitimate instance of participating in the patient's neurotic pattern and then reflecting on the participation in a way that sheds light on his problem. I would further maintain that such "errors" cannot be eliminated by being "better analyzed," but only by staying so distant from the patient that one does not participate very much with him—the price of which is not learning a good deal that it is necessary to learn. The opprobrium attached to such reactions by therapists in the traditional psychoanalytic literature probably motivates many therapists not to notice such deviations from the model when they occur. Supervisees hide them from their supervisors, experienced analysts hide them from themselves, and understanding of the typical course of therapeutic interaction is constrained by efforts to ward off (unnecessary) guilt.

vation and phenomenology to the ongoing events of his life and to the consequences of his own behavior.

Additionally, while usually focused particularly on characterological patterns that are pervasive, persistent, and complexly related to unconscious motives and defenses, I am nonetheless continually ready to entertain the hypothesis that any particular pattern may have more "give" than I initially estimated. Even where evidence of manifold interconnections leads me to think in terms of images such as "deeply rooted," I will test out how much change might be brought about by rather direct and simple interventions or suggestions. Thus, with one patient whose loneliness seemed to me in part due to continually relating to people in terms of his achievements and credentials rather than sharing with them what he really felt, I suggested he go a whole day without mentioning to anyone a single accomplishment or "impressive" thing about himself. Another man was advised that his fear that others will crumble if he is critical or competitive might be more likely to change if he began to try out more direct and expansive behavior in his day-to-day interactions instead of telling me, in the sessions, of his history and "personality structure."

Such "simple-minded" interventions or suggestions usually are not sufficient (as most behavior therapists also recognize). But occasionally they generate a surprising momentum, and frequently they help to clarify just how intimately the pattern is tied to various other features of the patient's way of living. Even the simple matter of whether the patient tries out the suggested change, quite apart from whether it has any impact, can provide a very useful perspective on what one is up against.

At various points in the course of the therapy I am likely to utilize, as well, any or all of the behavioral assessment methods discussed earlier in the chapter. I find it particularly useful to ask the patient to systematically attend to and record some particular pattern of behavior and its context. Sometimes such a request is treated solely as a means of exploring or assessing some aspect of the person's difficulties. At other times such systematic recording is an accompaniment of the patient's carrying out some specific therapeutic assignment of the sort discussed in the chapters that follow. Generally I find that such requests for systematic observation do not seriously disrupt the tone of the therapeutic interaction or make more interpretive work, based on empathic listening, problematic. I am, throughout, someone who listens, who manifestly and explicitly wants to help, who frequently maintains I can be most helpful by listening more and trying to understand and sense the emotional currents, but who is obviously willing to make direct suggestions when I think they may be useful.°

My work reflects the view that, in contrast to what one might conclude from the behavior therapy literature, there is a vast storehouse of insightful observations and useful conceptual tools that have evolved in the development of psychodynamic thought. While these concepts and observations require much more rigorous evaluation than they have typically received, they can be discarded altogether only at great peril to one's effectiveness as a clinician. Additionally, I would maintain that much therapeutic learning does take place within the patient-therapist relationship and that that relationship, when it combines the twin features of engagement and reflection, provides a unique opportunity for relearning, which cannot readily be replaced by relying solely on learning to be different in one's everyday milieu. Further, on the basis of both clinical experience and the findings of research on perceptual learning, cognitive restructuring, and so on (see Leeper, 1970), I believe behavior therapists have underestimated the therapeutic value of insight into or clarification of the issues in one's life (especially when that insight is into current inclinations and alternatives, rather than primarily historical in focus).

Yet I am also struck by the unspectacular success rate and inordinate time and expense of traditional therapies, and the promise and logic of the methods developed by behavior therapists. Since my interpretive comments do not pretend that the patient's reactions to me have nothing to do with me, but address themselves to the patient's idiosyncratic reactions (both overt and hidden) to whatever it is that I am doing (or whatever anyone else is doing, or represents), I find that using the assessment and intervention methods of behavior therapists does not interfere with interpretation, sensitive clinical listening, or explicating unconscious processes. The patient will have (conscious and unconscious) reactions to the use of such methods, as he has such reactions to *not* offering structured assistance, and in either case it is important to clarify these reactions. It need not be anomalous for some part of the therapy to consist mainly of the therapist's listening, concentrating on feelings, and occasionally commenting, and other parts to be characterized by the therapist's active efforts to implement change, based on his accrued understanding. Most human relationships show different features at different times.

---

° This is in contrast to the position of some dynamic therapists who maintain they can be most helpful by not taking on the explicit role of "healer" (see Paul, 1974) and by not having a stake in whether the patient changes.

Without the aid of useful clinical concepts and without paying attention to affective and communicative subtleties, assessment of the patient's problems is seriously hampered. Also, as illustrated in the case of shyness discussed earlier, premature efforts to bring about specific change, based on normative assumptions instead of immersing oneself in the patient's world, can be problematic. So too, however, can be the rejection of all efforts to provide systematic assessment and to complement the clinician's subjective impressions with other sources of data. And even more limiting are efforts to place the entire burden of therapeutic change on the valuable but nonetheless limited effects of clarification or understanding alone, or even on the experience of a new, more open, reflective, and regenerative relationship with the therapist.

The behavioral contributions discussed in this chapter have been primarily those explicitly conceived of as assessment methods. The intervention methods discussed in the next few chapters will be seen to be very valuable ways of *using* the kinds of understanding arrived at by the assessment methods described in this chapter to bring about meaningful therapeutic change.* Further, as we shall see, change and assessment feed upon each other, for as an individual begins to confront what he fears, or to interact with others in a different way, the possibility of a new understanding of where he stands, where he comes from, and where he might go is greatly increased.

---

* The intervention methods may be viewed as a way of enhancing the process of "working through," once an initial understanding is achieved by patient and therapist (provided, of course, that working through is not conceived of exclusively in terms of gaining more and more understanding).

# 8

# The Reduction of Fears:
# Foundations of Systematic
# Desensitization and
# Related Methods

THE analysis presented in Chapter 6 suggests that reduction of inappropriate anxiety is central in bringing about therapeutic change in neurotic problems. In that chapter we saw that many of the problems patients bring to psychotherapists can be understood as deriving from fears initially learned in the childhood state of extreme helplessness and dependency. These early experiences of fear-learning exert their influence not by any direct continuation of impulses or defenses as concrete things in a particular walled-off area of mental geography, but, as discussed in Chapter 4, by skewing the course of further development. Early fears, and the desperate efforts made by the child to diminish them, lead to particular kinds of experiences and adaptive strategies which leave the developing individual vulnerable to particular classes of stresses that others might take in their stride.

Thus, for example, if a person learns at an early age to depend on aggressive conquest and domination of others to relieve intense feelings of fear and vulnerability, he will be threatened to an inordinate degree by the prospect of failure or by any sensing of inclinations on his part to approach another in an open, trusting, or dependent fashion. Similarly, the person who has learned to quell intense anxiety by being loveable, nice, or harmless, and to place himself in the hands of a strong and reliable protector, will be inordinately threatened by signs of disapproval or loss of interest by the other, or by sensed inclinations within himself to react angrily or expansively or to threaten in any other way his "right" to the other's protection.*

As Dollard and Miller (1950) point out, traditional psychoanalytic therapies probably achieve their effect largely through the extinction of the unrealistic fears that motivate neurotic behavior. By facilitating expression of feared thoughts and feelings, and enabling them to be expressed in a situation where no punishing event is experienced, the analyst fosters the extinction of the inappropriate fears at the heart of the patient's neurosis.

In principle, such an approach to changing fear-motivated problematic behavior seems sound. Studies such as those of Miller (1948) provide a reasonable basis for conceiving of fear as a response (or a cluster of responses—see Lang, 1971) learned in certain situations, and like other responses studied by psychologists, it should be expected to be extinguished if reinforcement consistently fails to occur. A variety of research findings, however, suggest that extinction of anxiety is no easy matter and presents problems that extinction of other kinds of responses does not.

Miller's own research, for example, illustrates quite clearly how resistant to extinction strong fears can be. In one study (Miller, 1951) animals trained to press a bar in order to escape from a compartment in which they had previously been shocked continued to exhibit this habit for many trials without shock. The avoidance response, and presumably the fear that motivated it, did eventually begin to show signs of extinction, but only after a very long time. One animal continued to

---

* It should be noted that such an analysis does not necessarily contradict Mischel's (1968) demonstration that variability in behavior from situation to situation is far greater than had been recognized by many early theorists. The patterns noted above may be called out only in certain situations, rather than be evident in every aspect of the person's life. What is important in the present context is that where such behavior is motivated by avoidance of anxiety, it is likely to be somewhat peremptory and rigid, and not as finely attuned to subtle changes in environmental events as are behaviors learned on a different basis (cf. Wachtel, 1973a, b; Mischel, 1973b).

*improve* his avoidance responding (reinforced by fear reduction only; °
no shocks were administered) for 200 trials before even beginning to
show a decreased speed of bar-pressing, and the graph presented by
Miller indicates that responding continued, though at a slower speed,
beyond 600 trials.

Solomon and Wynne (1954) reported similar findings in experiments
with dogs. Their animals maintained avoidance behavior for 500 or
more extinction trials, and Solomon and Wynne were led to conclude
that fear learning is partially irreversible. Others, too, have reported
extraordinary persistence of fear-motivated behavior in the face of no
external reinforcement (e.g., Brush, 1957; Seligman and Campbell, 1965;
Sheffield and Temmer, 1950; Sidman, 1955).

## WOLPE'S EXPERIMENTS ON FEAR REDUCTION

Wolpe (1958) found conditioned fears and avoidances to be similarly
resistant to extinction. Cats that were subjected to painful electric shocks
in an experimental cage were subsequently found to be extremely resistant to being put in the cage, showed many signs of intense anxiety
when forced into the cage, and refused to eat in the cage even after as
much as three days without food. Further, these anxiety reactions were
evident not only in the cage in which shock had occurred but also,
to varying degrees, at the sight of the experimenter, at the sound of an
auditory stimulus that had accompanied the shock, and in a number of
rooms other than the one in which shock occurred, but that shared some
stimulus properties with the "scene of the crime."

As is now well known, Wolpe found that he could eliminate these
anxiety reactions by relying on a procedure that involved feeding the
animals in a situation resembling the most feared one only to some extent. If a situation was chosen for which the anxiety responses were mild
enough, the anxiety did not inhibit eating. After the animals had eaten
for a while in a situation just slightly similar to the one in which they
had been shocked, they could then be put in a slightly more similar
one and be found able to eat in that one. Gradually they could be introduced to situations increasingly similar to the original scene of the
shocks, until finally they could be introduced to the original scene and

---

° The relation of fear to avoidance is somewhat different in some recent accounts
(e.g., Seligman & Johnston, 1973).

would eat rather than freeze or try to run. Thus it seemed that a portion of the anxiety was removed at each step of the continuum (or "hierarchy," as it came to be called) of situations increasingly similar to the scene of the trauma. A rather efficient way of eliminating fear and avoidance behaviors seemed to be available that did not take hundreds and hundreds of trials to accomplish its ends.

Wolpe reasoned that the procedure was effective because, by choosing to begin with a situation that shared some properties with the original but in which anxiety did not inhibit eating, he had created circumstances in which the eating inhibited anxiety instead. This active inhibition of anxiety was seen as enabling the anxiety to be unlearned and the bond between the previously frightening cues and the anxiety response broken. Having removed the anxiety from a portion of the cues, the animal could now be placed in a situation with a somewhat larger proportion of the fear-provoking cues. Whereas previously, in that situation, anxiety would have inhibited eating, now eating would inhibit anxiety, and so anxiety would be eliminated as a response to some further features of the fearful situation. In this fashion, the *reciprocally inhibiting* effects of anxiety and eating could be utilized to remove the anxiety from increasingly larger portions of the originally frightening complex of stimuli, until the original situation itself ceased to be evocative of anxiety.°

This experimental work, and the theory Wolpe used to account for it, became the basis for a number of innovative clinical methods for the reduction of neurotic anxiety in humans. Particularly prominent in the clinical repertory of behavior therapists are the methods known as systematic desensitization and assertive training. Assertive training will be discussed in Chapter 10, where I will try to place its procedures in a rather different clinical and theoretical context from that in which it was originally conceived. Systematic desensitization will be a major focus of the present chapter, as well as the following one. We will look at some of the evidence for the efficacy of systematic desensitization with various kinds of problems, at the variety of related procedures that have at times been given the label of systematic desensitization, at theoretical rationales for these procedures that vary from the one originally proposed by Wolpe, and at the relation between desensitization (and other behavioral anxiety-reducing methods such as flooding) and the methods of psychodynamic therapists. Particularly in Chapter 9, we will look at some of the problems encountered in the clinical use of

---

° A more detailed examination of Wolpe's theoretical position will be presented later in this chapter.

systematic desensitization, and the ways in which the methods and perspectives of the psychodynamic approach can contribute to dealing with these problems.

In applying the findings of his animal studies to the treatment of human neuroses, Wolpe made a number of important changes that seem to have had great clinical utility but that are also the source of considerable controversy. One such change, not so commonly remarked upon, was his use of the clinical interview for data gathering.

The early animal experiments were rather clear instances of a behavioristic methodology (within the expanded meaning of the term brought in by Hull and other mediational behaviorists). Directly observed behavior, or inferences tied to close observations in the orthodox tradition of behavioristic experimental psychology, provided the basis for the conclusions Wolpe reached.

No such methodological strictures limited Wolpe's clinical reports with human neuroses. There he relied heavily on the patient's reports of his earlier experiences, on the patient's description of his current feeling state, and on the patient's report of how things in his present life were going.

Locke (1971) has argued cogently that systematic desensitization is not in fact a behavioristic methodology, and recent efforts to refute his contention have been unconvincing (Eysenck, 1972; Waters and Mc-Callum, 1973). Indeed, as it is actually practiced by experienced and sensitive behavioral clinicians, systematic desensitization (and the behavioral analysis that precedes it) relies on introspection to such an extent that it might be viewed as the grandchild of Titchener as much as of Watson. Some have even contended that the skill the patient develops in attending to and articulating his subjective experience is a prime factor in the therapeutic efficacy of the systematic desensitization technique.

Other changes from the procedures in the animal experiment have also been of considerable import and the source of much theoretical debate. In addition to introducing interview methods and introspective reports in his work with human patients, Wolpe also, in many cases, had his patients *imagine* the situations they were afraid of rather than actually introducing concrete physical stimuli, as he did in his animal studies. It is, in fact, this imaginal desensitization that is most often referred to in the literature when the term "systematic desensitization" is employed, and that has been the focus of the most extensive research scrutiny. The closer parallel to the original animal experiments—presenting actual concrete stimuli—while not an uncommon procedure, is not really the "standard" way of proceeding with systematic desensitization, and it is designated by the special term *"in vivo* desensitization."

The practical advantages of using imagined scenes are obvious. Few therapists could have available in their offices all the stimuli patients might possibly be afraid of, as well as graded versions of them, so that patients could be gradually introduced to progressively more difficult items along a hierarchy of fearfulness. In our imaginations, we can, while sitting in a chair or lying on a couch, encounter an enormous range of experiences, with countless variations and intensities.

The equivalence of instructing a patient to imagine and presenting a concrete stimulus to an animal has been seriously questioned on a number of grounds, however, both theoretical and practical. Both problems and advantages are associated with the introduction of imagination, which requires more complex conceptualizations than were utilized to deal with the animal experiments. I shall examine a number of these as we proceed through our examination of the clinical use of systematic desensitization.

The other major variation from the animal studies that Wolpe introduced in working with his patients was to substitute relaxation for eating as the reciprocal inhibitor of anxiety. Training in deep muscle relaxation was not the only response used by Wolpe to inhibit anxiety (see Wolpe, 1958, 1969 for a detailed account of his procedures), but, like the use of imagery, it has come to be viewed as the "standard" version of systematic desensitization, and it is the referent for the term in most of the clinical and research reports in the literature. Therefore, in discussing systematic desensitization in the rest of this book, the reference (unless otherwise stated) will be to a procedure * in which (1) the stimuli that evoke the patient's anxiety are sought out; (2) one or more hierarchies are drawn up, representing dimensions along which the patient's fearfulness varies from very little to a great deal; (3) the patient is trained in deep muscle relaxation; and (4) while deeply relaxed, he is asked to imagine an item low on the hierarchy. He imagines it for a number of seconds, repeating it if it causes him anxiety and going on to the next item on the hierarchy if he experiences little or no anxiety. In this fashion

---

* The reader is urged to notice when the systematic desensitization *procedure* is being referred to and when the desensitization *model* is. Reference to the latter will apply to a wider range of procedures.

he proceeds until he can imagine the originally most distressing item on the hierarchy with little or no anxiety.*

## DESENSITIZATION AND DYNAMIC THERAPY

Wolpe's procedure seems on the face of it quite different from the way of proceeding typical of most dynamic therapists. Yet in some respects there are substantial areas of overlap, which make a distinction—if still real and important—not as hard and fast as is typically implied. For one thing, as I have noted above, skillful clinical interviewing is essential for the success of both approaches. The therapist must be able to elicit from the patient descriptions and reactions that will enable the relevant sources of anxiety to be identified, and he must have the skill and knowledge to know what the data elicited mean. The behavior therapist, no less than his psychodynamically oriented counterpart, must be trained to *notice* that a patient's symptoms seem to worsen whenever his mother-in-law visits and that, despite his initial claim that he likes her and is comfortable with her, his speech becomes hesitant when she is discussed, his body tenses, his hand forms a fist, and he changes the subject.

The emphasis, in Wolpe's procedure, on gradual exposure to increasingly threatening images also overlaps considerably with the approach of many dynamic therapists. Under such rubrics as "dosing of anxiety," "timing of interpretations," "allowing the patient to set the pace," "interpreting only what has already become preconscious," and so on, dynamic therapists are often trained to create conditions under which the patient is initially exposed to images and thoughts that are only minimally threatening and is gradually exposed to contents progressively more disturbing. "Wild analysis" (Freud, 1910), in which the patient is confronted very early with ideas and images that are deeply repugnant to him, is frowned upon in most psychodynamic quarters these days.

Wolpe's use of relaxation and other counter-anxiety responses also has its counterpart in psychodynamic approaches. Wolpe himself (1958) has suggested that the successes achieved by dynamic therapists are in large measure due to the anti-anxiety responses evoked by the presence

---

* There are, of course, many other aspects to the procedure, many other problems and special issues encountered, and many variations even within the "standard" procedure. Some of these matters will be taken up in this and the following chapter, but the reader interested in the traditional practice of systematic desensitization is advised to consult Wolpe (1969) or some other more strictly behavioral text.

of the therapist as a calming, protective, help-offering figure.* A number of features of dynamic approaches seem to contribute substantially to such a calming effect. For those analytic therapists who use the couch, the reclining posture and resultant muscular relaxation may itself be expected to contribute to the reduction of anxiety.† Additionally, the therapist's accepting, non-punitive reaction to the patient's revelations of thoughts and acts of which he is ashamed adds to the therapist's general tendency to be an anxiety-reducing social stimulus. Modern psychoanalytic writings on the need to establish a working alliance in order for painful interpretations to have a therapeutic effect seem also to reflect the conclusion, from a quite different direction, that a positive emotional climate must be the background for exposure to that which evokes considerable anxiety.

### DIFFERENCES BETWEEN DESENSITIZATION AND DYNAMIC APPROACHES

The above discussion should not be construed to mean that systematic desensitization and dynamic therapies are so alike that the differences between them can be ignored or that all therapists really do the same thing. Anyone reading a transcript of a substantial segment of analytic psychotherapy and of Wolpe doing systematic desensitization would have no trouble telling which was which. Wolpe systematically focuses on one thing at a time far more than the typical dynamic therapist, who is especially concerned throughout the entire course of therapy with exploring the significance of incidentals and asides, even if this implies a somewhat less monotonic advance in any one direction. Additionally, Wolpe's therapy usually (though not always) attempts to supplement the anxiety-reducing properties of the therapeutic relationship with *explicitly trained or instructed patient responses* for this purpose. Further, therapists employing systematic desensitization tend to place greater emphasis on exposing the patient (either directly or through imagery) to cues associated with environmental events that evoke anxiety, whereas dynamic therapists tend to emphasize affective and motivational states as providing the most salient cues in evoking anxiety and defensive reactions. Here again, however, as with the other distinctions noted above, the difference is one of degree rather than an absolute one. Therapists of almost all theoretical predilections, from Freudian to Wol-

---

* He, of course, also claims that the therapeutic effects which are mustered by dynamic therapists are not nearly as great as those brought about by the explicit use of his procedures. This issue will be examined shortly.

† This and other features of the procedure that are calming to most people, can, of course, *increase* anxiety for some people, depending on the particular personal meaning to the patient at that point.

pean, recognize that humans are responsive to both inner and outer events.

Thus, while systematic desensitization represents a substantial departure from earlier psychotherapeutic methods, it need not be thought of as an approach that is utterly alien to what earlier methods involve. This seems especially to be the case when one considers that, as we shall see below, the success with systematic desensitization spawned a wide variety of efforts by behavior therapists to reduce anxiety directly through the application of learning principles. Some of these efforts vary considerably from the original desensitization procedure, and the necessity of such apparently crucial features as relaxation or gradual movement through the hierarchy has been called into question. The definitional question of at what point these therapeutic procedures no longer should be designated as "systematic desensitization" need not concern us here. Behavior therapists have experimented with a family of related though differing procedures for reducing maladaptive anxiety. Our concern here will be to see if we can articulate more clearly than do the labels now extant just where the various therapeutic efforts of "dynamic" and "behavioral" therapists are divergent, equivalent, or complementary.

## EFFICACY AND APPLICABILITY OF SYSTEMATIC DESENSITIZATION

The evidence for the therapeutic value of systematic desensitization is too substantial for dynamic therapists to ignore—but it is too incomplete for behavior therapists to be complacent about it. Although there have been many controlled experiments establishing the efficacy of systematic desensitization-type procedures in reducing fear, the large majority of these have dealt with "analogue" phobias (see below), such as fears of snakes, mice, or spiders in students solicited for the purposes of research. There is some systematic evidence for the efficacy of systematic desensitization with a wider range of problems and in individuals self-defined as patients who sought out therapeutic assistance rather than volunteering for a study. This evidence (discussed below) provides substantial support for the use of systematic desensitization with at least some clinical problems. But for the majority of kinds of problems for which systematic desensitization has been reported as effective, the evidence consists essentially of case reports.

Thus, for a wide range of complex human neuroses, the behavior therapist justifying his use of systematic desensitization is to a considerable extent in the same boat as the dynamic therapist justifying his way of proceeding. When it comes to evidence that their procedures are useful for complex interpersonal problems, concerns about death or illness, insomnia, nightmares, and a host of other clinical problems, both must essentially rely on the reports of clinicians who have achieved success with similar kinds of cases. And such reports are subject to a host of familiar problems (for example, the likelihood that unsuccessful cases are not similarly reported, or the possibility that the change that occurred was due to factors other than the specific therapeutic procedures: for example, placebo effects, effects due to the therapist's personality rather than his method, effects due to concurrent events external to the therapy—meeting a new mate, getting a new job, and so on. (See Paul, 1969a, Bergin, 1971, and Kiesler, 1966, for more extensive discussion of these issues.)

The situation is not quite comparable, however, when evaluating the case reports supporting systematic desensitization and those supporting psychodynamic approaches. The case reports relevant to the two approaches tend to have different characteristics, with different strengths and weaknesses. Additionally, any case report must be evaluated in the context of the body of evidence of which it is a part, as explicated below.

Regarding the first point, it will be obvious to the reader versed in the literature of the two approaches that case reports describing the use of systematic desensitization tend to differ from psychodynamic reports. A number of features tend to enhance, at least to some degree, the evidential value of the systematic desensitization reports. For one thing, they generally describe a change occurring in a shorter period of time; and, roughly speaking, the less time the treatment took, the less time there was for an external event to have occurred that was actually responsible for the change. So much occurs over the course of a five-year analysis that it becomes extremely difficult to sort out which life events were themselves a product of therapeutic progress, and which were happy occurrences that fortuitously occurred during the time the patient was in treatment. (Did the treatment help the patient be more "open" to a new relationship, or did the "right person" just "happen" to come along and help the patient change and so on?)

Additionally, the relationship between the therapeutic intervention and the change that occurs tends to be more direct and obvious in the case of systematic desensitization, making the causal connection seem more compelling (though obviously far from conclusive). The focused nature of the treatment also limits the degree to which "shotgun" change measures can reveal a therapeutic effect simply because all aspects of functioning tend to fluctuate and *something* is bound to be better after treatment than it was before. The less symptom-oriented nature of dynamic therapies makes it possible to report, as a treatment success for a particular patient, that he is less frequently depressed *or* freer sexually *or* more able to enjoy friendships, and so on. Such changes might be reported as valuable concomitant changes in a report of systematic desensitization, but change in the target symptom is clearly the major criterion of success or failure, and the effect of the treatment on *that one measure* is crucial.*

It should be noted, however, that the broader focus of the typical psychodynamic case report has certain advantages as well, and enables the reader to consider some issues more fully than does the typical case report on the use of systematic desensitization. Consider, for example, the detection of the influence of events external to the therapy, as described above. Though such intercurrent events may be less likely in the shorter time span covered by the typical desensitization case report, when they *do* occur they may be more likely to be omitted from such a report and hence not to be subject to the reader's evaluation. This is due to the more focused nature of both the treatment and the report. Once a focused course of systematic desensitization for, say, claustrophobia, or a fear of illness is begun with a patient, the fact that he meets a new girl friend a week or two after desensitization begins is more likely not to be reported to his behavior therapist than to a more traditional therapist; and even if reported to the therapist, it may well be excluded as "irrelevant" to the written report. The wider net cast by the dynamic therapist, despite its danger in generating false positives in reports of change, does have the advantage of making a broader range of data (though perhaps a more biased and idiosyncratic selection) available to the reader who wishes to consider alternative ways of understanding what has occurred. Additionally, it enables the evaluation of hypotheses by the use of convergent observations as a supplement to the

---

* To draw an analogy to statistical analysis, reports of improvements in dynamic case reports are in some respects similar to running numerous t tests, capitalizing on the likelihood that one will be "significant," whereas the narrower criterion for the effectiveness of an effort at desensitization is like running only a single t test and standing or falling with it.

experimental method, which has limitations as an exclusive method for investigating neurosis and psychotherapy (see Wachtel, 1973b, in press).

Turning now to the second point noted above in evaluating case reports on systematic desensitization—the context of the body of evidence of which it is a part—we are led to consideration of those fears and behavior disorders where there *has* been systematic evidence of the effectiveness of desensitization. Case reports extending the range of applicability of the desensitization approach gain credence to the degree that problems not too different from the one reported in the single case have been shown to be aided by such an approach in well-controlled studies. The range of problems presented by patients seeking therapy is so diverse one could hardly expect that all such problems would be examined in systematic outcome studies. Let us see, then, just what sorts of difficulties have been the object of systematic treatment and study.

THE ISSUE OF ANALOGUE STUDIES

As noted above, by far the largest number of studies have been devoted to the reduction of fears of snakes, spiders, insects, rats, and so on, with the snake in a commanding lead over his four-, six-, and eight-legged competitors. The effectiveness of systematic desensitization in reducing such fears has been fairly well documented (see Paul, 1969b), though adequate comparisons with traditional therapeutic procedures have been few (see below).

There are many reasons for the choice of snake phobias and the like for study by behavior therapists. Certainly not the least of these is the convenience, for research purposes, of focusing on a well-defined fear for which behavioral avoidance measures are easily obtained (for example, whether the subject will approach the snake and pick it up), on which the ubiquitous college sophomore can initially be assessed by questionnaire and then solicited for further study, and so on. Additionally, however, snake phobias have been a favorite target for symbolic or ideological reasons. With the keen eye for psychoanalytic excesses and absurdities noted earlier, behavior therapists have been fond of quoting statements such as that of Fenichel (1945) to the effect that "the sight of snakes provokes penis emotions." Snake phobias are often chosen, then, to refute the presumed psychoanalytic view that all the world is a disguise for phallic symbols. In this regard it is an interesting footnote to the debate that Freud himself did not regard fear of snakes as based nearly as much on the kind of symbolic processes that he viewed as relevant to most other phobias. He specifically chose snake fears to illustrate those kinds of fears that are essentially "normal" and perhaps even due to a phylogenetic inheritance, and he regarded fear of snakes as quite different from real phobias, which seem "unintelligible" and hence require interpretation to be understood (Freud, 1917).

In many of the studies of fear reduction in snake phobias, systematic desensitization has been found to be an effective procedure when compared to groups receiving no treatment, various control groups designed to assess placebo effects and effects of getting attention from professionals per se, and control groups designed to examine the effectiveness of various parts of the desensitization procedure in isolation (see next section). These studies suggest that in at least some instances the systematic desensitization procedure can be effective in reducing fears, but their relevance to the treatment of the fears evident in patients coming for psychotherapy has been seriously questioned by sophisticated behavior therapy researchers.

Bernstein and Paul (1971) have clearly highlighted the problems met in generalizing from such studies to actual clinical problems. Like Bandura (1969, p. 432), they have pointed out that though investigators often pay lip-service to the limitations in their procedures, the majority nonetheless go on to draw conclusions totally unwarranted from their findings. Much of the literature in this area has been building cumulatively on this shaky foundation.

Bernstein and Paul note a number of interrelated difficulties with the majority of these "analogue" studies. For one thing, the subjects of the study are rarely individuals distressed enough to seek treatment. Rather, they tend to be volunteers recruited from college classrooms. In contrast to patients in actual clinical settings, who often are distressed enough by their problem to pay a good deal of money to be helped, these subjects often have to be induced to have their "problem" treated by giving them credit toward fulfilling a course requirement—or even by paying them to be treated. Since receipt of these benefits depends upon their being sufficiently "phobic," they may well be motivated to report higher levels of distress than they otherwise might (if, for example, the inducements were being offered to people with moderate fears but not full-blown clinical "phobias"). In contrast to Bandura's (1969, p. 432) contention that "the incidence of snake phobias is relatively high," Bernstein and Paul suggest that only a rather small percentage of college students are really afraid of snakes to a degree that would have any clinical relevance.

Even where behavioral avoidance tests are used (tests of subjects' actual approach behavior in the presence of the "phobic" object), there is room for a great deal of latitude, especially since initial assessment is concerned with *not* being able to approach a presumably feared object, something far easier to fake than the opposite. Bernstein and Paul discuss a variety of factors that render these tests rather useless in most of the studies reported. As with many of the fancy methodological efforts in this area, they are icing on a moldy cake.

Not only does the frequent use of subjects not really very distressed by their "phobias" make it difficult to know if more severe problems could be similarly helped, it also makes it impossible to know if even the same *process* is involved. As we shall soon see, for example, a number of studies have suggested that treatment requirements for very intense fears may differ from those for moderate ones. Bernstein and Paul point out that because of the way the typical "analogue" study is conducted, the expectancies induced in subjects and the social pressures inherent in the experimental procedures may well account for more of the changes observed than does genuine reduction of fear. Moderate avoidances are far more subject to the effect of such variables than are really intense fears.

The relevance of these analogue studies has been objected to on another ground as well, one which Bernstein and Paul do not accept. From the point of view of many dynamically oriented clinicians, true clinical phobias are seen as integrally related to more extensive, generally less evident personality difficulties. Many of these clinicians might well acknowledge that a fear of snakes might develop, the origins of which were essentially independent of the individual's personality dynamics. (For example, the fear might be due to modeling of parental fears, or to traumatic experiences with a poisonous snake that led to fears that generalized to harmless ones.) But they would contend that such a fear is of a very different sort than the fears of most of the phobic patients seen in the clinic, and thus that the study of the first kind of fear has little bearing on the second, *even if the fear really is very intense.*

This is a difficult but important issue. To be sure, the objection is based upon and to a certain degree *assumes* a theoretical position that behavior therapists tend to call into question (that is, the assumption that real clinical phobias, unlike simple fears, are a result of such processes as symbolization and displacement). On the other hand, the distinction is based on a good deal of clinical observation. To dismiss it out of hand is a risky procedure, especially in light of reports such as that of Feather and Rhoads (1972), in which, for a number of cases, traditional desensitization treatment did not work, whereas a modification of the desensitization procedure based on dynamic conceptions of phobia was successful. Clearly it is essential (though not sufficient), in evaluating the cogency of this distinction between kinds of phobias, to consider what hard evidence there is for the efficacy of systematic desensitization in a wider range of complaints closer to those actually seen in clinical practice, and it is to this research that we turn next.

OTHER OUTCOME STUDIES

One of the most widely cited studies in this area is that of Paul (1966). In keeping with his criticisms noted above, Paul's own study attempted to focus on individuals whose anxiety was strong enough to be clinically relevant. The subjects of the study experienced strong performance anxiety in a public speaking situation. Paul compared the effectiveness of systematic desensitization with that of "insight-oriented psychotherapy," identified as primarily neo-Freudian and Rogerian in orientation. Also included were an attention-placebo control group, a no-treatment "waiting list" control group, and a no-contact control group. The group receiving systematic desensitization showed significantly greater reduction in anxiety than any other group on self-reports of distress, on blind behavior ratings of their performance, and on physiological measures. The "insight therapy" group and the attention-placebo group also showed a significant decrease in anxiety compared to the no-treatment controls, on the self-report and behavior rating measures. The insight and placebo groups did not show improvement, however, on the physiological measures, and improved consistently less than the desensitization group on all measures. The insight and placebo groups did not differ from each other.

Paul's study is frequently cited as evidence of the superiority of systematic desensitization over traditional therapeutic approaches. It does suggest that when "insight-oriented" therapists accept the task of producing a limited focused change in a brief period of time, they may not do as well as could be done using systematic desensitization.* The therapists in Paul's study apparently regarded such a goal as appropriate to their traditional methods, and presumably a significant portion of traditional therapists do also, according to some of the figures on treatment duration that Paul cites. Paul's comparison is of little relevance, however, in comparing systematic desensitization with psychoanalysis or intensive, psychoanalytically-oriented psychotherapy. The latter two are long-term treatments with broader therapeutic aims. They would not

---

* Even this conclusion is probably too general to derive from Paul's study. As discussed below, there is considerable question as to how comparable Paul's subjects were to the variety of patients seen in psychotherapy. With regard to these people, and the specific problem focused upon, systematic desensitization was the superior treatment.

be expected by their practitioners to produce much change in any specific aspect of the patient's life in the first six sessions.

It is sometimes argued that it is no saving grace for psychoanalysis that it could accomplish in several years what systematic desensitization achieves in six sessions. Such an argument does not take into account that psychoanalysis (or intensive dynamic psychotherapy) does not *try* to do what desensitization did in the six sessions. Its goals are far more extensive, touching on many aspects of the person's life. It is directed not just to the more obvious sources of distress in the person's way of living, but also to the reexamination of compromises that currently feel comfortable to the person but may be limiting the possibility for greater satisfaction and development. It thus tries to do *more* in a longer period of time, not just the same.

The issue of differing goals seems particularly germane to the implications of Paul's comparative study when one considers that Paul's explanation for the superiority of systematic desensitization emphasizes that desensitization provides more focused exposure to the "cues of prime importance." From this perspective, it is not surprising that this more focused kind of treatment achieves good results in reaching a focused goal. How it might compare with intensive psychodynamic therapies in the more ambitious goals they aim for cannot be answered from Paul's study. This is a matter for which the available literature provides little that is conclusive.

If Paul's study is not very relevant as a comparison with intensive psychodynamic therapy, it does seem to provide a clear demonstration that systematic desensitization is an effective and efficient way of reducing a kind of anxiety other than an isolated fear of snakes or other small animals. The comparability of the disturbances of Paul's subjects to those shown in typical clinical cases is not, however, unequivocal. Paul administered a battery of paper and pencil tests to students taking a public speaking course required for graduation, and he asked the students to indicate if they would be interested in obtaining free help with whatever difficulties and anxieties they experienced in the speech situation. Those who requested treatment in response to this solicitation and who scored high on a scale of performance anxiety and low on a falsification scale were contacted.

As Paul describes this group, they do seem much closer to the kinds of individuals typically seen in psychotherapy than do the subjects of most "snake phobia" studies. Paul reports:

> The subjects' degree of anxiety was strong to severe in most cases, and was reported to be of two-to-twenty-years duration. In addition to high perform-

ance-anxiety scores, the subjects reported many problems characteristic of anxiety, for example, nausea, mental confusion, "black-out," vertigo, tremors, excessive perspiration, accelerated pulse rate, rigidity, speech disturbances, tension, headaches, insomnia, depression, avoidance behavior. Anxiety was seldom reported to be restricted to the speech situation, although it was usually more severe in that setting. In most cases anxiety was present in almost any social, interpersonal, or evaluative situation: competing in contests, answering roll call, meeting strangers, taking examinations, making appointments and dates, bidding at auctions, and carrying on casual conversation. ( Paul, 1966, p. 26)

Several features of Paul's selection procedure raise some question, however, about just how comparable his subjects were to those typically seen by psychotherapists. For one thing, Paul reports that students who had entered treatment elsewhere prior to being contacted or who dropped the speech course were excluded from the study. These two excluded groups would actually appear to be the individuals most severely disturbed by their anxiety.

The exclusion of those who had already sought therapy not only leaves out of the study a group of individuals likely to be particularly comparable to the kinds of individuals seen in clinical settings, it also highlights that the individuals who did participate in the study *had not* sought out therapy for their problem. Some of these latter individuals may of course have refrained for economic reasons, or been ignorant of the possibility they could be helped, and some might have been on the verge of seeking help. But the fact remains that the subject population of the study was in part *defined* by an absence of any effort to seek therapy for their problem.°

The second excluded group, those who had dropped the course, also would seem to be a group likely to have been particularly distressed by the strain of facing the public speaking task. One might partly determine whether this was the case by examining Paul's unpublished data to see whether this group gave different answers to the battery of tests administered. But (for differing reasons) neither behaviorists nor psychoanalysts are likely to give too much credence to such paper and pencil self-report measures. It would also be of interest to know whether this excluded group, as well as the group excluded for seeking therapy, was a sizeable proportion of the students originally contacted. Even if their number was small, however, they are important in highlighting for

---

° That they did respond positively to the questionnaire item asking whether they desired help does not seem to be a strong counter-argument. Fully 54 percent of the students in the course answered "yes" to that question. There is a difference between agreeing to participate when solicited for therapy and actually seeking therapy out.

us the kind of group that was studied: students with performance anxiety who did not seek therapy for it (and in fact had had no previous psychological treatment of any sort [p. 25]) and were not so distressed as to drop the course.

Paul's reasons for excluding these two kinds of individuals seem obvious and reasonable, given the design of his study, and his description (above) suggests that, anyhow, he may well have obtained a group of individuals with significant interpersonal anxiety roughly comparable to what is seen in a traditional clinical practice. The applicability of his findings to more typical clinical problems and populations (and more typical clinical goals) cannot, however, be assumed without question. Let us, therefore, turn to some of the controlled studies on actual clinical problems.

An interesting study was reported by Moore (1965) on the treatment of severe asthmatics. Subjects received either systematic desensitization, relaxation only, or relaxation plus direct suggestion. A decrease in reported attacks was associated with all three treatments, but only systematic desensitization led to significantly improved respiratory functioning in actual physical measurements. No comparison with psychodynamic therapy was undertaken.

Studies that have compared systematic desensitization to dynamic therapies have tended to support the value of the former, at least in obtaining certain focused results more quickly, but practical difficulties encountered in such research have made it difficult for firm conclusions to be drawn. A number of comparative studies have been performed by Marks, Gelder, and their colleagues at the Maudsley Hospital in London. These studies have the merit of being among the very few comparing behavioral treatment of definite clinical disorders with traditional treatment. They have, however, been seriously criticized (Paul, 1969a).

Three of the studies (Cooper, 1963; Cooper, Gelder, and Marks, 1965; Marks and Gelder, 1965) were retrospective studies, in which cases that had been treated by behavioral methods over a period of years were compared to another sample of completed cases, matched on a number of variables. The retrospective nature of the studies created a number of problems, discussed by Paul. The studies suggested some superiority for the behavior therapy methods (not all behavior therapy patients received systematic desensitization) over a mixture of traditional methods with different patients (drugs, ECT, abreaction, and leucotomy as well as psychotherapy). The success rate was lower, however, than that obtained in analogue studies, and there was some tendency toward relapse after a time. In one of the studies (Marks and Gelder, 1965), all the behavior therapy patients were individuals who had received systematic desensitization, and the symptoms were divided into agoraphobia and "other phobias." With the specific phobias, the advantage for desensitization was substantial: all eleven showed signs of improvement, while only three out of ten psychotherapy patients were similarly described. The agoraphobic patients treated by desensitization also did better than the traditionally treated group, but the difference was not so great, and desensitization was not so effective for these patients. That the results for behavior therapy were only moderately positive might be attributable to the fact that most of the behavior therapy had been administered by inexperienced therapists. The whole series of studies, however, with its reliance on retrospective material, was exploratory in nature, and the conclusions drawn are subject to qualifications.

These same authors also reported several prospective studies characterized by random assignment of subjects to either desensitization or dynamic therapy prior to treatment. This corrected for one of the major limitations of the earlier studies. In one of the prospective studies (Gelder and Marks, 1966), severe agoraphobics were assigned to treatment either by traditional psychotherapy or systematic desensitization. Seven out of ten patients in each group were judged as showing some improvement, but all had some residual agoraphobia, and some of the progress had diminished on later assessment. The study certainly provides no evidence for the superiority of desensitization, and as Eysenck and Beech (1971, p. 572) note, "these results are much less satisfactory than those obtained with non-psychiatric subjects." *

A second prospective study, by Gelder, Marks, and Wolff (1967), compared desensitization, group psychotherapy, and individual psychotherapy for the treatment of phobic outpatients with over eight years average duration of disturbance. Some indications of superiority for systematic desensitization were obtained, though most of the differences were nonsignificant. These two prospective studies have also been criticized in considerable detail by Paul (1969a), but many of the criticisms have been countered by Marks (1969, pp. 212–13).

Marks concluded, on the basis of both controlled research and clinical experience, that systematic desensitization was of substantial value in that small minority of actual patients whose problems were similar to those of the volunteer subjects in analogue experiments, and could "occasionally be of limited value, e.g., in reducing an agoraphobic's fear

---

* Later work by Marks and his colleagues suggests that while desensitization is not a very effective procedure with agoraphobics, another behavioral method (flooding) is quite useful (Marks, 1975).

of travelling to work despite his retention of multiple other phobias." Desensitization, he noted, "is often costly in time and limited in effectiveness," and he recommended that "psychotherapy is indicated in any phobic disorders complicated by disabling interpersonal problems." Lazarus and Serber (1968) and Wolpe, Brady, Serber, Agras, and Liberman (1973) have also noted that systematic desensitization is of value only with certain specific kinds of problems.

More recently, the results of an important study were reported in which the effectiveness of behavior therapy with the *full range* of patients seen in a typical outpatient clinic was evaluated and compared with the effectiveness of brief psychoanalytic therapy (Sloane, Staples, Cristol, Yorkston, and Whipple, 1975). The study did not examine the efficacy of systematic desensitization per se (the behavior therapists used a variety of techniques), but it is of interest in relation to the present contribution in that both dynamic and behavioral approaches were shown to be effective and neither showed a clear superiority. Thus, while the study does not bear on the present notion of an integration between the two approaches, it does support the view that both are of real value in dealing with typical clinical problems.

## EFFECTIVE COMPONENTS OF SYSTEMATIC DESENSITIZATION

In the preceding section, systematic desensitization was discussed rather globally, as if it were a single technique. In fact, Wolpe's innovation has spawned many offspring, and has opened up a wide range of therapeutic possibilities. Some of these varying, but related, approaches differ quite considerably from Wolpe's own original approach. The theories that have been advanced to understand the efficacy of these various methods have also been diverse.

Most important for the purposes of the present volume, different variations in conception and procedure are more or less compatible with the approach of dynamic therapists. Let us therefore look next at the evidence bearing on just which forms or aspects of systematic desensitization are clinically useful.

### THE ROLE OF RELAXATION

Typically, an integral feature of systematic desensitization is training in deep muscle relaxation and the pairing of relaxation with images from the patient's anxiety hierarchy. The studies cited in the previous section were primarily concerned with evaluating the efficacy of just such a way of proceeding. But despite the widespread use of relaxation training and pairing of images with relaxation, the role of relaxation in anxiety reduction through systematic desensitization is an issue that has generated considerable controversy. This controversy bears importantly on the feasibility and value of the integrative effort undertaken here.

Empirically, muscle relaxation has seemed to be a critical component in fear reduction in some studies but not in others. Davison (1968), in a widely cited study, found substantial reduction of avoidance behavior when fear-relevant images were paired with relaxation, but not when the same images were not paired with relaxation (nor when relaxation was paired with images irrelevant to the subject's fear). This study is frequently cited as evidence for the necessity of pairing the frightening images with relaxation.

Davison himself noted, however, an important factor which tempers the conclusion that exposure to the fearful images without relaxation is ineffective.[*] Specifically, only the relaxation-plus-imagery subjects themselves controlled just what hierarchy items they were exposed to and for how long. As in the standard desensitization procedure, these subjects were told to terminate the image if it became aversive; they did not go on to the next highest item on the hierarchy until they could experience the previous one without anxiety. In contrast, the exposure-only group did not have such control over what they experienced. In order to assure that the two groups had equal exposure to the relevant imagery, each subject in the exposure-only group was paired (or "yoked") with a matched subject in the exposure-plus-relaxation group. Just which item they were asked to imagine and for how long was determined not by *their* experience of the image but by the experience of their counterpart in the standard desensitization group. Unlike the latter subjects, those in the exposure-only group could not terminate an image when it became distressing, nor did their moving on to the next item depend on their having mastered the previous one.

This difference in control over what they were exposed to has several important implications. For one thing, control per se seems to be anxiety-reducing and lack of it aversive. (See Mowrer and Viek, 1948; Goldfried,

---

[*] It may also be noted that, as discussed below, Davison has subsequently presented some of the most cogent arguments for an *alternative* to the counter-conditioning model represented in his early study. The issue of effective exposure to the anxiety cues, emphasized in the present discussion of Davison's study, is consistent with his current emphasis on the role of exposure to the feared cues in reducing anxiety (Wilson and Davison, 1971).

1971; Goldfried and Merbaum, 1973.) Additionally, the lack of control of the exposure-only subjects over their exposure to an aversive situation may have defeated the very purpose of the "yoking" design: to assure equal exposure on the part of subjects in the two groups. This is likely for the following reasons.

The standard desensitization subjects accumulated all of their exposure time to the images in a state of relative comfort, since they terminated the image if it became aversive. The exposure-only subjects, on the other hand, although ostensibly exposed to the same images for the same time, in many instances were imagining while feeling quite uncomfortable with the image. This was so because (a) their yoked partner's pattern of tolerance was not likely to be highly correlated with their own, and (b) subjects in this group were experiencing considerably more anxiety throughout the imaging procedures (a difference that *could* be due to the efficacy of relaxation but that could also be due to the control factor noted above). Thus, while spending the same amount of *time* imagining each image as their standard desensitization counterparts, a good portion of that time was spent imagining something distressing to them. Davison notes that "[c]ooperation in this obviously unpleasant task was obtained through friendly but cogent reminders that such visualization was important for the experimental design." One must wonder, however, how vividly they imagined the distressing scenes, especially since the experimenter had no way of directly determining the degree of their compliance with this essentially subjective task, and since they would be highly motivated *not* to picture something that they were experiencing as distressing.

Furthermore, even apart from their motivation for avoiding (or at least attenuating) the images, the exposure-only subjects might have shown impaired attention to the details of the image as a result of being exposed to an aversive event that they could not control. In a study conducted by the present author (Wachtel, 1968), a threat with which subjects could not cope had restricting effects on their attention that were not evident when they were able to exert some control over the aversive possibility. The situations in the Wachtel and the Davison studies differed quite considerably, making a clear application of the findings to this situation impossible. But the substantial literature on the effects of anxiety upon attention (e.g., Easterbrook, 1959; Korchin, 1964; Wachtel, 1967) suggests that one must be cautious in assuming that subjects imagining something while anxious were as fully attentive to all its stimulus elements as subjects who logged their time with the image only when it was not disturbing.

The issue of just what constitutes effective exposure to sources of anxiety will concern us considerably as we proceed. For now, though, let us continue our examination of the role of relaxation by turning to a study that did *not* use a yoking design. Schubot (1966) examined issues very similar to those in Davison's study, but allowed subjects in both the exposure-plus-relaxation and the exposure-only groups to control their own exposure and progress up the hierarchy. For subjects with only moderate anxiety, relaxation was found to be irrelevant to anxiety reduction. Exposure to the distressing images without harmful consequences was sufficient. For *highly* anxious subjects, however, relaxation did seem to be a critical factor in fear reduction. Others (e.g., Vodde and Gilner, 1971) have also suggested that it is only with severe anxiety that relaxation is particularly valuable. Some of the theorizing about the role of arousal in anxiety reduction (e.g., Crowder and Thornton, 1970; Lader and Mathews, 1968) seems to have similar implications. This seems an important issue for further study, especially with genuine clinical populations. Most of the studies bearing on the role of relaxation have been analogue studies, with the same problems of generalizability noted earlier in discussing outcome studies.°

Looking at the overall body of research done on the role of relaxation up to the time of his book, Bandura (1969) concluded that relaxation was often a valuable *facilitative* factor in anxiety reduction through systematic desensitization, but that it did not appear to be a *necessary* one. Rachman (1968), too, concluded that muscle relaxation per se was not a necessary component of systematic desensitization. Rachman does stress, however, *mental* calm or relaxation as a necessary feature, and argues that the utility of relaxation of the musculature is that it is often an effective way of bringing about the necessary mental state. Rachman, who earlier had been a proponent of the need for muscle relaxation (Rachman, 1965), based his revised view on such evidence as reports of considerable therapeutic progress with minimal relaxation training, therapeutic results with *in vivo* desensitization without relaxation training at all, poor correspondence between patients' reports of calmness and physiological measures of muscle tension, and studies using curare that showed flaccid musculature and anxiety as not necessarily incompatible.

As Rachman notes, his view is consistent with the theoretical position put forth by Lader and his colleagues in England (Lader, 1967; Lader and Mathews, 1968; Lader and Wing, 1966). These authors view de-

---

° Different populations or different kinds of problems may not only make change more or less likely, the *process* of change may be different as well.

sensitization as a means of creating optimal conditions for habituation, by allowing the individual to be exposed to the upsetting stimulation in a state of low central nervous system arousal. According to their theory, reactivity to stimuli habituates relatively rapidly under low arousal, whereas in states of high arousal, habituation is slow or nonexistent, and reactivity may even be increased. This conception accounts well for much of the findings on desensitization and has had considerable heuristic value as well. (See, for example, Watts's [1971] interesting study, which is derived from the habituation view.) Eysenck and Beech (1971) suggest that the habituation view may have difficulty handling reports of effective fear reduction with *in vivo* desensitization, but Watts's work suggests a possible reconciliation. The issue of arousal level during exposure seems an important one for clinical purposes, but one whose implications for how to work with particular patients or on particular problems are not yet clear. (Cf. Crowder and Thornton, 1970; Lader and Mathews, 1968; Marks, 1972, 1975; Van Egeren, 1971; Watts, 1971.)

Rachman suggests that his reconceptualization in terms of mental calm is consistent not only with a habituation theory, but with Wolpe's theory of reciprocal inhibition as well. To some extent this does seem to be the case. Though Wolpe pioneered the use of a modified form of Jacobson's (1938) relaxation training in desensitization, and though he has continued to be a strong proponent of the use of muscle relaxation, he has never suggested that muscle relaxation per se is essential. Muscle relaxation is but one of several ways Wolpe has recommended to bring about a state antagonistic to anxiety. Assertive responses, sexual responses, positive imagery, and so on have been treated by Wolpe as having effects quite equivalent to relaxation and as being even more appropriate and useful in particular clinical situations. Wolpe's theoretical writings, however, have stressed events occurring at the level of the autonomic nervous system, whereas both Rachman's (1968) interpretation of the available data and the findings deriving from habituation theory tend to implicate the reticular arousal system as a more important locus of anxiety-reducing processes.

RELAXATION AND RECIPROCAL INHIBITION THEORY

Close examination of Wolpe's theoretical position, and of alternative conceptualizations of the role of relaxation, is important for our purposes, because several features of Wolpe's explanation of desensitization effects would seem to severely limit the compatibility of his approach with that of dynamic therapists. In Wolpe's accounts of systematic desensitization, the principle presumed to underlie the effectiveness of the procedure is that of *reciprocal inhibition*. In the early discussions of systematic desensitization, reciprocal inhibition was advanced as a neurological mechanism explaining why, for example, feeding a frightened animal in a situation eliciting only moderate anxiety could facilitate the elimination of the anxiety. The explanation, based on Sherrington's (1906) neurology and Hull's (1943) learning theory, goes as follows.

Following Hull, Wolpe assumed that extinction of any response was due to the generation of an inhibitory state (reactive inhibition) analogous to fatigue. This reactive inhibition builds up with each unreinforced effort, leading to a temporary suppression of the response. This can become permanent by a process of conditioned inhibition, in which cessation of responding is reinforced by reduction of this aversive fatigue state. According to Wolpe, anxiety responses are also extinguished in this fashion. However, Wolpe views anxiety as essentially an autonomic response, and claims that autonomic responses generate only a very small amount of reactive inhibition. Thus, since extinction in this view depends upon the buildup of reactive inhibition, anxiety is extinguished exceedingly slowly.

From this fatigue theory of extinction, the efficient elimination of anxiety would seem to require some other form of inhibition functionally equivalent to reactive inhibition. Reciprocal inhibition was postulated as fitting the bill. Wolpe extrapolated from Sherrington's observation that the evocation of one reflex can reciprocally inhibit another (for example, contraction of the extensor muscles of the arm produces a reciprocal relaxation of the flexor muscles). He argued that sympathetic and parasympathetic responsiveness are reciprocally inhibitory, that anxiety was a sympathetic discharge, and that therefore evocation of parasympathetic reactions could reciprocally inhibit anxiety and hence hasten its elimination.

Wolpe's explanation in terms of inhibitory processes at the level of the autonomic nervous system has been challenged frequently in recent years by other writers in the behavior therapy literature (e.g., Bandura, 1969; Wilson and Davison, 1971; Delprato, 1973; Waters, McDonald, and Koresko, 1972). These challenges, and the alternative explanations offered, are of considerable importance for our purposes, because they provide a framework potentially far more useful to an effort to integrate dynamic and behavioral points of view.

Wolpe's explanation of systematic desensitization emphasizes a rather mechanical and automatic effect of pairing stimuli and responses under the right set of conditions. The role of relaxation in his theory is essen-

tially one of producing the appropriate physiological state to bring about
the reflexive inhibitory mechanism. In contrast, a number of other writers on the subject (e.g., Wilson and Davison, 1971; Vodde and Gilner,
1971; Delprato, 1973) have suggested that relaxation may facilitate the
reduction of anxiety not through any direct neurological mechanism but
by *enabling the person to expose himself to that which he is afraid of.*
Wilson and Davison note that

> phobics are, by definition, people who typically avoid their respective feared
> objects. In order to encourage them to expose themselves to what they fear,
> it may be necessary not only to create a situation that is graduated, beginning
> with relatively mild "doses" of the phobia, but also to reduce still further the
> distress to be elicited by stimuli far along the generalization gradient by pro-
> viding the person with a comforting anti-anxiety response, like relaxation.
> Since progress up the hierarchy is traditionally controlled by the client, he
> should be more likely to confront aspects of his fear if he is bolstered in some
> way, for example, by knowing how to relax. (p. 12)

In Wolpe's view, sheer exposure to threatening images is of relatively little value. In fact, Wolpe warns that such exposure can *increase*
anxiety; that if the patient's relaxation is not sufficiently deep and/or
he is exposed to images too far along the hierarchy, the anxiety will
reciprocally inhibit the relaxation rather than vice versa. In this view,
it is almost entirely a matter of which response will win out over the
other; and if conditions are not arranged so as to assure that it is the
anti-anxiety response that at that point is stronger, things will only be
made worse.*

According to Wilson and Davison (1971), however, "this integral part
of the clinical lore in behavior therapy is contradicted by the well-
established phenomenon of experimental extinction," and this in fact is
one basis for these authors' emphasis on exposure rather than reciprocal
inhibition. Such an emphasis, as we shall see shortly, provides an important wedge into the problem of how concepts and methods of behavior therapists and dynamic therapists can be brought to bear on
each other.

Wolpe says little about the conditions limiting or facilitating exposure
to what is feared, other than to emphasize that it is important that the

* Indeed, from this viewpoint, Wolpe's comment that traditional dynamic therapies
achieve success in about 50 percent of cases by inadvertently providing the conditions
for reciprocal inhibition (Wolpe, 1958, p. xi) seems rather surprising. If the danger
of premature exposure to high anxiety items and of insufficient production of an
anxiety-inhibitory state were so substantial, the deterioration effect that Bergin (1971)
reports occurring in a percentage of dynamic treatments should be the typical
outcome.

patient be capable of fairly vivid imagery. Discussions of this topic tend to treat vividness of imagery as a fairly global, traitlike (though somewhat trainable) attribute. One sees little discussion of the possibility that some images, particularly threatening ones, may be harder to imagine vividly than others, nor of the possibility that the primary value of relaxation may be in dealing with just that problem. In Wolpe's model, exposure to the threatening cues per se is treated as a relatively simple and uncomplicated matter, and the issue is largely reduced to whether such exposure occurs in the presence of a sufficiently anxiety-inhibiting state for it to be therapeutic. As I shall discuss further shortly, for psychodynamic therapists the question of how to arrange full and adequate exposure to the most important anxiety-arousing cues is a very crucial one and one whose answer is far from simple. Wilson and Davison's emphasis on exposure, and on relaxation as a means for assuring that adequate exposure occurs, suggests a framework that well incorporates the range of findings thus far accrued from studies of desensitization, and that further suggests intriguing possibilities for integrating these findings and methods with those deriving from psychodynamic investigation.

HIERARCHIES AND GRADUAL APPROACH

Most of what has been said thus far about the role of relaxation can be seen to hold as well for gradual progression up the hierarchy. Originally, Wolpe developed the method of hierarchy construction in order to ensure that the patient is always exposed to a situation only slightly anxiety-provoking, so that the anxiety could be inhibited by the relaxation response. Intense anxiety could not be readily inhibited, and it was therefore viewed as necessary to start with mildly disturbing items and to neutralize their impact first. It was assumed that the reduction in anxiety would then generalize up the hierarchy so that the (now somewhat diminished) anxiety evoked by the next most distressing item would now become capable of being inhibited by relaxation. In such fashion, items high on the hierarchy, reactions to which were originally incapable of being inhibited by relaxation, could gradually be approached and neutralized by the successive neutralization of portions of the original anxiety reaction. (Some experimental evidence of the generalization of anxiety reduction up the hierarchy has recently been obtained [Lomont and Brock, 1971; but cf. Grossberg, 1973; Van Egeren, Feather, and Hein, 1971].)

Hierarchy construction was thus originally conceived within the framework of Wolpe's reciprocal inhibition theory of systematic desensitization. Wilson and Davison's (1971) alternative interpretation in terms of exposure, however, is relevant to hierarchy construction in much the same way as it is to relaxation. These authors treat both aspects of systematic desensitization as "tactical maneuvers . . . rather than as indispensable theoretical ingredients" (Davison and Wilson, 1972, p. 28). Starting with minimally threatening images facilitates the patient's exposing himself to an aspect of his experience that he might run from if confronted initially in its full intensity. Only if some exposure to the dimension of threat in his life is achieved can extinction of the anxiety occur. If the patient is very anxious about some aspect of his experience, tolerance for exposing himself to progressively more salient and disturbing features of this class of experiences may well be dependent upon the extinction of anxiety achieved with the easy items generalizing to more difficult related items. But Davison and Wilson's explanation of why such a way of proceeding can be tactically efficient is rather different from Wolpe's account of the role of hierarchies.

The most important implication of the Wilson and Davison version is that *other* ways of assuring exposure to the area of threat should be equally useful. Wilson and Davison's conceptualization seems readily able to encompass, for example, reports of effective anxiety reduction via *flooding*, whereby subjects are exposed to the most anxiety-provoking images right away, rather than being gradually led along a hierarchy. So long as the individual is really exposed to the threatening cues or images, extinction should be expected to occur.° With flooding, however, the therapist must be much more active in assuring that the patient is in fact vividly experiencing the threatening material, since the patient's motivation to avoid or attenuate exposure is much higher than when he is encountering items of only mild threat.

At the present time, it is not possible to specify very precisely when gradual approach up the hierarchy is important and when it is unnecessary or even an impediment to the therapeutic process. The increasing number of positive reports regarding flooding strongly suggest that gradual approach is not always essential or the method of choice, and it is important that flooding can eliminate anxiety as well as avoidance behavior. (See Marks, 1972, 1975; Rachman and Hodgson, 1974; Riccio and Silvestri, 1973.) But for many patients, gradual approach may well serve

---

° Aspects of habituation theory, noted earlier in the chapter as a potentially important complement to the exposure view, suggest that additional parameters are also relevant in determining whether flooding will be helpful. Duration of exposure also seems a potentially critical parameter. (See Baum, 1970; D'Zurilla, Wilson, and Nelson, 1973; Staub, 1968; Sue, 1975.)

as a useful tactical maneuver along the lines suggested by Wilson and Davison for facilitating patient exposure to areas of threat. Further, it is far from irrelevant that such an approach tends to be considerably less distressing for the patient who is participating in the treatment. This is important not only in terms of its immediate humane effects but also in assuring that the patient is not stressed into premature termination of treatment.

OTHER PROCESSES IN SYSTEMATIC DESENSITIZATION

Gradual approach up the hierarchy and pairing of anxiety cues with relaxation are not the only features typically occurring in systematic desensitization, though they tended to be stressed in the early literature for reasons of theoretical predilection. A number of other possible sources of therapeutic gain from the procedure have been considered in recent years. Several authors, for example (e.g., Leitenberg et al., 1969, 1971; Barlow et al., 1970; Wagner and Cauthen, 1968), have pointed out that the typical desensitization procedure involves the therapist's reinforcing the patient for approaching what is feared, either in imagery or in real life. It has been suggested that the therapist's approving reaction to the patient's progress up the hierarchy, rather than or in addition to the anxiety-reducing factors discussed above, is responsible for the change that occurs.

Davison and Wilson (1973) have more recently reviewed the research on this operant conditioning view of systematic desensitization and have found it far from convincing. They similarly find lacking in solid evidence the view that the effects of systematic desensitization are primarily due to the subject's expectancy of therapeutic progress (e.g., Marcia, Rubin, and Efran, 1969; Wilkins, 1971) or to the subject's cognitive reinterpretation of his fearfulness upon observing himself behaving nonfearfully (Valins and Ray, 1967). As they note, it is one thing to show that a subject's mild aversion to snakes can be mitigated by making him think his heart rate is no longer responsive to snake pictures, and quite another to fool a terrified individual into thinking he has been mistaken in believing he is afraid. Not surprisingly, there is little evidence for the latter.

Davison and Wilson do not dismiss these social-cognitive factors in systematic desensitization, nor do they dismiss the variety of other "relationship" considerations that have been put forth as relevant. Rather, they argue that these cannot be reasonably understood as factors that exclude the role of the kinds of processes discussed earlier in this chapter. Davison and Wilson, like Bandura (1969), argue for a multiple approach to fear reduction and elimination of avoidances that includes both the use of specific technical procedures that have proved useful, and the development of a clinically sound relationship with the patient. (See also Goldfried and Davison, 1976; Lazarus, 1971.)

## SYSTEMATIC DESENSITIZATION AND MERGING
## FANTASIES

One final explanation of the effect of systematic desensitization will concern us in this chapter. It is a particularly novel view, one hard to reconcile with the point of view of most of the work that has been done. Nonetheless, the study upon which it is based, though preliminary, is impressive, and it follows from a large body of other empirical work that has received far too little attention, considering its rather startling implications.

Silverman, Frank, and Dachinger (1974) treated insect-phobic individuals with a procedure inspired in some ways by systematic desensitization but differing in important respects. Based on considerations deriving from psychoanalytic theory and from earlier findings in Silverman's programmatic research, for relaxation training they substituted exposure to a tachistoscopically flashed stimulus—the verbal message "Mommy and I are one" for the experimental subjects and the message "People walking" for the controls. On measures of both subjective discomfort and behavioral approach, subjects in the experimental group improved significantly more than control subjects. Though no comparison with traditional desensitization procedures was done in this initial study, the findings seem to have important implications. Since the only thing that differentiated the experimental and control groups was the content of the subliminal stimulus—experimenter bias or demand-characteristic differences do not seem likely, since the experimenter was blind as to what stimulus had been placed in the tachistoscope and (at least consciously) so was the subject, by virtue of the brevity of exposure (.004 seconds)—the differences in improvement would seem to be due to the effect of the stimulus and/or the fantasies, affects, and so on that it stimulated. Silverman's hypothesis that fantasies of merger with the therapist as mother substitute underlie the effectiveness of systematic desensitization is consistent with, but certainly not required by, the data of this initial study, as he clearly recognizes. But even the finding that such a message, without being consciously perceived, could play a role in fear reduction is an extremely provocative one, and one that suggests that our understanding of how fears are reduced is far from complete.*

---

* Silverman has reported a substantial series of studies using tachistoscopic stimulation that is free of many of the problems found with such research in the early 1960s and that provides rather startling support for a variety of psychoanalytic formulations. These studies must be addressed by behavioral critics who claim there is no experimental evidence for unconscious processes (and they indeed present—I think not insurmountable—challenges even to the present version of psychodynamic theorizing [see Silverman, 1971, 1972, 1976; Wolitzky and Wachtel, 1973]).

# 9

# *Anxiety Reduction Through Exposure: Clinical Issues*

$\mathbb{T}$HE findings and arguments considered in Chapters 6 and 8 together lend themselves to the view that analysts and behavior therapists have each, in different ways, found means to help patients overcome anxiety by exposing themselves to disturbing thoughts, situations, and images. Behavior therapists practicing systematic desensitization have emphasized gradual exposure and relaxation training, procedural features that enable the patient to gradually accumulate exposure to what he would otherwise avoid. As we've seen, analysts in some respects use similar methods. They use these methods, however, much less systematically or completely than do behavior therapists. Instead, relaxation and gradual exposure are essentially adjunctive features for analytic therapists, whose main method of facilitating exposure to sources of threat is to interrupt the patient's typical ways of avoiding exposure by "interpreting" the patient's defenses.

As we have seen in the past few chapters, neither behavior therapists nor analysts—with important exceptions—have tended to conceptualize what they do primarily in terms of facilitating exposure to usually-avoided sources of anxiety. The emphasis on reciprocal inhibition or counterconditioning, on the one hand, and insight or emotional understanding, on the other, has led to apparently disparate methodologies and conceptual strategies, which, in their own terms, seem alternative and irreconcilable. By instead emphasizing the central importance of creating conditions that foster exposure, we are enabled to see that systematic desensitization and much that is done by dynamic therapists are complementary ways of achieving the same therapeutic end, and to consider how the particular strengths of each approach can be combined in overcoming disturbing anxiety.*

## VALUE AND LIMITS OF SYSTEMATIC DESENSITIZATION

The research reviewed in the last chapter indicated that in certain kinds of clinical problems, systematic desensitization makes a decided contribution in alleviating neurotic distress, and that evidence for symptom substitution or other signs of adverse consequences is not often obtained. The applicability of systematic desensitization, however, was seen to be considerably more limited than had first been thought. Thus despite the very definite advance in treating anxiety provided by the development of systematic desensitization, alternative methods are still frequently needed. Deciding precisely what other means to use (and particularly in what ways these other means will draw on traditional psychodynamic methods and in what ways they may be fruitfully viewed as variants of systematic desensitization) requires us to consider in more detail why systematic desensitization has turned out to have lesser applicability than was originally anticipated.

The answer is not immediately obvious. In many respects, systematic desensitization seems an eminently sensible and rational way of proceeding with the therapeutic task of exposing the patient to what he is afraid of. Training in relaxation and the gradual approach up a hierarchy of exposures both seem very useful technical devices for enabling the patient to expose himself to what he fears instead of avoiding it as he has done in the past. The minimization of distress brought about by these technical aids would seem to have value both procedurally and

* My argument here should not be taken as a blanket refutation of the role of either counterconditioning or understanding. The degree to which these are useful concepts for understanding how people overcome irrational anxiety still remains a fruitful area for further research. What I am emphasizing here is that effective exposure is one very crucial consideration that theorists of both persuasions have not fully exploited. It enables us to see a broad area of convergence, however the other specific therapeutic processes may differentiate methods.

ethically. On the one hand, this relatively comfortable approach to exposing the patient to what he fears makes it less likely that he will terminate therapy prematurely in order to avoid its travails. On the other, it is important in its own right that the procedure is a humane one; one is not doing something painful to the patient "for his own good." Many psychotherapeutic procedures are frustrating and painful, and it is certainly preferable if comparable results can be obtained without such a price.

Another advantage of the desensitization procedure is that by the nature of its clearly defined focus, it is easy to assess whether one's efforts are working. Instead of having to wait several years to see if there has been a sweeping characterological change, one can know if one's therapeutic intervention is being effective by monitoring the patient's anxiety reactions to a clearly defined class of events. Although cases have been reported in which hierarchies with hundreds of items have been presented over a great length of time, Lazarus and Serber (1968) recommend that the therapist "re-examine the appropriateness of desensitization whenever appreciable results are not forthcoming after five or six sessions." Such a view (if practicable) lends itself to far greater therapist accountability than is traditional in psychotherapy, and to a greater possibility of the therapist learning from his experience and not committing himself irrevocably to an inappropriate strategy with his patient.

The clearly defined focus characteristic of systematic desensitization is perhaps its most reliable defining feature * and probably the most important source of its superiority to traditional methods, when such superiority is found. Paul (1966) has suggested that the principles that account for anxiety reduction with systematic desensitization are the same as those operating in more traditional interview or relationship therapies,† but that desensitization is a more efficient application of those principles because of its more focused nature:

> Instead of allowing the client to introduce haphazardly, with varying degrees of attention, symbolic anxiety-generating cues, the desensitization procedure attempts to systematically arrange the learning contingencies. Competing stimuli and responses are reduced to a minimum. The situation is constructed to limit external stimuli; and through the relaxation procedure, internal and

---

* Recall that therapeutic efforts have been reported, and described as variants of systematic desensitization, in which neither relaxation nor gradual approach up a hierarchy have been employed.

† In this respect, Paul's view is surprisingly similar to the one presented in this book.

proprioceptive stimuli are brought to a minimum. With the decrease in competing events, the therapist can direct the client's attention specifically to the cues of prime importance. (p. 89)

But despite this appealing rationale, systematic desensitization is *not* always so efficient. In part this is because many anxiety reactions are intimately related to deficiencies in social skills and other problems of maladaptive overt behavior. This issue will be examined in Chapters 10 and 11, where we will consider various ways of facilitating the patient's learning more satisfying and effective interpersonal behavior, as well as how failure to sufficiently ensure such learning can frequently undermine therapeutic efforts. Paul, too, acknowledges the importance of the patient's learning more effective ways of dealing with life situations, and that such learning does not automatically follow from the desensitization of anxiety. He contends, however, that although "additional work" may be required to prevent the anxiety from being reestablished as a result of maladaptive patterns of interaction, "in practice, the systematic desensitization procedure should provide an efficient and useful treatment technique *in almost any case in which anxiety is prominent.*" (p. 9; italics added)

In my view, Paul's prescription extends the applicability of desensitization well beyond the arena in which it has proven effective and, I would venture, beyond where it is likely to. For, in addition to the limits placed upon the utility of desensitization by the need to consider maladaptive overt patterns of interaction, there are also limits placed by the therapist's limited control over what cues the patient is really exposed to. The notion that "the therapist can direct the client's attention specifically to the cues of prime importance" is a highly idealized one. For certain patients and certain kinds of anxieties (particularly those in which the anxiety cues are largely situational and external), the systematic desensitization procedure does seem to facilitate exposure. But in many cases, the therapist's limited control over what a patient imagines, and how vividly he does so, requires that methods other than those typical of desensitization be employed to ensure sufficient exposure.

The weakness of the analogy between exposing an organism to a stimulus and requesting a person to imagine something has been stressed by a number of writers on the subject (e.g., Breger and McGaugh, 1965; Weitzman, 1967). Weitzman's observations are particularly interesting. He interviewed six patients after each of a cumulative total of about 200 desensitization sessions to inquire into precisely what they did imagine. He reports,

Without exception, when closely questioned, patients reported a flow of visual imagery. The initiating scene, once visualized, shifted and changed its form. Moreover, these transformations took place continuously and, when the imagining was terminated by the therapist, had produced images which were quite removed in their content from the intended stimulus. These contents, and the transformations they exhibit, compel a characterization as a form of spontaneous and apparently autonomous fantasy familiar to many dynamically oriented therapists . . . [p. 305]

Weitzman thus contends that the therapist does not control the content of the patient's imagery very closely when he asks the patient to picture an item on the hierarchy. The patient may use the therapist's words as a starting point, but his experience during the silent period of imagining ranges far from what the therapist expects, and in directions that are largely determined by the patient's unique configuration of motives, conflicts, memories, and associations.

Weitzman's contentions have not gone unchallenged. Davison and Wilson (1973), for example, report that in their extensive clinical experience with systematic desensitization, they have "seldom if ever found evidence for Weitzman's observations." Possibly the differences are at least in part due to different implicit communications given by different therapists. Lazarus's (1968) suggestion, however, that the patient be asked to describe precisely what he experiences with each instruction to imagine (instead of the older instruction merely to signal by raising a finger if he feels anxious) seems predicated on the view that one cannot assume that the scene imagined is necessarily the scene the therapist intended.

Not only may the patient's images wander, or the contents vary from what is intended, they may also vary considerably in vividness. This is an extremely important matter and one very difficult to assess. Even apart from overall individual differences, each of us can probably recall subjective experiences of imagining that vary in vividness and intensity across a wide range. Some images or recollections are hardly more than saying words to oneself, while others are almost dreamlike in their reality and intensity. Clearly, the degree to which the patient is exposed to a substantial portion of the stimulus elements involved in his fear will likewise vary. Even in the simplest of cases, one would certainly expect a greater reduction in, say, fear of snakes if the patient, especially with a high hierarchy item, were vividly experiencing the shape, the movement, the scaliness, the color, and so on of a snake than if he were merely, in effect, saying to himself the words "a snake is very close to me." This problem is routinely acknowledged in writings about systematic desensitization, but little has been written directly about it.

To some extent, where practical, the problem of the quality of the patient's exposure to the target cues can be dealt with by real-life (*in vivo*) exposure. In recent years there have in fact been a number of reports that suggest greater efficacy with real-life exposure than with imaginal desensitization, or that question the early assumption that the effects of imaginal desensitization will fully generalize to the real-life situation (e.g., Agras, 1967; Barlow, Leitenberg, Agras, and Wincze, 1969; Davison, 1968; LoPiccolo, 1969; Marks, 1969; Sherman, 1972).

Even where real-life exposure is used, however, it is necessary to recognize that what cues the individual is effectively exposed to depends strictly not on what is *presented* but on what is *perceived*. The two may not always be that closely related. The problem is less acute when real-life rather than imaginary cues are utilized, but it is still a very real one. People vary greatly in what they "notice," and when the cues are anxiety-provoking, then idiosyncratic "defensive" ways of perceiving are of particular importance. (See Erdelyi, 1974; Wolitzky and Wachtel, 1973.) This latter consideration could be seen as a factor in favor of the desensitization method, which tries to ensure exposure at low levels of anxiety. But the entire issue of the quality of the patient's exposure to what is "presented" requires a recognition of the limits of the glib S-R terms in which desensitization is frequently discussed, and the introduction of more complex epistemological and clinical conceptualizations.

Perhaps even more importantly, the *in vivo* solution is much less practical when the most important cues evoking anxiety are not external ones but rather cues associated with the person's own thoughts and affective reactions. As we saw in Chapter 6, there is good reason to believe that it is anxiety in response to just such events that is centrally involved in most neuroses requiring psychotherapy. In such cases, the distinction between imaginal desensitization and *in vivo* desensitization becomes rather ambiguous. The therapist cannot "present" the stimulus to the patient in the way he can bring a dog into the room with a dog phobic or bring a claustrophobic patient into a tiny windowless room. The stimuli must be produced by the *patient,* just as they are with imaginal desensitization. They are thus not directly observable by the therapist. Furthermore, they are difficult cues to produce intentionally.

Giving instructions to someone to intentionally produce an affective state often creates confusion and the experience of paradox. In fact, some behavior therapists attempt to deal with anxiety that is unyielding to traditional behavioral methods by utilizing precisely this paradoxical property of efforts to intentionally produce affective states. The patient is requested, instead of trying to quell his anxiety, to try to make himself as anxious as he can. At times he finds that in response to such a request, he is unable to become very anxious, and by this effort to become more anxious his anxiety is reduced. At the Summer Institute in Behavior Therapy conducted by Joseph Wolpe and his staff, I saw this method of "paradoxical intention" (Frankl, 1960) used with impressive effects with several agoraphobic patients.

When the patient's anxieties are evoked largely by his own thoughts and feelings, then ensuring therapeutically adequate exposure to the source of threat presents a considerable dilemma. The cues to which the patient must be exposed are cues that only he can produce, which are difficult to produce intentionally, and which furthermore, because of his anxiety, he is highly motivated *not* to produce. If the patient's problems are due to the anxiety evoked in him when he becomes sexually aroused, or angry, or inclined to rely on others, then in order for that anxiety to be extinguished he must be exposed to the cues associated with aroused sexuality, or anger, or dependency. If he habitually engages in maneuvers to prevent the arousal of such feelings (defense mechanisms or security operations), then he will not be able to get the exposure necessary for extinction of the anxiety.

One could, in principle, contend that even with such sources of anxiety, it is possible to distinguish between imaginal and *in vivo* desensitization—that while the therapist can't expect the patient to get angry or sexually excited on request, he can ask the patient to *imagine* such a state of affairs. Such a distinction, however, while perhaps logically correct, is likely to be of little value clinically, for the problem of the vividness or "realness" of what the patient imagines is an especially acute one in such circumstances.

Unless the experience in imagination is a good approximation to the actual feared experience, little benefit is to be expected from imaginal desensitization. Paul (1966), for example, in the study discussed earlier, made a point of instructing his therapists to be sure the patients imagined the situation as it would appear if they were in it. They were to see the things around them that they would see if they were there. They were not to see themselves in the picture, for then they would be viewing it from outside themselves rather than as a real experience of being there. Paul's good results with desensitization are substantially attributable to the care with which he assured that his subjects' exposure through imagery would be realistic. Requesting someone who is not feeling something to imagine that he is does not seem a very effective way of achieving comparable vividness and reality.

Such a solution is especially problematic when, as is so often the case, the patient does not acknowledge that he does or even could feel that way. If his fear of certain of his own thoughts or feelings leads not only to particular distressing symptoms or characterological difficulties, but also to a hesitance to recognize those very thoughts and feelings as part of his own behavior, it is difficult indeed for him to imagine them with any vividness or reality. The patient may try to be cooperative with the therapist—the hard-driving, ulcered executive can try to picture himself openly longing for succor, or the shy Salvation Army worker with frequent panic attacks can try to picture herself lusting after truck drivers—but the success of such an effort is not likely to be impressive.

In the above discussion I am of course depicting what is traditionally referred to as defenses, which render important thoughts, motives, and affective reactions unconscious, and the patient's resistance to recognizing these things about himself. Behavior therapists frequently reject such concepts as unfounded and unnecessary. Upon close discussion of actual clinical observations, however, the objection is usually seen to be not about whether anxiety can lead people not to notice how they are reacting, or not to notice the basis for their actions, but rather about precisely what *kinds* of things are going on unnoticed and/or what kinds of inferences to make. (For example, the same woman may be seen by one clinician, with one set of assumptions, as not noticing that her behavior is motivated by a wish for a penis, and by another clinician as not noticing that she gets upset when men exhibit their freedom and power, or that, despite her claim that this is not an issue for her, it is at such times that she gets depressed, gets a headache, or—again without noticing—acts in a sabotaging way toward their efforts.)

The objection by behavior therapists to concepts like defense tends also to be about the theoretical language used to describe these observations. Behavior therapists object particularly strongly, for example, to terms like "the unconscious," with its seeming implication of an autonomous homunculus whose actions in turn require explanation. Here again, as in so many respects, the differences between dynamic and behavioral views are not nearly as great as seems at first, especially when it is recognized that, regarding the first objection (level of inference), many non-Freudian dynamic thinkers would also be skeptical about literal penis envy. And regarding the second objection (the theoretical language of psychoanalysis), many modern psychoanalytic writers have as little use for reified concepts like "the unconscious" as any behavior therapist.* (See particularly Schafer, 1972, 1973a, 1973b.)

## DEALING WITH INTERNALLY GENERATED FEARS

The difficulties in using the standard systematic desensitization procedure when the patient fears his own thoughts or inclinations do not leave the clinician helpless in such cases. There are a number of ways, other than standard desensitization, by which behavior therapists have dealt with such cases, and of course the methods of dynamic therapists are particularly designed to deal with just such problems. I will discuss in later chapters how such methods as modeling, behavior rehearsal, shaping, and others can contribute to helping patients overcome fear of their own reactions and inclinations. At this point, we will look at methods that emphasize facilitating exposure to the cues that unrealistically signal danger. Specifically, we will look at variations of the desensitization and flooding models and how they can be combined with the way of proceeding that derives from psychoanalytic inquiry.

Weitzman (1967) has suggested that at times the standard desensitization procedure itself can accomplish the task of overcoming anxiety aroused by the patient's own thoughts and impulses. He argues that, from a psychoanalytic perspective, the particular stimuli or situations that are feared may be viewed as symbolic "carriers" of the impulse. Whether the patient acknowledges the impulse or not, by exposing himself to the feared phobic object or by doing so in imagination, he is of necessity exposing himself to the arousal, at least indirectly, of the feared impulse. Thus, when his anxiety is reduced, it is not just accidentally conditioned anxiety that has been extinguished but the signal anxiety that had led the patient to view his impulses as dangerous.

Weitzman's speculations about why systematic desensitization works are interesting. They suggest that where anxiety generated primarily by the arousal of particular thoughts or impulses leads also to fear of some clearly definable external event or object, the former may be treatable through a focus on the latter. Such a use of the traditional systematic

---

* Again, it should be clear that I am not suggesting that there are *no* substantive differences between dynamic and behavioral views. In actual practice, the differences between what inferences are made can be quite substantial. It is the combination of compatibility and difference which motivated this book.

desensitization procedure has its limits, however. Firstly, as even more strictly behavioral writers have pointed out (e.g., Wolpe, Brady, Serber, Agras, and Liberman, 1973):

> Systematic desensitization is a less fruitful approach to a person's fears if these fears, after a systematic behavioral analysis, are found to be ill-defined and not clearly connected with specific stimuli: 'I don't know what I'm afraid of. One day it's a bridge, the next day it's going to work.' Patients who are panphobic or whose fears change their configuration frequently and without apparent external stimuli are poor candidates for systematic desensitization. (p. 963)

Secondly, even where one or several clearly defined phobias are identifiable, desensitization to images of the external phobic objects is not always helpful. Chapter 7 noted the reports of Feather and Rhoads in which desensitization to external images had little efficacy, whereas a modified form of desensitization, using images of the acting out of forbidden fantasies, yielded good results.

It may be of value to consider Feather and Rhoads's approach somewhat further at this point. Feather and Rhoads's approach is based on the view that only a small percentage of cases can be understood in terms of accidental pairing of neutral external cues with cues that evoke anxiety. More often, they suggest, anxiety is most directly provoked by the arousal of a particular drive or impulse, and other symptoms are understandable in terms of the relation to the arousal of the drive.

> For example, in cases of multiple phobias in the same individual, the feared objects or situations often seem unrelated either by symbolism or physical similarities. If the seemingly different feared situations all represent occasions for a specific drive to be heightened, then a parsimonious explanation of multiple phobias is at hand. Otherwise, one would have to postulate multiple etiologies, such as a series of unrelated, accidentally conditioning events.
>
> An important practical implication of this view is that successful intervention at the level of the drive should generalize to all of the phobias that are maintained by that drive. In operational terms, one might apply the behavior therapist's technique of systematic desensitization to the drive-related imagery underlying the avoidance behavior rather than to images of the environmental stimuli being avoided. One would then expect modification of all the drive-related phobias. (p. 501)

Their clinical procedure begins with two to five diagnostic interviews. These interviews focus especially on the history of the symptom, but make use of all the kinds of material that psychodynamic therapists have typically utilized (e.g., dreams, fantasies, slips) and aim at achieving a psychodynamic formulation. They particularly rely on asking the patient what the worst thing is that he can imagine happening in the situation he fears, and pursue this until the patient gives a vivid, concrete description. Usually the patient describes a fantasied antisocial act. The patient is then trained in relaxation, and a hierarchy of "graded fantasies of enacting the relevant impulses" is constructed. Along with the imaginal desensitization, the patient is required to begin gradually to confront the real situations that he fears.

As their procedure developed, Feather and Rhoads altered some features of this approach. For one thing, they began to use hierarchies less and less, instead encouraging the patient, while relaxed, to imagine the worst thing he could. Thus in this respect, their approach began to shift from a desensitization model to one that resembled flooding or implosive therapy in many ways. The patients did not simply experience anxiety, however. They were also encouraged to *enjoy* imagining acting in an extreme antisocial way—that is, to *gratify* the impulse in fantasy. Feather and Rhoads report smiling and loud laughter accompanying some of this imagining. Often, however, the patients also reported guilt at such expression, even in fantasy, of violent or antisocial inclinations. The therapist's emphasis then was on aiding the patient in discriminating between fantasy and consequential action. In fact, the central explanatory notion in Feather and Rhoads's account of their work is that of fostering the discrimination between fantasy and reality. The patients are seen as having trouble distinguishing between the consequences of wishes and of overt acts.

Feather and Rhoads's explanation thus stresses a process more akin to insight than to extinction through accumulated non-reinforced exposure. The insight stressed, however, is not insight into the childhood origins of the problem but, rather, insight about the differential consequences of fantasied actions versus real ones. Insight of this latter kind is not that readily distinguished from extinction, which has also been interpreted at times in terms of discriminating a change in contingencies. It does seem, however, that at least in some of the cases reported by Feather and Rhoads, the change may have been mediated by a fairly rapid cognitive restructuring. Some of the patients changed considerably, despite resistances that led to rapid termination of the treatment.

Resistances were, in fact, found frequently by Feather and Rhoads (see Rhoads and Feather, 1972). Patients came late, missed sessions, failed to carry out therapeutic assignments, and so on. The technique was altered in some cases to deal with these behaviors, which were also viewed as deriving from transferential reactions to the therapist. The issue of resistance will be apparent as an implicit theme in much of this book. It is an important topic and one that has been insufficiently addressed in the behavior therapy literature. Whether the term "resistance" is accepted or not, most practicing behavior therapists will acknowledge the not infrequent occurrence of behaviors that run counter to the desirable course of therapy. Much of the clinical skill of the behavior therapist involves figuring out how to enlist the patient's cooperation in carrying out the therapeutic assignments they have agreed upon.


## INTERPRETIVE METHODS AND EXPOSURE TO ANXIETY CUES


The difficulties that may arise in enlisting patient cooperation for any particular technique, as well as the problems noted earlier in creating conditions in which the patient will actually be exposed to the most crucial anxiety cues, make it desirable for the therapist to have available a variety of interventions for this purpose. In that way he can suit his approach to the current needs and inclinations of his patient. The anxiety-reducing techniques we have considered thus far in the last chapter and in the present one have shown considerable promise and, in my view, should be included in the therapeutic armamentarium of almost all therapists. Where applicable, they appear to be capable of achieving more rapid change in specific aspects of patients' distress and maladaptive behavior resulting from anxiety than is generally achieved by traditional methods. In some cases, particularly where therapeutic goals center on changing one or several discrete and readily isolated features of the patient's behavior or emotional life, these techniques may, after appropriate assessment is undertaken, prove sufficient to bring about important and enduring changes. In many other cases, these techniques may prove of considerable value as one aspect of the therapeutic effort, introduced at a particular point in the context of a more prolonged and extensive therapeutic process. For a number of reasons, however, some of which should already be evident, I do not regard these newer procedures as a *replacement* for the more traditional interview- or relationship-focused therapies (though their availability and effectiveness should place our understanding of the more traditional methods in a new light, and should alter as well the way in which they are employed).

Most of the following discussion will be addressed to ways in which traditional therapeutic modes may also accomplish the task of exposing the patient to anxiety cues and extinguishing the maladaptive anxiety.

But the discussion should not be taken to imply that psychodynamic methods are nothing but an alternative form of desensitization. To avoid this implication, it seems useful first to emphasize something which, however obvious, can be readily overlooked in a discussion of psychodynamic interviewing that is couched largely in the language of extinction and desensitization—namely, that traditional psychodynamic methods have many more goals and effects than simply to extinguish anxiety through accumulated exposure to what has been frightening and avoided. The possibility of changing troubling problems is greatly enhanced, for example, when the troubled person is given the opportunity to participate in a relationship in which the other person (the therapist) is not simply reacting to him or pursuing his own interests and inclinations * but, rather, is attempting to reflect upon what is happening between them both and to encourage the patient to reflect as well. Patterns can thereby be detected that may be seen to be important in other current relationships in the person's life but that have not been discerned or understood, because both parties have been immersed in what has been happening in such a way that they react somewhat automatically and without identifying clearly just what is going on.

The detection of such interpersonal patterns is difficult, especially when they are subtle and/or where defensive mislabeling and misperceiving is prevalent. When the therapist is actively involved in implementing a technique, or convincing the patient to do something, it may be hard for him to also be able to notice the fine details of the emotional minuet in which they are engaged. Only by allowing a portion of his time to be spent largely in just listening to what the patient spontaneously brings up, or in attending to the vicissitudes of the relationship, is the therapist likely to be maximally perceptive. Especially in cases where the patient's complaint is not a clear-cut or delimited one but is rather on the order of "I don't seem to get involved with people" or "Men lose interest in me after a point" or "I don't feel real or genuine most of the time," such detection of relational subtleties is likely to be crucial. To be sure, as noted previously, it is important to discover more concrete referents for these rather vague complaints. But one of the best ways to do so is to notice what happens right there in the consultation room. Often the patient does not know what to look for in his day-to-day interactions until the therapist has helped by saying something like, "You know, when I

---

* To some extent, of course, both of these things do occur, but (it is hoped) considerably less than in other relationships—not because the therapist is a better or more selfless person than others, but because the therapeutic situation is structured to facilitate this happening.

smiled at you just now you turned away," or, "It seems to me that whenever I say something complimentary, you manage to find a note of criticism in it."

These and other therapeutic aspects of the traditional therapist's stance and attitude are discussed more fully elsewhere in this book. My current reliance on the traditional patient-therapist relationship as the basis, or context, in which my use of specific behavioral interventions is rooted, is based on my continuing respect for the variety of ways in which such a relationship can be helpful. (It is also based on my evaluation, discussed in Part One, that the really valuable features of such a relationship are not undermined by the use of more active and explicit intervention techniques.) Thus, I would see great value in retaining many of the features of traditional psychotherapeutic modalities even if they did not serve as another means of accomplishing desensitization. Part of the value of desensitizing or extinguishing in this way is, in my view, that these other therapeutic aspects are also brought into play. At this point, however, I wish to discuss how the traditional therapeutic interview may at times actually be a more appropriate vehicle even for the specific task of extinguishing anxiety than is desensitization, and to examine the technical details of how such a use of the interview is maximized.

The conditions under which desensitization is of limited effectiveness have already largely been considered. We have noted, with Wolpe et al. (1973), that systematic desensitization tends to be ineffective with multiple or shifting fears and with vague complaints that are not readily articulated in a few focused interviews. We have also considered the limits placed on systematic desensitization when the patient's fears center on his own thoughts and inclinations, and have seen that this is quite frequently the case. Sometimes either or both of these difficulties can be dealt with by the behavioral technique of flooding, as both Wolpe et al. (1973) and Marks (1972) suggest. Immersing the patient in a cacophony of distressing images can at times enable the multiple sources of his anxiety to be covered and can evoke a range of feelings that might be more readily warded off with the gentler and more gradual desensitization approach.

With some patients, however, and at certain stages of the therapy with many more, flooding, too, is ineffective or inappropriate. As with most of the methods discussed thus far in this chapter, flooding is likely to be perceived by both patient and therapist as a discrete, isolatable technique, something introduced in addition to or on top of whatever relationship exists between patient and therapist. In this respect, it is likely to be experienced in a rather different way from the activities of the therapist in more traditional, interpretive therapies, however much the latter may in fact also contain "techniques." Some individuals find such use of explicit techniques a jarring interruption of a relationship that is unique in their experience, and they object to it as artificial, dehumanizing, and so on. It is likely that therapists who practice from an exclusively behavioral framework underestimate the prevalence of this kind of difficulty, since such patients are least likely to seek out a behaviorally oriented therapist. Goldfried and Davison (1976), who discuss the vicissitudes of the patient-therapist relationship more extensively than most behavior therapists, note that patients who are rather dependent follow their directions far more readily than do more independent individuals.

In addition to patient objections to the use of explicit techniques (objections which may be based, in varying degree, either on sincere value commitments that have largely developed apart from the patient's anxieties and conflicts, or on motives and influences that justify viewing them as resistances of the patient), flooding as a formal behavior therapy technique may be difficult because the patient does not acknowledge the real sources of his anxiety—or even that anxiety is involved at all. Thus, a patient who shows abundant evidence of anxiety over sexual feelings, and many of whose problems can be understood as reflections of avoidance behaviors motivated by this anxiety, may attribute his loneliness to being "too choosy" in selecting women, to his dislike of parties, to his heavy work burden, and so on. He may continue to complain, while opposing as silly, or off the mark, any effort to deal therapeutically with his complaints. Or a patient with several sources of strong anxiety may continually shift his description of his behavior and his complaints from session to session: "No, that's not really it. I think I really am assertive enough after all. My problem is I can't sustain a work effort. . . . No, work isn't the problem. If only I could meet a girl. . . . You really have a stake in that girl business. It seems to me my trouble with my mother is much more important."

Similarly, the patient may complain that the therapist is pushing too hard, not listening to him, and so on. Or he may claim he can't imagine what he's being asked to imagine, because "I don't have a good imagination" or "I don't believe this is really what my problem is about" or "I feel silly pretending." Alternatively, he may bring in crisis after crisis to divert the therapist and keep things at the stage of "just talking." Or he may keep picturing the wrong thing, "misunderstand" the therapist's instructions, and so forth. In some instances, such difficulties can be overcome by firm insistence.* But it is particularly difficult to do this when the patient reports that he "can't" picture what is being requested no matter how hard he tries, or that he experiences the image coldly and without feeling.

When any or all of these difficulties arise, it can be useful to recognize that traditional psychotherapeutic modalities do also provide opportunities for exposure to the cues that evoke anxiety, and that, in fact, when the cues at issue are response-produced cues—concomitants of the patient's own thoughts, feelings, and inclinations—the traditional methods may be the most effective exposure technique of all. This is especially the case when this aspect of the procedures (that is, exposure to anxiety cues) is recognized and consciously and intentionally used by the therapist in order to maximize its effect.

Typically, the dynamic therapist listens for latent themes and coherences and for signs of resistance and avoidance, and comments to the patient about what he perceives. These comments are usually viewed as interpretations, which elucidate meaning and enable the patient better to understand the forces and events in his life. To be sure, this is one of the effects of these comments. But they also have the effect of bringing the patient face to face with what he has been afraid of; thus irrational fears can be reduced.

The therapist's comments act in several ways to facilitate exposure to the anxiety-arousing cues, and to increase the efficiency of the therapy in extinguishing anxiety and avoidances. The slow rate of extinction of fear-motivated behavior found in the experiments cited above (pp. 147–48) can be understood as a result of the establishment of a situation in which avoidance of the anxiety-provoking cues was freely permitted. In experiments where avoidance behavior was interfered with and contact with the fear-provoking cues thus increased, extinction proceeded much more rapidly (see Baum, 1970). Interpretation of resistances in traditional psychotherapy can be seen as a clinical analogue of this "response-prevention" procedure. The therapist's comments about the patient's avoidance of certain topics or about other actions that attenuate his exposure to the therapeutically relevant experiences serve to interrupt the patient's avoidance efforts.

Interruption of defenses or resistances by the therapist can have the dual effect of facilitating the patient's recognition of just what the real issues and real sources of anxiety are, and of bringing him into closer contact with what he fears. Facilitating insight and facilitating exposure can

---

* Some of the practical and ethical issues involved in the therapist's persuading or insisting will be discussed in Chapter 12.

go hand in hand, for it is by experiencing the frightening thoughts and tendencies first-hand, rather than by abstract reasoning, that therapeutically useful insights are achieved.

For example, one patient complained that he didn't feel close to anybody, had not fallen in love, felt lonely, and so on, yet he kept himself largely unaware of how he actually went about preventing himself from deepening his attachments to others, or even that he did so in an active way. He was a tall, blond, muscular young man who had been a popular member of the California surfer set before coming to New York and embarking on a successful career in public relations. He knew many women, but he felt restless and discontent and longed to care for someone in the way he saw others do with such apparent gratification. In the abstract he would acknowledge that it must be "his" problem, but he was reluctant to see what he did to maintain the problem. He preferred to focus instead on why any particular woman was not really the right one to get involved with. Such a focus was, in fact, not only a way in which he obscured the nature of the problem; it was also one of the ways in which the problem was maintained. One of the things he did to keep from getting close to a woman was to search out her shortcomings and selectively focus upon them, until his not getting involved with *this* woman seemed perfectly natural and due to his perceptiveness, not to his problem.

Thus, this man had little real understanding of how anxiety over closeness influenced the life pattern that distressed him and brought him to therapy, and this despite his willingness to avow on various occasions, "I guess I must be afraid to get close to anyone." As in most clinical cases outside of the movies, the insight that the patient needed to achieve was not a blinding flash of recognition regarding something he had been completely unaware of before, but rather a more consistent and more fully experienced sense of something grasped only in a fleeting or facile manner theretofore. His understanding of his fears over getting closely involved with another person was "intellectual" rather than "emotional" because, though in some sense he was aware that he was anxious about such matters, the awareness was a kind of inference or logical deduction from his observations of his own behavior and from his knowledge of the psychology that has permeated the popular culture. He had rarely actually *experienced* the anxiety, because his avoidances were so efficient. One is reminded of the analogue experiments with animals, where avoidance behaviors become so rapid and efficient that the animal seems never to show the various signs of anxiety that were evident in the early learning of the avoidance behavior. One could imagine, if the animal could talk, that it would say: "Me afraid of the black compartment? Don't be silly. I haven't felt afraid in months. I just like running into the white compartment."

The patient described above had a number of ways of avoiding the experience of close and increasing contact with another person, and hence of the anxiety such contact could arouse in him. As already noted, one way he did this was to focus his attention upon the shortcomings of whomever he began to involve himself with, and to attribute the dissolution of that *particular* relationship to the properties of the other, while avowing in the abstract that *in general* he did have a problem with closeness. By repeatedly pointing out this combination of actions on his part, I sought to disrupt the efficiency of this avoidance pattern. My aim was to call attention to the fact that *he* was *doing something*, thus directing his thoughts away from what was wrong with *her* and toward his own perception as an activity. As part of this strategy it was hoped that, in focusing his attention on his own actions, he might begin to notice the anxiety that motivated them and, gradually, the feelings and yearnings that set the anxiety off.° By thus altering the focus of his attention (hopefully *in vivo* as well as in the sessions) he could begin to be exposed more to the cues associated with the arousal of loving and dependent feelings, rather than restricting his gaze to the other person's warts. Thus, effective exposure to the anxiety cues for purposes of extinguishing the anxiety, and interpretation of feelings and defenses for purposes of experiential understanding, can be seen as two sides of the same coin.

Two other important, and related, avoidance maneuvers came to light in an early session in which the above patient was telling me of having had a rather profound experience, while smoking marijuana with a woman older than himself, of longing for mothering from her and feeling that she in fact could be a good mothering figure for him. As he began to describe what sounded like an important and meaningful experience with this woman, I recalled some of his opening words in telling me about her: "This is about the third time I've seen her. I probably won't see her again many times. . . ." These words, said in passing without emphasis, seemed in retrospect very important, suggesting a tendency to move on as soon as someone began to touch him. I commented that having just heard his description of what went on between them, I was now struck by his earlier statement that he thought he would not see her again very much. This theme was to become an important one in its own right

---

° More speculatively, the possibility might be considered that in redirecting his attention away from her and toward himself, his skill in quickly finding the rationalizable flaws in the other person might be diminished, as skill in finding a hidden figure would be disrupted when attention was frequently being directed elsewhere.

in the course of our work. But in the present session it was shunted aside by the introduction of a second avoidance maneuver right in the session, one which also became a crucial focus for subsequent work. In response to my comments he said, "Yes, it was a profound experience, but I can have it with other people, too." What began to emerge, and became clearer in subsequent sessions, was a pattern of diluting his experience with any one person by viewing people as equivalent or interchangeable. Through his eyes no one was unique: common features were sought which had the effect of reducing his need for or commitments to any one person—he could always get the same thing elsewhere.

As I pointed out to him, what seemed to me at issue was not the accuracy or logic of his view (he might well be largely correct in any particular judgment), but rather the function his view served. It would regularly occur when he began to move toward more intimate contact with another person, and it would have the effect of diminishing that intimacy. The point was, as I repeatedly emphasized, that *other* thoughts were logical or correct at that point, too—for example: "That was really fun," or "I really felt good being with her," or "She understands me well." Yet the thought that tended to occur to him when reflecting on such an experience was, "She's not the only one I could have such an experience with."

Interestingly, it was not only in reacting to a more intimate experience with a woman that he utilized such a defensive maneuver. The session discussed above began as follows:

P:  I don't quite know what to talk about today.
T:  I was thinking we had quite an important session last time.°
P:  You were? What was that important?
T:  Do you recall what the session was about?
P:  I'm not sure. Was it the session where . . . me not knowing how to show vulnerability and to . . . really experience insecurities and inadequacies? It's hard for me to put each session into perspective. Each one seems really profound to me. If there's something you felt was really important about that last one, I should know about it.

In this illustration, it is particularly clear how "each one seems really profound" readily becomes implicitly "none of them mean anything to me" or "there was really nothing very special about it." (Incidentally, this brief segment also illustrates how the patient used language to keep himself from experiencing while appearing to himself to be cooperating and involved. His glib use of words like "vulnerability," "insecurity," and

---

° My attempt to deliberately introduce a focus, instead of relying on his own associations, will be discussed later in the chapter.

"profound" tended to rob these words of affective connotation even when describing something for which they were appropriate.) In meeting these and a number of other ways in which he worked to blunt or attentuate the arousal of feelings that would be frightening, I had to repeatedly call attention to and interrupt the smooth running-off of avoidance sequences in order to enable him to have effective contact with the experiences he was afraid of (and/or to enable him to really understand that he actually was afraid and was avoiding). He would repeatedly reinterpret things to subtly shift the focus and meaning back to familiar territory.

Thus, later in the same session, I was saying that he was fooling himself in thinking that he simply had higher standards and was waiting to get involved until someone came along "where it could be really special, sort of all-encompassing." I was emphasizing that the problem was really not that the right person hadn't come along, but that he in fact worked very hard at staying uninvolved, that he did things to keep it that way. The following interaction then ensued:

P:   I don't know. I mean, I think you're absolutely right, but . . .° You see, what I say to myself is now I'm looking for someone to get involved with, and . . . you know, that's why I married Joan [a woman he had married with considerable ambivalence, and more out of a sense that it was a good thing to do at that point than out of strong feeling for her. They were subsequently divorced after two years], because I said to myself I'd been through so many women and I tried to get involved with one and I couldn't, and no one's perfect so can I stay with this woman and marry her and get involved with her, because you can get involved with anyone.

T:   That sounds like commitment, but I think there you were doing the same thing again.

P:   Yeah, in what way?

T:   Because when you say you can get involved with anyone, again it's saying all people are equivalent, interchangeable.

P:   Except she was a lot nicer in a lot of ways than a lot of other women.

T:   O.K. But if you're putting it, if you're thinking in terms of well, you can get involved with anybody . . .

P:   Yeah.

T:   . . . you're already making her just anybody. That's a way of staying uninvolved. Sure, we've talked about the element of choice, of choosing to commit yourself to someone, but if you're doing it with the feeling that "I'm just choosing anybody arbitrarily," then you're not really commit-

---

° "You're right, but . . ." was a repeated leitmotif in the therapy, and one which I think the reader can see is quite consistent with the other aspects described.

ting yourself, you're not really focusing on what is unique, what feels special about this person.

P: Well, let's take Carole, for example [his current girlfriend]. I mean, Carole is very special in many ways. There are a lot of reasons why she's the appropriate woman for me, but there are also lots of ways in which she's not the appropriate woman for me, and some of those are very important ways, so I'm conflicted about Carole.

T: Right now I'm not really talking about Carole, or about this woman Friday night. [This refers to the older woman mentioned earlier in the session. I am struck in going over the transcript of the session that she had remained nameless to this point.] You're again looking at what are the properties of this woman or the properties of that woman. But there are things *you do* that account more for why you're not involved with anyone.° That's the key to it, not this woman or that woman or where to look.† What am *I* doing, how is it that after all these years and all the women I have met, I've never really felt I love anyone? What am *I* doing?

P: It could be just that I haven't met the right woman yet.‡ I mean, I know there was a long period in my life when I steered away from any woman I could get involved with, I just steered away from them altogether, and I've tried to not do that anymore, but, I don't know, I'm gonna look for someone.

T: I think there's an intermediate step that we're trying to work on today, which is what are the things you've been doing all along to keep yourself from getting involved. Because one of the things that we're seeing is that right after a moment of feeling involved, almost the next thought is "well, this isn't going to last very long, I don't want to see her very often," and when somebody is involved in a meaningful experience with you, you say to yourself "someone else could have given me that, too."

In this last comment of this sequence, I am again directing the focus toward his avoidance techniques, here seemingly even at the expense of discouraging his effort to try to get close to someone. This decision was largely based on the resiliency of his defensive maneuvers, the manifold

° Here I am again bringing him back to the focus introduced earlier (see p. 194). Notice how skillfully and unobtrusively he has moved away from that focus. The therapist must maintain a constant vigilance to keep the focus maintained.

† To some extent here I seem to have gotten drawn into his defensive operations. Here it is *I* who am saying, in a sense, that no particular woman matters and who am encouraging a kind of narcissistic focus instead. To be sure, I am also encouraging him to look at what he is doing, in hopes of interrupting the sequence that keeps his problem going, but the tone of my phrasing is noteworthy, because such unwitting collusion with patients' defenses is so frequent, and probably inevitable, in an active therapeutic engagement (see Levenson, 1972).

‡ If the reader has gotten a feel for the way things go, working with this patient, he will vicariously experience frustration at this comment by the patient. I hope, however, that he is not surprised or overly discouraged. Patterns such as this are not usually changed in just a short time. The periods between such comments will gradually lengthen—or so one hopes.

gross and subtle ways in which he could initiate variations in his avoidance maneuvers in order to prevent or attenuate the experience he was trying to ward off. Until these sequences became a little less efficient and automatic, I felt he would gain little from simply going out and "trying." His effort would be unsuccessful.

Unlike the relatively simple response-prevention procedures in analogue experiments (where the avoidance is usually a simple physical act), in clinical cases such as this, one must rely largely on pointing things out, gaining the patient's attention, trying to interject different thoughts and perspectives in the sequence of his acts of attention. The patient usually prevents the anxiety that experiencing closeness would bring about by acting in a way such as to prevent the full development of frightening feelings and by organizing attention in a way such that he does not notice when tendencies to move toward, share with, and count on another person do develop.* Cues not perceived cannot cause anxiety. The avoidance behaviors displayed by this patient, as in a great many clinical cases, are primarily cognitive—ways of thinking, of perceiving, or organizing attention, of interpreting events. Most of them operate so automatically and efficiently (in the short run) that they are not experienced as avoidances but as thoughts and perceptions guided simply by the obvious realities of the situation.

By raising questions about these cognitive acts, calling attention to them, and making the patient self-conscious about them, they become a little less automatic, a little less smooth; and some exposure to what they were supposed to ward off can occur. One can understand this in terms analogous to slowing down an animal's jumping out of a chamber in which he had been shocked.† Or one can understand it in more traditional clinical terms of interpreting defenses and resistances, making the patient more conscious of his defensive activities, and so on. In either case it should be clear that a psychodynamic, interpretive approach such as that illustrated in the therapy segments above—other portions of the therapy were more frankly behavioral—can, among other things, have the effect of disrupting the ways in which the patient prevents himself from

---

* It should be understood that I have not, in this example, attempted to present all the evidence that the experience of closeness is in fact a major source of anxiety for the patient, though much that I have presented is suggestive in this regard. Nor have I attempted in this brief presentation to specify in detail just what kinds of psychological events are included in the catchall phrase, "getting close to another person"—something which I feel should be done in considerable detail in the course of actually dealing with such a problem.

† It is extremely difficult, in a case like this, to do the clinical equivalent of stopping his jumping out altogether, though in other instances imaginal flooding can at times come close.

making contact with the experiences he fears and hence from the possibility of learning that they are not as dangerous as he thinks.°

Explicit consideration of the response-prevention and extinction aspects of traditional therapeutic modalities can also lead to interventions that depart more substantially from typical clinical practice than do the excerpts above, which are closer to common psychodynamic practice than to clinical innovation. For example, consider the following intervention with another patient, who was also rather aloof and lonely. In this case, it seemed clear that his feeling of isolation was based in large measure on a hesitancy to communicate to others anything that might be viewed as a sign of weakness or not being in control of things. Because of this, he was unable to really share with others his more genuine concerns (or even his genuine joys and pleasures), because he always had to "manage" what he was presenting, to screen and control it so as not to open himself up to the ridicule he anticipated. He was a successful attorney and a glib talker and could manage his image rather successfully most of the time, but he was becoming increasingly unhappy over how little other people meant to him, how unsatisfying his continuing round of making acquaintances and impressing them was becoming. He was originally largely unaware of how extensively and compulsively he managed his image, and of how this management related to his initial complaint of nagging depression, loneliness, and meaninglessness. At the point of the present example, however, he had begun to recognize it to some extent.

In the session of interest here, he began by saying he intended to tell me about his inadequacies but noted that it was difficult to do so today, as he felt very much on top of things today. He nonetheless began to present a list of limitations and concerns, but in a tone that communicated clearly that he really wasn't feeling very concerned about any of it. I tried to find a way to make some emotional contact possible, and at one point noted that by his use of "maybe" and "perhaps" in describing feelings of inadequacy (for example, "maybe I feel I'm not adequate enough sexually"), he distanced himself from the feeling he was talking about.

Here, for the first time in the session, his gift of gab failed him and he fell silent, then began to talk softly and hesitantly, and for the first time seemed touched by what was going on. It became clear to me, and it was somewhat acknowledged by him, that his previous confessions of inadequacy were really all in areas in which he was quite competent,

° I say "possibility" here because, as will be discussed in Chapter 10, the interacting set of events that leads to and maintains neurotic character development may make reaching out to others *in fact* aversive, unless other changes are initiated as well.

and that he could sense that others did not really take his confessionals seriously. Thus, for example, he said that he worried about how he measured up to others as a professional success (he was well on the way to becoming a partner in a prestigious Wall Street law firm) and that at dinner parties he sometimes felt that he was not as good a conversationalist as others (he was an exceedingly glib and articulate person). While his expression of concern about these matters was not wholly a ploy, and he did at times make himself quite miserable with these worries, he tended to actually talk about them only at those times when he was really feeling rather confident.

In contrast, my comment about his using "maybe" to distance himself touched a concern he was much more loathe to express, a matter he was almost never confident about—his inability to be emotionally genuine and expressive. Being concerned that he was *really* at the bottom of the barrel in this respect, and quite fearful that others would see it and scorn him, he almost never talked about this, with me or with others. It thus seemed very important to me to enable him to experience the sharing of this concern with me and to experience that it did not lead to the rejection and scorn he anticipated. I focused on this matter and made a point of letting him know that I was hearing him say he felt helpless and inadequate about being emotionally locked up, inexpressive, unable to share with and relate to others. Even where he was only tangentially communicating such feeling I picked it up, emphasized it, and brought home to him that I wasn't hearing the abstract complaint of a successful man who would like some emotional icing on the already rich cake that was his life (the tone he usually adopted about this issue—which was, after all, not wholly denied but was in fact his presenting complaint). Rather, I indicated, I was hearing an unhappy and desperate man crying out for help, feeling lost and helpless and almost in tears about his inability to experience normal human relatedness and feeling.

In this, I was gilding the lily somewhat, overdramatizing relative to what he was letting himself experience; but I wanted to maximize his experience of being in the presence of another person who was perceiving something he *really* felt inadequate about and yet who was still sympathetic and respectful toward him. This was stressful for him, and in various ways he tried to reinterpret or qualify what I was saying, but he nonetheless did have an extended experience in the session of, so to speak, being in the shock chamber so that he could begin to see that the shocks wouldn't come. That is, his maneuvers to sidetrack me weren't working, he did perceive me as seeing him as feeling inadequate, and he was gaining more experience in learning that this would be tolerable. At the end of the session I made explicit what I thought had been going on, that he had managed to let me really see him feeling inadequate—and not about something he secretly felt he was good at—and that if he could begin to expose himself to this perceived danger more and more, it was likely he could learn that it would not really lead to the rejection and humiliation he had all his life thought it would. At this, he started to say, "I see what you mean, but, . . ." and I had the strong feeling he was about to try to undo the experience, to make me think he did not really feel all that inadequate and unable in this regard. I therefore interrupted him, told him what I thought was about to happen, and insisted that I did not want to hear what he had to say at this point. I indicated that whether I was correct or not, I was experiencing him as telling me he really was worried that in this area he just couldn't make it, and that I thought it would be useful for him to spend the next two days knowing that someone important to him was seeing him that way (and discovering that this knowledge could be combined with respect and liking for him).* He tried once or twice to interject a "but," with an air of simply correcting my logic or making something a little clearer, but I maintained firmly that, right or wrong, I was going to stay with my view of things till the next session, that I would listen then to what he had to say but, for now, he would have to bear my seeing him in this way.

Whether it was related or not I cannot be sure, but two sessions later he told me he liked me and wanted to get closer to me, and it was said not in his usual manner—glib and/or "emotional" in a transparently displayed way—but with clear signs of struggle, hesitantly and with genuine feeling. In any event, apart from whether what I did was wise or correct, it should be clear that the particular way in which the session progressed, and particularly what I did at the end, would not have been likely had I not been doing dynamic therapy with extinction and response-prevention models in mind.

Response-prevention is, of course, not the only aspect of traditional clinical practice that can serve to bring the patient into contact with the

---

* There is an interesting paradox here that is common in this sort of work. To the degree that he was really communicating how inadequate he felt about being emotionally closed off, he was in fact being expressive. By sharing with me his feeling that he couldn't share, he was in a sense putting the feeling of failure to the lie. Yet the effect was very different than his other expressions of inadequacy about things he really could do. Also, my feeling of respect and liking for him was in fact stronger than usual at that point, for he *was* sharing with me and being genuine. It was somewhat true that his being closed off made it hard to like him or take him seriously. Yet by acknowledging it, he was transcending it, and in effect his cries that he was heartless made him human.

cues associated with frightening thoughts and feelings. The likelihood that the patient will think particular thoughts or feel particular feelings, for example, is altered simply by the therapist's directing attention to those thoughts and feelings. For example, in the first case discussed above, the experience and expression of close, intimate feelings toward the motherly woman the patient had spent the evening with could have been facilitated by inquiring into what happened between them as well as by pointing out how he had pulled away. In fact, the expression of some of those feelings (with the chance for some of the anxiety to be extinguished, and so for more of the feelings to be disinhibited) might well have proceeded more rapidly in the session itself had the former strategy been followed. The latter strategy was chosen largely for its effect outside the sessions, where it was hoped that focusing on his avoidances would make them less likely to be smoothly and automatically run off in his day-to-day affairs. Finding the optimal balance between encouraging expression and discouraging avoidance—complementary strategies but, as this discussion illustrates, different actual operations at times— is a complex matter, which will be discussed more fully in Chapter 11.

There are several reasons why the expression of frightening feelings is facilitated when the therapist says such things as "Tell me more about your experience with this woman," or "It sounds like she's a really good mother." Firstly, there is an attentional or associational effect. Simply directing the patient's attention to a particular aspect of his experience alters the flow of his associations and reactions. Additionally, the patient's wish to please the therapist can play a role in keeping the patient in somewhat uncomfortable territory that he might otherwise leave. The therapist, by his questions and comments, indicates interest in certain thoughts and feelings, and the patient may therefore be more willing and able to focus on them than he otherwise might be. Further, the therapist's expression of interest indicates that he is not afraid to look at and hear about things that frighten the patient. By thus modeling fearlessness regarding these matters, and an inclination to approach them, the therapist helps the patient to approach and be less afraid.

The foregoing discussion suggests that most of what the dynamic therapist does can be understood in terms very similar to those that provide the rationale for behavior therapy techniques.* I have argued, however, that in many instances the prominence of anxiety associated with response-produced cues, and of avoidances that are subtle alterations of perception, attention, affect, or attitude, create problems for more formal

---

* I do not, however, wish to suggest that this is the *only* useful way to understand the therapist's activities (see below).

behavioral means of insuring exposure to anxiety cues, such as desensitization or flooding. Further, anxiety-motivated alterations of experience (defenses) often lead the patient to conceptualize his problems and to react in such a way as to make cooperation with formal methods difficult, especially early in the therapeutic effort. We have seen that the operations by which the therapist goes about facilitating insight and those by which he facilitates exposure to anxiety cues overlap substantially. Thus, there are times where the changes brought about by use of traditional procedures (or slight modifications of them) bring the patient to a point at which he is now able to cooperate more fruitfully in the more focused kind of exposure methods that behavior therapists have developed. Behavioral methods seem particularly valuable for accomplishing what dynamic therapists have regarded as the "working through" stage of therapy, a stage that may well take the greatest amount of time and effort, but that usually requires, as well, a good deal of preliminary exploration to give both patient and therapist a clear picture of what is involved.

Just how much exploration is needed and how much time is required to achieve sufficient understanding of the patient's problems has been a matter of some disagreement. In a symposium on the role of learning in psychotherapy (Porter, 1968), Lazarus and Kubie, from a behavioral and psychoanalytic perspective, respectively, differed considerably on how readily the major themes and issues in a case could be discerned. The view of many psychoanalytic therapists, that sufficient understanding for extensive therapeutic change can only be achieved over a very long period of time, is intimately linked to the historical or genetic emphasis in psychoanalytic thinking. The analyst's claim that he really doesn't know all he needs to know even after many months, and that further exploration is essential, is likely to make him sound either dull or ingenuous to the more behaviorally oriented clinician, who finds he can get a fairly clear picture of the key issues much sooner. But the analyst's demurrer is based on his view that it is essential to know the childhood experiences that led to the patient's current dilemma. To recapture the events of childhood, to discover crucial developmental experiences and the private, disavowed fantasies of the patient's early years, does indeed take a great deal of time and effort. Regarding the *current* dynamics—the defenses, warded-off wishes, and troubling behavior patterns currently in evidence—the analyst would, I think, be confident much earlier that he has a fairly comprehensive picture. Thus, from the present point of view, which deemphasizes the role of genetic understanding in the therapeutic effort, the phase of the therapy that is primarily characterized by "exploration" ends earlier (though some further exploration, discovery, and reconceptualization goes on throughout, and this kind of activity may become predominant again at several later points in the therapy). Concomitantly, working through or acting on the implications of the understanding receives proportionately greater emphasis.

The perspective developed here also suggests less reliance on the process of free association than is true in most psychoanalytic writings or in Dollard and Miller's account of therapy. I would agree with Fromm-Reichmann's (1950) contention that at our present stage of knowledge, it can be inefficient and wasteful to place heavy emphasis on free association when we can predict, with some accuracy, what things are relevant and what are diversionary or beside the point. This does not mean that all associational methods of inquiry or of eliciting feelings should be eschewed, but that their use has to be considered in the context of what stage of therapy the patient is in, what the therapist already knows about the patient's problems, what alternative methods of inquiry and intervention are available, and what countervailing considerations are relevant.

At times, asking the patient to let his thoughts drift with some particular idea or image can be a useful way of understanding the significance of something puzzling or unclear. As a brief, specific intervention I myself ask for associations quite a bit in my work. Additionally, I frequently try to let the patient take the lead, rather than introduce topics myself. This both encourages independence and responsibility on the part of the patient and helps to assure that the concerns addressed in the therapy are those of the patient rather than the therapist. And often, in response to a patient's question, I do respond with another question or a reflection rather than a direct answer. This traditional clinical technique remains a very valuable way of discovering concerns and feelings about which the patient is embarrassed or conflicted and which he is both trying to communicate and trying to disguise by asking the question. In such instances, answering the manifest question can have the effect of discouraging the patient from more directly expressing what had been on his mind, because the answer might make his concern seem "silly" or "wrong." Alternatively, inquiring into the feeling or concern that led to the question, instead of answering it directly, can have the effect of inviting the patient to share with the therapist whatever the patient was tentatively hinting he would like to express. It can demonstrate that the therapist is not afraid of what the patient feels and does not need to hide behind the facade that the manifest agenda may represent.

Often, however, I do answer patients' questions quite directly, and find that my willingness to take the patient seriously on his own terms and not to automatically hide behind the therapeutic mask pays rich rewards in the progress of the work. Clearly there are complex matters of clinical judgment involved in deciding when to answer and when to reflect. And it must be recognized that when the therapist does not routinely do one or the other, each time he makes a choice in either direction, it will be construed by the patient as having some particular meaning. Nonetheless, however much it complicates the therapist's task to not regard his appropriate aim as limited to "exploring," I would maintain that it is essential that he not so restrict his view of what he actually does. Thus, though there is value in letting the patient take the lead, there are times when the therapist has a quite clear idea of where things should go—and where, as in the examples above, the patient may gain needed corrective experiences if the therapist quite actively and explicitly points to the direction it would be fruitful to pursue.

Where the therapist is confident, for example, that exposure to particular cues will aid in extinguishing anxiety that is important in the patient's problems, there is little point in encouraging more or less random exposure in its stead, in the hope that *perhaps* what is discussed that way will also be relevant, or that further exploration will yield new understanding. However valuable it is to be open to expanding and correcting one's view of what is going on, it does not make sense to continually sacrifice treatment for the sake of diagnosis. As with the patient, the therapist, too, must not only understand but at some point must *act* on the basis of that understanding.

## DESENSITIZATION, EXPLORATION, AND INSIGHT

The preceding discussion emphasized how the procedures of traditional interpretive or conversational therapies can facilitate extinction of anxiety through unreinforced exposure to anxiety-provoking cues. I have tried to indicate how, with certain kinds of patients and certain kinds of anxiety cues (notably, response-produced cues), interpretive methods may be more effective than standard desensitization in effectively exposing the patient to the conditions that frighten him. Extinction through repeated unreinforced exposures, however, is not the only way in which unrealistic anxiety can be diminished. Dynamic therapists, of course, have stressed for years the role of insight or of new and clearer understanding in bringing an end to unrealistic anxieties based on faulty assumptions about the world and about the consequences of one's own thoughts and actions. In recent years, many behavior therapists have also recognized the importance of restructuring one's view of things, and have discussed the need for cognitive models of maladaptive behavior and behavior change to supplement the more strictly conditioning models that originally guided their work.*

Bandura (1969), for example, has suggested:

> The overall evidence would seem to indicate that emotional behavior may be controlled by two different stimulus sources. One is the emotional arousal self-generated by symbolic activities in the form of emotion-provoking thoughts about frightening or pleasurable events. The second is the response evoked directly by conditioned aversive stimuli. The former component would be readily susceptible to extinction through cognitive restructuring of probable response consequences, whereas elimination of the latter component may require repeated nonreinforced exposure to threatening events either directly or vicariously. (p. 304)

Wolpe (1969) and others have similarly distinguished between directly conditioned and cognitively mediated anxiety responses, and have suggested that different treatment strategies are needed when one or the other predominates.

A number of behavior therapists have made important contributions in recent years toward developing an approach to cognitive restructuring. (See Goldfried and Davison, 1976; Goldfried, DeCenteceo, and Weinberg, 1974; Lazarus, 1971; Mahoney, 1974; Meichenbaum, 1973, 1974.) Some of this work bears similarities to the approach described in the present volume. Much of it, while compatible with the present approach, represents distinctive points of view that contribute to therapeutic effectiveness in highly original ways. In much of this work, the influence of Ellis's (1962) rational-emotive approach is strong. The present approach differs from work based on the rational-emotive model in placing considerably greater emphasis on the kinds of phenomena that psychodynamic therapists have discussed in such terms as resistance, defense, intellectualizing, and isolation. It is my guess that much of the success that has been obtained with methods derived from the rational-emotive approach is due to their frequent combination with graded real-life assignments in carrying out more "rational" behavior, and that the rational argument per se frequently has its effect in motivating the patient to try

---

* One should note well, however, Davison and Wilson's (1973) warning that some of the work that is self-described as "cognitive" is best understood as reflecting a mediational S-R approach, rather than a more fundamental departure from the perspective of conditioning theories.

new ways of interacting with others, rather than primarily through directly correcting faulty assumptions or aspirations. For facilitating new understanding of and new perspectives on one's life, I would suggest that greater attention should be paid to defensive attenuation of the impact of statements with which the person may manifestly agree.

In my own work, I have tended to use more traditional means to approach the task of helping the patient understand more clearly the events of his life and the compexities of his aims and feelings. Thus, while I frequently view interpretive comments from the exposure-facilitating perspective stressed above, at other times my prime purpose is to aid the patient in *understanding* the choices and assumptions he makes and where they may be related to his problems. At times this understanding, and the correction of faulty assumptions, may be facilitated by considering aspects of the patient's history; but, as I have indicated earlier, I share with most behavior therapists (and some dynamic therapists as well) the conviction that focusing mainly upon contemporary events and reactions will most fruitfully provide the kind of understanding that leads to change.

In pursuing the goals of exploration and insight through such traditional means as free association, interpretation, and reflection of feelings, I have found that features of the desensitization procedure can also be useful and integrated into the process. Not only can traditional means be used as an alternative form of desensitization, but aspects of desensitization can be used as an alternative means of facilitating insight as well. (See also Singer, 1974; Weitzman, 1967.)

One does not find much discussion in the behavior therapy literature of how the procedures associated with desensitization can contribute to furthering self-understanding. Perhaps this is a result of the theoretical context and psychological climate within which systematic desensitization developed. When the images patients experience are viewed solely as "stimuli" presented to the patient as part of the regimen prescribed by the therapist, and not as significant products of the patient's imagination (potentially carrying valuable information about his motives, feelings, and assumptions about the world), the opportunities for using such images are limited.

An example of the use of relaxation and/or directed imagery may illustrate how these methods can aid psychodynamic exploration and help the patient to see things he previously had kept hidden. On one occasion, a patient was discussing his tendency to communicate to others the message that he was unimportant and could readily be ignored. As a result of the work of the previous few sessions, he had become more acutely aware of this tendency and had begun to notice some of the ways in which he did this. In the session under discussion here, he began to recognize that he did this particularly when he was beginning to have a strong positive impact. He described this in connection with two different business encounters, and said that he had the feeling this was not such an uncommon experience for him. I asked him if he could think of any other instances, and he recalled an incident in which he was having dinner with several people, including a woman, Laura, who had been influential in getting him his present job. She had made a flattering comment about something he had said, and then he felt uncomfortable. As he put it, he had been going along feeling involved in the conversation, not self-conscious, "and then someone says something which makes it clear I'm doing well, and I become self-conscious and begin to fuck up."

I asked him how he felt when Laura said she was impressed with what he had been saying; he said it was hard to answer, he just felt asinine. I asked him to imagine right now sitting at the table and holding forth, and Laura saying "John, that was very impressive." I asked him to try to immerse himself in that image and see what he experienced. He said it was hard to do this, and I urged him to try to picture it in as vivid and concrete detail as he could, indicating I would wait silently while he got into the experience and noticed what he felt. After a while he said, "I would have asked myself if she was shitting me, putting me on."

I commented that one of the things that seems to happen, then, is that he wonders when he's being taken for a ride. I asked him to imagine the situation again, but this time to imagine himself knowing she really meant it. I again waited silently, and after a while he said, "The first thing I want to do . . . I can imagine that, and I feel uncomfortable, feel I have to say something to justify her opinion. I would want to say something else, and now I'm feeling very self-conscious, very constrained, and I would say something stupid."

I listened with interest at what he told me, and then said that maybe we could approach the anxiety in a way similar to systematic desensitization (which we had used previously). I suggested he relax, and then try to imagine the situation very vividly. I asked him to imagine Laura saying she was very impressed and his knowing she really meant it. "And now imagine that all you do is say 'thank you,' nothing else. Just hold that image and try to stay with it."

He sat silently for a while, then said, "You know what came to mind? The need for a cigarette. In the old days, when I smoked, I would have said thank you, then taken a cigarette to distract myself."

I asked, "What happened this time when you just said thank you?"

He said, "I had the feeling something else was supposed to happen. I like the idea of not having to respond after accepting the compliment. But I felt tense, like something else was supposed to happen."

I asked him to again imagine exactly the same set of events. I explained that I hoped that by exposing himself to the situation a number of times he would be able to take the edge off the anxiety.° I again encouraged him to imagine himself just accepting the compliment, staying with it and being there behind what he said.

This time he said, "Actually, before, when I began to think about it, about that suggestion of just being very calm in responding to this, it actually brings up a strong erotic thing, there's a strong erotic element in my response to this, which occurs to me before I actually begin to visualize the situation: which surprises me, because I really don't respond to her erotically. I mean, she's very attractive, but she's really too much of an anxiety object . . . Now I can see sticking my hand out and touching her instead of wanting the cigarette." As he said this he burst out into loud, uncontrollable, nervous laughter.

I commented that part of the anxiety he experienced in the situation might be that when she complimented him, it felt like a come-on.

"There's something I'm supposed to do, you know, when someone says to me 'that was pretty good.' I'm supposed to repeat the performance and do it twice as good this time."

"So this time you felt two things? You felt pressure to repeat it and you felt an erotic feeling for her?"

"No, no, actually I didn't feel the first. That is, when I really, you see, when I think I'm really responding to this situation in a relaxed way, that is, not feeling any pressure to perform, then I really do feel some sort of sexuality which is not, which is somehow different, but I think that's a consequence of the fact that I'm not feeling too much anxiety. I'm visualizing the situation without too much anxiety, and the feeling was just sort of sitting there. I didn't expect it."

There was still a good deal of work needed in exploring the erotic feelings that were stirred in the patient in that situation (which he didn't recognize when the situation actually occurred), and in facilitating a still more experiential, less intellectualized sense of those feelings and of their relation to his self-effacing manner. But the session did have the feeling for both of us of a "breakthrough" that greatly aided the thera-

---

° This was, of course, not all that was involved. I was also implicitly modeling an alternative way of handling such situations. Additionally, as discussed below, transference fantasies are probably mobilized by proceeding in this way and play a role in bringing about change.

peutic work. It is possible, of course, that he would have come upon these feelings just as soon without the use of relaxation and directed imagery, or that a price was payed for achieving understanding in this particular fashion, even if it did occur sooner than it otherwise might have.

Certainly, as discussed in Chapter Seven, the use of this or any other explicit intervention by the therapist can stir a variety of fantasies and feelings in the patient. It does not seem to me, however, that such reactions are necessarily harder to "analyze" or "resolve" than those the patient has to the way the more strictly interpretive therapist conducts the session (cf. Silverman, 1974). Depending on whether the patient is more prone to experience others (especially authorities) as manipulative, controlling, or knowing better than he what he ought to do, or to see them as depriving, mysterious, or unwilling to lend a hand, problems may be posed for one approach or the other. But in either event, it is possible in most cases to help the patient sort out where he is perceiving the interaction in an idiosyncratic, selective, or distorted way, especially if one takes the view that the patient's transference reactions are not just the playing out of something from the past but a reaction to present events guided by schemas that are characterized by both assimilation and accommodation.

choose not to change; the therapist has no right to tell the patient what to do; and so on. These kinds of issues will be discussed in some detail in Chapter 12. In this chapter, I will discuss some of the ways in which the therapist *can* facilitate action based on the patient's new understanding, and why I believe it is often a practical necessity to do so if enduring change is to occur. This discussion of the practical realities is, for me, a necessary prelude to consideration of the ethical issues, for a sensible system of ethics must be based on some conception of the anticipated consequences of alternative choices of action (or inaction).

One of the reasons why the traditional view has been maintained for so long is that sometimes patients do change, after a point, simply from better understanding their own desires and their life situation. A clearer view of what one faces, or a perceptual-cognitive reorganization that suggests a whole different range of alternatives, can be a very powerful force for change.

Frequently, however, understanding is not followed by a changed way of living. I have already discussed some of the limitations of the explanation that understanding did not lead to change, in some cases, because it was intellectual rather than emotional. Here it may be added that even if this were an adequate conceptualization, one could in such instances still ask why, if one grants the value of emotional insight, the therapy has gone on for years and years and not been able to bring change about. It is not an adequate answer to say the patient was resistant. If he was resistant to what the therapist was doing, then the therapist should have been doing something different.

The perspective developed in Part One suggests that one of the things the therapist must do differently in many cases is to make more direct efforts to instigate and guide new behavior patterns than is traditionally done in dynamic therapies. A number of considerations all point in this direction. First of all, as I have discussed at several points, actions sustain structures. The persistent modes of thinking and perceiving and related motivational tendencies which analysts have observed in great detail are not preserved simply by the configuration of forces in a hypothetical psychic apparatus. They are kept going in important ways by the consequences of patients' day-to-day actions in living. These consequences include both the responses evoked in others by the patient's behavior (for example, the hostility evoked by a paranoid attitude, which confirms the patient's suspiciousness and perpetuates the cycle) and the relatively direct effect of the patient's actions upon how he experiences his own motives, his self-worth, and so on. (For example, the patient may not ask for things, out of a fear of being too "demanding" or "voracious."

This may lead to considerable deprivation and the build-up of intense desires, which in turn confirms the sense of himself as dangerously over-demanding and starts the whole cycle going again.) *

Through such processes, the work of the analytic session can readily be undermined by the neurotic living that goes on between sessions and, so to speak, repairs the neurotic structures that were partly dismantled in the session. Formulations that regard change in neurotic patterns of inter-action as a by-product of changes in self-perception and motivational states, and therefore not the direct responsibility of the therapist, fail to consider sufficiently the degree to which change in either one of these poles of human experience (that is, either self-perceptions *or* overt action patterns) is part and parcel of the process of change in the other. If the analysis presented in this volume is correct, then even where therapeutic efforts that spurn direct intervention in the patient's day-to-day behavior *are* successful, they probably take longer than they should and achieve somewhat less than they might. Further, it is likely that when they do work, they do so because the patient's environment is very encouraging of those new interaction efforts that do get instigated by the interpretive work of the sessions; thus, even here, new actions are aiding intrapsychic change as well as vice versa. As will be discussed shortly, however, there are likely to be many aspects of the patient's life context that hinder rather than foster such changes.

A second, and related, consideration that points to the importance of therapist efforts to directly monitor and guide new interaction patterns by the patient involves the constraints upon insight brought about by desperate clinging to old modes and old relationships. When the patient has closed off many options in his daily living and has come to seek his gratifications from very few people and in highly stereotyped ways, he may be frightened to question and reflect upon his feelings about these relationships. If he can begin to take small steps to live his life differ-ently, he can begin to examine and reflect somewhat more freely.†

---

* Short-cut terms like "build-up of desires" should not be taken as an endorsement of hydraulic or energic models. One can account for the same phenomena in largely cognitive terms, such as emphasizing how memories of past slights and deprivations, comparisons with what others have, and other factors can intensify (not necessarily consciously) one's current longings, increase what would be needed to feel satisfied and have one's just deserts, and so on (see Klein, 1967).

† These first steps are almost certain to be gross and sporadic. It is difficult to accomplish finely tuned interpersonal accommodations, or to be prepared to deal in a persistently progressive way with all the possible setbacks, unless clearer understand-ing of the issues in one's life is also developing. Considerable blurring of the realities of one's transactions with others and experience of self is almost always a feature of neurotic patterns of living. This has been emphasized, in somewhat different terms, by many behavior therapists in the cognitive or broad-spectrum wing of the behavior

I have previously discussed this sort of issue (Wachtel, 1975) in the case of a young man whose intense conflicted ties to his mother played a major role in keeping him from establishing meaningful ties to anyone else. It was almost impossible for him to examine his feelings toward his mother because, since he was so overwhelmingly dependent upon her, he didn't dare risk losing what he did have by psychically trespassing beyond the bounds of permissible thought and feeling that his mother had established. Attempts by his therapist to resolve the patient's ties to his mother, by insight into their origin and meaning, foundered because the intensity of the ties themselves stood in the way of insight. My discussion of how the case might have been successfully approached suggested the use of methods of the sort discussed in the last two chapters and later in this chapter. That particular case was a quite extreme instance of the situation where the very problems the therapist intended to explore were an impediment to exploration. The patient was of the sort usually labeled "borderline" or "not a good analytic case." However, as the following discussion indicates, impediments to achieving change through insight alone may be important in a far wider range of cases than would be expected from traditional assumptions.

## IMPEDIMENTS TO CHANGE IN DAILY LIFE

For a number of reasons, reactions from others that are counter to the patient's growth and change may be more common than is generally suggested in psychoanalytic writings. Not infrequently, those who become involved with the patient on a long-term basis do so to satisfy rigid neurotic needs of their own, and have a stake in keeping the patient involved in the same interaction pattern. This phenomenon in itself is not new to traditional therapists (though the arguments in this chapter and elsewhere in this book, that such current sources of feedback are probably a more potent source of resistance than the traditionally emphasized intrapsychic ones, are likely to be quite controversial in some circles). Students of neurosis and/or marriage have long been familiar with such classic pairings as the know-it-all husband and the take-care-of-me wife, the pair of fearful people who reassure each other that others' more ad-

---

therapy movement; and even among the neo-Skinnerians, there are fewer and fewer who insist on focusing solely on overt behavior, without regard for cognitive set, attention, or other organismic variables.

venturous lives are superficial, the "busy" pair whose mutual fear of sharing and intimacy comfortably mesh, the hostile overbearing wife whose husband's identity is that of an abused martyr, and numerous other combinations equally (and equally sadly) familiar. Not only in marriage, but in any long-term relationship of some degree of importance and some degree of voluntarism in whether it is continued, one must ask if those who complement the patient's neurotic behavior patterns do so at least in part out of a need to participate in such an interaction (or, in other language, whether something about an interaction which would seem to be aversive might actually be reinforcing).

INDUCED DEVELOPMENT OF COMPLEMENTARY NEEDS IN PARTNERS

Less frequently noted in the psychodynamic literature is that even where the other person enters into a relationship with the patient because of its *non*-neurotic aspects and *in spite of* the neurotic ones, it is important to consider the likelihood that human adaptational flexibility may interact virulently with human neurotic rigidity. By this I mean that the individual who is attracted to a partner largely for the partner's non-neurotic qualities may at first try to change the neurotic patterns but, finding them inflexible and still being interested in the relationship, he may begin to adapt to these patterns, perhaps even to find ways in which he can derive some pleasure or benefit from them. Over a period of time, if he is really good at making a virtue of a necessity, he may increasingly bring a certain side of himself to this relationship and fulfill needs here that other relationships don't as readily permit to be gratified. Thus, after a while, the partner's adaptational efforts may lead him to construct a relationship with our patient such that he does begin to have a stake in keeping things going as they are. His adaptive resolution of the problem of how to get the most out of a relationship that is gratifying but marked by neurotic annoyances may help keep the other person locked into neurotic patterns of living.

Needless to say, I am not suggesting that all of the above efforts, adaptations, and gratifications need be in awareness. Nor am I suggesting that the partner, even where he has strong needs to perpetuate the neurotic features of the relationship, does not suffer in some way for his participating in this mess, and would not benefit from a change in the interaction pattern if one could be arranged. I am merely emphasizing that the partner may be motivated by short-term considerations to resist the changes in the patient and may—again, not necessarily consciously —try all sorts of ways to undo them.

INVOLUNTARY CONFIRMATION BY PARTNERS OF
PATIENTS' NEUROTIC PATTERNS

The various contingencies just described are in contrast to a substantial
number of other cases in which the clinical evidence does not justify any
emphasis on the partner's *needing* the patient to be neurotic, yet in which
the partner is nonetheless, perhaps unwittingly or even unwillingly, an
accomplice in perpetuating the patient's neurotic pattern. In such instances, the partner experiences largely pain and frustration in response
to the patient's neurotic behavior, yet is induced to behave in ways that
help keep it going.

The sexual partner of a patient who is strongly conflicted about sexuality, for example, is likely to respond to the patient's tentative, anxiety-
ridden advances with a good deal of tension and discomfort of his or her
own. The partner may be quite capable of responding fluidly and sen-
sually with other partners, but with our patient sex is stiff, clumsy, and
not really much fun. The partner may genuinely desire that the patient
be freer and more expressive sexually, yet be unable to respond to the
patient's awkwardness other than in ways that, by making their sexual
encounter largely tense and joyless, actually keep the patient's anxieties
going and make him again unable to give, or receive, sexual pleasure.

Similarly, someone involved with an aggressive, suspicious individual
may genuinely wish he would drop his guard and be more loving and
trusting. Yet the constant assault of suspicion and hostility may make it
hard for the partner not to react with anger or withdrawal, and hence
strengthen the patient's view that others can't be trusted or relied on.

In another kind of situation, the overly dependent individual may
elicit behavior from others in which they assume what should be his
responsibilities and thereby do not allow him to develop his own resources sufficiently so that his dependency can begin to diminish.
Though in this latter type of process the "giver" is often satisfying his or
her own needs ( viz., the classic picture of the overprotective mother ), the
dependent person's demands are often a genuine pain in the neck instead; yet the person who is entangled with him may be strongly pushed
toward just the behavior that will keep the annoying dependency going.

FAILURE TO NOTICE CHANGE

In still other instances, those who interact with the patient help keep
old patterns going when they fail to notice the initial changes that occur.
Frequently our expectations guide our perceptions to such a degree that
we continue our old way of categorizing and responding to others' be-

havior even in the face of fairly considerable change in that behavior. Once we have labeled someone as "shy" or "insincere" or "uninteresting," a great many behaviors that would in other circumstances be viewed differently are likely to be seen as consistent with our ongoing picture of the person. Eventually, if the patient's changed behavior persists, the change is likely to get through to those who interact with him. But often the lack of initial response from others can be discouraging, and the changed behavior does *not* persist. The patient goes back to his old ways, others' perception of him remains unchanged or even strengthened, and the conservative effects of perceptual expectations keep the repetitive cycles from changing. In those instances, it is important to help the patient persist through the early stages until others do begin to provide different feedback.°

### DEFICITS IN SOCIAL SKILLS

Perhaps the most important reason for needing special techniques to guide the patient's overt behavior—important both because it is so pervasive and because it is so rarely discussed in traditional accounts of therapy—is that the conflicts and inhibitions that typically are at the core of the patient's problems lead very regularly to specific deficits in the learning of social skills. When the conflicts and inhibitions are reduced and the patient begins to try to put into practice his new understanding, the deficit remains, and his first efforts to act differently are often crude and ineffective. Instead of encountering newer and more positive responses from others, he may instead experience rebuff or disdain. Thus punished instead of rewarded, he may be discouraged about trying again or even have his earlier fears and "unrealistic" fantasies strengthened.

Many writers on therapy explicitly disavow concern with this problem. They assume that the patient knows what to do and how, but does not do so because of inhibition and conflict—or that if for some reason he does not know, he can easily and quickly learn. Thus the patient who complains that he does not know what to say to people at parties, or how to put his foot down in a way that does not get dismissed, or how to approach a girl without seeming overly aggressive or excessively awkward, is viewed as manifesting a kind of resistance, and it is expected that he will rapidly discover he is able to do these things effectively once his conflicts are resolved.

---

° In Chapter 11, I will discuss how the therapist, too, can impair the process of change by being insufficiently aware of the change that has already occurred.

Such a view, I would contend, fails to take sufficiently into account just how complex and prolonged is the process whereby we learn to achieve the interpersonal behaviors appropriate to an adult in our culture. It is easy to overlook this long and difficult process because it is so gradual and because, once achieved and exercised daily, its manifestations seem inherently "obvious." Yet if one looks at the social behavior of children and adolescents, one is struck by the succession of forms that social actions take and the inappropriateness of any of these earlier forms for an adult.

Thus, adults, like children, can feel left out of a conversation and wish to have the conversation directed to them or be about them. But whereas at age two my son could count on a positive response when he said to us, "Don't talk to Daddy, Mommy, talk to Kenny" or "Talk about me," an adult wanting the same thing would be ill-advised to express it in quite the same way. Children must go through a long process of learning how to effectively channel and express their feelings. Their initial crude efforts would be readily discouraged were adult standards of moderation, articulate expression, or subtlety applied to them. Fortunately, the expectations brought to bear in evaluating the child's response are usually geared to his developmental stage, so that he can achieve satisfying interactions throughout the many years in which his behavior gradually evolves into its adult form.

But where neurotic inhibitions have interfered with this gradual learning process and kept it from proceeding in normal fashion, the adult who in the course of therapy begins to express a need he has largely inhibited for years is likely to do so in a way that lacks the fine tuning of typical adult behaviors and resembles to some degree the cruder efforts of children. As therapists, when we are faced with unmodulated and inappropriate anger in a patient who had previously been defending against such feelings, or unrealistic demands for attention and devotion from someone who had been compulsively independent, we are likely to be pleased that *some* change is occurring and not to be put off by the less than optimal form these early expressions take. The set we adopt as therapists enables us to respond empathically and encouragingly to behavior in our patients which we often would not tolerate in our friends. And our unusually understanding and growth-oriented way of experiencing things in this unique kind of situation can easily lead us to overlook how others, engaged in a different kind of relationship, might respond to this kind of behavior.

When the poignant struggle we observe in our sessions does not lead to the progress in the patient's way of living that we hope for, it is probably often because other figures in the patient's life are not nearly as encouraging of these first crude efforts as we are. In addition to having a stake in old ways, as discussed above, these figures also (not really inappropriately) employ different standards than we do in reacting to the patient's behavior; and in their reactions, they may again teach the patient that expression of what he is feeling is dangerous. Sometimes the negative reaction comes from an explicit aversion to the crudity or lack of modulation of the patient's behavior, as when a sexual advance does not conform to the cultural rituals that the other person is accustomed to. At other times, the disappointing and inhibition-strengthening reaction is a result of insufficient skill, intensity, or persistence, as when a previously meek person risks speaking up and asserting himself, but once having stuck his neck out does not know how to handle the other's reaction and retreats in acute humiliation.

Such kinds of failure experiences can result either from explicit ridicule or put-down or from the shame that comes when others don't even notice one's efforts to reach out or speak up. Thus, the person who tries to be a more active participant at parties by sharing in a joke-swapping session, instead of just listening and feeling impotent as he had previously done, may stumble or mess up the punch line. He may even fail to complete the first sentence, since getting the floor when several people are eager to be "on" next requires a sense of timing and a kind of assertive persistence if two people start talking at once and it is rightly your turn. If the patient stops after three words and the other person who began simultaneously keeps talking, or if he starts while people are still laughing at the last joke and thus isn't heard, or if he waits until someone else has already begun the next joke, he may feel as humiliated by his not having managed to get the attention of the group as he would by having gotten the floor, muffed the joke, and been explicitly ridiculed.

Because all of these varied kinds of discouraging consequences of unskillful social behavior can feed back to undermine therapeutic change, it is important not only to monitor the patient's efforts to apply his new understanding in his daily life (I would contend that in *every* case one should pay a good deal of attention to such efforts and their consequences) but also in many cases to focus with the patient on training social skills and developing an explicit program of practicing and applying them. A useful model for doing this is provided by the method behavior therapists call assertive training, and by applications and extensions of its various components.

## THE ASSERTIVE TRAINING APPROACH

By assertive training I am referring here to a multifaceted approach to bringing about new, more effective interpersonal behavior. It tends to include such (not necessarily mutually exclusive) methods as role-playing anticipated real-life interactions in the sessions, practicing desired behaviors in the sessions (perhaps with successive approximations to some appropriate criterion), modeling by the therapist of effective ways of dealing with particular situations, and setting up a graded series of real-life tasks for the patient to perform in shaping his interpersonal skills and altering his ongoing relationships. As we shall see, "assertive training" is by now a misnomer, and at times a misleading one; the methods that originally were developed to facilitate being able to stand up for one's rights have been (or can be) extended to apply to almost every kind of inhibition in effective transactional behavior (for example, meeting members of the opposite sex, expressing feelings of love, requesting help, engaging in easier or more genuine conversation with friends, and so on).

### FORMAL RESEARCH

There has been much less formal, systematic research on assertive training than on systematic desensitization, and for good reason. Assertive training, as it is practiced clinically by skilled practitioners, is a much less mechanical and routinized procedure than systematic desensitization, and is much more poorly approximated by experimental analogues. I have had the opportunity to observe some particularly outstanding clinicians engaged in assertive training, and what I observed bore little relationship to what is studied in the experimental literature. (In fact, as I shall elaborate below, it is particularly in observing skilled behavior therapists using assertive training and its extensions that one sees the striking convergence between good clinical practice from a sophisticated behavioral approach and the practices of the more active interpersonal dynamic therapists.) In contrast, when one watches the clinical practice of systematic desensitization, one has the sense that, despite the necessity to make particular idiosyncratic accommodations to the particularities of any given patient, one is watching a procedure rather similar to what is utilized in the analogue studies.

Thus, studies that focus upon standardized applications of what in practice is a highly flexible and individualized treatment procedure are of questionable value in guiding clinical activity. They have provided much less guidance regarding essential and unessential components than is the case for systematic desensitization. For example, a study by McFall and Twentyman (1973) suggests that modeling, which is typically one of the major components of clinical assertive training, does not produce an increment in performance beyond the level achieved by simply providing a general set of instructions about how to be more assertive and an opportunity to rehearse assertive behavior. Additionally, they found that covert rehearsal (in imagination) was fully equal to actual overt practice of the desired behavior. Their subjects, however, were not patients seeking treatment but, rather, student volunteers (see Chapter 8). Their focus was not on building or elaborating complex interpersonal skills, but rather on a very narrow range of behavior: the ability to say no to "unreasonable" requests (a definition that was not easy to provide without considering the idiosyncratic personal meaning of events to each subject). Their procedure was a standardized tape recording that in no way accommodated to the particular nature of any subject's difficulty, to his progress through the program of training, or to his progress in applying in his life situation what he learned from the training program. And, apart from all the above limitations, the assessment of the effects of all of this in real-life behavior was both quite short-term (one month at the longest) and equivocal (showing up on only one of several measures in several studies).* Whether, therefore, modeling might be of value when, as in many clinical situations, one is working on more complex interpersonal skills than just saying no; whether it would be useful if employed in a highly individualized way geared to the particular patient's needs, attitudes, specific deficits, and progress rather than presented in a standardized way; whether it is more important with a more seriously impaired patient population than with student volunteers; and whether it is helpful in bringing about more enduring change, are all questions that research of this sort does not answer.

---

* My intent here is not to criticize a few isolated researchers or their efforts. McFall and Twentyman, for example, are quite sophisticated about what they are doing and discuss the compromises they had to make intelligently and openly. Rather, I am trying to illustrate why formal research has provided little dependable guidance for clinical practice in this area. If I differ with McFall and Twentyman, it is not in seeing the compromises any more clearly but in my estimate of whether the compromises make questionable the strategy of approaching these questions through analogue research with standardized procedures. The same is essentially the case regarding the Goldstein et al. (1973) study discussed below, though here it is particularly puzzling why researchers so keenly aware of the limitations of studying non-clinical *populations* would, when studying a more appropriate group, in turn choose inappropriate *behavior*, in the sense of again requiring some *other* study to know if what one has found has any clinical relevance whatsoever.

Further, in order to compress the range of observations into standardized procedures, research of this sort tends to be minimally attentive to the effects of the reciprocal feedback systems that I have stressed in this book and that, in principle, should be of central concern to behaviorally oriented clinicians and researchers. McFall and Twentyman report, for example, that their subjects behaved more assertively but *without conveying a more assertive impression*. This is quite an intriguing incidental finding in light of the kinds of considerations presented earlier in this chapter (e.g., pps. 216–217), and might reflect a kind of process that after a while would tend to undermine any changes that occurred by limiting the kind of new feedback that could support new behavior. The strategy of comparing standardized procedures discourages examining such issues, leading the investigator to look at the "outcome" of an experimental "input" without considering the interpersonal processes that mediate both the overall group effects and the observations that vary from the group norm (again, despite the fact that such processes are very much at the heart of what social learning theory —as opposed to the experiments that tend to be done in its name—would point to).*

Another study, which did focus on a real clinic population, yielded somewhat similar findings: elaborate modeling procedures were not superior to simple instructions to behave more assertively and the provision of a rather minimal degree of modeling (Goldstein et al., 1973). Yet this study, motivated by the recognized need for the "systematic use and evaluation [of modeling procedures] in clinical contexts" (p. 31), looked only at these patients' answers to a series of "What would you do if . . ." kinds of questions. The researchers conclude, "One would do well to compare such interventions not only on such intermediate criteria (for example, changes in verbal behavior) as were used in our investigations but also on more ultimate criteria, such as changes in patient independent behavior in his real-life environment." (p. 41) Such an extension is indeed needed.

Other systematic studies on aspects of the assertive training model tend to be similarly ambiguous with regard to their implications for clinical practice. Lacking clear guidelines as to essential and inessential components, practitioners have tended to develop a rather complex approach, with a number of features whose rationales are convergent and complementary.

---

* For further discussion of some of the ways in which experiments may skew what is observed, see Wachtel (1973a, b).

CLINICAL RATIONALE FOR ASSERTIVE TRAINING

In Wolpe's (1958) early writings on this topic, assertive training was conceived of as primarily a way of getting the patient to emit behavior incompatible with anxiety. Thus, within the reciprocal inhibition model, assertive behavior played a role similar to that of muscular relaxation, and assertive training could in a sense be viewed as a variant of systematic desensitization. Certainly one of the consequences of successful assertive training is that the patient is less anxious. The reduction of anxiety, however, now tends to be seen as part of a complex set of interacting processes and not only a result of direct deconditioning. Wolpe's pioneering efforts in this area have led to considerable further developments, both by him and by others, that have led to new understanding of the possible ways of using assertive training and related methods. It is now recognized that as the patient learns to interact with others more appropriately, skillfully, and effectively, he receives quite different feedback from others, which contributes to more positive feelings about himself and to reduction of anxiety; its also helps create a context in which adaptive behavior is made increasingly likely. Additionally, as will be discussed below, the assertive training procedures can also be an important aid in facilitating insight. When the process goes well, the anxiety reduction, better feedback, clearer understanding, and more adaptive behavior all enhance each other in a positive version of the kind of spiralling emphasized throughout this book.

As the framework for conceptualizing assertive training has broadened and become more sophisticated, so too has its clinical practice. At one time it may perhaps have been justified to object to the assertive training approach as overly mechanical, or as an inappropriate effort to teach the patient to react as the *therapist* would, in accordance with *his* values and personal style rather than the patient's. This is, however, not at all an accurate description of assertive training as it is practiced today by sensitive clinicians who understand the complexities of how the development of adaptive interpersonal behavior may be either impaired or facilitated.

In fact, far from imposing the therapist's values or preferences upon the patient, skillful use of assertive training can have as one of its valuable consequences the facilitation of the patient's own self-understanding and ability to act in terms of his own inclinations rather than others' wishes. One of the things that most struck me when I first observed behavior therapists using assertive training in complex cases, was that in some instances what they were doing could readily be seen, in the language of dynamic therapists, as facilitating the expression of what the patient was preconsciously leaning toward. I have, for example, observed several instances of patients being aided by behavior therapists in dealing with an overbearing, intrusive, hypercritical mother. Some therapists tended to simply tell the patient what to do ("You ought to say to her . . ."). Others, however, in dealing with very similar clinical problems, were more likely to say to the patient things like, "It sounds like you'd like to tell her in no uncertain terms to stop opening your mail, but something keeps you from doing so. You shrink back from it at the last minute and tell yourself it's not important." Such comments were often followed by patient statements such as, "Yeah, I guess I really would like to tell her off, maybe more than I realized. But you don't know my mother! That's easier said than done."

This combination of a kind of insight (which, as in dynamic therapies, is much more likely to be gradual and almost obvious by the time it is expressed and genuinely experienced, rather than sudden and dramatic) with an expression of the difficulty of putting it into practice is a very common one, seen by both dynamic and behavioral clinicians, and is often the consequence (in either case) of what is essentially the interpretation of a conflicted action tendency. Effective behavior therapists, no less than analysts, address themselves to just such tendencies; and like analysts, their impact tends to be greatest when their focus is on those tendencies that the patient is just beginning to acknowledge but is still also motivated to retreat from or deny. The behavior therapist doesn't tend to talk about interpretations or insights, and certainly doesn't refer to preconscious urges, but in practice the skilled practitioner does in fact pick up what the patient is himself inclined to do but may be only scarcely aware of until it is voiced.* Further, not only does he address himself to the patient's incipient actions, but focusing on such tendencies frequently makes it possible in later sessions to discern still other conflicted action tendencies that had previously been associated with even more intense anxiety and the avoidance of which had strongly influenced the person's style of life. (The psychoanalytic reader will recognize this as similar to the familiar sequence whereby continued interpretation of

---

* Among the behavior therapists whom I have observed doing assertive training, I have been particularly struck by this kind of clinical radar in Arnold Lazarus of Rutgers and Alan Goldstein of the Temple University Department of Psychiatry. It is a pleasure to acknowledge here the role that observing these two outstanding clinicians had in helping me to see many of the convergences discussed here, though they are by no means responsible for the idiosyncratic way in which I have construed their work.

that which has become preconscious leads to progressively "deeper" trends that had once been unconscious and defended against.)

Thus, the sensitive application of assertive training procedures can begin with efforts to clarify the patient's conflicts using probes and statements not always distinguishable from what many dynamic therapists would try. Where the assertive training model begins to lead in a somewhat different direction is in its way of dealing with the patient's demur in the above illustration ("But you don't know my mother! That's easier said than done."). Even here, the two approaches at first tend to be rather similar. Most therapists, of whatever persuasion, would want to know what the patient anticipates the mother would do. But whereas many dynamic therapists would seek, through a series of interpretations, to expose highly unrealistic repressed infantile fantasies (which they would view as the most influential factor in maintaining the patient's inhibitions), the therapist utilizing the assertive training model would take a different course. Rather than restricting himself to interpretations, and assuming that appropriate action will eventually follow adequate understanding, he would make an early effort to foster the occurrence of real-life actions, and would expect new understanding to follow—not just as an epiphenomenon, but as part of a synergistic process in which actions and feedback continually effect understanding and one's understanding continually generates some kind of effort at action. Such is certainly the view of action and understanding underlying the use of assertive training within the active interpersonal approach propounded in this book, and it is what I take to be the view of many more strictly behavioral clinicians as well.

Within the assertive training model, the new real-life actions are fostered both by events within the session and by planned experiences outside the session. Usually both are used, but not necessarily: occasionally, real-life actions are planned without any special preparation in the sessions; at other times, within-session work leads to "spontaneous" effective actions by the patient that were not explicitly programed but that are effective enough for such explicit planning to become unnecessary.°

---

° Sometimes, of course, valuable real-life change occurs with *no* explicit focus by the therapist on how the patient might handle his current life situation. The traditional psychoanalytic model of therapy emphasizes such instances, viewing overt behavioral change as a by-product of therapy not directly addressed by the analyst. My guess is that in most instances where psychoanalysis is helpful, one important factor has been the analyst's not quite explicit (perhaps even covert and guilty) efforts to guide the patient in taking adaptive action in addition to helping him understand; and my interest in assertive training reflects my belief that this is done better when it is explicit and systematically followed through.

In Wolpe's early accounts of assertive training (see Wolpe, 1958), it appeared that providing the patient with a few simple rules for effective action usually sufficed to establish effective behavior and reverse neurotic patterns. In my own experience, and judging from the work of behavior therapists whom I have observed, this is not very frequently the case. Very often, quite considerable attention must be paid to carefully planning and monitoring the patient's actions with regard to the particular therapeutic goal, as well as to developing the appropriate behavior patterns through work in the sessions.

### NEED FOR GRADUALISM: CASE ILLUSTRATION

Regarding the need, in many cases, for the patient's therapeutically relevant actions in his everyday life to be quite carefully planned out, the following illustration is fairly typical of the kinds of problems encountered. The patient, Mr. Jones, was a man of 38 who had been divorced several years ago and who was feeling lonely and depressed. He had met his wife when he was quite young, had had a rather clinging relationship to her, and still felt quite at a loss as to how to live without her and how to meet other women. The latter was a particular sore point for him. He had met his wife when they were both in school, and felt he didn't know how to meet women any other way. His school years were long behind him and his job brought him into contact almost exclusively with men.

At a certain point in the therapeutic work he began to feel it was time for him to meet a woman, and it seemed appropriate to begin working explicitly toward the development of skill and comfort in meeting women, striking up a conversation, asking for a date, and so on. (Recall that the view presented earlier in this chapter posits that such difficulties are not only the result of current inhibition and conflict, but also frequently reflect a real learning deficit that resulted from having avoided the relevant earlier experiences that gradually build social facility.) Mr. Jones at first had no idea where he could meet women. When encouraged to inquire, he found out about several bars where men of his particular socioeconomic and ethnic group went to meet women; and although he felt some anxiety about this, it seemed to him the most comfortable or compatible of the alternatives available. We talked some about his anxieties, and his reluctance to try. I encouraged him to do so, suggesting we examine how he could go about it step by step. Rather than plunging right in, and facing the likelihood of both intense discomfort and awkward, unsuccessful efforts, he was encouraged to work toward gradually building up comfort and familiarity with this new situation. This made sense to him, and it was agreed that on the first occasion he would simply go in, look around, get a feel for what the place was like, and leave; he would feel no obligation even to say hello to anyone, much less strike up a real conversation, get someone's phone number, or the like.

It was hoped that in this fashion, by introducing him to the bar in a non-pressured situation, he could start out with a feeling of comfort in that setting (that is, the cues associated with the physical setting would not become anxiety cues, and any further efforts there would not be based on a compounding of an already tense situation). It was planned that if he did feel any tension while there, he would remind himself that he was not going to approach a woman that day, and it was further planned that if tension occurred on this first occasion he would stay with the same goal the second time he went; he would not go on to the next step until he could sit in the bar with comfort. Once this was achieved, it was expected that further incremental steps would be taken, such as just saying hello, then engaging in a five-minute conversation, then asking a woman for her phone number, calling her for a date for dinner, and so on—again with each step being repeated until it was more or less anxiety-free before going on to the next stage.

After the first visit to the bar, Mr. Jones was elated. He had always been terrified of such places, and was very pleasantly surprised at how the removal of performance demands had made it comfortable for him to go in. He was eager to go on to the next step, and confident that "I'll have this thing licked in no time." He was cautioned not to go *too* fast, and reminded that it was precisely his not pushing himself to perform that had enabled him to do well in round one.

Apparently, however, the warning was not strong enough. The next occasion went fine; he felt comfortable there, said hello to one or two women, and left feeling very good. But the session after the third visit to the bar, he came in very depressed, talking about missing his wife, how no one could ever replace her, and so on. After inquiring into this for a while, it came out incidentally that at the bar the night before he had met a woman, danced with her several times, and gotten her phone number. Closer examination revealed that she had been the initiator, had said hello, asked him to dance, and offered her number, saying "call me tomorrow night." As we further reconstructed the evening, it turned out that Mr. Jones had first felt great and decided there was no need to continue at the slow and gradual pace we had agreed upon. He started to fantasize an intense affair with this woman, then became anxious, feeling he was getting in over his head and would have to meet all sorts of demands and expectations. He began to think of his ex-wife, with whom, until shortly before his divorce, he had worked out a comfortable—if not very gratifying—*modus vivendi* based on mutual tolerance of each other's limitations. Feeling unable to cope with the current situation, and longing for the safety of the lost relationship, he sunk into a depressed and despairing state which was relieved only when the events of the night before were clearly sorted out and he resolved to go back to the gradual pace originally worked out. At that prospect he now felt some anxiety in comparison to his initial foray, but felt optimistic and ready to proceed to grasp control for himself.

This kind of occurrence—the patient going too fast and then becoming very anxious and discouraged—is not uncommon in efforts of this kind. The therapist must walk a thin line between encouraging the patient's spontaneous efforts and enabling him to begin to trust his own impulses and inclinations, on the one hand, and trying to assure that he goes at a pace that is likely to be rewarded and not to lead him into humiliating experiences, on the other. As I have gained experience in working this way, however, it has increasingly seemed to me that in most cases it is probably best to err somewhat on the side of caution. When one is encouraging a patient to enter into territory he regards as dangerous, it is terribly important that he not have a bad experience, and unlike situations where the person fears something external or inanimate (such as heights or subways), interpersonal encounters are always unpredictable and dependent upon others' responses. As discussed earlier in this chapter, when a patient goes into an encounter unprepared to deal with all its ramifications, he can at times come out worse off in terms of therapeutic progress than if he had not ventured at all. To the therapist whose training was in a more open-ended style of working, the stress on structuring and pacing may seem uncomfortable, perhaps even controlling or obsessional at first. But it can be richly rewarded in terms of gains for the patient.

## SYSTEMATIC DESENSITIZATION, FLOODING, AND ASSERTIVE TRAINING

The above discussion should bring to mind parallels between assertive training and systematic desensitization. In fact much of what has been described can be viewed as a kind of *in vivo* desensitization. Cues associated both with the situation itself (the bar, the presence of women, and so on) *and with one's own intentions* ° are anxiety-provoking to varying degrees, and the patient is introduced to them in a graduated fashion. But whereas the necessity for graduated exposure in systematic desensitization has been cogently questioned (see Chapter 8), gradualism is crucially important in assertive training. With the kinds of anxieties for which systematic desensitization is appropriate (anxiety with regard to situations toward which no action can be taken or is required), there is reason to believe that a flooding model may be as effective, perhaps even more so. With interpersonal problems that require an appropriate response from the patient, however, the flooding model is usually entirely inappropriate.

The need for gradualism in this connection is perhaps most dramatically illustrated not by an explicit instance of assertive training but by an approach that bears considerable resemblance: the sex therapy of impotence (Kaplan, 1974).† This approach is based on the view that psychogenic impotence is the result of anxiety in the sexual situation. This consists very largely of performance anxiety, but in some cases it also includes fears of harm to the penis during intercourse, or other such fears familiar to psychodynamic clinicians. The therapy is based on gradually introducing the patient, step by step, to increasingly more difficult (and/or more arousing) situations, assuring all along the way that pressure to perform is removed and that the patient does not proceed to the next step until sensual pleasure rather than anxiety is clearly the dominant affect in the previous step. Thus, initially the patient and his partner might just caress one another in non-genital areas, being instructed to concentrate only on the pleasurable sensations and not to go on to more explicitly sexual behavior no matter what. When this had become pleasurable and comfortable, they might go on to gently stimulating each other's genitals (with intercourse still proscribed). Only after a gradual process of associating all of the steps on the path to intercourse with pleasure and arousal rather than anxiety would they attempt intercourse. In such a fashion the anxiety that inhibits erections

---

° This latter source of anxiety is extremely important. The same place can be safe or dangerous, depending on what one intends to do. Assertive training, in dealing with interpersonal situations, brings the clinician forcefully to recognize the importance of cues associated with intentions or motivational states. This is probably why the clinical thinking of behavior therapists who are particularly involved with assertive training has seemed to me so compatible with that of interpersonal dynamic therapists.

† Sex therapy is not discussed in any detail in this volume because Kaplan's discussion provides both an excellent description and a view of the relation to psychodynamic approaches that is largely, though not entirely, consistent with my own view.

is gradually eliminated, and erections appear spontaneously at some point in the process.

In contrast with this desensitization-like model, consider what a flooding model of dealing with this anxiety might be like. If instead of being gradually introduced to increasingly more challenging sexual situations, the patient were instructed to confront the most difficult one right away, he would get nowhere. The anxiety would inhibit erection, and his fear of failure would be confirmed again. Further, whatever fears he had of being harmed if he had a stiff erection and entered the vagina could not be extinguished, since he would first have to have the erection to try it; and *not* being able to get an erection in that situation is precisely why he sought therapy! *

While perhaps not as dramatic or as obvious, with most instances of assertive training, too, the aim is to enable an inhibited response to occur as well as to reduce anxiety (obviously the two are often mutually supportive). In similar fashion, the response may simply not occur if the starting point is too difficult. With the problems requiring assertive training, the patient is not just being exposed to external stimuli, which can presumably be "administered" in any intensity; he needs to be exposed to cues associated with *his own responding,* and if the therapist-created or therapist-encouraged situation is one in which the response does *not* occur, then the patient has not been at all exposed to the situation he *really* fears (that of being there *and doing something*).

Further, in most instances of assertive training it is not enough to just do *something.* The patient must respond in a way that is effective, that gets reactions from others that are rewarding and likely to strengthen the tendency to continue in that direction.† This is a reason not only for encouraging the patient to proceed gradually in his *in vivo* encounters, choosing challenges he can handle, but also for much of the within-session work that is an important part of most assertive training. It is to this latter aspect that we turn next.

---

* One could of course use a flooding model in fantasy (for example, instructing the patient to imagine either being ridiculed for failing to get an erection or being frightened of harm while erect and in the vagina), but most sex therapists find *in vivo* procedures far more effective for treating sexual problems.

† "Rewarding" here does not necessarily mean "positive" in the sense of pleased, friendly, or explicitly encouraging. Sometimes the patient's intent is to upset or defeat someone, and an angry response could be rewarding, whereas a friendly or tolerant smile could be frustrating or even humiliating.

## IN-SESSION ASPECTS OF ASSERTIVE TRAINING

Assertive training, as has been noted, usually consists both of planned actions in the patient's everyday situation and specific experiences within the therapeutic session. The latter most often relies on various aspects of role-playing to achieve its effects. The simulation, within the session, of situations encountered in the patient's day-to-day activities has a number of functions in the therapeutic effort. It deals with the problem of the patient's vulnerability to others' responses by letting the patient first try out new behaviors in the safe context of the therapeutic relationship, where the therapist is in a position to assure that they will be met with a positive response. It enables the therapist to see more clearly and vividly just what the patient actually does in the situations which give him trouble. It enables the *patient* to gain a new perspective on his behavior, especially if audio or video tapes are available. It facilitates *behavior-rehearsal,* the systematic practicing and development of new adaptive patterns of interaction. And it permits *role-reversal* (that is, the therapist playing the part of the patient and the patient the part of someone he interacts with) and thereby both the possibility of the patient's gaining understanding of what it feels like for someone to interact with him (if the therapist plays the role in the way the patient usually does) or of alternative ways of dealing with situations that give him trouble (if the therapist, in the patient's role, *models* alternative behavior).

Let us consider first the provision of a safe place to try out new behaviors. The value of such a haven for experimentation should be obvious from the discussions earlier in this chapter. The difference between the therapist's set to accept and encourage new and more adaptive behavior, however crude, and the set of people not in the therapeutic role to expect appropriate adult behavior is crucial to recognize. The therapeutic setting provides a unique opportunity to try out new ways of being without the dangers usually inherent in such efforts.

Even for the therapist, it is not always easy to respond in a way that encourages the patient's gropings toward a life style that is more rewarding and expressive of his convictions and inclinations. Wolf (1966) has lucidly described how the therapist can be drawn into the patient's neurotic patterns and confirm or strengthen them rather than working against them—or in the terms introduced earlier in this book, how the therapist can become an "accomplice" in the patient's neurosis. An important part of the therapist's training involves sensitizing him to the subtleties of nonverbal communication, so that cues can be identified and articulated instead of leading to automatic responses. This disengagement from the kind of automatic reciprocity that keeps neurotic patterns going is also facilitated by the way the therapist structures the relationship with the patient so as to be able to listen and reflect. (Chapter 11 will discuss some additional considerations that can aid the therapist in assuring that he in fact does encourage the patient's new efforts, rather than inadvertently working to make them less likely.)

Because the therapist's training and his stance of participant-*observer* enable him to respond (it is to be hoped) in a more growth-facilitating way, some of what is achieved in assertive training by way of providing a place to safely try out new ways of living is provided in traditional therapeutic efforts as well. The patient can try things with the therapist he wouldn't dare outside; this is encouraged both by the atmosphere of acceptance that the therapist tries to create and by his interpretations, which demonstrate a readiness on his part to notice and deal with incipient behaviors that the patient might otherwise brush aside and that others in relation to him might be unlikely to pick up on. This can be very helpful, but its value is often limited in traditional approaches by a reluctance on the part of the therapist to directly address the problem of transfer or accommodation to the conditions in the patient's daily world. Without explicit efforts to bridge the gap between the nurturant therapy relationship and the more demanding world outside, there is a good chance that the patient will learn to discriminate and act one way with the therapist and another with everyone else. The therapist then has the conviction—correct as far as his (within-session) direct experience of the patient is concerned—that the patient has become freer, more open, more healthy and genuine; yet in the patient's day-to-day living, change is far less extensive. If this occurs frequently, it accounts for why therapists can be sincerely convinced that they are having a major impact, whereas research confirmation of their effect remains more equivocal—patients may *really* change a great deal with the therapist, but not nearly so much in other contexts.

Some traditional therapists are well aware of this problem and do pay a good deal of attention to what actually goes on in the patient's daily life. In many instances, this kind of informal monitoring may be quite sufficient. The patient has gained enough clarification of issues, or reduction of anxiety, or understanding of the necessity for changed behavior to go and try the change, and has enough sense of what he has to do to have a fair chance of succeeding. Certainly not every patient needs formal assertive training.

For many patients, however, more explicit and detailed attention to building new interaction patterns is needed; and even where it is not essential, it would lead them to faster or more extensive change. It is not only a matter of the patient not *knowing* the most appropriate or effective way to deal with the situation. I do think that this is often the case—that for the reasons discussed above, the patient's conflicts and inhibitions have frequently limited the possibility of his observing and assimilating how people behave in various situations. But even where the patient does in a certain sense "know" what to do, this knowledge may not be available or usable in a way that enables him to act effectively. The patient may be able to describe what is called for, but not to put it into practice. Or he may be able to manifest assertive behavior with his wife but not with his boss, or vice versa.

Gradually structuring real-life efforts and playing out some of these interactions in the session may enable anxiety about taking action in particular settings to be desensitized and may facilitate the translation of implicit action patterns into manifest actions in new settings or contexts. The effect of assertive training in such instances may be less one of teaching something new than of acting as a kind of *releaser* of knowledge that has been stored somehow, but not in a way that is readily translatable into behavior. The person who has difficulty saying goodbye, for example, has certainly had a good deal of opportunity to observe others saying goodbye. But he may continue to experience himself as not knowing how to do so, until an opportunity to rehearse in nonthreatening circumstances gives him a chance to integrate the representations of his observations with action patterns and interpersonal cues. He may then "learn" much more quickly than the person who has to master a kind of interaction about which he has really picked up very little, even in a strictly passive-observer mode. Thus, while not necessary in all cases, role-playing and behavior rehearsal may, for a variety of reasons, be important in enabling the patient to take effective action.

Role-playing procedures are also of value in giving the therapist a picture of the patient's style in a way which no amount of description of the "So then I said that I didn't like what he was doing" variety can convey. The value of this kind of direct observation is, of course, one of the reasons the therapist is trained to be attentive to just what the patient does with him, including the style and inexplicit communications that accompany and sometimes modify or even reverse the explicit message the patient thinks he is conveying (for example, the glint of pleasure or triumphant stubbornness in the patient's report that he has "tried" to do what the therapist suggested but finds that he "can't"). But as I have noted, it is essential that the therapist also have a vivid picture of how the patient is with others (especially since some kinds of interactions of importance in the patient's life may *not* be replicated in his relationship with the therapist.° And for this, role-playing is an invaluable therapeutic aid. Detailed inquiry into an exact sequence of events, especially if the patient has been asked to keep actual written records made as soon after the event as is feasible, are of course also of great value in this respect, and at times quite sufficient. In many instances, however, one discovers something in seeing the patient actually play out just what he said and how he said it that is masked in the patient's reporting of the event.

The difference between reporting and acting is sometimes vividly illustrated in the patient's hesitancy to role-play. On several occasions patients have protested to me that they did not want to role-play because it was too "artificial," and in each instance they came rather quickly to recognize that what they feared was in fact precisely the opposite— that playing out what occurred (or could have occurred—see below) made it *too real*. In fact, one must at times be cautious in role-playing precisely because of this. The patient can feel exposed and stripped naked when his "I told her off" or "I told her to stop doing it" is revealed, when finally played out, as a rather ineffectual statement, undermined by tone of voice, frequent "uhs" and hesitations, an obsequious posture, and so on; or when he says "I told her I really loved her," and in role-playing the interaction it becomes clear that genuinely affectionate statements stick in his craw, and in response to the question "Tom, do you really care for me" he literally cannot say "Yes, I really love you" without making a face or tensing up as if a punch were about to be thrown at him.

For this reason, patients will frequently, when role-playing is introduced, slip away from it at first. Elaborating the above illustration to include its early vicissitudes, the therapist after explaining role-playing, and indicating that he is playing the part of the patient's wife, says "Tom, do you really care for me?" Tom says "I would say to her that I do, but she'd complain." Therapist: "Don't tell me what you *would* do.

---

° As I have argued elsewhere (Wachtel, 1973b), the generalizability of emotional interaction styles is probably greater than many social learning theorists would expect from their experiments, but not so great that it can automatically be *assumed* that everything of importance in the patient's life will necessarily become evident in the transference.

I'm Jane. Talk to me. Tom, do you really care for me?" Tom (turning away, looking slightly disgusted): "Yes." Therapist (still as Jane): "You don't say it like you mean it." Tom: "Yeah, that's what she says, and I usually . . ." Therapist (interrupting): "You're again telling me *about* what you'd say. I'm Jane. Tom, you don't say it like you mean it." Tom: "It's very hard for me to answer her when she says that." Therapist: "How do you feel when she says it?" Tom: "Angry, pushed." Therapist: "OK, I'm Jane. Tell me how you feel." Tom: "Jane, when you do that it really turns me off. Maybe if you didn't ask me so often I'd be able to say it spontaneously without feeling like a puppet . . . (then, in a tone that indicates he is now talking to the therapist as therapist) Gee, I wonder what would happen if I really said that to her." Therapist: "Let's play it out a little further and see how it would feel. How do you picture her reaction?"

As the last part of the interchange indicates, the role-playing procedure can be a way of increasing the *patient's* understanding as well as the therapist's. The exploration, observation, and rehearsal aspects of the role-playing procedures are not sharply differentiated in practice, and the same sequence in the session can be viewed from several perspectives. Not only can the patient gain understanding from observing his behavior in role, under circumstances more favorable to self-observation than the often pressure-filled real encounters (especially where audio or video tape recording permits detailed retrospective examination); he can also gain considerable insight into those he must deal with, and into his impact on others, by engaging in *role-reversal* procedures.

Behavior therapy writings do not tend to stress this aspect of role reversal. Behavior therapists tend to introduce role reversal for other reasons, such as to enable the therapist to gain a clearer picture of the behavior of significant others by having the patient act it out, or to provide the therapist with an opportunity to model more effective behavior in the course of playing the patient's role, or perhaps to enable a shy patient to ease his way into role-playing by playing the role of someone else instead of acting his own part.* Role reversal can, however, be a very useful way of facilitating certain kinds of understanding on the part of the patient.

In one case, for example, a patient, Mrs. Brown, reported that her husband was like a rock, completely immovable, and that there was no

---

* This may seem to some readers counter-intuitive. One might expect the patient to be more self-conscious having to portray another person than just acting himself. In my experience, however, patients do at times find it easier to begin role-playing via role-reversal and feel less that they are "laying themselves on the line."

kind of leverage she could exert on him to induce him to be more attentive to her needs. No amount of discussion or interpretation seemed to make much dent in this. There was a kernel of truth in her view. He was a rather impassive, unresponsive man. But she could not see how her own submissive, unassertive manner made it easy for him to ignore her requests. When she did begin to act somewhat more assertively, as a response to my continuing focus on this topic, she did not persist very much, and her husband was able to continue in his pattern of walking away or remaining silent without answering her. Her sense of things was that no matter how forcefully and persistently she asked, he would remain very comfortable ignoring her. I asked her to act out his role, with me playing hers, suggesting that this might give me a sense of what it was like for her to interact with him. In role, I said "Edward, there's something I want to talk about with you that's very important to me." She said, out of role, "He wouldn't answer me." I, out of role, said "Don't tell me what he would do. You be Edward. Give me a hard time so I'll know what it's like." Then, again in role: "Edward, there's something I want to talk about with you that's very important to me." Mrs. Brown, in role, remained silent, looking bored and inattentive. I then continued, in role, "Edward, what you're doing now is exactly what I want to talk to you about. Whenever I want to talk to you you just look bored and don't respond. That has got to stop." Mrs. Brown then came out of role again and said "That wouldn't have any effect on him at all. He'd still ignore it." I again indicated that I wanted her to *do* what Edward would do instead of *telling* me what he would do, and again began the same interaction. This time she stayed in role a bit longer and then again came out of role and insisted Edward would not respond. I had to continually press for her to stay in role and be the resistant Edward as my playing-out of Mrs. Brown's role gradually increased the pressure on Edward to change.

Finally, an interesting thing happened. I had just said, in role, to Edward (Mrs. Brown), "Edward, you've been used to me asking for something and then backing off very shortly. I'm not backing off this time. I want you to respond to what I'm saying, and I'm going to sit here and wait till you respond." I sat there staring at Edward (Mrs. Brown) very intently. She remained silent for about thirty seconds, fidgeting a great deal, and suddenly burst out into uncontrollable nervous laughter. When she regained her composure, she said, "I guess it's not so easy to be Edward, especially if I were to be firm with him. I never did confront him the way you just did." She now recognized that her frequent coming out of role just before was due to how uncomfortable it was to be Edward opposite an insistent wife who wanted some response from him, and she elaborated for the rest of the hour on her new sense of what Edward must experience, and how she had made it easy for him to ignore her. In the next session she reported having had her first meaningful, really personal conversation with Edward in many years.*

Actually, role-reversal can not only facilitate the patient's understanding of the experience of those he interacts with, it can also be a way of furthering self-understanding at times. Earlier in this chapter it was discussed how the adept behavior therapist can point the patient toward expressing just those things that the patient is on the verge of sensing in himself. I may add here that often this sense is imparted to the patient not in the form of an explicit interpretation or suggestion, but in the course of the therapist's modeling of the patient's part in a role-reversal procedure. When the therapist models the way the patient *has* acted, the patient can be helped to understand his impact on the other person; when the therapist models how the patient *might* act, the patient may gain some insight into himself, into what he is on the verge of feeling inclined to do.

Most accounts of modeling in the literature tend to stress not this insight-facilitating aspect but rather the presentation to the patient of a picture of how to cope, which he can then use to deal more effectively with the situations he encounters. (See Bandura, 1969, 1971 for a detailed account of the use of modeling for behavior change.) As discussed earlier, however, such instructional use of modeling is most effective, and most desirable, when the behavior being modeled is congruent with the style, values, and aims of the patient. The instructional and the self-exploratory aspects of the modeling procedures are really quite compatible and complementary. Both are evident in the clinical work of accomplished behavior therapists, though probably many would benefit from a more explicit consideration of these issues.

Role-playing procedures also aid the development of social interaction skills by providing opportunities for shaping of appropriate behavior (see Chapter 11) and for behavior rehearsal—the practicing of particular ways of interacting and of dealing with specific anticipated problematic situations in the safe context of the therapist's office and with the opportunity to "take it from the top" if it does not go right. I have al-

---

* Obviously there was more to Mrs. Brown's situation than just what is described here. It was important, for example, to understand why she stayed with Edward and felt up to the present that leaving him was impossible; there was also a host of other things to determine about what kept them both locked into this pattern of (non?) interaction.

ready discussed the various reasons why the patient's initial efforts toward change are likely to be crude and ineffective, and how this can lead to discouraging consequences if these actions are first tried with people who are not trained or set to focus on how the patient has begun to change rather than on whether his behavior fully matches normal adult standards of reasonableness and competence. By rehearsing with the therapist, where specific aspects of the new behavior can be examined in detail and tried in various ways without punishing consequences, the patient can make it much more likely that when he does put his therapeutic learning into practice in his day-to-day living, he will meet with gratification and success.

It is this *rehearsal* perspective on role-playing, and its concomitant concern with structuring and monitoring the actual interactions that the patient attempts in his daily life, that tends to distinguish the use of role-playing in assertive training from its use in the context of such approaches as Gestalt therapy or psychodrama. The latter approaches bear many similarities to what I have described, but tend to be concerned primarily with the use of role-playing to facilitate *insight* and far less with the planning of a structured therapeutic regimen in the patient's manifest interpersonal behavior. These approaches share with most psychodynamic approaches the assumption that genuine insight will lead spontaneously to more adequate and adaptive behavior. As I have indicated, I believe that this is frequently not the case, and that in-session practice and structured efforts in the patient's daily life can make a critical difference in the success of the therapeutic effort.

# 11

# *Reinforcement and*

# *Interpretation*

───────────

Traditional accounts of psychotherapy frequently stress that the therapist should refrain from advising the patient or selectively approving of or rewarding certain of his actions. Such a view appears with great regularity in both the psychodynamic and Rogerian literature, yet it is difficult to know how seriously it is taken. In my experience, most therapists acknowledge, when pressed, that they cannot refrain completely from making their preferences known or directing the patient toward certain choices and not others; but they say one should do so as little as possible, and they indicate that they are able to avoid such influencing most of the time.

In contrast, behaviorally oriented writers frequently assert both that the therapist is always, and necessarily, reinforcing his patients' behavior, and that he *should* do so. Their objection to the traditional approach is largely based on the view that traditional therapists reinforce *ineffectively*, that they are not systematic enough in how they administer reinforcements.

## RELATION BETWEEN THE PRESENT APPROACH AND OTHER REINFORCEMENT APPROACHES

Probably the most explicit, best known (and to some, most notorious) use of reinforcement principles occurs in therapeutic programs such as token economies (Ayllon and Azrin, 1968). In such programs, principles derived from research on operant conditioning are rather directly applied to altering specific target behaviors. This work differs in a number of respects from the behavioral methods discussed thus far, and it differs as well from the ways of using reinforcement principles that will be stressed in this chapter.

For one thing, token economies occur of necessity within the context of institutions and depend for their success upon the control that total institutions can exercise over access to rewards (see Goffman, 1961). (In this respect, the typical classroom can be regarded as a *time-limited* total institution; for a part of the day, the teacher exercises a kind of control similar to that of a hospital or prison staff, and hence can make use of similar behavior control methods if he chooses.)

Related to this difference in context is a variety of ethical issues that may well be different from those raised by other methods, in which control over what happens to the other person does not seem to be as complete or as explicitly exploited. To be sure, not all such programs are set up by authorities who independently decide what behavior the subjects should evidence and what rewards to administer (in some school applications, in particular, it is not uncommon for the students and teacher to negotiate just what will be expected by each party and what contingencies will be established). A good case can also be made for the view that there is always *counter-control,* that the subject is never simply the passive recipient of a set of interventions by the experimenter or therapeutic agent.* Nevertheless, the issues raised by such programs are sufficiently problematic to merit special consideration. It is possible that they may be viewed simply as special cases of more generally relevant ethical considerations, but the specifics of token economy programs are such that some readers may find them unacceptable in a way that other applications of reinforcement principles are not.

In addition, such programs have tended to be undertaken from a strictly Skinnerian point of view that allows little possibility for the kind of integration explored in this volume. Though the token economy could, in principle, be approached differently (see Greenspan, 1974), it is likely to be one of the last behavioral techniques to be integrated with traditional psychotherapeutic approaches.

For these reasons, I do not intend to discuss token economies any

---

* A famous cartoon in the *Columbia Jester* depicted a rat in a Skinner box bragging to a compatriot that he had trained the experimenter to give him a food pellet whenever he pressed the bar.

further in this chapter.° Moreover, I wish to explicitly *distinguish* between the token economy approach and the use of reinforcement principles considered here. I ask the reader to try to put aside his feelings (positive or negative) about token economies, or about Skinner's social philosophy, and to look afresh at the implications for psychotherapeutic change of our knowledge of how we take into account the consequences of our behavior.

For somewhat similar reasons, I also do not intend to discuss the use— even in the context of individual therapy outside of institutions—of such concrete reinforcers as cookies or M&Ms. Such practices may well have a place with certain kinds of individuals, especially where more natural social influences are theretofore lacking, and as a transitional step *toward* greater sensitivity to human interaction (see Chapter 4 of Bandura, 1969 for an excellent discussion of this issue). But (if I may be permitted a gastronomic nightmare) M&Ms are red herrings, and the specific kind of use of reinforcement principles that seems to me most relevant to the integration I am pursuing in this book is best considered on its own merits.

Somewhat closer to the focus of the present chapter, though still distinct from it, is work such as that of Allen et al. (1964). These authors report a successful effort to intervene in the shy, isolated behavior of a nursery school girl. When they were first consulted, the girl tended to spend very little time with other children. They observed that when she isolated herself, the teachers, who were concerned about her, would try to reassure and comfort her and to induce her to play with the others. On those infrequent occasions when she did approach the other children, the teachers felt less need to attend to her. The authors hypothesized that adult attention was a powerful reinforcer for this little girl, and that the contingencies in the classroom were such that she was in effect being reinforced for being apart from other children and that the reinforcement was being withheld when she approached them. They therefore advised the teachers to reverse the existing contingency—to attend to her *only* when she moved toward the other children and to ignore her when she was alone.

The results were very clear. When the new contingency was instituted, her time spent with other children increased markedly. When, in order to ascertain whether their explanation of the change was correct, the authors instructed the teachers to return to the old contingency—to

---

° For an excellent discussion of the achievements and problems of such an approach, see Davison (1969). See also Levine and Fasnacht (1974).

attend to her when she was alone and sad but to ignore her when she was with the other kids—the child's behavior reverted to its former patterns. Reinstituting the new contingency again was quickly followed by an increase in her social play, and on follow-up a year later she had maintained this new behavior and appeared to be a healthy, happy, outgoing little girl.

This work differs in a number of respects from the kinds of operant approaches discussed earlier. It is concerned with a more social form of behavior, and the reinforcements it employs are social reinforcements. It is based on a careful analysis of the human interaction that was occurring prior to the appearance of the psychologist on the scene. Efforts such as this, or the more complex analyses by Patterson of reinforcement patterns in families (see Patterson, 1974), reveal the utility of a reinforcement perspective for understanding the often surprising consequences of such human phenomena as sympathy, compassion, anger, or moralism. Their therapeutic effort is based on correcting the untoward consequences of the patterns of reinforcement previously existing in the "state of nature" of the client's environment.

Inquiry, and even intervention, of this kind is not foreign to psychodynamic practitioners, especially in working with children. Examination of the kind of behavior encouraged by the parents (often without the latter's recognizing that they are doing so or how they are doing it) has been important in much traditional therapeutic work with children, as has been instructing the parents how to respond to the child in a way that will encourage a different direction to the child's behavioral development.

Work such as that of Allen et al. or Patterson differs from traditional child-therapeutic work primarily in two respects, one (to my mind) positive, the other negative. On the positive side, their work involves far more elaborate and explicit consideration of reinforcement contingencies and the implications and guidelines developing from laboratory research in this area. As part of this trend, they are keenly aware of the difficulties in observing and categorizing behavior, and of the need for extensive and careful observation within the setting in which the problem is manifested.

On the negative side, my main reservation about this work is that it applies only one perspective to the behavioral events it deals with, and that it is likely to miss a good deal because of this narrower perspective. One critical issue that remains unresolved is whether a price is paid for the gains achieved with respect to the target behavior. Did the child described above, for example, learn to go through the motions of relating to others, to cover over her real feelings in order to win desperately needed approval from parental figures, and was she therefore being launched on a life course of dissimulation and alienation when the root causes of her isolation could instead have been uncovered and resolved? Allen et al. do provide some data which bear on such a question: first of all, after a time her behavior persisted even without the continued maintenance of reinforcement by teachers; presumably, after being encouraged to spend more time with other children, she was enabled to overcome her anxiety with them and to learn ways of relating that persisted because they were intrinsically gratifying. Secondly, the authors did attempt to assess the general quality of her affective development, and they report that, far from showing problems in some other area, she seemed generally happier and more confident.

It is hard to know, however, how much confidence to place in such reports. Clinicians operating from an exclusively operant perspective are not trained to detect subtle signs of conflict or to evaluate the subjective, experiential element of people's lives. To be sure, when no negative effects are discerned by the investigator, the burden of proof is on the challenger who argues that a sharper observer would come to different conclusions (Wachtel and Arkin, mimeographed). But confidence would be greater were a broader perspective applied to the evaluation, as well as to the work in general.

The approach I wish to emphasize here involves substantial consideration of the consequences that follow the patient's actions, and it owes a great deal to the explorations of more exclusively operant workers. The present approach differs from theirs, however, in a number of important respects. (1) It looks to a far greater extent at non-obvious, non-conventional reinforcers that are often disavowed as such by the person who seeks them (for example, hurting others, or gratifying a sexual fantasy). (2) It emphasizes multiple and conflicting reinforcers. (3) It tries to combine examination and utilization of response consequences with interpretation and facilitation of the patient's understanding (and to show in what respects many behavior therapists already do so and where, from my point of view, they stop short). I will consider the effects of clear and explicit reinforcements, but also the importance of more subtle ones; and I will look both at how one takes into account the reinforcement contingencies operating in the patient's daily life situation, and what the contingencies are (and should be) in the therapeutic session. An important part of this will be the reinforcement aspects of interpretations—both the reinforcements that inadvertently occur and those that should be explicitly used.

## REINFORCEMENT AND "STIMULUS CONTROL"

Reinforcement is frequently discussed by behavior modifiers in terms of the rhetoric of "stimulus control." A kind of inexorable effect of reinforcement contingencies and reinforcement schedules seems to be implied, which makes the individual human being merely the locus of a set of forces impinging upon him. Such a view is uncongenial to many psychotherapists, who are reluctant (a) to view the everyday social behavior of their patients (or themselves) in such terms, and (b) to explicitly try to "control" their patients in this way. It is therefore important, if one wishes to argue for an integration of a reinforcement perspective with traditional clinical approaches and conceptions, to point out that this is not the only way to view reinforcement.

Bandura (1969) points out, for example, that reinforcements may be conceived of as *informative* events, which convey (to a being who can judge and anticipate) just what consequences will result from various courses of action. Views of reinforcement that stress *incentives* rather than any kind of direct and automatic *control* are increasingly prominent even among "hard-headed" researchers (e.g., Bolles, 1972). Apparently, not only is such a view more respectful of man as a choosing agent, it also fits the data better.

## REINFORCEMENT IN THE PATIENT'S LIFE CIRCUMSTANCES

As noted in Chapter 10, failure to recognize the powerful influence of the patient's daily experiences outside the therapy room can seriously undermine whatever progress is made in the sessions. Optimal therapeutic effort requires knowledge of the reinforcement contingencies that the patient experiences in his day-to-day living. This knowledge is often quite difficult to tease out, because behavior is frequently maintained by a quite irregular pattern of reward. Indeed, a good deal of research suggests that behavior that is rewarded very sporadically and irregularly is more stable than behavior that is rewarded each time it occurs and that therefore disappears rather quickly when the typical result is not soon forthcoming.

The persistent patterns of behavior that are of most concern to the clinician are thus likely to be on an irregular schedule of reinforcement and therefore not easy to connect with a particular outcome. It is much easier to identify a connection between a pattern of behavior and a particular consequence when the latter regularly follows the behavior. When the sequencing is irregular, so that the behavior often occurs without the critical outcome (and, often, the outcome of concern occurs without the prior occurrence of the particular behavior—rarely is a particular reinforcer obtained only by one kind of behavior), the observer can readily fail to discern the connection between the response and the particular outcome the occasional occurrence of which maintains it.*

Sometimes this problem can be dealt with by careful and systematic observation and recording, either by the patient or by a trained observer. Both possibilities can yield useful information in particular circumstances, though each has important practical limitations. Another approach to the issue, useful at various stages in formulating a picture of the patient's life, follows from recognizing that, ultimately, the reinforcement contingencies that are relevant in maintaining behavior are the contingencies *as perceived by the individual*. What maintains behavior is the patient's expectation (not necessarily conscious) that a particular way of acting is instrumental in attaining some desired goal—not the "objective" facts of what follows what. For this reason, efforts to observe or infer the patient's fantasies, whether from TATs, dreams, free associations, or what have you, can be of considerable value in highlighting the relevant contingencies, and they may lead the therapist to notice a relevant (though occasional) behavior-outcome sequence that might otherwise go unnoticed (for fantasies are not always unrealistic; often they are subjective probability estimates of contingent outcomes, and they may be variations of the actual contingent relationships which are observable). Attention to both fantasy and the actual contingencies in the person's life is necessary in order to understand what maintains his behavior.

---

* The greater persistence of behavior that has been only intermittently reinforced, and its tendency to go on for a long time without further reinforcement, is quite relevant to consideration of notions of internalization. It is possible that phenomena such as guilt that persist despite the absence of external rebuke or punishment may be usefully understood in terms of infrequent intermittent reinforcements. Greenspan (1975), in his monograph on operant conditioning and psychoanalysis, provides some interesting discussions of reinforcement schedules and structure formation in the psychoanalytic sense. Greenspan's approach differs substantially from the present one, however, in viewing reinforcement contingencies as influencing behavior without the individual's mediating cognitions and organizing processes. Thus, unlike the present approach, his does not stress reinforcements as *perceived* but as "objectively" presented.

ASSURING THAT ADAPTIVE BEHAVIOR IS REINFORCED

As Chapter 10 stressed, it is important that the patient's efforts to act in a more adaptive and expansive way meet with success. In order to make this more likely, an approach was suggested in which care is taken to structure the patient's efforts in such a way that he is not taking on a challenge for which he is not prepared. The gradualism in the tasks and encounters into which he enters was likened in that chapter to the gradualism evident in systematic desensitization. In the present context it may be noted that this gradual approximation to the kind of functioning eventually desired is akin, as well, to the notion of "shaping" in the literature on operant conditioning.

As Bandura (1969, 1974) has pointed out, many Skinnerians are overly reliant on shaping, a method that is more necessary and appropriate in animal research than in working with human subjects. With animals, often the only way to communicate what is required is to reinforce some approximation to the criteron behavior that is fairly likely to occur, and gradually to "up the ante" as closer approximations to the criterion become more probable. With humans, one can often simply instruct the person as to the behavior desired, or model it.*

With humans too, however, shaping, or something akin to it, can be useful. A knowledge of the circumstances in which the patient is living can suggest to the therapist that the patient's current level of skill in interpersonal transactions will lead to success in certain kinds of efforts (or with certain people) and failure in others. With this in mind, the therapist can encourage the patient to extend himself in some directions and urge caution or patience in others. In this way, the patient can gradually build both adaptive skills and a sense of optimism and confidence. Reinforcement is not just a way of guiding or rewarding behavior, it is also a way of *sustaining* behavior in a particular direction, of maintaining a mood that will make discouraged abandonment of the effort less likely.

UNNOTICED REINFORCEMENTS

In considering the need for the patient to be reinforced for his efforts, it is important to recognize that, as stated earlier, the effective reinforcements are the reinforcements as perceived by the individual, not as "presented" in an "objective" fashion. Sometimes the reinforcing events

---

* As Bandura has also noted, exclusive reliance on shaping may be inefficient even with animals. In animal studies, too, modeling may frequently be sufficient to get across what the required behavior is.

are not recognized as such by the patient, but do act to sustain the behavior they follow. This is essentially what is meant by "unconscious gratification," and the aspects of experience that can function in this way are manifold. Many questions remain as to whether or in what ways such unacknowledged reinforcers differ in their effects from consciously acknowledged rewards or aims. (Cf. Brody, 1972; Spielberger and De Nike, 1966; Bandura, 1969; Silverman, 1972.)

At other times, the patient's failure to recognize that some desired event is a contingent consequence of his own behavior can impede progress even though, "objectively," the behavior is being rewarded. Such an occurrence was evident in the case of Mrs. Brown, discussed in Chapter 10. After the experience described in that chapter, in which she gained insight into how easy she had made it for her husband to ignore her, Mrs. Brown began, with the help of continued role-playing, to be more assertive with him. From her reports of her interactions with him it was clear that a good deal of change was occurring and that her new behavior was having substantial impact. It was also clear, however, that she was not experiencing her efforts as being successful and was becoming discouraged at what she perceived as a lack of effect.

Initially she had described her husband as literally unwilling to say even one word to her when the topic even approached feelings. After several sessions of role-playing and applying it in practice, they had had conversations of 10 or 15 minutes duration that dealt with some important issues between them. While such a level of interaction is, to be sure, still rather limited and far from what one would finally hope to see occurring, the change was nonetheless quite notable and rather directly at odds with her initial prediction that he would not budge an inch nor respond even with a single sentence. Yet this change, which two weeks before she had said could not be achieved "even with an elephant gun," now seemed to her not worth noticing at all. She could focus only on how far they still had to go, not at all on how far they had come.

Now, such a way of construing her experience can be understood in a number of ways. Traditional dynamic considerations, for example, are certainly relevant. Her not noticing the change could be seen as at least in part a motivated pattern of behavior, reflecting an overdetermined stake in old modes of adaptation and a fear of the feelings and inclinations that might be stirred by substantial change. In addition to this "resistance" view of what occurred, a more cognitive emphasis is also possible. New events that differ only slightly from expected events to which one has adapted are likely to be assimilated to old schema, and if the incremental changes continue to be small, it may be some time before the person realizes that a substantial amount of change has occurred.

Approaches to the problem of the patient's not experiencing any real effect from his or her efforts can also vary. At times, it is most appropriate to deal with the kind of difficulty presented by Mrs. Brown by interpreting her resistance and working on clarifying various fears and gratifications that motivated her non-perception. Sometimes, however, a simple and more direct approach is quite effective, and while it may not address some of the related issues, it may enable the particular change to occur more rapidly and hence to set in motion a reverberating set of events. Thus, one might ask a patient like Mrs. Brown to keep a written record of the length and content of her conversations with her husband. By this simple expedient she would be confronted concretely with the change that is occurring from interaction to interaction, and it would then be harder for her to ignore the progress that is being made. It would of course still be possible for her to deride the extent of the change, and more explicit resistance interpretations might also be required. But the direct technical intervention is at times quite useful and, as I have argued, need not interfere with also proceeding interpretively.*

WHAT IS REINFORCING FOR WHOM?

It is important to be clear that when behavior that is apparently being reinforced does not continue or increase, it is not always a result of the patient's not noticing the contingencies. Frequently the patient does notice the contingencies, but his or her aims (either conscious or unconscious) are different from the "average expectable" aims that are being assumed. To some extent, this is an issue that has been of concern both to behaviorally as well as dynamically oriented writers. Mischel (1973b), for example, has stressed a view of behavior therapy as concerned with the unique, idiosyncratic features of the patient's personality, including the particular reinforcers that are appropriate for him. The Premack principle (Premack, 1965) of permitting the person to engage in high-frequency behaviors as a reward for behaviors of lower frequency is similarly a basis for behavior therapists to focus upon the unique reinforcing events for any individual. Nonetheless, if one observes behavior therapists at work, or examines the case studies in the behavioral literature, it is clear that there has been a far greater tendency by behavior therapists than by dynamic therapists to assume that what the person

---

* For still another aspect of the problem of people not experiencing rewards as following from their own actions, see the important work of Seligman (1974).

wants are the things that are culturally standard (see Chapter 7). Behaviorally oriented clinicians and researchers have made their greatest contribution in elucidating the effects of the *scheduling* of rewards (regardless of content) and in indicating how explicit consideration of rewards and punishments can play a role in therapeutic strategy. The psychodynamic tradition has provided far more consideration of the often surprising range of events that seem to be sought by different people.

Frequently it is assumed that praise is an excellent all-purpose reinforcer, and, of course, praise is often something people strive for and feel rewarded by. But the motivational properties of praise are far more complicated than is frequently assumed. At times, for example, praise carries with it an implicit demand for more, and even better, accomplishments in the future. I have seen a variety of unfortunate patterns of living that had their origin in parental use of praise in such a way as to keep the developing child on an accelerating treadmill. In the context of their families' communication patterns, "That's very good" was experienced by these children as "I care whether you achieve. You got this far, so now I expect the next step." As young adults, these patients rejected the inexorable demands they had striven to meet, but they could leave the treadmill only by a frantic leap, a radical rejection of all achievement striving and all seeking after praise. This left them paralyzed and isolated, and it puzzled those who reached out to them with more benign positive responses, only to be treated as insincere taskmasters.

A related kind of way in which praise can become aversive is when a person is praised for qualities he does not have. In such instances, the praise can have the effect of calling attention to the defect and, particularly if it comes from a parent, can lead to a feeling that one is not being seen for who he really is, because who he really is is not good enough. The parent, needing to see the child as perfect, does not praise in an appropriate and realistic way that includes recognition and acceptance of the child's limitations, but praises *everything* in a way that implies that everything *must* be praiseworthy. One man, for example, who despite considerable talents struggled for quite some time to achieve a sense of being accepted and respected, was praised by his father for his physique and athletic prowess at a time when he was painfully thin and a mediocre athlete. Though not clearly articulated by him at the time, the effect of praise such as this seems to have been to leave him feeling that he *ought* to be an "all-American" type and that his intellectual talents were of little value (even though these, too, were praised by his father). In later years, it was very hard for him to believe that praise was based on genuine respect and a correct perception of him. This is related to the issue of the perceived "sincerity" of praise, or other interpersonal reinforcers and will be taken up further later in this chapter.

I have spoken thus far of "praise" rather globally. Though at times, as in the first set of cases just described, almost all praise is experienced as tainted, more frequently a discrimination is made so that some praise is valued and other praise is not. Thus, for example, an individual may find praise for his or her intellect very rewarding, but praise for appearance discomfiting (or vice versa). Or praise from a peer may be valued highly and praise from an authority mistrusted, or signs of "respect" may be valued and signs of being "liked" taken as reflective of weakness.

Quite frequently, the reinforcement being sought is more specific than such global concepts as "praise," "attention," or "positive regard" would suggest. A hypochondriacal patient, for example, for whom the attention he receives is an important factor in maintaining his preoccupation, will not necessarily readily change if the "same" reinforcement (attention) is offered for acting in a more mature and independent fashion. Careful observation may suggest that it is not "attention" that is reinforcing for him, but "attention-for-passivity" or "attention-for-suffering." Such specificity in the content of reinforcement may be overlooked when one's clinical work is based on laboratory-derived models in which one rather global motive (such as hunger) is artificially made prepotent, and the scheduling rather than the content of the reinforcements thereby is made the predominant concern.

UNCONSCIOUS MOTIVES AND CONFLICTS

The last example leads us to the most important, and most controversial, aspect in defining and accounting for non-normative reinforcements. In exploring clinically why a patient seeks attention-for-suffering more than attention-for-achieving, one frequently finds that the end sought is a kind of compromise and that understanding this aim and its vicissitudes requires inferring a number of motivational tendencies that the patient does not acknowledge and that conflict with each other. Among these tendencies, inferred from aspects of overt behavior as well as from dreams and fantasies, are some that are antisocial, childish, or at odds with the person's conscious sense of what is right and worthwhile. Demonstrating the importance or validity of inferences about unconscious motives or the role of conflict is not a simple or straightforward matter. It requires consideration of a variety of criteria for "proof," and a complex web of interlocking observations. The reader who is implacably opposed to the use of such concepts is unlikely to be persuaded by any presentation of the issues that is of less than book length itself, and I know of no fully satisfactory single work on the topic to which the reader can be referred. Various discussions in this volume and elsewhere (Wachtel, 1973b, in press) point to some of the issues that seem to me relevant, but they hardly constitute "proof." A definitive presentation of the necessity for concepts of unconscious motivation and fantasy seems to me both needed and possible—but despite all that has been written on this topic, no work has yet appeared that presents the logic of inference, the clinical data base, and the controlled research findings in a maximally effective way. Those of us who are persuaded of the value of such concepts base our view on a range of observations and considerations that is hard to organize or summarize. The following description of how to make use of reinforcement concepts in the therapy hour is primarily directed to clinicians who find at least some kind of notion of unconscious motive and conflict to be appropriate; but the reader who is more skeptical in this regard may nonetheless find that, perhaps with some change of language, much of what follows is relevant to his concerns as well.

## REINFORCEMENT IN THE THERAPY SESSION

The image of the therapist who does not respond contingently, who can communicate "unconditional positive regard" irrespective of what the patient is doing or saying, is probably not a very realistic one. Truax (1966), for example, in a widely cited analysis of tapes of a successful therapy by Rogers, has reported findings that suggest that even this vigorous opponent of contingent reinforcement does respond differentially to different kinds of patient statements, and that those kinds of statements that are followed by empathic or accepting therapist statements tend to increase in frequency.

Bandura (1969) cites a number of other studies also suggesting that unconditionally acceptant behavior by the therapist is "virtually impossible," and further argues that to the degree that it is, "abundant social responsiveness provided on . . . a 'nonconditional' basis can neither create nor maintain beneficial personality characteristics." (p. 77) Several considerations are relevant in evaluating such a claim.

### THE ROLE OF NONCONTINGENT ACCEPTANCE

First of all, it should be recalled that no therapeutic effort is likely to be successful if it is based on a faulty understanding of the patient's experiences and the factors that determine them. A correct understanding is not easy to obtain. Dynamic therapists have, of course, made achieving and imparting such understanding almost coterminous with what they view the therapist's skill and mission to be. But behavior therapists too often regard the achievement of a thorough and accurate behavioral analysis as the major task for the highly trained professional, and at times even regard the implementation of the therapeutic regimen as a lower-level task that can be accomplished by technicians with far less training.

Achieving a clear understanding of the patient's experiences, dilemmas, and life style may be greatly facilitated by a largely noncontingent, acceptant approach by the therapist. Unless the patient trusts the therapist a good deal, he is unlikely to reveal to him the full complexity of his psychological functioning, especially those aspects of himself that clash with social taboos or self-imposed standards of adequacy or worthiness. There is much that is secret and vulnerable in all of us, especially those of us at the point of entering psychotherapy. From conscious withholding, to unnoticed selective reporting and remembering, to prolonged and active efforts at self-deception, we all have ways of presenting ourselves that are likely to hide just those things most relevant in maintaining our neurotic problems. Only with a good deal of experience with gradually revealing more and more "dangerous" things to the therapist, and finding them accepted, is the patient likely to reveal what is necessary for a full understanding of his problems. This is, of course, a basic tenet of traditional psychotherapy, and the analysis of Dollard and Miller (1950), discussed in Chapter 6, makes it clear that such a view is readily understandable in learning theory terms.

Additionally, it is important to recognize that even where the therapist has the intention of relying heavily on the use of differential reinforcement, he must have significant reinforcements to dispense if he is to have an influence. Here again, the heavy emphasis on *contingencies* and *schedules* in operant research has led many operant-oriented behavior therapists to be less attentive to the issue of *what* is reinforcing, a matter far more complex when one is dealing with troubled human beings than with laboratory animals, or even with humans in the artificial constraining influence of the psychological experiment. Understanding just which events are reinforcing is essential. Not every nod or "uh huh" or "good" from any person will be particularly desirable. It is only when the therapist becomes a highly valued figure that his approval becomes a powerful motivating force. One of the ways in which this happens is for him to be for some time a warm, accepting figure who does not make demands or require that the patient work, conform, or pretty himself up in order to be heard respectfully and attentively.

But if such a noncontingent, accepting attitude seems important for the success of the therapeutic effort, it may also be the case that feeling free to actively intervene at a later stage may be an important guarantor of the therapist's ability to *be* noncontingent in the beginning. Findings such as those of Truax (1966), which suggest that unconditional acceptance is not so easily achieved, may reflect the difficulty of doing so when the entire burden of the therapeutic enterprise rests on it. Therapists who permit themselves no explicit influence upon the patient's behavior may be more prone to attempt such influence subtly and covertly. Therapists who expect to exert active efforts to bring about change at a later point, on the other hand, may more readily be able to hold efforts at influence in abeyance until they have a clearer picture of the patient's difficulties and a firmer relationship based on empathy and acceptance. Such therapists may well be able to listen and respond noncontingently in the early stages of the therapy. Empirical research along these lines would be very useful.

### THE NATURE OF THE THERAPIST'S REINFORCEMENTS

To grant that the therapist does, and perhaps even should, act in such a way as to exert a systematic influence upon what the patient does, says, or even thinks seems to open a Pandora's box of ethical and tactical questions. The former will be discussed primarily in Chapter 12. At this point I wish to look a bit more closely at just what kinds of events and processes are being referred to when the therapist is described as "reinforcing" the patient's behavior.

As the earlier discussion on "stimulus control" should make clear, this is hardly an unambiguous, cut-and-dried issue. The therapist does not dispense a pellet that automatically strengthens whatever behavior has just occurred (nor, probably, does the laboratory worker have his effect this way, though for him such a conception does not lead to quite as thoroughly misleading expectations). The most obvious and probably the most frequent way in which the therapist is influential through selective and contingent responding is by approving of the patient's actions, saying "that's good," and so on. Such therapist comments are often rewarding in their own right and serve as well to provide the patient with information as to whether his actions are of a sort to help solve his dilemma. But several problems associated with the therapist's approving of the patient's actions are worth pointing out.

First of all, I have noticed in my observations of behavior therapists that there is a rather common tendency to make praise too effusive. Frequent and exaggerated responding with "beautiful!" "marvelous!" "that's wonderful!" and the like can have the effect of cheapening the value of the therapist's comments, rendering them largely ineffective. A kind of psychological inflation occurs in which, figuratively, a wheelbarrow full of "beautifuls" by the therapist has very little currency in the patient's psychological economy. Extensions of adaption-level theory (Helson, 1964) into the personality realm suggest that such effusive praise can be assimilated to become a kind of baseline, requiring still greater reactions for there to be any impact.

In more everyday language, it may simply be noted that when the therapist praises too frequently and too effusively, he may be experienced as insincere.

In a related vein, it is important that the therapist's criteria for what merits praise be reasonably related to the patient's own criteria. To be sure, one of the important problems many patients present is that they have overly strict criteria for what is praiseworthy, and the therapist should not duplicate the standards of a harsh superego. But some accommodation must be made to what is experienced as a meaningful advance *by the patient*. When the therapist wishes to train the patient to be less strict with himself and more receptive to incremental advances, he would be well-advised to couch his praise in ways that explicitly acknowledge the patient's own differing standards. Thus, in responding to a report of a pleasant conversation with a woman by an isolated man who is also harshly deprecatory of his own "feeble" efforts, it would likely be a mistake to respond with "Beautiful, that's really great." Rather, the spirit of one's response might be: "In the past you've reacted to something like this by dismissing it and feeling that if you didn't go to bed with her, then you're a failure. But I really think it's important to recognize that you did take a step, and did so effectively and with pleasure."

It is also important to recognize that, as noted earlier, praise can be experienced as punishing. Not only is this the case when it implies demands, as discussed previously, it is also so at times in situations such as the one just described. If, by over-praising, the therapist appears to the patient to be naive, to not understand, or to be insincere, this can be very distressing to the patient as a sign that he has lost the hope of a relationship he can respect and count on. Additionally, in a not infrequent number of cases, praise or approval can be frightening as a sign that the therapist is getting too close. Closeness can be a threat if it comes before the patient feels ready for it, perhaps at a time when he still feels it is likely to make him open up and become vulnerable to being hurt later. Sullivan's (1953) discussions of the "malevolent transformation" and Guntrip's (1969) of "schizoid" phenomena are very relevant in this regard.

Finally, profuse and ostentatious praise can be problematic because the patient can come to view his adaptive behavior as done solely to get the therapist's praise and can fail to develop a sense of intrinsic satisfaction from behaving in a more adaptive and expansive way. When such is the case, the new behavior is likely to stop when praise from the therapist is no longer forthcoming, and is thus unlikely to be sustained very long after the therapy is terminated. As was noted earlier, reinforcement no longer seems well understood in terms of an automatic stamping-in of responses as a function of the stimuli that contingently follow. The effects of reinforcement seem better understood in terms of the complex interactions of cognitive and motivational variables. Among the factors increasingly recognized to be important is the person's *attribution* regarding his own behavior. If he perceives his behavior as occurring only in the service of some extrinsic reward, he is far more likely to revert to earlier patterns when that specific reward is not available than if he experiences himself as acting that way because he *wants* to. (Cf. Bowers, 1974; Levine and Fasnacht, 1974.)

MORE SUBTLE AND UNRECOGNIZED REINFORCEMENTS

Thus far I have been discussing relatively explicit and clear-cut reinforcements by the therapist—praise, encouragement, approval, and so forth. Often, however, the therapist may act in rewarding or punishing ways that are less intentional or obvious but that nonetheless have an important influence upon the patient. Such reinforcing events present less problems from an attributional point of view—the patient is likely to be unaware that he is responding to them, and hence unlikely to attribute any change in his behavior to their effect—but they present another problem much more difficult to deal with: since they are subtle and generally not consciously intended, they are less subject to the therapist's control and hence capable of conflicting with his conscious therapeutic strategy.

There has been relatively little systematic study of these influences, though they are casually acknowledged to exist by most therapists. As social beings we are influenced by and attuned to far more than the explicit verbal messages others offer. Tone of voice, posture, gesture, rhythm, and a variety of other dimensions of people's behavior can exert an enormous influence upon us, as the skillful actor or orator is well aware. But rarely are all these aspects of our communication to others in fact skillfully under conscious control. Only in a highly treasured myth does the therapist's attention hover evenly at all times; being mortal, we therapists are sometimes acutely responsive and sometimes adrift in a daydream. Frequently this is somehow communicated to the patient, and if systematically related to his behavior, it can influence that behavior to change or persist. Similarly (if face-to-face), variations in our eye contact, a stifled yawn, a leaning forward or backward, a half-conscious glance at the clock, or an intermittent brushing of lint from one's trousers can serve the same function as a "very good" or a "that's wrong."

If the patient is on the couch, some of these communication media are not in operation, but there are plenty of others, and their significance is probably enhanced by their exclusivity. Not only tone of voice, style of phrasing, or selectivity in content can serve as guides or goads. Perhaps loudest of all is silence. In the classical psychoanalytic situation, silence is an extraordinarily important communication medium. Though it is the typical background or context for the patient's associations, and hence seemingly as unobservable as is the sea by the fish who swim in it, it is a turbulent and changeable sea whose currents can be sensed by the patient and can influence his associations and his feelings. There are hostile silences, accepting silences, baffled silences, and depriving silences, and each has its own impact.

To be sure, the silence does not exert its influence upon the patient directly, without mediation by the patient's expectations and fantasies. A silence that reflects the therapist's fear of what he might say can be experienced by the patient as a sign of calm acceptance of what he has just communicated; similarly, a silence that reflects sympathetic, interested listening and an effort to understand what the patient means before responding can be experienced as a spiteful withholding of help.

But in even the most "fully analyzed" of therapists, there are likely to be patterns to his silence—or rather, to his silence and talking, for what makes silence significant is that the therapist is not always silent. Sometimes he talks and sometimes he does not, and in some sense he is constantly deciding and choosing to do one or the other. There have been few, if any, studies of the systematic relation between various kinds of patient behaviors or communications and the occurrence of speech or silence by the therapist. My hunch is that therapists who would volunteer to participate in such studies would be shocked (and enlightened) by what was discovered, and that aspects of the patient's behavior would be found to correspond reliably to the pattern discerned (and perhaps would be found to change if the therapist, alerted to what he had been doing, began to behave differently).

Put simply, we say "yes" and "no" in far more ways than we are usually willing to acknowledge, and while these responses are by no means omnipotent, they are heard; and their impact is substantial. The associations that travel along paths laid out in the patient's inner world of fantasy, memory, and desire are guided as well by road signs plentifully posted by the therapist.

## REINFORCEMENT IN INTERPRETATION

These subtle, nonverbal reinforcing features of the therapist's behavior are particularly important and intriguing as they interact with the interpretive aspect of the therapist's activity. Our understanding of what the therapist is really doing, and why he succeeds (or fails) is, I believe, considerably enhanced by recognizing how much of what is intended as a relatively neutral effort to explicate or clarify serves as well to influence through encouragement, criticism, and so on.*

### INTERPRETING DEFENSES AND RESISTANCES

One of the important developments in psychoanalytic technique that accompanied increased interest in the ego was the rule that one interprets resistance or defense before interpreting impulse. This was in many ways a very sound bit of clinical advice. Not only does premature, unprepared interpretation of an unconscious trend have little convincing impact (it may even *increase* resistiveness, make the person *less* likely to experience the impulse as really his), but also, focusing upon the defensive activities is a prime way of making the patient aware of an-

---

* As discussed below, this perspective should not be taken to suggest that interpretations are *nothing but* reinforcements.

other equally important aspect of himself that he has failed to fully appreciate and that is of great importance in his life. Further, as discussed in Chapter 9, calling attention to a defensive activity can be a way of interrupting its effective functioning, and hence allowing to emerge that which it is warding off.

Thus with a very obsessional individual, for example, it is not likely to be very useful to make "deep" interpretations without first working on how he makes *any* interpretation simply an "interesting" idea, which he may evaluate for its logical fit to the data but which does not lead him to experience a previously rejected aspect of himself or to be motivated to change. Pointing out to the patient how his choice of words, his measured tone, or his diligent examination of alternatives serve to curtail certain experiences can be very valuable. With one man, for example, I found that simply pointing out over and over again how he always referred to his experiences in terms of "perhaps" ("perhaps that means I'm angry," "perhaps I don't really care for her," and so on) eventually led not only to a reduction of this particular behavior but also (and here I am, of course, only guessing at the causal link) to an opening and enrichment of his experiencing as well.

But this time-honored bit of clinical strategy can lead to serious problems if it is not tempered by another consideration that is essentially one of reinforcement and shaping. The considerations discussed below are probably (implicitly or explicitly) evident in the work of a good many traditional dynamic therapists, but I have also heard a number of experienced colleagues discuss their work in ways that suggest that they are not sufficiently attuned to these matters; and in supervising beginning therapists, I have seen quite substantial neglect of these matters on their part. Perhaps because student therapists are especially likely to follow the "letter of the lore," they may be prone early in their work to interpret defenses almost relentlessly and may particularly need to be shown the rewarding or punishing aspects of their "interpretations."

Consider, for example, an obsessional patient such as described above. The dynamically trained clinician is likely to be keenly attuned to subtle as well as gross manifestations of the patient's defensive strategy. He will notice the wide variety of ways in which the patient can seemingly be dealing with significant emotional issues but in such a way as to render them relatively devoid of affect. If such a patient does begin to take a small, tentative step in the direction of fuller experience of a conflicted trend in his personality, it is likely still to be with noteworthy hedging and intellectualizing. Attuned to this less obvious aspect of the patient's behavior (and perhaps prouder of his ability to detect this defensive activity than the change in content, which even the non-clinician might notice) and guided as well by the clinical maxim that the defense is interpreted first, many clinicians would be prone to focus primarily on the warding-off aspect of the behavior. The patient might be told that he is referring to his anger at his mother as if it were some "thing" he were examining rather than something he felt, or that his tone of voice did not seem to reflect the anger he said he felt, or that the phrase "somewhat annoyed" that he used seemed to take back what he was trying to say. All of this might be true, yet clinically the wrong thing to say.

I would suggest that what is most important to consider, with regard to the balance of expression and defense, is the direction of the change from his previous behavior that this instance represents. Thus, if he had been talking more openly and affectively, and then shifted somewhat in an intellectualizing direction, it would be important to be attuned to this and to "interpret the defense." But if he had previously been *even more* intellectualized than he was at the moment, I would contend that it is a mistake to focus on this aspect of his behavior. To do so is to implicitly convey the message that his change toward more open expression was not good enough and is likely to have the effect of discouraging further efforts in this direction. To say instead something like "You're talking about your anger toward your mother with more feeling than you had before" (even if he is also still being considerably more intellectualized than most) is likely to have the opposite effect. It is an accepting encouragement of his change toward more open expression; rather than leaving the patient feeling frustrated and inadequate, it enhances his sense of being able to change and to cope with his anxiety. It is likely to lead to further efforts along the same lines.

Recently, a student therapist whom I was supervising reported to me the following incident. The patient was a teenage girl who had considerable difficulty in accepting that she had any role in what happened to her and who, partly because of her stance of passivity and her self-pitying attitude, had had rather little success with boys. In a session reported to me, the patient indicated that boys had been treating her more nicely recently. From the context, it was clear that this was a result of some changes she had made in how she related to them, yet she reported the change in a tone which suggested that she had nothing to do with it. The student therapist was sensitive to this and said to her, "You say it as if you had nothing to do with it," to which the patient (characteristically) responded, "It doesn't matter what I do, you don't think it's good enough."

I suggested to the student that the same point could have been made in a way that built upon and encouraged the step that the patient had taken by responding instead with, "Well, I guess you were doing something right to get that response from the boys." (I might have regarded the student therapist's comment as appropriate if it had been made at a stage in the therapy when the patient had largely given up her tendency to see herself as a passive observer of her own life, and the patient's comment were a return to a previous maladaptive mode; here, however, the patient is reporting an important advance, even if it is reported rather grudgingly.)

In a related vein, an extremely self-critical and self-deprecating patient told me in a session of having been riding in a car with another person when the car broke down on the highway. Having recently been reading a book on auto repairs for women, she was able to figure out what was wrong and said what she thought to her companion. It was clear that she enjoyed being able to do this, and enjoyed telling me about it as well. In the telling, she also went on to say that this was the only thing she knew about cars, that basically she was very ignorant. Such a statement was consistent with her defensive minimizing of her own achievements and her efforts to keep a tight rein on expansive and pleasurable feelings. On another occasion I might well have wanted to call attention to how she hedges her expressions of pride and competence. In this instance, however, it seemed important to me not to engage in a discussion of where she fell short, even if my perception was in a certain sense "correct." Instead, I simply said that I could see she took pleasure in her competence on this occasion and was glad to see that she was now allowing herself this. My decision as to what to say was based on my view that the incident had represented a meaningful step for her, and I wanted to respond in a way that was positive and encouraging, rather than following her report of this change in her behavior with a negative comment. As interpretations, both commenting on her pleasure or commenting on her hedging (or mentioning both aspects) would be accurate. But recognizing that what was an interpretation from one perspective could be viewed as a reinforcement from another led to the particular choice I made.

### SHAPING AND REINFORCEMENT

In the above discussion I am implicitly drawing upon the operant concept of shaping. Often the ultimately desired behavior (for example, with the obsessional, the rather direct expression of feeling unhedged by obsessional modifying and undoing) is not within the person's current repertoire of behaviors, and it is necessary initially to choose a less desirable approximation to the ultimate criterion in order to reinforce the trend or direction to his behavior that will eventually lead to the more fully satisfactory activities. As he begins to shift his behavior in the desired direction, the criterion for reinforcement is changed in the direction of closer approximation to the final goal behavior. Thus behavior by the patient which at one point draws the comment, "You seem to be talking straighter to me today," might at another elicit only silence, and at still another elicit a "defense interpretation" (for example, "You sound like you're telling me what makes logical sense to you, rather than what you're really feeling").

The point, then, is not that one never interprets defenses or points out to the patient how he is evading the task of honest self-confrontation and expression. Rather, the issue is whether the particular way of putting it that you hear at any given moment represents progress (even if minimal), stalemate, or retreat. The particular expression must be understood not only as a particular mix of expressiveness and defensiveness, but as a point in a sequence of behavior whose meaning for the therapeutic process cannot be understood out of context. In a seminar early in my postdoctoral analytic training, the late Harry Bone expressed considerable concern over clumsy comments by therapists that could crush the first tiny sprouts of a new way of being and prevent the later flowering of a richer, more expansive way of life. Bone was at that point interested in and emphasizing the relevance for analytic work of Rogers's approach, but his lesson has at least as much Skinner in it as Rogers. The former would have had little impact on psychology had he required of the organisms he reinforced that they measure up right away. Shaping can certainly be described in ways that reflect a cold, manipulative stance, but it can also be understood in terms of patience, of understanding what an individual is up to at any point, and of gentle encouragement of incremental progress toward a desired goal. And it is no more "true" that the patient is still being defensive than it is that he is taking a step in the direction that will lead him away from self-constriction and distortion.

The rule of interpreting defense before impulse can now be viewed from a somewhat different perspective. Early in the therapeutic work (or in work on some particular issue), the patient is likely to manifest the far from satisfactory compromise he has tried to get by with for some time. At this time, it is useful for the therapist to focus primarily on how the patient is defending, both enlightening the patient on this matter and implicitly discouraging the further use of this mode of experiencing and relating. As the balance shifts, and the patient begins ever so slightly to modify his defensive activity, the therapist can shift his interpretive comments so as to highlight the shifting balance and the value of the change. Thus, here he might either note the reduction in defensiveness or increased directness of expression, or respond directly to the content, along the lines of "I hear you telling me more today about how angry your mother can make you at times." As in traditional descriptions, he refrains from making his comments "too deep," staying with what the patient is ready to notice and experience.

Most likely, progress will be far from monotonic. The patient will either stay on a plateau for a while, trying out the new compromise that the therapist has just reacted to encouragingly, or perhaps even retreating to the previous, more elaborately defensive behavior that had been implicitly punished by interpreting it. (He can do this for a great many reasons, one of the most important of which is a temporary spontaneous recovery in the level of anxiety that was largely responsible for the nature of the presenting compromise. See Chapter 6.) At this point, the therapist can again start pointing out the defensive aspect of the behavior (whether in the case of a retreat or of a lingering plateau that threatens to stagnate the therapy), with, it is hoped, the effect of again leading to slightly less defensive behavior. When this happens, he can again direct his remarks to the change or to the new content that begins to emerge. Thus, from this perspective, whether the therapist interprets content or defense depends largely on whether the patient has just moved in the direction of more openly expressive behavior, has been standing for a while on a plateau, or has been retreating from a previously achieved position.

As the therapeutic work proceeds, the patient is, one hopes, more likely to be moving in ways counter to his previous defensive mode, and so content interpretations are more likely to be appropriate. The therapist is, of course, *interpreting;* that is, to some extent, he is explicating aspects of the patient's behavior that the patient himself did not fully recognize. But to be effective, the interpretation must still be fairly close to the patient's experience and capable of being acknowledged by the patient. Thus, the interpretation still has the implicit message, "I sense that you are reaching out to tell me such and such and am pleased to hear it." Though interpretations later in therapy are "deeper," they are no less bound by the rule that they are not likely to be useful unless they are fairly close to what the patient can then deal with. They are "deeper" more from the frame of reference of where the patient started than from where he is now.

Defense interpretations do not disappear at this late stage. Therapeutic progress is inevitably variable, and there are times at all stages of therapy when the patient is retreating from expansiveness and direct expression rather than groping toward it. At these times, defense interpretations are still appropriate. They may be expected to occur less frequently at the late stage of therapy, but they do not disappear altogether.

Budding (if still far from satisfactory) adaptive changes can be undermined not only by clumsy interpretations by the therapist, but by the patient's own evaluations as well. Many patients will, because of their own defensive style, react with self-criticism whenever they have started to take a positive step. The motivations for such a pattern can be manifold, and depending on what they are, the appropriate strategy for intervention will vary to some extent. But in almost all instances it is important for the therapist to find some way of calling attention to the progress the patient is making and not to be distracted by the patient's focus on self-deprecation.

On more than one occasion I have had the experience of seeing a patient make a good deal of progress on some aspect of his problems and then finding myself mired in a tangle of new, elusive complaints, seemingly reflecting "deeper" layers of the personality and carrying either the implicit or explicit message that the previous progress was superficial and based on denial of the underlying weakness or even rottenness of the personality. Usually, what was happening would not be clear at first, because the new focus either emerged gradually or seemed a response to some external event that could not have been predicted. But when, in wrestling with my own discouragement and sense of stagnation, I have recalled the previous period of movement and begun to refocus in that direction, interesting things have tended to happen. Not infrequently, the seemingly deeper and more genuine soul-wrenchings have turned out to be a diversion which seemed best understood as a distraction from the new behaviors and feelings that were beginning to become evident in the period of progress. Sometimes just a simple comment like "Despite all this I get the sense you've continued to be more direct with people" has done the trick. On other occasions, it was necessary to focus a good deal on the fear of what was emerging and on the defensive nature of the current pessimism before the crisis was passed.

In retrospect, these episodes have seemed like crucial choice-points or tests in which the sincerity of my interest in the patient really living differently was being sorely tried. Having based his whole life on the view that he had to behave in a particular way, at any price, in order to be accepted, he was not ready to trust my good faith easily. The discouraging diversion seemed designed to give me an "out," to let the new ways of feeling and acting sink back into the sea unless I made a special effort to retrieve them again. Therein would my commitment be demonstrated.

Such a maneuver is a dangerous one for the patient, for failure on the part of a therapist to see such a pattern can result from far more than just lack of genuine acceptance of the patient's new way of being. The patient's skill in disguise, or the therapist's lack of skill in noticing it, can lead to a snowballing of pessimism and failure even if the patient is wrong in thinking that he dare not really carry through on the new patterns. I have begun to wonder if one or more such periods of testing by means of pessimistic retreat may not be essential in almost every deep psychotherapeutic change, and I have begun both to look more carefully for when such a pattern may be beginning and to ponder whether past failures may have been due particularly to failure to detect just such retreats and to maintain a focus on the matters where change had begun to occur. Regularly asking oneself what aspects of the patient's unproductive patterns of living have begun to change and being sure to keep the patient noticing such changes may be a valuable antidote to such puzzling and discouraging unraveling of the therapeutic skein.

### INTERPRETATION AND UNDERSTANDING

Discussion of the various ways in which comments usually viewed as interpretations may be seen in terms of reinforcement should not be taken as negating the traditional role of such comments. It is rare for someone to come for psychotherapy who does not—and does not need to—gain a clearer, more encompassing sense of his own desires and of the assumptions that guide his pursuit of those desires. The conditions of our upbringing—both those specific to Western industrial society and those deriving from the simple biological fact that humans are helpless and dependent when young and unable to comprehend the world very well—assure that we will become afraid of various of our thoughts and feelings and will develop and present a picture of ourselves that is incomplete and at least somewhat inaccurate. Much human misery is the result of building life strategies on the basis of a mistaken view of self and world, hedged by fears no longer appropriate to the full-grown person. The interpretive process in psychotherapy provides an opportunity for reexamining the basis for our way of life. Statements made by the therapist in the course of this re-examination inevitably are experienced as rewarding or punishing, and have an important role in leading to change by virtue of this. But unless such statements also further our understanding of what we are about, their positive effect is likely to be limited.

In my own work I find that, even since my commitment to the value of active intervention, I spend a good deal of time in this kind of interpretive, clarifying effort. This reflects both my continuing belief that clearer self-understanding and deeper experiencing are of value in their own right and my sense that empathic, interpretive activity by the therapist frequently plays a major role in bringing about other kinds of change as well. For some patients, this way of working seems to be all they really need; and for a number of others, it is all they will accept, particularly early in the work. Even when explicit behavioral techniques play a major role in the treatment effort, I find the interpretive, clarifying aspect of the work to be critically important, not only in facilitating the patient's understanding but also in establishing a relationship in which he can count on me as someone interested in knowing all of him, not just what he has learned to "present."

*Ethical Considerations*

# 12

## *Some Questions of Ethics and the Image of Man*

To many traditional therapists the methods I have been discussing are unacceptable, even if they work, because they are seen as manipulative and demeaning of human dignity. The methods of the traditional therapist are seen, in contrast, as fostering the autonomous development of the patient's inherent potential, enabling him to grow according to his own innate plan or express his true self. The therapist's role is seen not as an influencer but as a kind of psychological midwife, present during the birth, possessed of useful skills, but in attendance mainly to see to it that a natural process does not go awry.

While this analogy expresses, I think, the spirit in which many therapists like to think they operate, it has its limitations. The patient's life history has brought him to a point where one can be fairly certain that the birth would not occur at all without the participation of the therapist. But, to stay within the metaphor, the traditional therapist would insist at the very least that he does not and cannot function like an obstetric surgeon performing a Caesarian; the birth cannot occur with the patient asleep and operated upon.

The view that behavioral methods are completely alien to the spirit of the psychotherapeutic enterprise is based, I believe, on both an exaggeration of the midwife aspect of the traditional therapist and an exaggeration of the surgeon-like qualities of the behavior therapist. On the one hand, traditional therapists have generally not come to terms with their role as influencers of their patients' behavior. And on the other, they have failed to recognize how much the success of the behavior therapist's efforts depends on his establishing an active, cooperative relationship with the patient in which, far from being asleep and acted upon, the patient must be doing things in order to change.

Part of the responsibility for the erroneous picture so commonly held regarding the work of behavior therapists must be attributed to the writings of behavior therapists themselves. Although more recent writings on such matters as self-control and on the therapeutic relationship in behavior therapy have begun to correct the picture, the behavioral literature has tended to talk of control of behavior and manipulation of variables in a way that does make their work and point of view sound cold, mechanical, and antithetical to conceptions of human choice and freedom. Such a picture is no doubt partly a reaction to the excessive *denial* of influence so common in the traditional therapeutic literature, and a reaction as well to the less than stringent standards of evidence that the traditional literature frequently employs. But in trying to be rigorous where the previous literature is perceived as sloppy, behavior therapists have often adopted a very narrow view of science and a "hardheaded" rhetoric that is poorly suited to express the gains in freedom and richness of experience that their methods can in fact help to bring about.

I will argue in this chapter that all therapists, of whatever persuasion—if they are at all effective—influence their patients. We are never just observers or interpreters. I will further argue that it is a false dichotomy to oppose structure, manipulation, and control to freedom, autonomy, growth, and choice. The same set of events can be seen through one lens as behavior determined by a variety of influences and through another as choices made in response to a variety of alternatives; neither view is a truer one. Freedom, autonomy, and choice, I will argue, are not antithetical to influence, advice, or direction, either philosophically or in practice.

There are many questions that can (and should) be raised about the *nature* of the therapist's influence. For example, is his influence being exerted in a direction that is in the patient's interest or in the service of the therapist's needs? Are some good ends, such as a reduction in the patient's anxiety, being achieved at the expense of other good ends, such as the patient's enhanced vision of the possibilities that life offers and an increased sense of self-directedness? Is the patient being fully informed of the kind of influence the therapist wishes to exert and the kind of ends being sought? Is the patient's choice being excessively influenced by a fear of displeasing the therapist rather than by what he himself would really prefer? These and other matters will be discussed, and I will point out instances where using behavioral methods makes these dilemmas more difficult (as well as ways in which they can ease some dilemmas that traditional methods make more acute). But I will insist that behavioral methods do not introduce influence or control into a situation in which there was none before. Psychotherapy is a situation in which one human being (the therapist) tries to act in such a way as to enable another human being to act and feel differently than he has, and this is as true of psychoanalysis as it is of behavior therapy.

## A PSYCHOANALYST'S VIEW OF BEHAVIOR THERAPY

Let us pursue these issues further by considering the depiction of behavior therapy by a particularly articulate psychoanalyst, Allen Wheelis. Wheelis (1973) describes behavior therapy as "a type of coercive treatment in which the therapist acts as agent for society, and the goal is adjustment." Though depicting behavior therapy as "less extreme" than brainwashing or lobotomy, he views it as essentially similar and contends that "[a]ll such treatment takes the person as object and seeks to achieve the desired change by manipulation." (pp. 103–04)

Wheelis goes on to say the following:

> We are in no position to comment on the efficacy of behavior therapy as generally practiced, but in principle we know it works. People may indeed be treated as objects and may be profoundly affected thereby. Kick a dog often enough and he will become cowardly or vicious. People who are kicked undergo similar changes; their view of the world and of themselves is transformed. The survivors of Hitler's concentration camps testify that the treatment received did have an effect. Nor find we reason to doubt the alleged results of Chinese thought-control methods. People may indeed be brainwashed, for benign or exploitative reasons.
>
> Behavior therapy is not, therefore, being contrasted with self-transcendence in terms of efficacy; the contrast is in terms of freedom. If one's destiny is shaped by manipulation one has become more of an object, less of a subject, has lost freedom. It matters little whether the manipulation is known to the person upon whom it acts. For even if one himself designs and provides for those experiences which are then to affect him, he is nevertheless treating himself as object—and to some extent, therefore, *becomes* an object.
>
> If, however, one's destiny is shaped from within then one has become more of a creator, has gained freedom. This is self-transcendence, a process of change that originates in one's heart and expands outward, always within the

purview and direction of a knowing consciousness, begins with a vision of freedom, with an "I want to become, . . ." with a sense of the potentiality to become what one is not. One gropes toward this vision in the dark, with no guide, no map, and no guarantee. Here one acts as subject, author, creator. (pp. 104–5)

Wheelis, in this passage, is not very different from a great many psychotherapists in their view of behavior therapy. Indeed, with his analogies to kicked dogs and Nazi concentration camps, his rhetoric here is riper than most and his rejection of behavioral methods, however efficacious they might be in bringing about change, seems even more absolute. What makes Wheelis's description so useful as a point of departure is that in almost every other passage of his small gem of a book he presents arguments that are strikingly consonant with those of the present volume, and that are precisely the sort of considerations that led me to turn toward behavioral methods.

Wheelis, for example, through most of his book avoids the false dichotomy between freedom and determinism which leads many to conclude that if such means of "control" are utilized, the patient's "freedom" is reduced. Wheelis states:

> Being the product of conditioning and being free to change do not war with each other. Both are true. They coexist . . . What makes a battleground of these two points of view is to conceive of either as an absolute which excludes the other. For when the truth of either view is extended to the point of excluding the truth of the other it becomes not only false but incoherent. We must affirm freedom and responsibility without denying that we are the product of circumstance, and must affirm that we are the product of circumstance without denying that we have the freedom to transcend that causality to become something which could not have been previsioned from the circumstances which shaped us. What destroys the behaviorist's argument is not the evidence marshalled to demonstrate that we are controlled by the environment—that is utterly convincing—but the use of that evidence to deny freedom. (pp. 87–88)

I could not agree more. Indeed, I have made a very similar point myself in a different context (Wachtel, 1969, pp. 653–54). If the behaviorist uses his data to "prove" we are not free, he is engaged in a fool's errand. For whether man is free is not an empirical matter, not something that can be settled by a set of observations; it is a point of view, a way of looking at things, a way of making sense out of whatever observations are made.

But it is precisely for this reason that I reject the view that to use the findings of behavioral research and the methods that have grown from them is to abandon concern with human freedom and choice. Questions of choice and responsibility are complemented by such work but never precluded. It is always appropriate to view man as choosing; the question is, what are the choices or alternatives that are available? The phobic perceives himself as having had available the options of approaching what he fears and thereby experiencing excruciating terror, or avoiding what he fears and thereby necessarily restricting his life. With systematic desensitization, a third alternative is available. He can commit himself to engage in a disciplined set of experiences that can enable him to re-expose himself to what he has feared without having to undergo the terror. Systematic desensitization is, of course, not the *only* other alternative that might be found, either among formal therapeutic modalities or among possible strategies of living and coping. This is not my point. Rather, I wish to stress that such a method does provide one extra alternative that the individual might find a more attractive and workable choice, and that *he does have a choice.*

In Wheelis's view, even if engaging in such a procedure may be freely chosen, that is not sufficient to legitimatize it. "For even if one himself designs and provides for those experiences which are then to affect him, he is nevertheless treating himself as object—and to some extent, therefore, *becomes* an object."

Here, I think, Wheelis loses track of his earlier insights into conditioning and freedom as complementary perspectives. One does not become an object by being exposed to particular contingencies or conditions. All of us are at once conditioned and free and can no more eliminate the one than the other. Rather, the issue lies in the spirit in which the procedure is undertaken. Does the patient, in a spirit of helplessness, turn himself over to someone else who will tell him how to be saved? Or does he, out of desire to expand the boundaries of his life, seek out someone who can teach him how to develop the skills (say, in muscle relaxation or in structuring exposure) that can enable him to move beyond his phobic limits? The difference between the two is crucial, and the therapist operating within the framework I have described would be as concerned with helping the patient to see in which spirit he is approaching the procedure as he would with helping the patient learn the procedure itself. But he *would* be concerned with the latter as well; for as Wheelis himself makes clear, enhancing the experience of freedom and the richness and wholeness of one's life is not achieved by a *denial* of causality but by an *understanding* and *acceptance* of the causal nexus so that, from another perspective, one can use it to transcend it. The man who deconditions himself *can* make an object of himself thereby. But he can also use the procedure to be *less* an object, to be less at the mercy of his past history and more able to step forward into an expanding range of future choices.

More difficult problems seem to be raised by operant methods. Desensitization, after all, is a procedure limited in its focus to the reduction of anxiety. It is thus relatively easy (at least for me) to see it as in the service of freedom. For anxiety is one of the greatest *restrictions* on freedom; a method that enables its constricting influence to be diminished enables the person to perceive and explore more freely. Reinforcement contingencies, on the other hand, are not used exclusively to diminish anxiety but can be applied to any aspect of the person's behavior, to his choice of wife, job, religion, or political party, as well as to his courageous approach to an object feared since childhood. Moveover, those who use operant methods often do describe their work rather exclusively in terms of control, and subscribe to Skinner's (1971) view that freedom is only an illusion. Additionally, operant methods can seem to convey the message that the patient should not do what he intrinsically wants to do but should either be swayed by some material reward or engage in behavior because the therapist prefers it. Thus the dangers of conformity or alienation from one's innermost self seem here combined with the dangers that have existed throughout history when one individual or group uses rewards and punishments to influence the behavior of others; even if one restricted oneself to examples where the dispenser of rewards and punishments had good intentions, one could compile a rather chilling list.

These considerations should be taken seriously. To my mind, for example, the kinds of procedures that have been developed for systemically applying reinforcement contingencies in institutional settings are so subject to abuse that their use is rather questionable. Where they can be shown to be effective and where it is clear that there are no alternative ways to rescue the subject from a life that is miserable, empty, or destructive, they may be justified. But as a routine part of how society deals with deviant behavior, this particular approach raises very serious ethical questions.

Even apart from its use in institutions, where some people have a great deal of power over others, the deliberate use of reinforcement contingencies to bring about therapeutic change seems to raise serious problems. Are we ever justified, some ask, in helping people by manipulating them?

To frame the matter in terms of manipulation, however, is already to prejudge the issue. In some contexts, the term "manipulate" can have the rather benign connotation of working with skill and dexterity; but when it is raised in discussions of psychotherapy, its connotation is almost always that of one of its secondary dictionary definitions: ". . . to control, manage, or play upon by artful, unfair, or insidious means, especially to one's own advantage." * This hardly seems a humane way to treat another human being. If one instead speaks of the therapist as obligated to make a maximum effort to use his knowledge, skills, and understanding to help the patient free himself of a destructive cycle of events, the same message may be experienced rather differently. The therapist can indeed get across his approval or his questioning of a patient's behavior in the spirit of a puppet master pulling strings. But it is also possible, and legitimate, for the therapist to view what he is doing as honest communication in which the patient receives feedback both as to how another person experiences what he is doing and as to whether, on the basis of the therapist's experience and training, this seems to be a step toward freeing himself of the patterns of behavior that have brought him to therapy.

Confusion arises because reinforcement is viewed by many—proponents and opponents alike—as somehow having an inexorable controlling effect upon the person's behavior and rendering him incapable of choice, reducing him to an automaton or duly wound mechanism. The Skinnerian metaphysic is implicitly accepted by many traditional therapists, who seem to feel that if reinforcements are found occurring in the therapy room, then freedom has been checked at the door. I find more compelling Wheelis's arguments, noted above, for free choice and environmental control as complementary perspectives. Even when being "reinforced," people are making choices. There is no inexorable force making the patient do what the therapist finds desirable and somehow overriding his "real" desires. The therapist's reaction is one of many consequences the patient may consider in choosing a course of action.†

Reinforcements appear to have inexorable effects in Skinnerian experiments, because the organism has had imposed on it a state of deprivation which makes unlikely that anything else will seem worth considering other than what brings food (if the subject is a starved animal) or "privileges" (if the subject is an inmate on a token economy). It is the reinforcing agent's power to physically deprive that gives his reinforcements their seemingly inexorable power. And it is his power to impose

---

* *Webster's Third New International Dictionary of the English Language Unabridged.* Springfield, Mass.: G. & C. Merriam Co., 1971.

† See below (pp. 280–83) for a discussion of the question of whether the *therapist's* preferences, in particular, have a special power because of the transference that develops.

major deprivations upon uncooperative subjects that should be viewed with alarm—not the contingent nature of his response.


## INFLUENCE AND ABUSE

The distinction between contingent reactions by the therapist and the power to effect major deprivation if cooperation is not enlisted is important. Not only is it relevant to considerations about reinforcements, it also points to a larger distinction that is relevant to considering the use of systematic desensitization, modeling, role-playing, helping guide and structure real-life interactions, and—significantly—interpretations. The larger distinction is between influence (which is inherent in any human relationship) and abused power or control (which is both an exaggeration and a perversion of influence). In an effort to avoid the latter, some therapists have attempted to disavow the former as well. They have claimed that the therapist should, and can, have no interest in the patient choosing any course of action over any other or even in whether the patient changes or feels better as a result of the therapeutic contact, but should be interested only in furthering a process of self-understanding.°

Influence in itself, however, cannot be avoided, nor is there any reason why its avoidance, or even minimization, should be the goal of a humane facilitative interaction. Indeed, being able to be influenced is an essential part of living. The man whose choices are not responsive to what goes on about him, who cannot be influenced, is hardly alive at all. And the therapist who has no influence might as well not be there.

Shapiro's (1965) description of the obsessive-compulsive personality depicts a person who is minimally influenced by others, who maintains his direction regardless of what is said by the other. He shows vividly how barren such a life is. The healthy personality does not make his choices of alternative courses of action solely on the basis of some "inner" promptings; he is alive to all the potential cues that are available to help him gauge the realities of his situation and the potential consequences of

---

° What complicates matters is that the process of self-understanding is viewed as having the result, when it works right, of leading to feeling better and to a change toward more adaptive and satisfying behavior. Thus the question of whether the process of understanding is really the sole or overriding goal, and specific behavior changes really not sought, does not have to get addressed. In fact, when the latter does not occur, the former tends to be assumed to have been faulty or incomplete. Thus the therapist can claim he does not care about behavior change and yet remain in business.

his actions. The therapist who tries to remove himself as a source of such cues does not thereby change the nature of the patient's choice from one of adjustment or conformity-to-external-standards to one of true inner-directedness; he merely removes one possible (and potentially very valuable) source of information from the array that the patient will examine before deciding.

In fact, the very distinction between external influence and genuine, inner-directed behavior is one fraught with confusion. To be sure, the distinction points to something crucially important. There is indeed a vast difference between the person who has a firm sense of who he is and what he wants, who lives his life with a feeling of zest and wholeness, and the person who senses himself as yielding now to this pressure, now to that, rarely feeling sure he wants to do what he is doing or caring very deeply about anything. Numbed, alienated, docile, or "unreal" people seem in fact to represent the particular darkness of our time, and any therapy that can deal with symptoms but not with such ways of living has serious shortcomings. But to address this issue in terms of inner determinants versus external influences, and to suggest that avoidance of therapist influence is the path to genuineness and inner integrity is, I believe, a serious mistake.

Neither patient nor therapist can get a clearer picture of the "inner" man by removing "outside" influences. We are not *things*, separable from and describable apart from the world we live in. We are alive, and we live in a world we are *alive to*. Free association or focusing upon bodily sensations or tensions can aid in self-understanding, but such methods are most useful when viewed as part of a process of becoming clear about one's experience of the events of one's life, not as a look at some inner world apart from these events. The therapist inevitably becomes part of the patient's world, becomes an influence upon what he wants and how he sees things. This influence is not a contaminant, preventing him or the patient from seeing what the patient is *really* like. It is part of the process of living, of continually assimilating and accommodating to new events. Only when self-understanding is implicitly confused with knowing the properties of an inert object is such an influence viewed as antithetical to deep self-knowledge. The therapist need not fear that what he says will matter to the patient; the danger is that it will not. The patient's task is to *use* what the therapist does, to consider it, to take it into account. If he blindly follows, if he uses it without reflection, if he merely placates the therapist or seems to become but a carbon copy or pale reflection, then it is the therapist's responsibility to point this out, loudly and clearly. But it is *not* his responsibility to not be taken into account at all. Indeed, it is his responsibility to try his hardest to be sure this does not happen.

## AUTONOMY, REACTIVITY, AND RESPONSIVENESS

In a related vein, therapists are sometimes hesitant to try to explicitly influence their patients because of a commitment to a view of man as an autonomous agent and a repugnance toward the view, propounded by some behaviorists, of man as merely reactive, nothing but a bundle of reflexes tied together by their accidental occurrence in the same package of flesh. Those opposed to this reactive model of man have tended to emphasize autonomy as a central concept. Enhancing autonomy is frequently presented as a paramount goal by therapists opposed to behavior therapy; and Skinner (1971) in his attack on traditional views of man, uses the term "autonomous man" frequently to characterize the traditional humanistic view.

In the service of enhancing the patient's autonomy, the therapist is frequently cautioned against introducing, or letting become apparent, his own preferences, reactions, or ideas about dealing with life situations. The patient is encouraged instead to discover *his own* inclinations and approach to problems. Such a prescription, to be sure, is based on important considerations. As discussed above, there is indeed a real and important difference between solutions and life patterns passively absorbed from another and those that are grounded in the person's unique experiences and that bear his own individualized stamp. But where does the uniquely personalized, genuinely owned preference or strategy come from? Again, I would insist that the person does not just reach "inside" to discover something "there" all along. He constructs or creates his solutions, and he does so not in isolation but as part of his contact with the events he perceives about him.

The therapist, by minimizing the availability of clues about what he thinks or feels, may (possibly) be able to reduce to an insignificant degree the patient's taking his (the therapist's) views and preferences into account in making his decisions. But this has little bearing on how autonomous the patient's decisions become. The patient's autonomy *from the therapist* may be increased thereby, in the sense that he is less likely to make choices solely on the basis of what the world looks like to the therapist. But his choices will then reflect *other* sources of guidance and influence that the patient is in touch with. The choices are never just "his."

This is *not* to say that man is just a product of external forces, or that we must accept the "realism" of Skinner. Rather, the issue is that "autonomy" is a poor banner under which to wage a battle against a purely reactive view of man. The concept of autonomy has too many connotations of isolation or separation from alien forces. It lends itself to a not clearly articulated conceptual strategy of dealing with those who say "it's all environment" by saying "damn the environment, it's the inner man that counts."

To be sure, such a false dichotomy is not totally or explicitly accepted by those for whom autonomy is an important concept. Sophisticated psychoanalytic writers have been crucially concerned with issues of autonomy in relation to both environmental and endogenous events, and with the relation between these two aspects of autonomy (see Holt, 1967b; Rapaport, 1958). Moreover, psychoanalytic ego psychology *generally* has attempted to transcend the false dichotomy between outer and inner and to show how our behavior and experience can be understood in terms of *both* who we have become and what is happening around us now. I have suggested throughout this book, however, that this effort has not been as successful as is typically claimed, and I would suggest that the emphasis on autonomy, even relative autonomy, reflects the lack of resolution of this issue in psychoanalytic thought (and in the thought of many purportedly interpersonal and existential therapists whose thinking and practice is in this respect not so fundamentally different from the psychoanalytic model).

Autonomy is always couched in terms of autonomy *from*. It reflects a view of individuals as separate units whose dynamics or motives can be understood apart from the person's context, and who can discover what is really within by ceasing to be distracted by things external. From a concern with autonomy it is but a short leap to a concern with limiting the influence and guidance of the therapist. But the same humanistic concern—with a way of life that is genuine, integrative, and not merely reactive or conforming to the demands and views of others—can be couched in terms of freedom *to* rather than freedom *from* (Fromm, 1941). Instead of counterposing to the Skinnerian reactive man a model of autonomous man, one can suggest a model of *responsive* man.

The term "responsive" seems to me to convey far more satisfactorily what I take to be the shared humanistic concerns of therapists who are opposed to the model of man (and of human interaction) that takes as a given that we are inevitably "controlled" by environmental forces and that the only issue is whether the control has good effects. Unlike autonomy, responsiveness as a therapeutic goal does not have a connotation of isolation or separateness, but rather quite the opposite—it implies an aliveness, an in-touchness or in-tuneness that is (or should be) the hallmark of the person who has benefited maximally from a therapeutic experience. As the dictionary suggests, being responsive is the opposite of being apathetic, impassive, or unaffected. The responsive person is certainly open to influence and to the contingencies that his environment offers. But this openness is very different from the susceptibility to environmental control postulated by proponents of purely reactive models of man. The responsive man actively selects, filters, and organizes the input he receives. He is influenced by what occurs around him; but he is not blindly shoved around, helpless and uncomprehending.

With this image as the guidepost for therapeutic strategy rather than that of autonomy, the therapist might be less reluctant to try to guide and structure the patient's experiences or actively introduce procedures that can reduce anxiety through exposure. His aim is not to enable a pristine separation of outer from inner influences but, rather, to enable the person to be more fully alive to the possibilities life offers, unfettered by fears based on untested childhood conceptions or by deficits in social learning that continue to lead to the kinds of life experiences that further truncate the chance to correct them. He still is staunchly opposed to a view of man as merely reactive and to treating people as if they were. But he does not regard autonomy *from* undue influence to be as rich a goal as responsiveness *to* the events of one's life, and he views the latter goal as frequently aided by methods some therapists eschew in the name of autonomy.

## IMPLICATIONS OF TRANSFERENCE

It may be objected that while the approval of another person, or his communication that you seem to be on the right track, may *generally* be but one of many consequences that one can consider, and hence not necessarily coercive or unduly restrictive, special considerations are introduced in the context of psychotherapy. There, it is sometimes maintained, a state of affairs is created in which the therapist's word does have a very special, almost overriding power, much as the directives of a parent have for a young child. The analogy is, of course, not accidental. I am referring here to the concept of transference, which suggests that the therapist does come literally to be the recipient of feelings and attitudes previously directed by the patient toward his parents when he was a child. For the therapist, then, to use the power that has been transferred to him by virtue of his participation in the role of therapist—to influence the patient not by directing himself to the patient as a rational choosing adult, but by playing upon the childish fears and longings that are evoked by the therapeutic process—would seem to be an abuse of the trust that has been placed in him.

Several considerations are relevant here. Firstly, it must be recalled that the therapeutic relationship within which I am advocating guidance, direction, or reinforcement is not the classical psychoanalytic relationship but, rather, the kind of working relationship described throughout this book. One of the major premises of the approach described here is that a regressive tranference neurosis is not necessary to achieve maximal personality change, and the relationship established is consistent with that view. Patient and therapist are active collaborators in this approach, often explicitly discussing goals and how to achieve them. In such a context the therapist's role is largely demystified, and the likelihood of his becoming the recipient of powerful regressive urges is greatly diminished. Hence, his influence is rather that of an expert (Sullivan) or rational authority (Fromm) than that of an irrationally feared or revered parental figure.*

Additionally, the demystification itself serves to increase the patient's role as an active chooser rather than an object being worked upon. He is not prone in his participation in the therapy, and his contribution is not limited to the expression of actionless fantasy. He is responsible for taking real-life action, for observing his actions and the consequences they bring, and for full and open discussion with the therapist of the events of his life and his feelings both within and outside the consultation room. The therapist, in turn, has the responsibility of sharing with the patient his understanding of the patient's goals (including conflicted and unconscious aims and strivings) and his sense of how they can be reached.

Strong feelings are experienced toward the therapist, as they are toward anyone who plays a major role in one's life, especially one involving the sharing of intimate matters. But the therapist's strategy is not one of using silence and ambiguity to intensify those feelings and revivify childhood emotions. Rather, it is one of continually trying to clarify and sort out the feelings generated as they develop, to accept and articulate the feelings of the present adult rather than trying to recreate the feelings of the long-ago child.

* Clearly, I am referring here to relative, not absolute, differences.

Part of the very special influence that the therapist seems to have in psychoanalytically oriented therapies may actually be due to the interpretive, nondirective stance that is adopted to avoid such influence. If I am correct that the therapist inevitably views certain actions by the patient as more helpful and appropriate than others, and that this gets communicated in some way to the patient, then a manifestly nondirective stance can have the effect of rendering the therapist's influence hidden and harder to come to terms with. One is reminded of Laing's (1969) description of how parents frequently can disguise their telling a child what to do by couching it in a statement of what they perceive the child to be like (for example, "You're a good boy. You're nice to your little brother and love him.").

Such a stance may be very effective, but for reasons quite different than its enhancing the patient's ability to sort things out and to make clear conscious choices. Implicit and unacknowledged influence can be very powerful, and can open the person to change, because the person's critical faculties are not fully engaged. The process may well be akin to what goes on in cognitive dissonance studies, where compliance is obtained without the experience of sufficient justification, or in studies deriving from attribution theory, in which the person concludes he must be feeling something since he is acting as if he did. It also seems understandable in terms of the kind of paradoxical double-binding communications described by Haley (1963). In contrast, communicating one's preferences openly and explicitly leaves the patient knowing more clearly where he stands and what is going on. He may still feel pressure and anxiety in response to the therapist's expectations, but he is potentially in a better position to sort out where his own preferences may differ from those of the therapist.

It is sometimes contended that when the therapist explicitly indicates to the patient what he thinks the patient should do, the patient is likely to feel he has disappointed the therapist if he does not do what is suggested. Further, since in such an instance the therapist really has indicated an investment in a particular behavior by the patient, the feeling of disappointment cannot be resolved by interpretation. There is, however, a vast and crucial difference between the therapist's feeling disappointed that the patient did not do something, and the therapist's being about to give up on the patient or withdraw from him. For many patients, it is the failure to make just this distinction that is very much at the heart of their difficulties. If the patient does disappoint the therapist, but experiences it as a catastrophic occurrence signifying a dangerous loss of contact with a needed figure, this issue can then be examined, with resolution more possible precisely because the often implicit messages of expectation and preference have in this instance been explicit and discussable. The opportunity for the patient to learn experientially that it is possible to disappoint someone and yet maintain a close and genuine relationship may in fact be one of the most valuable things the therapy can provide.

## EXPLORATION AND SELF-UNDERSTANDING

In another variation of the themes and issues discussed thus far, some therapists will readily acknowledge that they are, and even intend to be, sources of influence with their patient; but they will insist that the influence should be restricted to the promotion of self-understanding.° Thus they will feel quite comfortable acknowledging that, as they interpret a defense, they hope that this will have the effect of the patient's giving it up and thus coming to a clearer sense of himself. Perhaps they will even acknowledge that their silence in response to a patient's expression of feeling or to an implicit or explicit question is a technique or device (manipulation?) designed to bring about a particular experience in a way the patient can no longer deny. But they will still staunchly oppose any attempt to extend the effort at influence to the realm of day-to-day behavior, and even in the session they will be uncomfortable with asking the patient to do anything (such as desensitization or role-playing).

Frequently, in this context, psychotherapy is described as a process of *exploration*, leading to self-discovery. A number of things make this metaphor an appealing one for many therapists. On the one hand, it conveys a sense of excitement, of a bold adventurous journey of the sort undertaken by historical figures admired for their courage and daring and viewed as living life to the fullest. Yet at the same time, along with this connotation of risk-taking, action, and pushing forward to new territory, the term "exploration" or "exploratory" can convey a reassuringly tentative sense of forestalling action or decision until more is known, of looking around, digging here, sniffing there, taking everything in. In this

---

° There is a precedent for this view in Freud's writings. Freud was quite explicit about the need to persuade and convince the patient, and even about using the positive transference to this end. But the persuasion was in the service of changing the patient's view of himself, not for the purpose of influencing his day-to-day behavior.

sense, viewing therapy as an exploratory process seems gentler than images that stress intervention; it suggests, as well, the virtues of openness and readiness to accept whatever turns up. Finally, I would suggest, the terms "exploratory" or "exploration" have been appealing because they are usefully ambiguous regarding the role of the therapist and his relationship to the patient. At one moment the exploration metaphor can connote a sense of shared excitement and risk, of "we're in this thing together." At another, the same metaphor can be used to suggest that the patient must voyage on a lonely journey into the unknown where no one can really follow. The therapist's reluctance to provide conventional or technical assistance is then seen as in the service of not distracting from this all-important journey into the heart of darkness.

The problem with the exploration metaphor as a central characterization of psychotherapy (apart from its considerable ambiguity) is that the kind of exploration undertaken in psychotherapy is rather fundamentally different from the kind that led to discovery and knowledge of unknown lands. In the latter instance, the discovery is of something that has existed in the state in which it is finally encountered long before the explorer arrived, and that is describable quite apart from the actions of the explorer or the process of exploration. In the former, the act of exploring changes what is there to be discovered; what the psychic explorer does changes who he is.

To be sure, there are considerations suggesting that the distinction is not an absolute one. Developments in science and philosophy in our century rightfully leave us skeptical that *anything* can be observed in such a way that the act of observing does not change it. Nothing that we see is just "there." From the moment the first Dutchmen set foot on the peaceful, verdant island of Manhattan it was already in the process of becoming something rather remarkably different. And of course when explorers discover a culture that had previously had no contact with what we call civilization, they are inevitably observing that culture in transition, no matter how stable it had been for centuries before the moment of contact. Moreover, inverting our perspective, we must also recognize that there certainly is a sense in which the patient in psychotherapy does discover some previously unnoticed things about himself in a way that is at least roughly analogous to the geographic explorer's tracing a river to its source.

Nonetheless, the differences are substantial enough that the exploration metaphor should be used only with considerable caution. It seems to me that this metaphor has contributed to an unhelpful restriction on psychotherapeutic intervention. In attempting *self*-exploration or *self*-

discovery, it is particularly crucial to be aware that what one is discovering is not inert—that far more (and far more instantaneously) than with rivers or forests, or even than with the customs of a tribe, the process of observing does change what is observed. In some respects, of course, this is a central premise of most psychotherapists (including myself): that insight contributes to change, that seeing what one is really like can help *change* what one is like. But to satisfactorily understand the distinction between self-exploration and exploring territory in a literal sense, it is necessary to go still further. The complexity of the relationships between observer and observed, the way in which what the observer does changes who he is and thus what he can discover about himself and what he is likely to further do—all this sets psychotherapy apart from other kinds of exploration.[*]

The psychic explorer's discoveries are severely limited if he tries to confine his observations to what has been "there inside" all along. And he is unlikely to change very much if he expects the changes in his day-to-day living to follow the completion of his inner journey. Some of the most important insights or self-discoveries are achieved only after the person begins to act in a new way in his daily life. The traditional meaning of exploration in psychotherapy tends to be something quite apart from any emphasis on behavior change. Indeed, the idea that the therapist should make a direct effort to make it more likely that certain specific changes occur in daily living is often actively rejected by therapists in the name of exploration and self-knowledge. In doing so, self-knowledge may actually be limited rather than increased.

The view that insight may follow as well as lead to behavior change is one that is not unfamiliar to nonbehavioral therapists. Alexander and French (1946) attempted major revisions in psychoanalytic technique with this notion as one of their guiding principles. Indeed, one of Alexander's last writings (Alexander, 1963) suggests that he saw quite clearly

---

[*] The limits of the exploration metaphor—at least to the extent that it evokes images of exploration of territory—are related to the limits of a psychology that relies heavily on concepts implying things extended in space rather than events extended in time. Mischel (1973b) has suggested that there is a surprising similarity between behavioral and existential models of man, in that both stress what people *do* rather than properties they *have*. He distinguishes this emphasis from that of psychodynamic theorists, who emphasize structures and internal states and seem less concerned with what the person actually does in various situations. Mischel's point is well taken, though it is overstated in some respects (Wachtel, 1973a, b). Schafer's (1973) action model for psychoanalysis does express the essential concepts of psychoanalysis in terms of what people do (though his conception of the range of things we do and the ways in which we do them is far broader than Mischel's), and it will be interesting to see whether, if it begins to be employed to a substantial extent, it will lead to a different sense of how to proceed with psychotherapy.

the potential coherences between psychoanalytic methods and insights and those that were beginning to accrue from work guided by learning theory orientations.

Interestingly, however, some of those who have seen most clearly the mutually reciprocal relation between understanding and the undertaking of new courses of action have nonetheless been staunch opponents of behavioral methods that could help facilitate such a process. Again, Wheelis (1973) is a particularly interesting examplar, providing a view of neurosis and change that I find extraordinarily congenial with my own— yet coming to a resoundingly negative conclusion about behavioral methods.

Wheelis notes that though the correlation between an inner feeling and the way one lives may not be evident at first, "no such feeling can be independent of behavior; and if only we find the connections we may begin to see how *a change in the way we live will make for a change in what we feel.*" (p. 112; italics added) He describes also how the taking of direct action brings about further insight and recognition of previously submerged aspects of the self. Throughout, he stresses the crucial role of changed behavior as part of the *process* of change and not just as an outcome; and he stresses, as well, how difficult it is to initiate and sustain the new behavior.

> Personality change follows change in behavior. Since we are what we do, if we want to change what we are we must begin by changing what we do, must undertake a new mode of action. Since the import of such action is change it will run afoul of existing entrenched forces which will protest and resist. The new mode will be experienced as difficult, unpleasant, forced, unnatural, anxiety-provoking. It may be undertaken lightly but can be sustained only by considerable effort of will. Change will occur only if such action is maintained over a long period of time. (p. 101)

Thus, for Wheelis, useful insight and genuine self-knowledge are not things that go on apart from the struggle to be different, and the success of the former depends crucially on the success of the latter. Further, the achievement of a sustained new course of behavior is seen by him as extremely difficult. He has keen insights into how entrenched modes of action tend to maintain themselves, to create conditions in which any other way of acting becomes extremely hard to sustain. But he leaves little place for the therapist to help the patient in this difficult struggle. The patient must "[grope] toward this vision in the dark."

Wheelis's arguments suggest to me, however, that the therapist can (and should) play a more active role in helping the patient to behave differently, and that far from limiting his self-understanding and sense of responsibility for himself, such help can greatly facilitate the process of self-knowledge and of struggling for integrity. If new behavior is not just the dessert but the meat and potatoes of changing one's identity and achieving self-knowledge, then facilitating the occurrence of new behavior is a crucial responsibility for the therapist whose humanistic goals are to be maximally achieved.

Wheelis is correct in stating that sustaining new behaviors that are counter to one's previous life style is extremely difficult, and he makes clear that the gains attained by most patients in the kind of approach he advocates are, while important, far from spectacular. He does not make the leap, however, to advocating that since behavior change is so difficult to achieve and since it is so intimately a part of furthering self-understanding as well, the therapist ought to *help* the patient attain behavior change. Nor does he suggest that the therapist's responsibility does not stop with interpreting, but extends to using his understanding of the principles of behavior to make the change as easy as possible for the patient to achieve. As I have discussed above, this is partly because of his view that the methods available somehow turn the person into an object. Additionally, though relatedly, his emphasis on the patient's lonely struggle, and the view that there is no way to make the struggle easier, derive from the assumption that all that the (ethical) therapist can offer is insight. Wheelis is certainly right in stating that the therapist's help "will be of no avail if he is required to provide a degree or kind of insight which will of itself achieve change" (p. 102), and his description of the folly in the therapist's striving for earlier and earlier reconstructions in response to the patient's lack of change is thoroughly consistent with the message of the present book. Like Wheelis, I too feel that instead of trying to do the job for the patient with more and more brilliant insights, one must ask the patient why he keeps waiting for his therapist's statements to do something to him and ask what he himself intends to do about his problem.

But insights into psychodynamics need not be all that the therapist has to offer. It is now well recognized that warmth, support, and caring—or their absence—can play a crucial role in determining whether the patient does or does not take the steps that lead toward change. Less frequently grasped is that so, too, can a crucial role be played by the offering of technical assistance based on a thorough understanding of the probable consequences of various kinds of occurrences. Far from necessarily representing an approach that minimizes self-knowledge, this latter kind of therapeutic assistance can be a crucial link in making likely that such self-knowledge does develop and deepen. By using desensitization or related methods to help the person expose himself to what he has fearfully avoided and/or rationalized; by helping him to plan and structure encounters in his daily life that are likely to be rewarding and to facilitate growth; by helping him to role-play and practice new modes of behavior in the safe environment of the therapist's office; by making very clear to him when you think he has taken a step that will lead him out of his dilemma, and letting him know you are pleased—by these and related technical measures the therapist can make the new behaviors that generate new insights less of a Herculean task that only a few can achieve. When he refuses to offer such assistance, he is not on the side of insight or self-knowledge, but simply on the side of things having to be difficult.

## THE ETHIC OF THE LONELY STRUGGLE

Few therapists, of course, explicitly try to make things difficult for their patients, and few would recognize themselves as sternly moralistic. Yet there is much in the assumptions and ground-rules underlying traditional psychotherapeutic work that does seem to smack of the puritanical, and this despite the fact that acceptance of the patient's sexual, aggressive, and other "antisocial" feelings is a very real and very important part of the typical therapeutic relationship.

These days, warmth and caring are a much more obvious and acceptable (indeed essential) feature of the relationships established by most therapists than they were in the days when the "blank screen" model predominated and the importance of frustration played a leading role in writings on psychoanalytic technique. There is still, however, a strong reluctance to provide direct assistance, and an assumption that "lending a hand" is somehow crippling or limiting. The term "supportive therapy" is a tainted one. Lending support to any substantial degree is done only when the patient's resources are seen as impaired, and it implies a therapeutic pessimism in the sense of an acceptance of more limited goals.

I would suggest that therapy is "supportive" therapy to the extent that its outcome is continued reliance on the therapist for direction and affirmation. But if dependence on the therapist is the path to independence, then support has very different implications. Efforts by the therapist to direct and structure a set of experiences for the patient to approach are perfectly consistent with the aim of major personality change. What is crucial is not whether the therapist provides help and support along the way, but whether he establishes a relationship that aims toward its own dissolution.

The emphasis on change from "within" and on the therapist's refraining from showing the patient how to deal with specific problems, teaching him skills, or taking direct action to help relieve him, as in systematic desensitization, all seem to reflect the highly individualistic spirit that pervades our culture. Though in many respects psychoanalytic therapists tend to be social critics, most end up at least implicitly endorsing one of the fundamental (and in some ways highly problematic) tenets of our society—its emphasis on each man doing for himself. This ethic, though it certainly has its strengths, and though it is probably at least in some ways linked to the value we place on individual rights and civil liberties, is also largely responsible for a number of very unfortunate features of American life. Though this kind of individualism can, as in pioneer days, be associated with a considerable sense of community, at present it seems contributory to the loss of such a sense—a loss that is so prevalent in contemporary American life.

The anomie and "I don't want to get involved" attitude—and its corollary, the fear that the streets are not safe because no one will come to your aid—is the dark shadow of the ethic that each man should take care of himself. The therapeutic ethic that it is somehow antihumanistic and demeaning to suggest to a patient a structured course of action he might follow, or to introduce him to a regimen of systematic desensitization, has disturbing parallels to the Reagan welfare ethic, with its claim that providing direct assistance to able-bodied men and women is crippling. It is certainly not unimportant that the psychotherapeutic version of this ethic lacks the selfish, harsh, and mean-spirited quality that its more extreme political counterpart exhibits. The spirit of the latter is, "My parents groped their way out of the pit without any help from anyone else; let 'those people' do it too; it's good for them." In the former, genuine humane concerns are far more readily apparent. But I believe that there are very real similarities that are not usually noticed, and that, unwittingly, many therapists who criticize behavior therapy as an agent of cultural norms are themselves upholding one of the basic tenets of our capitalist society, when they stress change based solely on autonomous action and deride the need for direct assistance from others. In a culture with a greater sense of community, in which mutual assistance rather than rock-ribbed self-reliance were more the norm, the goals and methods of militantly individualistic psychodynamic and humanistic psychotherapists might appear quite different. It is, after all, just as human to be able to turn to others as it is to stand alone.

In a related vein, it may be noted that the emphasis on autonomy, independence, and self-knowledge in much writing on psychotherapy is correlated with a decreased emphasis on the relief of suffering per se, and sometimes even with strong opposition to measures that can provide such relief. To be sure, this emphasis is in part a function of theoretical considerations that suggest that direct efforts to relieve suffering may produce less permanent or complete relief in the long run (and much of the present volume constitutes a critique of important portions of this theorizing). But in addition, there is often a sense in which what is communicated is that relief from symptoms or anxiety is not as noble an aim as enhancement of the development of the individual, and that the former ought to be subordinated to the latter.

This attitude does not in itself reflect an insensitivity to human suffering. The hope is that if the patient can bear the suffering for a period of time, the outcome can ultimately be both relief of suffering *and* fuller development of the self; and the view that this is preferable to symptomatic relief alone is far from an inhumane one. It is probably only the rare therapist who shows signs of outright contempt for those practitioners who choose to devote the majority of their efforts to relief of symptoms or for those patients who choose such a goal (though in personal discussions I have encountered such an attitude at times). But there is a danger, I believe, that in opposing direct intervention into troubling reactions and patterns of living, in the name of autonomy or freedom, the keen edge of one's commitment to the simple relief of suffering as a worthy goal in its own right can be dulled. There are times when bearing pain for a while is necessary if more lasting or more extensive improvement is to be achieved. But there is no special moral virtue in bearing pain, and helping someone achieve self-understanding is in itself no more or less worthy a goal than helping him stop hurting.

## THE ISSUE OF SYMPTOM REMOVAL

Rapid intervention to help the patient alter troubling behavior is sometimes opposed for a reason related to those discussed thus far, but distinguishable from it: the view that symptoms are a communication, and that taking away symptoms can be like asking the patient to shut up.

While I would take issue with the view that all symptoms are necessarily communications (or even with the view that all "symptoms" are really "symptoms"; sometimes the difficulties that patients complain about are not symptomatic of a broad characterological pattern or life style but are, rather, relatively specific bits of faulty learning or experience), it is certainly very often the case that a symptom is a signal that may alert us to a debilitating or self-betraying way of life. Freud discovered early in his career that attempting to take away symptoms without dealing with the issues in living that led to them was likely to be futile; the symptoms would recur, or others would take their place. As psychoanalytic thought and practice have developed, it has become clear that another alternative, possibly even sadder in the long run, is also a possible result of purely symptomatic treatment: the patient may be calmed, returned to his prior state of no-acute-distress, and condemned to a life in which dissatisfaction and meaninglessness have become so much the norm that it hardly hurts at all.

Frequently, the use of behavioral methods to deal with problematic behaviors is confused with the kind of "symptom removal" Freud wisely abandoned. But there is a quite considerable difference between, on the one hand, such practices as hypnotically suggesting away a hysterical symptom without exploring its basis and, on the other, using systematic desensitization to enable a person to begin to approach something he has fearfully avoided, or using assertive training to aid a person to *express* his dissatisfaction (or affection) instead of keeping it hidden and suffering in some directly or indirectly related way.

To be sure, there are certainly behavior therapists who use these methods simply to get someone to behave in ways more comfortable for those around him, or to relieve the most acute distress without addressing more fundamental issues. But (1) this kind of use of behavioral methods is not all that effective (see Lazarus, 1971); (2) it is certainly not the kind of use of these methods that is being advocated in the context of the active-intervention psychodynamic therapy I have been discussing in this book; (3) it is not how these methods are used even by many strictly behaviorally oriented therapists, who base their interventions on a rather thorough behavioral analysis and reject the view that the symptom is the neurosis; and (4) there are times when purely symptomatic relief, even at the possible price of failing to fully address the communicative aspect of the symptom, may be justified (which is again the issue of relief of suffering as an important goal per se).

In most instances, behavioral methods, when properly used, are not at all properly characterized as "symptom removal." These methods, as I have

# PART TWO

*The Relational World*

# 13

# Introduction to Part Two

―――――――

Ⅰ N the years since *Psychoanalysis and Behavior Therapy* was first published, the separate paradigms it aimed to integrate have continued to evolve. At the same time, the cyclical psychodynamic point of view the book espoused has developed as well, both bringing in new perspectives to weave together with those originally addressed and reworking its formulations and clinical strategies in light of these new ingredients and of clinical experience. My aim in Part Two is to describe these new developments and elaborate on their implications, both theoretically and clinically.

The term "relational world" in the present title refers to several different foci of the new material: the developments in psychoanalytic object relations theory and in the broader "relational" point of view in psychoanalysis, the wider world of relationships addressed by the family systems perspective, and the still broader social relations embodied in the psychological impact of the society at large and the habits, values, and assumptions it engenders.

Chapter 14 describes the evolution of the psychotherapy integration movement over the past two decades. At the time *Psychoanalysis and Behavior Therapy* was first being written, a number of important contributions to integration had already appeared, but it would have been a prime example of hyperbole to label them part of a "movement." Today, circumstances are quite different. Aided considerably by the galvanizing effects of the founding of the Society for the Exploration of Psychotherapy Integration, efforts at psychotherapy integration are today quite accurately described as a worldwide movement of considerable influence. Reviewing the directions this movement has taken in the past two decades, the chapter attempts to sort out its main currents.

Chapter 15 concerns itself with new developments in psychoanalytic thought that bear significantly on the prospects for integrating psychoanalytic perspectives with those of other orientations. It focuses especially on the articulation and elaboration of what has come to be called the "relational" thrust in psychoanalysis and situates cyclical psychodynamics within that emerging paradigm.

Chapter 16 addresses an equally significant development within the orientation that I referred to in the original edition simply as "behavior therapy." Today, for many of its theorists and practitioners, this orientation is better described as "cognitive–behavioral." The chapter examines in detail the implications of the cognitive shift for the integrative effort depicted here, finding some perhaps surprising complexities.

Chapter 17 explores a significant extension of the integrative model first presented in *Psychoanalysis and Behavior Therapy*—the introduction of a family systems perspective into the evolving approach. Only as the writing of *Psychoanalysis and Behavior Therapy* was being completed did it become clear that the circular and contextual model of cyclical psychodynamics had important affinities with the circular and contextual model employed by family therapists. Chapter 17 describes the ways in which the two models converge and the ways in which a systemic perspective adds further clinical and theoretical power to the cyclical psychodynamic integration.

Chapter 18 describes another important new emphasis within the cyclical psychodynamic approach since the original publication of *Psychoanalysis and Behavior Therapy*. In recent years, close attention to the language used by the therapist has been a central feature of the approach—addressing both the unwitting ways that therapists may couch their comments in a fashion the patient experiences as discouraging or as a source of shame and the ways that therapists may creatively employ phrasings and constructions that facilitate the patient's viewing herself differently and taking action to resolve and overcome her difficulties. The communication strategies outlined in this chapter are relevant to therapists practicing from a range of orientations. For the therapist specifically oriented toward an integrative approach, they permit a more "seamless" integration in which the separate parts are so thoroughly woven together that the boundary between what belongs to one orientation and what belongs to another is difficult to demarcate.

Finally, Chapter 19 examines the current status and future directions of the cyclical psychodynamic approach. It begins by considering the respective contributions of logical and conceptual analysis, clinical observation, and systematic empirical research as the foundations for the cyclical psychodynamic point of view. It then turns to the ways in which the vicious circle analysis at the heart of the clinical approach presented in this book has been extended to larger social questions such as the psychological and ecological consequences of a consumer way of life and the painful impasse between the races in our country. Ultimately, its aim is to make clear that the unnecessary misery created by psychological disorder and the unnecessary misery resulting from social arrangements that are unjust or rooted in self-deception are not completely separate phenomena but rather manifest a similar vicious circle structure and derive from similar cognitive and motivational tendencies. Moreover, individual psychological distress and frustration contribute to maintaining dysfunctional social arrangements even as such social arrangements contribute to creating and exacerbating individual psychological distress. Here again, we see not simple or readily separable linear strands of causality but the same complex, recursive pattern that it is the aim of this book to illuminate in all spheres of human experience.

more and more frequent at meetings of the American Psychological Association and of other major professional organizations.

Perhaps most significant, a thriving organization has emerged to provide a professional home and identity to the increasing number of therapists, theorists, and therapy researchers who are exploring the synergistic possibilities of crossing the boundaries between schools. That organization, the Society for the Exploration of Psychotherapy Integration (SEPI), currently has members in 27 countries on 5 continents. SEPI's increasing influence and prestige; its publication, beginning in 1991, of the *Journal of Psychotherapy Integration;* and the opportunities for interchange SEPI has provided among thinkers of widely disparate views have all been major facilitators of the remarkable growth in interest in integrative approaches in recent years. Increasingly, important contributions to psychotherapy integration have been issuing from all over the globe (e.g., Fernandez Alvarez, 1992; Mirapeix, 1995; Opaso, 1992; Ryle, 1990).

I will not, in this chapter, attempt to offer a comprehensive history of that growth and evolution. Several excellent accounts of this history have appeared in recent years (e.g., Arkowitz & Messer, 1984, in press; Goldfried, 1995a; Goldfried & Newman, 1992), and two major handbooks provide a comprehensive overview of the entire field of integrative psychotherapy and psychotherapy integration (Norcross & Goldfried, 1992; Stricker & Gold, 1993). Rather, I wish to examine a number of questions and issues that have emerged since the original publication of *Psychoanalysis and Behavior Therapy* that bear on the entire project of integrating competing approaches to psychotherapy.

Although the virtual quantum jump in receptiveness to integrative ideas in the early 1980s was no doubt influenced both by key writings on integration in the preceding years and by the founding of SEPI, our understanding of the remarkable changes in the attitude of therapists toward considering the potential contributions of other approaches would be incomplete without consideration of the substantial changes that have developed *within* the competing schools. At the time the writing of *Psychoanalysis and Behavior Therapy* began, Freudian drive theory (as modified by psychoanalytic ego psychology) was the dominant paradigm in American psychoanalysis. Correspondingly, behavior therapy, which was just beginning to show the influence of a cognitive perspective, was still largely an outlook characterized by stimulus-response and conditioning models, and by a commitment to the "behaviorism" that had dominated American academic psychology for several decades.

Today, both psychoanalysis and behavior therapy have changed significantly. The most influential and creative currents in contemporary psychoanalytic thought are likely to be framed in "relational" rather than "drive" terms (Greenberg & Mitchell, 1983; Mitchell, 1988, 1993). "Two-person" models that acknowledge more fully the presence of the therapist in the room and his or her powerful impact on the patient's experience and associations have, for many analysts, replaced the "one-person" model in which the patient's associations are viewed as deriving preponderantly from "within" and from the past (see, e.g., Aron, 1990; Messer & Warren, 1995; Modell, 1984). Behavior therapy has evolved in new directions as well. Today, the term "cognitive behavior therapy," once viewed as practically an oxymoron, is accepted by the majority of practitioners of this orientation as the most accurate and appropriate depiction of how they work. Although they remain committed to examining in detail their clients' actual behavior and its relation to its environmental context, today's cognitively oriented behavior therapists place great emphasis on their clients' thoughts and organizing assumptions.

Moreover, substantial change has been evident not only in psychoanalysis and behavior therapy—the two main components whose integration was the original aim of the cyclical psychodynamic approach—but in a third major orientation to psychological difficulties that was scarcely mentioned in the original edition but has increasingly become an important constituent of the cyclical psychodynamic model. It became apparent toward the end of working on *Psychoanalysis and Behavior Therapy* that the model being developed, with its strong emphasis on vicious circles and understanding people in context, had many affinities to the models that guided work in family therapy. In part, the absence of a family systems perspective in the original formulations of *Psychoanalysis and Behavior Therapy* reflected simply the difficulty of putting together even *two* points of view that were seen as antithetical by their proponents (and a concomitant absence of masochism on the part of the author). But the difficulty of including a family systems perspective derived as well from the particulars of how family systems concepts were originally framed. Family therapy, like behavior therapy, developed in significant degree as a challenge to and protest against the dominance of psychoanalytic thinking in our society's approach to mental health problems. The objections to psychoanalysis by family therapists were of a different sort than those of behavior therapists and derived from different concerns and premises, but they were as intense and profound. In particular, many early family therapists were strongly opposed to *individual* psychotherapy of any kind. Here again, however, considerable evolution and maturation can be discerned. Increasingly, the methods and viewpoints developed by family therapists are being applied in a variety of contexts, *including* work with individuals (e.g., Wachtel & Wachtel, 1986), and the stark rejection of all other points of view is increasingly regarded as ideological excess.°

Adding to all of these changes within the primary paradigms in the field are larger social and economic trends that are profoundly influencing the thinking and the practice of psychotherapists. Not all of these influences are salutary. In many ways sound clinical judgment is being pushed aside by an excessive emphasis on bottom-line thinking that reflects deeply troubling currents in our society and profound self-deceptions among Americans about the real sources of well-being in their lives (Wachtel, 1989). But one potentially more positive result of these new pressures has been to shake up old habits and assumptions, and to increase the receptiveness of therapists to ideas from outside their original orientation. It has also led many therapists to experiment with models of *brief* therapy, in which the older orthodoxies often are less deeply ingrained or even are directly challenged.

The trend toward briefer therapies is by no means an unmixed blessing. Spurred as it so substantially is by accounting rather than clinical concerns, it has put patients at the mercy of economic considerations, at times offering them considerably less help than they really need or requiring them, even when helped, to settle for less extensive change than they would have achieved under less budget-focused clinical thinking. It has, however, led some therapists to reexamine the assumptions under which they work, with the consequence not only that some patients are helped more quickly than they once would have been—virtually everyone, after all, would prefer to diminish her suffering or unhappiness sooner rather than later—but also that even those patients continuing to receive long-term therapy may encounter a therapist more innovative and flexible than he or she would have been a decade before.

## INTEGRATION AT WHAT LEVEL?

A central point at issue among contemporary proponents of integration in psychotherapy concerns whether integration should take place pri-

---

°A fourth significant thread in the tapestry of the psychotherapies, the experiential/humanistic therapies, also has evolved during this period, and important integrative efforts have appeared incorporating the experiential perspective (e.g., Greenberg & Safran, 1987; Safran & Segal, 1990). These developments have interesting potential points of intersection with the evolving cyclical psychodynamic model presented in this book, and they will be discussed in the following chapters. But they have not as yet been as central in the evolution of the cyclical psychodynamic approach.

marily at the level of practice or at the level of theory. While both must, of course, proceed together to at least some degree—theory divorced from practice tends to become too abstract and lacking in what might be called responsibility, and practice divorced from theory becomes a hodge-podge of techniques that lack a rudder to guide them through the rough storms any psychotherapy can encounter—nonetheless, there are clear differences in emphasis among differing integrative approaches.

Arkowitz (in press) has suggested that approaches to integration in psychotherapy can be usefully divided into three main strands—"technical eclecticism," "the common factors approach," and "theoretical integration." Technical eclecticism is the least theoretical of the three. Indeed, Arnold Lazarus, perhaps the best known proponent of technical eclecticism, is rather pointedly critical of what he views as a frequent overreliance on theory by psychotherapists (e.g., Lazarus, 1989a, 1989b, 1992, 1995). Nonetheless, even Lazarus's work is in fact significantly guided by theory—in his case, social learning theory—and what he objects to is in essence the use of *other* theories, which he believes are overly speculative, wrong, or both. Other prominent proponents of technical eclecticism (e.g., Beutler & Clarkin, 1990; Beutler & Consoli, 1992; Clarkin, Frances, & Perry, 1992) are not as explicitly opposed to theory as Lazarus, but they share the view that patients are best served by an approach that actuarily matches specific procedures with specific patient characteristics and that places the emphasis on empirically derived relationships more than on the guidelines offered by a theoretical focus.

What places the technical eclectics in the integrative camp is not really an effort to find commonalities, convergences, or syntheses, but simply their willingness to look in all directions for techniques that work rather than limiting their search to those produced by only one orientation. The self-described technical eclectics are aptly named. They are indeed eclectics, not integrationists. Or, to use a metaphor first introduced at a SEPI meeting by Harold Lief, their commitment is to desegregation, not integration.

## THE COMMON FACTORS APPROACH

The second broad trend identified by Arkowitz, the common factors approach, is not as atheoretical as technical eclecticism, but largely confines its theorizing to a limited domain or area of convergence between approaches. The common factors approach is most strongly rooted in the persistent finding that, all in all, different approaches to therapy tend to yield more or less similar results with the majority of patients (e.g., Elkin et al., 1989; Elkin, 1994; Lambert & Bergin, 1994; Luborsky, Singer, & Luborsky, 1975; Shapiro & Shapiro, 1982; Smith, Glass, & Miller, 1980). Although this seeming similarity could be legitimately challenged on a number of grounds—for example, insufficiently sensitive or poorly focused measures that do not capture the differential impact of different approaches; the danger of lumping together disparate patients into a spurious "average" that masks the ways in which particular methods do well with certain kinds of patients but not with others (the heart of the technical eclectics' view); and the difficulty in assuming that all practitioners of a particular "approach" are in fact doing the same thing—proponents of the common factors approach believe it is most prudent and appropriate at our current level of knowledge to explore the possibility that the results really are equivalent. They posit that despite surface differences that appear quite substantial, the essential therapeutic processes called into play by the various therapies are more or less the same. In effect, the different therapies are really different packages for the delivery of the same therapeutic ingredients.

Certainly the most influential figure in the initial development of the common factors approach was Jerome Frank (e.g., 1961, 1973, 1982). On the basis of both the findings of his research at Johns Hopkins and a broad study of interpersonal influence in diverse cultures, Frank concluded that common processes underlie not only the various types of psychotherapy but other processes of profound human influence as well. He saw similarities in the underlying mechanisms of influence processes as diverse as shamanism, faith healing, Communist "thought reform," and the placebo effect in medicine. In addressing psychotherapy specifically, Frank concluded that, "features common to all types of psychotherapy combat a major source of the distress and disability of persons who seek psychotherapeutic help. The source of this distress may be termed demoralization—a sense of failure or of powerlessness to affect oneself and one's environment." The attributes shared by all approaches in combating this demoralization, Frank suggested,

include certain features of the therapeutic relationship and the setting, and a particular conceptual framework linked to certain activities. In conjunction, these features intrinsic to all psychotherapies help the patient to clarify his symptoms and problems, inspire his hopes, provide him with experiences of success or mastery, and stir him emotionally. *Although the achievement of these aims requires a conceptual framework and certain ac-*

*tivities linked to it, the specific content of these may be largely irrelevant*
[italics added]. (Frank, 1973, p. xvi)

Frank notes that his thesis does not deny that for certain specific kinds of psychological distress or certain types of patients there may be advantages accruing to particular techniques. But he maintains that with the exception of relatively few disorders, such as circumscribed phobias, the evidence available thus far does not encourage this conclusion. He adds, moreover, that even when there appears to be a differential effectiveness for a particular approach, "it may depend on the differential ability of the technique to mobilize certain features common to all" (Frank, 1973, p. xvi). Among the common features especially emphasized by Frank as helpful in overcoming the demoralization are an emotionally meaningful relationship with a helping person in whom the patient can confide, a setting designated as a place for healing, a rational conceptual scheme or myth to explain the patient's symptoms and emotional distress, and a ritual through which symptoms may be resolved.

More recently, there has been a considerable acceleration of efforts to examine the common factors in psychotherapy, both conceptually and empirically. Goldfried (1980), in a paper that has been a central influence on the common factors approach, has suggested that the pursuit of common factors needs to address the issue of what level of abstraction is most suitable to this approach to integration. Goldfried argues that we are unlikely to find much common ground at the level of abstraction of the therapist's overarching theoretical framework or fundamental philosophical stance, and that different but equally problematic impediments face any effort at rapprochement at the level of specific techniques, where comparisons are unlikely to reveal more than "trivial points of similarity" (p. 994). Theorists' efforts should concentrate instead, Goldfried suggests, on an intermediate level of abstraction, encompassing what he calls "clinical strategies." It is here that we are likely to find that therapists of different persuasions are doing something genotypically similar even when appearing phenotypically quite disparate. Particularly emphasized by Goldfried are the therapist's efforts to enable the patient to engage in new, corrective experiences and the offer of feedback to the patient to enable him or her to develop increased awareness of thoughts, feelings, and actions and the relation between them.

Goldfried's aim is not simply to find convergences, but to clarify the similarities *and* differences between therapeutic approaches. Under-

standing where seemingly differently oriented therapists seek essentially similar aims or evoke similar processes points us toward what may
be the most effective and essential features of all therapies, and raises
at least the possibility of finding ways to administer the active ingredients in more effective ways. But knowledge of the specific contributions of the different approaches is essential as well to an understanding of the full range of therapeutic methods and processes potentially
available. Moreover, a key feature of Goldfried's empirical investigations is that the link between therapeutic outcome and particular activities by the therapist may be different in different therapeutic approaches. In one study, for example, Goldfried (1991) found that
psychodynamic and cognitive–behavioral therapists provided interpersonal feedback to equal degrees, but that such feedback was more
strongly related to positive outcome for the psychodynamic therapists
than the cognitive–behavioral therapists. Thus, it appears that the context within which a procedure is used may give different meaning to
the same procedure; a "common factors" approach need not assume either that all crucial factors are common, or that factors that operate
over a range of therapeutic approaches always operate in the same way
or have the same meaning (Goldfried, 1991; see also, Jones, Cumming,
& Horowitz, 1988; Karasu, 1986; Messer & Warren, 1995; Safran &
Messer, in press).

Nor, it is evident, need common factor approaches be largely atheoretical as are technical eclectic approaches. Indeed, one prominent
line of research presented by Arkowitz (in press) as a protoyptical example of the common factors approach (Prochaska, 1984; Prochaska &
DiClemente, 1986; Prochaska, Rossi, & Wilcox, 1991) is categorized by
Norcross & Goldfried (1992) as an example of theoretical integration.
The different takes on this work become understandable once it becomes clear that Prochaska and DiClemente's "transtheoretical" approach seeks precisely a *theory* for common factors (Prochaska & Di-
Clemente, 1992. Theirs is a common factors approach in that it is rooted
in an examination of common change processes and common stages of
change across therapies. What they offer is a theory, but a theory of the
commonalities. Much the same can be said about the work of Beitman
(e.g., 1987), who also stresses the stages of change common to different therapeutic approaches, and who also offers what might be called
a mid-level theory, in his case guided by the explicit principle of "keep
it simple" (Beitman, 1992). Similarly, Orlinsky and Howard (1987),
though rooting their work in a careful examination of empirical research
every bit as painstaking as that of the technical eclectics, are less hesi-

tant to offer a theoretical framework for integrating those findings. Their theoretical effort, however, is focused on the search for underlying common factors.

## THEORETICAL INTEGRATION

I will focus most closely on the third of Arkowitz's categories of integrative approaches, theoretical integration, for obvious reasons: *Psychoanalysis and Behavior Therapy* is often cited as a prime example of such an approach. This is not to say that the cyclical psychodynamic approach described in this book eschews all features of the other two approaches. Like technical eclecticism, the approach presented here seeks to make use of research indicating what kinds of interventions work best with what kinds of difficulties. (Indeed, one key impetus for my initial foray outside the bounds of the therapeutic procedures I had been taught in my doctoral and postdoctoral training was a conviction that it was incumbent upon me to pay attention to the accumulating evidence that behavioral interventions were indeed helpful to people in very specific and demonstrable ways.) And like the common factors approaches, my aim includes understanding the fundamental processes that underlie the success of therapeutic work of diverse orientations. (The discussion below, for example, of the central role of exposure to anxiety-provoking experiences that have previously been avoided clearly reflects an interest in common factors.)

But the cyclical psychodynamic approach, much like the approach of assimilative integration proposed by Messer (1992) and by Stricker and Gold (1996), with which it shares many premises and commitments, aims for something further as well. It seeks not only to see what works and what is common in the currently extant approaches, but also to point toward a new emergent approach through a close examination of the theoretical underpinnings of the separate approaches and through the construction of a more encompassing and overarching theoretical framework to guide both therapeutic work and our understanding of personality development and dynamics. I am in strong agreement with Kurt Lewin's maxim that "there is nothing so practical as a good theory."

It has been increasingly emphasized by philosophers of science that the theories people hold profoundly influence what they see as well as what they do. In the current jargon, facts are theory-laden. Thus, integrative efforts that aim only for breaking out of the bounded set of methods employed by any particular approach, or even for reaching an understanding of the common processes that underlie diverse methods and interventions, may be seen to be incomplete. These efforts expand the walls of the tunnel, so to speak, but they do not really eliminate the tunnel vision. The current fashion for "manuals" notwithstanding, effective psychotherapy is never a simple matter of following rules. Every case inevitably introduces new wrinkles—virtually every *session* does—and without the creative application of *imagination* by the therapist, the work is unlikely to be very successful.*

One of the limitations of the separate school approach is that each of the theories that guide clinical work according to a particular school facilitates imagination in certain ways but cramps it in others. When psychotherapy was dominated by competing schools, observations deriving from *other* schools (including observations regarding the efficacy of the other school's *methods*) were excluded from the theoretical perspective that clinicians brought to bear.† Regularities observed daily by behavior therapists were simply ignored by psychoanalysts; phenomena and connections observed regularly by analysts were banished or forbidden entry by behavior therapists, and so forth.

As a consequence, proponents of each school virtually became blind to the observations of the other, as if their antennae were simply not tuned to that band. This much the technical eclectic and common factors approaches contribute to overcoming. It is part of the desegregation referred to above. An important contribution of the advocates of these approaches has been to reintroduce proponents of each school to the observations of the other. But their task has been incomplete for two reasons.

First, they have called attention primarily to *techniques*. Less emphasized have been the observations that support and lead to the techniques, the body of findings and theories that form the crucial background for each school's choice of techniques in particular situations.

---

*Perhaps the limiting exception to this observation is the application of systematic desensitization to a simple phobia. Often (though by no means always) the rather routine application of the procedure, in technician-like fashion, can achieve impressive results. But two things must be borne in mind: (a) Even where successful, such mechanical application of a "technique" may forgo an opportunity for even greater therapeutic gain (see, for example, Wachtel, 1991a); (b) Even where the *application* of the technique procedes rather routinely and mechanically, the *decision* to use the technique should be based on a thorough understanding of the complexities of the case and how the symptom fits within the larger context of the patient's life and psychological organization.

†This is still the case for those practitioners whose commitments and outlook remain strongly tied to a single school.

Precisely because they have not aimed to achieve a thoroughgoing reworking of theory, they have left out much that could be useful.

Second, even attending to the observations underlying each approach and advocating a greater catholicity in this realm is insufficient. A further crucial task is to examine how the observations which had previously been excluded can give new meaning to the observations that had already been within the approach's purview. Theoretical formulations, after all, are not simply descriptions of reality. Today it is generally acknowledged that theoretical formulations are constructions, imaginative choices, that never directly represent reality.* When new observations are added to the mix, the entire Gestalt is likely to look different, and thus the picture we draw to connect the dots, as it were, is likely to be different from the picture we drew based on a more circumscribed observational field. Efforts at theoretical integration, being more explicitly attentive to examining and reworking the conceptual foundations underlying the different approaches, are more likely to alert one to the need for reformulating even one's understanding of familiar observations as unfamiliar observations are introduced.

It is worth noting that particular theoretical formulations endure not, because they work but because they work "well enough." That is, we "sort of" notice that they do not always fit, but if they seem to catch the majority of fish that swim by, that seems sufficient. Unfortunately, it often seems that if our catch has any heft at all, that is sufficient to persuade us that in fact we are catching *all* the fish, or at least all that are fit to eat (or to persuade ourselves that only those fish we are able to catch *are* fit to eat).

The aim of a theoretical integration, and certainly of cyclical psychodynamics, is explicitly to examine and reconstruct the theoretical foundations of clinical work as well as the practice. It is hoped thereby to tune the clinician to notice a broader set of regularities. The limitations of the school-oriented theories are obvious—they are rooted only in a subset of the available data, and to a significant degree they reflect virtually a commitment to ignoring data with the wrong pedigree. But the limitations of putatively atheoretical approaches, such as technical eclecticism, may be even more insidious, because such approaches look more open and "innocent." As I noted above, even those who claim to be suspicious of theory, and to stake their therapeutic efforts on an "empirical" foundation, nonetheless inevitably are guided by theoretical

*This is equally true, of course, for an integrative theory such as cyclical psychodynamics.

premises for what they see and do not see, think to do and do not think to do. This is not in itself problematic; as with everyone else, their theory may be facilitative as well as a source of blinders. But it is perhaps most incumbent on those whose view of theory stresses disproportionately the ways in which theory can lead us astray, to be alert to the dangers of keeping theory in the background. For when it is kept hidden, like an embarrassing relative one would rather the world not notice, theory is not eliminated but simply unexamined and, thereby, rendered especially capable of leading us on a voyage of its own making without one's realizing what has happened. If, as Santayana has suggested, those who cannot remember the past are condemned to repeat it, those who do not attend to theory are condemned to be its unwitting slave.

My concern, however, is not just negative—to avoid the untoward effects of either excessive allegiance to a particular theoretical system or denial altogether of theory's inevitably powerful impact. It is also *constructive*—to construct a theory that is shaped by (and gives shape to) the data emerging from therapists and researchers whose work is at once consequential and limited by the fact that they ignore each other's contributions. How must we conceptualize if we recognize both the ways that early object relations shape our lives and the ways in which current reinforcement contingencies do; the role of cognitions and the role of family structure; the impact of social phenomena such as racism or poverty and the impact of such private phenomena as conflict and defense? Such a conceptual framework can enable us not only to reconcile putting together interventions that appear incompatible from the framework of their separate original theoretical underpinnings, but also to develop new interventions and new understandings unlikely to have been thought of if we confine ourselves to looking through the more narrowly focused lenses of the separate theories. Theory, that is, not only rationalizes after the fact but points to new facts and new connections, and, by virtue of stimulating new interventions and interactions, in essence *creates* new facts, brings forth phenomena that would otherwise not have materialized.

## CRITIQUES OF THEORETICAL INTEGRATION

The conceptual program of theoretical integration has not gone unchallenged. Writing in an edited volume in which proponents of integration and skeptics exchanged views (Arkowitz & Messer, 1984)—a volume whose appearance reflected the growing interest in, and influence of, integrative thinking—Cyril Franks (1984) argued that psychoanalytic and behavioral perspectives were "fundamentally incompatible" and that "integration is impossible at the conceptual level without doing injustice to quite different but equally cherished notions about methodology that are held by behavior therapists and psychoanalysts." He suggested as well, though noting that there is a lack of evidence for evaluating this claim, that "in the long run, advancement in clinical practice is more likely to emerge out of programmatically and rationally derived techniques spawned within a clearly articulated system than out of an indiscriminate deployment of whatever seems to work, regardless of its origin" (Franks, 1984, p. 230).

It is worth noting, to begin with, that Franks' second point is in fact entirely consistent with the aims of theoretical integration in general and the cyclical psychodynamic approach in particular. It is precisely what distinguishes theoretical integration from technical eclecticism that the former aims for a "clearly articulated system" rather than "an indiscriminate deployment of whatever seems to work." However, it must also be noted that the kind of clearly articulated system toward which the cyclical psychodynamic approach aims is significantly different from that advocated by Franks. For Franks, only data that have been koshered, not only by a particular methodology but also by particular ideological affiliations, are acceptable. That is why he places such emphasis on "origins." Data deriving from psychoanalytic sources are deemed unacceptable and can therefore comfortably be ignored. All psychoanalysts, in Franks' view, share "an acceptance of a methodology and a definition of science and its acceptable yardsticks that are quite alien to the behavior therapist" (p. 231).*

Thus, it is not simply a clearly articulated system that Franks advocates but a clearly articulated system *rooted in the exclusion of data from sources outside the system.* And it is this exclusion that is challenged by the cyclical psychodynamic approach. To be sure, there are almost certainly aggregate differences in the epistemological preferences of psychoanalysts and behavior therapists. *On average* or *as a group,* they adhere to different criteria. But it is also the case, as I have seen repeatedly in observing the work of behavior therapists and discussing cases with them, that good behavior therapists are attentive to

---

*Franks argues as well that all psychoanalysts employ the model he attributes to them, "even though [they] might think otherwise" (p. 231). This raises the intriguing question of whether Franks assumes that, for those who "think otherwise," their underlying assumptions are unconscious.

impressions gained in clinical practice and base their clinical work on far more than what has been demonstrated in the laboratory. And it is the case as well that considerable data have been collected by psychoanalysts or in the service of exploring psychoanalytic hypotheses that utilize the standard methodologies of psychological science (e.g., Barron, Eagle, & Wolitzky, 1992; Luborsky, 1996; Luborsky & Crits-Christoph, 1990; Masling, 1983; Shevrin, Bond, Brakel, Hertel, & Williams, 1996; Singer, 1990).

According to Franks, "Those of us who have encountered both the behavior therapist's painstaking attention to precise but sometimes trivial detail and the psychoanalyst's willingness to have a ready explanation for virtually everything will readily appreciate the vast gulf between the two systems" (1984, p. 232). In these characterizations, Franks does manage to be evenhanded; both behavior therapists *and* psychoanalysts come off badly. But he does not capture very well the complexity of the real world diversity among both groups.

Franks's strategy for pruning the data does make consistency easier; there are fewer disturbing new observations that do not quite fit. But while that may be a plus for the mental serenity of the narrow-gauge theorist, it is scarcely a spur to new thinking. It is the challenge from outside our assumptive world that spurs creativity and new ideas. Forced to change one's conceptualization by unexpected or unfamiliar data, one is then in a position to notice and think to look for *new* data that one otherwise would not have encountered.

The stereotypes that Franks employs to foreclose the question of how to transcend the limitations of particularistic approaches are not restricted to epistemology. To be sure, epistemological questions are the primary ones Franks instructs his border guards to ask in strictly enforcing the boundaries between psychoanalytic and behavioral approaches; but clinical questions too are framed by him in such a way as to preclude *a priori* the possibility of combining or integrating perspectives. In psychoanalysis, Franks asserts, "direct behavioral intervention is never acceptable" (1984, p. 232).

It is certainly not difficult to find psychoanalysts who would agree with Franks on this last point. But the issue is not nearly as categorical or without ambiguity as Franks presents it as being. In the very same volume as Franks' comments, for example, Merton Gill (1984a), one of the most thoughtful and influential psychoanalysts of his generation, suggested that, although direct behavioral intervention was not compatible with psychoanalysis, such intervention might well fit within the purview of psychodynamic psychotherapy. Indeed, Gill argues,

That psychodynamic techniques and techniques of direct behavioral intervention can be combined is no longer in question. They can be and are being combined. The combination differs from how psychodynamic therapists ordinarily work, in the abandonment of the stricture against direct behavioral intervention that was adopted from psychoanalysis. (p. 180)

Gill does join Franks, as it were, in excluding such interventions in psychoanalysis per se. Indeed, he offers a somewhat similar rationale. Franks comments that

it is difficult to see how the behavioral goal of direct intervention can be combined with a primary concern for therapeutic experience of the relationship in terms of prior subjective and often symbolic patterns. (pp. 232–233)

Gill seems to concur when he states that

it is hard for me to see how a therapy centrally concerned with a hierarchy of imagined situations to promote desensitization, for example, can be combined with a central concern with the patient's experience of the relationship that is designed to show how that experience is influenced by the patient's prior expectation. (p. 182)

In fact, however, not only can the two approaches be combined, but Gill himself provides very useful theoretical input and clinical guidelines in this regard. To begin with, he notes that the implications of using behavioral interventions vary depending on whether the therapist examines how doing so is experienced and given meaning by the patient, and he states quite explicitly that the approach described in this book does do just that. Moreover, the central thrust of Gill's writing in the last years of his life (e.g., Gill, 1982; 1994) was to argue that the analysis of the transference was not well pursued by the analyst's attempting to remain so neutral or anonymous that he or she had no discernible impact on the patient's experience. Gill not only thought such a goal quixotic, but argued that the insistence on such a stance by many analysts actually interfered with the effective analysis of the transference.

The analyst's actual behavior, attitudes, and demeanor, even the inevitable variations in when she comments or asks questions and when she sits and listens, will always have an impact on the patient's experience (cf. Greenson, 1967; Wachtel, 1993b). The contention that the patient's transference reaction simply "emerges" or "unfolds" from within, with the actual events between the patient and therapist as at most a "hook" or "trigger" for reactions simply lying in wait and virtually destined to spring forth is not only false in Gill's view as it evolved, but clinically counterproductive (cf. Wachtel, 1982). Contrary to what is often assumed, the patient is not more likely to ward off exploration of her inner experiences if the analyst gives her an "excuse" by providing a rationale for that experience in terms of what is actually transpiring; rather, acknowledgment of the analyst's role is likely to enable the patient to feel freer to own up to, and to be more interested in exploring, her own (Gill, 1982).

Such a position is also more respectful of the patient's experience. Its thrust is not to invalidate the patient's perception by attempting to persuade her that her perception comes from the past and from her unconscious rather than from what is really going on. Rather, it regards the perception as coming both from the patient's inner imperatives and proclivities and from what is really happening. What becomes the focus of exploration is the patient's characteristic way of making sense of what occurs, rather than simply the patient's "distortions." The analyst, in Gill's approach (which in this respect has much in common with the approach described in this book), attempts to understand how the patient indeed might see what transpired in the way she did (that is, to see it as one valid and plausible possibility), but raises the question with the patient of whether there are also *other* ways to understand the experience. That the patient's interpretation of events has been shaped by earlier experiences and that many of the shaping forces are unconscious remains a central assumption. But because the account is not reductionistic, because it does not attempt to persuade the patient that her reaction is nothing but the effect of past experiences and unconscious proclivities, the patient is likely to feel more respected and taken seriously, and thus to be more receptive truly to explore rather than either to resist overtly or comply superficially.

The underlying assumptions of this approach are constructivist. Gill challenges the notion that the analyst has seen the interaction accurately or correctly and the patient, out of transference, has "distorted" it. Rather, each has a perspective on events that reflects how he or she has constructed events, and the aim is not so much to correct the patient's misperceptions as to broaden the range of ways she may construe experience. Interestingly, this constructivist emphasis, which is paralleled by other important contributions in the recent psychoanalytic literature (e.g., Aron, 1996; Hoffman, 1991, 1992; Mitchell, 1993; Schafer, 1980, 1992; Spence, 1982; Stern, 1992), is shared as well by important contributions from cognitive and cognitive–behavioral perspectives (see, for example, Feixas & Neimeyer, 1990; Fernandez Alvarez, 1992; Guidano, 1991; Mahoney, 1995; Neimeyer & Mahoney, 1995; Ryle, 1990).

## DEFINITIONS AS GATEKEEPERS

It should be apparent that much of the controversy over the possibility of an integration between psychodynamic and behavioral or cognitive–behavioral approaches comes down to matters of definition. As I noted in a paper in the same volume as the Franks and Gill papers, "It is not very difficult to argue against an integration of psychodynamic and behavioral approaches. All one has to do is to define psychodynamic and behavioral in the right way, and they will indeed be incompatible" (Wachtel, 1984, p. 31). Franks, we have seen, defines each approach in a way that declares its essence to be an exaggeration of the modal epistemological presumptions of each group. If we accept his definitions, his way of framing what are the key issues, the two approaches certainly do appear to be incompatible.

But defining the essence of the two approaches in this way is tendentious and misleading. Epistemology and research methodology are not the sole concerns of either group, and as we have seen, there is more overlap even on these counts than Franks acknowledges. Moreover, the differences in epistemological preferences that do exist overall between the two groups do not necessarily constitute arguments against integration. The very fact that psychodynamic and behaviorally oriented therapists root their approaches in such different databases contributes to the need for an overarching framework to encompass the observations accruing from both. As I have put the matter in a different context,

> the tendency for proponents of psychodynamic theories and proponents of behavioral and social learning theories to base their formulations on rather different data bases, with neither addressing the full range of observations that are encompassed by the other . . . is a severe limitation on the adequacy of either theory alone. . . . Psychodynamic theorists tend to regard the experiments which form the basis for social learning formulations as mostly trivial. They are viewed as sidestepping significant phenomena in the quest for a specious certainty. Moreover, the generalizability and applicability of the experimental findings to real-life circumstances outside the laboratory are seen as questionable; the assiduous application of experimental controls in one setting disguises the leaps of faith required in applying those findings to contexts that are sometimes radically different. Behaviorally oriented clinicians and investigators, on the other hand, tend to hew to an epistemology that is dismissive of uncontrolled clinical observation and to attempt to found their theories on experimentally verified propositions.

> There is a measure of truth in each side's attacks on the other's data base, but the sum of their assaults adds up to the inadequacy of either alone and

the need for the tempering of one with the strengths of the other, both epistemologically and in the focus of their observations. (Wachtel, 1994, p. 51)

Gill's definitions, too, present a challenge to integration; but because they are more rooted in the actualities of what therapists think and do—and thus, ironically, are more empirical than those of Franks, who anchors his definitions in abstract ideological and epistemological stances—they can be more readily probed and explored. (Franks's definitions, in contrast, can really only be accepted or rejected; they are more closed or conclusory.) For Gill, the key distinction between psychoanalysis and psychodynamic psychotherapy has to do with how thoroughly the interaction between patient and therapist or analyst is examined. It is certainly true that Gill is skeptical to say the least regarding whether, when direct behavioral interventions are employed, such examination can be sufficiently thorough to merit the term "psychoanalysis." He acknowledges that *some* analysis of the meaning of the intervention to the patient can be achieved if the therapist is so inclined—and it is precisely because my own approach is to explore that meaning that he supports the efforts described in this book, so long as they are described as an integration of psycho*dynamic* and behavioral approaches—but he demurs when the integration is depicted as one between psycho*analysis* and behavioral or cognitive–behavioral approaches.

In part, Gill's position seems to reflect a vestigial allegiance to a distinction that has been almost sacred in the psychoanalytic community, that between "psychoanalysis" and "psychotherapy" (cf. Wachtel, 1987, Chapter 12). But his definitions and distinctions lend themselves just as readily to a depiction of a continuum as to a sharp dichotomy. The analytic situation, Gill states, "is an interaction from the first minute. . . . Analysis is not an absence of interaction; analysis is an *analysis* of interaction. And the difference between psychoanalysis and psychotherapy is that in psychoanalysis you make every effort you possibly can to analyze the interaction; in psychotherapy, sometimes yes, sometimes no" (Gill, personal communication, 1991).

Several questions remain unresolved in this way of framing the issue. Making "every effort you possibly can" to analyze the interaction is not as unambiguous a directive as it might first appear to be. You cannot, after all, spend *all* your time analyzing the interaction or there would be no interaction to analyze (or only a very peculiar one consisting of unceasing efforts to address the implications of what was said—or not said—a moment before). This would not only leave the analyst frantically racing to keep up with a moving target, but would lead both participants into a hall of mirrors in which the patient's experience would likely be one of frustration and bewilderment.

"Making every effort you possibly can" to analyze the interaction cannot mean trying to do *nothing but* analyzing the interaction. There may still be some analysts who routinely respond to every question by the patient with an interpretation rather than an answer, or who even hesitate to express sympathy at the death of a loved one for fear this will create an "unanalyzable" event, but fortunately such behavior is now very far from the analytic mainstream.

Clearly Gill's intention is not to endorse such a caricature of analysis. Indeed, a key thrust of his efforts was to question the sclerotic habits that had, in some hands, become "proper" psychoanalytic technique. Rather, the essence of Gill's message must be understood to be that one *acknowledges* that one is doing many things other than interpreting—indeed, that one is doing many things *even when* interpreting, for interpretations are always given in some affective tone, they are given sometimes and not others, they are shaped by motives of which the analyst is never fully aware, and so forth—but that one remains consistently interested in understanding the *meaning* those interactional dimensions have for the patient.

It is certainly true that Gill was much less confident that the meanings could be disentangled sufficiently when the meaning of introducing a behavioral intervention was considered rather than when the focus was on the meaning of the tone of voice of an interpretation or the patient's experience of the analyst's motive for interpreting her behavior in a particular way. But that was largely a matter, I suggest, of what he was familiar and comfortable with. For, in fact, it is probably easier to disentangle the meaning to the patient of suggesting the use of systematic desensitization to help deal with her phobia than of the analyst's covert affect in making an interpretation. The latter has no less impact and is no less meaningful in Gill's scheme of things; but because it is closer to home for the analyst, and also because it is enmeshed with a clinical tradition in which the very idea that the interpretation is an intervention or an interaction has been denied—this, indeed, is one of the notions Gill was most intent on challenging—it is extremely complicated to "resolve."

In any therapy that is guided by psychoanalytic or psychodynamic premises (including those therapies that are labeled as "psychoanalysis" rather than "psychotherapy"), the task one confronts is inevitably to find the proper balance between examining the interaction and interacting with the patient in other ways. Finding that balance in an optimal way requires a sophisticated understanding of the interpenetrating relation between the two terms. Specifically, it is essential to understand that examining the meaning of what has just transpired is itself a form of interacting and can be examined in its own right for the meaning *it* has to the patient. It is one way to interact with the patient, but attempting literally to do nothing but analyze the interaction is both impossible and farcical.

## MESSER AND WINOKUR'S CRITIQUE OF INTEGRATION: THE ISSUE OF VISIONS OF REALITY

Perhaps the most sophisticated and challenging critique of theoretical integration has been offered by Stanley Messer and his colleagues (see, e.g., Lazarus & Messer, 1988; Messer, 1986, 1992; Messer & Winokur, 1980, 1984). In some ways, Messer's analysis overlaps with those of Franks, Gill, and others in focusing on the contrasting belief systems of psychoanalytic and behavior therapists. But Messer brings an innovative approach to the discussion by introducing the "visions of reality" associated with the four key mythic forms—romantic, ironic, comic, and tragic—as articulated by Northrup Frye (1957) in his influential contribution to literary analysis. Frye's analysis was first applied in the psychotherapeutic realm by Schafer (1976) to spell out the aims and assumptions that guide psychoanalytic work. Messer and Winokur (1980) then further extended this analysis by using it as a basis for distinguishing the visions of reality of psychoanalysts and behavior therapists. Behavior therapy, they argued, is rooted in the comic vision, in which:

> Conflict is viewed as centered in situations, and it can be eliminated by effective manipulative action or via the power of positive thinking. Endings are happy ones free from guilt and anxiety. Security and sexual gratification, comfort and worldly success are, finally, achieved. This description of the comic mode is a remarkably close fit to the language and concepts of behavior therapy. (Messer and Winokur, 1980, p. 823)

Psychoanalysis, in contrast, is viewed by Messer and Winokur as characterized by the complex interweaving of all four visions, with the tragic and ironic visions figuring particularly prominently. The latter two visions of human life, Messer and Winokur argue, are largely antithetical both to the comic vision and to the worldview of behavior therapists that is so closely related. As a consequence, the therapist who would wish to combine them is at best confronted with a circumstance similar to that of the alternating images that characterize some of the experiments derived from Gestalt psychology. One can see the profiles or the cup, but not both at once; the very act of seeing things one way supresses the alternative perception.

Although, as elaborated below, potential distortions are introduced by applying the scheme of the four visions of reality to the comparison of psychoanalytic and behavioral therapy (stemming in part from the authors' clearly greater sympathy for the former than the latter), there is much in Messer and Winokur's account that seems to me insightful and clarifying. Particularly when they move from the generalized discussion of the visions of reality to consideration of the concrete choices introduced by any clinical case, Messer and Winokur illuminate usefully the often unrecognized background assumptions that shape the options therapists see as available and the goals and methods they see as appropriate. Here and in Messer's later contributions (e.g., Lazarus & Messer, 1988, 1991; Messer, 1986), one gains a vivid sense of the differences in the ways clinicians of the two schools approach clinical choice points, set goals, and bring their values into play in the clinical process.

Nonetheless, it is essential to note a number of aspects of Messer and Winokur's analysis that are potentially misleading and that provide a falsely negative picture of the prospects for integration. To begin with, Messer and Winokur's analysis shares a limitation already discussed in considering the critique of Franks. They treat a real and substantial difference between the modal tendencies of the two groups of therapists as if it were an essential or intrinsic difference. That is, although *on the average* psychoanalytic and behavioral therapists differ in the ways Messer describes—and though indeed the differences are not just statistical subtleties but pervasive and robust—overlap does exist. Moreover, the exceptions to the general tendency are not just cases of therapists being illogical or manifesting ignorance of the essential foundation of their own orientation. Many, rather, are expanding the envelope, pushing against the self-imposed limits of their native tradition to discover new ways of applying its methods and resources.

To be sure, Messer and Winokur's analysis is closer to the bone, as it were, than Franks'. That is, Franks' emphasis on epistemology and research methodology does not capture well the concerns that are most focal to clinicians—of either school—in the course of their daily clinical work. Franks, in effect, mistakes the preoccupations of a subset of academics for the issues that occupy center stage in the deliberations and choices of practitioners. Messer and Winokur, in contrast, root their analysis in observations of clinicians at work and in considerations that are part of daily clinical decision making. Nonetheless, their account as well dichotomizes too sharply, treating readily discernible group differences in the proclivities of behavior therapists and psychoanalysts as if they were *sine qua nons*. Perhaps not surprisingly, given that the authors' own orientation is psychoanalytic, it is particularly in characterizing the worldview of behavior therapists that exaggeration and oversimplification slip in. Many behavior therapists fit easily into their portrayal; many others do not.

A second difficulty with Messer and Winokur's account is that there is something biased and misleading about the very categories they employ to contrast the two approaches. The problem does not lie with the categories per se; for purposes of literary analysis, they are useful and illuminating. Indeed, even in the psychological realm they have proved useful; their adaptation by Schafer (1976) to highlight the interweaving perspectives and assumptions that underlie psychoanalytic work added to our understanding of the complexities of psychoanalyst's choices and the values and assumptions that (sometimes in conflict) contribute to them. But something odd happens when these same categories are applied in the context of Messer's analysis. For when they are used to *compare* the worldviews of psychoanalysis and behavior therapy, problematic biases and distortions are introduced.

First, in Messer and Winokur's account, psychoanalysis is depicted in terms of the interacting influence of four different visions of reality, whereas behavior therapy is treated as fully encompassed by only one. This alone plays into the stereotype of behavior therapy as simplistic, though it is merely an artifact of the way Messer and Winokur have sliced the pie. Second, compounding matters, the one vision attributed to behavior therapy is labeled as "comic." Messer and Winokur are careful to indicate that comic in this context is not intended to imply "funny," "in a light vein," or "not serious." But the very term, especially when presented as the only vision through which behavior therapists view the world, inevitably implies a lack of seriousness. Subtly, the message in part becomes, "psychoanalysis and behavior therapy cannot be integrated because one is serious and complex and the other is superficial and silly."*

---

*To be sure, I believe that Messer and Winokur did not explicitly set out to convey such a message. But psychoanalysts most of all should be aware of the influence of connotations that convey something quite other than the official "manifest content."

It is important to note that over time Messer's views about the possibilities of integration have evolved. His later writings on this theme, while remaining committed to an essentially psychoanalytic approach, and continuing to explore the obstacles to integration posed by divergent visions and assumptions held by therapists of different orientations, cautiously endorse the positive value of integrating some aspects of other approaches. Messer now advocates an "evolutionary" or "assimilative" integration in which "techniques and concepts from one therapy do indeed find their way into another, and get incorporated within its slowly evolving theory and mode of practice." He cautions, however, that these importations should be "very selective" and "carried out in such a way that they fit comfortably into the larger theoretical context" (Lazarus & Messer, 1991, p. 153).

## CONCLUDING COMMENTS: WHAT IS AN INTEGRATION?

Perhaps most important to understand is that arguments showing that psychoanalysis and behavior therapy are *different* do not imply that they cannot be integrated. Indeed, were they not different in significant ways, the pursuit of integration would be pointless. It is precisely because each approach introduces perspectives and emphases that the other does not that an integration of the two holds the promise of being more useful than either separately. Moreover, it is their difference as well that makes an effort at integration interesting and challenging. Putting together elements that are already widely viewed as compatible is scarcely much of a feat.

The total set of procedures, theories, and philosophical assumptions that presently constitutes behavior therapy (even cognitive–behavior therapy) is indeed incompatible with the total set of procedures, theories, and philosophical assumptions of psychoanalysis. The gulf that Franks, Messer, Lazarus, and others have described does exist in various ways. But it is possible to selectively extract significant elements of each and combine them into a new synthesis that shares important (and largely nonoverlapping) features with each of its constituent approaches, but has its own structure and its own internal coherence. That new synthesis will almost certainly resemble each of its constituents more than they resemble each other independently, but it is a new, third procedural and conceptual entity, and it is likely to include not only elements that derive from its original components but new features and new assumptions as well that derive from the requirements and the experience of working within what, increasingly, is a new and different framework.

As I put it in an earlier reply to the arguments of Messer and Winokur,

> The fallacy in most arguments against integration is a failure to appreciate that a synthesis is a different entity than either of its constituents. It is a clinical and theoretical approach with its own structure. It can be selective in what aspects of each approach it incorporates, drawing upon what seems potentially useful in constructing a new synergistic strategy, rather than upon what proponents of each as *separate* therapies regard as most important. The major constraint is that the elements must not be incompatible in the context of the new structure. (Wachtel, 1984, p. 47)

That, at least, is the aim of the kind of integrative effort that has come to be labeled *theoretical integration*. At this point, theoretical integrations, such as cyclical psychodynamics, resemble their constituent elements in numerous and obvious ways. Quite possibly, as cyclical psychodynamics and other integrative efforts evolve, their unique and emergent features will become increasingly central. In principle, that is a development to be welcomed; it is particularly the aim of efforts at theoretical integration such as cyclical psychodynamics—moreso than either technical eclecticism or the search for common factors—to be generative in just this way. This prospect should, however, introduce a note of caution as well. As different integrative schemes develop their own particular characteristics, the danger emerges of their evolving into "schools" themselves. It would be ironic and damagingly self-contradictory if this were to happen.

Those of us who are proponents of integrative approaches must be alert to the possibilities for borrowing from our fellow integrationists as well as from the established "schools." It is inevitable that different approaches to and styles of integration will persist; people differ in temperament, personality, cognitive style, and fundamental philosophy, and it is precisely the aim of the integrative movement to respect those differences and acknowledge their validity. A single, lock-step integrative approach is essentially a contradiction in terms. But at the same time, "integrating the integrations" must be a continuing task as well. High walls or barbed wire fences between approaches make especially little sense if one is an integrationist.

SEPI's full name (Society for the Exploration of Psychotherapy Integration) is far from mellifluous, but it was chosen carefully. The rhythm of the name would be far more pleasing without the "extra" word *Exploration,* but the organization itself would not. What has made SEPI conferences events that continue to surprise those used to professional meetings where ego and stance-taking pervade is the uncommon degree to which people actually listen to each other. The *exploration* of psychotherapy integration—including both the examination by proponents of integration of our own assumptions and the shortcomings in our own arguments and approaches and the welcome participation of skeptics with enough interest to explore their skepticism even as they offer us their reasons for it—has been the lifeblood both of SEPI as an organization and of the integrative movement itself.

In a similar vein, it was no accident either that *Psychotherapy Integration* rather than *Integrative Psychotherapy* became part of the organization's name. Whereas the latter can seem to imply a single approach and a finished product, the former implies a process. Psychotherapy integration is a continuously ongoing process in which more and more therapists, researchers, and theorists are participating. Through the integration of their efforts as well—that is, of clinical experience, empirical data, and conceptual inquiry and synthesis—the open-ended effort we call psychotherapy integration will hopefully continue to evolve.

# 15

# *The Changing Visions of Psychoanalytic Therapists: Object Relations, Self Psychology, and the Relational Paradigm*

THE versions of psychoanalytic thought that were primarily addressed in the original edition of *Psychoanalysis and Behavior Therapy* were classical Freudian thought (including its modifications in psychoanalytic ego psychology) and interpersonal theories such as those of Horney and Sullivan. In the ensuing years, other perspectives have become increasingly prominent in American psychoanalytic discourse, particularly the "self psychology" that has evolved from the work of Heinz Kohut and his followers and the variety of related perspectives that are generally referred to as object relations theories. These latter two perspectives, along with interpersonal theory, have been depicted by Greenberg and Mitchell (1983; Mitchell, 1988, 1993) as constituting a broadly "relational" perspective that contrasts in significant ways with the "drive/structure" theory of classical psychoanalysis and psychoanalytic ego psychology. I wish in this chapter to clarify how the new developments in relational thinking in psychoanalysis bear on the synthesis offered in *Psychoanalysis and Behavior Therapy.*

The interpersonal point of view was the first relational theory to take hold on these shores. Its impact on psychodynamic thought was substantial, but most of the influence was indirect or unacknowledged; the interpersonal perspective was rather widely viewed as of only peripheral influence in psychoanalytic quarters at the time *Psychoanalysis and Behavior Therapy* was written (Wachtel, 1982). Although proponents of the ideas of Sullivan and Horney usually described themselves as psychoanalysts, the term "psychoanalysis" frequently tended to evoke images within the profession that were limited to the Freudian version and its direct heirs. For this reason, much of the discussion in the book used the broader term "psychodynamic" rather than psychoanalysis or psychoanalytic, but the very title of the book may have led to some confusion (see Wachtel, 1984).

Today, things are quite different. Psychoanalysis is more open to diversity than ever before in its history. Factional strife, to be sure, has not entirely disappeared, but there is a genuine exchange of ideas between analysts of different persuasions to a degree that not long ago would have seemed impossible. The major psychoanalytic journals regularly include, in the same issue, contributions written from classical, ego psychological, self psychological, and object relational points of view, and categorizing analysts as to which grouping they belong is not always easy today. Current psychoanalytic writing offers a rich but potentially unstable mixture of models and insights deriving from sources once rather isolated from each other. The results can sometimes be confusing; contemporary psychoanalytic theorizing at times unwittingly mixes models that retain the hermetic vision of psychic fragments sealed off from influence by the perceptual world (the "woolly mammoth" model discussed in Chapter 3) and concepts rooted in an appreciation of the continuing transactional impact of our ongoing experiences with other people. But the entire enterprise is evolving rapidly, and the possibility of contradictory formulations developing along the way is more than compensated for by greater openness that spurs creativity and questioning of orthodoxy. Perhaps most germane to the theoretical issues discussed in this book, the very term "psychoanalysis" now refers to a considerably wider range of models and concepts. The exploration of new and expanded implications of psychoanalytic ideas addressed here, confusing when the term "psychoanalysis" so strongly evoked images of the Freudian drive model, now fits more readily within an expanded psychoanalytic discourse that views the boundaries of what is and is not psychoanalytic much less restrictively.

## THE ASCENDANCY OF OBJECT RELATIONS THEORIES

Amidst the diversity that presently characterizes psychoanalytic thought, a discernible central tendency or common thrust is nonetheless apparent. As Greenberg and Mitchell (1983) have put it, "The common 'landscape' of psychoanalysis today consists of an increasing focus on people's interactions with others, that is, on the problem of object relations" (p. 2). Such a depiction would seem to ease still further the path of integration pursued in this book. Both behavioral approaches and family systems approaches are focally concerned with people's interactions with others. To discern possible points of convergence between these approaches and a version of psychoanalytic thought that shares that concern would seem a considerably easier task than to find links to versions of psychoanalysis in which such a focus is missing or less central.

Matters are not as simple as they might first seem, however. To equate "object relations" with a "focus on people's interactions with others," although in one sense quite accurate, is in another rather misleading. For although virtually all conceptualizations that fall under the rubric of object relations attend to *something* about the impact of human relationships on our psychological development, by no means are object relations concepts necessarily centered on our *interactions* with others (see below). There is a vast difference between conceptualizations that emphasize the tangible transactions between actual people and conceptualizations that emphasize what are called "internal" object relations.

Much confusion can result from failing to note the specific sense in which the term is being used. Contemporary object relations theories encompass a wide range of ideas about relationships, development, personality structure, and the process of psychotherapy. In the hands of some authors, "object relations" is indeed virtually synonymous with "relations with other people." Used this way, the concept is relatively experience-near and subject to reasonably satisfactory assessment by observing how people actually live. For others, the label "object relations" connotes an approach that stresses not so much our actual interactions with actual other human beings, but rather our ties to inner "presences," emotionally charged images that, although they in some way derive from our concrete experiences with other people, are primitive, fantasy laden constructions that may bear little relation to the events and persons that might be discerned by an adult observer. In this theoretical vein, to say that we are attached to our objects means that, however varied or promiscuous our manifest daily behavior might appear, our fundamental aims entail maintaining the symbolic and fantasied ties to the inner "presences" that represent our earliest attachments.

Thus, maintaining a tie to "Mother," for example, may have little to do with behavior toward the individual whose name appears on one's birth certificate. Maintaining the "inner" tie, indeed, may well require defying and disappointing *that* Mother, even physically separating oneself from her or cutting off contact with her altogether. That is, in some versions of object relations theory, it is not the contemporary ties to actual people that matter but the fantasied ties to images from very early in life—images that do not bear a one-to-one correspondence to the biological entity one consciously learns to call Mother, but rather embody fragments of experience organized around representations of selfness, otherness, and the relation between them. Such formulations are not entirely isolated from clinical observation or empirical assessment—Fairbairn's (1952) conceptualizations, for example, which are among the most abstruse in the entire literature, derive very considerably from his observations of how fervently children who have been abused cling to and justify the abusing parent. But formulations that stress the patient's "inner world" or "internal" object relations present a considerably greater danger of introducing a closed system mode of thought that is virtually impossible to disconfirm.

In general, cyclical psychodynamic formulations are more closely related to clinical observation than are many versions of object relations theory. Although cyclical psychodynamics does not share the strict operationism sometimes espoused by Sullivan (but often contradicted or, depending on one's point of view, transcended, in Sullivan's actual clinical formulations and in those of contemporary interpersonalists), its inferences are considerably less speculative and more anchored in concrete clinical phenomena than object relations formulations tend to be. Nonetheless, object relations concepts have increasingly found their way into cyclical psychodynamic accounts, and recent presentations of the cyclical psychodynamic approach (e.g., Wachtel, 1993b) describe means of addressing, in concrete and specific clinical detail, what might be thought of as internalized objects (see especially pp. 236–255). This is one sense in which the point of view presented in this book is part of the broadly relational thrust in psychoanalytic thought articulated by Greenberg, Mitchell, and others. (Other ways in which cyclical psychodynamics fits within the relational rubric should be apparent as well, as I proceed.)

One of the main ways in which the cyclical psychodynamic account differs from that offered by most object relations theorists is in its view of psychological development as a process of continuing and continuous development rather than as a splitting off of "primitive" psychological tendencies in such a way that the tendencies become part of an "inner world" largely impervious to the impact of daily experience with actual others. This does not mean that the cyclical psychodynamic approach ignores the clinical phenomena emphasized by object relations theorists. Rather, the "infantile" or "archaic" fantasies and attachments that object relations theorists stress are reworked theoretically in order to illuminate how they are part of a complex interactional system. As in the reworking of classical Freudian formulations earlier in this book, the key to this reworking entails examining how the intrapsychic experience varies with, and symbolically represents, the individual's concrete experiences with other people. In addition, the development of these intrapsychic structures and processes is understood in terms of a continuous and progressive back and forth between intrapsychic structures and actual life events and interpersonal transactions, rather than in terms of encapsulated and discontinuous developmental events. This reworking is consistent with accumulating research findings on the process of psychological development (Zeanah, Anders, Seifer, & Stern, 1989).

## THE IMPACT OF KOHUT AND THE PSYCHOLOGY OF THE SELF

A second new thrust of great moment for the evolution of psychoanalytic thought in recent decades—and converging in interesting ways with the approach depicted in this book (though certainly also differing in significant ways)—has been the self psychology developed by Heinz Kohut (e.g., 1971, 1977, 1984) and elaborated by his followers (e.g., Basch, 1983; Fosshage, 1992; Goldberg, 1983; Lichtenberg & Kaplan, 1983; Ornstein, 1991; Stolorow & Lachmann, 1980; Wolf, 1988). At the heart of Kohut's reformulation of psychoanalytic theory was the conclusion that the essence of his patients' psychological experience "was not an aggressive or sexual fantasy, wish, or drive but, rather, a struggle to express the need for responses that would evoke, maintain, or enhance their sense of self" (Bacal, 1995, p. 354). The implication of this reframing, according to Bacal, was "a more collaborative and less adversarial quality to the therapeutic process than that which is informed by the more traditional analytic perspectives" (p. 355).

Why this should be is especially well articulated by Basch (1995), who begins his discussion with a striking example that captures—for me, chillingly—an all too common (mis)understanding of what psychoanalytic work entails:

> A candidate I was supervising presented the following excerpt from his patient's material: Once on the couch, the patient said, "Well, I did it. Did you see the papers?" The patient was referring to a major achievement that had come to fruition after much planning, hard work, and anxiety and was now being publicly acknowledged and celebrated. "Of course, I said nothing," the candidate assured me. After a minute or so of silence, the patient associated, in an angry tone, to his ungiving, emotionally distant father.
>
> I asked the candidate, "What were you thinking during the patient's silence?" "I wondered what he was trying to get away with," my student replied. "What do you mean, 'trying to get away with'?" "You can't give in to the patient," was the reply. (Basch, 1995, p. 367)

Basch refers to this stance by the analyst as part of the "ritual of abstinence" that characterizes much psychoanalytic work: "whatever the patient wants or seems to want in the way of a response must, on principle, be thwarted" (p. 368). He asks why it is that such an unfacilitative stance would make sense to large numbers of analysts, and traces the foundations of this idea to the theory of dammed up libidinal and aggressive instincts and the conception of the patient as seeking surreptitiously to discharge these instinctual energies. Unwitting gratification by the analyst or failure by the analyst to be firm and steady enough to prevent such gratification would momentarily permit the patient to feel better, but at the cost of leaving the repressed mental contents intact and of vitiating the motivation to address the more difficult, but more enduringly beneficial, task of working through the defenses against these impulses and enabling them to find a stable, ego-syntonic mode of expression. As Basch put it, depicting the position that Kohut's views transcended,

> Only through the frustration engendered by the analyst's silence would the repressed needs, in some derivative form, become focused on the analyst and, once so transformed, be open to interpretation and genetic reconstruction, a process that lifted the repression and left the patient now free to deal with life as he would have been able to do had his neurosis not interfered with the normal development of the ego. (Basch, 1995, p. 369)

Kohut's approach, in contrast, posits that it is not fundamentally the discharge of instinctual gratification that the patient seeks but the affirmation of his efforts to feel whole, worthy, and efficacious. In clinical practice, this implies a rather different stance toward the patient and the experiences and inclinations she communicates in the course of the therapeutic work. Reviewing Kohut's book, *The Restoration of the Self* in the *Journal of the American Psychoanalytic Association*, Stein (1979) notes the "austere and demanding discipline" that characterizes psychoanalytic work and regards Kohut's approach as compromising that to some degree.

Further amplifying the basis for the difference in viewpoint between Basch and Kohut on the one hand, and Freudians such as Stein on the other, Aron (1991) noted that from the vantage point of Freudian drive theory, therapy must be carried out in an atmosphere of abstinence and renunciation.

> The patient must give up infantile wishes, renounce unconscious longings, abandon strivings after childhood sexual objects, and all of this must be done in an atmosphere of deprivation. The analyst must always be careful *not* to gratify transference wishes, because if gratified these wishes would no longer push for satisfaction (discharge) and therefore there would be no motivation (energy) with which to uncover repressed memory. (p. 91)

Freud, Aron points out,

> often wrote that once the unconscious conflicts between impulses and defense were made conscious, then, in the light of secondary process thought, the patient would have to *renounce* or *condemn* the infantile wishes. Waelder (1960) wrote that once the drive was recognized as part of oneself, it would be condemned, "consciously denied gratification," so that after a while it would gradually be "given up." ... This is consistent with references in Freud's writings to the analyst's having to "persuade" patients to "abandon" particular infantile strivings, as well as to his description of the need to induce the patient to "adopt our conviction . . . of the impossibility of conducting life on the pleasure principle." (p. 88)

Followers of Kohut take a very different view of what is required to achieve a therapeutically useful stance toward the patient. Much like the cyclical psychodynamic view that underlies this book, they reject the idea that the patient's basic impulses are essentially antisocial and regressive and that therapeutic change entails the renunciation of those impulses. Rather, from the perspective of self psychology, when such impulses appear they are viewed as "disintegration products," results of the failure of the self to thrive and be facilitated rather than direct expressions of our most fundamental, undisguised nature (Kohut, 1977).

To be sure, from the vantage point of cyclical psychodynamics, there are difficulties with some aspects of the conceptual framework of self psychology. Self psychologists place considerable stock in the concept of developmental arrest, positing that failures on the part of the parent early in life to empathize with the needs of the developing child lead her to get "stuck" in an early mode of experiencing herself and, in important respects, to fail to go beyond the developmental level of an early childhood self structure. My objections to the concept of developmental arrest are perhaps best captured by the title of a paper I delivered a few years ago: "Development Is Never Arrested, but Sometimes It Is Put on Probation." The point I wished to make was not that people cannot persist in rather childlike ways and fail in important respects to "grow up"—that certainly happens—but rather that thinking of this phenomenon as "developmental arrest" offers an excessively static and hermetic account that begs the most important and interesting question: What has to keep happening for this to persist?

Also problematic is that the emphasis on developmental arrest is part of a psychology of deficits. Something is *missing* in the patient, something is damaged or faulty. Wile (1984) has articulated this dimension of Kohut's work especially forcefully. In a paper that acknowledges the ways in which self psychology does point to more humane and respectful formulations regarding the patient than had been previously typical of psychoanalytic discourse, Wile nonetheless shows how the emphasis on deficits can be subtly but significantly demeaning. Wile (1984) reformulates Kohut's observations in ways that address the same clinical phenomena from a more affirmative vantage point (see also, Wachtel, 1993b). Even Basch (1995), in the paper discussed above, which is otherwise highly consistent with the spirit of this book, sees the major part of his patient's difficulties as deriving from deficits—indeed, from deficits that are "earlier" than those stressed by Freud (p. 371). Here again, it seems, the model of the encapsulated past intrudes on an otherwise progressive point of view.

In contrast with the emphasis on arrest and deficit, there is much in self psychology that is not only salutary but also highly consonant with the approach described in this book—for example, self psychology's emphasis on empathy and respect for the experience of the patient, and its recognition of the inevitable imperfections of the analyst or therapist, with the consequent understanding that progress in the work comes from dealing with mistakes, not from avoiding them. Indeed, central to how self psychology understands therapeutic change is the therapist's acknowledgment of the inevitable breaks in empathy that occur, along with the therapist's efforts to address with the patient the meaning of such experiences. Of special importance in providing a ba-

sis for reconciling the self psychological perspective with that of cyclical psychodynamics was the recognition by Kohut and his followers that
the need for the participation of others to maintain a sense of self is
not just a pathological phenomenon. Rather, the need for what self psychologists call a "selfobject" is a central psychological characteristic of
the human species, evident throughout life. Such a perspective is in
marked contrast to the emphasis on deficits and developmental arrests
that reflects the more intrapsychic and pathocentric model from which
self psychology evolved.

## THE CONCEPT OF A "RELATIONAL" PARADIGM

The impact of the developments just described has been considerably enhanced by a further development that has brought these various efforts into productive contact with each other and highlighted the
convergences among them. That further development is the introduction of the concept of a "relational" approach to psychoanalytic theory
and practice, encompassing not only object relations theory and self
psychology but the interpersonal approach that, for many years rather
at the periphery of psychoanalytic thought (Wachtel, 1982), has
reemerged as an important contributor to the ferment and development of psychoanalytic ideas.°

The watershed event in the development of the concept of a relational paradigm was the publication of Greenberg and Mitchell's (1983)
volume, *Object Relations in Psychoanalytic Theory.* Its title notwithstanding, the book was not only about object relations theories but about
self psychology and interpersonal theory as well, and, most of all, about
what all three types of theory have in common and how they jointly di-
verge from Freud's drive theory.

The essential thesis is stated with particular clarity by Mitchell in his
1988 volume, *Relational Concepts in Psychoanalysis:*

> The relational-model theories which have dominated psychoanalytic think-
> ing of the past several decades are varied and heterogeneous—they differ
> from one another in many significant respects. Yet they draw on a common
> vision quite different from Freud's and, taken together, have changed the

---

°Having become a part of "where the action is" in psychoanalysis seems to have
stirred greater creativity among interpersonal analysts, who have in recent years
introduced a variety of useful contributions to psychoanalytic discourse (e.g.,
Ehrenberg, 1992; Levenson, 1983; Lionells et al., 1996).

nature of psychoanalytic inquiry. We are portrayed not as a conglomerate of physically based urges, but as being shaped by and inevitably embedded within a matrix of relationships with other people, struggling both to maintain our ties to others and to differentiate ourselves from them. In this vision the basic unit of study is not the individual as a separate entity whose desires clash with an external reality, but an interactional field within which the individual arises and struggles to make contact and to articulate himself. *Desire* is experienced always *in the context of relatedness,* and it is that context which defines its meaning. Mind is composed of relational configurations. The person is comprehensible only within this tapestry of relationships, past and present. (p. 3)

Further elaborating on these trends, and on Mitchell's interpretation of them, Frank (1990) noted that, "From this perspective, different observers have characterized the central mechanism of analytic change according to three dimensions of the 'relational matrix,' that of interpersonal transactional patterns, attachment to others (object-ties), and the self-organization" (p. 739).°

The contention that a coherent relational paradigm has evolved, and that it is conceptually distinct from Freudian drive theory, has not gone unchallenged. For example, object relations concepts—so central to the relational paradigm—are contested territory, claimed by Freudians as well as by avowed relational theorists (e.g., Bachant & Richards, 1993; Kernberg, 1988; Pine, 1990; Rangell, 1985; Sandler, 1992; Spruiell, 1988). Moreover, not all writers who identify with the relational camp disavow concepts that derive from drive theory (e.g., see Aron, 1995; Benjamin, 1991). Greenberg and Mitchell have captured a very important convergence in contemporary psychoanalytic thought, but the dust has not yet settled and the implicit factor analysis, as it were, is not yet complete.

## ONE-PERSON AND TWO-PERSON MODELS

A related, though not identical, concept to that of the relational point of view is the articulation of a two-person model of psychoanalytic understanding in contrast to the one-person model of classical psychoanalytic thought. Modell (1984), who has done much to bring the two-

---

°To my knowledge, Frank's paper was the first in the literature to relate the prospects for integrating active methods into psychoanalytic technique to the articulation of a relational paradigm.

person perspective into focus, notes that in some ways this perspective has been a part of psychoanalysis for a long time. He cites, for example, Balint's (1950) explicit acknowledgment of what should have been obvious from the first day a patient free-associated on Freud's couch— that psychoanalytic theory and technique deal with events occurring between two people and not simply within one. Modell also acknowledges as an important forerunner of the contemporary two-person perspective Winnicott's (1960) famous statement that there is no such thing as a baby, only a baby and a mother.°

An important feature of Modell's own contribution was to articulate the implications of a two-person model in the context of more recent developments in psychoanalytic thought, and to point out the ways in which the one-person versus two-person issue has been fudged by some analysts, who attempt to address the real world of relations between actual people via the strictly intrapsychic concept of "internalized" object relations. Writers such as Klein, Fairbairn, and Kernberg, Modell suggests, pay great attention to the "object," but they introduce a measure of incoherence when they "attempt to preserve the classical viewpoint of psychoanalysis by referring not to the actual object but to the representation of the object in the mind" (1984, p. 17). Modell further notes the fallacies in equating these "internal" objects with the actual objects with which people interact.† Real people are their own center of agency, responding to and evaluating others' actions toward them (and even feelings about them, as they are revealed in actions and nonverbal behavior); internal objects, in contrast, are not people with minds of their own, but "fantasies" that are part of people's own minds.

Thus, some versions of object relations theories lend themselves well to the more comprehensive integrative approach described in this book, but some do not. The cyclical psychodynamic approach, especially as it has evolved since the original publication of *Psychoanalysis and Behavior Therapy* (e.g., see Wachtel, 1993b), is compatible with much that has emerged from the object relations tradition, as it is compatible with much that has derived from self psychology. In certain respects,

---

°Reflecting the highly politicized way in which influence in psychoanalysis is dispersed and acknowledged, Modell gives only passing acknowledgment to Sullivan, whose interpersonal theory was perhaps the first fully elaborated two-person theory based on essentially psychoanalytic premises and remains one of the most thoroughgoing explorations of the implications of a two-person perspective.

†I leave aside at this moment the inelegance and potentially problematic connotations of referring to *persons* as "objects." Let us, for now, recall the pleasantly benign phrase, "the object of my affection" as a way of reminding ourselves that, at its best, this mode of theorizing emphasizes that we *care* about people, even if it does so in a language that obscures that meaning unnecessarily.

it is even compatible with those versions of object relations thinking that Modell has perceptively revealed to be one-person psychologies in two-person clothing. Those theories do address important elements of the unconscious fantasies that motivate and guide people, and, as should be apparent to the reader of this book, such fantasies are an important concern of cyclical psychodynamic theory. In addition, even the one-person versions of object relations theories stress the powerful role in our psychological lives of our attachments and connections to others, a focus that is close to the heart of cyclical psychodynamic theory as well.

The cyclical psychodynamic approach is, however, especially compatible with those versions of object relations and self psychological thinking that are genuinely two-person psychologies. Cyclical psychodynamics attempts to understand people in the context of the key relationships that form the foundation of their lives. Moreover, it highlights the ways in which even the "deepest" and most private experiences can be seen as responses to the actual transactions that create the tone and texture of the person's daily experience. To be sure, the "response" is by no means a simple stimulus-response (S-R) connection, nor is it necessarily linked to the situation by any conventional or socially expectable meaning. As does any psychodynamic approach, cyclical psychodynamics explores the unique meanings people attribute to experiences, which may well be expressed in a disguised and symbolic fashion. But in understanding the private and idiosyncratic, the "intrapsychic structures" that are the focus of most psychodynamic accounts, cyclical psychodynamics nonetheless attempts to examine how those structures are related to the ongoing life experiences of the individual. The structures are not ignored, but they are contextualized.

In the therapeutic relationship itself, this emphasis leads not only to a two-person conception of the therapeutic relationship but to a two-directional view of the causal structure relating the intrapsychic creation of meaning to the actual therapeutic transaction. That is, the therapist's behavior is not simply assimilated into the patient's internal world—the powerful pull of preexisting psychic structures casting its shadow upon the behavior and characteristics of the therapist in relentless and virtually inexorable fashion. Rather, alongside what indeed are powerful (though *not* inexorable) pulls from the past and from "within," are influences of the therapist's behavior *upon* the patient's internal structures, and influences of the *patient's* behavior upon those of the therapist. The total picture is one of continuing and reciprocal influence, a vicious circle of the sort already familiar to the reader of this book. The two persons in the room mutually shape each other's behavior and experience, and the skill of the therapist, from this perspective, is not simply in seeing how the patient's inner world creates the same experience over and over again, but in seeing how the patient and therapist together have participated in the pattern through which the patient recreates her inner world itself over and over again.

The focus is not symmetrical; both patient and therapist are primarily attending to how the patterns of *the patient's* life are replicated.* But the inevitable participation of the therapist in that process of replication—even as she also participates in a process of reflection and examination designed to interrupt that replication—is a necessary implication of a two-person perspective.


## KENNETH FRANK'S EXPLORATIONS OF ACTION TECHNIQUES IN PSYCHOANALYTIC THERAPY: LINKING CYCLICAL PSYCHODYNAMICS AND THE RELATIONAL PARADIGM

In an important series of papers, Frank (1990, 1992, 1993) presented an approach to integration that is closely related to that described in *Psychoanalysis and Behavior Therapy*, but that usefully amplifies the implications of relational theories for such an integration. Action-oriented techniques are used by Frank not only to promote adaptive behavior, but also, following Sandler's (1976, 1981) terminology, to modify the enactments that play a significant role in perpetuating problematic psychic structures. In this, Frank draws as well on the interactional perspective on psychoanalysis described by writers such as Ehrenberg (1992).

In addition to conceptualizing the role of cognitive–behavioral methods as a means of modifying problematic enactments, Frank suggests that "the therapist's use of action-oriented techniques may also be understood as a structure-building technique if, working within a developmental arrest framework emphasizing the self-organization, the therapist conceptualizes the work in terms of actively supplying selfobject functions that are eventually internalized" (1993, p. 537). He does not emphasize this self psychological formulation, however, because his own orientation draws much more heavily on object relations and interac-

---

*A similar process, of course, can be found in the life of the therapist as well (no matter how "well analyzed" she might be). But the place to explore that process in similar detail is in *her own* therapy. The ways the therapist's idiosyncracies and proclivities shape the interaction must be considered, of course, but generally they remain a crucial part of the ground, with the patient's patterns viewed as figure.

tional frameworks than on the developmental arrest model of self psychology.

Frank (1993) notes that a number of contemporary psychoanalytic thinkers have begun to experiment with informal versions of active techniques, often under the rubric of "psychoeducational" methods. Both Gedo (1988) and Basch (1988), for example, point out the importance of skill deficiencies in people's difficulties and of the need to restore competent coping skills. Introducing the more focused and structured behavioral–cognitive techniques, Frank argues, thus builds upon techniques that are already being used informally by many analysts, but offers them in a more powerful form.

Frank's aim is to highlight how a thoroughgoing two-person perspective can open the therapist's eyes to a much wider range of intervention possibilities, but he also points out that often this potential is not fully realized. A variety of conservative assumptions and old habits serve to constrain practice in ways actually more consistent with the older one-person model. Focusing on the implications of the two-person model and of newer relational conceptions of psychoanalysis, Frank builds a case for active intervention in psychoanalytic therapy that is rooted both in cyclical psychodynamic theory and in object relations and self psychology perspectives. Frank's framing of the arguments for active intervention in the language of relational theory helps further to clarify the convergences between relational perspectives and cyclical psychodynamics. It also makes the case for using active interventions in a psychodynamic therapy in terms that are familiar and evocative for psychoanalytic therapists and, as he implies, in terms that may elicit less resistance.

Frank's sophisticated clinical and theoretical discussions contribute importantly to the project of integrating active intervention into psychodynamic practice and also to the integration of the cyclical psychodynamic approach with other relational points of view. In general, the reader of this book will find Frank's papers an invaluable addition to the literature on psychotherapy integration and an important extension of the cyclical psychodynamic point of view. There is one respect, however, in which his characterization can leave the reader with a misleading picture of the cyclical psychodynamic view: He depicts it as "minimizing intrapsychic formulations" (p. 546) and "playing down the role of inner structure and intrapsychic exploration" (p. 537). Because Frank's is a very affirmative account of cyclical psychodynamics and one based, in almost all other respects, on a very sophisticated understanding of the theory and its implications, it is very likely that Frank's mis-

reading of the theory in this one regard reflects a fairly common misconception. It thus seems useful to treat Frank's depiction in this respect as an opportunity to clarify further the nature of cyclical psychodynamic theory and its aims. I shall quote here at length from my
published comments in response to one of Frank's papers:

> If by intrapsychic one means an "inner world" that is conceived of as in no
> way in touch with the world of daily events, then it is correct to say that I
> minimize such formulations. But as Frank himself points out, analysts of a
> variety of orientations are increasingly appreciating that intrapsychic
> processes are better understood as part of an ongoing process of transaction
> with others and that interpersonal and intrapsychic are not really alterna-
> tives but rather two poles of a single interactive or dialectic process. Un-
> derstood this way, the approach I advocate in no way "minimizes intrapsy-
> chic formulations." Rather, what it does is *rework* or *recast* those
> formulations precisely for the purpose of transcending the misleading di-
> chotomy between interpersonal and intrapsychic.
>
> . . . [F]ar from playing down the role of inner structure, [cyclical psy-
> chodynamics] has had as one of its central aims to reconceptualize just what
> inner structure is. . . . What makes early relationships so fateful is their
> *twofold* effect on later experience. First, as psychoanalytic accounts have
> tended to stress, they create the schema or template through which later ex-
> periences are interpreted and understood. Through multiple and complex
> processes of filtering, sifting, and reorganizing, new experiences are given
> meaning in terms of previous experiences and the expectations, biases, fears
> and wishes they have engendered. Reality, we might say, is encountered only
> through the midwifery of fantasy. Because interpersonal and affective events
> are inherently ambiguous, there is substantial latitude for the retrofitting of
> experience to expectation.
>
> But there is a second way in which the past casts a shadow over the pre-
> sent that is equally crucial to appreciate but has received less attention in
> psychoanalytic quarters. As powerful as is the purely assimilative role of un-
> conscious fantasies and expectations, as forcefully as they twist the arm of
> experience until it cries uncle and declares, "Yes, I see once more in this
> new encounter what I have always seen," the power to effect such tenden-
> tious redescription of the events of daily life does have its limits. We could
> not survive until adulthood, much less function effectively enough to afford
> an analyst's fees, were this not the case.
>
> As foggy and idiosyncratic as our view may be of what actually transpires
> between us and other people, it is far from arbitrary or blithely autonomous.
> As Gill (1982, 1983), Hoffman (1983), and others have argued, even the most
> seemingly idiosyncratic transference reactions are rooted in the actual events
> between patient and analyst, and this is the case in our interactions with
> other people in our lives as well. Were others persistently to react to us in

ways that differ from our transferential expectations—transference here referring not just to what transpires between patient and analyst but rather to the pervasive tendency *in all facets of our lives* to experience the present in light of the past and its residue in psychic structures—those expectations would gradually be modified. The past is not an all-powerful dictator in the realm of the psyche but rather one powerful lobby in a system characterized, with homage as much to Montesquieu and Madison as to Freud, by a division of powers. The actual characteristics and intentions of the other, and the social context within which the transaction occurs, also insist on having their due; and the transference lobby, as it were, must settle for the same portion of the pie in the realm of the psyche that the corporate lobby must content itself with in the politics of the nation—enough to do a good deal of mischief but, fortunately, not an absolute.

But just as the corporate interests' influence is exercised not just by muscle alone, but is further magnified by the effects of advertising and the media more generally on the public's perception of what it wants (so that some of what should be negotiated is conceded, some of the force of opposition dissolved), so too in the psychic realm is the influence of the past magnified by the defection of its opposition. That is, where the actualities of the present could, in principle, provide at least some degree of counterbalance to the transferential impact of the past, where a persistent difference between what is expected and what actually happens could gradually chip away at the edges of those expectations, often this does not materialize. Instead, it seems, the opposition caves in and *confirms* the expectation, not just in the distorted eyes of the transference-blinded perceiver, but even as might be seen by a hypothetical unbiased observer (a concept, of course, that is a fantasy in its own right, but a useful one).

For our interpersonal perceptions are directed not to inert objects but to reactive beings, who respond to how they are being perceived. When we perceive a benign or friendly smile as mocking or an expression of interest as something vaguely insidious or sinister, we begin to *change* the other person's attitude, not just in fantasy but in actuality. Initially perhaps it is only the considerable ambiguity of interpersonal affairs that enables us to perceive the other as mocking. But when, three, four, five, or more times, we persist in seeing a darker side to the friendly gesture, and—almost inevitably—convey that perception in some aspect of how we respond to the other (either grossly or subtly), that begins to take its toll. The other will not forever remain benignly interested and friendly in the face of such mistrust (if not outright hostility); before long he or she *will* begin to feel rather unfriendly, thereby "confirming" the first person's suspicions, since indeed the other does "show his true colors" after a while (cf. Wachtel, 1981). Thus do prophecies become self-fulfilling and transferences become fixed and seemingly embedded in the psyche as a kind of supremely independent variable, stubbornly tucking reality into its procrustean bed. (Wachtel, 1993b, pp. 590–592)

## WHAT IS A "PERSON" IN THE TWO-PERSON MODEL?

Confusion about the role of intrapsychic factors in two-person theories has not been limited to considerations of cyclical psychodynamic
theory. What is largely missed in much of the contemporary debate over
one-person and two-person models is that two-person models are models of two "one persons," as it were. That is, the two-person model does
not leave out the structural and dynamic features of concern to one-
person models. Rather, it *understands* those features differently, and
understands them in context. Each participant in any two-person model
that is in any meaningful sense psychoanalytic or psychodynamic brings
to the interaction a host of already structured psychological proclivities
that powerfully and (to a significant degree) predictably influence just
how she interprets what happens. But, she *is* interpreting what happens, not just reeling off something inside ready to be triggered, something that simply "emerges" or "unfolds" (Wachtel, 1982).

When Mitchell (1993, p. 475) writes, "The crucial question is how
one conceives of, and prioritizes, the relationship between one-person
factors and two-person factors, between fantasy and actuality, between
past and present," he is pointing to much the same considerations I am
pointing to. This way of putting it, however, seems to me to concede
just a bit too much and, potentially, to contribute to the very confusion
it is designed to address. Reference to the complementary influence of
one-person factors and two-person factors too readily lends itself to the
misunderstanding that two-person factors are only external and must
be *combined* with one-person factors to include intrapsychic influences.
I would prefer to point out that the two-person model itself considers
fantasy, the past, and so forth, but does so in a fashion that places these
influences in a larger, more comprehensive and integrative framework.°

The very terms "one-person model" and "two-person model," as clarifying as they have been in some ways in the historical development of
psychoanalytic thought, can also introduce confusion. The terms, by
their very nature, make dichotomous understandings and images likely.
Much the same is true for the terms "interpersonal" and "intrapsychic,"
as they are usually presented as opposing pairs; what is missed is that

---

°One should bear in mind, however, Mitchell's warning (p. 468–469) that each
theorist thinks he or she is being more comprehensive, is taking into account all
the factors the others do plus something else. The reader will have to use her own
judgment in evaluating these claims here and elsewhere.

a thorough interpersonal account—certainly a thorough interpersonal *psychoanalytic* account—must include the intrapsychic characteristics of each individual. Or at least it must include the phenomena that are usually *labeled* as intrapsychic. However (cf. Schafer, 1976), these phenomena are understood not as "inside," and certainly not as locked away in some region inaccessible to the light of day, but as the personal, subjective, idiosyncratic, meaning-constructing side of the transaction between two subjectivities. (I shall have more to say about this in Chapter 17. It is part of why family therapy does not simply *replace* psychoanalysis or individual therapy.)

## MERTON GILL AND THE ANALYSIS OF THE TRANSFERENCE

The work of Merton Gill (1982, 1994) on the analysis of the transference was a particularly important development in elaborating the implications of the two-person model. Although beginning in, and continuing to largely identify with, the Freudian camp, Gill increasingly adopted formulations deriving from interpersonal and relational models and emphasized the difference between a one-person model, which he concluded was inaccurate and inadequate, and a two-person model, which opened up new theoretical and therapeutic possibilities.

Gill's clinical work and writing increasingly focused on the analysis of the transference, a focus which in his hands had implications both convergent with and divergent from the approach described in this book. On the one hand, although sympathetic in principle to the idea of incorporating more active methods into the practice of psychoanalytically informed *psychotherapy,* he viewed such methods as antithetical to the aims of *psychoanalysis* (Gill, 1984a), and, implicitly at least, he largely adhered to the traditional view that the latter was invariably the more powerful method for any patient with whom it could be applicable (cf. Wachtel, 1987, Chapter 12). In large measure his reservations about the use of active-intervention methods in psychoanalysis proper derived from a belief that active-intervention methods were incompatible with what he viewed as the overriding aim of psychoanalysis—analyzing the transference continuously and to the greatest extent possible.

On the other hand, Gill's conception of what it means to analyze the transference differs considerably from more traditional conceptions that stress the "distortion" in the patient's perception and the need for the analyst to keep as low a profile as possible in order to persuade the patient that her perceptions derive from her own psychic interior and not from what is actually transpiring (cf. Greenson, 1967; Gill, 1982; Wachtel, 1981). Indeed, as I will try to show, a good case can be made that Gill's own arguments provide powerful support for the view that active interventions do *not* preclude thorough transference analysis.

To begin with, Gill stated unequivocally that "the notion of an 'uncontaminated' transference is a myth," and that the reluctance of many analysts to interact with their patients

> implies a failure to be fully aware that because analysis takes place in an interpersonal context there is no such thing as non-interaction. Silence is of course a behaviour too. Nor can one maintain that silence is preferable for the purpose of analysis because it is neutral in reality. It may be intended to be neutral but silence too can be plausibly experienced as anything ranging from cruel inhumanity to tender concern. It is not possible to say that any of these attitudes is necessarily a distortion. (Gill, 1984b, p. 168)

The patient, Gill suggests, is always responding to something real about the analyst, but she is always responding "in her fashion," as it were. That is, the fact that there is some "real" basis for the patient's perception does not preclude effective transference analysis. Such analysis, in Gill's view, should proceed on a "perspectival" foundation— that is, on the assumption not that the patient's perception is wrong or distorted but that it is only one of many perspectives on what happened, one of many ways that what transpired could be understood or experienced. The analysis of transference thus need not—indeed should not— proceed on the assumption that the patient's reaction had nothing to do with reality but rather that the patient's reality, the patient's characteristic way of construing events, is both valid and limited at once. To be sure, the particular perspective the patient brings to bear on these events derives from her previous history and, very largely, is rooted in unconscious mental structures. That much Gill shares with traditional psychoanalytic thought. But for Gill it is erroneous to try to persuade the patient that her history and unconscious proclivities alone account for her perception. It is erroneous clinically or tactically, because invalidating someone's experience is a poor way to get her to listen. And it is erroneous epistemologically, because it denies the equally influential role of the actual events in generating the perception. The patient's transference experience is neither entirely idiosyncratic nor simply a "realistic" response to what actually happened; it is *her* way of perceiving *this* situation.

Certainly, a therapeutic process must go beyond the articulation of an infinite number of specifics. The patient must reach a generalization that she can carry with her to new experiences, and the primary dimension of that generalization involves her own contribution. In sum, we might say, the focus ends up largely on her contribution. Almost in the way that evoked potentials are measured by cancelling out the interfering noise of other ongoing neural events, the image ultimately achieved by transference analysis entails a kind of cancelling out of the specifics of each situation.* But there is no shortcut through that process. If we attempt in *each* situation to cancel out the role of actual events, if we immediately "cut to the chase," as it were, we end up in endless contradictions and we end up generating needless resistances. What is needed is an understanding of the patient's inclinations *across* situations, but not *without* situations or *independent* of situations.

Transference analysis proceeds best, Gill suggests, when the analyst "approaches the transference in the spirit of seeing how it appears plausibly realistic to the patient" (Gill, 1979, p. 280). Thus, for example,

> A patient's statement that he feels the analyst is harsh . . . is, at least to begin with, likely best dealt with not by interpreting that this is a displacement from the patient's feeling that his father was harsh but by an elucidation of some other aspect of this here-and-now attitude, such as what has gone on in the analytic situation that seems to the patient to justify his feeling. (Gill, 1979, p. 265)

Indeed, in Gill's view,

> it is so important to make a transference interpretation plausible to the patient in terms of a current stimulus that, if the analyst is persuaded that the manifest content has an important implication for the transference but he is unable to see a current stimulus for the attitude, he should explicitly say so if he decides to make the transference interpretation anyway. The patient himself may then be able to say what the current stimulus is. (Gill, 1979, p. 279)

The radical implications of this position—one that Gill and I share—can be especially appreciated if one compares them to Gill's own formulation of several decades before (Gill, 1954), which had been one of the most widely cited arguments bolstering the so-called classical stance in psychoanalytic practice. The very effort to minimize interaction with the patient that Gill criticized in 1984, the empty and mythical em-

---

*There are exceptions to this cancelling out, however, that are very important. See the discussion below of the important role of the patient's understanding how her transferential proclivities are related to relational and affective events.

phasis on neutrality and anonymity, had as one of its key justifications
Gill's formulation that:

> The clearest transference manifestations are those which recur when the an-
> alyst's behavior is constant, since under these circumstances changing man-
> ifestations in the transference cannot be attributed to an external situation,
> to some changed factor in the interpersonal relationship, but the analysand
> must accept responsibility himself. (Gill, 1954, p. 781)

From such a vantage point, active interventions would indeed seem
to "muddy" the transference, make it impossible to analyze or resolve,
because the analyst would be "really" doing something instead of staying constant and in the background. Those analysts who remain fixated,
as it were, on formulations such as Gill's from the 1950s can see little
basis for utilizing active-intervention techniques without utterly abandoning an interest in transference—or, put differently, without giving
up psychoanalysis altogether.

From Gill's later vantage point, however, in which the analyst is *always* "really" doing something, and in which that fact is not an obstacle to transference analysis but an essential dimension of it, the objections to active intervention become much weaker. Gill himself, to be
sure, never went the extra step to become an advocate of active intervention (though he was at least sympathetic enough to the effort to be
a member of the original Professional Advisory Board of SEPI). But
the thrust of his work in the last decade or so of his life contributes
much conceptual support for such efforts.*

## "CONTAMINATION?" OR EVENT TO ANALYZE

The various trends and developments just described further bolster
the case for the introduction of active intervention techniques into a

---

*Indeed, as Frank (1993) notes, Gill's later formulations have a great deal in
common with the cyclical conceptions that guide the present work. Gill, for example, increasingly emphasized the ways in which intrapsychic and interpersonal
factors mutually influence each other. As he put it, "The intrapsychic patterns not
only determine selective attention to those aspects of the external world which
conform to them, but the individual behaves in such a way as to enhance the likelihood that the responses he meets will indeed confirm the views with which he
sets out. This external validation, in turn, is necessary for the maintenance of those
patterns. . . . It is this last insight that psychoanalytic theory often ignores, postulating instead an internal pressure to maintain the intrapsychic patterns without
the significant reference to the external world" (Gill, 1982, p. 92).

psychoanalytically informed integrative psychotherapy and bring the integration described in this book closer to the mainstream of psychoanalytic thought. As Frank (1993) has put it, "compared with the blankscreen conception of the psychoanalytic situation, the interactional emphasis often associated with relational points of view lends itself effectively to an integrative approach" (p. 536). Elaborating on this point, Frank notes that introducing action techniques within the one-person model of classical psychoanalytic thought presents serious issues of incompatibility. Within that model, he points out, "the analyst must remain outside, rather than 'contaminate,' the field. Analytic material is thought to develop spontaneously, and, through free association, to express endogenous conflicts; thus the 'actuality' of the analyst must be minimized" (p. 550).

In contrast, the two-person model views transference as *always* a joint product of the patient's intrapsychic proclivities and the actualities of what transpires between patient and therapist. The essence of the relational or two-person model is the recognition that interpersonal and intrapsychic are not antithetical; rather, each perspective is meaningless and vacuous without the other. As Gill has articulated, attention to the impact of the therapist's real actions and characteristics does not diminish our ability to help the patient see her own unconscious inclinations and conflicts; it *activates* that ability. Moreover, not only does such respect for the reality of what is transpiring not interfere with the exploration of fantasies about it, it widens the scope of that exploration and of the understanding achieved. The richness of our understanding of unconscious images, fantasies, fears, and desires is expanded considerably when they are understood *in relation to* the world of daily experience. Pitting reality and fantasy against each other in a simplistically dichotomous way impoverishes our understanding of both. It is the intertwining power of fantasy to shape our perceptions of reality and of daily realities to shape our ongoing fantasies that must most of all be appreciated by both participants in the psychotherapeutic enterprise. Knowing not only *what* her fantasies are but *when* they are activated—that is, in response to what relational configurations and affective contexts—both deepens and broadens the patient's insight and most effectively assures that those insights will be incorporated into her daily life and become an impetus for change. The fictional disappearance of the therapist from the equation, the erasure of the relational context, hampers the patient's gaining the full range of insight she needs. From a fully potentiated relational framework, the analyst's introduction of active methods should be seen not as a "contamination" of the transference but as one more event to analyze.°

## CYCLICAL PSYCHODYNAMICS AS A RELATIONAL THEORY

The developments in psychoanalytic thought described in this chapter largely parallel, or complement, the perspective of cyclical psychodynamics that guides the entire book. Although there are certainly differences—sometimes significant differences—between the cyclical psychodynamic approach and that of theorists and therapists operating from viewpoints such as object relations theory or self psychology, it should be apparent to the reader that cyclical psychodynamic theory is a version of the theoretical tendency that Greenberg and Mitchell (Greenberg & Mitchell, 1983; Mitchell, 1988) have labeled as relational. Indeed, in the present theoretical climate, it may be less confusing to depict cyclical psychodynamics as a relational theory than as an interpersonal theory, the rubric utilized in the original version of *Psychoanalysis and Behavior Therapy*.

This in no way implies a rejection of the interpersonal formulations emphasized in the original edition of *Psychoanalysis and Behavior Therapy* or of the interpersonal perspective in general. Those formulations still seem to me to provide a sound foundation for psychotherapeutic work in general and psychotherapy integration in particular. Rather, my preference at this point for the term "relational" has two roots.

First, as noted above, there has been considerable confusion about what is meant by the term "interpersonal." The perception that an interpersonal perspective is antithetical to concern with the phenomena usually labeled as intrapsychic remains widespread.† The cyclical psychodynamic version of interpersonal thought, however, was never con-

---

°Frank notes the convergence in this regard between the implications of perspectives such as Gill's (e.g., 1982, 1983) and Aron's (1990) and the viewpoint of cyclical psychodynamics that guides the work described in this book.

†In part, this misunderstanding can be attributed to Sullivan's tendency at times to state his positions in exaggerated and needlessly provocative ways. But in sum it represents an almost perverse misreading that reflects the politics and sociology of psychoanalysis much more than its substance or content.

ceptualized in opposition to intrapsychic factors. Fantasies, unconscious motivations, conflicts, affect states, conceptions or representations of self and other, all were significant elements of the cyclical psychodynamic model from the very beginning. What *was* true—and remains true—is that the cyclical psychodynamic model does not conceptualize these phenomena as manifestations of an autonomous realm lying behind or underneath the facade of daily life and experience—constituting the real power behind the throne, as it were. Rather, from the vantage point of cyclical psychodynamics, the putatively intrapsychic and interpersonal are seen together as part of a mutually interpenetrating and mutually shaping and sustaining relationship between fantasies, fears, and desires on the one hand and the actions and experiences of living and interacting with people on the other.

So pervasive among psychoanalytic thinkers is the false antithesis between interpersonal and intrapsychic, however, that, as noted above, the crucial role of "intrapsychic" factors in cyclical psychodynamic theory has not always been recognized, and the theory is sometimes seen as omitting such factors. The term "relational" has the advantage of not generally being understood as excluding the intrapsychic. Consequently, less confusion is introduced if cyclical psychodynamics is thought of as a relational theory than if it is depicted as an interpersonal theory.

A second reason for conceptualizing cyclical psychodynamic theory as part of the broadly relational trend depicted by Greenberg and Mitchell is that it encourages efforts to incorporate developments in the other relational perspectives within the evolving integration that is the continuing project of the cyclical psychodynamic approach. Many of the developments in object relations theory and self psychology have been framed in a way that does not fully transcend the limitations of the "woolly mammoth" version of the encapsulated past; fragments of self experience or representations of objects are presented as split off remnants from the past, powerfully influencing our ongoing experiences but barely influenced themselves by those experiences. The cyclical psychodynamic model provides a means of reworking these concepts and observations in terms that are freer of one-person and woolly mammoth conceptualizations. Such reworking will in fact render them more fully relational, as well as illuminate how they are compatible with—and can enrich—active interventions designed to enable the individual to grow beyond the impasse that has constrained her efforts to express fully the development of her differentiated self and her relatedness to others.

## THE "WOOLLY MAMMOTH" TODAY

It is important to be clear that the point of view depicted in Chapter 3 in terms of the "woolly mammoth" model of archaic remnants preserved in their original form and impervious to modification from new input is not just a relic of the early years of psychoanalytic thought. From a range of psychoanalytic perspectives, it remains a persistent assumption and one of the persistent sources of opposition to active intervention and the integration of behavioral and other active methods into the psychoanalytic process. Adler (1993), for example, in discussing Frank's (1993) arguments for active intervention (based largely on a cyclical psychodynamic model), notes that "active—as opposed to *interpretive*—attention to maladaptive patterns of behavior has traditionally been relegated to the periphery of technical concern in the psychoanalytic literature" (p. 581), and he essentially affirms this repudiation of active methods on the basis of a woolly mammoth formulation. Adler depicts relational models as "naively environmentalist," and states as the distinguishing hallmark of a contemporary Freudian perspective,

> the idea that repressive and defensive barriers established by the end of the oedipal period of development isolate vital portions of the infantile inner world. This more or less archaic area of psychic life will not thereafter be exposed to the same transformational and maturational impact of experience as other sectors of the personality. This does not suggest that these primal repressions cease to influence development . . . but only that the elemental contents of core conflicts and repressed experience resist the transformational influence of ongoing experience. (Adler, 1993, p. 585)

The resemblance of this formulation to what I depicted as the woolly mammoth model in Chapter 3 should be obvious.

In a similar vein, Arnold Richards, the editor of the *Journal of the American Psychoanalytic Association*, criticizes Mitchell (1988) for substituting for the idea of early experience "structuring psychic life" a view of patterns of relating that are repeated in varying forms throughout the course of development. Richards objects to emphasizing "needs that are active throughout life" rather than the structuring role of very early experience, and regards as unsatisfactory any account in which the decisive role of early experience is not the result of their "lay[ing] down structural residues which remain fixed" (Bachant & Richards, 1993, p. 444).

The woolly mammoth model, it seems, is alive and well. Far from being a straw man, it continues to provide a central justification for resisting innovation in psychoanalytic technique, especially innovation that includes looking outside the bounded world of psychoanalysis itself in order to see if therapists of other orientations might have something to contribute. The cyclical psychodynamic approach continues to provide an alternative model that accounts for the same set of observations but does so in a way that also addresses observations left out of the woolly mammoth versions and in a way that points to a wider range of potential therapeutic interventions.

# 16

# *From Behavior Therapy to Cognitive–Behavior Therapy*

═══════════

THE developments in psychoanalytic thought depicted in the last chapter have been paralleled in the years since the original publication of *Psychoanalysis and Behavior Therapy* by equally significant changes in the theories and practice of behaviorally oriented clinicians. This chapter addresses these developments and examines their implications for the theoretical and clinical approach presented in this book.

## THE EMERGENCE OF COGNITIVE–BEHAVIOR THERAPY

When a number of prominent behavior therapists organized a symposium on "Cognitive Processes in Behavior Modification" for the 1968 meetings of the American Psychological Association, they explicitly confronted what was then the "predominant conceptualization of the 'Behavior Therapies' as conditioning techniques involving little or no cognitive influence on behavior change" (Goldfried, 1995b, p. 7). A little more than two decades later, Craighead (1990) found that 69% of the members of the Association for the Advancement of Behavior Therapy identified themselves as cognitive–behavioral in orientation, whereas only 27% identified themselves as behavioral. Today, as Goldfried and Davison (1994) note, "Most therapists who use behavioral interventions routinely make use of cognition in their assessment and interventions" (p. 282).

This remarkable shift in the identifications and conceptualizations of behavior therapists—or, as most now prefer, cognitive–behavioral therapists—obviously has important implications for the integration proposed in this book. Although cognitive perspectives had already begun to emerge among behavior therapists at the time *Psychoanalysis and Behavior Therapy* was being written, they were still far from the mainstream. On the one hand, Bandura's version of social learning theory (e.g., Bandura, 1969), which incorporated cognitive concepts quite considerably, had already become a significant theoretical foundation for many behavior therapists, and Mischel (1973) had further amplified a perspective on personality in which cognitive factors figured prominently. These developments were noted and discussed in the original edition. However, reflecting the primary thrust of behavior therapy at the time, they were not at the center of the analysis presented.

A number of important beginning efforts toward introducing a more cognitive or mediational approach to the therapeutic process itself were also noted (e.g., Goldfried & Davison, 1976; Goldfried, DeCenteceo, and Weinberg, 1974; Lazarus, 1971; Mahoney, 1974; Meichenbaum, 1973, 1974), but they too were still largely at the periphery of behavioral practice at the time *Psychoanalysis and Behavior Therapy* was being written. Indeed, Arnkoff and Glass (1993) reported that the early proponents of cognitive perspectives in behavior therapy were regarded as "heretical" and that after the publication of Mahoney's (1974) influential and scholarly argument for a cognitive point of view, he was warned by some behavioral colleagues to "cease and desist" if he wished to remain in good standing in the movement. As late as the mid-1970s, there was a movement to totally exclude cognitively oriented presentations from the meetings of the Association for the Advancement of Behavior Therapy (Arnkoff & Glass, 1993, p. 666). This effort did not succeed, however, and it was not long before the cognitive point of view became not only acceptable but dominant. To a degree that would have appeared very unlikely when *Psychoanalysis and Behavior Therapy* was being written (and that, of course, would have required a different title to the book), behavior therapy has become cognitive–behavior therapy.

The addition of a cognitive dimension to behavior therapy certainly enhanced its effectiveness and comprehensiveness. Behavioral treatments became "lengthier, more comprehensive in scope, and considerably more sophisticated" than they had been originally (Hersen, 1983, p. 5). Moreover, as Fishman and Lubetkin (1983) have noted, the emphasis of behavior therapists' clinical efforts shifted from a narrow focus on particular techniques addressing specific symptoms and narrowly defined problems to a broader focus on developing the coping skills and capacities to deal effectively with the problems life presents. Glass and Arnkoff (1992), in reviewing the history of behavior therapy, noted that the influence of cognitive perspectives—as well as the demands of more complex cases as behavior therapy became established as a truly clinical discipline—rendered the original "narrow-band definitions" of behavior therapy insufficient to capture the range and complexity of cognitive–behavioral practice.

But what enhances cognitive–behavior therapy as a separate therapeutic orientation does not necessarily augment its contribution to an integration of psychodynamic and behavioral or cognitive–behavioral approaches. The cognitive perspective filled an important gap in behavioral theory and practice, but the gap it filled was not one that existed in psychoanalysis. Psychoanalysis already had a point of view that stressed complex internal mediating structures and processes. What it needed, where its gap lay, was precisely in the realms in which behavior therapy had originally staked its claim—for example, in the application of active interventions focally directed at particular sources of anxiety and particular problematic interactions with others.

Thus, many of the innovations introduced by cognitive–behavior therapists were largely redundant from a psychoanalytic vantage point. Moreover, as I shall describe below, in large measure they were not as fully developed or as comprehensive as the psychoanalytic models. This is not to suggest simply that psychoanalytic models are superior. Rather, my point here is twofold: The mediational concepts of cognitive therapists are not likely to be especially appealing or exciting to psychoanalytic therapists, and those mediational concepts do not add important dimensions that are left out of standard psychoanalytic practice, as do the more behavioral features of cognitive–behavioral therapy. They are, one might say, enhancers of behavior therapy, but not necessarily enhancers of a psychodynamic–behavioral integration.

## TOWARD A MORE DIFFERENTIATED ANALYSIS: COGNITIVE THERAPY? OR COGNITIVE–BEHAVIORAL THERAPY?

The foregoing is not intended to suggest that cognitive concepts and methods are in no way useful in a psychodynamic–behavioral integration. One must be cautious about making blanket claims in a realm where there is so much complexity and diversity. No more than psychoanalysis is cognitive–behavior therapy just "one thing." The relevance of the new cognitive perspectives for the integration proposed in this book must be examined in a differentiated way that takes account of the variations. My point thus far is simply a warning that what might seem at first blush to be an unambiguous advance for the cause of integration in fact requires careful and discriminating scrutiny.

In certain respects, to be sure, the cognitive turn in behavior therapy further eases the path toward integration. An approach that views people as guided by complex mediational structures is obviously more compatible with a psychoanalytic point of view than one that hews to a strictly conditioning model. However, as we shall see, developments that ease the path of integration conceptually can nonetheless create obstacles clinically. To understand how and when this can happen, we must consider some of the differences in the ways that cognitive perspectives have been introduced.

It is worth noting, to begin with, that there are differences in how cognitively oriented therapists conceive of themselves, with some identifying as "cognitive therapists" and some as "cognitive behavior therapists." The sources of these differences in self-designation are multiple. In large measure they reflect personal tastes, loyalties to particular groups and individuals, and what might be thought of as guild concerns. In part, they reflect the differing intellectual origins of different groups of therapists. The backgrounds of the originators of cognitive therapies include some whose original training was psychoanalytic (e.g., Beck, Ellis) and some whose background was primarily in behavior therapy (e.g., Mahoney, Meichenbaum, Goldfried, Davison). Those in the latter group, along with their students and followers, are more likely to describe themselves as cognitive–behavioral.

As Arnkoff and Glass (1992) noted, the differences in identifying labels frequently reflect differences in the way therapists situate themselves in the field at large and in its history. Opinions differ, for example, over whether cognitive therapy should be seen as an evolution within behavior therapy or constitutes a revolution signifying a completely new point of view. Not surprisingly, those who hold to the latter view are more likely to use the term "cognitive therapy" than "cognitive behavior therapy."[*]

[*]It should be noted that the labels have different histories and different implications outside of North America. In Latin America, for example, therapists whose approaches dovetail most with the approach presented here tend to call themselves cognitive therapists rather than cognitive–behavior therapists, and it is the former that are more closely associated with constructivist rather than rationalist perspectives and with a more open, less ideological viewpoint.

To be sure, the labels do not provide a very reliable guide to what these therapists actually do. But whereas the overlap between self-designated cognitive therapists and cognitive behavior therapists is very considerable, certain differences in outlook and orientation do correlate with the labels at least to some degree, and these differences—regardless of label—have in fact rather substantial implications for the compatibility of contemporary cognitive approaches with the integrative approach proposed here. It is to these more substantive differences that I now turn.

## COGNITION AS THE FUNDAMENTAL DIMENSION VERSUS COGNITION AS PART OF A COMPLEX WHOLE

In principle, all therapists recognize that cognitions can be both causes and effects: How we think about things influences how we experience them and what we do, but at the same time what actually happens to us also influences how we think about things. There are considerable differences, however, in the degree to which the two halves of this circular process are emphasized. Some cognitively oriented therapists, having come to recognize the crucial and significant role of cognition, seem to go still further and accord cognition a special status that relegates all other factors to the background. As Coyne (1992, 1994) noted, there is a disturbingly pervasive tendency toward what he called "cognition über alles" in the realm of cognitive therapy, a tendency to posit cognitions as *the* causal factor and to treat all other factors as epiphenomena.

To be sure, there is indeed a sense in which how we ultimately interpret an experience determines the meaning it has for us. We may interpret an adversity as a challenge, or think about a success in such a way that it signifies only greater demands and the prospect of a bigger fall later. Our capacity to interpret events "in our fashion" is indeed impressive. Therapists of all persuasions recognize this, from psychoanalysts to cognitive therapists to narratively oriented family therapists (e.g., White & Epston, 1990). Focusing on this side of our psychological functioning becomes problematic only when it crowds out all other perspectives, when "it's only true if we think it's true" becomes a kind of mantra that virtually severs the link between our thoughts and the actual events of our lives.

There is certainly considerable truth, as well as therapeutic value, in conceptualizing what brings people to therapy as the persistence of particular ways of seeing things that leave us feeling bad about our lives again and again. But it is essential as well to understand that those ways of seeing things have consequences. They lead us to actually construct our lives on a different basis from people who see things in a different way. And in turn, the actual life we have constructed influences how we continue to see things. Similarly, how we view things certainly influences how we feel, but it is equally the case that how we feel influences how we view things. The way we see the world is a constantly evolving product of our experiences and our various (affective, cognitive, and behavioral) proclivities, and each facet of this complex set influences all the others even as it is influenced *by* them.

Most cognitive therapists acknowledge these mutual and reciprocal causal networks, at least in principle, but some retain a sentimental attachment to the idea that cognitions are, to borrow from Orwell, "more equal" than the other links in the causal chain. Ellis (1962), for example, regards therapeutic efforts that directly challenge the irrational syllogisms that he views as at the heart of things, as a more complete and "elegant" solution than efforts—also, to be sure, within the purview of Rational Emotive Therapy (RET)—that rely more on the direct experience of behaving differently in the world. Beck's approach, too, places considerably greater emphasis on the ways that cognition influences other psychological processes than on the reverse, although in practice his approach also relies quite considerably on the consequences of actually behaving differently in the world.°

My concern about this bias on the part of some cognitive therapists derives from several sources. To begin with, one of the key ways in which cyclical psychodynamics differs from earlier psychoanalytic models is in its strong emphasis on the reciprocal influences of so-called internal and external events and its related conviction that for any theory to give special priority to only one part of what is most essentially a circle is problematic. (It is in large measure the increasing recognition of this reciprocal causal nexus on the part of some relational psychoanalytic thinkers [e.g., Aron, 1996; Frank, 1993; Mitchell, 1988, 1993] that

---

°In actual clinical practice, even therapists who describe themselves as cognitive therapists rather than as cognitive–behavioral are likely to make considerable use of active behavioral interventions (Kendall & Bemis, 1983). Indeed, there is much reason to think that it is these direct attempts to confront the individual *experientially* with the fears and difficulties in her life—rather than verbally or rationally— that are the most effective ingredient in the putatively cognitive therapies.

marks the convergence between cyclical psychodynamics and the broader relational trend in psychoanalytic thought.)° When cognitive therapists repeat the very overemphasis on "internal" factors that for so many years (problematically) characterized the psychoanalytic perspective, it is neither an advance nor a development that facilities the assimilation of a cognitive perspective into the evolving integrative cyclical psychodynamic perspective.

Cognitive and cognitive–behavioral therapies at their best entail a close interweaving of attention to the client's governing assumptions and psychological structures on the one hand, and efforts to intervene in the affective and behavioral dimensions of her difficulties on the other. But there is a danger in cognitive therapy that parallels one in psychoanalysis: an overvaluation of words and an excessively intellectualized approach to the therapeutic process. In both therapeutic traditions, it is certainly possible (and legitimate) to say that when that happens it betokens bad clinical work. But it is also the case—in both traditions—that such a miscarriage of the therapeutic process is far from rare.

Much of the impetus for the integrative effort described in this book derived from a dissatisfaction with the ways that aspects of traditional psychoanalytic practice could constrict the more *experiential* dimensions of the change process, which seemed to me crucial. What appealed to me about behavioral measures was not only their attention to overt behavior—a useful but far from exclusive focus of behavioral approaches in any event—but also their potential to enhance the *experiential* dimension of the therapeutic work. Although behavior therapists were typically viewed by psychoanalysts as mechanistic technicians, part of what attracted me to their work was the way their methods could in fact bring people into more direct, experiential contact with the objects of their fears and the experiences with which they had difficulty.

Both cognitive and psychoanalytic therapies have dimensions that are designed to counter whatever inclinations toward dry intellectualization might develop. In the psychoanalytic tradition, the analysis of intellectualization is a standard part of the work whenever such tendencies are evident. Indeed, it was psychoanalysis that first conceived the very concept of intellectualization as a defensive process against direct experience of that which makes us uncomfortable. Among cognitive therapists,

---

°It should be noted, however, that not all theorists who fit within the general "relational" rubric show such awareness of reciprocal causality. One project I hope to begin before too long is a thorough examination of the range of relational theorists in order to sort out those who continue to hew to the model of the encapsulated past and those who have achieved a more thoroughly transactional model.

the safeguard against sterile intellectualization lies in the use of the behavioral measures that are ubiquitous not only in explicitly labeled cognitive *behavior* therapy but in virtually all putatively cognitive therapies.[*]

These protections notwithstanding, the danger of arid intellectualization remains in some forms of psychoanalysis and some forms of cognitive therapy. Every therapeutic approach, one might say, has certain fault lines, certain directions in which the therapy is most likely to go awry. Dryly intellectualized therapy is indeed bad therapy from the vantage point of virtually all practitioners of these two approaches, but that does not mean that such bad therapy is all that rare. In cognitive therapy, the danger of being dryly intellectualized increases when the therapist is too concerned about "elegant solutions" or overstresses the way clients *think* about their lives.[†]

Now, to be sure, few who have seen films or tapes of Albert Ellis's clinical work would describe him as being "dryly" anything. He is surely a vivid and distinctive personality. But most of Ellis's followers have softened the tone of RET quite considerably, and when one considers the "kinder and gentler" versions of RET, the concerns raised here do seem especially relevant. In considering the transition from Ellis's version of RET to that of his followers, one must wonder how much of the tang is in the harangue. If one persists in being "rational" without the distinctive (but, in many therapists' view, problematic) tone of Ellis himself, what is left in RET seems much more R than E. (It is noteworthy in this regard that Ellis has recently taken to calling his approach RE*B*T (rational emotive *behavior* therapy). This more explicit recognition of the crucial role of actual lived behavior (and not just how we think about it) seems to me a potentially useful advance in this point of view.

## RATIONALIST AND CONSTRUCTIVIST VERSIONS OF COGNITIVE THERAPY

Arnkoff and Glass (1992) highlight an important distinction that can further aid our understanding of the implications of different versions

---

[*]Kendall & Bemis (1983), examining the actual practice of cognitive and cognitive–behavioral therapies, concluded that behavioral influences tend to predominate.

[†]Family therapy, Gestalt therapy, less cognitive versions of behavior therapy, and so forth also have their fault lines. The most likely ways for the therapy to go wrong differ from approach to approach, but no approach enters the fray without vulnerabilities. Knowing the vulnerabilities is the first best defense.

of cognitive and cognitive–behavioral therapy for the integrative effort described in this book. The cognitive approaches introduced by Ellis and by Beck have been described as *rationalist* cognitive approaches in contrast to the *constructivist* approaches that have emerged in more recent years, represented by the work of such theorists and therapists as Feixas and Neimeyer (1990), Feixas and Villegas (1993), Fernandez-Alvarez (1992), Guidano (1987, 1991), Guidano and Liotti (1983), Mahoney (1990, 1995), Neimeyer (1986), and Neimeyer and Mahoney, (1995). As Arnkoff and Glass point out,

> Constructivist theories differ from rationalist theories such as RET in philosophy of science, in theories of psychopathology and change, and in some important clinical aspects (Mahoney & Gabriel, 1987). Whereas rationalist cognitive theories assume that the therapist can know the true state of affairs through logic or sensory observation, constructivist theories posit that each person creates his or her own reality. Therefore, a constructivist therapist cannot presume to know "the" truth and simply pass it on to the client. Constructivist theories emphasize developmental processes, limiting themselves in therapy to the current state or presenting problem less than do the rationalist therapies. (p. 669)

The greater compatibility of the constructivist approaches with psychodynamic ways of thinking should be obvious. It is manifested, in fact, in a variety of ways. To begin with, we may simply note that a constructivist point of view has increasingly been gaining ground within psychoanalytic circles as well. Analysts of a number of persuasions have offered constructivist formulations and arguments, some associated with the *hermeneutic* turn in psychoanalytic thought, some with the increasing emphasis on *narrative,* and some in the context of reevaluating the appropriate clinical stance to the perceptions the patient reports (e.g., see Hoffman, 1991, 1992; Messer, Sass, & Woolfolk, 1988; Mitchell, 1993; Schafer, 1980, 1992; Spence, 1982, 1993; Stern, 1992). In addition, the constructivist version of cognitive therapy largely eschews an enormous obstacle to the compatibility of psychoanalytic and cognitive–behavioral points of view that is posed by the rationalist version. In the more rationalist forms of cognitive therapy, the patient's way of thinking tends to be regarded as simply "irrational" and in need of correction. The therapist, in contrast, is seen as in touch with how the world "really" is, and takes as his or her task to impart this healthier and more realistic way of thinking to the patient. Such a stance is in stark contrast to the way that most psychoanalytic therapists view the work they do, and represents, in effect, still another basic difference in the visions that guide therapists of the two persuasions. Indeed, it should be evident to the reader of this book that such an outlook by an influential subset of cognitive and cognitive–behavioral therapists represents a far greater obstacle to integration than did the worldview that underlay earlier noncognitive versions of behavior therapy.

Responding to a very similar set of considerations, Kenneth Frank (1993) framed his argument for a similar integration to that offered in this book entailing as an integration of psychoanalytic therapy and *behavioral–cognitive* therapy rather than cognitive–behavioral therapy. As he explained it,

> I have been unable to find a satisfactory solution to certain methodological incompatibilities between psychoanalytic and strictly cognitive interventions, related to the therapist's stance. Specifically, analytic techniques typically expand and elaborate the subjective experience of the patient, while cognitive techniques involve a persuasive attempt directly to influence the patient's beliefs and thought processes through reason. Accordingly, recent psychoanalytic formulations related to the benefits of viewing the patient's productions as "plausible" (Gill, 1982) cannot easily be reconciled with a stance resulting in a therapist's efforts to "correct distorted cognitions." That is why I have chosen to reverse the customary terminology ("cognitive–behavioral") in describing the endorsed application of action-oriented techniques in this approach. (pp. 542–543)

The difficulties noted by Frank are greatly diminished in the more constructivist versions of cognitive therapy. In those approaches, the aim is very similar to that described by Frank—not to persuade the patient that her way of thinking is "incorrect" or "irrational," but to help the patient examine how she thinks and perceives, to help her recognize that her way of framing things represents but one possible way of construing her experience and to help her explore the implications, and even the origins, of the way she has chosen and with which she has become familiar.[*] Both rationalist and constructivist versions of cognitive therapy are often framed in terms of helping the patient approach her experience as a "personal scientist." But whereas the former embodies a kind of science that is strictly a hypothesis-*testing* approach (and, indeed, one in which the therapist's view of her own hypotheses regarding what are productive and accurate ways of thinking admit of little

---

[*]This is not to suggest that cognitive and psychoanalytic approaches to this kind of exploration are identical. But it is important to recognize that they represent variations on a theme rather than the almost unbridgeable gulf between approaches that dismiss the patient's current thinking as irrational and simply attempt to "correct" it, and approaches that attempt to *understand* the patient's way of seeing things and then to examine or expand it.

doubt), the latter reflects a hypothesis-*generating* version of science, characterized by curiosity, reflection, and the real possibility of new and emergent hypotheses that replace those originally held by both parties.

Another important way in which constructivist and rationalist cognitive therapies differ is that in the latter, strong emotions, especially strong negative emotions, are seen primarily as a problem to be controlled, whereas in the former, such emotions are viewed as central to grasp and understand in order to facilitate the client's process of self-knowledge and self-reorganization (Arnkoff & Glass, 1992). The therapeutic relationship is conceived as a safe context in which the client may engage in self-exploration and in the exploration of her attachments to others. Clearly, this strand of cognitive therapy has far more affinities with psychoanalytic approaches than does the more "rationalist" orientation.°

## FROM "WORDS" TO "SCHEMAS"

Much of the early work on the cognitive dimension of psychological difficulties emphasized what people said to themselves that perpetuated their difficulties. The focus was relatively close to the surface and to consciousness. An almost magical power was given to words, and frequently a syllogistic conception of psychological structure was either explicitly or implicitly assumed. Over the years, both clinical experience and a more sophisticated understanding of cognitive psychology have changed this emphasis substantially. As Goldfried and Davison (1994) noted, the emphasis on things that clients "told themselves" that characterized the early years of cognitive behavior therapy has increasingly yielded to "a movement in the direction of seeing these self-statements as manifestations of more implicit meaning structures [that] cannot readily be measured directly, but are instead reflected by such indirect indicators as misperceptions or selective recall" (p. 295). The greater convergence between this latter conception and the approach and point of view of psychodynamic therapists should be obvious. This evolution thus parallels that from more rationalist to more constructivist approaches to cognition as a trend pointing toward convergence and compatibility.

In a similar vein, Meichenbaum and Gilmore (1984) noted that cognitive–behavioral therapy has increasingly paid attention to such phenomena as covert reasoning and covert emotional biasing, as well as to schemas and core organizing principles. In their view, "We can see in

°Interestingly, perhaps the most prominent proponents of the rationalist approach, Ellis and Beck, were originally trained psychoanalytically, in contrast to the backgrounds of most of the key figures in the constructivist approach.

these unconscious domains many points of similarity with the concept of unconscious function offered by psychodynamic theories. It is important to understand that in cognitive behavioral assessment, therapy, and research, what is not conscious is seen as being highly significant. This is a reversal of the original behavioral point of view, and deserves emphasis" (p. 290). To be sure, Meichenbaum and Gilmore see significant differences, even today, in the ways that the two broad paradigms conceptualize and work with unconscious processes, but they anticipate interesting possibilities for further exchange between proponents of the different approaches "as the passions that separate therapeutic approaches subside and the logical analysis of techniques and concepts are [sic] undertaken" (p. 291).

Today, concern with schemas and meaning structures has replaced the earlier focus on mere words for large numbers of cognitive and cognitive–behavioral therapists. It is likely that, at least to some degree, this emerging emphasis will contribute further to the possibility of integration of cognitive and psychodynamic approaches. At this point, although convergence is increasing, uses of schemalike concepts still vary quite considerably, and many cognitive therapists' use of such concepts bears only slight resemblance to the kinds of meaning structures and organizing schemes conceptualized by psychodynamic theorists. In recent years, however, there has been increasing use of the schema concept by psychodynamic theorists to express and clarify psychodynamic concepts (e.g., Horowitz, 1991; Wachtel, 1987) and a tendency for some schema-focused cognitive approaches to address issues and pursue questions that were once virtually the exclusive province of psychoanalytic inquiry (e.g., Young, 1991). It is still not infrequently the case, to be sure, that the term "schema" may be used so differently by therapists of differing orientations that the commonality is more apparent than real. But the conceptualization of schemas, especially when understood as hierarchically organized and characterized by varying degrees of accessibility to consciousness, provides useful common ground for cognitive and psychodynamic thinkers to explore.

## RELATIONAL PERSPECTIVES IN COGNITIVE–BEHAVIORAL THERAPY

Still another development that bears quite substantially on the prospect for an integration of psychoanalytic approaches with the evolving cognitive–behavioral paradigm is the increasing attention being paid by cognitive–behavioral therapists to the therapeutic relationship. This is a development that is accelerating and is much to be welcomed, but it is still not well developed in the general cognitive–behavioral realm. In perhaps the most comprehensive examination of relationship influences in cognitive and cognitive–behavioral therapy, Safran and Segal (1990) concluded that there has been

> a fundamental imbalance in cognitive approaches to therapy, an imbalance that has seriously detrimental impact on practice. Because the therapeutic relationship or nonspecific aspects of therapy are less tangible and more difficult to operationalize than specific cognitive and behavioral techniques, cognitive therapists tend to see them as less important. Although in recent years they have begun to pay more attention to the therapeutic relationship, they still tend to see it as something separate from the active ingredients of therapy, as a prerequisite for the change process rather than as an intrinsic part of it. (pp. 4–5)

Safran and Segal's conceptualization, in contrast, puts relational factors at the very heart of the process of cognitive therapy, and their approach interfaces with psychodynamic points of view in a number of interesting and useful ways. Whereas some versions of cognitive therapy seem to be dryly intellectual and overly focused on rationality and on words, their approach places considerable emphasis on *experiential* disconfirmation of problematic interpersonal schemas. Although in some ways this notion overlaps with the more conventional cognitive dictum of teaching the patient to be a "personal scientist," its connotations are somewhat different, and at the very least it represents a way of framing the process to which psychodynamic therapists are likely to be more receptive. Whereas the "personal scientist" framing can readily signal to psychodynamic therapists an approach that is overly intellectualized and devoid of affect—and can, moreover, lead some cognitive therapists to that way*—the emphasis on *experience* in Safran and Segal's conceptualization points in quite a different direction. Indeed, Safran has been one of the most vigorous proponents of the importance of *emotion* in psychotherapy (e.g., Greenberg & Safran, 1987, 1989; Safran & Greenberg, 1991).

Further contributing to a cognitive–psychodynamic bridge in Safran

---

*It should be clear that by no means does the "personal scientist" concept necessarily imply such a bloodless approach. Not only is scientific investigation itself now understood as a process far less affect-free than was once thought, but in the hands of many cognitive therapists the metaphor of the personal scientist means precisely an experiential confirming or disconfirming. Nonetheless, it is not difficult for an unbiased observer to detect a significant thread in cognitive therapy that *is* more bloodless than other therapeutic approaches, and Safran and Segal's version differs substantially in this regard.

and Segal's approach is the central role they give to the therapeutic relationship and to what psychodynamic therapists would call working with the transference. The experiential disconfirmation that is central to their approach is understood as taking place in the context of the relationship between patient and therapist as much as in the life situations the patient has come to therapy to work on. Safran and Segal's conceptualization in this regard draws heavily on attachment theory. Noting that the theorizing of Bowlby (1969, 1973), as well as the research of Ainsworth (1982), Main (1983), and others suggests that the capacity to engage in exploratory activities depends on a secure sense that the attachment figure will be available and responsive when necessary, Safran and Segal suggest that in therapy the patient needs similarly to develop trust in the therapist's reliability and availability before she can engage in the explorations that are crucial to the therapeutic process.

Paralleling Safran and Segal's (1990) emphasis on experiential disconfirmation is attention to what they call "decentering." As they depict it,

> Decentering is a process through which one is able to step outside of one's immediate experience, thereby changing the very nature of that experience. This process allows for the introduction of a gap between the event and one's reaction to that event. By developing the capacity to observe oneself and one's own reactions, one begins to distinguish between reality and reality as one construes it. (p. 117)

The potential points of convergence between this conceptualization and the psychoanalytic concept of fostering the observing ego should be evident.

Finally, apropos of the distinction discussed above between rationalist and constructivist versions of cognitive therapy, Safran and Segal advocate an approach that emphasizes expanding the patient's awareness of how she constructs reality rather than directly challenging the patient's assumptions or arguing the patient out of presumed errors. As with many therapists operating from the vantage point of attachment or object relations concepts, their focus is on the patient's "internal working model." Indeed, their very definition of what a cognitive approach entails is likely to sound quite familiar and compatible to many psychoanalytic therapists—an emphasis on "the way people construct representations of their experience" (Safran & Segal, 1990, p. 10).°

---

°A recent valuable paper by Wolfe (1995) points to a related dimension of convergence: the representation of the self.

## CONCLUDING COMMENTS

In considering the implications of the developments discussed in this chapter, it is useful to note that the introduction of a cognitive perspective into behavior therapy is not as radical a change in the *reality* of behavior therapy as it is in the ideology. Although the pioneers in cognitive–behavior therapy encountered considerable opposition within the behavior therapy establishment of the time, and although they did achieve a quite substantial reworking of the formal conceptual underpinnings of behavior therapy and a significant shift in practice as well, behavior therapy was never as exclusively "behavioristic" as it was portrayed by either its proponents or its critics (in this connection, see again Part One of this book).

Certain strands of the behavior modification branch of the behavior therapy movement did come close to being an ideologically pure behavioristic approach. But in large measure that was possible only because these efforts were applied primarily to unwilling, or at the very least to less than fully voluntary, subjects. The mentally retarded, prisoners, chronic schizophrenics in the days when such individuals were relegated to back wards rather than to the streets and homeless shelters,° these were the focus of most behavior modification efforts, and it was at least an instance of truth in labeling that this approach was called "behavior modification" and not "behavior therapy." Behavior therapists usually worked with people who sought their help, and right from the start they approached their patients or clients as conscious subjects or agents, people with intentions and feelings who could say what they wanted, what felt good or bad, and so on. Moreover, behavior therapy paid considerable attention not only to what people said about their experience but to images, interpersonal strategies, and, increasingly, to "self-talk," the bridge, one might say, between behavior therapy and cognitive–behavior therapy.

This is not to suggest that the emerging cognitive emphasis in behavior therapy did not have a significant impact on clinical practice. Although not as discontinuous with previous behavioral approaches as is sometimes suggested, the changes were real and substantial. The irony lies in the observation that this movement toward a more cognitive version of behavior therapy—which on the surface seems so much more

°Some things change without improving.

compatible with the thinking of psychoanalytic therapists—may actually hold less appeal to the proponent of a behavioral–psychodynamic integration than the earlier, less cognitive approach. It largely remains the *behavioral* aspects of cognitive–behavior therapy—aspects that, as discussed above, are also well understood in many respects as *experiential*—that may most effectively be adapted by psychoanalytic therapists seeking to assure that their therapeutic efforts do not become overly abstract and intellectualized.

Indeed, it is these same behavioral elements that are the best safeguard against cognitive therapy's becoming bloodless and lost in thought. It is my strong conviction that it is precisely the combination of exploration of a person's underlying, and often not very clearly or consciously articulated, assumptions, on the one hand, and active behavioral interventions, on the other hand, that accounts for the documented effectiveness of cognitive approaches. But because I view the psychoanalytic model of intrapsychic process and structure as more penetrating and comprehensive, I regard the approach to such a combination through an integration of psychodynamic and behavioral perspectives to be a more promising route than the integration of behavioral interventions with the simpler and more limited model of internal structure offered by theorists such as Beck or Ellis.

There are, of course, drawbacks as well to the more elaborate psychodynamic model. Some versions of psychoanalytic thought are utterly baroque and virtually untestable. In certain respects the cognitive model plays things closer to the vest, trading off profundity for certainty, or at least for greater testability. But it is a great mistake to distinguish too sharply between cognitive and psychoanalytic conceptualizations on this account. On the one hand, there has been much more empirical investigation of psychoanalytic formulations and assumptions than is commonly recognized (e.g., see Barron, Eagle, & Wolitzky, 1992; Luborsky, 1996; Luborsky & Crits-Christoph, 1990; Masling, 1983; Singer, 1990). Conversely, much of the underpinning of cognitive approaches constitutes simple and unexamined "common sense" rather than truly empirically validated propositions.*

It is certainly true that the experimental investigation of cognition, both by experimental psychologists and by researchers in the new field of cognitive science, has yielded impressive advances. However, cognitive therapy cannot validly borrow the prestige of these scientific ef-

---

*It is worth noting in this regard that it has been the function of psychoanalysis—and indeed of the entire enterprise of science—precisely to question apparent common sense.

forts. Most of their findings have little to do with the practice of cognitive therapy; indeed, many of the commonsense assumptions underlying cognitive therapy harken back to centuries-old cultural presumptions about rationality that are among the casualties of the more rigorous study of cognition in recent decades. Moreover, the easy assumption of the therapist's rationality and realistic view of life, and of the patient's *ir*rationality and *un*realistic view, flies in the face both of contemporary philosophy of science and of empirical findings that suggest that in certain respects, for example, depressed individuals are more realistic than nondepressed individuals (e.g., Taylor, 1989).

Focusing also on depression, Coyne and his colleagues (e.g., Coyne & Gotlib, 1983, 1986), in a series of papers highly critical of cognitive approaches and especially of the assumption that the key to psychological difficulties is the patient's irrational or unrealistic attitude, have argued that not only does such an approach presumptuously assume that reality is the way the therapist sees things, but it also ignores very real differences in the actual circumstances encountered by depressed individuals and people who are not depressed. Behaving in a depressed manner, they point out, has interpersonal consequences that create a truly different set of life experiences for the depressed person. Their account of the vicious circle encountered by the depressed individual—whatever the origins of the pattern, once it begins, being depressed creates circumstances that keep one depressed—has many affinities with the cyclical psychodynamic model presented in this book.[*]

All in all, the relation between the emergence of cognitive behavior therapy and the integrative framework originally presented in *Psychoanalysis and Behavior Therapy* is multifaceted and at times almost paradoxical. In certain respects, the increasing importance of a cognitive perspective in behavior therapy clearly augments the compatibility of psychodynamic and behavioral conceptualizations. But in others, it may surprisingly impede such compatibility. The most promising prospects for further integrating a cognitive approach into the evolving cyclical psychodynamic model seem to lie in the direction of the more contructivist versions of cognitive therapy. The work of writers such as Davison and Goldfried, Feixas, Fernandez Alvarez, Guidano, Liotti, Ma-

---

[*]Coyne's critique of the cognitive model has itself been criticized as replacing an overemphasis on cognition with a dismissive *under*emphasis (e.g., Safran & Segal, 1990). Gotlib and Whiffen (1991), in a paper that retains much of the perspective of Gotlib's earlier collaboration with Coyne, offer an account of depression that addresses both the value and the limits of a cognitive perspective, treating cognitive distortions as real but as only one of numerous mutually interacting factors that contribute to and maintain the problematic pattern.

honey, Meichenbaum, Safran, and others holds out intriguing possibilities for further cooperation and convergence. The banner of constructivism does not carry with it a connotation in which affect is implicitly relegated to the periphery or in which the work may be sidetracked by mere words, logical syllogisms, or gratuitous assumptions by the therapist that he or she is more "rational" than the patient. Moreover, constructivism is a point of view in which the conceptualizations of cognitive therapists and psychoanalytic therapists naturally converge.

Significant differences can be found, to be sure, among the constructivist models put forth by cognitive therapists and those proffered by psychoanalysts. However, in contrast to the problematic prospects for an effective integration of psychodynamic perspectives and the more rationalist versions of cognitive therapy, the possibilities for achieving meaningful progress toward synthesis through constructivist visions are real and exciting. In principle, constructivist approaches are at once empirical and open to the complexities of subjectivity, prepared to take the patient's view of the world seriously even while questioning it, open to affective experience rather than focused on controlling it, and committed to expanding the patient's consciousness rather than devoted to teaching the patient the "right" way to think. In the evolution of both cognitive and psychoanalytic approaches toward such a vision, we may see the most fruitful path toward integration in the coming years.

# 17

## Including the System

As its name implied, *Psycho-analysis and Behavior Therapy* focused primarily on the interface between two key schools of thought, both predominantly directed toward work with individuals. Given the almost universal attitude at the time the book was being written that psychoanalytic and behavioral approaches were rather thoroughly incompatible, demonstrating their potential convergence and synergy seemed quite enough of a challenge. As work on the integrative effort proceeded, however, what emerged was a model—cyclical psychodynamics—that seemed to provide a foundation for a more thoroughgoing integration as well.

The rationale for active intervention within a psychodynamic context points clearly, for example, to the compatibility of the cyclical psychodynamic framework with the third broad strand of individual psychotherapy, the "experiential."° As I noted in the previous chapter, a significant part of the appeal of behavioral methods as a complement to psychodynamic exploration was precisely their capacity to make the therapeutic work more concretely experiential. The conventional labels, and the lines of division created by ideological imperatives rather than

---

°Although all three of these strands—psychodynamic, behavioral, and experiential—have been applied to work with couples, families, and groups, their main purview has been psychotherapeutic work with individuals. I refer to them here as "strands" because clearly there are multiple "schools" within each of the three, sometimes sharply differentiated from and antagonistic toward each other. That is the reason why some observers have been able to identify as many as 400 different "brands" of therapy (Karasu, 1986).

clinical observation, can obscure crucial features of each approach that do not immediately fit the label. In fact, important aspects of some behavioral approaches are experiential, just as significant elements of some explicitly (and, indeed, appropriately) labeled experiential approaches are behavioral.*

Perhaps even more significant—because it points to still more wide ranging integrative possibilities for understanding and intervention—is the convergence between the cyclical psychodynamic model and that of family systems approaches. Like behavior therapy (and like most experiential approaches as well), family therapy originated very largely as a challenge to psychoanalysis, which, in the period in which family therapy first became an important force on the therapeutic scene, was clearly the dominant paradigm. Although a number of the key originators of family therapy had been trained psychoanalytically (e.g., Ackerman, Bowen, Minuchin, Whitaker), the early evolution of family therapy, much like that of other approaches, entailed a process of differentiation, in which the differences from the psychoanalytic viewpoint—indeed, from almost all individual viewpoints—were primarily emphasized. Many leading figures in family therapy conceived of the "circular" model of the family systems perspective as a radical break from the "linear" model of approaches like psychoanalysis.†

There is a significant kernel of validity to this view. Many aspects of psychoanalytic thought are indeed framed in ways that make a synthesis between psychoanalysis and more systemic approaches quite difficult. The cyclical psychodynamic model that is the focus of this book, however, is itself framed in a way that emphasizes circular transactions and recursive processes, and thus lends itself to an interface with family systems approaches much more readily. Indeed, elaborating why and how systems models are more compatible with the cyclical psychodynamic approach than they are with other psychodynamic models helps to clarify further the nature of the cyclical psychodynamic model itself.

Although the convergences between the cyclical psychodynamic model and many of the key assumptions underlying family therapy now

---

*For greater attention to this particular convergence, see Safran and Segal (1990). An interesting clinical illustration of this aspect of the process of psychotherapy integration may be noted in Greenberg's (1990) contribution to a videotape series in which several integrative therapists interviewed the same patient. This series may be of particular interest to readers of this book, because the present author was also one of the therapists who participated in this project, and my session with this patient (Wachtel, 1990) illustrates rather well the clinical approach presented and updated in this volume.

†I will discuss the meaning and implications of circularity and linearity in more detail below.

seem quite clear, they became apparent to me only as I was complet-
ing work on *Psychoanalysis and Behavior Therapy*. A full-scale exploration of the integrative possibilities between individual psychodynamic
approaches and family systems approaches was not undertaken until
some years later (Wachtel & Wachtel, 1986). My aim in this chapter is
to provide a concise overview of the ways in which the two models interface and to explicate the clinical implications that derive from such
an amalgam.

## ANTIPATHIES AND ATTEMPTS AT RECONCILIATION

It would not really be far-fetched to suggest that Freud was the first
family therapist. The very idea that the psychological dynamics within
the family, and the charged relational vectors between parents and children, were the source of neurotic misery throughout life was one of the
great insights of psychoanalytic investigation.

Yet it is also true that from the inception of the modern family therapy movement, sometime around 1960 or so, family therapists have in
large measure been hostile to psychoanalysis, viewing it is an outmoded
individualistic paradigm that it was family therapy's destiny to transcend.

Analysts in turn have returned the favor, often regarding family therapy as manipulative or insufficiently attentive to the psychological
depths, or simply regarding it with the disdain and lack of interest generally accorded a younger sibling.

There have been exceptions, to be sure. As noted above, a number
of the early leaders of family therapy had previously received psychoanalytic training, and some of them continued to inject psychoanalytic
perspectives into their work as family therapists. And from the psychoanalytic end, significant numbers of analytically trained clinicians
also practice family therapy, although usually with a sense that their
family therapy work is a rather different kind of enterprise, that practicing both kinds of therapy entails wearing two quite different hats.

More recently, a number of authors have attempted syntheses and
combinations that go beyond mere willingness to do two different
things, each valid but separate. Particularly important contributions to
a true integration of individual and systemic perspectives have been offered by Feldman (1992), Gurman (1981), Kirschner and Kirschner
(1986), and Pinsof (1983). Ester Shapiro's (1994) *Grief As a Family
Process*, although focused, as its name implies, particularly on dealing

with grieving and loss, offers an extraordinarily powerful and sensitive integrative approach that can be adapted to a much wider range of human issues. It also has the virtue of integrating not only individual and systemic points of view, but a cultural perspective as well.°

A number of recent efforts at synthesis have particularly centered on object relations theory as the bridge and have seen the concept of projective identification as the link between the internal object relations of concern to the psychoanalyst and the manifest object relations of concern to the family therapist (e.g., Scharff & Scharff, 1987, 1989; Slipp, 1984, 1988). The cyclical psychodynamic approach to integration of individual psychodynamic thinking and family systems thinking takes a different tack. I do see projective identification as one useful concept in understanding how the dynamics of the individual and the dynamics of the family are linked. But I believe that an approach to integration rooted in the cyclical psychodynamic perspective, with its emphasis on vicious circles and ironies, provides a fuller and more illuminating framework for synthesis.

The analysis of vicious circles enables us to gain a different perspective on the phenomena that psychoanalysts have usually conceptualized in terms of fixation and developmental arrest. Concern with fixation and arrest does create obstacles to an integration of the approaches of psychoanalytic and family therapists. Such a way of conceptualizing the persistence of certain seemingly anomalous features of psychic life directs attention away from the details of the person's present life. The relational systems in which the person participates seem, from the vantage point of these conceptualizations, a mere stage on which is acted out a script already written in childhood. A certain degree of editing or improvisation may be acknowledged, but the basic outlines are viewed as pretty well set, and the impact of the new setting on the actors is minimized.

To be sure, the *observations* on which concepts of fixation and arrest are based must be addressed. On close observation, many patients do seem to think and act in ways that seem aptly described as "infantile," and it is understandable that these observations would lead to the

---

°As this book went to the printer, another interesting effort to build a bridge across the divide between individual (especially psychoanalytic) and family therapy appeared, Mary Joan Gerson's (1996) *The Embedded Self: A Psychoanalytic Guide to Family Therapy*. As its name implies, it is not an explicitly integrative effort as much as a work designed to introduce family systems thinking to psychoanalysts, but its view that psychoanalysis and family therapy stand as figure and ground to each other is a useful contribution to the emerging movement toward synthesis.

assumption that something got "stuck," remained unchanged despite changing circumstances. Similarly, there is much reason to think that early experiences are of crucial importance in development; early patterns often do tend to persist. The problem arises when a form of linguistic slippage enters in that packs conceptualization and observation together in a confusing stew, and makes the separation of the two—troublesome under any circumstances—especially difficult. When the patient's problem is described as "from age 2," or even as "pre-Oedipal," observations about the content and the cognitive–affective features of her thinking and behavior are stated in a way that implies a direct relation, virtually unmediated by later events or by current circumstances, between the psychological state of the earliest years and the present psychological state. It is this way of conceptualizing that is, with some accuracy, described as "linear."

However, these conceptualizations—which can lead the therapist away from a focus on the way the patient now lives, and toward a search for the kernel of the patient's problems in the distant past—are not the only way to approach the observations on which they are based. Those observations must be included in any viable clinical approach. Accounting for them, however, does not require the concepts of fixation and developmental arrest and the clinical and theoretical baggage they bring.

The focus on vicious circles that is characteristic of the cyclical psychodynamic approach does not ignore the past, but it examines in much more detail how the past is carried forward into the present. Like other psychodynamic theories, cyclical psychodynamics emphasizes a person's unconscious wishes, fears, fantasies, expectations, conflicts, images of self and other, and so on. Rather than viewing these as part of an "inner world" separated from the daily world of lived experience, however, cyclical psychodynamic formulations lead us to look at how the internal state (wishes, fears, fantasies, expectations, conflicts) both leads to and results from the network of concrete experiences with others that constitutes the structure of daily life. Such an approach is acutely attentive to the details and subtleties of intrapsychic processes but conceptualizes those processes in a way that highlights their connection to the systems of mutual interaction that give form and tone to a person's life structure.

The unconscious wishes and fantasies are in no way epiphenomena in such an account, but neither are they the exclusive fundament or what "really" lies beneath the world of manifest interactions. Rather, the focus in the cyclical psychodynamic approach is on tracing the ways in which each individual's organizing psychological structures lead her to experience herself and others in certain ways, and hence to act in certain ways, which in turn leads others to act toward her in relatively predictable and consistent ways that, more often than not, serve to maintain the same organizing psychological structures and help to start the process all over again. (Many examples of how this proceeds can be found throughout this book, and also in Wachtel, 1987, 1993b and Wachtel & Wachtel, 1986.)

From this perspective, neither the system nor the individual is primary. Feedback works in both directions, and each participates in the life of the other and, indeed, defines who and what the other is. As family therapists frequently point out, how one "punctuates" a description is often arbitrary, but it is also often highly consequential. Psychodynamic theorists tend implicitly to punctuate the sequences by starting with the individual; family therapists tend to start with the system. When this is simply a matter of convenience, it is not problematic; the nature of language is such that we have to start somewhere. The problem arises when—from either end—the punctuation is mistaken for ontology. When either pole of the dialectic is taken as more real or fundamental, false incompatibilities appear that confound efforts to bring to bear the widest range of observations and interventions.

## INTENTIONAL AND UNINTENTIONAL PATTERNS: WHEN THE SOLUTION BECOMES THE PROBLEM

Further understanding of the possibilities for an integration of psychodynamic and family systems perspectives is aided by a consideration of the role of irony in the patterns that constitute people's lives. Most psychoanalytic accounts of the relation between individuals' intrapsychic lives and their transactions with the people around them emphasize the direct expression of motivations; what occurs is what was intended. The individual may well experience dismay at what transpires, but that is because the intention has been unconscious, not because the outcome was unintended. At times, for example, individuals may repeatedly find themselves in situations that are distressing and that, over and over, turn out badly for them. From an external perspective, the negative outcome may seem entirely predictable. Yet for the individual encountering it, it comes each time largely as an unpleasant surprise, indeed even in many instances as something that "happens to" him.

One common approach to these repeated unpleasant surprises—often raised when I have depicted the cyclical psychodynamic account to psychoanalytic audiences—is embodied in Freud's concept of the repetition compulsion. From the point of view of the concept of the repetition compulsion, two different motivational strands may be posited. In one, related to Freud's more abstruse conceptualization of the death instinct, and to the more concrete psychological motivation of masochism, the aim is self-punishment. From this vantage point, the repeated occurrence of failure or frustration or pain is most directly viewed as unconsciously sought or desired; the aim is self-harm. From another angle—probably the more dominant perspective on the repetition compulsion these days—the primary aim posited is mastery. The individual has suffered a painful experience, and (usually unconsciously) aims to master the experience by bringing it about intentionally. In *Beyond the Pleasure Principle,* Freud offered the prototypic instance of this in the example of a small child who was distressed by his mother's leaving—an event over which he had no control—and who then engaged in an interesting repetitive game. The child would throw a wooden toy over the side of his crib, while continuing to hold onto a string to which the toy was attached. When the toy had disappeared from his view, he would utter a sound that Freud understood to represent the German word "fort" or "gone." He would then pull the toy back up by the string and excitedly hail its return with the word "da" or "there." Freud took this repetitive game to represent symbolically the mother's repeated appearance and disappearance, a pattern that is originally experienced passively, but is controlled actively in the game.

Examples of this same dynamic later in life tend to be more complicated. Often they entail repeatedly getting into a kind of relationship that has been disastrous (and that may have roots and parallels in experiences of childhood), each time with the (largely vain and often unconscious) hope that "this time" it will be different, this time I will master the experience or change the outcome." Thus, from the point of view of this conceptualization, it is not the entire sequence that is craved—what is desired is the same beginning but a different ending, one might say—but the situation in which the individual finds himself is indeed thought of as unconsciously sought.

The concept of projective identification similarly emphasizes the individual's intention to produce the outcome of which he or she complains. Unacceptable and conflicted feelings are attributed to, and even induced in, the other, with the aim of simultaneously gratifying them through an unconscious identification with the presumed holder of the feeling and controlling or opposing them with reactions of criticism or revulsion toward the other for allegedly harboring the unacceptable feeling.

To be sure, in emphasizing the ways in which seemingly unwanted outcomes and experiences are in fact unconsciously intended, psychoanalytic accounts do not view the motivations as simple or unconflicted. Conceptualizations of conflict, after all, are at the very heart of the psychoanalytic enterprise. But, as will be apparent very shortly, the cyclical psychodynamic conception of how that conflict is reflected in the actual events of people's lives differs in important ways from that of most other psychoanalytic accounts.

Although there is room in the cyclical psychodynamic account for concepts such as projective identification or unconscious strivings for mastery, from a cyclical psychodynamic vantage point, irony plays a far greater role in the impasses that bring people to psychotherapy than is commonly recognized. Consequently, cyclical psychodynamic theory places considerable emphasis on the ways that people's actions bring results that are quite at odds with what they have intended and on the circumstances in which such ironic consequences are not simply occasional and accidental but quite regular and predictable. In this, the cyclical psychodynamic perspective has much in common both with the theories of Karen Horney (see Wachtel, 1987, Chapter 21) and with a prominent theoretical thrust in family therapy. Although some family therapists do make use of concepts such as projective identification (e.g., Framo, 1981; Skynner, 1981; Stierlin, 1977), a central observation guiding the work of many family therapists is captured in the phrase "the solution becomes the problem" (Watzlawick, Weakland, & Fisch, 1974). From such a vantage point, the causal nexus of psychological difficulties is infused with irony. What we end up with often is not what we intended but precisely what we were trying to prevent. And, in these instances, this happens not because in fact we secretly wanted what we say we are trying to avoid, but because the predictable consequences* of our actions are not equivalent to—or automatically reduceable to— the *aims* of those actions.

This is certainly not to say that directly motivated and intended consequences do not occur. Human beings could not survive as a species, after all, if we could not, most of the time, come reasonably close to producing the consequences we were seeking. In the more familiar or

*The consequence is predictable, of course, not from the vantage point of the individuals who blindly repeat the problematic pattern over and over, but from the vantage point of the observer not trapped in the pattern.

surface features of our lives, this is so obvious and pervasive as to be trivial. Moreover, even with regard to the more puzzling and distressing experiences that bring people to therapists, the degree to which these experiences fulfill needs and reflect motivations of the person who is dismayed by them is likely to be considerably greater than is initially recognized. This is the case not only because the motivations are often unconscious but because they are complex and conflicted as well. The pervasiveness of conflict in psychological life means that a given act or experience may reflect any particular motivation only partially or may be a compromise that is the resultant of several competing motivations. This state of affairs makes it difficult to disentangle the motivations behind the patterns therapists confront and easy to overlook the ways in which—however complexly and conflictually—they reflect the individual's intentionality.

Nothing in the above discussion of irony and unintended consequences is meant to contradict these points. I do aim, however, to place some constraints on such formulations, to render imputations of unconscious intention of consequences the individual claims to find distressing a little less automatic or reflexive. From a cyclical psychodynamic perspective, as in much family systems thinking, ironic consequences are a very regular feature of psychological life, and a considerable increment in understanding is achieved when we examine as well the ways in which our very efforts to banish certain experiences from our lives can actually contribute to bringing them about. The reader has seen, in earlier examples, how efforts to ward off anger can bring about a way of life that generates still more anger, how the narcissistic individual's efforts to ward off feelings of emptiness and fraudulence by puffing himself up create still further feelings of emptiness and fraudulence, and so forth. Without an understanding of how desperation can feed on itself and of how people may be plagued by the very experiences they have organized their lives around avoiding, therapists are likely to be baffled and frustrated in their efforts to be helpful.

## CIRCULARITY, LINEARITY, AND SYMPTOM SUBSTITUTION

Much of what has been discussed in this chapter has addressed, from one perspective or another, the issue of circular versus linear models of human behavior and experience. Among family therapists who see little prospect or utility in an integration of psychoanalytic and family systems models, this issue is perhaps the most strongly emphasized. It is the conceptualization of circularity of causation that is most typically cited in arguments that family therapy approaches represent a new paradigm in the mental health disciplines.

The emphasis of family systems theorists on circularity and their strong sense of the contrast between their approach and those they view as linear is well captured by Lynn Hoffman (1981) in an influential text exploring the foundations of family therapy:

> Mental illness has traditionally been thought of in linear terms, with historical, causal explanations for the distress. . . . But if one [sees the troubled individual] with his or her family, in the context of current relationships, one [begins] to see something quite different. One [sees] communications and behaviors from everybody present, composing many circular loops that play back and forth, with the behavior of the afflicted person only part of a larger, recursive dance. (pp. 6–7)

This observation, in one form or another, is the key foundation of almost all approaches to family therapy: When one has sufficient opportunity to observe the context in which problematic behavior actually occurs, it appears to make sense rather than to be an anomaly to be explained by a fault within the individual that keeps her responding to the past rather than to what is actually transpiring before her eyes; the apparent irrationality or inappropriateness is a result of viewing the behavior or experience out of context.

Family therapists are usually critical of perspectives that locate the difficulty "within" a particular individual. When a member of a family manifests psychological symptoms, he or she is depicted by family therapists as the "identified patient." This term is meant to suggest that although this particular individual is the one who manifestly "has a problem" and is therefore brought into contact with the mental health system, the problem really resides in the system as a whole. One person in the family (or sometimes more than one) in effect carries the burden for the difficulties in the system as a whole. An observation reported widely in the family therapy literature in this regard is that when the symptoms of the identified patient are treated by individual means, with the systemic problem left untouched, another family member may begin to manifest symptoms. This newly symptomatic family member takes the place of the former identified patient, but more fundamentally nothing has changed. The underlying pattern that is creating the symptoms persists.

Interestingly, this formulation, frequently introduced as a critique of psychoanalytic treatment approaches, is a first cousin of the critique that psychoanalysts often raise of behavior therapy; it is the "symptom substitution" hypothesis writ large. In both instances, it is a combination of useful observation and perceptive conceptualization on the one hand, and mythic overstatement and misunderstanding or caricature on the other. We have seen in Part one that the psychoanalytic critique of behavior therapy as likely to lead to symptom substitution is both empirically unfounded and rooted in a misconception of what behavior therapists actually do.

The symptom substitution hypothesis originated in observations that when treatment was based on simple suggestion that a symptom would disappear, the results were often short-lived; the symptom would either recur, or another would take its place. To be sure even under such treatment regimens, symptom substitution is by no means an invariable consequence. Symptoms, for example, are at times a response to a crisis that was temporary, and the treatment of the symptom through simple suggestion could for some patients provide a face-saving rationale for letting go of the no-longer-necessary symptom. But it is likely that in the days when virtually the only alternative to psychoanalytic treatment was such direct suggestion, the phenomenon of symptom substitution was not uncommon. Behavior therapy, in contrast, is not a means of "taking away" the symptom but is a genuine *treatment* of the symptom. Often, it entails not avoiding the source of the patient's fears but providing a means of more effectively confronting those fears, of achieving exposure to what is frightening, and eventually attaining a measure of mastery.

But just as the symptom substitution hypothesis has been misused and overused by psychoanalysts, it can be similarly overzealously applied toward psychoanalytic treatment, as when the very idea of individual treatment is seen as necessarily leaving untreated the real underlying problem, conceived of as invariably systemic. To be sure, psychoanalytic treatment can at times proceed in a way that is insufficiently attentive to the larger systemic dynamics in which the patient's difficulties are embedded and of which they are a part. This can at times yield changes, even in a "successful" treatment, that have an impact on other family members that is not necessarily benign. But understanding when psychoanalytic treatment—or any individual treatment—is (or is not) likely to exacerbate difficulties for other individuals in the system requires further consideration of the interaction between intrapsychic and systemic processes.

Psychoanalysis is a highly individualistic form of treatment, whose roots in and parallels to the underlying assumptions of our social and economic order are insufficiently appreciated (Wachtel, 1989). Much as our legal system frequently promotes an approach to divorce and separation that is highly adversarial and magnifies and exacerbates tensions, so too can the focus of individual psychodynamic therapy promote an approach that portrays parents, spouses, and others in intimate relationships with the patient as adversaries. Campbell (1992), reviewing published descriptions by therapists of the significant others in their patients' lives, found that over 90% of the depictions were negative. Parents, for example, were described as "highly critical and intrusive," "distant and emotionally barren," "withholding and abandoning," "prohibitive," and "rejecting."

This feature of individual psychotherapy—by no means exclusive to psychoanalysis—can be quite problematic at times, and the family systems perspective offers a useful corrective in several respects. To begin with, although it is certainly helpful for the patient to understand the ways in which actions and characteristics of her parents and other significant figures in her life have had a negative impact on her development, a focus that attempts to grasp empathically only the patient's experience and does not also attend to how the world looked through the eyes of the other becomes adversarial and eventually counterproductive. The lesser, but not insignificant, danger is that it can contribute to disharmony in the patient's interactions with others, to a kind of *folie à deux* in which patient and analyst see everything from a perspective in which the patient is always right, and the actual relationships in the patient's life deteriorate as a result. This is a lesser danger only because good analysts tend to be aware of it; when the analyst or therapist is not, the negative consequences of such a stance are considerable. The more subtle and pervasive danger is a failure to appreciate the degree to which one's identity and sense of self are built upon identifications. If the parents, or even current key relationship figures, are viewed too negatively, the sense of goodness of the self becomes a casualty. There are times when a patient's upbringing has been so bad that there is little choice but to help her create a positive identity in opposition to her origins. But this is a difficult task to achieve and, wherever possible, is aided by inclusion (to whatever degree is feasible and honest) of an appreciation of what she did get from parental figures who, despite all their failings, can usually also be understood as struggling with their own conflicts and pressures and who likely imparted some qualities that can be valued.

Sometimes the absence of positive identification figures that emerges from an individualistically conducted treatment is countered by the analyst's presenting *herself* as an identification figure. Much of the recent offerings on technique emerging from the object relations and self-psychology approaches largely amount to this. In certain circumstances and in certain respects, this can be a useful strategy, but it can also contribute to fostering still further alienation from the "natural" identification figures in the patient's life. Although there is certainly something to be said for the therapist presenting herself as a "good object" for the patient to internalize—especially since this approach has led to a more empathic, available, and nurturant therapeutic stance—it is important not to overvalue or overestimate the therapist's impact on the patient. The most important objects in the patient's life remain those she grew up with and those with whom she now spends her other 23 hours. The therapy, if it is going well, has a powerful impact, and the therapist becomes indeed an important person in the patient's life. But when the therapist attempts to make up for the deficiencies in the rest of the patient's life by how caring and empathic she is, the therapy is based on a very faulty foundation.

The strategy of family therapists implicitly addresses a number of the difficulties I have just described. Although many of these therapists would not think in terms of the patient's identifications (or even accept the idea that a single individual can be "the patient"), their aim is usually to aid people in working out their difficulties together, in relation to each other rather than apart from each other. This does not imply a superficial emphasis on "togetherness" or an automatic preference for merger rather than autonomy; a key concept in family therapy thinking is that some families are "enmeshed" and for such families boundaries must be strengthened, not dismantled (Minuchin, 1974). Rather, the essence of the family system perspective is that however close or distant family members may appear to be, however much they may either ignore or interfere excessively, they are inevitably part of a network of relationships that plays a crucial role in the lives of all network members. The therapist becomes a part of that network as soon as she enters the lives of any of its members, but she cannot substitute for them. She can only be a catalyst for changing what they do for (or to) each other.

## CONCEPTUALIZING THE ROLE OF HISTORY

Childhood is seen by virtually every influential psychological theory as a crucial period in shaping the patterns of interpersonal transaction and personal experience that constitute an individual's personality. The patterns established early most often persist in significant and fateful ways. The theories differ substantially, however, in their accounts of *how* the impact of childhood experiences is manifested throughout the life span and how the continuity so frequently observed is mediated. In some theories, the traces or structures deriving from early experiences are in some way "laid down" or "internalized," and then persist as an influence that directly affects behavior and experience thenceforth. In others, the impact of early experience is mediated by a myriad of intervening events in which the individual's evolving characteristics and the interpersonal world in which they are manifested continuously shape each other. As Bateson (1972) has put it, individuals who regularly interact with each other engage in a process of "coevolution." The impact of each upon the other is mutual rather than unidirectional, as is the causal relation between individual behaviors and the characteristics of the group or system of which they are a part. The individual's history is not a result of a linear influence of early, determining events, but rather reflects the way in which those early events influenced how the individual entered into later encounters, which in turn shaped still other choices and experiences, in a virtually infinite series. Early experiences are anything but inconsequential in this sort of account, but their importance is acknowledged and incorporated in a way that does not diminish the equally great import of the continuingly evolving context. It is not a matter of some sort of 50–50 split of the variance, but of an evolution and interpenetration in which the absolutely and utterly crucial role of each is not diminished by the similarly decisive import of the other. They are not pitted against each other, but rather reinforce and define each other.

Theories characterized by such accounts may be described as field theories. Such theories do not ignore the role of history or of the past. Rather, they view that role as being embodied in the present in the form of a field of forces that includes in the here and now the total impact of all the previous theres and thens in which each individual has participated.

Both family systems theories and cyclical psychodynamic theory may be seen in essence to be field theories. Moreover, both are theories in which the continuity between past and present is understood as a recursive process in which often very substantial stability and continuity can be discerned, but in which that continuity must be understood in terms of the dynamics of the systems that have come into play. Those dynamics, when stability is the manifest property, depend on an underlying homeostatic process in which feedback tends to bring the sys-

tem back into the pattern from which it has deviated, much as a ther-
mostat keeps the temperature relatively constant despite the ever-
present occurrence of deviations from the temperature to which it is set.°

## THE INDIVIDUAL AND THE SYSTEM

Apropos of the discussion in Chapter 15, the distinction between a
one-person psychology and a two-person psychology must be extended
when considering the contribution of family therapy. Rickman (1957)
has suggested that "the whole region of Psychology may be divided into
areas of research according to the number of persons concerned. Thus
we may speak of One-Body Psychology, Two-Body Psychology, Three-
Body Psychology, Four-Body Psychology, and Multi-Body Psychology"
(p. 123). Balint (1950), in discussing this point, noted that "almost all
[the terms and concepts of psychoanalysis] were derived from studying
pathological forms hardly going beyond the domain of the One-Body
Psychology" (p. 124). Family therapy, in contrast, is an approach that
builds its terms and concepts from a "multi-body psychology," but the
way different family therapists carry out this program varies quite considerably, and the neglect of a multi-body psychology by psychoanalysts
may be paralleled by a neglect of a "one-body psychology" by some
family therapists.

In the family therapy literature, the most common focus is on sets
of three. The concept of "triangulation," a complex process in which
pairs of individuals attempt to work out their individual conflicts and
their conflicts with each other through involving a third person, figures
prominently in practically every version of family therapy. But the exact focus of actual clinical work can differ substantially from one family therapy approach to another. Theories within the family therapy domain about the origins of children's symptoms, for example, most often
stress the way the child has been triangulated by the parents, but in actual practice, the child is often ignored and the triangle collapses into

---

°Recently, influential critiques of the concept of homeostasis have appeared in
the family therapy literature. These critiques highlight that homeostasis is neither
a necessary outcome nor one that is somehow "intended" by the system, and, in
pointing to ways in which homeostasis is only one potential result of a system's
functioning, they point to new possibilities for intervention and change. The expanded understanding of the range of ways that system dynamics can be manifested should be seen as complementing but not replacing or eliminating the concept of homeostasis, which remains crucial for understanding the dynamics of
continuity that so often keep people locked into highly problematic patterns.

work with the couple alone (E. Wachtel, 1994). This can entail conceptualizations, to use the terminology just introduced, of a two-body nature (i.e., the interaction between the spouses) or of a three-body variety (when the triangulation of the therapist by the couple is emphasized).

E. Wachtel's (1994) child-in-family approach is strongly rooted in a systems conceptualization of the difficulties the family reports with the child, but although it pays considerable attention to the two-body, three-body and multi-body dynamics, it does not ignore the one-body dimension. Put differently, systems theory is viewed, as in the present approach, not as replacing or transcending the study of individuals but as complementing it. The individual must indeed be understood in the context of the important systems within which she participates, but her characteristics as an individual are not thereby ignored. In E. Wachtel's child-in-family approach, the behavioral and psychodynamic dimensions of the child's difficulties (and, importantly, of the child's strengths and potentials) have a prominent place, even as both of these dimensions are understood in a way that is thoroughly infused with an appreciation of their inevitably systemic interconnection. Thus, in place of the common reduction of child work to couples therapy, the child-in-family approach includes attention to the couple dynamics, but extends the therapist's attention in both directions to a concern with the one-body properties of the child herself and the three-body dynamics of triangulation. Moreover, the latter process is conceived of not just as a screen for diversion by the couple from their problems with each other, but as a process in which the child, as a real person with distinct and impactful psychological characteristics of her own, is a full and active participant. In this respect, the child-in-family approach converges with important trends in the literature of child development that stress the reciprocal and mutual influence between parents and children (e.g., Stern, 1985; Sameroff, 1983, 1987; Zeanah et al., 1989; Beebe & Lachmann, 1988).

With regard to the relative contributions of individual and systemic influences, the thrust of cyclical psychodynamic work with adults has much in common with the child-in-family approach just described for work with children. Here too, the psychodynamic and behavioral dimensions are interwoven with attention to context and system, and the assumption is that insights into the role of systems do not *replace* what we know about individuals but rather *expand* that knowledge.

Writings about family systems can be almost maddeningly abstract at times, retreating into what Coyne (1982b) has described as "epistobabble," a pretentious, jargon-filled prose that can make even versions of psychoanalytic writing that are "deep in the heart of cathexis" seem crystalline. Moreover, quite apart from style, the emphasis on general systems theory (von Bertalanffy, 1950, 1969) by some writers on family therapy obscures the significant differences between the "systems" that are identified by family therapists and the other varieties and levels of systemic phenomena that general systems theory unifies. Clearly, general systems theory represents a major achievement of twentieth century science, pointing to unities and commonalities in the properties of systems of a very diverse nature. And indeed, the general systems perspective illuminates aspects of the interpersonal and behavioral systems in which human beings engage that are both important and not immediately obvious. Understanding their properties as systems is a major contribution.

At the same time, however, it is crucial to be attentive to the very special nature of these particular systems. Unlike other systems, the "parts" of family systems are entities with intentions and feelings. It is possible, to be sure, in discussing, for example, the body as a system reflecting complex interactions of cells and organs, to point to feedback and interaction, and even in a certain sense "sensitivity" to the "communications" between the cells and organs, but it would stretch the metaphor beyond all coherence to talk about what the liver wants or how the pancreas feels about what the kidneys are doing. In family systems, however, it is *crucial* to consider what Johnny wants or what Billy feels about what Sarah is doing. We are parts of a system, but we are parts like no other parts; accounts in which we are effectively reduced to kidneys, cell nuclei, or gears are simply inadequate.

Carl Whittaker has captured an important aspect of this point in his much quoted comment, "You can't hug a system." As important an advance as systems conceptualizations represent, unless our approach to systems acknowledges the very special nature of individual human beings, the ways in which they differ from all other "parts" of systems, systems thinking will be a dead end. Good family therapists, of course, know this and include sensitivity to the individuals either in the intuitive background that enables their systemic interventions to work or, to varying degrees, in their explicit theoretical formulations. What has made the full articulation of the interface between individual and systemic perspectives difficult has been the often acontextual way in which important insights about the experiences and dynamics of individuals have been framed. Much of what this chapter and this book have been about is the construction of a fully contextual psychodynamic model that reflects the same kind of cyclical, recursive emphasis found in systems formulations, and that consequently provides a bridge between conceptualizations at the two levels.

## ACCOMPLICES, SYSTEMS, AND THE CAST OF CHARACTERS

A key element in the bridge that cyclical psychodynamics provides is the concept of accomplices introduced in Chapter 4. I have suggested elsewhere (Wachtel, 1991b) that

> understanding how people change requires first understanding how neurosis is a joint activity, a cooperative enterprise of a most peculiar sort. Without the participation of the cast of characters in a person's life—or, to put it differently (since nothing in human behavior occurs in a vacuum) with *different* participation of significant others in the patient's life—the neurosis would not continue. Indeed, one might even argue that the process whereby others are continually recruited into a persisting maladaptive pattern *is* the neurosis. (p. 22)

Such a conceptualization focuses the clinician's attention on the individual's motives, conflicts, perceptions, and anxieties, and the behavior that flows from them, at the same time that it points toward the system of transactions with others of which the individual is a part. Attention to the behavior of others within such a framework does not direct the focus away from the individual but expands our understanding of her and of the life patterns that in large measure constitute her unique personality. Indeed, much of what it means effectively to understand a person—and especially to understand her in a way that aids in promoting therapeutic change—is to understand how, mostly without awareness and often even without any direct intention, she in effect selects, recruits, and trains the accomplices in her life.

### MEETING THE CAST OF CHARACTERS

Within the cyclical psychodynamic approach, the understanding of the interpersonal context for the patient's difficulties, and of the ways she recruits and interacts with accomplices, comes from several sources. Much of our understanding of these factors and processes comes simply from the patient's descriptions of her experiences with other people. The therapist operating from a cyclical psychodynamic perspective is clearly interested in such accounts, but is attentive as well to how people punctuate and edit them in ways that may obscure the concrete details. She is therefore likely to include as part of her listening and inquiry a variety of prompts designed to elicit and recapture those details ("What did she say in response to that?" "What did you do at that point?" "How exactly did the fight start?" etc.).

In addition, much is learned from the experience of patient and therapist together in the room. Notwithstanding the emphasis on concrete details of who said what to whom, the focus of a cyclical psychodynamic inquiry is equally on the affective experience of both participants, and for such understanding, attention to the transference and countertransference is invaluable. By attending to the patient's experience in the here and now of the therapy relationship, and by attending to her own experience in relation to the patient, the therapist can gain an immediacy as well as an intimacy of understanding that cannot be achieved in any other way.

As discussed in earlier chapters, however, as valuable as is the insight the transference and countertransference offer into the patient's interpersonal style and emotional life, there are limitations to this source of data as well. A broad sample of the patient's spectrum of interpersonal and affective experiences is tapped by a skillful exploration of the transference and countertransference experiences, but not the entire range. A key emphasis of the cyclical psychodynamic approach (as, in certain ways, a key emphasis of family systems thinking) is on the specificity of people's responses. We do not respond simply to the call of inner voices that will "emerge" or "unfold" come what may (Wachtel, 1982). We respond to the ways that particular interpersonal configurations call forth particular aspects of our complex and largely unconscious potential. This is what makes taking into account the specifics of the family system and of the characteristics of the accomplices in the patient's life so important. It is also what makes the transference–countertransference configuration, as crucial as it is, not utterly sufficient. As Gill (1982, 1994), Mitchell (1988, 1993), and others have pointed out, the real properties of the therapist always play a role in what transference experience the patient will manifest, and no therapist is possessed of all properties. It is true that there will be times when even a rather vigorous and confident therapist will be hesitant (or at least hesitant enough to evoke the patient's set of reactions to such an interpersonal configuration). Similarly, a young and attractive therapist may look haggard some days, even a shy therapist may convey genuine comfort and confidence in the session on many occasions, and so on. Nonetheless, although each individual is multifaceted, no individual is infinite or universal. Each therapist will elicit different sides of the patient's personality. Therapists are not equivalent or interchangeable, not merely screens for the patient's projections.

Thus, there are cases where what we learn from the patient's reports of her interactions with others and from our direct experience in the transference–countertransference transaction is insufficient or misleading. At times, an opportunity to meet directly the key figures in the patient's life and, to some degree, to observe how the patient interacts with them is invaluable. Family therapists, of course, have this opportunity regularly, but the individual therapist often does not. From the vantage point of many individual therapists, that is neither an accident nor (as they perceive it) a handicap. The very rationale of the therapist's approach may exclude the participation of others in the patient's session. The exclusivity of the relationship—both for its "hothouse" effects on the transference and as it reflects a commitment to seeing the world through the patient's eyes alone—is seen by some therapists to be central to what is curative. From the perspective of cyclical psychodynamics, there is also much to be said for a sharp focus on the patient's experience and on the relationship that evolves between patient and therapist. But there is also room for the careful inclusion of others in the work, even when the work remains individual psychotherapy.

CONDUCTING THE CAST OF CHARACTERS SESSION

The question of when it is best to see a patient individually and when it is preferable to see a couple or family as a whole is a complex one that cannot be addressed here. Suffice to say that both modalities have their place. The focus here will be on a narrower question: If one is working with an individual, when and how does one bring in other key figures from the patient's life? There are doubtless many answers to these questions. Those that have emerged from work undertaken from a cyclical psychodynamic perspective point in the following directions (see Wachtel & Wachtel, 1986, for a more detailed account of when and how to conduct a "cast of characters" session):

(a) The idea of meeting important members of the "cast of characters" in the patient's life may be introduced by the patient or by the therapist. In the former instance, the patient may possibly be responding to signals from the therapist that she is receptive to the idea. Patients in more traditional therapies may pick up that such an idea is impossible or unacceptable and may not broach it; within the more flexible framework of cyclical psychodynamics, the idea is both more likely to occur to the patient and more likely to be expressed. If the patient does not suggest it, but the therapist thinks it might be useful, then she can broach the topic, both offering her rationale for why it might be useful and listening to any hesitations the patient may have. Some patients have initial misgivings that change when the issue is explored and the nature of the proposed sessions is clarified. Others decide they would rather not have such a session, and their wish is, of course honored. In such instances, the mere introduction of the idea can still be useful, for it often evokes considerable new material, both in the transference and with respect to the person whose possible visit is being discussed.

(b) In the cast of characters sessions under discussion here, the patient is present. These are not sessions alone with a spouse, parent, or other figure, but sessions in which the other person, or people, and the patient *jointly* meet with the therapist. I have occasionally had sessions alone with a family member, when both the patient and the other person have requested that. But those are a different sort of session, even though they share many of the same ground rules. The most crucial technical point in such instances is to make absolutely clear to both the patient and the family member that the therapist's commitment regarding confidentiality does not mean that she will hold confidential from the patient what is told her by other family members. It is made clear to family members that they should not tell the therapist anything they do not want the patient to know about. I cannot work with a patient and have "secrets" from her. The family member must know, and even more important, the patient must know that the patient will be privy to everything that is said. (The patient's own confidentiality is, of course, preserved; the family member is not made privy to what the patient had told me in the sessions.)

(c) In conducting the cast of characters session, much of the most important work is done before the other person ever comes to a session. To begin with, the patient's feelings about introducing another person into a session must be thoroughly explored. Of importance to examine are not only the patient's hesitations and anxieties, but also her hopes and expectations. The former (hesitations and anxieties) are more likely to be appreciated as important to explore; most therapists recognize that one should never introduce another person into a session unless the patient's feelings about it have been thoroughly worked through. It is easier to overlook the need to explore the patient's hopes and expectations. Part of why cast of characters sessions are useful is that they can at times mobilize a powerful set of feelings, and those feelings can include strong anticipations by the patient that something special will happen. To raise false hopes and expectations can be traumatizing to the patient when they are dashed. It can be damaging as well to the therapeutic relationship and to the patient's trust and confidence in the therapist. The idea that the therapist will protect and guide the patient in her dealings with another person with whom she has had an important but conflictual relationship can exert a very powerful pull, and stir unrealistic expectations, and these too must be worked through.*

It should, of course, be understood that working through these feelings does not necessarily mean that the patient is unambivalent. Certainly, one should never go ahead with such a session if the patient feels something is being forced on her or is passively acceding to something about which she has considerable doubt. But often ambivalence is a state that therapy helps us deal with better, not something that is eliminated. Often it is precisely the capacity to bear and work with—not eliminate—complex and mixed feelings that is the gain therapy yields.

(d) Occasionally, the aim of the cast of characters session is to work on an issue between the patient and significant others that is impeding the progress of the therapeutic work or to ward off possible systemic resistance by making the system more hospitable to change. Giving family members an opportunity to participate in a session in which their perspective is heard can help to defuse potentially adversarial situations. In all cast of character sessions (not only those aiming to ward off a potential problem), the therapist aims to make the guest feel heard and respected. Part of the preliminary work with one's patient entails clarifying this. Especially where the individuals invited to the session have been a source of difficulty for the patient, it is important that the patient understand that listening respectfully to the other is not "changing sides."

Most often, however, the aim of these sessions is more one of reconnaissance than intervention. Frequently, the cast of characters session provides a useful additional perspective on the patient's history. A sibling or parent may have a different take on the nature of the family the patient grew up in or on a particular key event the family encountered. The sessions also afford the therapist an opportunity to form her own impressions of the key individuals in the patient's life. Is mother as critical, or distant, or self-sacrificing as the patient has seen her? Is

---

*To be sure, therapists *can* use their skills to help people resolve difficult and conflictual relationship issues, and obviously that is sometimes aided by work together with the other in the presence of the therapist. But to turn an individual therapy into couples or family therapy raises complexities that are often difficult to resolve, and that is not what is being described here.

father as warm, or weak, or domineering? The therapist may, as well, gain a useful perspective from these sessions on how the patient interacts with key others.

To be sure, this extra evaluation must not be undertaken in the spirit that the therapist's perception or that of the guest in the session is more realistic or accurate than that of the patient. Such a view is problematic epistemologically, ethically, and pragmatically. Rather, as discussed in more detail in the next chapter, the therapist's task is always simultaneously to listen to and validate the patient's view of things and to help the patient expand her perspective and consider alternatives. That is the set with which these potential alternative stories are listened to as well. They are a means to expand the patient's perspectives and increase her range of ways of viewing matters; they most decidedly should not be viewed as a means of checking up on the patient or contradicting her.

A useful product of these sessions as well is that the other people in the patient's life become more real and human. This not only affords a more three-dimensional understanding but helps to counter the tendency to blame the patient's significant others. Almost inevitably, the individual one is seeing as a patient does (and even should) become the hero of the story to some degree, but it is important to balance this with a broader perspective so that the others do not correspondingly become the villains. As discussed above, such a perspective is likely ultimately to be counterproductive to the patient's own interests. The cast of characters session is a useful counterpoise to such a development.

(e) A crucial element of the cast of characters interview for the therapy process is the feedback in the session or sessions that follow. That feedback includes both the therapist's input to the patient and the patient's account to the therapist of how she experienced what transpired. Exploring the patient's experience of the session can be of great value. Some important questions to ask include the following: Did the other act in a way that seemed to the patient fairly typical? Does she think the therapist was able to get a reasonably accurate impression from the session of the other person and of how that person and the patient interact with each other? Did the patient have any feelings about how the therapist conducted the session? What was it like to share the session with someone else? What might the therapist have missed about what went on?

Most patients, not surprisingly, are curious about the therapist's impressions of the guest in the session. (Some, however, prefer not to hear the therapist's reaction. It is important not to impose feedback on a patient who does not wish it at that time, although obviously the patient's hesitancy to find out is important clinical information that may enter into the work at a later point.) In general, it is unusual for the therapist's view of the other people in the patient's life to be radically altered by such sessions. Most often, the picture the therapist has of the other, or of the patient's way of interacting with him or her, will be modified only in subtle (but often quite useful) ways. Real surprises are uncommon, although obviously important when they occur.

Communicating one's impressions to the patient requires the same kind of sensitivity that any part of the therapeutic process requires; one must find a way to be honest and tactful at once (see Wachtel & Wachtel, 1986, for more detailed discussions of how to deal with the many complex challenges presented in this phase of the therapeutic work). The skill of the therapist lies very largely in transforming raw impressions—whether negative or positive—into therapeutically effective communications. That is a skill that is crucial not only to the specific clinical context addressed here, but to the entire success of the therapeutic enterprise. It is to this topic, as it is manifested in a variety of therapeutic situations and approaches, that we now turn.

# 18

## Bringing Integration to the Heart of the Therapy: An Integrative Approach to the Therapist's Language

═══════

IN the early stages of an integrative effort, the separate components are likely to remain discrete and identifiable. They are combined but not really synthesized. What emerges is, to be sure, more than the sum of the parts, but the parts themselves remain largely untouched by virtue of being put together with other elements that derive from very different sources.

It is not likely to be long, however, before something more interesting and thoroughgoing happens. When assumptions and methods come into close contact with other assumptions and methods that were previously alien, subtle changes begin to appear in all of the constituents of the evolving synthesis. Something much like this happened in the evolution of the approach described in this book.

In the initial stages of the integrative effort described in this volume, the therapy looked at some points like a fairly standard interpersonal version of psychoanalytic therapy; at other points what could be seen was a fairly standard version of systematic desensitization, assertiveness training, or some other behavioral method. As befit my own origins in the psychoanalytic approach, psychodynamic forms predominated, but both "parts" could be seen. After awhile, however, several things began to happen. First, the tone and style of the behavioral interventions began subtly to change. One might say they took on a psychoanalytic "accent." This became evident fairly early, and can be seen in a number of the clinical illustrations in Part One (e.g., pp. 207–210). In a variety of ways, the behavioral methods began to be themselves a source of psychoanalytic insights, and the way I approached those methods conveyed clearly to the patient that I was interested in learning about anything that occurred to her in the process and about her experience while participating. The point was not just to do the various exercises and techniques—though of course that was a very important part—but also to avail herself of the opportunities these newer methods afforded for further self-understanding and for exploring the experiences and associations they stimulated.

It was not just the behavioral parts of the work that were affected by the new context in which they were incorporated; the psychoanalytic parts of the work changed as well. Increasingly, thinking and practicing integratively made me aware of other dimensions to the process of psychoanalytic exploration and interpretation besides those usually discussed in the psychoanalytic literature. Interpretations, for example, are also ways of *exposing* the patient to the forbidden and of conveying to the patient alternative ways of behaving in challenging life situations. Moreover, notwithstanding prevalent contentions regarding neutrality, what is said (or not said) by psychoanalysts and other supposedly nondirective therapists almost inevitably has elements of reinforcement and direction (see, in this connection, Greenson, 1967, p. 273; Truax, 1966; Wachtel, 1987; and Chapter 11 of this volume).

What has emerged in my work over the years is a more "seamless" integration (Wachtel, 1991a) in which it is increasingly difficult to say which moments are the psychodynamic moments and which are the behavioral or systemic. The nature of the way each is employed is shaped by the others, and what can be seen is more truly a synthesis. To be sure, as its name implies, the cyclical psychodynamic approach is still most distinctively guided by a psychodynamic point of view, but it is a psychodynamic view in which systemic and cognitive–behavioral elements fit comfortably. Perhaps the realm in which this more thoroughgoing synthesis is most evident is in the concrete details of what the therapist actually says to her patients.

The clinical recommendations offered in the original edition of *Psychoanalysis and Behavior Therapy* included a few guidelines for how to frame comments to patients, but largely focused on the integration of the specific active intervention methods developed by behavior therapists into an exploratory psychoanalytic approach to therapy. As I began working in an increasingly integrative mode, however, a focus on precisely what the therapist says, and on ways of conveying our message that are therapeutic (as well as on an understanding of ways that are not), took center stage. Several years ago, I devoted an entire book to this topic (Wachtel, 1993b), describing in great detail ways in which the things we say to our patients and clients are or are not therapeutically helpful, and articulating a series of strategies for making our communications more useful to the patient in his or her efforts to change. It is attention to this dimension of the therapeutic work that presently constitutes the cutting edge of the cyclical psychodynamic approach, and I turn to it now.

## BOTH PARTIES TALK IN THE "TALKING CURE"

Psychotherapy is the "talking cure," but for many years it was discussed and taught as if only one of the two parties talked. Enormous attention was paid to what the patient said, but much less to the words of the therapist. The therapist, in the more exploratory or expressive forms of treatment, was primarily taught to listen.

For many years, this emphasis reflected in part the very substantial disparity in how much actually was said by the two parties. The therapist's job, it was thought, was mainly to listen, and only occasionally to say something. It was thus somewhat understandable that so much more attention would be paid to the nuances of what the patient said. Her words were the primary medium of the treatment, with the therapist's words serving only as an occasional counterpoint. Moreover, it was the patient's communications that were seen as needing to be understood. Unravelling the meanings of the patient's communications very largely *was* the therapy in the minds of many therapists. The therapist's words were simply a means of conveying the understanding achieved, and if the understanding was correct, it was usually assumed, what to say and how to say it would follow rather directly and automatically.

Today this view of the therapeutic process is increasingly untenable. To begin with, therapists probably talk more today than they once did. I cannot cite an empirical study comparing the number of words spoken by therapists in the 1950s and the 1990s, but increasingly the therapeutic process is conceived of as a dialogue, as a process characterized by the interaction between two people. Virtually silent analysts have probably not completely disappeared, but they are viewed as almost as laughable by the majority in the psychoanalytic community as they (continuingly) are by the cartoonists of the *New Yorker.* Today's psychotherapists—even today's psychoanalysts—both speak and acknowledge to their supervisors that they speak.

Even more significant, perhaps, attention to countertransference is much greater today. Where once countertransference was very largely viewed in terms of error, of ways in which the therapist's unconscious was leading her astray, now countertransference is viewed as an essential tool of the therapy. Therapists are encouraged not to expunge their countertransferences but to attend to them. This presents the therapist with a more difficult and complex task, but one that has the potential to enrich the therapeutic process. The therapist must, in a certain sense, both trust and mistrust her reactions simultaneously. The original thrust of viewing countertransference feelings with suspicion, of examining oneself for irrational reactions to the patient based on longstanding unconscious inclinations, still stands; the new emphasis on the positive value of countertransference is not an excuse for self-indulgence on the therapist's part. Yet at the same time, countertransference reactions are now seen as an extremely valuable source of understanding of the patient and of the world the patient creates. Once the therapist has examined her reactions in light of what she knows about her own biases and proclivities,* she is in a position also to consider how her experience of the patient can enable her better to understand the experiences of other key figures in the patient's life, who—as emphasized throughout this book—contribute very significantly to the texture and quality of the patient's daily experience. She is also better able to grasp empathically what the patient herself is experiencing, which often is more clearly understood via the emotional reaction evoked in the therapist than by a more intellectual process of inference.

In a therapeutic climate in which the pervasive influence and importance of the countertransference is emphasized, attention to the impact of the therapist's participation in the process can be understood as more essential. The more the therapy process is understood as a mutual, two-person interaction, the more important it is to understand the impact of the therapist's words on the patient's experience. If the patient's experiences and associations are no longer viewed simply as "emerging" or "unfolding" from some pristine and previously inaccessible recesses of the mind (Wachtel, 1982), but rather are understood

---

*It should be obvious that this new emphasis on the positive uses of the countertransference makes it even more urgent that one's own psychotherapy be a part of every therapist's training.

as powerfully affected by the therapist's participant-observation, then the influence of the therapist's comments is crucial to take into account. Moreover, not only must the therapist's influence be taken into account in order properly to understand the patient; the impact of her remarks on the prospects for change is crucial as well. The framework articulated in this book points to a wide range of influences contributing to the ability of the patient to change troubling life patterns. Self-understanding (both spontaneously achieved in the process and aided by the therapist's interpretations) is certainly an important part of the change process, but the analysis presented here points to many other factors contributing to change as well.

Notwithstanding the important contribution of exposure-focused methods such as systematic desensitization and flooding or such processes as behavior rehearsal and modeling that can be mobilized by a variety of methods discussed earlier in this book, the vast majority of therapeutic interventions employed by psychotherapists across all orientations entail a kind of conversation. The therapist's impact is most frequently manifested through what she *says* to the patient or client. It remains one of the great gaps in the literature on psychotherapy that detailed examinations of the impact of this staple of the therapeutic process are few and far between. Such examination has recently been undertaken from a cyclical psychodynamic point of view (Wachtel, 1993b), and my aim in this chapter is to bring the reader up to date on the general thrust of this effort.

## THERAPISTS' UNWITTINGLY ACCUSATORY COMMENTS

The language therapists use in their theoretical discussions with each other obscures the language they use when they talk to patients. In theory, the therapist is neutral. Her comments convey neither permission nor prohibition, neither praise nor rebuke. They simply tell the truth.

Closer inspection, however, suggests that in fact the vast majority of comments therapists make are *not* neutral, that they give subtle indications of the therapist's approval or disapproval and that they are likely either to enhance or diminish the patient's self-esteem. It has been a central theme of the cyclical psychodynamic approach in recent years to examine these messages in detail and to find ways of conveying what the therapist has observed or understood that enhance rather than diminish the patient's sense of self.

Such an emphasis in no way entails an abandonment of the search for truth. Rather, it embodies a growing recognition on the part of philosophers, psychologists, and others that truth—especially in human affairs—is multifaceted and perspectivistic. The viewpoints that incorporate this recognition are often described by such terms as constructivist or postmodern, and they include a wide variety of doctrines and claims, some of which are quite consistent with the point of view that guides this book and others of which depart quite substantially (see Anderson, 1995, for a useful overview of these varied, yet related, trends). Most apposite in the present context is the appreciation that even though it is largely true that a significant goal of the therapy is for the patient to overcome self-deceptions, and even though the therapist's ability to notice and point out those self-deceptions is a crucial feature of the process, nonetheless, the process of therapy is not one in which the therapist's view can be taken to be more correct or realistic than the patient's view. Rather, in a manner similar to Gill's views discussed in Chapter 15, the operating assumption is that there are multiple perspectives on the same events or experiences. Thus the therapist can make a contribution to expanding the patient's experience and awareness without this implying that she somehow sees reality more accurately than the patient does. The therapeutic task is not seen as entailing the search for a singular truth that the therapist must convey, even if it hurts. Rather, there are a variety of ways of understanding the patient's experience, and the therapist must choose which ones to convey, based not only on whether they are "true" or not, but also on whether they are useful.

At times, therapists' conviction that they are simply conveying the truth can serve to distract them from the impact of what they are saying. As Wile (e.g., 1984, 1985) has perceptively pointed out, many things that therapists say to patients are unwittingly accusatory or demeaning. In Wile's view, this tendency stems very largely from the ways that therapists think about their patients and about the therapeutic process. The practice of many therapists, Wile suggests, derives more than they realize from a set of unexamined assumptions from the early years of psychoanalysis, which persist implicitly not only in the work of later psychoanalysts, whose explicit theoretical ideas have changed very substantially since then, but even in the work of many therapists who do not think of themselves as psychoanalytic at all.

The persistence of the older model, Wile suggests, is evident in the pervasive tendency to view patients as "dependent, manipulative, narcissistic, hostile, symbiotic, controlling, masochistic, regressed, resistant, dishonest, irresponsible, pathologically jealous or competitive, engaged in game playing, or as refusing to give up their infantile gratifications and grow up" (Wile, 1982, p. 9). Interpretations made from this frame of reference, Wile argues, are "inherently pejorative."

The point, of course, is not that people cannot harbor such motives or act in such ways. They do, and any viable approach to therapy must take this into account. Rather, the issue is whether there is a better way to conceptualize these phenomena, a way indeed, that is more consistent with the explicit theories held by increasing numbers of therapists today, who are drawn to approaches that seem more humane, empathic, and attentive to the validation of the patient's needs and experiences—whether these be object relations and self-psychological points of view, humanistic and experiential models, or constructivist cognitive approaches.

Conceptualizing patients as narcissistic, manipulative, controlling, and so forth does not, of course, necessarily mean that what one says to them is similarly framed. Indeed, much of this chapter, as well as my earlier book, *Therapeutic Communication* (Wachtel, 1993b), is devoted precisely to examining how one can usefully put into words for the patient messages that, if phrased carelessly, could be experienced by the patient as critical and demeaning. One of the central points of this work is that what might nominally appear to be the same message can be presented in a multitude of ways, and that the way that is chosen has enormous impact. But we cannot convey the message in more constructive words to the patient until we do so to ourselves. If we think that the patient is "really" manipulative, primitive, and so on, it will be hard to find other words that effectively convey what we wish to, and especially hard to do so in a way that feels honest and genuine.

As I noted in discussing the writings of Basch and of Aron in Chapter 15, there is a still influential line of thought that views the therapeutic process as one in which "gratifying" the patient is a danger that will prevent necessary unconscious material from emerging in interpretable form. As part of this view, the patient is often seen as attempting to manipulate the therapist into gratifying primitive or infantile wishes, and it is the therapist's task not to be seduced into a counterproductive indulgence. Therapists operating from frameworks that do not derive from psychoanalysis are less likely to hold such a view in explicit form; but actual clinical practice depends at least as much on experiences in supervision and in one's own therapy as on the explicit theory one holds (Wachtel, 1993b), and unarticulated assumptions and practices can thus pass along unnoticed from generation to generation of supervisors and supervisees. In my experience, when I have presented the ideas about therapeutic communication that are the focus of this chapter to audiences that were not primarily psychoanalytic in orientation, most of them found much of what I had to say relevant to their own practices as well.

### A CLINICAL EXAMPLE

An observation reported in my book on therapeutic language (Wachtel, 1993b) was formative in shaping my views about the ways therapists speak to patients and the need to address this topic focally and explicitly. A student therapist, attempting to call the patient's attention to the meaning of her silences, said to the patient, "I think you're silent because you're trying to hide a lot of anger." When the class discussed this comment, several factors emerged as important. First, the therapist was uncomfortable with the comment as soon as she had said it. We had been discussing in the class the potentially critical implications of the things therapists say to their patients, and she sensed immediately that telling the patient she was "hiding" a lot of anger had an accusatory ring to it. Yet at the same time, she felt that the content of what she said was accurate and, for a variety of reasons, important to convey to the patient at that point. Moreover, both I and the rest of the class concurred on this.

What was especially striking was the response of the class to this clinical example. The students, although primed to deal with this very issue, found themselves coming up with alternatives that were themselves rather accusatory (e.g., "I think you're feeling very angry at me and the boredom is a cover," and "You're denying how angry you are"). Importantly, the difficulty the students had in finding a facilitative alternative that conveyed the same content was not a function of lack of aptitude. The students in the doctoral program in which I teach are a highly selected and exceedingly talented bunch, and the members of this class (including the student who made the initial statement) are individuals for whom I have great respect. Their difficulty here was not rooted in individual faults, but rather reflected unexamined and unrecognized features of what might be called the subculture of psychotherapy.

Finally, as the students' difficulties persisted, I suggested the following alternatives as examples of how to get the message across more effectively and less critically: (a) "I have the sense that you're angry but feel you're not supposed to be," or (b) "I wonder if you're staying silent because you feel you had better not say anything if what you're feeling is anger." These are, of course, but two suggested examples of many possible ways of conveying the idea. What differentiates them—and, once one has gotten the idea, their many cousins—is that rather than accusing the patient of hiding or denying, they convey an understanding of why it *makes sense* that she would be hesitant to express certain feelings. Moreover, the last two comments address the patient's *anxiety* about expressing anger and, at least implicitly, raise a question about whether the anxiety is necessary. Indeed, they are part of a general therapeutic tone that implies that maybe it is all right to be angry, that maybe anger is more acceptable than the patient had thought.

Such a view derives from a theoretical conception of the patient's conflicts that builds on the revised model of anxiety discussed in Chapter 6. The unwitting influence of very early conceptualizations on contemporary practice pointed to by Wile derives very largely from the period in which the central role of anxiety was not well understood. Without an appreciation that at the heart of patients' difficulties was anxiety about their own inclinations and experiences, there was a subtle tendency to see them simply as "harboring" or "hiding" unacceptable impulses. This was exacerbated by the gratuitous tendency to assume that our most fundamental nature was antisocial and had to be curbed to permit civilization to develop and be maintained,° and by the view that the underlying motivations for our behavior were "infantile" or "primitive." The result was a tendency to view the patient's task ultimately as one of renouncing her forbidden, antisocial impulses (see discussion of Dewald in Chapter 6 and of Aron in Chapter 15, as well as Wachtel, 1993b).

In contrast, the view guiding the approach described here sees the patient's task not as renouncing her most fundamental inclinations, but as more fully accepting them. To be sure, not everything we discover in the course of the psychotherapeutic process will be admirable. But the understanding suggested here is that when we get to the darker side of the patient's desires, we have not gotten to the heart of the personality but rather to the point where anxiety has wreaked its distorting effect. It is when people become afraid of more direct expressions of their desires and their nature, that more sinister and disruptive tendencies may develop. (This is part of what Kohut, 1977, was pointing out when he

---

°I call this view gratuitous because it does not derive from any empirical foundation but is rather an *ex cathedra* pronouncement about the fundamental ontology of human motives. As I have discussed elsewhere (Wachtel, 1987, 1993b), the fact that human beings can indeed be aggressive, destructive, or otherwise antisocial does not in any way require the assumption that such behavior is a reflection of our "real" nature and that manifestations of kind, caring, or considerate behavior are somehow derivatives, disguises, or sublimations rather than reflections of our nature as well, but of another side of that nature.

contended that the fundamental "drives" of classical psychoanalytic theory are in fact "disintegration products" reflecting not unadulterated, human nature but the effects of failures to create the conditions under which that nature can develop and thrive.) The alternative ways of framing the message that I offered the class derive from the view that the patient has already suffered from excessive self-alienation as a result of fear of experiencing her inclinations more directly. Thus, the aim of therapy is not to confront the patient with the truth (as a preliminary to enabling her to renounce the primitive or archaic desires she still harbors); rather it is to enable the patient to become less afraid of her desires and experiences, and therefore freer to explore them.°

FOCAL MESSAGES AND META-MESSAGES

From another (but not inconsistent) vantage point, the difference between the various comments generated by the class and the alternatives I finally proposed lies in what I have called their "meta-messages." As I have put it elsewhere,

> every overt message that the therapist intends to convey, every communication of a particular understanding of the patient's experience or dynamics (what I will call the *focal message*), carries with it a second message, a *meta-message* if you will, that conveys an attitude about what is being conveyed in the focal message. It is often in the meta-message—frequently unnoticed or unexamined—that the greatest potential for therapeutic transformation (or therapeutic failure) lies. (Wachtel, 1993b, p. 2)

## TOWARD A NEW DIRECTION FOR INTEGRATION

The students' response to my introducing these ideas, and particularly to the examples of alternative comments I offered, was a combination of surprise and recognition: What I suggested seemed perfectly obvious once I suggested it, but the experience was first a feeling of "Why didn't I think of that?" and second, a sense that they somehow had had an unrecognized mental set that impeded their coming up with similar kinds of phrasings. Spurred by the students' interest in and excitement about the topic, I began increasingly to focus on the details

---

°To be sure, there is a humane dimension even to the aim of renunciation. The governing notion is that when the patient rejects the forbidden desire *consciously,* the renunciation is more specific and limited, in contrast with the more sweeping self-rejection entailed in massive repression. Nonetheless, the difference in spirit between the contrasting understandings of the therapeutic process should be obvious.

of what they said to their patients, and to concentrate on this dimension in my own therapeutic work and in my writing. In the process, I found that the therapeutic work moved toward a fuller synthesis, in which the very distinction between the "parts" became more difficult to discern. In contrast to those aspects of the work in which discrete and identifiable behavioral interventions were introduced in the context of a psychoanalytically guided exploratory psychotherapy, the integration implemented through attention to the potential impact of particular ways of framing and phrasing one's comments derived from appreciation of how a comment could simultaneously accomplish psychodynamic and behavioral ends.

This new dimension of the integrative effort had diverse implications for therapists considering integration from different starting points. For therapists of a primarily psychodynamic orientation, for example, this dimension highlighted ways in which psychodynamic interpretations were interventions, whether or not they were recognized as such by the clinicians who used them. Interpretations did not just convey information to the patient about psychic contents; they conveyed messages of encouragement or discouragement, of approval or disapproval, or being understood or being diagnosed and viewed objectively and so forth. The implications, however, were equally significant for cognitive–behavioral practice. For, notwithstanding the mechanistic image of behavioral and cognitive–behavioral therapy that is advanced not only by opponents of behavior therapy but at times even by its advocates, the clinical practice of cognitive–behavioral approaches—as opposed to its fictional counterparts in the adversarial literature—entails a good deal of conversation and dialogue. Many of the considerations introduced here apply as much to the comments made by cognitive–behavioral therapists as they do in the context of a more psychoanalytically oriented therapy.

For example, a cognitive therapist who had consulted me for supervision reported saying to a patient, "It seems like you only take in the negative." Her aim in making this comment was to point out to the patient a cognitive bias, to show him that he attends selectively to negative input and ignores the positive. But the patient's experience of this comment was, "I can't seem to do anything right in your eyes."°

° It should be noted that this complaint on the patient's part was in certain respects an advance. He could, for example, have responded simply, "Yeah, I can't do anything right," which would, of course, have been one more instance of the very trend being pointed out—all he would have heard was what was wrong. In this sense, the fact that there was an element of complaint about the therapist, rather than his simply taking it all upon himself, was a positive sign. But as discussed next, the message could have been approached in a more therapeutically useful way.

In discussing the therapist's comment in the supervision session, I suggested that a preferable alternative for conveying what she wished to get across might have been, "Sometimes it seems to make you uneasy when you hear positive things about yourself. It's like it's dangerous to take it in, like you don't quite dare." This latter comment has a similar focal message, but its meta-message is significantly different in several respects. "You only take in the negative" is easily registered as pointing to a *failing* in the patient; only taking in the negative is something one should not do. In contrast, the second comment highlights the patient's anxiety; it addresses the *reason* he takes in the negative rather than the positive. In that sense it respects his behavior more and treats it as something that makes sense. At the same time, it also subtly conveys the idea that perhaps it is worth reconsidering whether it would be so dangerous to take in the positive.

## ATTENDING TO VARIATIONS IN THE PATIENT'S BEHAVIOR

There is another property of the second of the pair of comments just discussed that is also important to notice. The second comment states that the inclination to take in the negative rather than the positive happens "sometimes." Rather than viewing the patient as fixed or static, this version acknowledges the variability in his behavior. This is important for several reasons. First, it can be demoralizing to be told, whether directly or implicitly, that this is "the way one is." Highlighting the variability in the patient's way of being, that he only *sometimes* acts in a problematic way, helps the patient to see that there is more to him than just his problem.* Moreover, not only does such a way of communicating help counter demoralization (cf. Frank, 1973), it also is likely to contribute to the patient's receptiveness to what is being conveyed, to her hearing the message rather than warding it off.

Attention to variations in the person's functioning also can at times enable the therapist to address problematic behavior by calling attention to when it does *not* occur. Patients may evince considerable resistance to discussion of the ways in which they close off certain topics, change the subject, come late, and so forth. However, if one is attentive to the variations in their behavior, and calls attention to when they

---

*This is, of course, an especially important dimension to consider with a patient like the one being discussed here, who is inclined in any event to attend only to the negative side of what is being conveyed.

are being more open, or staying with the topic, or coming on time more regularly, they may begin to be able to address the entire topic without being as threatened or defensive. Thus, whereas the statement "you change the subject whenever the topic of feelings about your father comes up" may meet with an unreceptive response, the patient may be much more open to engaging a comment that states, "you seem more able today to stay with the topic of your feelings toward your father; I wonder what's enabling you to do that."

Such a comment has a number of advantages. First, apropos of the discussion above, it is less critical or accusatory. It addresses an instance in which the patient has succeeded rather than one in which she has failed. Moreover, it is less critical simply because it acknowledges that she does not always avoid the topic.° At the same time, calling attention to the patient's absence of avoidance here perforce brings her into closer touch with the fact that she does avoid at other times. The alternative formulations and framings presented in this chapter—although in certain ways "kinder and gentler"—do not avoid the harder issues. Quite the contrary: These framings are ways of enabling the patient to engage the harder issues. There is little value in "addressing" a topic or "confronting" the patient with it if the patient does not register it and carry forward an exploration that enables her to broaden and deepen her experience of the material being discussed.

Further, comments which attend to the variability in the patient's behavior and experience are actually more accurate and more comprehensive. It is rarely true that a person does *anything* all the time or in the same way. Comments that call attention not only to the general trend but also to its variations are thus not only frequently more readily heard, they also are a fuller representation of the truth. In addition, by contextualizing the behavior under consideration, they further understanding of the behavior in still another way. One understands oneself more fully if one understands not only that one tends to do something but also when one tends to do it (or when one tends to do it more or more intensely). Moreover, understanding when one does something aids very considerably in understanding why. That is, if one sees more clearly what kinds of circumstances bring out the behavior, what it is in response to, one has a better grasp of the *meaning* of the behavior.

---

°In other realms, what may be conveyed is that she doesn't always do $x$, $y$, or $z$ as much or as intensely or as thoroughly; the subtleties that a good therapist addresses do not necessarily fit into a dichotomous either–or formulation, but they almost always do fit into a formulation in which there are variations in the behavior or experience being addressed.

## ATTENTION TO VARIATIONS AND CONTEXT AS AN INTEGRATIVE THEME ACROSS ORIENTATIONS

In addition to the advantages discussed thus far, it is interesting to note as well that attention to variations in the patient's behavior and experience represents another potential point of convergence between the perspectives of cognitive–behavioral, family systems, and relational psychoanalytic therapists. Attention to context and to the way behavior varies with different circumstances is a central feature of the cognitive–behavioral point of view, as it is of family systems approaches. But it is also an important element in what distinguishes interpersonal and other relational versions of psychoanalytic thought from more classical formulations. Indeed, in a recent issue of *Psychoanalytic Psychology* devoted to the theme "Contemporary Structural Analysts Critique Relational Theories" (Sugarman & Wilson, 1995), a key thrust to the critiques entailed the claim that relational theories "skew toward social determination" (Wilson, 1995) and overly emphasize "external interaction" (Murray, 1995). In the view of these critics, relational perspectives err by moving so far in the direction of relating the patient's experience to real interactions with actual other people that they lose the depth of more classical psychoanalytic formulations deriving from the latter's attention to conflict and the "inner world." It will probably be apparent to the reader that I disagree with such an evaluation: In my view, not only do relational theorists generally include such considerations, but not infrequently they remain *too* enamored of concepts like "inner world." Nonetheless, it is certainly true that by and large relational versions of psychoanalytic thought are indeed more attentive to the ways our experience and behavior are responsive to input from others. Attention to ways in which psychological characteristics are not simply static properties of the person, but vary depending on a variety of contextual and relational configurations, is thus something that cuts across the various elements that make up the synthesis described in this book.

## THE IMPORTANCE OF BUILDING ON STRENGTHS

Attention to the variability of behavior and experience is part of a larger emphasis in the cyclical psychodynamic approach on building on the patient's strengths rather than focusing on her problems and difficulties alone. The conceptual foundation for psychotherapeutic work is typically rooted in the subdiscipline we call psychopathology or abnormal psychology. In some respects, this seems perfectly natural and sensible. Obviously, in order to help people, we need to know what is wrong. But we are severely handicapped in the helping effort if we do not also attend to what is right. The language and conceptual orientation of much clinical discourse is overly focused on pathology and insufficiently attentive to the patient's strengths. Much of our diagnostic vocabulary is disparaging and dismissive (see Wachtel, 1993b). A good part of what leads to the accusatory tone discussed above is related to this tendency.

It is important to understand that building on strengths does not imply ignoring or even minimizing difficulties. Once again, the issue is how to assure both that the message is really heard and that it is received in a way that does not leave the patient feeling worse about herself rather than better.° A key consideration is that both therapist and patient must see that there is indeed something to build on. All too often, I have heard diagnostic formulations, both by students and by experienced therapists, which if taken literally would seem to make a virtually unassailable case for the impossibility of the patient's improving. If one can already see the buds of a healthier way of being, even if they are obscure and none too robust, one is in a much better position to establish an effective therapeutic alliance and to help the patient develop some momentum for change.

At times what this entails is a version of the attention to variability noted above. It can be very useful, for example, for the therapist to notice small changes in a positive direction, and to inquire as to what enabled the patient to take those steps. This not only can be a useful foundation for exploring the more "negative" tendencies, as noted above, but it also can serve to encourage those useful steps that the patient *is* taking. Even the most entrenched pattern is unlikely to be so airtight that no positive exceptions ever come through, and helping that side of the patient to emerge is a crucial part of the therapeutic work.

At times, finding positive elements to build upon can be facilitated by just a slight change of focus. A student therapist described her work

---

°There are times, of course, when the process of therapy can *temporarily* leave the patient feeling worse. Confronting experiences one has shrunk from all one's life is not always a pleasant experience, and the path toward change often has brambles along the way. But not all of the pain patients experience in psychotherapy is contributory toward progress. Indeed, insufficient attention to the need to protect the patient's self-esteem, even while encouraging her to enter uncomfortable new territory and to dare to face uncomfortable truths, can be a powerful impediment to therapeutic success.

with a very self-depriving and self-critical patient and her difficulties in helping the patient break that pattern. The student was leaving the clinic to go on internship, and she wanted to arrange for the patient to be transferred to another therapist to continue the work. There were, of course, many issues raised by this—feelings of abandonment, anger, hurt, discouragement that they had not been able to accomplish all the patient's goals by the time the therapist left, etc.—and the therapist had addressed them sensitively and insightfully (as well as with an understanding that still more work on these issues was necessary). But in the session I wish to discuss here, a different issue had come up: Being transferred to a new therapist was experienced by the patient as a "luxury" rather than as something he needed.

This development offered the therapist an opportunity to address from another angle an issue that had been an important part of the work with this very self-depriving individual. She said to him, "How come you don't feel you deserve any luxuries?" The patient, in a typically self-critical fashion, said, "You're right. I shouldn't feel that way. I don't know what's wrong with me." This became the foundation for still further self-criticism, and the barely concealed hurt he felt at the therapist's "critical" remark was easy for her to see.

This example is particularly interesting because the therapist's comment was not an obviously critical one. Indeed, the therapist had been thinking of the very points being made in this chapter and had had in mind very consciously the meta-message, "It's OK for you to have luxuries."

To be sure, there is always a potentially critical dimension to questioning why someone does something (and although "how come?" is sometimes experienced by people as gentler than "why?", it is certainly a shade of the same color). Yet in most contexts, the therapist's statement would nonetheless be perfectly acceptable and experienced more as kind and sympathetic than as critical and about the patient's shortcomings.

The patient's experience of the comment as about his shortcomings was, to be sure, primarily a manifestation of the very pattern the therapist was trying to address. To a certain degree, "misunderstandings" of this sort are unavoidable, and they can even be the foundation for further therapeutic progress. Whether understood in the psychoanalytic terms of analysis of the transference or—in terms largely equivalent to the psychoanalytic understanding but more congenial to practitioners of other orientations—as an examination of the ways the patient construes and interprets events, the therapist's followthrough after such a response by the patient to what the therapist has just said can make

that response useful "grist for the mill." Indeed, avoiding all remarks
that the patient might experience as critical can mean avoiding the therapeutic process itself. It is often in just such examinations of how the
patient has experienced what we have said that the most effective therapeutic work is accomplished.

And yet, it is worth considering: Was there another way to convey
the same focal message that might have been experienced differently
by the patient? I suggested to the student therapist, for future reference in similar situations, the following framing of the comment: "Given
all the forces in your life that have worked against your being able to
permit it, it's impressive that you *have* been able to permit yourself
some luxuries. But this seems to be one situation that's still part of the
older pattern we've been working on, where you assume that you're not
permitted the luxuries that are OK for other people."

Such a comment would probably not completely eliminate the patient's tendency to find a way to criticize himself or to feel criticized.
Dealing with such repetitions in vivo is part and parcel of the therapeutic work. But, for a patient like this who needs a bit of extra help
in overcoming the tendency to construe his behavior self-critically, the
alternative version of the comment has a greater likelihood of establishing a beachhead for a more positive experience of himself. By highlighting that he does at times permit himself luxuries (and, of course,
doing so in a context in which allowing himself luxuries is treated not
as a presumptuous negative but as a healthy positive), the comment
starts, as it were, from higher ground. It points out his self-deprivation
in this instance against the background of his capacity to be different.
It thus is not only less harsh and discouraging, but also again raises the
important question of what enables him to be kinder to himself in some
instances and what makes it harder in others.

Two further considerations need to be discussed in this example before moving on. The first is relatively simple and should be obvious,
but it is nonetheless essential to note that such a comment is appropriate only if the patient really does show the alternative behavior some
of the time; empty reassurance is not likely to be therapeutic. But, apropos of the discussion above, patterns and tendencies in human behavior are rarely as fixed or monolithic as both patients and therapists are
sometimes inclined to assume. Highlighting the patient's hidden capacity to be different can contribute usefully to breaking the logjam.

The second caveat regarding the comment under discussion here
raises a more complex issue. It is not necessarily the case that the patient will experience it as positive that he has allowed himself luxuries

on some occasions. If the pattern of self-criticism is especially entrenched, pointing out that he has permitted himself luxuries on some
occasions could feel like a statement about his selfishness, presumptu-
ousness, and so forth. If there are indications that the patient does experience the comment this way, one of course must attend to it and—
in a fashion that is consistent with the principles described here°—point
this out to the patient at an appropriate time. In this sense, this "unfortunate" occurrence becomes simply another part of the therapeutic
work, another opportunity among the endless opportunities that are offered, to help the patient see the patterns in his life and change those
that trouble him. But although it is certainly not uncommon for the patient to construe an "innocent" remark in a fashion consistent with the
very difficulties being addressed, we are far from helpless in such an
eventuality. As I have attempted to show throughout this chapter (see
Wachtel, 1993b, for a more extended discussion), the ways in which we
frame our comments do make a difference. While it is certainly possible for the patient to construe the comment depicted in this example
as addressing a blameworthy tendency, it is nonetheless likely that the
implication that the therapist is pointing to something hopeful and positive also will be clear in the remark.

## THE ATTRIBUTIONAL DIMENSION TO THERAPISTS' COMMENTS AND INTERPRETATIONS

The example just described illustrates not just attention to the patient's strengths but another dimension of the framing of comments that
has become increasingly central to the approach described in this book.
It is an instance of what I have called "attributional" interpretations. In
a variety of ways, these comments attribute to the patient a degree of
understanding or a degree of change that the patient has not yet articulated to herself or has not yet given herself credit for.

The attributional aspect of the comment above is the phrase, "still
part of the older pattern we've been working on." By describing the behavior as part of the older pattern, it implies that it has more to do with
what was than with what is or will be. Moreover, the phrasing that describes the behavior as *still* part of the older pattern further implies a
process of change, but one that is not yet complete. (The implications

°That is, here too we must be concerned with conveying our message in a way
that is sensitive and constructive rather than blunderbuss "truth-telling."

of the word "still," of course, depend on the context. If one simply said, "You're still doing that," the connotation would be close to the opposite; it would highlight the *absence* of progress, as well as the therapist's discouragement or frustration. It is the entire comment that gives "still part of the older pattern" a link to change rather than stasis.)

The detailed examination of therapists' comments in *Therapeutic Communication* (Wachtel, 1993b) includes a variety of examples of comments that redescribe the patient's behavior in a way that highlights change. What makes these comments attributional comments in the sense that I am using the term is that they attempt to accelerate change by highlighting it. Whether the patient's attitude is part of the "older" pattern or is part of his present behavioral repertoire is a matter of emphasis or framing. In a sense, it is really both. That is, it has been his pattern (and thus is "old") but it also still is his pattern. But there are situations (not uncommon) in which describing the behavior as "what he does" (the implicit structure of most therapists' interpretations) can be discouraging or, at the very least, can fail maximally to contribute to change. In contrast, describing it as part of an *older* pattern that still *at times* persists can further the therapeutic process in several ways. First, it contributes to alienating the patient from the pattern. He is encouraged to experience it not as at the heart of who he is now but as a "remnant," a "residual," a "vestige" of something that really is *not* about who he is now but about something he has largely outgrown. (See Wachtel, 1993b, for further discussion of these variant forms of attributional comments.)

Additionally, depicting the behavior as a remnant of something old rather than as a present characteristic of the patient helps to encourage the patient and to give a kind of momentum to the change process. In essence, when one makes a comment of this sort, one hopes that it will become a self-fulfilling prophecy. That is, one hopes that *describing* it as old, residual, and increasingly infrequent will contribute to its *becoming* old, residual, and increasingly infrequent. In effect, one gives the patient credit for something that he has not fully achieved, in the hope that that credit will increase the likelihood that he will achieve it more fully. Elsewhere (Wachtel, 1993b), I have likened this process to a bank loan, wherein someone is given money with the understanding that receiving the loan will enable her to develop the resources to pay it back with interest.

### THE ISSUE OF SUGGESTION AND "EPISTEMOLOGICAL ANXIETY"

From another vantage point, what is being described here can be seen as a form of suggestion. In the early history of twentieth century psychotherapy, a key aim of Freud and other innovators was to distinguish their efforts from mere suggestion, which was at the time virtually the only alternative form of treatment. As a consequence, suggestion tended to be viewed rather negatively, even though it continued to be a significant element of all therapies, including psychoanalysis (cf. Frank, 1973). As I have examined in considerable detail elsewhere (Wachtel, 1993b), Freud struggled throughout his career to come to terms with the role of suggestion in the psychoanalytic process. His writings abound both with frank acknowledgments of the powerful and inescapable role of suggestion and with efforts to disavow or minimize that role. Often, the two trends are evident within a few pages of each other. At the heart of Freud's own concerns about suggestion was the desire to establish psychoanalysis on a firm empirical and epistemological foundation. If the experiences his patients reported were the product of suggestion rather than spontaneous and unbidden expressions of inclinations already present but previously warded off, his discoveries could be dismissed as artifacts. I have called this concern Freud's "epistemological anxiety" (Wachtel, 1993b).*

In a variety of ways, this continuing preoccupation of Freud's impeded the development of psychoanalysis as a therapeutic method. Psychoanalysis had the potential to develop the suggestive dimension of all therapeutic work in a much more sophisticated fashion than had previously been possible, as well as to incorporate the ubiquitous suggestive element into a therapeutic approach that went well beyond suggestion alone. Instead, the suggestive dimension continued to be acknowledged only grudgingly, and was resisted rather than integrated. Even in writings from a relational perspective, in which the overweening emphasis on insight has given way to an at least equal emphasis on the relationship itself as a curative factor, it is unusual to see the role of suggestion frankly acknowledged and explicitly turned to the advantage of the therapeutic effort.

In essence, the attributional interpretations developed from a cyclical psychodynamic vantage point approach the suggestive dimension of the therapeutic enterprise not as antithetical or threatening to a psychoanalytic approach but as an inherent part of the therapeutic process that has the potential to enhance the therapeutic impact of interpretations and insights and that can in turn be rendered more effective *by*

---

*For an understanding of the realistic foundations of Freud's concerns in this regard, see Grunbaum, 1984.

those insights. That is, sophisticated attributional interpretations, in contrast to the naive forms of suggestion that psychoanalysis replaced, build upon the understanding we have gained from psychoanalysis, and in turn enable that understanding to be used by the patient to change the patterns of thought and behavior that trouble her (see Wachtel, 1993b, for a fuller elaboration of the use of attributional interpretations and their relation both to suggestion and to the enhancement of therapeutic change more generally).

### ENABLING THE PATIENT TO "OWN" HER INSIGHTS

Another key aim of attributional interpretations is to help the patient to "own" the insights she achieves in the therapeutic work. Both from the vantage point of the patient's self-esteem and from the vantage point of whether the interpretation "takes," it is useful for the patient to feel that an insight achieved in the course of the therapy is *hers* rather than simply an idea she has taken on from the therapist. The structure of attributionally framed comments is designed to facilitate this process. It can be useful, for example, to preface comments designed to further the patient's understanding with phrases such as "if I'm understanding you correctly, what you're saying is," or "as we've both noticed," or "as I know has become increasingly clear to you." Here, as elsewhere, it is of course essential that one not simply "make up" such a framing. The patient will register such an effort as either insincere or just plain wrong. It is possible, however, to focus particularly on the aspect of what is being discussed that reflects the patient's own emerging understanding rather than on the specific contribution that comes from the therapist. This might be seen as a variant of the call that emanated from George Miller's 1969 presidential address to the American Psychological Association (Miller, 1969), in which he advocated "giving psychology away." Here, we might say, the aim is to "give insights away," to enable them to belong to the patient so that she may use and develop them and experience them as her own.

### USING ATTRIBUTIONAL INTERPRETATIONS TO POINT THE PATIENT TOWARD ACTION

In the process of interpreting or articulating the patient's as yet covert inclinations and experiences, the therapist not only helps to bring these tendencies to awareness, she also contributes to the form they take as they move closer to expression. Unconscious inclinations are often discussed as if they were fully formed and highly articulated wishes that just happen to be out of awareness. While there may indeed be a good deal of structure to mental activities out of awareness, much clinical evidence suggests that the therapist's view of the highly articulated wish that had once been unconscious is a matter of hindsight. The wish that finally emerges is not simply a pure product of the patient's unconscious, materializing like Hera from Zeus's forehead. The therapist's interpretations play a significant role in the way the wish or experience finally takes shape.

The view of the patient's unconscious inclinations as simply "emerging" or "unfolding" (Wachtel, 1982) obscures the therapist's participation in the process of the patient's moving from inchoate urges to social behavior. It also obstructs the therapist's vision of her potential role in helping the patient achieve her goals. The theoretical considerations advanced in this book suggest that a patient's difficulties are a product of cyclical patterns in which the responses of others to the patient's own behavior patterns play a crucial role. Consequently, it is often not enough only to examine and address intrapsychic factors; changes must take place as well in the patient's daily interactions with others if enduring and meaningful change is to occur. The way the therapist articulates the patient's incipient urges contributes to the form those urges finally take. But whether that contribution is a helpful or an impeding one is not foreordained.

The therapist cannot not have an influence upon the process, but she can render herself unaware of that influence. The prevalent mythology of "emerging" and "unfolding" deprives the therapist of the opportunity to reflect carefully upon the way her influence will guide the particularity of the patient's movement toward greater expression of previously warded off tendencies. When the therapist is able to see that the way she identifies the inclinations she perceives helps to shape those inclinations and how they are expressed behaviorally, she may more consciously work collaboratively with the patient to find modes of expression that will further the patient's deepest aims.

An attributional perspective can help the therapist to phrase her comments in ways that highlight the patient's own inclinations toward new, more adaptive patterns, and encourage the patient by emphasizing that she has already begun to evidence the desired changes. Attention to the attributional dimension can facilitate as well the dimension of modeling or identification that is still another way that the therapist, whether intentionally or unwittingly, can help point the patient toward adaptive action. (The therapist who is unaware of or denies this dimension of the work, of course, is less able to consciously consider among alternatives, and thus must rely on intuition rather than a clearly thought out therapeutic plan in assisting the patient in arriving where she intends to go.)

The patient's response to the therapist's structuring efforts, as to the therapist's modeling or pointing to potentially useful directions or actions, will again depend on the patient's sense of ownership of the new behavior or the new way of looking at things. If the new direction does not feel like "her own," if it still "belongs" to the therapist, its therapeutic value may be greatly reduced. Attention to the attributional dimension can be quite useful in this regard.

Thus, for example, comments that have a form such as, "it sounds like what you'd like to do or say is . . . ", have elements of traditional interpretation—indeed, many interpretations are phrased in such a way without the therapist ever giving a thought to the issues being raised in this chapter—but they also frequently have packed into them elements of advice. The therapist is, in effect, asking the patient to try on for size a particular way of behaving or expressing herself. If it "fits," if it feels consistent with who the patient feels she is, she can take it off the rack and make it hers. The element of advice in such a comment is not highlighted. "It sounds like what *you'd* like to do" attributes the inclination to the patient, treats it as something the patient has already come up with, even if it is only now being explicitly discussed.

It is of course crucial that the comment address something that the patient really would like to say or do. If the therapist's implicit suggestion is rooted in what the therapist would like to do in such a situation rather than in the patient's point of view, suggesting that it is the patient's desire would be disingenuous and inappropriate. Moreover, not only would such a maneuver be unethical, it would also likely be ineffective. The patient may superficially seem to comply (if that is her style), but the new behavior will not take root if it is not consistent with the patient's own inclinations. People often do not quite know how to give voice to what is immanent within them—that is why the input from a therapist can be so helpful—but they do know (if not always immediately, then before too long) when what the therapist has articulated is not really "them."

When such comments are appropriate and do prove helpful, they go beyond simply facilitating the patient's access to incipient inclinations that were previously out of awareness and help the patient link those inclinations to more specific possibilities for effective action. As I have put it previously discussing such comments, "The therapist, in effect, lends his ego to the patient at the moment of birth of the emerging idea, and thus helps to give it a shape more likely to fit with the most forward-reaching structures of the patient's psychological organization" (Wachtel, 1993b, p. 171).

## REFRAMING

From another perspective, many of the constructions discussed thus far, and especially the attributional comments, can be seen also as instances of what family therapists call reframing. Reframing is a concept that is rooted in an essentially constructivist epistemology. The therapist's job is not to "discover" or "uncover" a singular truth, but to examine the way the patient (or family) has *constructed* reality and to help the patient consider other constructions that may have rather different consequences for her life and for how she approaches the dilemmas she is facing. As Watzlawick, Weakland, and Fisch (1974) have put it, truth "is not what we discover, but what we create."

In many respects, reframings resemble what psychoanalysts call interpretations. They are alternative formulations, different ways of understanding or recoding the person's experience and the events of her life. Reframings differ from interpretations largely in the epistemological assumptions that underlie them. Typically, psychoanalytic interpretations have derived from what one might call a convergent epistemology: The aim is increasingly to converge on the "real" meaning of the patient's associations or her behavior, to discover the truth that is hidden behind the defensive disguises. Reframings, on the other hand, are based on a divergent view of truth or reality. The aim is to generate multiple versions of the patient's life story and to help the patient choose those that work better for her. For most therapists who employ reframing, concern with truth remains; reframing is not the writing of fiction. However, truth is seen as ambiguous and multiperspectived, and the *consequences* of viewing oneself or one's life in a particular way are emphasized. In effect the motto is, "If you don't like this truth about your life, pick another." The therapist's aim is not so much to discover or uncover as to create and construct, to offer a new lens through which the world looks more manageable and inviting.

Whether reframing is a close cousin of interpretation or only a distant relative depends on the spirit in which each is undertaken. If one considers the influential writings of psychoanalytic authors such as Gill (1982, 1994), Hoffman (1991, 1992), and Spence (1982), it is apparent that psychoanalytic interpretation can also operate from a largely divergent, constructivist epistemology. The emphasis by these writers on constructing a narrative and on offering alternative perspectives for the patient to examine overlaps substantially with the thinking that guides many family therapists' approach to reframing. The differences lie in part in the content of what is most likely to be focused upon (new ways of describing what an individual wishes for or fears, for example, or new ways of construing the way members of a family system interact with each other). They lie as well in how playful, fanciful, or "creative" the comment is. Some reframings, no matter how straightforward the therapist avows them to be, leave one with an impression that they are almost put-ons, that they are intended primarily to be provocative, to shake up the system in order to make a new reorganization more likely. If they are also efforts to expand on the stock of genuine truths about the individual or the system, they at the very least stretch the envelope of such truths close to the bursting point (e.g., see Selvini Palazzoli, Cecchin, Prata, & Boscolo, 1978; Watzlawick, Weakland, & Fisch, 1974; Weeks & L'Abate, 1982).

Comparing such creations to the alternative narratives and constructions of Gill, Hoffman, or Spence, one can discern readily the earlier roots of the latter authors in the more convergent approach to truth of psychoanalysis. Perspectives that may appear radical in the context of psychoanalytic discourse appear rather conservative from the point of view of the liberties taken in some reframings. (The terms radical and conservative in this context are not intended to correspond to any political positions that share those names. Nor do I intend a value implication in either direction. There is something to be said for each approach, but descriptively they do differ, even as, over much of the range of each, they overlap considerably.)

Reflecting the association of the reframing concept with family therapy, those comments that are most typically designated as reframings often have a strongly interpersonal flavor to them. Many seek to modify not so much the individual's view of herself but of significant others. Reframings can at times take the very same facts already noted by the patient, but cast them into a different meaning structure so that the implications of the facts are modified, both in terms of personal experience and in terms of how the person responds to them. This latter dimension, in turn, influences how the other person responds, contributing to change in the problematic pattern from both ends.

A good example of this kind of reframing was reported in Wachtel (1993b). Helping a patient resolve his conflicts with and about his wife was aided considerably by offering him another way to think of her. She was a socially anxious individual who was uncomfortable at parties with people she did not know well. He experienced her as "clingy" when they did go to parties, and the entire pattern of behavior was a source of considerable tension between them. A reframing of this behavior that proved helpful was to say, "Your wife seems to feel most relaxed when she's alone with you."

Interestingly, this comment does not contradict the patient's experience or argue with him, and yet it presents a quite different picture of her and their relationship. It takes the same facts he reports, but casts them in a way that gives them a positive connotation rather than a negative one. To state that his wife was more comfortable with him was the logical equivalent of the version emphasized by the patient up to then— that she was less comfortable with other people. But in making her comfort with him "figure" and her discomfort with others "ground," the psychological meaning of this two-sided fact was altered considerably.

## ATTENTION TO CONFLICT

A central feature of many of the principles and methods described in this chapter is a focus on the dimension of conflict in the patient's psychological life. Appreciating the importance of conflict is an important key to framing one's comments in a way that does not stir needless resistance or counterproductively end up lowering the patient's self-esteem. Many of the feelings and inclinations that need to be addressed in the therapeutic effort are potentially painful and humiliating. Increasing the likelihood that addressing them will nonetheless be a positive, growth-enhancing experience rather than one that stirs defensiveness or leaves the patient feeling shamed and diminished, depends considerably on seeing the person's full complexity, on recognizing and communicating that the trend being addressed is only a part of the patient's total psychological makeup.

It is a crucial part of skill as a therapist, I believe, not to get trapped into taking one side of the patient's experience as the whole. In part, this is a matter of understanding how anxiety may motivate the patient to forge a simplified view of herself that shaves off the rough edges of conflict. Such a view may provide some comfort to the patient in the short run, but ultimately it contributes to the perpetuation of the very difficulties that the patient wishes to resolve. In helping the patient to notice and experience the more hidden side of the conflict, however, it is essential that the therapist not make an equal and opposite error, as it were, by treating the hidden side as real and the more apparent side as false. Such a conception, whether explicit (as in some accounts of the "false self") or implicit and unwitting, can contribute significantly both to unproductive (if almost always unintended) harshness and to an imbalance that leaves further therapeutic work on a faulty foundation. What may be "false" is the patient's sense that what she experiences about herself is all there is to her; but an attitude by the therapist that dismisses as simply facade the traits and attitudes that the patient consciously values or that, at this point in her development, represent her experience of reality, is suspect both epistemologically and clinically.

Thus, for example, if the patient indicates she is pleased about an event or a relationship about which the therapist thinks the patient is actually quite dissatisfied, it is problematic to convey this in a way that implies that the patient is *not* pleased, that she is simply fooling herself. It is highly unlikely that there is *nothing* genuine about the emotion the patient is reporting. Any comment that has the implicit message, "You say you're pleased, but really you're very dissatisfied" is likely to be counterproductive. In contrast, a comment such as, "In some respects you're pleased, but I have a sense that you also have some doubts or dissatisfactions" is much more respectful of the patient's experience. It doesn't dismiss the conscious experience as sham or facade; rather it *expands* the patient's awareness and, in effect, conveys an expanded sense of the patient herself, a picture of a more complex and ample person rather than of one who simply fools herself and doesn't know what she is feeling.

Still further amplification of the dimension of conflict—consistent also with the discussion above of avoiding accusatory interpretations— might be conveyed in an amplified version of the preceding comment: "In some respects you're pleased, but I have a sense that you also have some doubts or dissatisfactions, but aren't quite sure it's OK to have them or to express them." This latter version addresses still a second conflict—that between expressing the doubts or dissatisfactions, or inhibiting them because they are not quite acceptable.

Most of the conflicts addressed in the course of therapeutic work come down to what Dollard and Miller (1950) have called approach–avoidance conflicts°—conflicts in which anxiety (or an anxiety equivalent such as shame or guilt) obstructs or inhibits an inclination that would otherwise be more evident or prominent. Being clear about the approach–avoidance structure, and helping the patient counter the constraining anxiety, helps considerably in formulating one's under-

°See Chapter 6 and also Wachtel, 1987, Chapter 5.

standing of what is happening in a way that addresses the complexity of her conflicted tendencies, yet still feels like being on the patient's side. In addressing various manifestations of "resistance," for example, it is easy to slip into an accusatory tone. Calling attention to the way the patient changes the subject, comes late, becomes silent, stays on the surface, and so forth, can all be delicate operations easily experienced by the patient as about her failure or about the therapist's being displeased with her. A more evenhanded addressing of both sides of the conflict helps to ease this sense of failure or disapproval without soft pedaling or backing off.

Thus, the patient may be much more able to hear comments about her coming late or missing sessions if they are stated in forms such as, "I know it's frustrating to you to be late, and that you've been getting caught in bad traffic recently, but I wonder if, as much as you want to get there, there are times when you're also uncomfortable about what we've spoken about." Such a way of putting it gives credence to the patient's own explanation rather than dismisses it, and acknowledges the truth in the patient's conscious experience, which is frustration rather than relief. But at the same time, it opens up the possibility of considering other aspects of what is transpiring as well. The point the therapist wants to make is presented not as something to replace the patient's explanation or experience, but to add to it. When the therapist's comment has what might be described as an "also" structure rather than an "instead" structure, the consequence is likely to be both greater receptiveness on the patient's part and less assault on the patient's self-esteem. Importantly, the comment is also likely to be more true. Far from it representing a shrinking from the harsh realities a successful therapy must address, it more fully and amply captures the reality that there is more than one side to the patient's experience. (In instances, of course, where there is reason to think that the patient does *not* feel frustrated, that the picture really is one of one-sided avoidance, a comment of the sort I am describing here would not be in order.)

In related fashion, comments therapists sometimes make about the patient "not really wanting to change" are usually problematically simplistic. The difficulty often begins with how the therapist *thinks* about the patient (to herself or in presenting the case at a case conference or in a supervisory session). In my experience, statements of this sort, at least in describing the patient to others, are far from rare, and I suspect that they are not that uncommon in communications to the patient as well. Certainly, as a supervisor, I have heard variations of "you don't really want to change" or "you want everything to get better without your changing" (though, to be sure, as I have become more explicitly interested in the exact details of what therapists say, my supervisees have either learned to say it better or learned not to tell me when they make comments to the patient of the sort just depicted).

In contrast, one can address the same tendency, in a manner that is again both more helpful and more precise, by being more careful about one's phrasing. It is usually much more accurate to say something like, "You want to change this pattern in your life, but there are also many things that you want to remain the same. It's hard to know what requires change, and it's tempting at times to keep on doing the same thing and to hope that somehow things will feel better," or, "As much as you want to change, it's hard to give up the old pattern. It doesn't feel safe to, and even if the old way doesn't work very well, it feels like the only thing that has worked at all." As I have noted elsewhere,

> It is the almost universal presence of a wish to change, alongside the wish to somehow keep on going just as one has, that gives poignancy to the phenomenon of resistance, and that makes it possible to attend to it without abandoning a commitment to empathic appreciation of the patient's experience of the world. It is because the patient is in *conflict* that he at once enlists your aid in changing his life and acts to impede that change. If one keeps the conflict in mind, it is often possible to find an opening wedge into change through the very process of empathizing. (Wachtel, 1993b, p. 138)

## CONCLUDING COMMENTS

The various strategies of communication and intervention described in this chapter and examined in more detail in *Therapeutic Communication* (Wachtel, 1993b) lend themselves to application in a variety of therapeutic contexts. I have especially emphasized their use within a psychodynamic approach both because that is the approach that is most quintessentially "the talking cure" and because, paradoxically, it is also the approach in which the impact of the therapist's words has in some respects been least examined. But clearly these strategies incorporate elements of and lend themselves to both cognitive–behavioral and family systems approaches, and their applications to other approaches are not difficult to discern. This broad applicability is an important feature of these therapeutic strategies and conceptualizations, but equally important is the way they lend themselves to a more fully integrated approach in which the very boundaries between the former "parts" begin to disappear.

It is unlikely that the evolution reflected in this chapter will ever result in an approach in which the origins, and even the separate identities, of different aspects of the therapeutic work will completely disappear. There are, for example, specific difficulties experienced by people in psychological distress that seem especially well suited for the application of particular discrete interventions, and the total withering away of the schools seems no more likely than the total withering away of the state. Nonetheless, it seems to me a noteworthy advance in the progress of integration that it is now possible, at various points in the therapeutic work, to weave together psychodynamic, cognitive–behavioral, and systemic perspectives so thoroughly that one cannot definitively say which approach is being manifested at such points. One of the difficulties therapists experience in trying to learn to work integratively is knowing how and when to "switch" from one approach to another in the course of the work. In part, such a concern derives from faulty premises that must be examined more closely; a good portion of my training workshops are directed toward enabling therapists to see how to make the transition back and forth from different modes of structuring the work in a fashion that feels smooth and consistent both to patient and to therapist. But it is certainly the case that as a therapist learns particularly to incorporate the strategies described in this chapter, integration becomes an easier task technically. Indeed, like Molière's *Bourgeois Gentilhomme*, who was delighted to discover he had been speaking prose all his life, therapists employing the strategies depicted in this chapter (see also Wachtel, 1993b) may find that, even without a specific intent to incorporate elements of other orientations, they can look back at the work they have been doing and recognize it as integrative.

# 19

## *Reprise and Future Directions*

T HE very aims of the point of view described in this book require that it be open-ended and continually evolving. The approach began as an integration of psychodynamic and behavioral perspectives. However, by the time *Psychoanalysis and Behavior Therapy* was completed, it was already apparent that the evolving approach had significant areas of compatibility with family systems thinking and could be enriched by explicating and developing the possibilities for integration in that direction. The first major presentation of that effort was *Family Dynamics in Individual Psychotherapy* (Wachtel & Wachtel, 1986). A subsequent application of a cyclical psychodynamic perspective to integrate psychodynamic, cognitive–behavioral, and systemic perspectives in work with children (E. F. Wachtel, 1994) and couples (E. F. Wachtel, 1993) has been developed by Ellen Wachtel.

At the same time that the compatibility of the cyclical psychodynamic approach with family systems thinking was being explored, it became clear that the nature of the original two elements in the integration was changing quite substantially. As described in Chapters 15 and 16, behavior therapy rapidly evolved into cognitive behavior therapy, while psychoanalysis was increasingly influenced by a two-person, relational perspective. The ways in which cyclical psychodynamics articulates with these developments is one of the central concerns of Part Two of this book.

As yet, there has been much less exploration of the ways in which the cyclical psychodynamic viewpoint can be further developed by including consideration of experiential perspectives such as those of

client-centered therapy, Gestalt therapy, and existential and phenomenological therapies (see, e.g., Greenberg & Rice, in press). I have, however, been intrigued by the hints of convergence in these directions that
have emerged from a number of exchanges at meetings of the Society
for the Exploration of Psychotherapy Integration (SEPI). Especially because my idiosyncratic take is that many of the experiential approaches—often depicted as a part of a "third way" that provides an alternative to psychoanalytic and behavioral methods and strategies—can
be seen as variant developments from an essentially psychodynamic
base, I am inclined to see them as potentially compatible with and
adding to the approach described here. (It should be recalled that one
of the chief attractions to me of integrating behavioral methods into a
psychoanalytically oriented therapy was that the former could help
make the latter more experiential.)*

Another potential area of convergence and integration entails the in-
corporation of group therapy into therapeutic work done from the vantage point of cyclical psychodynamics. The cyclical psychodynamic perspective emphasizes the contextual nature of psychological processes
and the ways in which people mutually shape each other's experience.
Such a viewpoint readily lends itself to exploring people's difficulties in
the context of therapeutic groups. At workshops I have presented, some
of the participants have seen affinities between the cyclical psychodynamic approach and Yalom's (1985) approach to group therapy. I have
been intrigued by these comments, but have not yet considered them
in any detail. Clearly this is a potentially fruitful area for further exploration.

Presently, the cyclical psychodynamic approach is largely characterized by what Messer (1992) has called "assimilative integration." Although behavioral and systemic concepts by now permeate the cyclical
psychodynamic point of view quite substantially, the approach is
nonetheless clearly most of all an offshoot of psychoanalytic thinking,
an attempt to imbue psychoanalysis with a dimension of active intervention and a greater consideration of context and the reciprocity that
characterizes all relationships. Although the integrative effort described
here has clear and weighty implications for practitioners whose identi-

---

*To be sure, behavioral methods are not experiential in the specific technical
sense in which many therapists of the experiential school use the term. But their
definitions of experiencing are not preemptive or exhaustive. If one moves from
the jargon or the proprietary concepts of a specific school to a broader concern
with attending to and clarifying subjective experience, I believe it is accurate to
describe participation in a variety of behavioral exercises as genuinely experiential.

fications are primarily systemic or cognitive–behavioral—indeed, cognitive–behavioral therapists have been among the most enthusiastic explorers of the potentialities of this new perspective—it may well have its greatest impact in coming years on the evolution of the psychoanalytic point of view. Especially with the increasing pressures on psychoanalytically oriented therapists to modify their practices in response to the economic pressures of managed care and other new developments in the health care industry, the availability of a model that is both psychoanalytic and rooted in explicit active intervention is likely to hold increasing appeal. As I have discussed previously in this book, the links between the psychoanalytic understanding of personality and the stances of neutrality and nonintervention seem to me artifactual rather than intrinsic.

## LOGICAL AND EMPIRICAL FOUNDATIONS OF THE CYCLICAL PSYCHODYNAMIC APPROACH

The theoretical propositions and clinical recommendations described in this book derive from a complex set of sources. In part, they derive from logical and conceptual analysis. For example, much of the foundation for developing conceptualizations drawing on observations and perspectives of more than one "school" entails examining whether the formulations of the different schools are as incompatible as their proponents have at times argued. Doing so includes such activities as carefully scrutinizing their logic, teasing out implicit assumptions, examining which of those assumptions are really essential for explaining the observations being addressed or as connective tissue for other crucial propositions, and probing the ways in which convergences are obscured because different terms are used by different schools for largely the same idea or observation or because the same term is used to mean something quite different in the different theoretical contexts. The reader will recognize all of these operations as central to the way the arguments of this book are constructed.

Logical and conceptual analysis underlies not only much of the orientation to theory of cyclical psychodynamics but also some of the clinical recommendations. The recommendations, for example, concerning how to phrase one's comments to the patient (see Chapter 18 of this volume or Wachtel, 1993b) derive considerably from a close examination of the comments' implicit messages that is at least in part pre-empirical. By pre-empirical I mean that these recommendations are based not simply on observations of "what works" (as might be undertaken by a technically eclectic approach to the therapist's language), but on a probing of the underlying messages and communicative structure.

To be sure, empirical examination of "what works" is ultimately essential. And even as a means of generating new ideas for treatment, there is a stage at which a well-conceived "fishing expedition"—in which properties of therapists' comments are rated and counted, and one simply sees which ones are associated with therapeutic gain for which patients in which circumstances—might usefully complement the approach to the study of therapeutic language emphasized here. The same empirical logic that has been used to address which "techniques" work with which patients or which disorders could similarly be applied to examine which modes or structures of communication work. It would take a bit more sophistication to go beyond just tallying already designated techniques and address matters such as style and mode of communication, but it could be done. Indeed, I will suggest a variant of this below in discussing the research possibilities implicitly generated by the cyclical psychodynamic approach. But the "pre-empirical" analyses discussed here are, at least to some degree, a necessary forerunner of such efforts. Without the conceptual work and the qualitative seeking after implicit meanings, there would not *be* the categories to examine actuarially in this domain.

CLINICAL OBSERVATION

A second source of the formulations and recommendations offered here, complementing logical and conceptual analysis, is direct clinical observation. Clinical observation has been central to theory development and clinical innovation and discovery for all psychodynamic approaches, and it is an important element in the evolution of the cyclical psychodynamic approach as well.

Clinical impressions, to be sure, are subject to many of the same vagaries of self-deception that psychoanalysts describe in their patients; psychoanalysts, after all, are just "patients" looked at from the other end of the telescope. But whereas caution about clinically derived formulations is appropriate, eschewing clinical observations altogether in the formulation of one's point of view is a formula for impoverishment. Continuing efforts to examine clinically derived hypotheses in more rigorous ways that address the tendency toward self-deception are essential. But attempting to root one's efforts as a therapist solely on formulations deriving from controlled experimental studies is not likely to be in the service of one's patients. Indeed, even in behavior therapy—a therapeutic approach that prides itself on being based on systematic empirical data—good clinical work requires considerable sensitivity to the subtleties that controlled experiments do not readily address. In their influential text on the practice of cognitive behavior therapy, for example, Goldfried & Davison (1994) noted that, "In all instances, a behavior therapist might be guided by a general principle, but he has to rely on his inventiveness as demanded by the clinical situation in order to translate that principle into clinical practice."

SYSTEMATIC EMPIRICAL RESEARCH

The third pillar on which the cyclical psychodynamic approach rests is systematic empirical research. This aspect of the theory's foundation may be less evident to the reader at first. Much of the research evidence is as yet indirect, and derives from findings originally obtained in efforts to test hypotheses deriving from other theoretical positions. Moreover, the importance of systematic empirical research to the cyclical psychodynamic point of view is likely to be obscured simply because my own participation in the research effort that underlies the approach described here has centered on organizing and giving theoretical coherence to already gathered data, or on pointing toward further data that need to be collected, rather than on collecting data myself. I have argued that the skills required for projects of data collection are not the same as those entailed in formulating hypotheses and making sense of the data, and that psychology has suffered as a discipline from a failure to be clearer about both the separate value and the relative independence of the two activities (Wachtel, 1980).

Physics, interestingly, has developed as a discipline with a quite different tradition. Theoretical physicists and experimental physicists play rather distinct, but crucially symbiotic, roles. Notwithstanding the extraordinarily expensive equipment that is often required for the empirical investigation of theoretical hypotheses in physics, I recall the words of a friend who was a theoretical physicist: "My only research tool is a pencil." (I have lost touch with this friend over the years, but I suppose that nowadays he also uses a computer.)

Whereas psychologists are often expected to collect the data themselves that substantiate their formulations, physics has thrived with a much greater division of labor. Theoretical physicists are by no means inattentive to or unconcerned about data; they just do not usually do the collecting. Both formulating theories and designing experiments are respected as activities that require great talent to do well, and either done at the highest level can win a physicist a Nobel prize.

In part, the difference between the way the two disciplines approach research derives from the greater ambiguity of the concepts of psychology and from the readiness of some psychological thinkers to advance theories with virtually no regard for empirical validation. Although some of the concepts of modern physics may seem extraordinarily fanciful, and although hypotheses have been framed for which no means of empirical validation yet exists, the links between theory and data are nonetheless less tenuous than they sometimes are in psychology. Some of Einstein's formulations, to take a famous example, could not be evaluated in light of data until methodologies were developed that were unknown at the time he worked them out. But his theories were never simply a matter of opinion or put forth as correct because of his "clinical experience" with the universe. Although highly intuitive in their nature and in their creation, they were always theories awaiting their data. Only when the marriage between the two was consummated could the viability of the theories be assured.

But if there is understandable reason for the suspicion toward theory often evident in the academic world of psychology, it is an error always to expect the theorist to be the one to gather the data that bear on the theory, or to evaluate the theory's empirical foundation solely in terms of the research programs it has specifically spawned. Particularly in the case of an integrative theory such as cyclical psychodynamics, much of the data that bear on its viability has been collected for other purposes.

## LINES OF RESEARCH EVIDENCE BEARING ON THE INTEGRATION OF PSYCHODYNAMIC AND BEHAVIORAL APPROACHES

The systematic research evidence bearing on the cyclical psychodynamic approach is of two sorts—research germane to the general project of integrating psychodynamic perspectives with those of other orientations and research that bears more specifically on the clinical approach of cyclical psychodynamics or on the cyclical theory of personality. In considering this research, I will first introduce some general considerations bearing on the overall integrative perspective that guides the work discussed in this book, and then present some of the evidence for more specific propositions, especially research examining the role of vicious circles, self-fulfilling prophecies, and interpersonal expectations.

LACK OF CLEARCUT EVIDENCE FOR THE GREATER OVERALL EFFICACY OF
ANY ONE APPROACH

A first line of evidence bearing on the cyclical psychodynamic point
of view is the data indicating that no one therapeutic approach has a
monopoly on therapeutic effectiveness (e.g., Elkin et al., 1989; Elkin,
1994; Shapiro & Shapiro, 1982; Smith, Glass, & Miller, 1980; Lambert
& Bergin, 1994). This fact alone certainly does not point to cyclical psychodynamics as the answer. It could as readily point to the search for
common factors discussed in Chapter 14, to other modes of theoretical or assimilative integration than cyclical psychodynamics, or to further inquiry into whether the absence of a general superiority of one
therapeutic approach over all the others might nonetheless obscure specific superiorities of particular approaches in particular symptomatic
and characterological contexts. Nonetheless, the findings to date do bear
very significantly on the cyclical psychodynamic project. If one particular approach had turned out to be generally superior to all others, this
would provide little encouragement for attempting to integrate the various approaches.

Strictly speaking, even the general superiority of one therapeutic orientation need not rule out the value of an integrative effort. It would
still be possible that one approach might show considerable overall superiority and yet therapeutic effectiveness might be enhanced by adding
elements of the "inferior" treatment. In the realm of orthopedic difficulties, for example, physical therapy alone might be consistently
demonstrated to be less effective than surgery for certain conditions
and yet could enhance the effects of the surgery considerably if "integrated" into the surgical treatment. Nonetheless, the absence of evidence of clear superiority for any particular school of therapy is at the
very least consistent with the aim of attempting to achieve a more powerful therapy via the route of integration.

EVIDENCE FOR PSYCHODYNAMIC CONCEPTS AND FOR THE EFFECTIVENESS
OF PSYCHODYNAMIC APPROACHES TO PSYCHOTHERAPY

The viability of an integration of psychodynamic concepts and methods with those of other approaches obviously depends on the validity
and effectiveness of psychodynamic approaches to begin with. Clearly
this chapter is not the place for an overall review of the evidence. Entire books have been written on the topic (see, for example, Barron,
Eagle, & Wolitzky, 1992; Fisher & Greenberg, 1985; Kline, 1972;
Luborsky, 1996; Luborsky & Crits-Christoph, 1990), and much research
in cognitive and social psychology as well bears quite directly on unconscious processes, self-deception, and other psychoanalytic ideas

(e.g., see Bowers & Meichenbaum, 1984; Curtis, 1991; Erdelyi, 1985; Uleman & Bargh, 1989). Indeed, many of the methodological strictures that constitute the very foundations of modern psychological research can be seen as implicitly incorporating the fundamental insights of psychoanalysis regarding our capacity for unwitting self-deception and for seeing what we wish or expect to see rather than what is impinging on our senses. Although it is true that many specific psychoanalytic hypotheses remain speculative or unconfirmed, the larger point of view that is the very essence of psychoanalysis—the untrustworthiness of conscious experience and the pervasiveness of complex processing out of awareness—has become a staple of psychological discourse even when that discourse is negatively inclined toward psychoanalysis (see, e.g., Greenwald, 1992; Kihlstrom, 1987; Nisbett & Wilson, 1977).

RESEARCH ON INTEGRATIVE THERAPEUTIC APPROACHES

In considering the efficacy of integrative therapeutic approaches, it has been easier thus far to demonstrate that such approaches are effective than to provide definitive evidence that they are more effective than single-school approaches (see, e.g., Barkham, Shapiro, & Firth Cozens, 1989; Brockman, Poynton, Ryle, & Watson, 1987; Glass, Victor, & Arnkoff, 1992; Hoffart & Martinsen, 1990; Nielsen et al., 1988; Nielsen et al., 1991; Shapiro & Firth, 1987; Shapiro & Firth-Cozens, 1990). Part of the difficulty in pinning down the contribution integrating approaches makes to improving outcome over what the outcome would have been with any of the components alone is that integrative therapy is not a unitary or redundant therapeutic approach. By its very nature, an integrative approach to therapy is likely to differ from patient to patient more than do single-school approaches (indeed, for therapists who advocate a more integrative approach to the therapeutic process, that is one of the reasons we believe that ultimately integrative approaches will yield additional benefit to a substantial number of patients).°

°I use the somewhat convoluted phrase "substantial number of patients" advisedly. Although I believe that for the majority of patients who seek psychotherapy the multiplicity of methods and perspectives of an integrative approach is of definite benefit, there is a significant subset of patients for whom a single-school approach is probably preferable. A patient seeking help with a simple phobia, for example, and not interested in working on anything else, is probably best served by a narrowly focused treatment such as systematic desensitization or flooding. What complicates matters, however, is that it is usually not so easy to be sure that the narrow goal is really all the patient wants to pursue. For exploring whether the patient's initial presenting goals are the most accurate representation of what she truly wants, or whether she has difficulty articulating (or feels guilty or anxious addressing) other dissatisfactions or potential therapeutic aims, a psychodynamic point of view is invaluable. Thus, even where the treatment ultimately decided upon may be a simpler, "single-school" treatment, an integrative perspective in the initial exploring and decision making is likely to be useful.

Put differently, integrative therapies do not lend themselves as readily to "manualization" as do approaches that are more procrustean in nature. The present climate for research funding is one in which the introduction of "manuals" is often virtually a prerequisite. This emphasis exercises a distorting effect in several ways. To begin with, except for its utilization within a few rather mechanically applied clinical methods, the concept of manuals is very largely a polite fiction. To be sure, in evaluating the effectiveness of a particular approach, it is important to be sure that that is the approach the therapists in the study are employing. For this, the so-called manuals have a certain degree of utility. By defining the parameters outside of which the therapist may be judged *not* to be practicing the approach under investigation, they do contribute to the precision of the research effort. But I refer to them as "so-called" manuals because in reality they do not—cannot—eliminate the need for almost constant creativity and innovation in the process of "following" them.

In the more exploratory and interpretive psychotherapies, virtually everything the patient says is "not in the manual." By this I mean that one needs to bring to bear a sensitivity to the specifics, to understand something that, at least in the particular form and emotional and historical context in which it now appears, one has never heard before. Only then can one creatively decide to see it as an instance of something one *has* heard before. Specification of criteria is important and appropriate for research attempting to determine the therapeutic effectiveness of a particular approach, but the notion that these are "manuals" has had the unfortunate effect of seeming to imply that doing therapy is simple or reducible to a scripted interaction.

Moreover, as if manuals alone could be used to teach psychotherapy (as—barely, in my experience—they can teach one how to use a new computer program), there have recently been rumblings from some quarters that doctoral programs in clinical psychology should be required to teach "manualized" treatments as a prerequisite for APA approval. Hidden agendas, cognitive slippage, and a magical overvaluation of words combine in such suggestions: Specifications that make sense in determining whether a therapist in a research study is reasonably close to what the researchers had in mind imperceptibly become the fantasy that there is something special or inherently efficacious about a therapy for which there is a manual.

The absurdity of the fetishism of manuals was particularly brought home to me recently when I discovered, in discussing the topic of manuals with some colleagues, that several objects in my office, which I had thought of as "books," were in fact—or at least also—"manuals" (I am reminded again of Molière's *Bourgeois Gentilhomme*).° One can indeed learn a good deal about the practice of therapy from reading such books—as I hope readers can from this one—but in choosing a therapist for myself or someone dear to me, I would much prefer that she regard what she has read as a book rather than as a manual.

These problems are especially severe if one attempts to apply the use of manuals to the study of an integrative approach. It is possible to develop a coding scheme to evaluate whether a therapist is using, for instance, both psychodynamic and cognitive–behavioral methods in any particular session—or preferably, and more sensibly, over a set of sessions—or to evaluate whether the therapy reflects the premises of cyclical psychodynamic theory. Such efforts are greatly to be encouraged, and would contribute significantly to efforts to determine whether in fact this or any other integrative approach contributes something useful over and above what a therapy of a single school can accomplish. But to attempt to create a "manual" for cyclical psychodynamic therapy is a fool's errand. If such a manual were to be viewed as a prerequisite for empirically investigating this approach, the result would be either to trivialize or utterly stymie such research.

If, on the other hand, one puts aside the question of manualization and the global evaluation of the cyclical psychodynamic approach, there are lines of inquiry that bear very directly on the clinical approach described in this book that can very productively be examined via systematic research. In particular, the aspects of therapeutic communication discussed in Chapter 18 and spelled out in more detail in Wachtel (1993b) lend themselves readily to empirical identification and investigation. For example, systematic ratings that capture the dimension of accusatory vs. faciliative communications or that address the use of the attributional dimensions I have described could be related both to the immediate response of the patient (process-outcome) and to outcome more generally. Studies focusing on this and other topics within the general realm of therapeutic communication (Wachtel, 1993b; Chapter 18 of this volume) could shed a good deal of light on important matters of therapeutic technique that are increasingly central to the integrative approach described in this book.

---

°I am not citing references here because I do not wish to appear to be criticizing particular individuals. The books were in my study because I respect the individuals who wrote them, and I do not hold them responsible for the misunderstanding and downright foolishness which others have introduced in fetishizing "manuals."

## LINES OF EVIDENCE BEARING ON THE SPECIFIC CONCEPTS
## OF THE CYCLICAL PSYCHODYNAMIC POINT OF VIEW

The heart of the integrative strategy of the cyclical psychodynamic point of view lies in its focus on vicious circles, self-fulfilling prophecies, and the evocative consequences of interpersonal expectations. Although the existing research on these topics has not generally been undertaken for the purpose of testing cyclical psychodynamic concepts, the findings of this research bear quite directly on the approach described in this book. Much evidence supports a cyclical view of personality dynamics in which intrapsychic factors and environmental influences (especially the behavior of others in response to our own behavior) reciprocally shape each other (see Blanck, 1993, Wachtel & McKinney, 1992, P. Wachtel, 1994, for fuller reviews of some of this evidence).

The vicious circles depicted throughout this book are perpetuated both by how people unwittingly get others to behave toward them and by how they interpret and perceive what has transpired. Researchers on expectancy effects and self-fulfilling prophecies have gathered evidence on both. One line of research examined people's tendency to see what they expect to see and to selectively remember what they have seen in a way that "makes" reality consistent with their expectations of others (Sherman, Judd, & Park, 1989). As Darley & Oleson (1993) put it in a recent review of the evidence for expectancies and self-fulfilling prophecies, "If a perceiver expects a target to 'be' altruistic, mendacious, clumsy, or graceful, then the expectancies may color the perceiver's judgments of actions by the target that are not actually altruistic, mendacious, clumsy, or graceful" (p. 48).

Moreover, the expectancy may not only color the way specific actions are judged or perceived, but also whether the action is viewed as typical or atypical of the person (Darley & Gross, 1983). Indeed, the tendency to attribute an individual's behavior to her own disposition (rather than, for example, to her response to others' behavior) is a crucial part of how expectancy biases and self-fulfilling prophecies are perpetuated. Such a tendency is widespread, and indeed has been depicted by Ross (1977) as the "fundamental attribution error."

Behavioral confirmation, the actual altering of others' behavior as a consequence of the expectations people hold of them, is a second dimension of the process of self-fulfilling prophecy that lies at the heart both of cyclical psychodynamic theory and of much contemporary research in social psychology and personality. Considerable evidence indicates that people do indeed induce in others the behavior they expect from them, regardless of whether that behavior is in fact the other's "natural" inclination (see, for example, Blanck, 1993; Bell & Harper, 1977; Buss, 1987; Coyne, 1976; Jussim, 1986; Kelly & Stahelski, 1970; Snyder, 1984, 1991; Snyder & Swann, 1978; Snyder, Tanke, & Berscheid, 1977). As one influential review of the literature on expectancies has put it, "To an important extent, we create our own social reality by influencing the behavior we observe in others" (Jones, 1986, p. 41).

We further shape our own social environment by who we choose to associate with. We cannot get everyone to act in accordance with our needs or expectations, but we can avoid those who do not and spend most of our time with people who do. A variety of studies indicate that indeed this is precisely what we tend to do (Emmons & Diener, 1986; Emmons, Diener, & Larsen, 1986; Gormly, 1983; Swann, Wenzlaff, Krull, & Pelham, 1992). With such an oversampling of expectancy-confirming "accomplices" (to use the term introduced earlier in this book), the circle becomes even tighter.

Most often, of course, these tendencies interact and support each other. Expecting certain behaviors, people act in ways that elicit those behaviors, and this in turn maintains the expectation and turns the wheel once more. In a study by Strack & Coyne (1983), for example, people who were at least mildly depressed were found to be more likely than nondepressed controls to anticipate rejection from the people they interacted with. Moreover, their way of interacting, based in part on those very anticipations, elicited reactions from those they interacted with that was judged as more depressed, hostile, and anxious. Not surprisingly, their interactional partners showed less willingness to interact with them again compared to the interactional partners of the nondepressed individuals. Other studies on depression have found similar kinds of skewed patterns in the interactions of depressed individuals with other people. The variety of findings seems best accounted for by an integrating formulation that again takes a cyclical form.

As a result of both experiences in childhood and patterns of cognitive bias and sensitivity (e.g., see Gotlib & Whiffen, 1991), depressed individuals anticipate, and as a consequence provoke, responses from others that are hostile, rejecting, alienating, or in other ways aversive or uncomforting. Such experiences, in turn, contribute to maintaining both the depressed individual's expectation of rejection from others and a selective sensitivity to whatever indications of rejection she encounters. This further increases the likelihood that she will continue to behave in ways that are dysphoric, critical, or otherwise disturbing to others, and thus more likely to elicit in them the responses that will perpetuate the depressive pattern.°

From another vantage point, the expectations we *think* others hold of us can shape our behavior, eventually leading to our perception of the other's view of us being "confirmed." In one study, for example (Curtis & Miller, 1986), research participants were (falsely) led to believe that another person either liked or disliked them. These false expectations led the participants to behave differentially in accord with the expectation and led the participants who anticipated dislike actually to be disliked more than the participants who thought they were liked. Thus, both the actual expectations people hold of an individual and the individual's *perception* or *assumption* of people's expectations can influence an individual's behavior. Once again, moreover, in real life the two operate in tandem—if we anticipate a certain attitude from someone, we are likely to act in a way that elicits that attitude, and in turn, the attitude elicited from that person serves to maintain the expectation of such an attitude from others or from that person again. As Robert Merton (1957), who coined the phrase "self-fulfilling prophecy," put it, "the specious validity of the self-fulfilling prophecy perpetuates a reign of error. For the prophet will cite the actual course of events as proof that he was right from the very beginning" (Merton, 1957, p. 477).

It should be noted that relatively few studies in the tradition of social cognition evince much concern with the complexities of where people's expectancies come from. (Indeed, often the expectancy is induced by the experimenter as part of the experimental procedure.) In everyday life, however, the sources of expectancies are both more varied and less controllable. One of the contributions of the psychodynamic tradition is its emphasis on the role of unconscious motivations in shaping expectancies; in part a person sees other people the way she needs to see them or she sees people as filtered through an experiential world that is shaped by unconscious beliefs or an internal working model of human relationships rooted in early experiences and coded in a fashion that is entwined with fears, wishes, and affective loadings. A more specific contribution of the cyclical psychodynamic version of psycho-

---

°It is clear that biological and social factors play an important role in depression as well, and a complete account of depression must take these factors into account. My aim here is simply to show how one particular subset of the total processes involved fits together in a cyclical pattern. Addressing the ways in which those factors omitted from this brief illustration can be conceptualized as part of a still larger pattern of reciprocal and interlocking relationships is beyond the scope of the present discussion.

analytic thought in particular is the linking of these "inner" determinants of expectations to the consequences of those expectations noted just above. The links between the seemingly irrational and out-of-touch-with-reality wishes, fears, and fantasies that have been the central concern of psychoanalysts and the self-perpetuating cycle of inner and outer events that makes those wishes and fantasies not really so out-of-touch if one studies the person's life closely enough is the special province of the theory elaborated in this book.

## CYCLICAL INTERACTIONS IN THE PROCESS OF DEVELOPMENT

Another fertile source of evidence for the processes at the heart of the cyclical psychodynamic conception of personality lies in the findings of recent developmental research. In contrast to formulations that stress fixation and developmental arrest, and view developmental questions as a matter of discerning at what "level" the person has gotten stuck, contemporary research has increasingly pointed to the role of reciprocal, interactive processes in the shaping of personality, as well as the self-fulfilling nature of the expectations that children and caretakers bring to the interaction. Stern (1985), for example, has emphasized that the developing child's expectations regarding social interactions play an important role as early as the second or third month of life. His discussions of what he calls "RIGs" (Representations of Interactions that have been Generalized) highlight both the power of these expectations and the ways in which they tend to be self-perpetuating.

Other prominent developmental theorists and researchers have also highlighted the cyclical and recursive nature of the developmental process. Brazelton's emphasis on reciprocity (e.g., Brazelton, Koslowski, & Main, 1974), Tronick's on bidirectionality (e.g., Cohn and Tronick, 1988), and Beebe and Lachmann's (1988) on mutual influence all point to a conception of development that parallels in interesting ways both the findings of the social psychological experiments discussed above and the overall cyclical conceptualization of cyclical psychodynamic theory. Expectations evoke responses consistent with those expectations, and what evolves between people is a product of context and reciprocal needs and perceptions, whether the people be two adults or a parent and an infant.

Summarizing their views on the implications of recent developmental research for psychodynamic theory and for clinical practice, Zeanah,

Anders, Seifer, and Stern (1989) offer a formulation that parallels quite closely the view of development offered in this book:

> [A] major paradigmatic shift away from the fixation-regression model of psychopathology and development is indicated. A new model that better fits available data is proposed instead. In this continuous construction model, there is no need for regression, and ontogenetic origins of psychopathology are no longer necessarily tied to specific critical or sensitive periods in development.... In the continuous construction model, patterns of internal subjective experience and patterns of relating to others are derived from past relationship experiences but are continuously operating in the present. (p. 657)

The "continuous construction model" (Zeanah et al., 1989) points, according to the authors, to a treatment approach that is multimodal and multidimensional (that is, integrative). As crucial as early experiences are in the view of these authors (who, after all, are noted as researchers on the very beginnings of development), it is precisely their understanding of the way development proceeds in those early years that leads them to regard the psychotherapy of adults as a process in which, especially through the transference relationship, attention is focused on the here and now rather than primarily on history. Because development is a continuous process rather than a road in which potholes prevent traffic from proceeding past certain points, what needs to be understood is how the person *continues* to create circumstances that perpetuate her difficulties. However large the potholes may be—and our early years offer us all formidable obstacles, to be sure—we somehow manage to move on. The detours we have taken are often much of the story of why we continue off course. But we must deal with where we have arrived—and where we presently are heading. To be sure, there needs to be room to mourn the wrong turns and curse the potholes that induced them. But "you can't get there from here" is not an attitude that facilitates therapeutic change.

Much of the developmental research just noted, bolstering the cyclical psychodynamic conception not only of developmental processes but of the ongoing dynamics of personality, has focused primarily on infancy. However, the evidence calling into question the fixation-arrest model and the picture of inherently irreversible effects of the first year of life—what Kagan (1979a) calls the "tape recorder" model of development—is not limited to infancy research. In a line of research that looks at the consequences much later in childhood of early circumstances and child rearing experiences that have been thought to yield permanent impairment, Kagan (1976, 1979a, 1979b; Kagan & Klein, 1973) has shown that quite different outcomes can result if context, expectations, and their transactional consequences are taken into account.

In a study of the cognitive development of North American and Guatemalan children, Kagan found that level of functioning in early childhood had very different implications for the later development of the North American children than it did for the Gualemalan children (Kagan & Klein, 1973; Kagan, 1976). The circumstances in which the Guatemalan children were raised were such as to suggest—by North American expectations—that they would show considerable impairment later in life. They were kept almost completely indoors for the first year of life in a small, dark, windowless hut. Toys or other stimulating objects were virtually absent, and interactions with adults were minimal. Instances of play or vocalization directed at the baby (whether by parents, other caretakers, or older children) amounted to less than ten percent of the time. (In contrast, such interactions occur 25 to 40 percent of the time in typical American homes.) And indeed, when assessed at a relatively young age, the anticipated impairment seemed evident; they were very passive and quiet and considerably behind their North American counterparts on a variety of developmental markers. At a later age, however, the seeming impairment had disappeared; their functioning was quite equivalent to that of their North American peers.

How can this be understood? Kagan's interpretation was that much of the seemingly lasting impairment that attends relative deprivation in our society is due to the expectations that follow the child as he or she develops. Guatemalan culture views the circumstances of these children's upbringing as perfectly normal. Moreover, Guatemalan views of "normal" development in children include an expectation of slow progress during infancy and a period of rapid developmental progress later in childhood. Expecting these children to thrive (despite their seeming both deprived and impaired according to North American perceptions), mothers and other adults in the Guatemalan villages treat these children as absolutely fine, and indeed, in response to this treatment—and to the expectation that *now* is the time to bloom—they respond accordingly and rapidly "catch up" to the North American children. Tests of Guatemalan children at ages ranging from 5 to 12 showed that, on culture-free tests of cognitive development, they were comparable to middle-class North American children, despite the fact that, when tested at various points in the first year of life, the Guatemalan infants seemed passive, emotionally flat, and markedly retarded.

As I have put it elsewhere, in discussing the explanation of these findings and their implications for the cyclical psychodynamic point of view,

> American children reared in as "deprived" a way as Kagan's Guatemalan children are an exception, a specially deprived subclass, and they are likely to continue in a deprived environment for many years. Moreover, they are likely to be perceived by those outside their family or social group as damaged, and to be *treated* as damaged even by those who treat other children in a facilitative way. In contrast, the Guatemalan children who are "understimulated" in the first few years of life, and who are perceived by American observers as "apathetic", "passive", or "timid", are not a special subgroup of their own society. They are "normal" children of "normal" parents and are perceived that way. They are thus in a position to respond adaptively and effectively to the stimulating experiences which their culture—with a different agenda and timetable—provides in later childhood. (Wachtel & McKinney, 1992, p. 360)

As I have noted in various contexts in this book, early experiences do have a powerful impact on how people's lives turn out. However, (consistent with Kagan's findings) they do so not because they irrevocably "fix" or "arrest" development, but because they are likely to initiate a chain of interlocking events that increase the likelihood of perpetuating aspects of the earlier experiences throughout the life cycle. First, early experiences shape our feelings, wishes, expectations, and potential interpretations of new experiences; then, as the research discussed in this chapter indicates, those expectations, inclinations, and anticipations in turn shape later experiences, both through the behavior they evoke in others and by inclining the subjective experience of that behavior in familiar directions even when the behavior itself does not fully conform. These factors alone make it likely that a roughly similar set of experiences will be encountered repeatedly—*not* just at the dawn of development. Moreover—as Kagan points out in discussing why in the North American context early deprivation and early poor performance are in fact linked to later impairment—in many settings the early circumstances are maintained quite apart from anything the individual suffering them might do or anticipate. The child brought up in a home with a depressed mother, or the lower-class child encountering a variety of deprivations early in life, will encounter the same deprivations over many years unless some unusual intervention occurs. The early deprivation, one might say, is linked to later impairment not so much because of its specific impact—or certainly not because of that impact alone—but because it is but the first of what might indeed be a lifelong series of such deprivations, impacting the individual's development over and over again. Where this is not the case—as in the changing environment encountered by the putatively deprived Guatemalan infants as they grow up—the harm that has been "internalized" seems to melt away. Where, as in the United States, the infant who is brought up in such circumstances is likely to be the child (and even the adult) who continues to encounter such circumstances—and who, furthermore, is stigmatized and thus encounters as well expectations of impairment from others he meets—the early experience looks more decisive and permanent.

The cyclical psychodynamic version of this developmental account builds on the observations of researchers such as Kagan, Rosenthal, and other developmental and social psychological investigators. It also adds another level of complexity by emphasizing as well the affective and motivational dimensions of the processes of expectancy confirmation and self-fulfilling prophecy, by highlighting the pervasive role of conflict, and by addressing the ambiguities and contradictions of subjective experience, the gradations of consciousness, and the defensive warding off of awareness of desires and experiences that are potentially uncomfortable.

## EXTENDING CYCLICAL PSYCHODYNAMICS BEYOND THE THERAPY ROOM AND INTO THE SOCIAL SPHERE

The vicious circle account that characterizes the cyclical psychodynamic point of view has relevance not only for efforts at integrating competing approaches to psychotherapy and understanding personality development, but also for the analysis of broader social patterns and problems. The sources of what might be called surplus suffering—the suffering that derives not so much from our being mortal beings with fragile bodies (for whom some suffering is therefore inevitable) but from our own actions and attitudes—are not limited to child rearing or close personal relationships. Such needless (though all too common) suffering derives as well from the social arrangements under which we live and the values and assumptions with which they are associated. Exploration of these sources of our discontents has increasingly been a concern of the cyclical psychodynamic perspective, complementing the more clinical focus from which the theory originated.

The first major effort to apply a cyclical psychodynamic perspective to the analysis of broad social questions was *The Poverty of Affluence*

(Wachtel, 1989). The major focus of that book was on the ways in which our psychological well-being, our experience of satisfaction and security, is being compromised by a preponderant and misguided focus on the economic side of our lives, the consequences of which are very poorly understood. The analysis in *The Poverty of Affluence* highlighted the irrationalities and misconceptions that have led us to misunderstand the role money and material goods play in our lives. As the data presented there indicated (see also Wachtel, 1993a, 1993b), society's assumptions about the relation between economic growth and the experience of subjective satisfaction or well-being are faulty. Contrary to the common wisdom, continuing economic growth and rises in personal and family incomes have *not* yielded a greater sense of satisfaction. Indeed, in certain respects, the pursuit of growth has undermined the foundations from which satisfaction and a sense of meaningfulness largely derive.

This is not merely a reflection of the old saw that money can't buy happiness. That idea, to be sure, is correct, however obvious it by now appears (and however much it continues nonetheless to be ignored). Summarizing the results of numerous psychological studies involving hundreds of thousands of subjects, Freedman (1978) concluded that, "Once some minimal income is attained, the amount of money you have matters little in terms of bringing happiness. Above the poverty level, the relationship between income and happiness is remarkably small" (p. 136).

What does matter, based on these studies, are things like love, friendship, being part of a community, being committed to or part of something larger than oneself. But, as *The Poverty of Affluence* detailed, it is these very things that are undermined by a way of life organized around growth and market transactions. With the idea of "more" as a key organizing principle of society, we experience stable incomes from year to year as "stagnation," and feel that we—and the system—have failed if we do not have more each year than the last, more than our parents, or more than other countries in the world.

Although a number of unique circumstances that existed during the decades immediately following World War II made these assumptions seem tenable for a period—though not necessarily conducive to a way of life that was both satisfying and sustainable—the events and realizations of recent decades have made these assumptions increasingly problematic. More and more countries are capable of competing with the United States economically and are expecting and demanding to live as we do. Moreover, we as a society are increasingly becoming aware of the environmental costs of unceasing growth. The pressures already being placed on a fragile ecosystem by those in the developed world are daunting. If that way of life were to be adopted by the billions in the less developed world—who, justifiably, see no reason why they should live less amply than we—the ecological consequences would be even more catastrophic. Already there is reason to question—once health, safety, and the future we are leaving for our children and grandchildren are taken into account—whether we are really better off after growth than we were several decades before.

Indeed, one of the central themes of *The Poverty of Affluence* is that the experiential consequences of economic growth have been so unsatisfying and even counterproductive that few people even appreciate that economically we *have* been growing. In fact, however, the economy has grown virtually ceaselessly through periods experienced as "hard times"—including the "stagflation" years of the Nixon administration, the inflation and "malaise" of the Carter years, the recession of the Bush years, and the current period of "downsizing" with its consequent economic insecurity and increase in the gap between the haves and the have nots. Through this all, the gross national product has consistently been higher each year than the year before. Equally consistent has been the widespread inability of people subjectively to register that in fact they can buy more (Duncan, 1975; Wachtel, 1996).

Understanding these observations requires us to take into account in still another way the key principle underlying the theoretical analysis in this book—the centrality of vicious circles in human affairs. In a wide variety of ways, our pursuit of ever greater economic growth results in a set of disamenities, pressures, and anxieties that are poorly understood because they are side effects of the very efforts we think are designed to make our lives better. Gearing up for competition, increased productivity, and "efficiency," we create powerful negative effects in our work life, family life, friendships, and sense of community (see, for example, Dominguez & Robin, 1992; Schor, 1991; Schwartz, 1994; Seabrook, 1990; Slater, 1980; Wachtel, 1989). Then, in an irony not unrelated to the ironic patterns discussed throughout this book, we attempt to assuage the feelings of distress and emptiness through still further efforts to "have" more and further demands on leaders to make the economy grow.

Because so many purchases are ultimately part of an effort to compensate for the very deprivations that our economic efforts impose on us, we find ourselves caught in a series of vicious circles. The more, for instance, we undermine community by choosing to move in order to get a "better" job or buy a "better" home—or the more we *have to* move because our system permits factories and offices readily to relocate because "efficiency" and "free enterprise" are valued more highly than preserving communities—the more we need to buy things to make up for what we have lost. So we begin subtly to define our goals in life in terms of a bigger house or a better car or even sending our kids to a "better" school (where, again, the apparent concern for their well-being does not consider the value to them of remaining in a stable community). Then, to achieve these constantly expanding needs and desires, we must be even more willing to work long hours, take an extra job, take the *best paying* job whether it leaves us the flexibility to spend time with our kids or not, and so forth. In turn, this puts a strain on our marriages or on family life and makes it difficult to find time to see friends. Then, given this state of deprivation, we feel we at least want to have nice things. And so the cycle begins again, each time with more of the things that make life meaningful falling by the wayside while more material goods accumulate (although, as noted above, we scarcely notice that we have accumulated very much).

Such a pattern in our lives—pervasive and yet barely noticed or articulated—bears a structure very similar to that highlighted throughout this book in discussing individual psychological disorder. This societal neurosis, as it were, is characterized, as are all neuroses, by a tendency toward self-deception in which the very causes of our distress are embraced ever more vigorously as they are fueled by the very distress they create. As *The Poverty of Affluence* tried to show, the vicious circle analysis that has proved so useful in understanding the traps and dilemmas that patients bring to their therapist has a useful role as well in understanding the still larger set of ironies and contradictions that characterize our society's dominant way of life.

## APPLYING THE VICIOUS CIRCLE PERSPECTIVE TO RACE RELATIONS

More recently, the cyclical psychodynamic perspective has been brought to bear on the study of race relations. In a book currently in progress, I have been examining the ways in which Blacks and Whites in America have been caught in a vicious circle, with each side unwittingly evoking in the other the very behaviors and attitudes they most fear and scorn—and then responding to that evoked behavior in ways that set the stage for eliciting it again. Many of the same processes discussed in the clinical portions of this book are evident writ large in this new sphere as well, and part of our difficulty in extricating ourselves from the impasse in which we all are caught is our failure to appreciate the circles and ironies that characterize our present circumstance.

Blacks and Whites tend to tell themselves different stories about how our society works, but both tend to tell stories that are linear and to see their own behavior and attitudes as simply a response to the behavior and attitudes of the other—"we" act this way because of how "they" act, with little attention to the ways in which how "they" act has to do with what "we" do. There is little room in each of the dominant narratives—there are, of course, numerous exceptions—for the way the world looks to the other. Both tend to be either-or, zero sum accounts, in which acknowledging any validity to the perception of the other seems to imply relinquishing the validity of one's own. There can be no resolution in this direction.

Drawing on the analyses of vicious circles, conflict, and defense that are at the heart of the cyclical psychodynamic viewpoint, one can fashion a different narrative that illuminates how *both* Blacks and Whites are caught in a pattern that locks us into mutual mistrust and resentment. From such a vantage point, there are uncomfortable truths on both sides that need to be incorporated into a more complex and comprehensive account of why we continue to be faced with the injustices, inequalities, dangers, and deprivations that characterize our wealthy yet troubled society.

Attention to circles and ironies shifts the focus from a discourse centered on blame versus purity to one in which shared responsibility and reciprocal participation predominate. This does not mean that no parties can be found at fault or that the weight of accountability must rest equally on all sides. For example, earlier comments about "punctuation" notwithstanding, in the case of race relations a clear starting point is evident: The historical facts of slavery and of subsequent severe discrimination make a vicious circle analysis morally suspect if this "linear" part of the causal sequence is not acknowledged. Moreover, it is essential to be clear that the solution to the problem does not lie in psychological directions alone. Efforts that are not rooted in political and economic initiatives to bring about greater equality and genuine opportunity are bound to fail. Nonetheless, it is also the case that unless we understand the ways in which, by now, we are dealing not directly with the impact of past oppression alone but with a complex set of mutual—and in some respects problematic—adaptations by both Blacks *and* Whites, we are likely to be unwittingly drawn into further perpetuating the painful patterns. The very political and economic measures we desperately need to implement will continue *not* to be implemented unless we can find a way to enable the majority who wield political power to understand the perceptions of the minority without having completely to give up their own take on reality. Appreciation of the ways that people get trapped in vicious circles, and of how we can be induced to perpetuate a pattern by the very actions we think are struggles against it, holds a key to extricating ourselves from the bind in which our history has entrapped us. The analysis of our racial dilemma that is currently being pursued from the vantage point that has guided this book is still a work in progress, but it is my hope that it can make at least a small contribution to the healing of wounds that have shown remarkable resistance to an easy cure.

## CONCLUDING COMMENTS

Further applications of the cyclical psychodynamic point of view to social problems will certainly be forthcoming. But it is important to be clear that such activities are not really separate from the analysis of psychotherapy and personality dynamics that has been the primary focus of this book. A central implication of the more contextual view of personality dynamics represented by the cyclical psychodynamic approach is that the social context must be taken into account synchronously with the more immediate interpersonal context. We live not only in families and relationships but in cultures and societies, and the effects of the latter are no less profound. Psychotherapy, it is increasingly being recognized, is an activity intimately tied to values, and those values do not appear out of thin air. Understanding the ways in which the social and cultural arrangements that define the contours of our lives shape (and in turn are largely maintained by) the more intimate details of daily living, is an essential next step in our understanding of how to diminish surplus human misery. Indeed, the linking of these still largely separate perspectives in the study of human behavior is likely to be the next major step in the advancement of integration in the human sciences.

# REFERENCES

Adler, E. (1993). Commentary on Frank's "Action, Insight, and Working Through" from the perspective of Freudian analysis. *Psychoanalytic Dialogues, 4,* 579–588.

Agras, W. S. (1967). Transfer during systematic desensitization therapy. *Behaviour Research and Therapy, 5,* 193–200.

Ainsworth, M. D. S. (1982). Attachment: Retrospect and prospect. In C. M. Parkers & J. Stevenson-Hinde (Eds.), *The place of attachment in human behavior.* New York: Basic Books.

Alexander, F. (1963). The dynamics of psychotherapy in the light of learning theory. *American Journal of Psychiatry, 120,* 440–448.

Alexander, F., French, T., et al. (1946). *Psychoanalytic therapy.* New York: Ronald Press.

Allen, K. E., Hart, B., Buell, J. S., Harris, F. R., & Wolf, M. M. (1964). Effects of social reinforcement on isolate behavior of a nursery school child. *Child Development, 35,* 511–518.

Anderson, W. T. (1995). *The truth about the truth: De-confusing and re-constructing the postmodern world.* New York: Putnam.

Andrews, J. D. (1966). Psychotherapy of phobias. *Psychological Bulletin, 66,* 455–480.

Arkowitz, H. (in press). Integrative theories of therapy. In P. L. Wachtel & S. B. Messer (Eds.), *Theoretical perspectives in psychotherapy.* Washington, DC: American Psychological Association.

Arkowitz, H., & Messer, S. B. (Eds.). (1984). *Psychoanalytic therapy and behavior therapy: Is integration possible?* New York: Plenum.

Arlow, J. A., & Brenner, C. (1964). *Psychoanalytic concepts and the structural theory.* New York: International Universities Press.

Arnkoff, D. B., & Glass, C. R. (1992). Cognitive therapy and psychotherapy integration. In D. Freedheim, H. Freudenberger, J. Kessler, S. Messer, D. Peterson, H. Strupp, & P. Wachtel (Eds.), *History of Psychotherapy* (pp. 657–694). Washington, DC: American Psychological Association.

Aron, L. (1990). One-person and two-person psychologies and the method of psychoanalysis. *Psychoanalytic Psychology, 7,* 475–495.

Aron, L. (1991). Working through the past—working toward the future. *Contemporary Psychoanalysis, 27,* 81–109.

Aron, L. (1995). The internalized primal scene. *Psychoanalytic Dialogues, 5,* 195–237.

Aron, L. (1996). *A meeting of minds: Mutuality in Psychoanalysis.* Hillsdale, NJ: The Analytic Press.

Ayllon, T., & Azrin, N. H. (1968). *The token economy.* New York: Appleton Century Crofts.

Bacal, H. A. (1995). The essence of Kohut's work and the progress of self psychology. *Psychoanalytic Dialogues, 5,* 353–366.

Bachant, J. L., & Richards, A. D. (1993). Review essay: Relational concepts in psychoanalysis. *Psychoanalytic Dialogues, 3,* 431–460.

Balint, M. (1950). Changing therapeutic aims and techniques in psychoanalysis. *International Journal of Psycho-Analysis, 31,* 117–124.

Bandura, A. (1969). *Principles of behavior modification.* New York: Holt, Rinehart and Winston.

Bandura, A. (1971). Psychotherapy based upon modeling principles. In A. E. Bergin & S. L. Garfield (Eds.), *Handbook of psychotherapy and behavior change* (pp. 653–708). New York: Wiley.

Bandura, A. (1974). Behavior theory and the models of man. *American Psychologist, 29,* 859–869.

Bandura, A., & Walters, R. (1963). *Social learning and personality development.* New York: Holt, Rinehart and Winston.

Barkham, M., Shapiro, D. A., & Firth-Cozens, J. (1989). Personal questionnaire changes in prescriptive vs. exploratory psychotherapy. *British Journal of Clinical Psychology, 28,* 97–107.

Barlow, D. H., Agras, W. S., Leitenberg, H., & Wincze, J. P. (1970). An experimental analysis of the effectiveness of "shaping" in reducing maladaptive avoidance behavior: An analogue study. *Behaviour Research and Therapy, 8,* 165–173.

Barlow, D. H., Leitenberg, H., Agras, W. S., & Wincze, J. P. (1969). The transfer gap in systematic desensitization: An analogue study. *Behaviour Research and Therapy, 7,* 191–196.

Barron, J. W., Eagle, M. N., & Wolitzky, D. L. (1992). *Interface of psychoanalysis and psychology.* Washington, DC: American Psychological Association.

Basch, M. F. (1983). The significance of self psychology for a theory of psychotherapy. In J. D. Lichtenberg & S. Kaplan (Eds.), *Reflections on self psychology* (pp. 223–238). Hillsdale, NJ: The Analytic Press.

Basch, M. F. (1988). *Understanding psychotherapy: The science behind the art.* New York: Basic Books.

Basch, M. F. (1995). Kohut's contribution. *Psychoanalytic Dialogues, 5,* 367–373.

Bateson, G. (1972). *Steps to an ecology of mind.* New York: Ballantine Books.

Beebe, B., & Lachmann, F. (1988). The contribution of mother-infant mutual influence to the origins of self and object representations. *Psychoanalytic Psychology, 5,* 305–337.

Beitman, B. D. (1987). *The structure of individual psychotherapy.* New York: Guilford.

Beitman, B. D. (1992). Integration through fundamental similarities and useful differences among the schools. In J. C. Norcross & M. R. Goldfried (Eds.), *Handbook of psychotherapy integration* (pp. 202–230). New York: Basic Books.

Bell, R. Q., & Harper, L. V. (1977). *Child effects on adults.* Hillsdale, NJ: Erlbaum.

Benjamin, J. (1991). Father and daughter: Identification with difference—A contribution to gender heterodoxy. *Psychoanalytic Dialogues, 1,* 277–301.

Bergin, A. E. (1971). The evaluation of therapeutic outcomes. In A. E. Bergin & S. L. Garfield (Eds.), *Handbook of psychotherapy and behavior change* (pp. 217–270). New York: Wiley.

Bernstein, D. A., & Paul, G. L. (1971). Some comments on therapy analogue research with small animal "phobias." *Journal of Behavior Therapy and Experimental Psychiatry, 2,* 225–237.

Beutler, L. E., & Clarkin, J. F. (1990). *Differential treatment selection: Toward targeted therapeutic interventions.* New York: Brunner/Mazel.

Beutler, L. E., & Consoli, A. J. (1992). Systematic eclectic psychotherapy. In J. C. Norcross & M. R. Goldfried (Eds.), *Handbook of psychotherapy integration* (pp. 264–299). New York: Basic Books.

Bibring, C. (1954). Psychoanalysis and the dynamic psychotherapies. *Journal of the American Psychoanalytic Association, 2,* 745–770.

Blanck, P. D. (Ed.). (1993). *Interpersonal expectations: Theory, research, and applications.* New York: Cambridge University Press.

Bolles, R. C. (1972). Reinforcement, expectancy, and learning. *Psychological Review, 79,* 394–409.

Bowers, K. S. (1973). Situationism in psychology: An analysis and a critique. *Psychological Review, 80,* 307–336.

Bowers, K. S. (1975). The psychology of subtle control: An attributional analysis of behavioral persistence. *Canadian Journal of Behavioral Science, 7,* 78–95.

Bowers, K. S., & Meichenbaum, D. (Eds.). (1984). *The unconscious reconsidered.* New York: Wiley.

Bowlby, J. (1969). *Attachment and loss* (Vol. 1), *Attachment.* New York: Basic Books.

Bowlby, J. (1973). *Attachment and loss* (Vol. 2), *Separation, anxiety, and anger.* New York: Basic Books.

Brazelton, T. B., Koslowski, B., & Main, M. (1974). The origins of reciprocity: The early mother-infant interaction. In M. Lewis & L. A. Rosenbaum (Eds.), *The effect of the infant on the caregiver.* New York: Wiley.

Breger, L., & McGaugh, L. L. (1965). A critique and reformulation of "learning theory" approaches to psychotherapy and neurosis. *Psychological Bulletin, 63,* 338–358.

Breuer, J., & Freud, S. (1895). Studies on hysteria. In *The standard edition of the complete psychological works of Sigmund Freud* (vol. 2). London: Hogarth Press.

Brockman, B., Poynton, A., Ryle, A., & Watson, J. P. (1987). Effectiveness of time-limited therapy carried out by trainees. *British Journal of Psychiatry, 151,* 602–610.

Brody, N. (1972). *Personality.* New York: Academic Press.

Brush, F. R. (1957). The effects of shock intensity on the acquisition and extinction of an avoidance response in dogs. *Journal of Comparative and Physiological Psychology, 50,* 547–552.

Buss, D. M. (1987). Selection, evocation, and manipulation. *Journal of Personality and Social Psychology, 53,* 1214–1221.

Campbell, T. W. (1992). Therapeutic relationships and iatrogenic outcomes: The blame-and-change maneuver in psychotherapy. *Psychotherapy, 29,* 474–480.

Chambless, D. L., Goldstein, A. J., Gallagher, R., & Bright, P. (1986). Integrating behavior therapy and psychotherapy in the treatment of agoraphobia. *Psychotherapy, 23,* 150–159.

Chapman, L. J., & Chapman, J. P. (1969). Illusory correlations as an obstacle to the use of valid psychodiagnostic signs. *Journal of Abnormal Psychology, 74,* 271–280.

Chein, I. (1962). The image of man. *Journal of Social Issues, 18,* 1–35.

Clarkin, J. F., Frances, A., & Perry, S. (1992). Differential therapeutics: Macro and micro levels of treatment planning. In J. C. Norcross & M. R. Goldfried (Eds.), *Handbook of psychotherapy integration* (pp. 463–502). New York: Basic Books.

Cohn, J. F., & Tronick, E. Z. (1988). Mother-infant face-to-face interaction: Influence is bidirectional and unrelated to periodic cycles in either partner's behavior. *Developmental Psychology, 24,* 386–392.

Cooper, J. E. (1963). A study of behavior therapy in thirty psychiatric patients. *Lancet, 1,* 411–415.

Cooper, J. E., Gelder, M. C., & Marks, I. M. (1965). Results of behavior therapy in 77 psychiatric patients. *British Medical Journal, 1,* 1222–1225.

Coyne, J. C. (1976). Depression and the response of others. *Journal of Abnormal Psychology, 85,* 186–193.

Coyne, J. C. (1982a). A critique of cognitions as causal entities with particular reference to depression. *Cognitive Research and Therapy, 6,* 3–13.

Coyne, J. C. (1982b). A brief introduction to epistobabble. *The Family Therapy Networker,* 6(July/August), 26–27.

Coyne, J. C. (1992). Cognition in depression: A paradigm in crisis. *Psychological Inquiry, 3,* 232–235.

Coyne, J. C. (1994). Possible contributions of "cognitive science" to the integration of psychotherapy. *Journal of Psychotherapy Integration, 4,* 401–416.

Coyne, J. C., & Gotlib, I. H. (1983). The role of cognition in depression: A critical appraisal. *Psychological Bulletin, 94,* 472–505.

Coyne, J. C., & Gotlib, I. H. (1986). Studying the role of cognition in depression: Well-trodden paths and cul-de-sacs. *Cognitive Therapy and Research, 10,* 695–705.

Craighead, W. E. (1990). There's a place for us: All of us. *Behavior Therapy, 21,* 3–23.

Crisp, A. H. (1966). Transference, symptom emergence, and social repercussions in behavior therapy: A study of 54 treated patients. *British Journal of Medical Psychology, 39,* 179–196.

Crowder, J. E., & Thornton, D. W. (1970). Effects of systematic desensitization, programmed fantasy and bibliotherapy on a specific fear. *Behaviour Research and Therapy, 8,* 35–41.

Curtis, R. C. (1991). *The relational self: Theoretical convergences in psychoanalysis and social psychology.* New York: Guilford.

Curtis, R. C., & Miller, K. (1986). Believing another likes or dislikes you: Behavior making the beliefs come true. *Journal of Personality and Social Psychology, 51,* 284–290.

Darley, J. M., & Gross, P. H. (1983). A hypothesis-confirming bias in labeling effects. *Journal of Personality and Social Psychology, 44,* 20–33.

Darley, J. M., & Oleson, K. C. (1993). Introduction to research on interpersonal expectations. In P. D. Blanck (Ed.), *Interpersonal expectations: Theory, research, and applications* (pp. 45–63). Cambridge, MA: Cambridge University Press.

Davison, G. C. (1968). Systematic desensitization as a counter-conditioning process. *Journal of Abnormal Psychology, 73,* 91–99.

Davison, G. C. (1969). Appraisal of behavior modification techniques with adults in institutional settings. In C. Franks (Ed.), *Behavior therapy: Appraisal and status.* New York: McGraw-Hill.

Davison, G. C., & Neale, J. M. (1974). *Abnormal psychology.* New York: Wiley.

Davison, G. C., & Wilson, G. T. (1972). Critique of "Desensitization: Social and cognitive factors underlying the effectiveness of Wolpe's Procedure." *Psychological Bulletin, 78,* 28–31.

Davison, G. C., & Wilson, G. T. (1973). Processes of fear reduction in systematic desensitization: Cognitive and social reinforcement factors in humans. *Behavior Therapy, 4,* 1–21.

Delprato, D. J. (1973). Exposure to the aversive stimulus in an animal analogue to systematic desensitization. *Behaviour Research and Therapy, 11,* 187–192.

Dewald, P. (1972). *The psychoanalytic process.* New York: Basic Books.

Dollard, J., & Miller, N. E. (1950). *Personality and psychotherapy.* New York: McGraw-Hill.

Dominguez, J., & Robin, V. (1992). *Your money or your life*. New York: Penguin.

Duncan, O. D. (1975). Does money buy satisfaction? *Social Indicators Research, 2,* 267–274.

D'Zurilla, T. J., Wilson, G. T., & Nelson, R. A. (1973). Preliminary study of the effectiveness of graduated prolonged exposure in the treatment of irrational fear. *Behavior Therapy, 4,* 672–685.

Eagle, M. N., & Wolitzky, D. L. (in press). Psychoanalytic theories of psychotherapy. In P. L. Wachtel & S. B. Messer (Eds.), *Theories of psychotherapy: Evolution and development*. Washington, DC: American Psychological Association.

Easterbrook, J. A. (1959). The effect of emotion on cue utilization and the organization of behavior. *Psychological Review, 66,* 183–201.

Ehrenberg, D. B. (1992). *The intimate edge: Extending the reach of psychoanalytic interaction*. New York: Norton.

Eisler, K. R. (1956). Some comments on psychoanalysis and dynamic psychiatry. *Journal of the American Psychoanalytic Association, 4,* 314–317.

Eisler, K. R. (1958). Remarks on some variations in psycho-analytical technique. *International Journal of Psycho-Analysis, 39,* 222–229.

Elkin, I. (1994). The NIMH Treatment of Depression Collaborative Research Program: Where we began and where we are. In A. E. Bergin & S. L. Garfield (Eds.), *Handbook of psychotherapy and behavior change* (4th ed., pp. 114–139). New York: Wiley.

Elkin, I., Shea, M. T., Watkins, J. T., Imber, S. D., Sotsky, S. M., Collins, J. F., Glass, D. R., Pilkonis, P. A., Leber, W. R., Dochery, J. P., Fiester, S. J., & Parloff, M. B. (1989). National Institute of Mental Health Treatment of Depression Collaborative Research Program: General effectiveness of treatments. *Archives of General Psychiatry, 46,* 971–982.

Ellis, A. (1962). *Reason and emotion in psychotherapy*. New York: Lyle Stuart.

Emmons, R. A., & Diener, E. (1986). Situation selection as a moderator of response consistency and stability. *Journal of Personality and Social Psychology, 51,* 1013–1019.

Emmons, R. A., Diener, E., & Larsen, R. J. (1986). Choice and avoidance of everyday situations and affect congruence: Two models of reciprocal interactionism. *Journal of Personality and Social Psychology, 51,* 815–826.

Epstein, S. (1962). The measurement of drive and conflict in humans: Theory and experiment. In M. R. Jones (Ed.), *Nebraska symposium on motivation*. Lincoln: University of Nebraska Press.

Epstein, S. (1967). Toward a unified theory of anxiety. In B. A. Maher (Ed.), *Progress in personality research* (Vol. 4). New York: Academic Press.

Epstein, S., & Fenz, W. D. (1962). Theory and experiment on the measurement of approach–avoidance conflict. *Journal of Abnormal Psychology, 64,* 97–112.

Epstein, S., & Fenz, W. D. (1965). Steepness of approach and avoidance gradients in humans as a function of experience: Theory and experiment. *Journal of Experimental Psychology, 70,* 1–12.

Erdelyi, M. H. (1974). A new look at the new look: Perceptual defence and vigilance. *Psychological Review, 81,* 1–25.

Erdelyi, M. (1985). *Psychoanalysis: Freud's cognitive psychology*. San Francisco: W. H. Freeman.

Erikson, E. H. (1950). *Childhood and Society* (Rev. ed.). New York: Norton.

Escalona, S. (1968). *The roots of individuality.* Chicago: Aldine.

Escalona, S. (1972). The differential impact of environmental conditions as a function of different reaction patterns in infancy. In J. Westman (Ed.), *Individual differences in children.* New York: Wiley.

Eysenck, H. J. (1959). Learning theory and behavior therapy. *Journal of Mental Science, 105,* 61–75.

Eysenck, H. J. (1972). Behavior therapy is behavioristic. *Behavior Therapy, 3,* 609–613.

Eysenck, H. J., & Beech, R. (1971). Counterconditioning and related methods. In A. E. Bergin & S. L. Garfield (Eds.), *Handbook of psychotherapy and behavior change* (pp. 543–611). New York: Wiley.

Fairbairn, W. R. D. (1952). *An object-relations theory of the personality.* New York: Basic Books.

Feather, B. W., & Rhoads, J. M. (1972). Psychodynamic behavior therapy: II: Clinical aspects. *Archives of General Psychiatry, 26,* 503–511.

Feixas, G., & Neimeyer, R. A. (1990). Constructivist contributions to psychotherapy integration. *Journal of Integrative and Eclectic Psychotherapy, 9,* 1–10.

Feixas, G., & Villegas, M. (1993). *Constructivismo y psicoterapia* [Constructivism and psychotherapy] (2nd ed.). Barcelona: PPU.

Feldman, L. (1992). *Integrating individual and family therapy.* New York: Brunner/Mazel.

Fenichel, O. (1940). Review of *New Ways in Psychoanalysis* by Karen Horney [Book review]. *Psychoanalytic Quarterly, 9,* 114–121.

Fenichel, O. (1945). *The psychoanalytic theory of neurosis.* New York: Norton.

Fenz, W. D. (1964). Conflict & stress as related to physiological activation and sensory, perceptual and cognitive functioning. *Psychological Monographs, 78*(Whole No. 585).

Fenz, W. D., & Epstein, S. (1967). Gradients of physiological arousal of experienced and novice parachutists as a function of an approaching jump. *Psychosomatic Medicine, 29,* 33–51.

Fernandez Alvarez, H. (1992). *Fundamentos de un modelo integrativo en psicoterapia* [Foundations of an integrative model of psychotherapy]. Buenos Aires: Paidos.

Fisher, S., & Greenberg, R. P. (1985). *The scientific credibility of Freud's theories and therapy.* New York: Columbia University Press.

Fishman, S. T., & Lubetkin, B. S. (1983). Office practice of behavior therapy. In M. Hersen (Ed.), *Outpatient behavior therapy: A clinical guide* (pp. 21–41). New York: Grune & Stratton.

Fodor, I. G. (1974). The phobic syndrome in women: Implications for treatment. In V. Franks & V. Burtle (Eds.), *Women in therapy: New psychotherapies for a changing society* (pp. 132–168). New York: Brunner/Mazel.

Fosshage, J. (1992). Self psychology: The self and its vicissitudes within a relational matrix. In N. Skolnick & S. Warshaw (Eds.), *Relational perspectives in psychoanalysis* (pp. 21–42). Hillsdale, NJ: The Analytic Press.

Framo, J. (1981). The integration of marital therapy with sessions with family of origin. In Gurman & Kniskern (Eds.), *Handbook of Family Therapy* (pp. 138–161). New York: Brunner/Mazel.

Frank, J. D. (1961). *Persuasion and healing.* Baltimore: Johns Hopkins University Press.

Frank, J. D. (1973). *Persuasion and healing: A comparative study of psychotherapy* (Rev. ed.). Baltimore: Johns Hopkins University Press.

Frank, J. D. (1974a). Therapeutic components of psychotherapy: A twenty-five year progress report of research. *Journal of Nervous and Mental Disease, 159,* 325–342.

Frank, J. D. (1974b). Psychotherapy: The restoration of morale. *American Journal of Psychiatry, 131*, 271–274.

Frank, J. D. (1982). Therapeutic components shared by all psychotherapies. In J. H. Harvey & M. M. Parks (Eds.), *The master lecture series* (Vol. 1): *Psychotherapy research and behavior change* (pp. 73–122). Washington, DC: American Psychological Association.

Frank, K. A. (1990). Action techniques in psychoanalysis. *Contemporary Psychoanalysis, 26*, 732–756.

Frank, K. A. (1992). Combining action techniques with psychoanalytic therapy. *International Revue of Psycho-Analysis, 19*, 57–79.

Frank, K. A. (1993). Action, insight, and working through: Outlines of an integrative approach. *Psychoanalytic Dialogues, 3*, 535–577.

Frankl, V. (1960). Paradoxical intention: A logotherapeutic technique. *American Journal of Psychotherapy, 14*, 520–535.

Franks, C. M. (1984). On conceptual and technical integrity in psychoanalysis and behavior therapy: Two fundamentally incompatible systems. In H. Arkowitz & S. B. Messer (Eds.), *Psychoanalytic therapy and behavior therapy: Is integration possible?* (pp. 223–247). New York: Plenum.

Freedman, J. (1978). *Happy people*. New York: Harcourt Brace Jovanovich.

Freud, S. (1887–1902). *The origins of psychoanalysis: Letters to Wilhelm Fliess, drafts and notes, 1887–1902*. New York: Basic Books, 1954.

Freud, S. (1895). Project for a scientific psychology. In *The origins of psychoanalysis: Letters to Wilhelm Fliess, drafts and notes: 1887–1902* (pp. 355–445). New York: Basic Books, 1954.

Freud, S. (1896). Further remarks on the neuro-psychoses of defence. *Standard edition* (Vol. 3, pp. 159–185). London: Hogarth Press, 1962.

Freud, S. (1905). Three essays on the theory of sexuality. *Standard edition* (Vol. 7, pp. 130–243). London: Hogarth Press, 1953.

Freud, S. (1910). "Wild" psycho-analysis. *Standard edition* (Vol. 11, pp. 221–227). London: Hogarth Press, 1957.

Freud, S. (1912). Recommendations to physicians practicing psycho-analysis. *Standard edition* (Vol. 12, pp. 109–120). London: Hogarth Press, 1957.

Freud, S. (1914a). Remembering, repeating, and working-through. *Standard edition* (Vol. 12, pp. 145–156). London: Hogarth Press, 1957.

Freud, S. (1914b). On the history of the psycho-analytic movement. *Standard edition* (Vol. 14, pp. 3–66). London: Hogarth Press, 1957.

Freud, S. (1917). Introductory lectures on psycho-analysis. *Standard edition* (Vols. 15–16). London: Hogarth Press, 1963.

Freud, S. (1923). The ego and the id. *Standard edition* (Vol. 19, pp. 12–66). London: Hogarth Press, 1961.

Freud, S. (1926a). Inhibitions, symptoms and anxiety. *Standard edition* (Vol. 21, pp. 87–172). London: Hogarth Press, 1959.

Freud, S. (1926b). The question of lay analysis. *Standard edition* (Vol. 20, pp. 183–258). London: Hogarth Press, 1959.

Fromm, E. (1941). *Escape from freedom*. New York: Holt, Rinehart and Winston.

Fromm-Reichmann, F. (1950). *Principles of intensive psychotherapy*. Chicago: University of Chicago Press.

Frye, N. (1957). *Anatomy of criticism*. New York: Athaneum.

Gedo, J. E. (1988). *The mind in disorder*. Hillsdale, NJ: The Analytic Press.

Gelder, M. G., & Marks, I. M. (1966). Severe agoraphobia: A controlled prospective trial of behaviour therapy. *British Journal of Psychiatry, 112*, 309–319.

Gelder, M. G., Marks, I. M., & Wolff, H. H. (1967). Desensitization and psycho-therapy in the treatment of phobia states: A controlled inquiry. *British Journal of Psychiatry, 113*, 53–73.

Gerson, M-J. (1996). *The embedded self: A psychoanalytic guide to family therapy*. Hillsdale, NJ: The Analytic Press.

Gill, M. M. (1954). Psychoanalysis and exploratory psychotherapy. *Journal of the American Psychoanalytic Association, 2*, 771–797.

Gill, M. M. (1963). Topography and systems in psychoanalytic theory. *Psychological Issues* [Monograph No. 10]. Vol. 3(2).

Gill, M. M. (1979). The analysis of the transference. *Journal of the American Psychoanalytic, 27* (suppl.), 263–288.

Gill, M. M. (1982). *Analysis of transference*. New York: International Universities Press.

Gill, M. M. (1983). The interpersonal paradigm and the degree of the therapist's involvement. *Contemporary Psychoanalysis, 19*, 200–237.

Gill, M. M. (1984a). Psychoanalytic, psychodynamic, cognitive behavior, and behavior therapies compared. In H. Arkowitz & S. B. Messer (Eds.), *Psychoanalytic therapy and behavior therapy: Is integration possible?* (pp. 179–187). New York: Plenum.

Gill, M. M. (1984b). Psychoanalysis and psychotherapy: A revision. *International Review of Psycho-Analysis, 11*, 161–179.

Gill, M. M. (1994). *Psychoanalysis in transition*. Hillsdale, NJ: Analytic Press.

Glass, C. R., & Arnkoff, D. B. (1992). Behavior therapy. In D. Freedheim, H. Freudenberger, J. Kessler, S. Messer, D. Peterson, H. Strupp, & P. Wachtel (Eds.), *History of psychotherapy* (pp. 587–628). Washington, DC: American Psychological Association.

Glass, C. R., Victor, B. J., & Arnkoff, D. B. (1993). Empirical research on integrative and eclectic psychotherapies. In J. Gold & G. Stricker (Eds.), *Comprehensive handbook of psychotherapy integration* (pp. 9–25). New York: Praeger.

Goffman, E. (1961). *Asylums*. New York: Doubleday Anchor.

Gold, J. R., & Wachtel, P. L. (1993). Cyclical psychodynamics. In J. Gold & G. Stricker (Eds.), *Comprehensive handbook of psychotherapy integration* (pp. 59–72). New York: Plenum.

Goldberg, A. (Ed.). (1983). *The future of psychoanalysis*. New York: International Universities Press.

Goldfried, M. R. (1971). Systematic desensitization as training in self-control. *Journal of Consulting and Clinical Psychology, 37*, 228–234.

Goldfried, M. R. (1980). Toward the delineation of therapeutic change principles. *American Psychologist, 35*, 991–999.

Goldfried, M. R. (1991). Research issues in psychotherapy integration. *Journal of Psychotherapy Integration, 1*, 5–25.

Goldfried, M. R. (1995a). On the history of therapeutic integration. In M. R. Goldfried, *From cognitive-behavior therapy to psychotherapy integration* (pp. 185–206). New York: Springer.

Goldfried, M. R. (1995b). *From cognitive-behavior therapy to psychotherapy integration*. New York: Springer.

Goldfried, M. R., & Davison, G. C. (1976). *Clinical behavior therapy*. New York: Holt, Rinehart and Winston.

Goldfried, M. R., & Davison, G. C. (1994). *Clinical behavior therapy* (Expanded Edition). New York: Wiley.

Goldfried, M. R., DeCenteceo, E. T., & Weinberg, L. (1974). Systematic rational restructuring as a self-control technique. *Behavior Therapy, 5,* 247–254.

Goldfried, M. R., & Merbaum, M. (Eds.). (1973). *Behavior change through self-control.* New York: Holt, Rinehart and Winston.

Goldfried, M. R., & Newman, C. F. (1992). A history of psychotherapy integration. In J. C. Norcross & M. R. Goldfried (Eds.), *Handbook of psychotherapy integration* (pp. 46–93). New York: Basic Books.

Goldfried, M. R., & Sprafkin, J. N. (1974). *Behavioral personality assessment.* Morristown, NJ: General Learning Press.

Goldstein, A. P., Martens, J., Hubben, J., van Belle, H. A., Schaaf, W., Wiersma, H., & Goedhart, A. (1973). The use of modeling to increase independent behavior. *Behaviour Research and Therapy, 11,* 31–42.

Gormly, J. (1983). Predicting behavior from personality trait scores. *Personality and Social Psychology Bulletin, 9,* 267–270.

Gotlib, I. H., & Whiffen, V. E. (1991). The interpersonal context of depression: Implications for theory and research. In W. H. Jones & D. Perlman (Eds.), *Advances in personal relationships* (Vol. 3, pp. 177–206).

Greenacre, P. (1959). The role of transference: Practical considerations in relation to psychoanalytic therapy. *Journal of the American Psychoanalytic Association, 2,* 671–684.

Greenberg, J., & Mitchell, S. A. (1983). *Object relations in psychoanalysis.* Cambridge, MA: Harvard University Press.

Greenberg, L. S. (1990). *Integrative psychotherapy* (Part 5) [Videotape]. Corona del Mar, CA: Psychological and Educational Films.

Greenberg, L. S., & Rice, L. N. (in press). Humanistic approaches to psychotherapy. In P. L. Wachtel & S. B. Messer (Eds.), *Theories of psychotherapy: Evolution and current status.* Washington, DC: American Psychological Association.

Greenberg, L. S., & Safran, J. D. (1987). *Emotion in psychotherapy: Affect, cognition, and the process of change.* New York: Guilford.

Greenberg, L. S., & Safran, J. D. (1989). Emotion in psychotherapy. *American Psychologist, 44,* 19–29.

Greenson, R. R. (1967). *The technique and practice of psychoanalysis.* New York: International Universities Press.

Greenspan, S. I. (1974). The clinical use of operant learning approaches: Some complex issues. *American Journal of Psychiatry, 131,* 852–857.

Greenspan, S. I. (1975). A consideration of some learning variables in the context of psychoanalytic theory: Toward a psychoanalytic learning perspective [Monograph No. 33]. *Psychological Issues, 9*(1).

Greenwald, A. (1992). New look 3: Unconscious cognition reclaimed. *American Psychologist, 47,* 766–779.

Grossberg, J. M. (1973). Generalization of extinction effects in fear scene hierarchies. *Behaviour Research and Therapy, 11,* 343–346.

Groves, P. M., & Thompson, R. F. (1970). Habituation: A dual-process theory. *Psychological Review, 77,* 419–450.

Grunbaum, A. (1984). *The foundations of psychoanalysis: A philosophical critique.* Berkeley: University of California Press.

Guidano, V. F. (1987). *Complexity of the self: A developmental approach to psychopathology and therapy.* New York: Guilford.

Guidano, V. F. (1991). *The self in process.* New York: Guilford.

Guidano, V. F., & Liotti, G. (1983). *Cognitive processes and emotional disorders: A structural approach to psychotherapy.* New York: Guilford.

Guntrip, H. (1969). *Schizoid phenomena, object relations and the self.* New York: International Universities Press.

Gurman, A. S. (1981). Integrative marital therapy. In S. Budman (Ed.), *Forms of brief therapy* (pp. 415–457). New York: Guilford.

Haley, J. (1963). *Strategies of psychotherapy.* New York: Grune and Stratton.

Hartmann, H., Kris, E., & Lowenstein, R. M. (1946). Comments on the formation of psychic structure. *The Psychoanalytic Study of the Child, 2,* 11–38.

Hatcher, S. L., & Hatcher, R. L. (1983). Set a place for Elijah: Problems of the spouses and parents of psychotherapy patients. *Psychotherapy, 20,* 75–80.

Helson, H. (1964). *Adaptation level theory.* New York: Harper and Row.

Hersen, M. (1983). Perspectives on the practice of outpatient behavior therapy. In M. Hersen (Ed.), *Outpatient behavior therapy: A clinical guide* (pp. 3–20). New York: Grune & Stratton.

Hoffart, A., & Martinsen, E. W. (1990). Exposure-based integrated vs. pure psychodynamic treatment of agoraphobic inpatients. *Psychotherapy, 27,* 210–218.

Hoffman, I. Z. (1991). Toward a social-constructivist view of the psychoanalytic situation. *Psychoanalytic Dialogues, 1,* 74–105.

Hoffman, I. Z. (1992). Some practical implications of a social-constructivist view of the psychoanalytic situation. *Psychoanalytic Dialogues, 3,* 287–304.

Hoffman, L. (1981). *Foundations of family therapy.* New York: Basic Books.

Holmes, D. S. (1974). Investigations of repression: Differential recall of material experimentally or naturally associated with ego threat. *Psychological Bulletin, 81,* 632–653.

Holt, R. R. (1965). A review of some of Freud's biological assumptions and their influence on his theories. In N. S. Greenfield & W. C. Lewis (Eds.), *Psychoanalysis and current biological thought* (pp. 93–124). Madison: University of Wisconsin Press.

Holt, R. R. (1967a). Beyond vitalism and mechanism: Freud's concept of psychic energy. In J. H. Masserman (Ed.), *Science and psychoanalysis* (Vol. 2, pp. 1–41). New York: Grune and Stratton.

Holt, R. R. (1967b). Ego autonomy re-evaluated. *International Journal of Psychiatry, 3,* 481–502.

Horney, K. (1939). *New ways in psychoanalysis.* New York: Norton.

Horney, K. (1942). *Self-analysis.* New York: Norton.

Horney, K. (1945). *Our inner conflicts.* New York: Norton.

Horowitz, M. J. (Ed.). (1991). *Person schemas and maladaptive interpersonal patterns.* Chicago: University of Chicago Press.

Hull, C. L. (1943). *Principles of behavior.* New York: Appleton-Century-Crofts.

Irwin, F. W. (1971). *Intentional behavior and motivation: A cognitive theory.* New York: J. B. Lippincott.

Jacobson, E. (1986). *Progressive relaxation.* Chicago: University of Chicago Press.

Jones, E. E. (1986). Interpreting interpersonal behavior. *Science, 234,* 41–46.

Jones, E. E. (1990). *Interpersonal perception.* New York: W. H. Freeman.

Jussim, L. (1986). Self-fulfilling prophecies: A theoretical and integrative review. *Psychological Review, 93,* 429–445.

References

Kagan, J. (1976). Resilience and continuity in psychological development. In A. M. Clarke & A. D. B. Clarke (Eds.), *Early experience: Myth and evidence* (pp. 97–121). New York: Free Press.

Kagan, J. (1979a). The form of early development: Continuity and discontinuity in emergent competences. *Archives of General Psychiatry, 36,* 1047–1054.

Kagan, J. (1979b). Family experience and the child's development. *American Psychologist, 34,* 886–891.

Kagan, J., & Klein, R. E. (1973). Cross-cultural perspective on early development. *American Psychologist, 28,* 947–961.

Kanfer, F. H., & Phillips, J. S. (1970). *Learning foundations of behavior therapy.* New York: Wiley.

Kanfer, F. H., & Saslow, G. (1965). Behavioral analysis: An alternative to diagnostic classification. *Archives of General Psychiatry, 12,* 529–538.

Kaplan, H. S. (1974). *The new sex therapy.* New York: Brunner/Mazel.

Kelly, G. A. (1955). *The psychology of personal constructs* (Vol. 1). New York: Norton.

Kelly, H. H., & Stahelski, A. J. (1970). Social interaction basis of cooperators' and competitors' beliefs about others. *Journal of Personality and Social Psychology, 16,* 66–91.

Kendall, P. C., & Bemis, K. M. (1983). Thought and action in psychotherapy: The cognitive-behavioral approaches. In M. Hersen, A. E. Kazdin, & A. S. Bellak (Eds.), *The clinical psychology handbook* (pp. 565–592). New York: Pergamon.

Kernberg, O. (1975). *Borderline conditions and pathological narcissism.* New York: Jason Aronson.

Kernberg, O. (1976). *Object relations theory and clinical psychoanalysis.* New York: Jason Aronson.

Kernberg, O. (1980). *Internal world and external reality.* New York: Jason Aronson.

Kernberg, O. (1988). Object relations theory in clinical practice. *Psychoanalytic Quarterly, 57,* 481–504.

Kiesler, D. J. (1966). Some myths of psychotherapy research and the search for a paradigm. *Psychological Bulletin, 65,* 110–136.

Kihlstrom, J. (1987). The cognitive unconscious. *Science, 237,* 1445–1452.

Kirschner, D. A., & Kirschner, S. (1986). *Comprehensive family therapy.* New York: Brunner/Mazel.

Klein, G. S. (1958). Cognitive control and motivation. In G. Lindzey (Ed.), *Assessment of human motives* (pp. 87–118). New York: Rinehart.

Klein, G. S. (1967). Peremptory ideation: Structure and force in motivated ideas [Monograph No. 18–19]. *Psychological Issues, 5*(2–3), 80–128.

Klein, M. H., Dittman, J. T., Parloff, M. B., & Gill, M. M. (1969). Behavior therapy: Observations and reflections. *Journal of Consulting and Clinical Psychology, 33,* 259–266.

Kline, P. (1972). *Fact and fantasy in Freudian theory.* London: Methuen.

Kohut, H. (1971). *The analysis of the self.* New York: International Universities Press.

Kohut, H. (1977). *The restoration of the self.* New York: International Universities Press.

Kohut, H. (1984). *How does analysis cure?* Chicago: University of Chicago Press.

Korchin, S. (1964). Anxiety and cognition. In C. Scheerer (Ed.), *Cognition: Theory, research, promise* (pp. 58–78). New York: Harper and Row.

Kuhn, T. S. (1962). *The structure of scientific revolutions.* Chicago: University of Chicago Press.

Lader, M. H. (1967). Palmar conductance measures in anxiety and phobic states. *Journal of Psychosomatic Research, 11*, 271–281.

Lader, M. H., & Mathews, A. M. (1968). A physiological model of phobic anxiety and desensitization. *Behaviour Research and Therapy, 6*, 411–421.

Lader, M. H., & Wing, L. (1966). *Physiological measures, sedative drugs, and morbid anxiety.* London: Oxford University Press.

Laing, R. D. (1969). *The politics of the family.* New York: Pantheon.

Lambert, M. J., & Bergin, A. E. (1994). The effectiveness of psychotherapy. In A. E. Bergin & S. L. Garfield (Eds.), *Handbook of psychotherapy and behavior change* (4th ed., pp. 143–189). New York: Wiley.

Lambert, M. J., Shapiro, D. A., & Bergin, A. E. (1986). The effectiveness of psychotherapy. In S. L. Garfield & A. E. Bergin (Eds.), *Handbook of psychotherapy and behavior change* (3rd ed., pp. 157–212). New York: Wiley.

Lang, P. J. (1971). The application of psychophysiological methods to the study of psychotherapy and behavior modification. In A. E. Bergin & S. L. Garfield (Eds.), *Handbook of Psychotherapy and Behavior Change* (pp. 75–125). New York: Wiley.

Langs, R. (1973). *The technique of psychoanalytic psychotherapy.* New York: Jason Aronson.

Lazarus, A. A. (1961). Group therapy of phobic disorders by systematic desensitization. *Journal of Abnormal and Social Psychology, 63*, 504–510.

Lazarus, A. A. (1968). Variations in desensitization therapy. *Psychotherapy: Theory, research and practice, 5*, 50–52.

Lazarus, A. A. (1971). *Behavior therapy and beyond.* New York: McGraw-Hill.

Lazarus, A. A. (Ed.). (1972). *Clinical behavior therapy.* New York: Brunner/Mazel.

Lazarus, A. A. (1973). Avoid the paradigm clash. *International Journal of Psychiatry, 11*, 157–159.

Lazarus, A. A. (1976). *Multimodal behavior therapy.* New York: Springer.

Lazarus, A. A. (1989a). *The practice of multimodal therapy.* Baltimore: Johns Hopkins University Press.

Lazarus, A. A. (1989b). Why I am an eclectic (not an integrationist). *British Journal of Guidance and Counseling, 19*, 248–258.

Lazarus, A. A. (1992). Multimodal therapy: Technical eclecticism with minimal integration. In J. C. Norcross & M. R. Goldfried (Eds.), *Handbook of psychotherapy integration* (pp. 231–263). New York: Basic Books.

Lazarus, A. A. (1995). Different types of eclecticism and integration: Let's be aware of the dangers. *Journal of Psychotherapy Integration, 5*, 27–39.

Lazarus, A. A., & Messer, S. B. (1988). Clinical choice points: Behavioral versus psychoanalytic interventions. *Psychotherapy, 25*, 59–70.

Lazarus, A. A., & Messer, S. B. (1991). Does chaos prevail? An exchange on technical eclecticism and assimilative integration. *Journal of Psychotherapy Integration, 1*, 143–158.

Lazarus, A. A., & Serber, M. (1968). Is systematic desensitization being misapplied? *Psychological Reports, 23*, 215–218.

Leeper, R. W. (1970). Cognitive learning theory. In M. H. Marx (Ed.), *Learning: Theories.* New York: Macmillan.

Leitenberg, H., Agras, W. S., Barlow, D. H., & Oliveau, D. C. (1969). The contribution of selective positive reinforcement and therapeutic instructions to systematic desensitization therapy. *Journal of Abnormal Psychology, 74*, 113–118.

Leitenberg, H., Agras, W. S., Butz, K., & Wincze, J. (1971). Relation between heart-rate and behavior change during the treatment of phobias. *Journal of Abnormal Psychology, 78,* 59–68.

Levenson, E. A. (1972). *The fallacy of understanding: An inquiry in the changing structure of psychoanalysis.* New York: Basic Books.

Levenson, E. A. (1983). *The ambiguity of change.* New York: Basic Books.

Levenson, E. A. (1992). Harry Stack Sullivan: From interpersonal psychiatry to interpersonal psychoanalysis. *Contemporary Psychoanalysis, 28,* 450–466.

Levine, F. M., & Fasnacht, G. (1974). Token rewards may lead to token learning. *American Psychologist, 29,* 816–820.

Lichtenberg, J. D., & Kaplan, S. (Eds.). (1983). *Reflections on self psychology.* Hillsdale, NJ: The Analytic Press.

Lionells, M., Fiscalini, J., Mann, C. H., & Stern, D. B. (Eds.). (1996). *Handbook of interpersonal psychoanalysis.* Hillsdale, NJ: The Analytic Press.

Locke, E. A. (1971). Is "behavior therapy" behavioristic? (an analysis of Wolpe's psychotherapeutic methods). *Psychological Bulletin, 76,* 318–327.

Loevinger, J. (1966). Three principles for a psychoanalytic psychology. *Journal of Abnormal Psychology, 71,* 432–443.

Lomont, J. F., & Brock, L. (1971). Stimulus hierarchy generalization in systematic desensitization. *Behaviour Research and Therapy, 9,* 197–208.

LoPiccolo, J. (1969). Effective components of systematic desensitization. Unpublished doctoral dissertation, Yale University, New Haven, CT.

Luborsky, L. (1996). *The symptom-context method: Symptoms as opportunities in psychotherapy.* Washington, DC: American Psychological Association.

Luborsky, L., Chandler, M., Auerbach, A. H., Cohen, J., & Bachrach, H. M. (1971). Factors influencing the outcome of psychotherapy: A review of quantitative research. *Psychological Bulletin, 75,* 145–185.

Luborsky, L., & Crits-Christoph, P. (1990). *Understanding transference: The CCRT method.* New York: Basic Books.

Luborsky, L., Singer, B., & Luborsky, L. (1975). Comparative studies of psychotherapy. *Archives of General Psychiatry, 32,* 995–1008.

Mahoney, M. J. (1974). *Cognition and behavior modification.* Cambridge, MA: Ballinger.

Mahoney, M. J. (1990). *Human change processes: Theoretical bases for psychotherapy.* New York: Basic Books.

Mahoney, M. J. (1995). *Constructive psychotherapy: Principles and practice.* New York: Guilford Press.

Main, M. (1983). Exploration, play, and cognitive functioning related to infant–mother attachment. *Infant Behavior and Development, 6,* 167–174.

Marcia, J. E., Rubin, B. M., & Efran, J. S. (1969). Systematic desensitization: Expecting change or counter-conditioning? *Journal of Abnormal Psychology, 74,* 382–387.

Marks, I. M. (1969). *Fears and phobias.* New York: Academic Press.

Marks, I. M. (1972). Flooding (implosion) and allied treatments. In W. S. Agras (Ed.), *Behavior modification: Principles and clinical applications* (pp. 151–214). Boston: Little, Brown.

Marks, I. M. (1972). Perspective on flooding. *Seminars in Psychiatry, 4,* 129–138.

Marks, I. M. (1975). Behavioral treatments of phobic and obsessive-compulsive disorders: A critical appraisal. In M. Hersen, R. Eisler, & P. Miller (Eds.), *Progress in behavior modification* (Vol. 1). New York: Academic Press.

Marks, I. M., & Gelder, M. G. (1965). A controlled retrospective study of behavior therapy in phobic patients. *British Journal of Psychiatry, 3,* 561–573.

Marks, I. M., & Gelder, M. G. (1966). Common ground between behaviour therapy and psychodynamic methods. *British Journal of Medical Psychology, 39,* 11–23.

Marmor, J. (1971). Dynamic psychotherapy and behavior therapy. *Archives of General Psychiatry, 24,* 22–28.

Masling, J. (Ed.). (1983). *Empirical studies of psychoanalytic theories.* Hillsdale, NJ: Erlbaum.

McFall, R. M., & Twentyman, C. T. (1973). Four experiments on the relative contributions of rehearsal, modeling, and coaching to assertive training. *Journal of Abnormal Psychology, 81,* 199–218.

McNulty, S. E., & Swann, W. B., Jr. (1991). Psychotherapy, self-concept change, and self-verification. In R. C. Curtis (Ed.), *The relational self: Theoretical convergences in psychoanalysis and social psychology* (pp. 213–237). New York: Guilford Press.

Meehl, P. E. (1973). Some methodological reflections on the difficulties of psychoanalytic research. *Psychological Issues, 8*(2, Monograph No. 30), 104–117. New York: International Universities Press.

Meichenbaum, D. (1973). Cognitive factors in behavior modification: Modifying what clients say to themselves. In C. M. Franks & G. T. Wilson (Eds.), *Annual review of behavior therapy theory and practice* (Vol. 1, pp. 416–431). New York: Brunner/Mazel.

Meichenbaum, D. (1974). Self-instructional methods. In F. H. Kanfer & A. P. Goldstein (Eds.), *Helping people change.* New York: Pergamon.

Meichenbaum, D. (1977). *Cognitive–behavior modification.* New York: Plenum Press.

Meichenbaum, D., & Gilmore, J. B. (1984). The nature of unconscious processes: A cognitive–behavioral perspective. In K. S. Bowers & D. Meichenbaum (Eds.), *The unconscious reconsidered.* New York: Wiley.

Menninger, K. (1958). *The theory of psychoanalytic technique.* New York: Basic Books.

Merton, R. K. (1957). *Social theory and social structure* (Rev. ed.). New York: Free Press.

Messer, S. B. (1986). Behavioral and psychoanalytic perspectives at therapeutic choice points. *American Psychologist, 40,* 1261–1272.

Messer, S. B. (1992). A critical examination of belief structures in integrative and eclectic psychotherapy. In J. C. Norcross & M. R. Goldfried (Eds.), *Handbook of psychotherapy integration* (pp. 130–165). New York: Basic Books.

Messer, S. B., Sass, L. A., & Woolfolk, R. L. (Eds.). (1988). *Hermeneutics and psychological theory: Interpretive perspectives on personality, psychotherapy, and psychopathology.* New Brunswick, NJ: Rutgers University Press.

Messer, S. B., & Warren, C. S. (1995). *Models of brief psychodynamic therapy: A comparative approach.* New York: Guilford Press.

Messer, S. B., & Winokur, M. (1980). Some limits to the integration of psychoanalytic and behavior therapy. *American Psychologist, 35,* 818–827.

Messer, S. B., & Winokur, M. (1984). Ways of knowing and visions of reality in psychoanalytic therapy and behavior therapy. In H. Arkowitz & S. B. Messer (Eds.), *Psychoanalytic therapy and behavior therapy: Is integration possible?* (pp. 63–100). New York: Plenum Press.

Miller, G. A. (1969). Psychology as a means of promoting human welfare. *American Psychologist, 24,* 1063–1075.

Miller, N. E. (1948). Theory and experiment relating psychoanalytic displacement to stimulus-response generalization. *Journal of Abnormal Psychology, 43,* 155–178.

Miller, N. E. (1948). Studies of fear as an acquirable drive: I: Fear as motivation and fear-reduction as reinforcement in the learning of new responses. *Journal of Experimental Psychology, 38,* 89–101.

Miller, N. E. (1951). Learnable drives and rewards. In S. S. Stevens (Ed.), *Handbook of experimental psychology* (pp. 435–472). New York: Wiley.

Miller, N. E. (1959). Liberalization of basic S-R concepts: Extensions to conflict behavior, motivation and social learning. In S. Koch (Ed.), *Psychology: A study of a science* (Vol. 2, pp. 196–292). New York: McGraw-Hill.

Miller, N. E., & Dollard, J. (1941). *Social learning and imitation.* New Haven: Yale University Press.

Minuchin, S. (1974). *Families and family therapy.* Cambridge, MA: Harvard University Press.

Mirapeix, C. (1995). Psicoterapia cognitivo analitica: Un paradigma de integracion en psicoterapia: Antecedentes, justificacion epistemologica, aspectos teoricos y tecnicos cognitive analytic psychotherapy: A paradigm for integration in psychotherapy: Antecedents epistemological justification, theoretical and technical aspects. *Revista de Psicoterapia, 20,* 5–43.

Mischel, W. (1968). *Personality and assessment.* New York: Wiley.

Mischel, W. (1971). *Introduction to personality.* New York: Holt, Rinehart & Winston.

Mischel, W. (1973a). Toward a cognitive social learning reconceptualization of personality. *Psychological Review, 80,* 252–283.

Mischel, W. (1973b). On the empirical dilemmas of psychodynamic approaches: Issues and alternatives. *Journal of Abnormal Psychology, 82,* 335–344.

Mischel, W. (1973c). Toward a cognitive social learning reconceptualization of personality. *Psychological Review, 80,* 252–283.

Mitchell, S. A. (1988). *Relational concepts in psychoanalysis.* Cambridge, MA: Harvard University Press.

Mitchell, S. A. (1993). *Hope and dread in psychoanalysis.* New York: Basic Books.

Modell, A. H. (1984). *Psychoanalysis in a new context.* New York: International Universities Press.

Montgomery, G. T., & Crowder, J. E. (1972). The symptom substitution hypothesis and the evidence. *Psychotherapy: Theory, Research and Practice, 9,* 98–102.

Moore, N. (1965). Behavior therapy in bronchial asthma: A controlled study. *Journal of Psychosomatic Research, 9,* 257–276.

Mowrer, O. H., & Viek, P. (1948). Experimental analogue of fear from a sense of helplessness. *Journal of Abnormal and Social Psychology, 43,* 193–200.

Murray, J. F. (1995). On objects, transference, and two-person psychology: A critique of the new seduction theory. *Psychoanalytic Psychology, 12,* 31–41.

Neimeyer, R. A. (1986). Personal construct therapy. In W. Dryden & W. L. Golden (Eds.), *Cognitive–behavioural approaches to psychotherapy* (pp. 224–260). London: Harper & Row.

Neimeyer, R. A., & Mahoney, M. J. (1995). *Constructivism in psychotherapy.* Washington, DC: American Psychological Association.

Neisser, U. (1967). *Cognitive psychology.* New York: Appleton-Century-Crofts.

Nielsen, G., Barth, K., Haver, B., Havik, O. E., Molstad, E., Rogge, H., & Skatun, M. (1988). Brief dynamic psychotherapy for patients presenting physical symptoms. *Psychotherapy and Psychosomatics, 50,* 35–41.

Nielsen, G., Barth, K., Haver, B., Havik, O. E., Molstad, E., Rogge, H., & Skatun, M. (1991). Unsuitable patients, or suitable therapy? *Tidsskrift for Norsk Psykologforening, 27,* 91–98.

Nisbett, R., & Wilson, T. (1977). Telling more than we can know: Verbal reports of mental processes. *Psychological Review, 84,* 231–259.

Norcross, J. C., & Goldfried, M. R. (Eds.). (1992). *Handbook of psychotherapy integration.* New York: Basic Books.

Opaso, R. (Ed.). (1992). *Integracion en psicoterapia.* Santiago, Chile: Ediciones Cecidep.

Orlinsky, D. E., & Howard, K. I. (1987). A generic model of psychotherapy. *Journal of Integrative and Eclectic Psychotherapy, 6,* 6–16.

Orne, M. T. (1969). Demand characteristics and the concept of quasi-controls. In R. Rosenthal & R. L. Rosnow (Eds.), *Artifact in behavioral research* (pp. 147–179). New York: Academic Press.

Ornstein, P. H. (1991). A self psychological perspective on conflict and compromise. In S. Dowling (Ed.), *Conflict and compromise* (pp. 133–171). New York: International Universities Press.

Patterson, G. R. (1974). A basis for identifying stimuli which control behaviors in natural settings. *Child Development, 45,* 900–911.

Paul, G. L. (1966). *Insight vs. desensitization in psychotherapy: An experiment in anxiety reduction.* Stanford, CA: Stanford University Press.

Paul, G. L. (1969a). Outcome of systematic desensitization: I: Background procedures, and uncontrolled reports of individual treatment. In C. M. Franks (Ed.), *Behavior therapy: Appraisal and status* (pp. 63–104). New York: McGraw-Hill.

Paul, G. L. (1969b). Outcome of systematic desensitization: II: Controlled investigations of individual treatment, technique variations, and current status. In C. M. Franks (Ed.), *Behavior therapy: Appraisal and status* (pp. 105–159). New York: McGraw-Hill.

Paul, I. H. (1974). *Letters to Simon: On the conduct of psychotherapy.* New York: International Universities Press.

Penfield, W., & Roberts, L. (1959). *Speech and brain-mechanisms.* Princeton: Princeton University Press.

Pine, F. (1990). *Drive, ego, object, self.* New York: Basic Books.

Pinsof, W. M. (1983). Integrative problem-centered therapy. *Journal of Marital and Family Therapy, 9,* 19–35.

Porter, R. (Ed.). (1968). *The role of learning in psychotherapy.* London: J. and A. Churchill.

Premack, D. (1965). Reinforcement theory. In D. Levine (Ed.), *Nebraska symposium on motivation: 1965* (pp. 123–180). Lincoln: University of Nebraska Press.

Pribram, K., & Gill, M. M. (1975). *Freud's "project" reassessed: Preface to contemporary cognitive theory and neuropsychology.* New York: Basic Books.

Prochaska, J. O. (1984). *Systems of psychotherapy: A transtheoretical analysis* (2nd ed.). Homewood, IL: Dorsey.

Prochaska, J. O., & DiClemente, C. C. (1986). The transtheoretical approach. In J. C. Norcross (Ed.), *Handbook of eclectic psychotherapy* (pp. 163–200). New York: Brunner/Mazel.

Prochaska, J. O., Rossi, J. S., & Wilcox, N. S. (1991). Change processes and psychotherapy outcome in integrative case research. *Journal of Psychotherapy Integration, 1,* 103–120.

Rachman, S. (1965). Studies in desensitization: I: The separate effects of relaxation and desensitization. *Behaviour Research and Therapy, 3,* 245–251.

Rachman, S. (1968). The role of muscular relaxation in desensitization therapy. *Behaviour Research and Therapy, 6,* 159–166.

Rachman, S., & Hodgson, R. I. (1974). Synchrony and desynchrony in fear and avoidance. *Behaviour Research and Therapy, 12,* 311–318.

Rangell, L. (1954). Similarities and differences between psychoanalysis and dynamic psychotherapy. *Journal of the American Psychoanalytic Association, 2,* 734–744.

Rangell, L. (1985). On the theory of theory in psychoanalysis and the relation of theory to psychoanalytic therapy. *Journal of the American Psychoanalytic Association, 33,* 59–92.

Rapaport, D. (1953). Review of J. Dollard and N. E. Miller's *Personality and Psychotherapy* [Book review]. *American Journal of Orthopsychiatry, 23,* 204–208.

Rapaport, D. (1958). The theory of ego autonomy: A generalization. *Bulletin of the Menninger Clinic, 22,* 13–35.

Rapaport, D. (1960). On the psychoanalytic theory of motivation. In M. M. Gill (Ed.), *The collected papers of David Rapaport* (pp. 853–915). New York: Basic Books.

Rapaport, D., & Gill, M. M. (1959). The points of view and assumptions of metapsychology. *International Journal of Psycho-Analysis, 40,* 153–162.

Reich, W. (1945). *Character analysis.* New York: Orgone Institute Press.

Rhoads, J. M., & Feather, B. W. (1972). Transference and resistance observed in behaviour therapy. *British Journal of Medical Psychology, 45,* 99–103.

Riccio, D. C., & Silvestri, R. (1973). Extinction and avoidance behavior and the problem of residual fear. *Behaviour Research and Therapy, 11,* 1–9.

Rickman, J. (1957). *Selected contributions to psychoanalysis.* New York: Basic Books.

Rosenthal, R. (1966). *Experimenter bias in behavioral research.* New York: Appleton-Century-Crofts.

Ross, L. (1977). The intuitive psychologist and his shortcomings: Distortions in the attribution process. In L. Berkowitz (Ed.), *Advances in experimental social psychology* (Vol. 10, pp. 174–221). New York: Academic Press.

Ryle, A. (1990). *Cognitive–analytic therapy: Active participation in change.* New York: Wiley.

Safran, J. D. (1991). *Emotion, psychotherapy, and change.* New York: Guilford.

Safran, J. D., & Greenberg, L. S. (Eds.). (1991). *Emotion, psychotherapy, and the change.* New York: Guilford Press.

Safran, J. D., & Messer, S. B. (in press). Psychotherapy integration: A postmodern critique. *Clinical Psychology: Science and Practice.*

Safran, J. D., & Segal, Z. V. (1990). *Interpersonal process in cognitive therapy.* New York: Guilford Press.

Saltz, E. (1971). *The cognitive bases of human learning.* Homewood, IL: Dorsey.

Sameroff, A. J. (1983). Developmental systems: Contexts and evolution. In W. Kessen (Ed.), *History, theories, and methods.* Vol. 1 of P. H. Mussen (Ed.), *Handbook of child psychiatry* (pp. 237–294). New York: Wiley.

Sameroff, A. J. (1987). The social context of development. In N. Eisenberg (Ed.), *Contemporary topics in developmental psychology* (pp. 273–291). New York: Wiley.

Sandler, J. (1976). Countertransference and role responsiveness. *International Revue of Psycho-Analysis, 3,* 43–47.

Sandler, J. (1981). Unconscious wishes and human relationships. *Contemporary Psychoanalysis, 17,* 180–196.

Sandler, J. (1992). Reflections on developments in the theory of psychoanalytic technique. *International Journal of Psycho-Analysis, 73,* 189–198.

Schachtel, E. (1959). *Metamorphosis.* New York: Basic Books.

Schafer, R. (1970). An overview of Heinz Hartmann's contributions to psycho-analysis. *International Journal of Psycho-Analysis, 51,* 425–446.

Schafer, R. (1972). Internalization: Process or fantasy? In *The psychoanalytic study of the child* (Vol. 27, pp. 411–436). New York: Quadrangle.

Schafer, R. (1973a). Concepts of self and identity and the experience of separation-individuation in adolescence. *Psychoanalytic Quarterly, 42,* 42–59.

Schafer, R. (1973b). Its place in psychoanalytic interpretation and theory. In *The annual of psychoanalysis* (Vol. 1, pp. 159–196). New York: Quadrangle.

Schafer, R. (1976). *A new language for psychoanalysis.* New Haven: Yale University Press.

Schafer, R. (1980). *Narrative action in psychoanalysis.* Worcester, MA: Clark University Press.

Schafer, R. (1992). *Retelling a life.* New York: Basic Books.

Scharff, D. E., & Scharff, J. S. (1987). *Object relations family therapy.* Northvale, NJ: Jason Aronson.

Scharff, D. E., & Scharff, J. S. (1989). *Object relations couple therapy.* Northvale, NJ: Jason Aronson.

Schmale, H. T. (reporter). (1966). Working through (panel report). *Journal of the American Psychoanalytic Association, 14,* 172–182.

Schor, J. B. (1991). *The overworked American: The unexpected decline of leisure.* New York: Basic Books.

Schubot, E. D. (1966). The influence of hypnotic and muscular relaxation in systematic desensitization of phobic behavior. Doctoral dissertation, Stanford University.

Schur, M. (1966). *The id and the regulatory principles of mental functioning.* New York: International Universities Press.

Schwartz, B. (1994). *The costs of living: How market freedom erodes the best things in life.* New York: Norton.

Seabrook, J. (1990). *The myth of the market.* London: Green Books.

Searles, H. (1966). *Collected papers on schizophrenia and related subjects.* New York: International Universities Press.

Seligman, M. E. P. (1974). *Helplessness.* San Francisco: Freeman.

Seligman, M. E. P., & Campbell, B. A. (1965). Effects of intensity and duration of punishment on extinction of an avoidance response. *Journal of Comparative and Physiological Psychology, 59,* 295–297.

Seligman, M. E. P., & Johnston, J. C. (1973). A cognitive theory of avoidance learning. In F. J. McGuigan & D. B. Lumsden (Eds.), *Contemporary approaches to conditioning and learning* (pp. 69–110). New York: Winston.

Selvini Palazzoli, M., Cecchin, G., Prata, G., & Boscolo, L. (1978). *Paradox and counterparadox.* New York: Jason Aronson.

Shapiro, D. (1965). *Neurotic styles.* New York: Basic Books.

Shapiro, D. A., & Firth, J. (1987). Prescriptive v. exploratory psychotherapy: Outcomes of the Sheffield Psychotherapy Project. *British Journal of Psychiatry, 151,* 790–799.

Shapiro, D. A., & Firth-Cozens, J. (1990). Two-year followup of the Sheffield Psychotherapy Project. *British Journal of Psychiatry, 157,* 389–391.

Shapiro, D. A., & Shapiro, K. (1982). Meta-analysis of comparative outcome studies: A replication and refinement. *Psychological Bulletin, 92,* 581–604.

Shapiro, E. (1994). *Grief as a family process.* New York: Guilford Press.

Shedler, J., Mayman, M., & Manis, M. (1993). The illusion of mental health. *American Psychologist, 48,* 1117–1131.

Sheffield, F. D., & Temmer, H. W. (1950). Relative resistance to extinction of escape training and avoidance training. *Journal of Experimental Psychology, 40,* 287–298.

Sherman, A. R. (1972). Real-life exposure as a primary therapeutic factor in the desensitization treatment of fear. *Journal of Abnormal Psychology, 79,* 19–28.

Sherman, S. J., Judd, C. M., & Park, B. (1989). Social cognition. In M. R. Rosenzweig & L. W. Porter (Eds.), *Annual review of psychology* (Vol. 40, pp. 281–326). Palo Alto, CA: Annual Reviews.

Sherrington, C. S. (1906). *The integrative action of the nervous system.* New Haven, CT: Yale University Press.

Shevrin, H., Bond, J., Brakel, L., Hertel, R., & Williams, W. J. (1996). *Conscious and unconscious processes: Psychodynamic, cognitive, and neurophysiological convergences.* New York: Guilford Press.

Sidman, M. (1955). On the persistence of avoidance behavior. *Journal of Abnormal and Social Psychology, 50,* 217–220.

Silverman, L. H. (1971). An experimental technique for the study of unconscious conflict. *British Journal of Medical Psychology, 44,* 17–25.

Silverman, L. H. (1972). Drive stimulation and psychopathology: On the conditions under which drive-related external events evoke pathological reactions. In R. R. Holt & E. Peterfreund (Eds.), *Psychoanalysis and Contemporary Science* (Vol. 1, pp. 306–326). New York: Macmillan.

Silverman, L. H. (1974). Some psychoanalytic considerations of non-psychoanalytic therapies: On the possibility of integrating treatment approaches and related issues. *Psychotherapy: Theory, Research and Practice, 11,* 298–305.

Silverman, L. H. (1976). Psychoanalytic theory: The reports of my death are greatly exaggerated. *American Psychologist.*

Silverman, L. H., Frank, S. G., & Dachinger, P. (1974). A psychoanalytic reinterpretation of the effectiveness of systematic desensitization: Experimental data bearing on the role of merging fantasies. *Journal of Abnormal Psychology, 83,* 313–318.

Singer, J. L. (1974). *Imagery and daydream techniques in psychotherapy and behavior modification.* New York: Academic Press.

Singer, J. L. (Ed.). (1990). *Repression and dissociation: Defense mechanisms and personality styles: Current theory and research.* Chicago: University of Chicago Press.

Skinner, B. F. (1971). *Beyond freedom and dignity.* New York: Knopf.

Skynner, R. (1981). An open-systems, group-analytic approach to family therapy. In Gurman & Kniskern (Eds.), *Handbook of Family Therapy* (pp. 162–181). New York: Brunner/Mazel.

Slater, P. (1980). *Wealth addiction.* New York: Dutton.

Slipp, S. (1984). *Object relations: A dynamic bridge between individual and family treatment.* New York: Jason Aronson.

Slipp, S. (1988). *The technique and practice of object relations family therapy.* Northvale, NJ: Jason Aronson.

Sloane, R. B. (1969). The converging paths of behavior therapy and psychotherapy. *American Journal of Psychiatry, 125,* 49–57.

Sloane, R. B., Staples, F. R., Cristol, A. H., Yorkston, N. J., & Whipple, K. (1975). *Psychotherapy versus behavior therapy.* Cambridge, MA: Harvard University Press.

Smith, M. L., Glass, G. V., & Miller, T. I. (1980). *The benefits of psychotherapy.* Baltimore: Johns Hopkins University Press.

Snyder, M. (1981). Seek and ye shall find: Testing hypotheses about other people. In E. T. Higgins, C. P. Herman, & M. P. Zanna (Eds.), *Social cognition: The Ontario symposium* (pp. 277–304). Hillsdale, NJ: Erlbaum.

Snyder, M. (1984). When belief creates reality. In L. Berkowitz (Ed.), *Advances in experimental social psychology* (Vol. 18, pp. 248–305). Orlando, FL: Academic Press.

Snyder, M. (1991). Motivational foundations of behavioral confirmation. In M. P. Zanna (Ed.), *Advances in experimental social psychology* (Vol. 25, pp. 67–114). New York: Academic Press.

Snyder, M., & Swann, W. B. (1978). Behavioral confirmation in social interaction: From social perception to social reality. *Journal of Experimental Social Psychology, 14,* 148–162.

Snyder, M., Tanke, E. D., & Berscheid, E. S. (1977). Social perception and interpersonal behavior: On the self-fulfilling nature of social stereotypes. *Journal of Personality and Social Psychology, 35,* 656–666.

Solley, C. M., & Murphy, G. (1960). *Development of the perceptual world.* New York: Basic Books.

Solomon, R. L., & Wynne, L. C. (1954). Traumatic avoidance learning: The principles of anxiety conservation and partial irreversibility. *Psychological Review, 61,* 353–385.

Spence, D. P. (1982). *Narrative truth and historical truth.* New York: Norton.

Spence, D. P. (1993). The hermeneutic turn: Soft science or loyal opposition? *Psychoanalytic Dialogues, 3,* 1–10.

Spielberger, C. D., & De Nike, L. D. (1966). Descriptive behaviorism versus cognitive theory in verbal operant conditioning. *Psychological Review, 73,* 306–326.

Spruiell, V. (1988). The indivisibility of Freudian object relations and drive theories. *Psychoanalytic Quarterly, 57,* 597–625.

Staub, E. (1968). Duration of stimulus exposure as determinant of the efficacy of flooding procedures in the elimination of fear. *Behaviour Research and Therapy, 6,* 131–132.

Stein, M. H. (1979). Review of H. Kohut, "The Restoration of the Self" [Book review]. *Journal of the American Psychoanalytic Association, 27,* 665–680.

Stern, D. B. (1992). Commentary on constructivism in clinical psychoanalysis. *Psychoanalytic Dialogues, 2,* 331–364.

Stern, D. N. (1985). *The interpersonal world of the infant.* New York: Basic Books.

Stierlin, H. (1977). *Psychoanalysis and family therapy.* New York: Jason Aronson.

Stolorow, R., & Lachmann, F. (1980). *Psychoanalysis of developmental arrests.* New York: International Universities Press.

Stone, L. (1961). *The psychoanalytic situation.* New York: International Universities Press.

Strack, S., & Coyne, J. C. (1983). Social confirmation of dysphoria: Shared and private reactions to depression. *Journal of Personality and Social Psychology, 44,* 798–806.

Stricker, G., & Gold, J. R. (Eds.). (1993). *Comprehensive handbook of psychotherapy integration.* New York: Praeger.

Stricker, G., & Gold, J. R. (1996). Psychotherapy integration: An assimilative, psychodynamic approach. *Clinical Psychology: Science and Practice, 3,* 47–58.

Sue, D. (1975). The effect of duration of exposure on systematic desensitization and extinction. *Behaviour Research and Therapy, 13,* 55–60.

Sugarman, A., & Wilson, A. (1995). Introduction to the section: Contemporary structural analysts critique relational theories. *Psychoanalytic Psychology, 12,* 1–8.

Sullivan, H. S. (1953). *The interpersonal theory of psychiatry.* New York: Norton.

Sullivan, H. S. (1954). *The psychiatric interview.* New York: Norton.

Swann, W. B., Wenzlaff, R. M., Krull, D. S., & Pelham, B. W. (1992). Allure of negative feedback: Self-verification strivings among depressed persons. *Journal of Abnormal Psychology, 101,* 293–306.

Taylor, S. E. (1989). *Positive illusions: Creative self-deception and the healthy mind.* New York: Basic Books.

Truax, C. B. (1966). Reinforcement and nonreinforcement in Rogerian psychotherapy. *Journal of Abnormal Psychology, 71,* 1–9.

Uleman, J. S., & Bargh, J. A. (1989). *Unintended thought.* New York: Guilford Press.

Valins, S., & Ray, A. A. (1967). Effects of cognitive desensitization on avoidance behavior. *Journal of Personality and Social Psychology, 7,* 345–350.

Van Egeren, L. F. (1971). Psychophysiological aspects of systematic desensitization: Some outstanding issues. *Behaviour Research and Therapy, 9,* 65–77.

Van Egeren, L. F., Feather, B. W., & Hein, P. L. (1971). Desensitization of phobias: Some psychophysiological propositions. *Psychophysiology, 8,* 213–228.

Vodde, T. W., & Gilner, F. H. (1971). The effects of exposure to fear stimuli on fear reduction. *Behaviour Research and Therapy, 9,* 169–175.

von Bertalanffy, L. (1950). An outline of general systems theory. *British Journal of the Philosophy of Science, 1,* 2–8.

von Bertalanffy, L. (1969). General systems theory and psychiatry: An overview. In W. Gray, F. J. Duhl, & N. D. Rizzo (Eds.), *General systems theory and psychiatry* (pp. 33–50). Boston: Little Brown.

Wachtel, E. F. (1993). Postscript: Therapeutic communication with couples. In P. L. Wachtel, *Therapeutic communication: Principles and effective practice* (pp. 273–293). New York: Guilford Press.

Wachtel, E. F. (1994). *Treating troubled children and their families.* New York: Guilford Press.

Wachtel, E. F., & Wachtel, P. L. (1986). *Family dynamics in individual psychotherapy.* New York: Guilford Press.

Wachtel, P. L. (1967). Conceptions of broad and narrow attention. *Psychological Bulletin, 68,* 417–429.

Wachtel, P. L. (1968). Anxiety, attention, and coping with threat. *Journal of Abnormal Psychology, 73,* 137–143.

Wachtel, P. L. (1969). Psychology, metapsychology, and psychoanalysis. *Journal of Abnormal Psychology, 74,* 651–660.

Wachtel, P. L. (1972). Cognitive style and style of adaptation. *Perceptual and Motor Skills, 35,* 779–785.

Wachtel, P. L. (1973a). On fact, hunch, and stereotype: A reply to mischel. *Journal of Abnormal Psychology, 82,* 537–540.

Wachtel, P. L. (1973b). Psychodynamics, behavior therapy, and the implacable experimenter: An inquiry into the consistency of personality. *Journal of Abnormal Psychology, 82,* 324–334.

Wachtel, P. L. (1975). Behavior therapy and the facilitation of psychoanalytic exploration. *Psychotherapy: Theory, Research and Practice, 12,* 68–72.

Wachtel, P. L. (1977a). Interaction cycles, unconscious processes, and the person-situation issue. In D. Magnusson & N. Endler (Eds.), *Personality at the crossroads: Towards an interactional psychology* (pp. 317–331). Hillsdale, NJ: Laurence Earlbaum Associates.

Wachtel, P. L. (1977b). *Psychoanalysis and behavior therapy: Toward an integration.* New York: Basic Books.

Wachtel, P. L. (1980). Investigation and its discontents: On some constraints on progress in psychological research. *American Psychologist, 35,* 399–408.

Wachtel, P. L. (1981). Transference, schema, and assimilation: The relevance of Piaget to the psychoanalytic theory of transference. *The Annual of Psychoanalysis* (Vol. 8, pp. 59–76). New York: International Universities Press.

Wachtel, P. L. (1982). Vicious circles: The self and the rhetoric of emerging and unfolding. *Contemporary Psychoanalysis, 18,* 273–295.

Wachtel, P. L. (1984). On theory, practice, and the nature of integration. In H. Arkowitz, & S. B. Messer (Eds.), *Psychoanalytic therapy and behavior therapy: Is integration possible?* (pp. 31–52). New York: Plenum Press.

Wachtel, P. L. (1987). *Action and insight.* New York: Guilford Press.

Wachtel, P. L. (1989). *The poverty of affluence: A psychological portrait of the American way of life.* Philadelphia: New Society Publishers.

Wachtel, P. L. (1990). *Integrative psychotherapy* (pt. 4) [Videotape]. Corona del Mar, CA: Psychological and Educational Films.

Wachtel, P. L. (1991a). From eclecticism to synthesis: Toward a more seamless psychotherapeutic integration. *Journal of Psychotherapy Integration, 1,* 43–54.

Wachtel, P. L. (1991b). The role of accomplices in preventing and facilitating change. In R. Curtis & G. Stricker (Eds.), *How people change: Inside and outside therapy* (pp. 21–28). New York: Plenum Press.

Wachtel, P. L. (1993a). Active intervention, psychic structure, and the analysis of transference. *Psychoanalytic Dialogues, 3,* 589–603.

Wachtel, P. L. (1993b). *Therapeutic communication: Principles and effective practice.* New York: Guilford Press.

Wachtel, P. L. (1994). Cyclical processes in psychopathology. *Journal of Abnormal Psychology, 103,* 51–54.

Wachtel, P. L. (1996). Overconsumption: Lessons from psychology for politics and economics. In D. Bell, L. Fawcett, R. Keil, & P. Penz (Eds.), *Political ecology: Global and local perspectives.* New York: Routledge.

Wachtel, P. L., & Arkin, A. (1980). Projective test assessment before and after behavior therapy. *Comprehensive Psychotherapy, 1,* 1–12.

Wachtel, P. L., & McKinney, M. (1992). Cyclical psychodynamics and integrative psychodynamic therapy. In J. Norcross & M. Goldfried (Eds.), *Handbook of psychotherapy integration* (pp. 335–370). New York: Basic Books.

Wagner, M. K., & Cauthen, N. R. (1968). A comparison of reciprocal inhibition and operant conditioning in the systematic desensitization of a fear of snakes. *Behaviour Research and Therapy, 6,* 225–227.

Waters, W. F., & McCallum, R. N. (1973). The basis of behavior therapy: Mentalistic or behavioristic? A reply to E. A. Locke. *Behaviour Research and Therapy, 11,* 157–163.

Waters, W. F., McDonald, D. G., & Koresko, R. L. (1972). Psychophysiological responses during analogue systematic desensitization and non-relaxation control procedures. *Behaviour Research and Therapy, 10,* 355–366.

Watts, F. (1971). Desensitization as an habituation phenomenon. I: Stimulus intensity as determinant of the effects of stimulus lengths. *Behaviour Research and Therapy, 9,* 209–217.

Watzlawick, P., Weakland, J., & Fisch, R. (1974). *Change: Principles of problem formation and problem solution.* New York: Norton.

Weeks, G. R., & L'Abate, L. (1982). *Paradoxical psychotherapy: Theory and practice with individuals.* New York: Brunner/Mazel.

Weitzman, B. (1967). Behavior therapy and psychotherapy. *Psychological Review, 74,* 300–317.

Wheelis, A. (1973). *How people change.* New York: Harper & Row.

White, M., & Epston, D. (1990). *Narrative means to therapeutic ends.* New York: Norton.

Wiggins, J. A., Renner, K. E., Clore, G. L., & Rose, R. J. (1971). *The Psychology of Personality.* Reading, MA: Addison-Wesley.

Wile, D. B. (1982). *Kohut, Kernberg, and accusatory interpretations.* Paper presented at the symposium "Do we have to harm clients to help them?" 1982 American Psychological Association Convention, Washington, DC.

Wile, D. B. (1984). Kohut, Kernberg, and accusatory interpretations. *Psychotherapy: Theory, Research and Practice, 21,* 353–364.

Wile, D. B. (1985). Psychotherapy by precedent: Unexamined legacies from pre-1920 psychoanalysis. *Psychotherapy, 22,* 793–802.

Wilkins, W. (1971). Desensitization: Social and cognitive factors underlying the effectiveness of Wolpe's procedure. *Psychological Bulletin, 76,* 311–317.

Wilson, A. (1995). Mapping the mind in relational psychoanalysis: Some critiques, questions, and conjectures. *Psychoanalytic Psychology, 12,* 9–29.

Wilson, G. T., & Davison, G. C. (1971). Processes of fear reduction in systematic desensitization: Animal studies. *Psychological Bulletin, 76,* 1–14.

Winnicott, D. W. (1960). The theory of the parent-infant relationship. In *The maturational process and the facilitating environment* (pp. 37–55). New York: International Universities Press.

Wolf, E. (1966). Learning theory and psychoanalysis. *British Journal of Medical Psychology, 39,* 1–10.

Wolf, E. (1988). *Treating the self.* New York: Guilford Press.

Wolfe, B. E. (1995). Self pathology and psychotherapy integration. *Journal of Psychotherapy Integration, 5,* 293–312.

Wolitzky, D. L., & Wachtel, P. L. (1973). Personality and perception. In B. Wolman (Ed.), *Handbook of general psychology* (pp. 826–857). Englewood Cliffs, NJ: Prentice-Hall.

Wolpe, J. (1958). *Psychotherapy by reciprocal inhibition.* Stanford, CA: Stanford University Press.

Wolpe, J. (1969). *The practice of behavior therapy.* Elmsford, NY: Pergamon Press.

Wolpe, J., Brady, J. P., Serber, M., Agras, W. S., & Liberman, R. P. (1973). The current status of systematic desensitization. *American Journal of Psychiatry, 130,* 961–965.

Yalom, I. (1985). *The theory and practice of group psychotherapy.* New York: Basic Books.

Young, J. E. (1991). Schema-focused cognitive therapy for personality disorders. In A. Beck & A. Freeman (Eds.), *Cognitive therapy for personality disorders.* New York: Guilford.

Zeanah, C. H., Anders, T. F., Seifer, R., & Stern, D. N. (1989). Implications of research on infant development for psychodynamic theory and practice. *Journal of the American Academy of Child and Adolescent Psychiatry, 28,* 657–668.

Zetzel, E., & Meissner, W. W. (1973). *Basic concepts of psychoanalytic psychiatry.* New York: Basic Books.

# INDEX

Assessment: behavioral features of integrated approach to, 143–145; behavioral methods of, 110–113, 143–145; in behavior therapy, 107; interaction in therapy used for, 138–140; therapy and, distinction between, 105–106

Asthmatics, desensitization therapy for, 163

Attention, anxiety and, 167

Attributional interpretations, 409–414

Autonomy of patient, 278–279

Avoidance behavior: anxiety and, 77, 81; anxiety reduction and, 192–198, 202–203; fear extinction and, 147–148; relaxation therapy in reduction of, 166; stopping-thinking response as, 84–85; See also Repression

Avoidance tests, behavioral, 158–159

Ayllon, T., 240

Azrin, N. H., 240

Bacal, H. A., 328

Bachant, J. L., 333, 348

Balint, M., 334, 382

Bandura, A., 46, 95, 107, 117, 158, 168, 170, 175, 206, 237, 241, 244, 351; on Dollard and Miller's work, 97–100; on identification of anxiety sources, 117–118; on reinforcement, 247, 251–252; on "underlying" determinants, 121

Bargh, J. A., 429

Barkham, M., 429

Barlow, D. H., 174, 182

Barron, J. W., 312, 365, 428

Basch, M. F., 328–329, 331, 337

Bateson, G., 381

Baum, M., 173n, 192

Beebe, B., 383, 435

Beech, R., 82, 120, 164, 169

Behavioral analysis, 106

Behavioral avoidance tests, 158–159

Behavioral–cognitive therapy, 359

Behavior confirmation, 432–433

Behaviorism, 7; See also Stimulus-response approach

Behavior therapists: as interviewers, 107–109; Dollard and Miller's work in view of, 94–102

Behavior therapy (behavioral approach), 4; active-intervention approach in, see Active-intervention approach; assessment stage of, 107; assessment-therapy distinction in, 105–106; cognitive or mediational approach, 351; definition of, 7; ethical issues in, see Ethical issues; evolution, 301; explicit techniques, patient objections to, 190–191; integration of psychoanalysis and, see Integration of psychoanalysis and behavior therapy; interviewing in, 107–109; observation methods in, 110–113; psychoanalysis and, see Behavior therapy and psychoanalysis; record-keeping and making charts or lists, 112; shift to cognitive–behavior therapy, 350–351; specificity in, 109–111; treatment of symptom, 378; Wheelis's critique of, 271–275; See also Behavior therapists; Interpersonal approach; and specific topics

Behavior therapy and psychoanalysis (psychodynamic therapy): Dollard and Miller's work, 95–96; internal versus external focus, contrast between, 115–120; interview methods, 107–109; limiting, behavioral methods seen as, 40; negative attitude to psychodynamic theorizing, behavior therapists', 95–96; specificity, 109–111; "underlying" problems vs. symptoms, treatment of, 120–121

Beitman, B. D., 306

Bell, R. Q., 433

Bemis, K. M., 355, 357

Benjamin, J., 333

Bergin, A. E., 155, 171, 309, 428

Bernstein, D. A., 158, 159

Berscheid, E. S., 433

Beutler, L. E., 303

Bibring, C., 39n, 40

Blanck, P. D., 432-433

Body ego, 33–34

Bolles, R. C., 244

Bond, J., 312

Boscolo, L., 416

Bowers, K. S., 72, 73, 75, 255, 429

Bowlby, J., 363

Brady, P., 165, 186

# ABOUT THE AUTHOR

$\mathbb{P}$AUL L. Wachtel is CUNY Distinguished Professor at City College and the Graduate Center of the City University of New York. He did his undergraduate work at Columbia, received his PhD in clinical psychology from Yale, and is a graduate of the postdoctoral psychoanalytic training program at New York University. Dr. Wachtel is the author of, among other books, *Family Dynamics in Individual Psychotherapy* (with Ellen F. Wachtel), *The Poverty of Affluence: A Psychological Portrait of the American Way of Life, Action, and Insight,* and *Therapeutic Communication: Principles and Effective Practice.* He has lectured and given workshops throughout the world on psychotherapy, personality theory and development, and the applications of psychological perspectives to social issues. Dr. Wachtel has served on the editorial boards of numerous journals spanning a variety of perspectives and concerns, including *Psychoanalytic Psychology, Journal of Marital and Family Therapy, Political Psychology,* and the *Journal of Social Distress and Homelessness.* He was one of the founders of the Society for the Exploration of Psychotherapy Integration.